THE BHARADVĀJAS IN ANCIENT INDIA

THE BHARADVĀJAS IN ANCIENT INDIA

THANESWAR SARMAH

MOTILAL BANARSIDASS PUBLISHERS
PRIVATE LIMITED • DELHI

First Edition: Delhi, 1991

ISBN: 81-208-0639-5

Also available at:
MOTILAL BANARSIDASS
41 U.A., Bungalow Road, Jawahar Nagar, Delhi 110 007
120 Royapettah High Road, Mylapore, Madras 600 004
16 St. Mark's Road, Bangalore 560 001
Ashok Rajpath, Patna 800 004
Chowk, Varanasi 221 001

This publication was financially supported by the Indian Council of Historical Research, New Delhi. The responsibility for the facts stated, opinions expressed or conclusions reached is entirely that of author and Indian Council of Historical Research accepts no responsibility for them.

PRINTED IN INDIA
BY JAINENDRA PRAKASH JAIN AT SHRI JAINENDRA PRESS, A-45 NARAINA INDUSTRIAL AREA, PHASE I, NEW DELHI 110 028 AND PUBLISHED BY NARENDRA PRAKASH JAIN FOR MOTILAL BANARSIDASS PUBLISHERS PVT. LTD., BUNGALOW ROAD, JAWAHAR NAGAR, DELHI 110 007

To those revered great souls

who taught me and

brought me up

FOREWORD

It is indeed a great pleasure to see that the Ph.D. dissertation of my pupil Dr. Thaneswar Sarmah goes under print. Dr. Sarmah began his study of the history of Bhāradvājas with the idea that he could set up a consistent picture of their families which originated from one single stem and branched into numerous families in different locales and times. However, he soon perceived the impossibility of the task which arose from paucity of definitely reliable chronological data and also from the Purāṇic fancy and hyperbole and consequently decided to focus his attention on the contribution of Bhāradvājas to Ancient Indian Myth and Ritual—also occasionally to Ancient India's law and history. Then, while he achieved his end, he discussed almost every bit of information, howsoever small, about various Bhārdvājas and about their writings and examined or weighed the same critically. His study of Bhāradvājas thus reveals a thorough and valuable picture of the contribution of Bhāradvājas to the making of Indian culture through passage of several centuries, from the hoary past to known past.

I should not fail to state that although Dr. Sarmah was inspired to take up the study of an ancient family of Seers of Ancient India by earlier studies of the Seers of Vedic times, he has revealed his ability to look at the problem steadily and as a whole. He studied the most ancient hymns of the Vedas, the ritualistic texts, the law texts—even late *Nibandhas*—and work on sundry subjects like Astronomy, *Śikṣā* etc. Also he studied ancillary literature of the Vedas, the Purāṇas and other works which supplied him historical, quasi-historical and mythical accounts of Bhāradvājas, together with the critical studies on these matters by modern scholars like Pargiter, Hazra, Pusalkar and P.L. Bhargava. And, what is particularly remarkable, Sarmah considered all these sources—primary and secondary—not only dispassionately but also boldly and with an open mind. He did not flag even a little when he controverted the views of the *savants* in the field. This is revealed in his somewhat laborious discussions on the histories of some particular individuals amongst Bhāradvājas, his discussions on the dates of the subfamilies of them, and also his explanation of the scanty and piecemeal mythical or other details which showed him some connected accounts. Indeed, imagination has served Sarmah, but only in a controlled and restrained manner.

I believe, Sarmah's work would usher in many more studies of Ancient Indian Seers' families and thereby our ancient heritage will be clearly underlined.

May I hope that this work of Sarmah is a fore-runner of many of his post-Ph.D. writings.

Retd. Professor of Sanskrit K. P. Jog
Deccan College and
Hon. Director of M.M. Dr. Kane Oriental
Research Institute of the Asiatic
Society of Bombay

Bombay
26 April 1989

PREFACE

This dissertation entitled 'The Bharadvājas in Ancient India' attempts to present a socio-historical study of the family of the distinguished seers. The work has been divided into two parts: Part I dealing with the socio-historical account of the family and Part II dealing with the significant contributions the family has made to Indian culture—it may nevertheless be mentioned that Part II does not present an over-all picture of the contribution of the Bharadvājas, rather it underlines some select aspects of the same.

While utilising the Vedic and Epico-Purāṇic sources for reconstruction of the family history of the Bharadvājas we have tried to ascertain the rationality of the sources and often faced paucity of actual historicity—particularly the sense of chronology which is the mainstay of history. As such while discussing the chronological problems either of the Bharadvājas or of the Bharatas—particularly of Divodāsa Atithigva—with a view to highlighting the date of the Ṛgvedic hymns, we had to depend mainly upon the date of the Mahābhārata War. We could not go into the problem of its date, its entirety as that discussion is only incidental. We have provided three tables of the genealogies of the early Bharadvājas and Bharatas up to the times of the Mahābhārata War (3100 B.C.) based on the Epic (MBh) and Purāṇas, independent of any modern authority. These tables, we hope, will help one to understand the historicity of the facts dealt with in this work and the relative chronology of the events of those times.

While dealing with the problem, we have tried to be forthright and given our independent consideration irrespective of hitherto established authorities and had often to be critical of some of them—we did so only when compelled by circumstances. We have nevertheless accepted opinions and findings of some scholars, when we found them suitable for our purpose. So also, we have drawn upon translations of some Vedic and post-Vedic works in pursuance of our objectives. Thus, we are indebted to and must pay homage to those *pūrvasūris* and express sincere gratitude to them. All the same, we may claim that our work does not lack in originality.

Since Vedic accents are not available, the quotations of mantras in Devanagari are without such accents for which our apologies.

ACKNOWLEDGEMENTS

It is my pleasant duty to acknowledge my indebtedness to many a person who assisted me in completing this Ph.D. dissertation and to publish it.

I am very grateful to the authorities of the University of Pune, particularly to Dr. S.D. Joshi, Director of the Centre of Advanced Study in Sanskrit, who granted me an opportunity to work as a Teacher Fellow for three and a half years (From July 27, 1977 to December 15, 1980) under the Faculty Improvement Scheme of U.G.C. (It may be casually mentioned here that Dr. Joshi taught me Grammar in the P.G. classes also during 1968-70 sessions.) I must not fail to thank the authorities of the Anandaram Dhenkial Phukan College, Nagaon, Assam, particularly to the then Principal, Late Md. Abdul Hye, M.A., LL.B., who kindly granted me study leave for Ph.D. work.

I am greatly indebted to my guide and teacher Dr. Keshav Pandurang Jog, now the Hon. Director of M.M. Dr. Kane Oriental Research Institute of the Asiatic Society of Bombay, the formerly Professor of Sanskrit and the Chief Editor of Sanskrit Dictionary on Historical Principles, Deccan College of Post Graduate Studies and Researches, Pune-6 (formerly Reader, Centre of Advanced Study in Sanskrit, Poona University, Pune-7); he spared no pains to see me complete my work (also he taught me lessons on the Gṛhyasūtras during the years 1968-70). To him I shall ever remain grateful and thankful. Also, I take an opportunity to thank Dr. R.P. Goswami, the then Librarian of CASS Library and his staff, who had always been ready to help me.

I must express my sincere gratitude to Dr. M.M. Sharma, Professor and Head of the Department of Sanskrit, Gauhati University, Guwahati-14, and Professor Suresh A. Upadhyaya, the Director, Post Graduate and Research Institute, Bharatiya Vidya Bhavan, Bombay-7, who inspired me to work on this Ph.D. thesis.

Besides, I must express my sincere thanks to (Retd. Profs.) Dr. G.B. Palsule, Dr. S.D. Laddu (my former teacher), Dr. V.V. Bhide, Dr. S.N. Shah, Dr. M.D. Pandit, Dr. Navathe, Dr. Ganesh Thite, (now Prof.) Dr. V.N. Jha, Dr. Shiv Kumar, Dr. S.K. Lal (all of the CASS, and Sanskrit Deptt. of Poona University), Dr. H.S. Biligiri and Head of the Department of Linguistics, Bombay University, (formerly Reader in Linguistics, Deccan College), Dr. M.A. Mehendale, Dr. N.M. Sen (Dr. Biligiri, Dr. Mehendale and Dr. Sen were my teachers), Dr. P. Bhaskar Rao, Professor, Department of Linguistics, Dr. H.C. Patyal (all of Deccan College, Pune-6) and Dr. S.K. Tiwari (of the then Maharashtra State Education Society, Pune-30 and now an officer, Kendriya Hindi Sansthan Guwahati) who by their anxious enquiries encouraged me to work hard to complete this thesis.

I thank my associates, Dr. S.P. Shrivastva, Prof. R.J. Deouskar, Dr. D. Kar, Dr. G.R. Pandeya, Dr. R.C. Misra, Dr. K.R. Tripathi, Dr. Nilima Mone, and Jayashri Sathe (who were co-research fellows at that time).

Also, I am grateful to my elder brother Shri Nripendra Nath Sarmah, Vyakarana Sastri who always have stood by me and encouraged me to pursue my higher studies; he boldly shouldered some responsibilities while I was away from home. I must not forget to thank my wife Shrimati Manomati Sarmah who braved all the sufferings during those years (1977-80) when I was away from home; she wished me success in my pursuit all the time.

I am also thankful to the authorities of Indian Council of Historical Research, New Delhi for their generous grant-in-aid towards the publication of my thesis, and Mr. N.P. Jain, Director, Motilal Banarsidass Publishers Pvt. Ltd., Delhi-7, for undertaking neat publication of this work.

AUTHOR

CONTENTS

ABBREVIATIONS

AA	Aitareya Āraṇyaka.
AB	Aitareya Brāhmaṇa.
AB	Ārṣeya Brāhmaṇa.
ABORI	Annals of the Bhandarkar Oriental Research Institute, Pune-4.
ABS	Atharvaveda Bṛhat Sarvānukrama.
Ag	Agni Purāṇa.
AgGS	Agniveśya Gṛhya Sūtra.
AIHT	Ancient Indian Historical Tradition by Pargiter.
AIOC	All India Oriental Conference.
AP	Atharvaveda Pariśiṣṭas.
APGS	Āpastaṁba Gṛhya Sūtra.
ApPitṛS	Āpastaṁba Pitṛmedha Sūtra.
APŚS	Āpastaṁba Śrauta Sūtra.
APŚSP	Āpastaṁba Śrauta Sūtra Pravarādhyāya.
AŚ	Artha Śāstra (see also KA).
AŚvGS	Āśvalāyana Gṛhya Sūtra.
AśvŚS	Āśvalāyana Śrauta Sūtra.
AŚvŚSP	Āśvalāyana Śrauta Sūtra Pravarādhyāya.
Aṣṭ	Aṣṭādhyāyī (with Kāśikāvṛtti) tr. by S. Basu.
AVC	Atharvaṇic Civilization by Karambelkar.
AVGB	Atharvaveda and Gopaṭha Brāhmaṇa, by M. Bloomfield.
AVP	Atharvaveda Paippalāda Saṁhitā.
AVS	Atharvaveda Śaunaka Saṁhitā.
AYV	Āyurveda.
BaudhGS	Baudhāyana Gṛhya Sūtra.
BaudhŚS	Baudhāyana Śrauta Sūtra.
BaudhŚSP	Baudhāyana Śrauta Sūtra Pravarādhāya.
BCSG	Bengal's Contribution to Sanskrit Grammar in the Pāṇinian and Cāndra Systems (part I) by K.C. Shastri.
BD	Bṛhaddevatā of Śaunaka.
Bd.	Brahamāṇḍa Purāṇa.
Bh	Bhāgavata Purāṇa.
BhārGS	Bhāradvāja Gṛhya Sūtra.
BhārPariS	Bhāradvāja Pariśeṣa Sūtra.

BhārPitṛS	Bhāradvāja Pitṛmedha Sūtra.
BhārŚikṣā	Bhāradvāja Śikṣā.
BhārDS	Bhāradvāja Dharma Sūtra.
BhārSS	Bhāradvāja Śrauta Sūtra.
BP	Bhāva Prakāśa of Bhāvamiśra.
BṛhU	Bṛhadarāṇyaka Upaniṣad.
Br	Brahma Purāṇa.
BUJ	Journal of Bombay University.
BV	*Bhāratiya Vidyā*, Bharatiya Vidya Bhavan, Bombay-7.
CAI	*Chronology of Ancient India* by S.N. Pradhan.
Ch.	Chapter.
ChU	Chāndogya Upaniṣad.
Comm	Commentary.
Comm. Vol.	Commemoration Volume.
CS	Caraka Saṁhitā.
CV	Caraṇavyūha.
DRg	*Date of the Ṛgveda* by D.R. Mankad.
DRV	*Der Rig Veda* by Geldner.
EBSGP	*The Early Brāhmaṇical Systems of Gotra and Pravara* by J. Brough (Translation of *Gotra Pravara Mañjarī*).
Ed	Edited by.
Edn	Edition.
ff.	following.
Fel. Vol.	Felicitation Volume.
fn.	foot-note.
GB	Gopatha Brāhmaṇa.
GPM	Gotra Pravara Mañjarī.
GPN	*Gotra Pravara Nibandha Kadaṁbakamam*, Ed. Chensalrao.
GS	Garga Saṁhitā (Purāṇic text).
HASL	*History of Ancient Sanskrit Literature* by Maxmüller (1926).
HCIP	*History and Culture of Indian People*, Published by Bharatiya Vidya Bhavan, Bombay-7.
HDS	*History of Dharaśāṣtra* by P.V. Kane.
HGAL	*Historical Geography of Ancient India* by B.C. Law (1976).
HIL	History of Indian Literature by M. Winternitz.

HOS	Harvard Oriental Series.
HR	*Hymns of the Ṛgveda* by Griffith (1973).
HSL(M)	*History of Sanskrit Literature* by Macdonell.
HSL(V)	*History of Sanskrit Literature* by C.V. Vaidya.
Hv	Harivaṁsa Purāṇa.
IVA	*India of the Vedic Age* by P.L. Bhargava.
IVK	*India of the Vedic Kalpa Sūtras* by Ramgopal.
JAOS	Journal of American Oriental Society.
JB	Jaiminīya Brāhmaṇa.
JUB	Jaiminīya Upaniṣad Brāhmaṇa.
KA	Kautilīya Arthaśāṣtra (see also AŚ).
Ka GS/KauGS	Kauśika Sūtra.
KB	Kauṣitakī Brāhmaṇa.
KŚS	Kātyāyana Śrauta Sūtra.
KS	Kāṭhaka Saṁhitā.
MBh	Mahābhārata.
Mbh	Mahābhāṣya of Paṭañjali.
MGS	Mānava Gṛhya Sūtra.
MSS	Mānava Śrauta Sūtra.
MS	Maitrāyaṇī Saṁhitā.
Ms	Manusmṛti (Manu Saṁhitā).
Mt	Matsya Purāṇa.
MU	Muṇḍakopaniṣad.
NA	Naigameya Anukramaṇī of SV.
Naigh.	Naighantuka.
Nir	Nirukta of Yāska.
NM	Nītimañjarī.
p	Page (Singular).
Pā	Pāṇini Ṣūtra (Pāṭha).
PB	Pancavimśa Brāhmaṇa (See TMB).
Pd	Padma Purāṇa.
PIHC	Proceedings of Indian History Congress.
PitṛS	Pitṛmedha Sūtra.
POIG	*Critical Studies in the Phonetic Observations of Indian Grammarians* by S. Varma.
Pp	Padapāṭha.
pp	Pages (plural).
PPOR	*Poet Philosophers of the Ṛgveda* by C.K. Raja.
PS	Pāṇinīya Śikṣā.
PS	Puṣpa Sūtra of Puṣparṣi.

PW	*Petersburg Sanskrit Wörterbuch* by Böhtlingk and Röth.
Raghu	Raghuvaṁśam of Kālidāsa.
Rām	Rāmāyaṇa of Vālmīki.
RP	Ṛgveda Prātiśākhya.
RPVU	*The Religion and Philosophy of the Vedas and Upaniṣada* by Keith.
Rt	Ṛktantra.
RV	Ṛgveda Saṁhitā.
RVVIS	*Ṛgveda*, published in Visveshwarananda Indological Series, Hoshiarpur.
RVVSM	*Ṛgveda*, Published from Vaidik Samśodhana Maṇḍala, Pune.
Sarvā	Sarvānukramaṇī of the RV.
SatyHirGS	Satyaṣāḍha Hiraṇyakeśī Gṛhya Sūtra.
SatyHirPitṛS	Satyaṣāḍha Hiraṇyakeśī Pitṛmedha Sūtra.
SatyaHirŚS	Satyaṣāḍha Hiraṇyakeśī Śrauta Sūtra.
Śānkh A	Śānkhāyana Āraṇyaka.
Śānkh B	Śānkhāyana Brāhmaṇa.
ŚānkhGS	Śānkhāyana Gṛhya Sūtra.
ŚānkhŚS	Śānkhāyana Śrauta Sūtra.
ŚB	Śatapaṭha Brāhmaṇa.
SBh	*The Sūtras of Bhāradvāja* ed. Kashikar.
SK	Skanda Purāṇa.
SP	Summary of Papers.
SR	(The) *Seers of the Ṛgveda* by Rahurkar.
SSG	*Systems of Sanskrit Grammar* by Belvelkar.
SV	Sāmaveda.
ṢḍB	Ṣaḍviṁśa Brāhmaṇa.
Taitt.	Taittiriya (school).
Taitt. P	Taittiriya Prātiśākhya.
TA	Taittiriya Āraṇyaka.
TB	Taittiriya Brāhmaṇa.
TMB	Tāṇḍya Mahābrāmhaṇa (See PB above).
TS	Taittiriya Saṁhitā.
V	Verse (singular).
Va	Vāyu Purāṇa.
VaikhGS	Vaikhānasa Gṛhya Sūtra.
VaikhŚS	Vaikhānasa Śrauta Sūtra.
Vam	Vāmana Purāṇa.

VD	Vedārtha Dīpikā of Ṣaḍguru Śiṣya.
VI	*Vedic Index* by Keith and Macdonell.
Vis	Viṣṇu Purāṇa.
VMH	*Vedische Mythologie* by Von Hillebrandt.
VMM	*Vedic Mythology* by Macdonell.
VMT	*Vedic Mythological Tracts* by Dandekar.
VP	Vājasaneyī Prātiśākhya.
VR (M)	*Vedic Reader* by Macdonell.
VR (B)	*Vedic Religion* by Bergaigne, Tr. into English by Paranjape.
Vv	Verses (Plural).
VVI	*Vaidika Vāṅmaya Kā Itihāsa* by Bhagavaddatta.
YN	*Yāska's Nirukta* by B. Bhattacharya.
YS	Yājñavalkya Smṛti.
YV	Yajurveda.

INTRODUCTION

A study of the Vedic culture would involve a consideration of number of its aspects *viz.*, its mythology, religion, philosophy, popular beliefs and superstitions, socio-political institutions and so on.[1] All these aspects show their gradual development as the Indo-Aryans (IA) kept on coming into this land in a number of waves of migrations and spread eastward in different settlements. These IA settlers lived in some scattered, even isolated, settlements and developed their own distinct family traditions, keeping, however, certain affinities with tradition of other families. This can be gathered from the hymns of the family Maṇḍalas of the RV, which are the earliest production in the world's literature; it is primarily a religious work, containing, of course, some historical traces—particularly in the so-called Dānastutis, the references in which to personal names, etc. may be said to be contemporary records of the age.[2]

The RV consists of a thousand and odd hymns which are divided into ten Maṇḍalas based on historical tradition.[3] The Maṇḍalas 2-7 are called Family Books (*Kula Maṇḍalas*), *i.e.* collections of the hymns by seers belonging to particular families. These families are: Gṛtsamada, Viśvāmitra, Vāmadeva, Atri, Bharadvāja and Vasiṣṭha. The eighth Maṇḍala contains hymns revealed to the members of the Kāṇva family and the Aṅgirases. The first Maṇḍala, too, is based on the same criterion, but it may be called a collection of the hymns of seers belonging to more than one family, and hence could be called a collection of smaller family books. The 9th and the 10th Maṇḍalas do not fall in the line with these Maṇḍalas.

Now, coming back to the early family books, we see that these family books were the contribution of the members of individual families. All those families are found to have followed and developed, in common, the cults of Indra, Agni and Soma. So also, they equally shared the same religious beliefs, mythology, magic, manners and customs. Nevertheless, each of the families distinguished itself from the rest in adhering to some uncommon cults or religious practices, mythology, (sometimes) magic and in having some special character of its own. It is noticed that members of all those families contributed a lot to the making of Indra,

Agni and Soma mythologies. The seers of these families vied with one another in eulogising the distinctive features or characteristics of these three gods. As a result, mythologies concerning these three gods swelled out of proportion. The mythologies of other gods, however important, were comparatively less popular. As such, the Aśvins, the Maruts and Uṣas appear in the second rank as regards the volume of their myths. There are some other gods who follow next. The Vedic seers belonging to each of those families contributed to the making of the mythology of all these gods. However, sometimes, one family appears to have specialised in the myth-making of one or two particular gods. Thus the Gṛtsamadas are found to have been devoted to Brahmaṇaspati (or Bṛhaspati) as their family deity, the Vāmadevas to the Ṛbhus, the Atris to the Maruts, the Bharadvājas to Pūṣan and the Vasiṣṭhas to Mitra and Varuṇa. The worship of each of these gods, within a particular family, was probably in keeping with certain traditions prevalent in that family. This sort of special worship of a particular god reveals some particular religious aspect maintained in that family's traditions. The Vāmadevas are found to be characteristically a family of mystic poets, while the Bharadvājas betray a pastoral-cum-warlike character. The Gṛtsamadas' worship of Brahmaṇaspati originated probably from ancestor worship.

This kind of worship, peculiar to each of those families, developed probably within the family or clan in certain peculiar conditions. For such a growth of each individual worship each of those families was probably keeping some distance from the others. Each family lived probably in a distinct settlement after its migration into this land and during that while, each adhered to and developed its peculiar worship of a particular deity and this gave rise to distinct mythology.

In spite of these peculiar cults followed in a family, all the families shared the common worship of Agni, Indra and Soma, who are conspicuous by their presence in every Vedic sacrifice. It is also natural that when each of these families adhered to the worship of a particular god and, side by side, shared the worship of Indra, Agni and Soma, all of them, later shared the worship of the gods who were earlier peculiar to some individual families. In other words, all the families made some adjustments with regard to their worship of the individual gods peculiar to themselves. As a result of these attitudes, they accepted the god/gods of another family and made some suitable adjustments in their religion and belief as well. Under such circumstances, mythology assumed new dimensions. Thus the family inheritance of the poetic compositions of a particular Maṇḍala does reflect the family heritage in respect of religion, mythology, magic, superstition, philosophy, ritual, manners and customs and so on.

The family of Bharadvāja is one of those who made significant contribution to the making of the Indo-Aryan culture and civilization. This family is represented by sixteen seers whose hymns are included in the extant Śākala Saṁhitā of the RV. The 6th Maṇḍala of the RV and a number of hymns in the 4th, 9th and 10th Maṇḍalas are ascribed to the members of the family Bharadvāja, the son of Bṛhaspati, who was the founder of this family. Although the Sarvā[4] ascribes to Bharadvāja Bārhaspatya as many as 59 out of 75 hymns which comprised the family book of the Bharadvājas, it is doubtful whether there is any hymn by that seer. It is rather possible that to some remote descendants of that family were revealed those hymns but were ascribed to their illustrious early ancestor. Other seers, Suhotra, Śunahotra, Nara, Garga and Ṛjiśvan are remote descendants of Bharadvāja Bārhaspatya.[4a] Śamyu may be said to be brother of Bharadvāja,[5] while Vītahavya's identity is even now doubtful.[6] The internal evidences sometimes go against the attribution of the hymns to them, yet we are to rely on the Sarvā, because no other source can help us to ascertain the ascription of the hymns to some ṛṣi or ṛṣis. Pāyu is said to be another son of Bharadvāja[7] and his name, unlike those of some other members of the family, is actually mentioned among those who received the gifts of the Bharata princes. One of these princes, Divodāsa, is mentioned in many stanzas of the 6th Maṇḍala and also in those outside the same.[7a] But it is possible to assume that most of the hymns were composed in the time of Divodāsa and Pāyu. Consequently, Bharadvāja, to whom majority of the hymns are ascribed, could probably be the father (or grandfather) of Pāyu. Thus, we consider Pāyu as an outstanding figure among the Bharadvājas who can provide some clue to ascertaining the time of the hymns of the 6th Maṇḍala.

The identity of Ajamīḍha and Purumīḍha among other seers, can be well ascertained although one cannot tell why their hymns were included in the Vāmadeva Maṇḍala (*viz.* the 4th) of the RV.[8]

The case of other seers is doubtful.[9] Nothing is certain about their relation to other Bharadvājas. In their case also we have simply to rely on the Sarvā.

Be that as it may, it is but a reality that the family was very much responsible for the growth and the development of ancient Indian culture. Particularly, the hymns of the 6th Maṇḍala bear the stamp of the Bharadvājas' age-old activities in the socio-political sphere of the early Ṛgvedic period. In their hymns in praise of Pūṣan and the cows,[10] they have left evidence of the pastoral stage of their family, while in a few Dānastutis they have preserved the unmistakable impression of the martial character of their family.[11] Of course, these hymns speak of an Atharvaṇic magic which they had successfully used in the time of war and that emphasized their relation with the Atharvāṅgirases.[11a] Their martial character is emphasized in the MBh. A legend in that Epic narrates how a Bharadvāja helped Divodāsa's son Pratardana to recover the kingdom of Kāśī from the clutches of the Haihaya-Vītahavyas.[12] Further, the legend of Droṇa Bharadvāja and his son Aśvatthāman who played prominent role in the Mahābhārata War, also, confirms our assumption that the Bharadvājas had more or less a martial character.[13] Again, the Epic tells us that the Bharadvājas upheld a long tradition of missiles and in this the Bharadvājas are comparable with the Bhṛgus whose war-like activities are equally well praised in the MBh.[14]

Another significant feature of the family is its connection with sociological problems. This family is probably one of those few families whose history shows traces of important social changes. One of these important changes is indicated in the legend of Bharadvāja's birth.[15] Bṛhaspati's sexual relation with Mamatā, the wife of his brother Ucathya, without any social inhibition or taboo probably hints at an age-old custom that was prevalent among the early IA people that may interest the student of social sciences.

Bharadvāja's alleged adoption[16] by Bharata, son of Duṣyanta, is also probably an event of still greater significance. Whether Bharadvāja himself was actually adopted or not will be discussed in the course of our study. We presume, however, that this alleged adoption had a far-reaching repurcussion on the socio-political structure within the families of the Bharadvājas and the Bharatas. It will be seen that many a Kṣatriya king was actually named as a seer of some Vedic hymns, and the term *rājarṣi* was probably more appropriate than merely *ṛṣi* in the case of Suhotra, Ajamīḍha, Mudgala, Divodāsa and Sudās etc. to whom the Sarvā ascribes some hymns. Their names figure in the genealogical list of the Bharatas—who were bifurcated into the Kurus and the Pāñcālas.[17]

It will also be seen that these Bharadvājas who were born in the line of the adopted son of Bharata gave rise to quite a large number of Kṣatriya Brāhmaṇas (*Kṣatropeta-Brāhmaṇāh*) some of whom contributed to the growth of the Vedic culture as seers or kings of royal seers. The Gargas, the Saṁkrtis, the Kaṇvas, the Mudgalas and the Mitrayus are some prominent examples.[18] This fusion of *brahman* and *kṣatra* is seen in the case of the Viśvāmitra also, who was a Kṣatriya by birth but later elevated into a Brāhmaṇa. But the case in hand shows a two-way traffic. One Bharadvāja was adopted by Bharata and he became a Kṣatriya, but subsequently he fathered both Brāhmaṇas and Kṣatriyas. This is definitely a proof of the flexibility that existed in the society of that age.

The study of this family may also help in deciding the relative chronology of a number of families of seers, *viz.*, the Kāṇvas, the Gṛtsamadas, the Viśvāmitras, the Vasiṣṭhas and the Vāmadevas. It is reasonable to expect that the relation of the Gṛtsamadas and the Kāṇvas to the Bharadvājas may be satisfactorily ascertained on the basis of the materials available directly,[19] whereas we may be able to find the relative positions of the others only in an indirect way.[20]

Turning again to the socio-political sphere, we see that each of the families maintained some sort of relation with some royal houses. There is no doubt that the seer-poets lived mostly in forest-huts and were engrossed almost all the while in ascetic and ritual practices, in the learning and teaching of all spiritual lore. But they could not keep themselves aloof from the socio-political developments taking place in the *Janapada* (country) in which Āśramas were situated. Often, the kings or princes rushed to them, seeking their guidance on the socio-religious problems, and sometimes even for succour in the event of war.[21] Some of the families of seers are found closely related to one or more princely families and have played vital role in shaping the history of the time, as they had occasion to witness action in battle, guiding the princes or maintaining the family line running in continuous succession.[22]

By way of example, we can point three important *ṛṣi* families who were attached to royal houses: (i) The Bharadvājas are found to have been closely related to the Bharatas, particularly to princes Divodāsa, Sṛñjaya's son Prastoka, and Cayamāna's son Abhyāvartin; the Bharadvājas, later served as their priests and military advisers and probably imparted instruction in the *śāstras* and *śastras* to some of those princes. (ii) Viśvāmitra's close relationship with Sudās in the early part of his rule is recorded in the RV 3, 53 and (iii) Vasiṣṭha's help to Sudās who was bounded by ten princes is vividly recorded in the well-known hymn RV 7, 18. The patron-priest relationship of the princes and the seers is portrayed in the Dānastutis 'eulogies of charity or gift' which can be taken as fragments of the historical records of the Ṛgvedic time. These historical traces are embedded in the hymns of the RV which mainly eulogise the gods and are religious in bias. Thus the Vedic hymns are of great interest to the student of history. He can regard them as history, and reconstruct from those the biography of a seer or a patron king or the history of that period. And, while doing this, he can derive additional help from other available sources such as the Epics and the Purāṇas.

The seers of the family Maṇḍalas of the RV, particularly Viśvāmitra, Vāmadeva, Atri, Bharadvāja, Visiṣṭha and Jamadagni are traditionally known as the seven seers and are, for their distinguished contribution, revered jointly. However, they originated from four main *gotras* (*mūlagotras*), Aṅgiras, Bhṛgu, Kaśyapa and Vasiṣṭha.[22a]

Another development of sociological significance to be noticed in the history of the family of Bharadvāja is the system of the *Gotra* and *Pravaras.*[23] This system of the *Gotra* and *Pravara* shows a three-fold trend: (1) In the early stages, the members of the family called themselves the Bharadvājas and adopted the three *ṛṣi-pravaras viz.*, Āṅgirasa, Bārhaspatya and Bhāradvāja. (2) In the next stage, some sub-families called themselves *Kevala* Aṅgirases. They adopted three or five *ṛṣi-pravaras* keeping Āṅgirasa alone at the head and replacing Bārhaspatya and/or Bhāradvāja by some new *ṛṣi*/*ṛṣis* nomenclature. (3) In the ultimate phase, some subclans of the Bharadvājas left the Āṅgirasa-fold and accepted the Bhṛgu-fold. Among them the Gṛtsamadas and the Mitrayus may be cited as examples.

In view of the significant role played by the seers in the making of the Vedic culture the information about the seers of the Vedic hymns or *mantras* has been emphatically considered as important ever since the beginning of the Vedic studies. BD[24] has pointedly emphasised the knowledge of the seers, metres, deities and the application of each of the Vedic *mantras* or groups of three *mantras* or of a hymn, as the case may be. It is significant to note that among these four aspects the knowledge of the seer occupies the first place.[25] Also, it has been further said that whosoever studies or recites a *mantra* without knowing its *ṛṣi*, *chandas, devatā* and *yoga* (or *viniyoga*) commits a sin.[26] Even modern critics of literary works attach primary importance to the information about the author. This practice has two reasons: (1) the knowledge of the biography of the author helps one to understand the circumstances or atmosphere prevailing at that time, and (2) the knowledge about the author's life and experiences leads one to appreciate his writing in a better way. This should hold equally good in the case of the seers of the Vedic hymns also. Sometimes, we find the background of the hymns given in the BD[27] which reports of the seer to whom the hymns were revealed. This would throw light on the environments and the psychological setting of the hymn or the *mantra* to 'seer'. A study of the groups of seers is, therefore, nothing but an attempt to search the environment and psychological background of the *mantras*.

The study of the history of a family of seers and the biography of an individual seer involves two types of literature—Vedic and Epico-Purāṇic. The Vedic literature, including the ancillaries, alone cannot give us positive results in the study of the lives of the Vedic seers. As such, one has to look into the Epico-Purāṇic sources and thereby achieve results, *viz*., a full picture of the seers under study. For long the study of the Vedas has been supplemented by that of the Epics and Purāṇas. A Purāṇic maxim says that "the study of the Veda should be amplified by (*i.e*. in the light of) Itihāsa and Purāṇa—because, the Veda is afraid of a man who has a little knowledge, for fear that he might harm it."[28] This maxim leads a student to make an effort at a quasi-historical, if not a historical interpretation of the Veda. For this, the Vedic personalities need be closely scrutinised in the light of the legends and genealogies of the kings and the seers mentioned in the Epico-Purāṇic sources. Such a study, it may be reiterated, is not of recent origin; it has its own history. Even a person of an early period like Yāska (approx. 9th century B.C.) has mentioned the existence of a school of *aitihāsikas*.[29] Naturally, therefore, this study of the lives and the thought of the Bharadvājas, who were seers of the Vedic hymns in general and the Ṛgvedic hymns in particular, will be based on a close scrutiny of the materials collected from the vast range of Vedic and Epico-Purāṇic literature which will be properly rearranged and analysed so as to have a clear picture of the sequence of events in the life of a seer and his family. This, we hope, will finally take the shape of a family chronicle.

Earlier, some scholars have attempted to study the lives of a number of individual seers and their families. Some of them are mentioned below.

K.K. Handiqui, C. Kunhan Raja, N.G. Chapekar, H.D. Velankar, V.G. Rahurkar, B.H. Kapadia, N. Bhargava, U.C. Sharma among others have brought out papers/works[30] on some individual seers and families. Among them, K.K. Handiqui attempted a study of the female seers of the RV.[31] Kunhan Raja conducted an elaborate research on the seers of the pre-Ṛgvedic and Ṛgvedic age in his work entitled *The Poet Philosophers of the Ṛgveda* (1963). N.G. Chapekar[32] wrote a number of papers on individual seers of the Vedas. Velankar[33] examined the family hymns of the family Maṇḍalas of the RV and compiled his findings in two papers. Rahurkar attempted a comprehensive study of all the RV seers in his book, *The Seers of the Ṛgveda* (1965). His work contains separate chapters on each of the families (including the Bharadvājas) of the RV, and their sketches.[34] Also, he has published a number of papers on individual seers as well. B.H. Kapadia's monograph entitled *Viśvāmitra* (1971) presents a brief account of the seers of the 3rd Maṇḍala only. N. Bhargava made a study of the Bhṛgus in her work (in Hindi) *Vaidika Sāhitya evam Saṁskṛti* (1972).[35] U.C. Sharma had a detailed investigation of two Ṛṣikulas, *viz. The Viśvāmitras and the Vasiṣṭhas* (1975).

P.L. Bhargava has, however, made a significant contribution to the study of the genealogies of the Vedic seers and kings in his work *India of the Vedic Age* (1971). He has successfully shown how much of the Epico-Purāṇic data corroborates and helps the reconstruction of the history of that period. His chapters[36] on select seers enable a student to appreciate their contribution to the development of Vedic culture.

Also, we cannot ignore the *Vedic Index of the Names and Subjects* (in two vols: first published in 1912 in the Harvard Oriental series, America) by Macdonell and Keith, which may be considered a pioneer in this field. This work sketches in brief the role of each of the Vedic seers and individuals. However, the work takes no notice of the Epico-Purāṇic sources and as such leaves scope for supplementary studies.

Pargiter's illuminating studies on the Epico-Purāṇic genealogies, *The Ancient Indian Historical Tradition* (first published in 1922) is indeed a mile-stone in this research. He has paid adequate attention to the study of the *ṛṣikulas*[37] and the royal dynasties.[38] But Pargiter's over-dependence on the Epico-Purāṇic sources is striking. It may be observed that, whereas Keith and Macdonell regard Purāṇas as baseless,[39] Pargiter accuses the Brāhmaṇic literature as lacking in historical sense and pays little attention to it.[40] Albeit this be so, the importance of Pargiter's work lies in his proper evaluation of the Epico-Purāṇic sources, rationalization of Purāṇic exaggeration, and synchronisation of the Brāhmaṇa and Kṣatriya genealogies. When these are studied along with the data available in the Vedic sources, one can expect positive and better results.

S.N. Pradhan's *Chronology of Ancient India* (1927), studies a few royal genealogies and criticises the Purāṇic sources, but has given correct names of a few kings and reconstructed the broken genealogies of royal dynasties with keen and ingenious skill. He was a torch bearer to many others similarly engaged. D.R. Mankad's monograph, *The Date of the Ṛgveda* (1952) is another work in the same strain. His observations are, however, based mainly on Pradhan's findings. V. Rangacharya's *The Pre-Musulman India, Vol. II* (Vedic India, Part I, 1937) seeks to reconstruct the genealogies of the dynasties of the pre-Bharata war, on the basis of the Vedic and Epico-Purāṇic data. Altekar in his paper "Can we Reconstruct pre-Bharata war History?" offers a study of select kings referred to in the Vedic literature with the help of the data supplied by the Epics and the Purāṇas.

Other notable works are: the articles of A.D. Pusalkar in *The Vedic Age*[41] (HCIP, Vol. 1, first published in 1951); *The Vedic History* (set in Chronology) by G.K. Pillai (1959), ***Bhārata-***

varṣa ka Bṛhad Itihāsa, Vol. 1 (1960) in Hindi by Pt. Bhagavedadatta, and *Āmacā Mahābhāratapūrva Rājakīya va Saṁskṛti cā Itihāsa* (1952) (in Marathi) by H.R. Diwekar. Recent noteworthy publications which deal with the data supplied by the Epics and the Purāṇas are: *Studies in the Proto-History of India* (1971) by D.P. Mishra; *History from the Purāṇas* (1975) by A.B.L. Awasthi; *Historical and Cultural Studies in the Purāṇas* (1978) by S.N. Roy; and *The Date of the Mahābhārata Battle* (1976) by S.B. Roy.

Again, a number of treatises on some aspects of individual Purāṇas have also appeared. Some of those are: *Matsya Purāṇa, A study* (1963) and *Vāmana Purāṇa, A study* (1964) by V.S. Agrawal; *Studies in Skanda Purāṇa*, Part I (1966), Part II (1975) by A.Bh. Awasthi; *Some Aspects of the Vāyu Purāṇa* (1933), *Matsya Purāṇa, A study* (1935), *Purāṇa Index* (3 vols—1951-52) by V.R.R. Diksitar; *Agni Purāṇa, A study* (1964) by S.D. Gyani; *Cultural History from the Vāyu Purāṇa* (1946) by D.R. Patil; *A Cultural Study of the Śrīmad Bhāgavata* (1969) by K.S. Tripathi; *A Cultural History from the Matsya Purāṇa* (1964) by S.G. Kantawala; *Studies in the Purāṇic Records on Hindu Rites and Customs* (first published in 1940); *Studies in the Upa-Puraṇas* Vol. I (1960), Vol. II (1963) by R.C. Hazra; and *Liṅga Purāṇa, A study* (1980) by N. Gangadharan. Among these only a few works have discussed the genealogies of the kings mentioned in the Purāṇas.[42]

Further, notice must be taken of the Kośas encyclopaedias (of the names of persons or places, etc.). These fall in the line with *the Vedic Index* by Macdonell and Keith. Notable among these are: *Prācīna Bhāratīya Caritrakośa* by Citrava Shastri (Marathi, 1963 and Hindi, 1964); *Mahābhārata Index* by Sorensen (1963); *Vālmīki Rāmāyaṇa Kośa* by R.K. Ray (1965); *Bhārata Manīṣa* by A.N. Sharma (Assamese, 1964); *Bhāratakośa* by H.N. Sharma Dalai (Assamese, 1977); *Puraṇika Kośa* by R.P. Sharma (Hindi 1973); *Purāṇic Encyclopaedia* by Vettam Mani (1975), and *Mahābhārata Kośa* by Ramkumar Roy (5 parts, 1964-82). All these works contain short but unconnected and non-committal accounts of the Vedic and the Epico-Purāṇic personages.

It is nevertheless regretable that the numerous works based on the Vedic and the Epico-Purāṇic sources, have little to say about the seers and sages of the Bharadvāja family. The so-called *Kośas* give us only brief sketches of some of the Bharadvājas. Bhagavaddatta,[43] Pradhan[44] and Mankad[45] also have taken casual and brief entries about the Bharadvājas. Only Pargiter[46] paid some attention to the Bharadvājas who appear only in some occasional discussions. His observations on Bharadvājas (among other Aṅgirases) are nevertheless, very striking. Rahurkar[47] devotes a full chapter to their family. He has given a broad biographical sketch of Bharadvāja Bārhaspatya against the socio-historical background in the Vedic and the Epico-Purāṇic sources. However, he has left unused material for the reconstruction of their family history. Most of the legends did not receive his full attention. What is more, all other seers of the family have been mentioned by him merely by name. S.D. Satavalekar also has given a brief pen-picture of Bharadvāja Bārhaspatya in his not-too brief *Introduction to the 'Bharadvāja Ṛṣikā Darśana'* (Hindi).[48] But he, too, did not take into account most of the materials recorded in the Epics and the Purāṇas. He has not discussed any other member of the family. F. Wilhelm appears to have made an attempt to collect the data on a number of Bharadvājas from the Brāhmaṇical Buddhist and Jaina sources in his *Politische Polemiken im Staatslehrbuch des Kauṭilya* (1960)[49] but had no consistent treatment. Even P.L. Bhargava deals with the seers of the Bhāradvāja family among the Aṅgirases but only briefly.[50]

Sources of our study

Two main sources must be mentioned: (1) Original or Primary which comprise texts, commentaries, glosses, etc. and (2) Secondary and Tertiary sources, critical of the primary ones. The latter can be divided mainly into two categories: (i) The Vedic and (ii) the Epico-Purāṇic. These are:

(*i*) Vedic
- (*a*) All the Saṁhitās, 'collections of Mantras',
- (*b*) All the Brāhmaṇas including the Āraṇyakas and Upaniṣads,
- (*c*) The Sūtra literature, and
- (*d*) The ancillary texts.

(*ii*) The two Epics:
- (*a*) The Rāmāyaṇa, and
- (*b*) The Mahābhārata.

(1) The Early Major Purāṇas:
 (*a*) Vāyu,
 (*b*) Brahmāṇḍa,
 (*c*) Matsya,
 (*d*) Mārkaṇḍeya, and
 (*e*) Viṣṇu.

(2) The late Major Purāṇas:
 (*f*) Bhāgavata,
 (*g*) Brahma,
 (*h*) Harivaṁśa,
 (*i*) Agni and
 (*j*) Brahmavaivarta.

Among the Vedic Saṁhitās, the RV stands the foremost and the material supplied by it has to be taken as the earliest information in regard to any individual or event. The RV Saṁhitā is primarily a literary work tinged with religious fervour. Whatever information (regarding a historical personage or incident) is gleaned from it is considered as the reflection or impression of some socio-political happening of those days. We can rely upon these, for they may be taken to have been narrated by the seers who could directly witness them.

The SV Saṁhitā derives all but 75 verses from the RV and thus claims no originality or quasi-historicity. The two Saṁhitās of the AV *viz.* the Śaunaka and the Paippalāda, also contain information, important from the cultural point view. The various Saṁhitās of the YV also present some material, sufficiently advanced in comparison with other Saṁhitās.

The Brāhmaṇas belonging to various Vedas are also considered veritable mine of reliable information, except at some places where the texts have described only myths, which can however be converted into legends about historical or semi-historical facts or persons. In many cases, nevertheless, they give some authentic information complementary to that of the Vedic Saṁhitās, the Epics, and the Purāṇas. Some Upaniṣads outline the *vaṁsas* of the teachers of Vedic lores; and thus supply some significant facts about the seers and the teachers.

The numerous Sūtras—mainly the so-called Kalpa-Sūtras—contain very important data. Some of the notable sacrificers and teachers of different schools are often mentioned in these texts, *e.g. Pravarādhyāya* or *Pravara-Kāṇḍa* or *Khaṇḍa* (appended to a number of Śrauta Sūtras). These texts list at length the *gotras* and *pravaras* of the Brāhmaṇa families, and, in some cases, of the Kṣatriyas, too. These gave rise to a class of literature called *nibaṅdhas* (descriptions of Brāhmaṇa families). These *Pravarakāṇḍas* are of immense use while dealing with the *ṛṣikulas* (families of seers).

The Vedic ancillaries form an important class of literature by themselves. Foremost among these, are the BD and the Sarvā that relate to the RV. The BD is replete with numerous important stories and legends. The BD narrates birth legends and abridges genealogies of the seers; these help us not only in interpreting the Ṛgvedic verses in proper perspective but also in reconstructing the biographies of individual seers and their family histories. Also it provides the background of some significant hymns. For examples, the BD gives a vivid legend of Pāyu extending timely help to the Princes Abhyāvartin Cāyamāna and Sṛñjaya, leading to the composition of the Saṁgrāma hymn (as we shall see later). The observations in the BD upon the *Dānastutis* of the RV are equally noteworthy. Sometimes, the Sarvā supplies remarkable details (*e.g.* Sarvā 2, 6, 52) about seers of the hymns in the 6th Maṇḍala. And the VD of Ṣaḍguruśiṣya provides a fuller exposition of the legends of the BD and this gives its importance. Besides this the Ārṣānukramaṇī attributed to Śaunaka, has a lot to say about the seers of the hymns. The other three Vedas, too, have their own Anukramaṇīs, *viz.* the Naigameya Anukramaṇī of the SV, the Vājasaneyī Sarvānukrama of the white YV and the Bṛhatsarvānukramaṇī of the AVŚ; these help us to identify authors of the *mantras*. They, however, lack in originality and follow the pattern of the Sarvā of RV.

Again, the various commentaries, *viz.* those of Skandasvāmin, Veṅkaṭamādhava and Sāyaṇa, establish the worth of their material.

The second type of primary works, the Epics and the Purāṇas, are valuable sources. The Rām of Vālmīki narrates the legends of the seers and the kings, particularly of the solar race. Among others, we have four narratives on Bharadvāja, and his spacious Āśrama; these are rich in details. The other Epic, *viz.* the MBh, provides a several accounts of more than one Bharadvāja, and two genealogical lists of the post-Bharata kings, right up to the Mahābhārata War. Its accounts of Suhotra Vaitithina help in reconstructing the genealogy of the Bhāradvāja family. But the two genealogies contained in MBh 1, 89 and 90 do not mutually agree on many points; and that raises fresh problems.

The Purāṇas are a dependable source for our study, in as much as they list not only the long genealogical tables of kings and *gotra* of the Brāhmaṇas, but also the legends of princes and seers. The early Purāṇas, however, do not agree with the later Purāṇas in respect of the genealogy of the Bharatas which overlaps that of the Bharadvājas. However, all the Purāṇas are in broad agreement. Further, the early Purāṇas, more or less, corroborate the genealogy given in MBh 1, 89 while the later Purāṇas endorse that in MBh 1, 90. Thus the researchers are bound to accept the authenticity of either genealogy in Purāṇas or the Epics. To us the early Purāṇic version, appears to be genuine and, therefore, authentic, and not that of the later Purāṇas. The merit of the early Purāṇas lies, further, in the fact that they more or less corroborate the evidence contained in the Vedic and the ancillary texts.

Again, the names of the seers, the sages and the kings are often wrong (probably due to poor knowledge of scribes) to such an extent that they baffle, sometimes, the investigator(s). Nevertheless, it is gratifying to note that the scholars like S.N. Pradhan[50] and F.E. Pargiter[51] have ably made some corrections. But a good many errors still await similar treatment.

Method and Approach

We have dealt with the materials collected from the various original texts from the RV to the Purāṇas. We have analysed these materials, correlated consistent data, and then reconstructed events and biographies. We have evaluated the Vedic evidences to see if it is supported by that from the Epics or the Purāṇas. We have made an attempt to overcome any apparent absurdity in every legend and explained the same in a way that it does not get out of contexts. Also, we have presented a rational analysis of events or legends in this dissertation. A critical assessment of every datum is also provided at the end of every item of information and conclusions drawn there from these.

We have already said that the Epico-Purāṇic texts need correction(s). In correcting a debased passage or name in the Epico-Purāṇic sources, we generally searched for a counter-part of the same from Vedic texts, for it is an accepted fact that they were preserved with meticulous care and were guarded from any error creeping into them it. Numerous Śikṣās and Prātiśākhyas speak volumes about it. So also the different *pāṭhas* (texts for reciting) of the Vedic *mantras* serve this very end. Thus, we can very safely rely upon a form found in the Vedic text, when in doubt about the one in the Epic(s) and the Purāṇas(s).

While examining numerous legends relating to persons bearing the same or similar name(s) we have taken into consideration the time, the place, the parentage, the descent and the contemporaneity of the person(s) related to him. This criterion is adopted by us for reasons stated in appropriate places. It may, however, be pointed out just here that (1) Bharadvāja is a proper name of a seer, who was the son of Bṛhaspati, and the progenitor of a family known after him. Thus, subsequently, his descendants adopted the partronymic Bhāradvāja (Where the initial vowel is long due to the suffix[51a] added to Bharadvāja). But the texts did not, at many times, observe this grammatical rule and pronounced the initial vowel as short one. Thus, in the course of time, there arose lot of confusion as to the persons having the same (patronymic) name(s). Further confusion was caused by dropping their proper names. A venerable sage or his descendants (who were equally honoured) were rarely called by their proper names, but were known only by their surnames. (2) A person called Bharadvāja cannot live, or continue to live, at the pre-Bharata age and also at the post-Bharata age or in the age of the Mahābhārata War. At the most, the life-span of and individual, in the Vedic age, was accepted as spread over a hundred years. Thus, it would be inconsistent to state that Bharadvāja, the priest of Divodāsa of the Kāśī dynasty, lived for a period covering more than 30 generations, each the span of being over 30 years. (3) Besides, each of the Bharadvājas, (i) associated with Divodāsa of Kāśī, (ii) the priest of Divodāsa, Sṛñjaya and Abhyāvartin, and (iii) one living at Prayāga at the Rāma age, are found to have lived in different localities and periods and associated with different persons. Although some of the seers lived a free-life and moved around wherever they liked, they could not be said to have lived in numerous places and at different times as the officiating priests of different Princes. Thus, the identifications of the persons of the same name may not be devoid of errors. They can, however, be called members of the family of Bharadvāja or his descendants.

In Part I of this dissertation we have presented detailed biographical sketches of those seers of the Bhāradvāja family who have made significant contribution to the Vedic culture. Together with them, we have also treated some sages (*munis*) to whom no hymn or *mantra* of any of the four Vedas was revealed. As such, we have deliberately given to this part the title 'The Seers and the sages of the Bhāradvāja family'.

In Chapter I, we have collected all the important textual evidences regarding the Bharadvājas. The references here are impersonal rather than personal, often relating to one or more persons—and these pose problems of identification. In certain cases, the criteria of time and space and of personal association are the determinants. Still, their identity remains shrouded in obscurity. Some of the material is shifted to other SECTIONS, READ DISCUSSION. In this Chapter, the references from the RV to the Upaniṣads are arranged in their chronological order. The section on the Rām is added to this Chapter. And a section on the seers mentioned in the hymns of the Bharadvājas is also included, findings of this section may prove useful subsequently.

In Chapter 2, we have grouped all Bharadvājas (from Epico-Purāṇic sources) whose sons and descendants are clearly mentioned. The most outstanding problems treated here are the legends of the birth of Bharadvāja Bārhaspatya and the adoption of Bharadvāja (Vidathin). We have viewed the two legends about him separately, unlike the versions of both the Purāṇas—Mt and Va.[52] And we justify our treatment of the subject. Another legend of importance is that of Bharadvāja, Divodāsa and Vītahavya. We have treated it just after Vidathins, as the Purāṇas treat the legend of the adoption of Bharadvāja (Vidathin) immediately after the legend of his birth referred to above. It would have been logical, had we placed Bharadvāja, the priest of Divodāsa of Kāśī, just after that legend, following Pargiter[53] that this Bharadvāja was the son of Bṛhaspati. Next to this legend comes that of Yavakrīta and his father Bharadvāja. We consider that this Bharadvāja was born earlier than the father of Srucāvatī and Droṇācārya. Because of the striking similarity of the legends of the births of Srucāvatī and Droṇa, they are placed in juxtaposition. The other legends, relating to some (other) Bharadvājas are considered in later sections, in view of the sequence of the texts or the lack of definite identity of persons.

In Chapter 3, we have treated all those seers whose hymns are included in the extant Śākala Saṁhitā of the RV. Precedence is given to those seers whose hymns comprised the 6th Maṇḍala, *i.e.* the Family Book of the Bharadvājas. Next rank seers of the hymns included in the 4th, 9th and 10th Maṇḍalas. While dealing with the first five seers, *viz.*, Suhotra, Śunahotra, Nara, Garga and Ṛjiśvan, we have followed the arrangement of their hymns in the 6th Maṇḍala and the Sarvā's reference to them. Pāyu is the sixth, because the BD[54] has provided us with some definite information about his relation with Bharadvāja and his hymn (*viz.*, the Saṁgrāma Sūkta), comes at the close of the 6th Maṇḍala. Next to Pāyu is Ajamīḍha followed by Purumīḍha (who are said to be descendants of Suhotra Bhāradvāja) and the seers belonging to the Aṅgirases. Their identity has helped us to give them priorities over the remaining seers—also said to be the Bharadvājas. As regards the identity of Vasu, Śiriṁbiṭha, Śāsa, Sapratha and Rātrī nothing is definitely known from any source—Vedic or post-Vedic. We have accepted them as the seers of the Ṛgvedic hymns on the basis of the statements in the Sarvā which may had traditional basis.

In Chapter 4, we have discussed Śaṁyu Bārhaspatya and Vītahavya Āṅgirasa. We did not talk about them in the last chapter, because they are nowhere called Bharadvājas. According to the Sarvā[55] and Va,[56] Śaṁyu is a son of Bṛhaspati; and probably a brother of Bharadvāja; hence his hymns are included among those of the other Bharadvājas. Therefore, we have assessed him separately in this chapter. To him we have added Vītahavya, whose identity is, in spite of our best effort, not yet correctly established. But he is called an Āṅgirasa and he is optionally said to be the seer of RV 6, 15 and is mentioned in RV 6, 15, 2 and 3. Hence, treatment in this chapter.

Chapter 5 deals with Divodāsa Atithigva *vis-a-vis* Bharadvāja. The Divodāsa issue had cropped up occasionally but could not be resolved earlier that would be digressing from the history of the Bhāradvāja family. But its addition, at least as an appendix was necessary to know the socio-political background of that family.

All these five chapters reconstruct the early history of the Bharadvājas and point to their socio-historical importance.

Part II of this dissertation contains a brief discussion on the legacy of the Bharadvājas. It would not be an exaggeration to state that this family has made contribution to almost all the aspects of our multi-faced culture; the topics here are representative of those. In this assessment, we have depended only on published sources of merit. Part II is divided into two chapters, one (Ch. 6) deals with Vedic themes, while the other (Ch. 7) deals with Post-Vedic survey of various contributions of the Bhāradvāja family.

In Chapter 6, Section (i)-(iii) we evaluated only the most significant contribution of the Bharadvājas from the RV Maṇḍala VI, *viz.*, the Pūṣan hymns 53-58, the family hymn(s), *i.e.* RV 6, 28 and 47; the Saṁgrāma-Sūkta, *i.e.* hymn RV 6, 75; and the Gosūkta (RV 6, 27).

In Chapter 6, Section (iv) we notice the Sāmans ascribed to the Bharadvājas while Section (v) Gṛhya deals with the Śrauta, the and the Pitṛmedha Sūtras the manuals of ritual. In Chapter 7, section (i) we discussed the Rājaśāstra or Science of Polity ascribed to the Bharadvājas.

In Chapter 7, Section (ii)-(iii) pertains to the phonetical observations in the Bhāradvāja Śikṣā and the Grammatical references of Bhāradvāja and Gārgya collected from different works on Grammar.

The next Section is based on the traditional information about Bharadvāja as the protagonist of Āyurveda.

Section (v) deals with the Garga Saṁhitā, which is thought to be a Pañcarātra text and narrates a number of the Kṛṣṇa legends in a Purāṇic style.

A chapter was proposed to be based on the Bhāradvāja Saṁhitā,[57] a Pañcarātra text on *Prapatti* 'devotion', but had to be dropped, as the text could not be procured from any source within time.

We have said above that Wilhelm collected the data on a number of Bharadvājas from Brāhmanical, Buddhist and Jaina sources in his *Politische Polemiken in Staatslehrbuch des Kautilya* (1960). However, for the present, we deal with the material collected from Brāhmanical sources only, relegating the other sources to a later research.

There are two appendices. The first appendix on Bāṣkala and Bāṣkali Bhāradvājas gives an idea of the Bharadvājas' contribution to propagation of the Vedic texts and their relation to the Bāṣkala

Śākhā of the RV. The second appendix outlines some facts about the Gotras and Pravaras of the Bharadvājas. It also lists their *gotras*. It is hoped that this appendix may provide a fuller picture of that family.

Notes and References

1. For works on different aspects of the Vedic culture, see our Select Bibliography.

2. Pargiter, AIHT p. 10.

3. Cf. HIL. Vol. 1, part 1 p. 50.

4. 2, 6, 1: *bārhaspatyo bharadvājah saṣṭham maṇḍalam apaśyat* 'Bharadvāja, the son of Bṛhaspati saw the sixth Maṇḍala'; this statement holds good for majority of the hymns wherein the seers are not specifically mentioned. For detailed discussion see Part I, Ch. 2, section (i).

4a. See Part I, Ch. 3, Section (i)-(v).

5. See Part I, Ch. 4, Section (i).

6. See Part I, Ch. 4, Section (ii).

7. See Part I, Ch. 3, Section (vi) and Part II, Ch. 1, Section (ii).

7a. See Part I, Ch. 5.

8. See Part I, Ch. 3, Sections (i), (vii) and (viii).

9. See Part I, Ch. 3, Sections (ix) to (xiii). Seers in these sections have definite historical background. The Sarvā, at different places, however, calls them Bhāradvāja and ascribes to them a number of hymns. Thus, we could not ignore the traditional view of the Sarvā which forms a pillar of Vedic studies.

10. Part II, Ch. 1, Sections (i) and (iii) discuss the Pūṣan-cult and mythology and the cow-worship and shows that the family of Bharadvāja was connected with pastoral tribe, even if they were not.

11. Some of the Dānastutis contained in RV 6, 27 and 6, 47, 22-25 are discussed in the Part II, Ch. 1, Section (ii) and the martial character of the family brought out therein.

11a. Hymns RV 6, 47, 26-31 and 6, 75 are of Atharvaṇic character and discussed in Part II, Ch. 1, Section (ii).

12. See Part I, Ch. 2, Section (iv).

13. See Part I, Ch. 2, Section (vi).

14. While making this statement, we had at the back of our mind the activities of Paraśūrāma. For details on the Bhṛgus see Sukthankar's "*The Bhṛgus and the Bharatas*", ABORI, 18 pp. 1-76 and also R. Goldman: *Gods, Priest and Warriors*, Introduction, pp. 1-8.

15. The legend on Bharadvāja's brith was detailed in Part I, Ch. 2, Section (ii) as also its sociological significance.

16. Our conclusion is that Bharata could not have adopt Bharadvāja Bārhaspatya at all. He might have met Vidathin Bhāradvāja, a descendant of Bharadvāja Bārhaspatya, probably for raising a son on his own wife by way of *niyoga*. See Part I, Ch. 2, Section (iii) Cf. also concluding remarks.

17. For a detailed discussion on the problem, see Pargiter's AIHT pp. 110-19.

18. See Part I, Ch. 3, Sections (ii), (iii) and (vii). Pargiter has devoted a full chapter on the Kṣatriya Brāhmaṇas; see AIHT, pp. 243-52.

19. See Part I, Ch. 3, Section (ii) and (vii) for the position of Gṛtsamada and Kaṇvas among the Bharadvājas.

20. The position of Vasiṣṭha and Viśvāmitra can be ascertained through the Bharatas.

21. See Part I, Ch. 2, Section (iv) and Ch. 3, Section (vi) for a discussion on how the Bharadvājas rushed to the help of Divodāsa of Kāśi and Abhyāvartin Cāyamāna.

22. Vidathin's adoption by Bharata or a possible *niyoga* through him is a pointer here.

22a. Read: मूलगोत्राणि चत्वारि समुत्पन्नानि पार्थिव ।
अंगिरा: कश्यपश्चेव वसिष्ठो भृगुरेव च ॥ (MBh 12, 165, 17; 12, 69, 11)

23. We have devoted chapter exclusively to the system of Gotra and Pravara and added to the bulk of the work as an appendix. Casually we have discussed this system in connection with a certain seer also.

24. BD 8, 135: ऋषिच्छन्दोदैवतादि ज्ञानं यज्ञादिषु श्रुतम् ।
तदाश्रित्य प्राणादृष्टिर्विहितात्रेति गम्यताम् ॥

25. Ibid 8, 138: ऋषिं तु प्रथमं ब्रूयाच् छन्दस्तु तदनन्तरम् ।
देवतामथ मन्त्राणां कर्मस्वेवमिति श्रुतिः ॥

26. Ibid 8, 136: अविदित्वा ऋषिं छन्दो दैवतं योगमेव च ।
योऽध्यापयेज्जपेद्वापि पापीयाञ्जायते तु सः ॥

27. For example, the BD gives the background of the hymns RV 6, 27; 47 and 75. See Part II, Ch. 1, Section (ii) for a detailed discussion on it.

28. Va 1, 201: इतिहासपुराणाभ्यां वेदं समुपबृंहयेत् ।
बिभेत्यल्पश्रुताद्वेदो मामयं प्रहरिष्यति ॥

29. Yāska quotes the Aitihāsika School thrice vide. Nir. 2, 16; 12, 1; 10.

30. Refer to our Bibliography for their works.

31. IA; 50.

32. See Bibliography, especially, of Papers and Articles.

33. "Family hymns in the family Maṇḍalas," ABBRS, 18, 1942.

34. SR pp. 89-113.

35. Read note 14 above.

36. IVA pp. 166-92.

37. AIHT pp. 184-243.

38. Ibid pp. 77-175.

39. VI 2, 187. Cf. A.B.L. Awasthi, *History from the Purāṇas*, p. 1, for comment on Macdonell and Keith's remark.

40. AIHT. pp. 2 and 9.

41. pp. 271-323.

42. D.R. Patil, K.S. Tripathi, Kantawala have briefly discussed the genealogies in their works.

43. *Bhāratavarṣa kā Bṛhat Itihāsa*, vol. 2 pp. 148 ff.

44. CAI pp. 1-19; only casual references in relation with Divodāsa.

45. DṚg. pp. 2 ff.

46. AIHT pp. 159-64; 220-24.

47. SR pp. 89-113.
48. Introduction, pp. 1-7.
49. pp. 174 ff.
50. *Op. cit.* p. 2 ff.
51. In the first few chapters, Pargiter has discussed similar problems in great detail, as also the names in Chapter XI, pp. 126ff of AIHT.

51a. Vide Pā 7, 2, 117: तद्धितेष्वचामादेः ।

52. Va 99, 135ff.; Mt 49, 17ff.
53. AIHT pp. 162, 220.
54. 5, 124-42.
55. Sarvā 2, 6, 44.
56. Va 71, 36-37.
57. The Bharadvāja Saṁhitā has been published in four different editions: (i) Mysore, Sadvidya Press, 1894 (Telegu script); (ii) ed. Khamaraja Srikrishna, Bombay, 1905. (Devanagari Script), (iii) Ananda Press, Madras, 1912 (*Devanagari* Script); (iv) ed. by Pancanadiya Vedanta Govindacarya Misra (with Hindi commentary by the Editor) Calcutta, 1922 (*Devanagari* script).

The work consists of 400 ślokas divided into four chapters. "In it *prapatti*, both as an attitude and as liturgical sacrament, is given marked attention" (Smith, Bibliography, p. 316).

The work may be summarised from Smith's Bibliographical notes pp. 316ff. thus:

Its Chapter 1 discusses *prapatti* 'good behaviour' and how sin is removed. Sage Bharadvāja in reply to the questions of the other sages says that *prapatti* is described in Vedas, Vedānta, Dharma and Pañcarātra. He defines it as a total dependence on a means of action offered to god, knowing that the desired object can only thus be attained. Then he describes *prapatti* in three categories. The sub-types of each of those three also are, stated there. Qualities of an *ācārya* and the qualifications of a *śiṣya* are enumerated. The next section deals with *vṛtti* 'general conduct' to be followed by a *prapanna* 'devotee'.

Chapter 2 deals with the procedure for Pañcasaṁskāras and the symbolism there of. The next chapter deals with the way of life of a *prapanna*. The habits of a *prapanna* include: daily worship, honouring the Vaiṣṇava Brāhmins, *prāṇāhūti* before meals, observing dietary rules, keeping up divine studies.

Chapter 4 deals with the things of a *prapanna* is expected to avoid. The *prapanna* has as his sole object in life the service of God. And to achieve that he is to avoid entertaining unorthodox ideas about his faith, he must resist deviations from his regular religious routine; he must abstain from spoiling his *puṇḍra* marks and take care not to sacrifice such gains as he may have, on account of his religious practices through carelessness.

According to Smith (Bibliography p. 316) the Bhāradvāja Saṁhitā presupposes Srivaiṣṇavism of Rāmānuja (1017-1137 A.D.) and hence the date of the work cannot be prior to the *ācārya*.

PART ONE

SEERS AND SAGES BELONGING TO THE BHĀRDVĀJA FAMILY: HISTORY

CHAPTER ONE

TEXTUAL EVIDENCES

(i) *Bharadvāja(s) in the Ṛgveda*

Bharadvāja is mentioned 19 times in the RV; twelve times in singular and seven times in plural.[1] Further, the derivatives *bharadvājavát*[2] 'like Bharadvāja' or 'accompanied by Bharadvāja' and *bhāradvāja*[3], a descendant of Bharadvāja', each occur once in RV. To these references may be added, only with grave doubt, one more *viz.*, RV 6, 26, 6 where 'metronymic' *vājineya* 'a son of Vājinī' occurs.[4]

Rahurkar[5] holds the view that the singular form should stand for the progenitor of the family, *i.e.*, Bharadvāja I, the *Gotrakāra* and the plural for the family or its members; and the derivative Bhāradvāja is to be taken in the sense of his descendants. While agreeing to the second and the third suggestions, we cannot concede the first, for it does not appear to be consistent. All the references to Bharadvāja in the singular form cannot be taken to mean Bharadvāja I, *i.e.* the progenitor of the family. For, a reference to a particular person should be considered on the basis of space and time and also of his association with someone else, *i.e.*, his parentage and descendance. Besides, while considering a Vedic poet-priest, one should consider his relation with the patron-king as a determining factor. Thus a reference to Bharadvāja even in the singular may be considered on the basis of these and allied factors.

Bharádvāja is said to be the originator to a *gotra, viz.*, Bhāradvāja, and it continued to be attached to the personal names of the descendants of that *gotra.* Everyone belonging to the family had definitely a personal name, but he was more often known by his family name or surname than by his personal name. Thus, in most of the cases, the personal names are lost to us, while different persons came to be known by the one and the same family name *viz.,* 'Bhāradvāja'. Here also difficulties arose. Sometimes, Bhāradvāja has been replaced by Bharádvāja. This sort of 'false identification' has misled some modern scholars like Pradhan[6] and Rahurkar,[7] for, they have not proved invulnerable to the tendency of offering such identification. This is why we do not agree to Rahurkar's first suggestion of interpreting an occurrence of the name 'Bharádvāja' in the singular. Indeed, it would be a serious lapse on our part, if we concede that a person outlives a number of other persons successively for several generations. It might be that Bharadvāja lived an unusually long life as is said in AB 1, 2, 6, or he lived for three spans of lives, each consisting of a hundred years, as we have seen elsewhere.[8] On the basis of some such passages we cannot say that the same Bharadvāja who lived prior to Bharata Dauṣyanti continued to live in the age of the Pāṇḍava Yudhiṣṭhira, to see the mortally wounded Devavrata Bhīṣma at the end of the Kurukṣetra war. Thus there is need to separate one Bharádvāja, living in the life span of Bharata, from the other, still alive after the Kurukṣetra war. While considering the Ṛgvedic passages we shall have to abide by some norms to arrive at nearly accurate results.

From a cursory look at the Ṛgvedic passages that mention Bharádvāja, it is clear that most of the occurrences are from the 6th Maṇḍala, only five other passages are from the 1st and 10th Maṇḍalas, while other seven Maṇḍalas are conspicuously silent about Bharadvāja! And curiously enough, those poets who have mentioned Bharadvāja outside the 6th Maṇḍala are also found to have belonged to the Āṅgirasa stock, to which the Bharadvājas also do.[9]

At RV 1, 112, 13 Bharádvāja is referred to by the poet Kutsa Āṅgirasa. The poet asks the Gods: "O Aśvins, by whatever aids you have protected Bharádvāja, the wise, by those (aids) do you protect us!"[10] The passage states that Bharadvāja was a protége of the Aśvins long before the poet Kutsa flourished and the twin divinities had extended their much sought help to the wise (*vipra*) Bharadvāja. Again, a Bharádvāja as a protégé of the Aśvins is mentioned in RV 1, 116, 8 along with Divodāsa. It is to be noted that this verse (*i.e.*, the hymn) is ascribed to the poet Kakṣīvat. Kakṣīvat is said to be the son of Dīrghatamas, the uterine brother of Bharádvāja Bārhaspatya. And it is probable that this Bharadvāja had certain relation with Divodāsa, who might have been a prince.[11] Thus it is difficult to say, whether Bharadvāja, mentioned by Kutsa is the same Bharadvāja who is mentioned together with Divodāsa by Kakṣīvat—even the age of the poet is to be considered in relation to the age of Bharadvāja and Divodāsa! It is also worth noting that there are two hymns, *viz.*, 62-63 in the 6th

Maṇḍala of the RV, which are dedicated to the Aśvins and ascribed to the seer Bharádvāja Bārhaspatya. At RV 6, 63, 10 the poet, while addressing the Aśvins, says that Purupántha gave Bharadvāja thousands of steeds. This is a solitary instance where Purupántha is mentioned[12] as the patron of Bharadvāja, for no other text refers to him. It is also probable that a junior member belonging to the family of Bharadvāja might have seen the hymn in question and referred to Bharadvāja and his patron Purupántha here. But (the) Bharadvāja, who was patronised by Divodāsa, as mentioned in RV 1, 116, 18, is to be distinguished from (the) one under the patronage of Purupántha in this verse.

RV 6, 16, 33 also mentions Bharadvāja. Here the poet (who according to the Sarvā 2, 6, 16 is Bharadvāja himself) asks the God Agni: "Give a far reaching and wide shelter to Bharadvāja, O conquering Lord! Send coveted wealth, O Agni!"[13] The other two passages showing Bharadvāja as a protége of Agni are RV 1, 59, 7 and RV 6, 15, 3 in the first Puruṇītha Śātavaneya and, in the second, Vītahavya are mentioned along with Bharadvāja. Puruṇītha is mentioned in RV 7, 9, 6 also. Macdonell and Keith[14] say that "Puruṇītha Śātavaneya ('a descendant of Śātavani') is the name of a sacrificer or perhaps a priest, a Bharadvāja in RV 1, 59, 7. It is doubtful whether he (Puruṇītha) is the same who as a singer occurs in yet another passage (*viz.* RV 7, 9, 6). The Purāṇic lists of kings or seers do not contain this name. His name is nowhere in the list of the *Gotras* of Bharadvājas.

Vītahavya is mentioned at RV 6, 15, 2, 3 and RV 7, 19, 3. The Sarvā 2, 6, 15 ascribes hymn RV 6, 15 to Vītahavya optionally with Bharádvāja. Nothing can be said with certainty as to whether Vītahavya was a singer-priest or a king.[15] Sāyaṇa gives two interpretations of the first passage; particularly the expression: *vītahavyāya bharadvājāya* where he takes *bharádvāja* as an attribute qualifying Vītahavya. He says: *bharadvājāya saṁbhṛtalakṣaṇāya vītahavyāya*' 'to Vītahavya who is known as possessor of food'. Here, Vītahavya is taken as a person possibly the poet of the hymn as suggested by Kātyāyana at the Sarvā 2, 6, 15. In the alternative interpretation, Sāyaṇa takes *vītahavya* as an attribute to Bharádvāja, (obviously accepting this second) as the poet of the hymn RV 6, 15, and he says: *vītaṁ gamitaṁ havyaṁ havir yena tādṛśāya bharadvājāya iti vā yojyaṁ* ("or it is applicable to Bharadvāja who has offered oblation").[16]

In the hymn RV 6, 48, ascribed to Śaṁyu Bārhaspatya, Bharadvāja is twice mentioned; the verse 7 runs thus: *bṛhadbhir agne, arcibhiḥ śukréṇa deva śocīṣā/bharadvāje samidhāno yaviṣṭhya revān naḥ śukra dīdihi/dyumát pāvaka dīdihi//* ("With your high flames, O Agni, with your bright glow, O God, kindled among Bharadvāja(s), O you youngest one, shine on us richly, O you white one, shine brightly, O you purifier").[17] That Bharadvāja was a devotee of Agni is established. At v. 13 of the same hymn, Bharadvāja is again referred to: *bharádvājāya áva dhukṣata dvitā́ dhenúm ca viśvádohasaṁ íṣam ca viśvábhojasaṁ* ("For Bharadvāja (O Maruts) you give two-fold (gift) namely you milked the cow that pours milk for all and food that gives nourishment to all").[18] *viśvádohas dhenú* 'the milch-cow yielding milk for all', constitute, as a matter of fact, *vāja* 'food, nourishment, strength, etc.' held by Bharadvāja, because of which he is so called. Similar ideas can be gleaned from yet some more verses. For example, at RV 6, 17, 14 it is said: *sá no vājāya śrávasa isé ca rāyé dhehi dyumáta índra víprān/bharadvāje nṛváta indra sūrín diví ca smaídhi pārye na indra//* (Which Velankar[19] translates as: "Such as you are, lead us, the glorious priests, to strength, fame, food, riches, oh Indra. (Bestow) on Bharadvājas rich patrons who are possessed of brave sons, oh Indra. And be ours, oh Indra, on the decisive day.").

Vāja is paraphrased here as *śravas* 'fame', *iṣ,* 'food' and *rāyaḥ* 'riches' etc. Indra is asked to bestow all these on the *vipras* 'wise' (Bharadvājas). A similar idea is conveyed at RV 6, 35, 4: *sá gómaghā jaritré aśvaścandrā vājaśravaso ádhi dhehi pṛkṣaḥ/ pīpihī́ṣaḥ sudúghām indra dhenúṁ bharádvājeṣu surúco rurucyāḥ//* (Velankar[20] translates as: "Such as you are, bestow on your singer foods which are accompanied by gifts of cows which are lovely, with horses, famous for their strength. Fatten our nourishments and also our easily milch-cow. Make them shine so as to be glorious among the Bharadvājas.") Here again *vāja* appears to have comprised many more material riches such as *gómaghā* 'riches containing cows' *áśvaścandrā* 'riches accompanied by lovely horses', etc. These indicate that Bharádvāja was really a possessor of all the worldly affluence and he desired to have more of the same for himself and his family. Bharadvāja possessed particularly riches (cows and horses) that made him prosperous. In the above-noted passages, Bharadvāja appears to be a devotee of Indra and the Maruts. Bharadvāja is mentioned again at RV 6, 65, 6 which is addressed to Uṣas: *ucchā divo duhitar pratnavánno bharadvājavát vidhaté maghoni*/ ("Light on us, O Daughter of Heaven, as in old days, for them as to Bharadvāja you did, O liberal Donor.") Bharadvāja is here taken as a standard for comparisons (*upamāna*) indicating that he was a person worthy of favour from Uṣas. The word *pratnavát* 'Liked in olden days' indicates that this Bharadvāja should belong to a period earlier than the period to which the poet belonged. But here the poet and the one under reference (Bharadvāja) are said to be one and the same person; this raises a doubt about the authenticity of the Sarvā's[21] ascription of the hymn to Bharadvāja. There may be a possibility that Bharadvāja, with whom comparisons are made may be the progenitor, while the poet of the hymn RV 6, 65 may be his remote descendant.

Now we have three passages in the RV,[22] wherein Bharadvāja and Divodāsa are mentioned side by side—these also hint at some sort of relation between them. In RV 1, 116, 18, Bharadvāja and Divodāsa are said to have enjoyed the favour of the Aśvins. Sāyaṇa accepts *bharádvāja* in the sense of *saṁbhriyamāṇa havirlakṣaṇānnāya yajamānāya divodāsāya*[23] ("for Divodāsa, the sacrificer, by whom food in the form of offering is being brought"). Chapekar[24] seems to have been bent upon accepting this interpretation. Once Röth[25] also went a step further and mixed up one with the other, but he could not prove this and his view was rejected by other scholars. Contrary to Röth's contention we have a passage (*viz.*, RV 6, 16, 5) which Velankar[26] translates as: "Do you (bring) these ample boons to Divodāsa, the presser (of Soma), and Bharadvāja who brings you gifts" (*tvámimá váryā purú dívodāsāya sunvaté*/ *bharádvājaya dāśúṣe*). The two words *sunvaté* 'to the presser of Soma' and *dāśúṣe* 'to one who offers oblation' can very well qualify either of the two persons separately or conjointly. It appears here that two terms signify two persons and distinguish one from the other. Thus Bharadvāja and Divodāsa are found here as two distinct persons, one offerer of oblation to God and the other the presser of Soma. A similar but more significant situation is presented in RV 6, 31, 4, where Divodāsa is qualified by the attribute *sunvat* 'pressing Soma' and Bharadvāja by *gṛṇat* 'singing (a hymn or prayer)'. Velankar[27] translates the verse as: "You battered down the hundred matchless forts of Dasyu Śaṁbara when you sought to give rich treasures to the sacrificer Divodāsa and the singer Bharadvāja, oh powerful God, brought by Soma".[28]

In both these verses (*i.e.*, RV 6, 16, 5 and 6, 31, 4) Divodāsa is qualified by *sunvat*, a sacrificer of Soma rite (lit. a presser of Soma), while Bharadvāja is qualified by the two adjuncts *dāśvas* and gṛṇat (in 6, 16, 5 and 6, 31, 4) indicating a mutual relationsip of the patron-sacrificer and poet-priest between the two. In RV 6, 31, 4 we have some more information about Indra's battering down the hundred forts of Dasyu Śaṁbara for the sake of Divodāsa and Bharadvāja. On the basis of the three passages discussed above, it is clear to us, that Divodāsa was a patron of Bharadvāja.[29]

Besides, there is a passage (*viz.*, 10, 150, 5) wherein Bharadvāja is mentioned along with Atri, Gaviṣṭhira, Kaṇva, Trasadasyu and Vasiṣṭha. Atri, Vasiṣṭha and Kaṇva are all well-known seers of RV Maṇḍalas V, VII and VIII. Gaviṣṭhira has been accepted as the personal name of an Atri and is mentioned as *ṛṣi* 'seer' in the RV and AV. He is referred to in AśvŚS 12, 14, 1 also. Trasadasyu is frequently mentioned in RV and is said to be the son of Purukutsa. However, we cannot establish any correlation among these people on the basis of this passage.

Now, we have a few passages, where the plural forms like '*bharádvājāḥ, bharádvājān, bharádvājeṣu* occur. These plural forms may easily be taken to mean the members of the family or immediate or remote descendants of Bharadvāja, the progenitor. In RV 6, 50, 15 Ṛjiśvan Bhāradvāja refers to his descendants: *máma nápāto bharádvājāḥ* ("my descendants, the Bharadvājas") which Sāyaṇa understands as *mama ṛjiśvanaḥ napātaḥ putrāḥ bharadvājāḥ bharadvājagotrajāḥ suhotrādayaḥ*[30] ("my descendants, *i.e.* Ṛjiśvan's descendants, are those Bharadvājas who have originated from the *gotra* of *Bharadvāja, viz.*, Suhotra and others"). Here Sāyaṇa's words *suhotrādayaḥ* appear to be exclusive of Ṛjiśvan, while in a similar instance in the Sarvā 2, 6, 52 *Suhotrādayaḥ* is taken to be inclusive of *Ṛjiśvan*. This complicates the matter and Sāyaṇa's knowledge about the Bharadvājas rests upon the Sarvā (among many other sources), so the last words of Sāyaṇa's statement quoted above appear to be erroneous. At RV 6, 47, 25 the Bharadvājas are said to have been honoured by Prastoka, the son of Sṛñjaya, who appears to be their patron.[31] In RV 6, 23, 10, a Bharadvāja poet says: "Thus, indeed, is Indra praised, when Soma is pressed among the Bharadvājas". Here the Bharadvājas should mean the members of the family, descended from Bharadvāja, not necessarily only his sons or grandsons, but also distant progeny. So, in 6, 25, 9 (=RV 10, 89, 7), the poet implores Indra: "May we, the Bharadvājas, obtain (riches) singing praises to you under your protection both at the break of the dawn and even now".[32] The poet here means to say that the descendants of Bharadvāja are the protégés of Indra and they are seeking his protection at the time of war. Further, at RV 6, 35, 4, the poet asks Indra, "to bestow foods on the singer, the foods, which are accompanied by the gifts of cows, lovely horses, famous for their strength". Again he asks the god to strengthen the nourishment so as to make the cows shine among the Bharadvājas. These Bharadvājas referred to here, are, either the descendants of Bharadvāja or the members of his family. The poet says at RV 6, 10, 6, that God Agni claims a good hymn from the Bharadvājas (*bharádvājeṣu dadhiṣe suvṛktím*). The Bharadvājas mentioned here are the descendants of Bharadvāja. At 6, 51, 12 mention is made of Bhāradvāja, who is certainly of the same lineage. The poet implores all the gods: "May I urge you, O gods, living in the Heaven. An invoker priest of Bhāradvāja family comes (to you) for favour. The sacrificer desiring wealth has honoured the family of the gods, with sitting and delighting in offerings".[33]

Now we can see if there is any possibility of identifying the Ṛgvedic Bharadvāja with any other Bharadvāja or those described in the Epics and Purāṇas. Before entering into a discussion of identifications, the possibility of having evidence in the RV of the existence of more than one Bharadvāja may be conceded. We can locate Bharadvāja on the basis of personal relations or associations with some princes or other individuals. We have seen above that one Bharadvāja was associated with Divodāsa Atithigva,[34] another with Purupanthā,[35] still another with Purunītha,[36] yet another with Śāṇḍa[37]. Each of these princes definitely ruled in different kingdoms or principalities. If so, one sage or seer could not probably serve each or all of them. A seer-cum-priest was not associated with a prince to guide him only for liturgical purpose, but also on secular and military matters. Besides, the princes had always rivalry among themselves; this resulted in wars. Thus, a single priest could never have served a number of princes belonging to more than one kingdom or principality at the same time. This fact thus militates against identifying one priestly-poet, associated with one prince, as being the same serving another prince. Pargiter[38] once argued that the princes had fixed settlements but not the seers. This might not be true in the case of a priest-cum-seer who was an adviser of a prince in all matters of war and peace. Hence our contention that the Bharadvājas associated with each of those princes (mentioned earlier as distinct persons) belonged but to the one and the same *gotra*. They appeared to some as a 'single' person because of the same surname they held without personal name. Therefore, a few Indian scholars[39] have accepted all these Bharadvājas as one and the same person. These scholars further identify Bharadvāja(s) described in the RV with Bharadvāja Bārhaspatya to whom the Sarvā (2, 6, 1) ascribes the 6th Maṇḍala on the one hand, and with the other Bharadvājas, *viz.*, the one who was priest of Divodāsa of Kāśī, and the other one of the Rām, on the other hand. It was Pradhan[40] who first took Bharadvāja of the RV, *i.e.*, the priest of Divodāsa as Bharadvāja of the Rām. And this Bharadvāja was again thought to be Bharadvāja, the priest of Divodāsa of Kāśī. His main argument was based on the fact that several Divodāsas bear the same name (*i.e.*, Divodāsa), that occurs in the texts of RV, MBh and Rām.

This process (of considering these Bharadvājas as the same person) found a strong support in Mankad, who in his short monograph the '*Date of the Ṛgveda*,'[41] has adduced arguments similar to Pradhan. Also, Rahurkar[42] lent support to the same thesis. This logic betrays a number of weaknesses,[43] making this identification unplausible and practically purposeless. However, Bharadvāja mentioned together with Divodāsa in RV may probably be Pāyu's father. This Pāyu is mentioned in RV 6, 47, 24,[44] and is said to have helped Sṛñjaya's son, Prastoka, and Abhyāvartin Cāyamāna, in their struggle against Vṛcīvants. Pāyu did so at the command of his father, Bharadvāja. Sṛñjaya and Divodāsa are said to have made gifts to Bharadvāja, on their victory over Vṛcīvants. Thus Bharadvāja, the father of Pāyu, appears to be a person chronologically nearer to the Sṛñjayas and the Bharatas of the Ṛgvedic age; and Bharadvāja must have been a remote descendant of Bṛhaspati's son Bharadvāja, the founder of the family.

(*ii*) *Bharadvāja*(*s*) *in other Saṁhitās*

A good number of passages from the Vedic Saṁhitās contain references to Bharadvāja together with some personages whose relation with our Bharadvāja can hardly be explained or specified. The persons belonging to various epochs of the Vedic period appear to have been grouped together because of their common allegiance to a particular god or gods. There are passages in the Vedas where we can make out a case of some relation between *a* Bharadvāja and a person or persons mentioned in the passages. A few of such verses, illustrating this point, are as follows:

A poet says (RV 10, 150, 5)[1]: "Agni protected Atri, Bharadvāja, Gaviṣṭhira, Kaṇva and Trasadasyu in the fight. Vasiṣṭha, the domestic chaplain, invokes Agni for obtaining his grace". Here different seers are shown to have a common god for worship and it is Agni of whom all of them were protégés. Atri is probably the seer of the fifth Maṇḍala, and the progenitor of the family of Atris, Gaviṣṭhira, a descendant of him and may be the seer of RV 5, 1. Kaṇva is the seer of RV 1, 36–43 and 9, 94; may be the son of Keśinī by Ajamīḍha; he originated the Brāhmaṇas called Kāṇvāyanas. Trasadasyu appears to be the son of Purukutsa and the seer of RV 4, 12; 5, 17 and 9, 110. Vasiṣṭha is the seer of the seventh Maṇḍala of the RV and the progenitor of the family of Vasiṣṭhas.

Similar statements regarding such mutually unrelated personages are found in other Vedas too. At AVS 4, 29, 5[2] it is said: "Let Mitra and Varuṇa save us from calamity, they who protected Bharadvāja, Gaviṣṭhira, Viśvāmitra, Kutsa, Kakṣīvat and Kaṇva." Here Viśvāmitra, Kutsa and Kakṣīvat are introduced in the place of Atri, Trasadasyu and Vasiṣṭha. Among the new entrants Viśvāmitra appears to be the seer of the 3rd Maṇḍala of the RV. Kutsa is one of those persons, whose names are frequently met with in the RV. And Kakṣīvat is the only person who appears to have some relation with the Bharadvājas. He is said to be the son of Dīrghatamas, who consorted a Śūdrā. He is a composer of RV 1, 116-125, 126, 1-5 and 9, 74. He is father of Ghoṣā Kākṣīvatī, a female seer of the Ṛgvedic hymn *viz.*, 10, 39-40. The same verse is repeated with minor alteration in the AVP 4, 38, 4[3] where Gaviṣṭhira is dropped and in his place comes Vadhryaśva. Vadhryaśva appears to be the father of Divodāsa and is mentioned in RV 6, 61, 1. These two, *viz.*, the father and the son, who were scions of the Bharatas, had some relation with the Bharadvājas, maybe, one of patron and priest. Here, all the persons—Bharadvāja, Vadhryaśva, Viśvāmitra, Kutsa, Kakṣīvat and Kaṇva—are said to be the protégés of Mitra and Varuṇa. The poet says: at AVŚ at 18, 3, 16[4]: "O Viśvāmitra, Jamadagni, Vasiṣṭha, Bharadvāja, Gotama, Vāmadeva—Atri hath taken (*grabh*) our *chardis* with obeisances: ye fathers of good report, be gracious to us". In this passage, a group of seven seers are addressed as 'fathers'. Three of them are for the first time introduced, *viz.*, Gotama, Vāmadeva and Jamadagni. Gotama and Vāmadeva are two distinguished seers belonging to the Aṅgirases and their hymns are included in the 4th Maṇḍala of the RV. Jamadagni is, however, a scion of the Bhṛgus, and author of a number of hymns in the RV. The Bharadvājas being a part of the Aṅgirases are loosely connected with Gotama and Vāmadeva, while Jamadagni's relation cannot be ascertained.

In a similar way a group of six seers are mentioned in AVP (2, 28, 5[5] and 5, 28, 4[6]) which says: "May Jamadagni and Kaśyapa sweeten it, may Bharadvāja produce sweet food to the recipient, may Gotama, Vasiṣṭha and Viśvāmitra increase our life!" We meet here all the six seers, whose names are strikingly enough retained intact in the later tradition also. Kaśyapa, whose name did not occur in the verses discussed above has been included in these two verses. In yet another verse, *viz.*, AVP 11, 2, 6[7] a number of seers are urged to destroy poison: "Atris, Aṅgirases, Gautamas know this tree by which Bharadvāja and Kaṇva destroy your poison." Here Atris, Aṅgirases and Gautamas may refer to their own families, while Bharadvāja and Kaṇva appear to be individuals. Except Atris, all belong to the larger group of the Aṅgirases. In the seven passages discussed above some fourteen seers belonging to different families are mentioned. Among them eight ṛṣis, including Bharadvāja, come from the stock of Aṅgirases. Kaśyapa, Atri, Gaviṣṭhira belong to Kaśyapa's family, Jamadagni to that of the Bhṛgus, while Vasiṣṭha and Viśvāmitra have their own. Some of them particularly Bharadvāja, Kaśyapa (and Atri), Vasiṣṭha and Viśvāmitra appear to be ancestors of their own respective ones. Among the Aṅgirases, Kakṣīvat, Kaṇva and Vadhryaśva appear to have certain relation with Bharadvāja by way of family tradition. Gotama and Vāmadeva are also closely related to each other, the former being the latter's father.

These miscellaneous references to the seers belonging to various families point to their hoary past. By their deeds and thoughts, they were highly respected by posterity. Most of them, who have made references to the seers mentioned above, definitely belonged to a comparatively later age. Thus they were respectful to their poet-seer forefathers. Also a prayer later on enjoined them to do so: *idáṁ namá ṛṣibhyaḥ pūrvajébhyaḥ púrvebhyaḥ pathikṛdbhyaḥ* "this salutation is made to the ancient poets who were born earlier and who have made path (for posterity)" (RV 10, 14, 15).[8]

The mention of the seers, in the same breath, not only indicates the origin of the worship of the forefathers, but speaks also of a common heritage handed down by them (*e.g.*, their contribution to the building of an enduring culture and civilization). They also punctuate the epochs of the development of thought within Vedic literature. Besides, we see a meeting point of the fathers leaving a heritage behind them, and of the descendants expressing their heartfelt gratitude to them.

(iii) *The Brāhmaṇic information of Bharadvāja*

The Brāhmaṇas also supply some scattered information about the Bharadvājas. The Ṛgvedic, Yajurvedic and Sāmavedic Brāhmaṇas have narrated some legends or myths while ascribing Sāmans to Bharadvāja. The AB 3, 49,[1] while describing the Ukthya alludes to a strife between the Gods and the Asuras thus: "In Agniṣṭoma the Gods took refuge, in the Ukthyas, the Asuras. They were of equal strength; they could not be discriminated. It was Bharadvāja, among the seers, who saw the Asuras taking refuge in the Ukthyas and pointed out, "These Asuras are resting in the Ukthyas; none of the Gods saw them (Asuras) there." Bharadvāja called to Agni "Come, I shall proclaim to you, O Agni, the other words." The other words are those of the Asuras. Agni rising up said to Bharadvāja, "What does this lean, tall, grey-haired one desire to say?" It indicates that Bharadvāja was lean, tall and grey-haired. He replied, "These Asuras are resting in the Ukthyas; and none of you have seen them there." Agni transformed himself into a horse and ran to them and beyond. That was the origin of the Śākamaśva Sāman, and that is why the Śākamasva/Sāman has its name.

This particular myth seeks to glorify Bharadvāja, associating him with the Gods in their endeavour to overcome the Asuras. He is singled out from among the seers as he was able to see the tricks played by the Asuras taking rest or hiding themselves in the safe *ukthya* rite. When he discovered the Asuras in the Ukthya, he pointed them out and Agni at once took note of it. Secondly, the myth gives us a bit of personal information of Bharadvāja that he was lean, tall and grey-haired. Probably, the narrator of the myth saw one Bharadvāja whose physical appearance was as stated here. This is said of Bharadvāja, the son of Bṛhaspati.

The TMB (15, 3, 6-7)[2] ascribes a Sāman called Adārasṛt to Bharadvāja. While commenting upon it, Sāyaṇa[3] describes another legend as a background of the origin of the Sāman as follows: "Bharadvāja was the domestic priest of the king Divodāsa. Once some hostile people surrounded Divodāsa and he could not find an escape route, he made fervent prayer to his priest Bharadvāja to help him come out of the clutches of his enemies. Bharadvāja did this for Divodāsa: the Sāman, named Adārasṛt which, when recited, provides a way out of difficulty for the person who recites it."

According to a legend a Bharadvāja was the priest of Divodāsa. The same Brāhmaṇa at 15, 3, 7[4] also mentions that Bharadvāja was the priest of Divodāsa. This Divodāsa probably was the king of the Kāśī dynasty and the father of Pratardana.[5]

AĀ (1, 2, 6)[6] says: "Bharadvāja was the most learned among the seers, endowed with a life of maximum length and the best of all ascetics."

That Bharadvāja lived a very long and extremely austere life is corroborated by the TB 3, 10, 11[7] which records an interesting legend as to how Bharadvāja learnt the Vedas from Indra. The legend speaks of the extreme austerity Bharadvāja observed for three full spans of his life. It runs thus: "Bharadvāja observed *brahmacarya* 'a strict life ensuring celebacy' while studying the lores continuously for three spans of life, each span consisting of a hundred years. As the third span of his life came to a close and Bharadvāja lay exhausted by his age, Indra approached him and addressed, "Bharadvāja, if I would grant you a fourth span of life, what would you do thereby"? He replied, "I would have continued to observe celibacy in the same way for securing Vedic knowledge." Thereupon, Indra drew his attention to the three hillocks that were ever unknown to him. Then from each of the hillocks Indra took (away) a handful of dust and presenting the same before Bharadvāja again spoke to him, "O Bharadvāja, (suppose) these three hillocks are the three Vedas; they are endless! What you have so far studied is comparable only to these handfuls of dust and the rest has remained unknown to you. Thus even now they stand fully unknown to you. Indeed you have known very little of them through your three spans of life! So, you should better give up this endless (pursuit of) your Vedic study. Come, I shall let you know this—all the sciences". Having said this, Indra told him of Agni which is called *Sāvitra.* Bharadvāja, then acquired from Indra full knowledge of the *Sāvitrāgni* and became immortal; he attained the world of light and bliss, and ultimately merged with the sun-god (*iyāya ādityasya sāyujyaṁ*).

These Brāhmaṇical texts emphasize the following few points: (*i*) Bharadvāja lived an unusually very long life; (*ii*) he practised austerity for the attainment of perfect knowledge of the Vedic lores; this also adds to his steadfastness and perseverence to his qualities; (*iii*) he was the most famous among the contemporary seers on account of his knowledge of the Vedic lores; (*iv*) he learnt the Vedas—attained the science of *Sāvitrāgni* from Indra, *i.e.*, there existed a relation of *ācārya* (or guru) 'preceptor' and *siṣya* 'pupil' between Indra and Bharadvāja; that is recorded elsewhere also.[8] At least it goes to hint at some communion between the God and his mortal pupil for the attainment of perfect knowledge.

The legend of the TB may be described as hyperbolic, since it presents the traditional view about the Vedas as 'endless'. No human agency is capable of exhaustively acquiring the knowledge of the Vedas. It is possible for an individual human being to acquire the knowledge of only some minute or small part of massive Vedic knowledge. The three hillocks represent the three Vedas (*trayī*, *viz.*, Ṛk, Sāman and Yajus) as a whole and the handfuls of dust taken therefrom form only a minute part thereof. Thus the attempt at knowing all the 'hillocks' of the three Vedas is futile; the *Sāvitrāgni vidyā* can be taken as a short-cut to an understanding of the teachings of all the Vedas and thereby attaining immortality.

(iv) *Bharadvājas in the Upaniṣads*

A number of the Upaniṣads, earlier and later, contain some information about the Bharadvājas. Among these only a few Upaniṣads, *viz.*, the Muṇḍakopaniṣad, the Bṛhadāraṇyakopaniṣad, and Praśnopaniṣad are known as the early Upaniṣads.[1] The remaining Upaniṣads, (*viz.*, Siddhāntaśikhopaniṣad, Tārasaropaniṣad, Gāruḍopaniṣad, Itihāsopaniṣad, Sarasvatīrahasyopaniṣad) are considered as later Upaniṣads. They may belong to the age of the Purāṇas. It is, however, difficult to give exact dates.[2]

In some of these Upaniṣads, the Bharadvājas are found as inquisitive seekers of secret or esoteric knowledge, while in others, they are in the chain of traditional *vaṁśas* of teachers receiving and transmitting the Upaniṣadic message. While most of the Upaniṣadic informations can be called legendary, one recorded in the Siddhāntaśikhopaniṣad, may be classified as mythical. In this Upaniṣad the fact of Bharadvāja's approach to Skandakumāra cannot have any historical or semi-historical authenticity.

The Muṇḍakopaniṣad (1, 1, 2)[3] says that one Bharadvāja, whose personal name was Satyavaha, received the teaching on the Brahmavidyā—highest knowledge—from an Aṅgiras and conveyed it to another Aṅgiras. Earlier, Brahmā is said to have delivered the teaching of Brahmavidyā to his eldest son Atharvan, who passed the same to Aṅgiras and the latter to Bharadvāja. It appears from this tradition that the message of the Brahmavidyā contained in the Muṇḍakopaniṣad was handed down to the seers of the family or families of the Aṅgirases from generation to generation. Needless to point out that the Bharadvājas are a clan belonging to the stock of the Aṅgirases. We come across, in this tradition, Satyavaha, as a descendant of Bharadvāja. But, on many an occasion, this name is lost to us. The persons are referred to by their surname or family name *i.e.*, Bharadvāja or Bhāradvāja that are freely used for many persons belonging to different ages. This creates confusion. While examining the texts—Vedic and post-Vedic—one has to face similar problem.

In Praśnopaniṣad (1,1. and 6, 1) we meet Sukeśā, another member of the family of Bharadvāja. This Sukeśā Bhāradvāja accompanied by Śaibya Satyakāma, Sauryāyaṇī Gārgya, Kauśalya Āśvalāyana, Bhārgava Vaidarbhi, Kabandhi Kātyāyana, (who were devoted to Brahman (*brahmapara*) and were seeking the Supreme Brahman, by taking *samits* 'sacrificial fuel-sticks' in hand, approached the venerable Pippalāda in the hope that he would tell them everything about Brahman (1.1)[4]. Then Sukeśā, the descendant of Bharadvāja, said to Pippalāda that one Hiraṇyanābha, the Prince of Kosala, once came to question him (Bharadvāja) about a person with sixteen parts; and this impelled him to come to Pippalāda (6, 1).[4a]

In this piece of Upaniṣadic information, Sukesā, a descendant of Bharadvāja, is contemporary of Prince Hiraṇyanābha of Kosala, and also of Pippalāda and others—that includes offsprings of Garga, of Aśvala, and of Kātya. Among them Gārgya is related to Bharadvāja. The Gargas are found to be remote scions of Bharadvāja Bārhaspatya and this Gārgya also must have belonged to the *Gotra* of Garga. Thus this Bhāradvāja may be chronologically placed several generations after Bharadvāja, the founder.

In the Siddhāntaśikhopaniṣad[5] one Bhāradvāja, mentioned thrice, is said to have approached Skanda (also known as Kumāra) with a request that he is to be imparted esoteric knowledge of Śaivism. He questioned Kumāra as to what was the resolution of the best of the devotees of Śiva like Skanda. Skanda agreed to convey the secret knowledge (of Śaivism): this is recorded in the Upaniṣad.

On being questioned, Skanda told Bhāradvāja about the real state of the mount Kailāsa. Here the personal name of Bhāradvāja is not given. This myth is significant since it tries to raise Bharadvāja to an eminent position among the seers.

Another Bhāradvāja, mentioned in the Tārasāropaniṣad[6], wants to know from Yājñavalkya the real nature of Tāraka, and he is satisfied with the answer. This Bhāradvāja sought Yājñavalkya's instruction on *mantras* by which Paramātman could be pleased to reveal his self. Yājñavalkya's answer made Bharadvāja happy.

This Bhāradvāja, as one in the Siddhāntopaniṣad, was also a member of the Bhāradvāja family. Without giving his personal name he is said to be a contemporary of Yājñavalkya, and of Janaka of Mithilā.

The Gāruḍopaniṣad[7] legend says that Brahmā delivered Gāruḍabrahmavidyā to Nārada, Nārada to Bṛhatsena, Bṛhatsena to Indra, and Indra to Bharadvāja. Bharadvāja in his turn taught the science of Gāruḍa to his disciples who desired (long) life. The relations of Indra and Bharadvāja[8] have been discussed above. The relation of the Bharadvājas with Indra, established in search of knowledge, is indeed found to be phenomenal.

In the Itihāsopaniṣad[9] also, one Bharadvāja is referred to as receiving the lore traditionally and passing the same on to many kings. Here he is stated to have benefitted from one Kaśyapa, Kaśyapa from one Puroga, and Puroga from Brahmāditya.

But we miss the personal name of this Bharadvāja, who is, however shown as one of high antiquity having been a student of Kaśyapa. But this is a later Upaniṣad. As such Bharadvāja's identity is in doubt.

In the Sarasvatīrahasyopaniṣad[10] 2, 1 Bharadvāja is said to be the seer of a *mantra*: *pra no devī, etc.* He is referred to in the Ārṣeyopaniṣad as the disciple of Vasiṣṭha, and the teacher of Gārgya in a list of twenty-four seers. Still, it is difficult to identify these Bharadvājas. The fact remains that all these Bharadvājas, as also other seers, were in search of knowledge and wisdom.

The Bṛh U has three lists of *vaṁśa*—the term *vaṁśa* here need not be confused with that in the Purāṇas. *Vaṁśa* does not at all point to the genealogy of the sages, born in a family; it indicates pupil-preceptor relations and a line of thinkers. This sort of succession relates only to spiritual or academic interest and not any other.

Now, turning to the first list of Bṛh U 2, 6[11] we find a Bhāradvāja as a student of one Āsuri. This Bhāradvāja is found in the 29th position (in succession) from Brahman. He appears to be a descendant of the Bhāradvāja family. This *vaṁśa* is repeated in Bṛh U 4, 6.[12] In the same list is found another Bhāradvāja as the pupil of one Pārāśarya and the teacher of one Gautaṃa; and this Gautama is teacher of another Bhāradvāja. The last one is said to be the teacher of one more Bhāradvāja, who appears to be the preceptor of another Pārāśarya. Both the Bhāradvājas might have belonged to the same family, because a father could function as a teacher for his son also, if the latter is well-merited to hold the tradition.

Among the students of the Śākhā of the Vājasaneyins (Bṛh U 6, 5[13]) two sons of some Bhāradvājī are included in the first two lists. They might have been remote descendants and members of the family of the Bharadvājas. This speaks of the chronological distance between the RV and the Bṛh U. It hints at the fact that the evolution of Indian thought took its own time to attain maturity.

In the *vaṁśas* recorded in Bṛh U more than once are mentioned a number of descendants of Bharadvāja engaged in spiritual pursuits and in learning and teaching. This tendency is reflected in the legends (TB 3, 10, 11, MBh 3, 135; 10-139, 18); some other

Bharadvājas are engrossed in the study of the Vedic lores. The *vaṁśas* in Bṛh U further shows that in pursuit of knowledge there was a free mixing of persons belonging to various families—something eternally embedded in Indian Culture since its inception. What has been stated in this section is only symbolic. This is important in the present context of education as well.

(v) *Bharadvāja in the Rāmāyaṇa*

In the *Rām*, Vālmīki depicts Bharadvāja and his hermitages on a broad canvas.[1] The *Rām* says that Bharadvāja enjoyed a prominent place among the seers of his time, and Rāma and Bharata paid him respects on more than one occasion. Rāma is said to have met the seer twice—once while entering the thick of the forest and again when returning to Ayodhyā after a lapse of fourteen years. Bharata met the seer on his way to Citrakūṭa and on his return home after meeting Rāma. Thus we have four places in the text of the Epic that describe Bharadvāja's four meetings with two of the scions of the Raghus. A brief résumé of those four meetings is given as follows:

The *Rām* 2, 54ff. describes that, accompanied by his brother Lakṣmaṇa and his wife Sītā, Rāma went towards Bharadvāja's Āśrama at Prayāga. They saw from afar the smoke that rose high in the sky. Seeing the soaring smoke they inferred that they were nearing a hermitage. At about noon of the day they arrived at the hermitage and saw Bharadvāja, the observer of the vows (*saṁśita-vrata*), gaining insight through *tapas* (*tapasā labdhacakṣusam*). He sat there, encircled by his pupils, and was himself attending to the mid-day Agnihotra (2, 54, 11-12). After Rāma paid due reverence to the sage he welcomed them and also offered them fruits (2, 54, 17-19). The sage let them know that he himself had already come to know about Rāma's exile, and requested them to stay in his hermitage (2, 54, 21-22). At this, Rāma very politely replied that his Āśrama was too near to Ayodhyā whose citizens would cause disturbance in the locality. So, at Rama's request, the sage advised him to establish their Āśrama at Citrakūṭa (2, 54, 28-32). However, on Ṛṣi's insistence, they spent that night in the Āśrama. Next morning, they proceeded to Citrakūṭa, and the sage performed the auspicious *svastyayana* ceremony which was customary before proceeding on a journey (2, 54, 36-43; 2, 55, 1–2). Having then shown the path leading to Citrakūṭa, the sage returned to his hermitage (2, 55, 3–10).

Later, Bharata followed Rāma's track leading to Bharadvāja's Āśrama in order to persuade him (Rāma) to return to Ayodhyā. Bharata asked Guha to guide him to his (Bharadvāja's) hermitage (2, 85, 5). Led by his *Purohita* Vasiṣṭha and followed by a huge army Bharata arrived at the Āśrama. When Vasiṣṭha approached the sage Bharadvāja, he stood up from his seat and commanded his disciples to fetch *arghya* for the honourable guest (2, 90, 4). As soon as Bharata bowed before the sage Bharadvāja, he recognised him as the son of king Daśaratha (2, 90, 5). After offering the *arghya* etc. to Vasiṣṭha, Bharata and others, Bharadvāja asked about the well-being of the members of the families of the guests (2, 90, 6). As the sage knew about the sad demise of king Daśaratha, he did not inquire about him (2, 90, 7).

The renowned sage Bharadvāja (*Bharadvājo mahāyaśāḥ*) then enquired about Bharata's intention towards Rāma (2, 90, 9–13). He felt pleased on Bharata informing him that he wanted to dissuade Rāma from the exile (2, 90, 14–20). The sage then requested Bharata to stay at his hermitage overnight (2, 90, 21-23) and also expressed his utmost desire to entertain Bharata and his retinue (2, 91, 1). At this, the Prince was hesitating to comply with his request, the sage asked Bharata to bring his soldiers also to the Āśrama (2, 91, 2–10). The great sage, then, entered his Agniśālā, sipped water and asked Viśvakarman, Gods, the Gandharvas and the Apsaras to entertain the Prince of Ayodhyā, *viz.*, Bharata, and his large retinue (2, 91, 11-22). When everything was ready, the sage requested Bharata to enter into the great hall built by Viśvakarman himself for the eventful entertainment (2, 91, 35). Through his severe penance, the sage made the whole garden of the heaven descend in his Āśrama for that night (2, 91, 47).

In the next morning when Bharata approached Bharadvāja, he asked the Prince whether the latter had sound sleep the previous night (2, 92, 2-3). At Bharata's request, the sage described to him the way leading to Citrakūṭa (2, 92, 10-14). When, at the hour of taking leave of him Kaikeyī, bowed before Bharadvāja, the sage wanted her identity (2, 92, 14-19). Bharata's reply injured her sentiments (2, 92, 25-28). At this the sage advised Bharata not to put any blame upon his mother, because the banishment of Rāma would result in the welfare of Gods and others (2, 92, 29-31).

Circumbulating the sage Bharadvāja, Bharata proceeded to Citrakūṭa.

After meeting Rāma at Citrakūṭa, on his return journey to Ayodhyā Bharata once more visited Bharadvāja (2, 113, 5). He again paid his due reverence to the sage. The sage asked him about his meeting with Rāma (2, 113, 7-8). Given the details, the sage admired Bharata's conduct (2, 113, 15-17).

After achieving the victory over Rāvaṇa, and effecting the release of his beloved wife Sītā from the custody of Rāvaṇa, Rāma returned to Ayodhyā after a lapse of fourteen years; he and Sītā called on Bharadvāja. It was the fifth day of their journey (6, 127, 1-2). When Rāma asked the sage whether he was aware of the current state of the affairs of Ayodhyā, the sage gave him firsthand information about Ayodhyā. The sage then admired Rāma for his truthfulness and expressed his delight over Rāma's victorious return to his kingdom. Also, he revealed to Rāma that all the happenings during those years and the activities of Rāma in the exile, were fore-known to him (6, 127, 3-16). After this conversation, Bharadvāja offered *arghya* to Rāma and Sītā, and asked them to stay overnight in the hermitage (6, 127, 16-17). Bharadvāja further granted a boon to Rāma, as Rāma desired, that all the trees standing on both the sides of the road to Ayodhyā should bear fruits which would emit mead all the while, even out of season (6, 127, 18-20).

It is further said in the *Rām* 7, 1, 6 that on Rāma's return from Laṅkā to Ayodhyā, Bharadvāja was present on the north direction to pay his respect to Rāma. It is also said in the *Rām* 7, 3, 3 that his daughter Devavarṇinī was married to one Viśrava. He is also said to have been present while Sītā took the oath of truth in the assembly of Rāma (7, 96, 4).

The *Rām* (1, 2, 4) says that there was a Bharadvāja among the disciples of the sage Vālmīki. He is said to have been present by the side of *Guru* on the bank of Tamasā, when Vālmīki uttered his pathetic words at the sight of the slaughter of the Krauñca bird.[2]

Vālmīki has depicted Bharadvāja and his hermitage not only on a broad canvas but also in glowing expressions. A good number of qualifying epithets are used by the poet who sought to bring out the innate qualities of Bharadvāja in the *Rām*. Bharadvāja is frequently referred to as a *muni*—'a thinker' (2, 54, 5; 19; 36; 89, 21; 91, 22; 6, 127, 1); a *mahāmuni*—'a great thinker' (2, 54, 27; 6,

127, 3); a *maharṣi*—'a great seer' (2, 91, 29; 36); a *paramarṣi*—'a supreme seer' (2, 91, 10). He was a *tapodhana*—'having the wealth of penance' (2, 91, 6); and a *taptatapas*—'one who has performed fierse penance' (2, 54, 3; 92, 9); a *mahātapas*—'one of great penance' (2, 90, 3; 92, 9). His *tapas* ('penance') is also mentioned in 6, 127, 16. His *tejas* ('prowess') is frequently mentioned (*e.g.*, 2, 91, 48-49) and he is spoken of as a *muni jvalitatejas* —'a thinker of burning prowess' (2, 54, 36); an *uttamatejas* 'one of best prowess' (2, 92, 4); a *mahātejas* —'one of great prowess' (2, 55, 3: 92, 9). According to Vālmīki, Bharadvāja was *satyaśīla*—'a person of truthful conduct' (2, 54, 37); *dharmajña*—'a knower of virtue' (2, 90, 6); *dharmātman*—'a person of virtue as his soul' (2, 54, 17); *mahābuddhi*—'a person of great intelligence' (2, 92, 29); *mahāyaśas*—'a person of great fame' (2, 90, 9); *dhīmat*—'a person possessed of intelligence' (2, 92, 8); *dhārmika mahātman*—'a virtuous person and a man of great soul' (2, 92, 8). He uttered only virtuous words (2, 54, 27). Bharadvāja's holding a banquet in honour of Bharata, the crown prince of Ayodhyā, with all pomp and grandeur with the help of the celestial nymphs, gods and demi-gods, speaks volumes of his penance and austerity. His meetings with the two Ayodhyā princes *viz.,* Rāma and Bharata hint at his hospitable nature and the human kindness he did possess. It also testifies to the fact that the sage was more or less concerned with the political development, in the royal court of Ayodhyā.

This Bharadvāja has been identified by D.R. Mankad[3] with Bharadvāja Bārhaspatya who composed nearly all the hymns of the 6th Maṇḍala of RV. While doing so, he solely depends upon the contention of S.N. Pradhan,[4] who says that (1) Bharadvāja of the *Rām*, and Bharadvāja of RV 'was' one and the same person, (2) he was priest of Divodāsa Atithigva who was brother of Ahalyā, the wife of Gotama and the mother of Śatānanda, the priest of Janaka of Videha, (3) Daśaratha and Divodāsa were contemporaries, (4) so also Rāma Dāśarathī and Pratardana (the son of Divodāsa) were contemporaries. However, ingenious may be these contentions of Pradhan and Mankad, to us there appear certain weaknesses: (1) Pradhan does not adduce any argument why Divodāsa of Kāśī dynasty should be identified with Divodāsa of Bharatas of the North Pāñcāla dynasty; (2) He also ignores the fact that Bharadvāja Bārhaspatya was a remote ancestor of

Divodāsa of Pāñcāla himself and thus Bharadvāja Bārhaspatya and Bharadvāja, the priest of Divodāsa, were two distinct persons separated by several generations; (3) besides, Vālmīki nowhere says that Bharadvāja depicted by him was son of Bṛhaspati; (4) and Vālmīki did nowhere mention Divodāsa by name. Thus it becomes impossible for us to agree with Pradhan and Mankad to identify Bharadvāja of the *Rām* with either Bharadvāja, the son of Bṛhaspati, or Bharadvāja the seer of the RV. We feel that this Bharadvāja was different from any other Bharadvāja.[5]

(vi) *The Primeval Seers mentioned by the Bharadvājas and their Inter-relationship*

In reconstructing the biography of a seer and the history of the family that originated from him, it is necessary to take note of the person or persons to whom the seer refers in his hymns. It is expected that an investigation or a survey of this type should reveal certain relation, intimate or otherwise, matrimonial or patrimonial, that our poet-seer might have had with those persons. Sometimes, it appears that the seer had occasion to mention his near relatives, particularly some ancestors, and at times he mentions some persons who were not at all related to him but just his predecessors to be reckoned with for their noteworthy achievements. Nevertheless, a survey of all those people helps one to establish facts regarding the poet's ancestry and to determine their chronology. It is, therefore, hoped that an inquiry of this kind should help one determine the poet's ancestry and the chronology of the persons related to him.

1. *Aṅgiras*

Among the notable persons mentioned by the Bharadvājas in their hymns, Aṅgiras stands the first. Aṅgiras is mentioned in the 6th Maṇḍala five times and he is frequently referred to in the other Maṇḍalas of the RV as well. In the 6th Maṇḍala his name occurs twice in the singular[1] and thrice in the plural.[2] Besides, the derivatives of the word *áṅgiras, viz., aṅgirasvát*—'like Aṅgiras'[3], *áṅgirasvant*—'accompanied by Aṅgirases'[4] and *āṅgirasāḥ*—'born among the Aṅgirases' (twice)[5] also occur in the Bharadvāja Maṇḍala four times. Except two of these, all others are found in the hymns ascribed to Bharadvāja.[6]

In the RV, the singular form *áṅgiras* always stands as an epithet of Agni, the fire god.[7] The two mentions in the 6th Maṇḍala (6,2, 10;[8] 16, 11[9].) must also refer to Agni as his epithet.

The plural form *áṅgirasaḥ* or its derivative form *āṅgirasāḥ* (pl.) can be taken to denote a number of persons, particularly, the poets who are either direct descendants of poet Aṅgiras, or the members of a certain School of thought founded by him.[10] A great number of poets with the patronymic Āṅgirasa have contributed to the bulk of the RV. "They may be the descendants of the great poets or their disciples and other members of the School known by the name of those great poets."[11] It is probable that Aṅgiras himself was a great poet of ancient times, but the extant text of the RV (Śākala Saṁhitā) does not give us any of his compositions. The RV has handed down to us the compositions of some younger generations which descended from the poet-seer Aṅgiras and his contemporaries, *viz.*, Bhṛgu, Atharvan, etc. A large number of Vedic poets claim to be Āṅgirasa, 'descendant of Aṅgiras'. They bear the family name Āṅgirasa and thus distinguish themselves from others, *viz.*, the Bhṛgus, the Atris, the Vasiṣṭhas, etc. That is why wherever we now meet the word *Aṅgirasaḥ* or *Āṅgirasaḥ* in the RV, we may infer immediately that some of the descendants of Aṅgiras or his disciples or their descendants are mentioned. The few verses in the 6th Maṇḍala, wherein the name Aṅgiras or its derivatives occur may be explained here to clear this point.

The poet Bharadvāja says at RV 6, 11, 3[12]: "Even Dhīṣaṇā which brings riches (to men), desires to worship the celestial tribes in (*i.e.*, through) you, for the sake of the singer, when the singer-priest, the flattering one, the most inspired among the Aṅgirases, recites the sweet (hymn) in his persuasion (of the gods)."[13] Also, the same poet says, at RV 6, 18, 5[14]: "Let our that companionship be for you—along with the Aṅgirases who are speaking in this way; you (Indra) killed Vala whom he was searching for, O Strong one; you burst all his forts and doors."[15] In another verse (6, 65, 5)[16] poet Bharadvāja says: "Now indeed, the Aṅgirases sing about you in the stall of the cows, O Dawn, sitting on the mountains as on a throne. They burst you open with their songs and with their adorations. The invocations to the gods done by the heroes become true."[17]

In RV 6, 11, 3 'the most inspired among the Aṅgirases' (*vépiṣṭho áṅgirasāṁ yád dha vipraḥ*), as indicated by Sāyaṇa,[18] is the poet Bharadvāja himself. Bharadvāja here intends to say that he is invoking god Agni as one poet, the most inspired among the Aṅgirases, *i.e.* he belongs to the clan of the Aṅgirases. Similar interpretation is possible in other two cases also. Particularly in the 3rd passage, (*i.e.* RV 6, 65, 5) where the poet says that 'the Aṅgirases sing about you' (*áṅgiraso gr̥ṇánti*), one can easily understand that the Bharadvājas are praising the Goddess Dawn. That means that the poet Bharadvāja considers himself as a descendant of Aṅgiras.

In the second verse (*i.e.*, RV 6, 18, 5), there is a little complication because of the allusion to the Vala myth. Elsewhere, the killing of a Vala is attributed to Indra.[19] In his strife against Vala, Indra is said to have the support of the Aṅgirases.[20] The word '*aṅgirasaḥ*' thus signifies more than one individual, because, in the RV the word is never seen to have been used definitely in the sense of the name of an individual who could be the centre of the group known as Aṅgiras. However, in the secondary (*taddhita*) formations like the one *aṅgirasvát* ('like the Aṅgiras')[21], the singular may denote the individual Aṅgiras, since the other words, used along with this, are all names of individuals. Similarly, the other secondary derivative *aṅgirasvān* ('companion of Aṅgiras')[22], also can mean an individual Aṅgiras. But when an individual is associated with a group of persons called the Aṅgirases, *aṅgirasvān* should be taken to refer to an individual in a group of Aṅgiras poets.

There is still another passage *viz.*, 6, 35, 5[23] where the poet Nara, a junior member of the family of Bharadvāja, says: "Today and for even in future I (choose) him, *i.e.*, Indra, as a great Power (*vr̥jánam*) since, Oh! Śakra, being brave, you are praised in spite of the strong gates (of Vala's cave). May I not slip away from the cow of the bright-milked (Indra). Inspire the descendants of the Aṅgirases owing to their prayer, O singer."[24]

Here it is very clear that the descendants of the Aṅgirases are none other than the Bharadvājas. The poet asks the god to inspire the descendants of his family, *i.e.*, the Aṅgirases alias Bharadvājas, to which he belongs.

In RV 6, 73, 1[25] Br̥haspati is regarded an Āṅgirasa—'a son or descendant of Aṅgiras'. Similarly RV 2, 23, 18[26] also, Br̥haspati, is called an Āṅgiras. Probably on the basis of such statements BD (5, 102-103)[27] says that Aṅgiras was the father of Br̥haspati, and Br̥haspati's son was Bharadvāja. And the Sūtras then give us the *pravararṣis* of the Bharadvājas as: 'Āṅgirasa, Bārhaspatya and Bhāradvāja'.[28] Then the Purāṇas vividly elaborate the genealogy of the descendants of Aṅgiras, Bṛhaspati and Bharadvāja.[29]

2. *Navagvas*

The RV mentions three groups of the Aṅgirases (*viz.*, the Virūpas, the Navagvas and the Daśagvas) as fathers in relation to Yama, the king of mortals.[30] Among these three groups, probably the Navagvas stand the foremost. The RV mentions them fourteen times.[31] Bharadvāja also refers to only Navagvas from the three groups, in the hymns ascribed to him.[32]

Sāyaṇa[33] takes the word *navagva* as a compound and splits it into two components, *viz.*, *nava* and *gva*; he derives *nava* from the root *nu* 'to praise' and *gva* from the root *gam* 'to go'. In order to justify this meaning, he alludes to the story how the Aṅgirases performed a grand sacrifice and how some of them attained the fruits in nine months and became known as the Navagvas, while, the others attained the fruits in ten months and came to be known as Daśagvas.[34] Thus the commentator believes that 'Navagva' means 'those who attain goal in nine (months).'[35]

Now Bharadvāja mentions the Navagvas in RV 6, 22, 2[36]: "Him indeed, did our ancient ancestors, the Seven Priests, the Navagvas, (worship) with their hymns, seeking to strengthen him who destroys his assailants, who is victorious, who stands firmly behind his bolt, whose speech is unoffending and who is the strongest."[37] Here Bharadvāja calls the Navagvas his 'ancient ancestors seeking to strengthen god Indra' (*naḥ pùrve pitáro návagvāḥ... abhí vājáyantaḥ*). The Navagvas' relation to Indra is similar to that of the Aṅgirases' to Indra. And this is because the Navagvas themselves form a group of the Aṅgirases. In RV 6, 6, 3,[38] the poet Bharadvāja says: "They, the heavenly Navagvas, who strike with boldness, subjugate the woods, being powerful (attackers)."[39] Here the Navagvas are to be identified with the flames of Agni. Their reference as the powerful attackers reminds us of their part in freeing the cows from Vala's cave (*Cf.* RV 10, 108, 8; 3, 39, 5 ab). Thus the similar relation to Indra of the Aṅgirases and the Navagvas and their role in the Vala-myth confirm the fact that the Navagvas formed an important part of the Aṅgirases. Once this is established, we are in a position to infer that they were associated with the Bharadvājas, as they also claimed to be the Aṅgirases.

3. *Uśija*

Uśija is said to be a son or descendant of Aṅgiras and Auśija is a patronymic derived from the name Uśija.[40] He is further said to be an ancestor of Bharadvāja, Dīrghatamas, Kakṣīvat, Ṛjiśvan, etc. In view of this opinion, it is significant that RV 6, 4, 6 mentions one Auśija, that may also mean 'a son' or 'descendant' of Uśija. However, all the scholars do not agree in their interpretation of the word *auśija*. Bergaigne[41] at one time noticed the word *uśija* as 'a proper noun in the making'. He noticed several passages of the RV,[42] where the derivative *auśija* occurs and was hesitant to regard this as a real patronymic in the way it is used with reference to Kakṣīvat in RV 1, 18, 1; 1, 112, 11 and to Ṛjiśvan in RV 10, 99, 11. On another occasion he further discusses the term with reference to Ṛjiśvan and rejected its patronymic sense.[43] Wilson[44] translates it as 'adored sun'. Velankar[45] also takes it as an adjective meaning 'zealous', 'eager', 'unfailing' etc. However, Geldner[46] appears to have accepted *auśija* as a proper name, *i.e.*, a patronymic term. Griffith[47] while translating the passage RV 6, 4, 6 takes the word in the sense of a patronymic and adds a note to his translation to say, 'Auśija: perhaps some contemporary priest who is regarded as bringing back delight by prayer and sacrifice.' Pargiter[48] has also examined the passages of the RV wherein the word *auśija* is used as a patronymic of Kakṣīvat Dairghatamasa and Vaidathina Ṛjiśvan, for he has come to the conclusion that Uśija was a common ancestor of the seers Kakṣīvat and Ṛjiśvan. He placed Uśija just below Aṅgiras and above Ucathya and Bṛhaspati.[49] This he has done on the basis of the evidence found in the traditional sources contained in the Purāṇas. Other scholars, who have opined that the word *auśija* does not signify any patronymic sense, appear to have neglected those traditional sources altogether. Pargiter's view has now been upheld by some Indian scholars[50] since he relies on both the Vedic and post-Vedic evidence, and also considered historical or semi-historical matters.

Therefore, it appears that Uśija was an ancestor not only of Ṛjiśvan and Kakṣīvat but also of all the Aṅgirases and the Bharadvājas. That explains why his name is read with reverence in the list of the *pravara-ṛṣis* of the Aṅgirases: *Kakṣīvatām āṅgirasaucathya-gautamauśija-kākṣīvateti*[50a] The eminent seer of the Kakṣīvats are: Āṅgirasa, Ucathya, Gautama, Auśija and Kākṣīvata."

4. *Bṛhaspati*

Bṛhaspati is praised as a god in eleven hymns.[51] Also he forms a pair with In dra in two hymns (RV 4, 49 and 7, 97). He is described in 193 verses of the RV. His name occurs about 120 times and in another form, *i.e.*, *Brahmaṇaspati* about 50 times.[52]

Bṛhaspati is described in the RV more as a god than as a poet or a mortal seer. Only in a few stanzas, he is referred to as a father,[53] which indicates that Bṛhaspati was probably a mortal and was later elevated to godhead. That raises a question whether there really was a mortal called Bṛhaspati and that he was elevated to godhead. To us, it appears probable that Bṛhaspati was in Vedic times, the name of a mortal also[54] (such as Viṣṇu, etc., of men, even in modern times). The Sarvā[55] also ascribes two hymns to a poet Bṛhaspati, probably noting such an ancient tradition that there was one person among the Aṅgirases called Bṛhaspati and that he saw the hymns.

We shall examine here only a few passages in order to establish that there is a *prima facie* case to prove that there was a mortal Bṛhaspati. In doing so, we shall examine briefly the texts from the RV to the Epics.

Among the gods, Indra and Agni are mentioned in association with Bṛhaspati.[56] Thus in the Vala-myth, (i) Bṛhaspati is Indra's associate and is said to have pierced Vala with his weapon[57] and (ii) Bṛhaspati is accompanied by the Aṅgirases[58] also—these Aṅgirases are mortals who were intimately connected with Agni as well. However, in this activity, Bṛhaspati's association with Indra, on the one hand and with the Aṅgirases and their different groups, on the other, is very significant.

In the RV 6, 73, 1[59] the poet Bharadvāja Bārhaspatya says: "Bṛhaspati, the son of Aṅgiras (*Āngirasa*), who is breaker of rock, the first born, possessing oblation, the holy one, growing in two places of earth, sitting in the shining place, our father, a bull, calls loudly on heaven and earth". Although Bṛhaspati is praised as god, here he is called an Āṅgirasa 'a son or descendant of Aṅgiras' (mentioned above) and 'our father'.[60] That he was an Āṅgirasa is further asserted in RV 1, 62, 2cd[61]: "Through whom (*i.e.*, Indra) our forefathers, the Aṅgirases, the knowers of the places and singers of the praises, found the cows (in the cave of Vala)". In the next verse (*i.e.*, in RV 1, 62, 3)[62] it is said: "When at the desire of Indra and the Aṅgirases (for the cows), Saramā found provision for offspring, Bṛhaspati cleft the mountain, found the cows; (at this) the heroes hailed the cows in triumph". Further, the Navagvas and the Daśagvas who form two distinct groups among the Aṅgirases are referred to in RV 1, 62, 4.[63] In RV 10, 14, 6, they are referred to along with the Aṅgirases as the *pitṛs*.[64] All these references point out that Bṛhaspati was probably at the head of the Aṅgirases and played a significant role in the recovery of the cows from Vala's cave. Bṛhaspati was most probably one among the Aṅgirases, *i.e.*, he was a descendant of Aṅgiras, as is suggested above (in RV 6, 73, 1). The poet Nodhas of the Aṅgiras family was also aware of this fact and, therefore, he praised the activities of the Aṅgirases who were led by Bṛhaspati in RV 1, 62. This assumption is supported by the statement in RV 2, 23, 18[65]; and Sāyaṇa interprets it accordingly: The poet Gṛtasmada says: "The mountain went asunder for your glory, when you set free the stall of the cows, O Aṅgiras. With Indra as your companion, you forced out the flood of waters which was enveloped in darkness, O Bṛhaspati."[66] The verse is addressed to Bṛhaspati. In *b* he is addressed as 'Āṅgirasa', as he is a descendant of Aṅgiras.[67] Here Bṛhaspati is said to have helped Indra against Vala (in *ab*) and Vṛtra (in *cb*). Sāyaṇa[68] interprets the first hemstitch as: *aṅgiraḥ āṅgirasa he bṛhaspate gavām āvarako valenādhiṣṭhitaḥ parvataḥ tava śriye āśrayanāthaṁ vyajihīta. vivṛtadvāratām agacchat* 'O Aṅgiras, *i.e.*, O descendant of Aṅgiras, O Bṛhaspati, you removed the veil of darkness, namely the mountain occupied by Vala, for your welfare.' And Veṅkaṭa Mādhava takes 'Aṅgiras' more clearly to mean 'one born in the family of Aṅgiras (*tvam aṅgirasāṁ kule jātaḥ*).[69]

In the RV, the Aṅgirases are mentioned as connected with Yama also. So also in two verses (*i.e.*, in RV 10, 13, 4 and 14, 3), Bṛhaspati is mentioned together with Yama. Varuṇa is the only god mentioned with Yama (RV 10, 14, 7). In RV 10, 14, 3[70] Bṛhaspati is urged together with the singers (*ṛkvans*), as Yama is urged together with Aṅgirases to rejoice in the *svadhā* oblation, which is generally offered to the *pitṛs* in contrast to the *svāhā* to the gods. RV 10, 13, 4[71] says: "For the sake of god(s) he chose death as his share. He does not choose for the sake of men, an eternal life. They sacrificed Bṛhaspati the seer.[72] Yama delivered his own dear body".

Thus, it becomes clear that there was one Bṛhaspati among the Āṅgirasa seers and he attained a place among *pitṛs*, too. His mention along with different groups of the Aṅgirases and also with

Yama goes to point to the fact that this Bṛhaspati was a mortal but he attained to a place like the *pitṛs* for good deeds. Among his exploits was, his battle with Vala and the release or recovery of the cows.

Besides this mortal Bṛhaspati, it is probable, that there was another Bṛhaspati who was symbol of piety and priesthood. And, in course of time, the Ṛgvedic poets made no distinction between the two; consequently there arose a lot of confusion.

Probably the mortal Bṛhaspati was connected with the kings of Vaiśāli,[73] and was Ucathya's and Saṁvarta's, brother. And he begot Bharadvāja from Mamatā, the wife of Ucathya.

It is also possible that this mortal Bṛhaspati was the seer of the hymns, RV 10, 71-72. The Sarvā (2, 10, 72)[74] calls him Bṛhaspati Laukya. The word *Laukya* means 'one belonging to the mundane world,'[75] to which the seer Bṛhaspati, belonged. This distinguishes him from a person belonging to the celestial world.

Also, it is probable that a mortal Bṛhaspati was elevated to godhead through a process of evolution. This deification of Bṛhaspati was done by the Āṅgirasa seers, for most of the references to and in the hymns in praise of Bṛhaspati are from what were visualised by the Āṅgirasa family. An ardent devotee like Gṛtsamada is also said to have been born in that family—he was later adopted by the Bhṛgus. He envisioned some hymns dedicated to the god Brahmaṇaspati, another form of Bṛhaspati, wherein the elevation of the mortal Bṛhaspati to the god Bṛhaspati was completely achieved.

5. *Kutsa*

Out of a large number of the Āṅgirasa seers who have made significant contributions to the making of the RV and other Vedas, Kutsa is another one mentioned in the 6th Maṇḍala four times.[76] His name occurs very frequently in other Maṇḍalas also, 40 times, in the RV.[77] Besides, one Kutsaputra and one Kutsavatsa 'probably meaning son of Kutsa' and 'one favoured by Kutsa' are respectively referred to in RV 10, 105, 11.[78]

In RV 4, 26, 1[79] Kutsa is called Ārjuneya—'the descendant of Arjuna'—(cf. RV 7, 19, 2; 8, 1, 11).

Kutsa is usually found to have been associated with god Indra in his war against the demons such as Śuṣṇa and Kuyava. In RV 6, 31, 3[80], the poet Suhotra Bhāradvāja says: "Befriended by Kutsa, do you fight the weak Śuṣṇa and Kuyava and ten more demons in a battle at the time of the sun-set"[81] (cf. RV 1, 103, 8; 2, 19, 6; 4, 16, 6; 7, 19, 2). In the second half of this verse, Indra is said to have won (lit. stolen away) the sun's wheel (*i.e.* the orb from the heaven) in company with Kutsa. The same myth is repeated in RV 6, 20, 5,[82] as well; it states: "The supporter of all life (namely the sun's wheel), was removed (to safety) away from the great demon (Śuṣṇa) when Śuṣṇa fell down dead at the fall of the Vajra. He made it most pleasant for Kutsa, who was his companion in the same chariot during (the battle for the) acquisition of the sun."[83] The poet Bharadvāja himself repeats this account at RV 6, 26, 3[84]: "You inspired Kavi for the acquisition of the sun's light; you slew Śuṣṇa for the sake of your worshipper Kutsa."[85] Thus it is clear that Kutsa was a protégé of Indra and for his sake, Indra killed Śuṣṇa and probably Kuyava also. Further Kutsa appears to have been associated with Indra's companion in his cosmic activity of stealing or winning the sun's wheel.

In the RV, there are a few passages where one Kutsa is said to have been defeated by Indra. In RV 6, 18, 13[86] the poet Bharadvāja says of this Kutsa that he was vanquished for the sake of one Turvayāṇa: "That deed of yours was well executed today, when you (subdued) Kutsa, Āyus, and Atithigva for him (*i.e.*, Turavyāṇa). (At that time) you laid low on the ground many thousand (of their warriors) and boldly carried off Turvayāṇa (from their midst)".[87] This is repeated in RV 1, 53, 10[88] wherein Āyus and Atithigva are also reported to have been defeated along with Kutsa for the sake of king Turvayāṇa (cf. RV 2, 14, 7; 4, 26, 1; 8, 53, 2). The above references conflict with the earlier statements that Kutsa was a protégé of Indra. This gives rise to the questions: 'Do all these references from the RV relate to one and same person? Or were there more than one Kutsa known to the Ṛgvedic poet-seers?' Rahurkar suggests a way to resolve this problem: Kutsa might have been "originally a devout follower of the Indra-cult, but in course of time, for reasons not explicitly mentioned in the RV, he turned antagonistic to that cult and was victimised by that god. ... Or it may be possible that Kutsa was originally anti-Indra, but that, after being vanquished by that god, he became an ardent convert to that cult."[89] As a third possibility he assumes that there might have been "two personalities—both called Kutsa."[90] To our mind, the final alternative is more probable.

Another Kutsa was seer of RV 1, 94-98; 101-115; 9, 97, 45-58.

He has mentioned (RV 1, 101, 1[91] Ṛjiśvan, whom we have identified as a poet of the Bharadvāja family.[92] In the hymn RV 1, 112 he refers to several Ṛgvedic personalities; *viz.*, Kaṇva (v. 5), Atri, Purukutsa (v. 7), Vasiṣṭha, Śrutarya, Kutsa (himself?), Narya (v. 9), Viśpalā (v. 10), Auśija Kakṣīvat (v. 11), Māndhātṛ and Bharadvāja (v. 13), and Śaṁbara, Atithigva (?), Divodāsa, Trasadasyu (v. 14) and some others. At verse 23, Kutsa, the descendant of Arjuna (Ārjuneya), is also named as the protégé of the Aśvins.

Now crops up the problem of mutual-dependence (*anyonyāśraya*). Because as we have seen above, Bharadvāja refers to Kutsa in three verses (*viz.*, in RV 6, 18, 3; 20, 5 and 26, 3) while Kutsa Āṅgirasa alludes to Bharadvāja (RV 1, 112, 13); so also, Suhotra Bharadvāja (in RV 6, 31, 3) while Kutsa refer to Ṛjiśvan (in RV 1, 101, 1). How could this be? All of them are protégés of Indra at different stages, and we do not know their chronological sequences. From the numerous references it appears that Kutsa Ārjuneya was a very famous seer and might have lived earlier. He may be considered as anterior to the Bharadvājas, the seers of the Ṛgvedic hymns. But he may not be considered as anterior to Bharadvāja Bārhaspatya. Kutsa, the seer of the extant Ṛgvedic hymns, probably was posterior to the Bhāradvājas, whose hymns are contained in the 6th Maṇḍala of the RV. The two Kautsas *viz.*, Sumitra and Durmitra,[93] might have been descendants of Kutsa Āṅgirasa, the seer of the Ṛgvedic hymns. Still, we think that Kutsa Ārjuneya was a member of the Āṅgirasa family and an ancestor of Kutsa Āṅgirasa. As the Bhardvājas form a part of the Aṅgirases, so their relation to different Kutsas is quite obvious and, among them, the posterior ones took it as their ardent duty to admire the activities of the anterior ones.

6. *Atharvan*

Atharvan is one among the ancient seers (*ṛṣayaḥ*) and forefathers (*pitaraḥ*) mentioned in the 6th Maṇḍala of the RV by the seers of the family of Bharadvāja. His name is given in the RV twelve times,[94] and in the 6th Maṇḍala alone, thrice.[95] Besides, the derivative *atharvavát* occurs twice in the RV (*i.e.* at RV 6, 15, 17 and 10, 83, 12). Moreover, words like *atharvyà* (RV 1, 112, 10) and *atharyá* (RV 7. 1, 1), also are noticed in the RV. Atharvan was, like Bhṛgu and Aṅgiras, an ancient poet whose hymns are not included in the extant Śākala Saṁhitā of the RV. Only two of his descendants, *viz*., Bhiṣak[96] and Bṛhaddiva[97] are said to be the seers of two hymns of the RV, *viz.*, 10, 97 and 120 respectively. But the extant Saṁhitās of the AV, *viz.*, the Śaunaka and the Paippalāda Saṁhitās contain a fairly large number of hymns ascribed to Atharvan, Aṅgiras and Bhṛgu.[98] Earlier, the name of that Saṁhitā is known to have been Atharvāṅgiras or Bhṛgvaṅgiras, and subsequently it came to have the title, Atharvaveda, which is far more significant.[99] As regards the substitution of Atharvan by Bhṛgu earlier, and then retention only of Atharvan hints probably at the growing influence of the Ātharvaṇic element in course of time.[100] Atharvan and Aṅgiras are said to represent two different aspects of magical practices, *viz*., *śānta* and *ghora,*[101] which were prevalent in the ancient Indian society. In the course of time, the Ātharvaṇic practice of *śānta* (also *bheṣaja*) aspect could retain its popularity and hold over the populace, while the *ghora* aspect of the Aṅgirases lost the ground. It may also be noted that the hymns ascribed to Aṅgiras and the Aṅgirases are, nevertheless, retained in the Saṁhitās, but the manuals pertaining to the ritual therein have rarely come to our hand. As regards the exchange of the two names (*i.e.* Atharvan for Bhṛgu), it is said that the Bhṛgus probably form a part of the Atharvans.[102] But there is no conclusive proof thereof.

The name Atharvan like those of Bhṛgu and Aṅgiras, is found to have been associated with the fire-cult, particularly, the art of kindling fire.[103] The poet Bharadvāja refers at RV 6, 16, 13, to Atharvan's kindling the fire: *tvam agne puṣkarād ádhy átharvā niramanthata/mūrdhnó viśvasya vāghátaḥ//*—"O Agni, Atharvan has churned you out from the lotus, from the head of everything."[104] Another poet Vītahavya also strikes the same note (RV 6, 15, 17), *imám u tyám atharvavád agním manthanti vedhásaḥ/ yám aṅkūyántam ānayann ámūraṁ śyāvyábhyaḥ//*—"Our priests, like Atharvan, churn out this Agni, whom they have brought from the dark-ones, *i.e.,* nights, the meandering immortal god."[105] The poet Garga Bhāradvāja, while appreciating the gifts of one Aśvatha at RV 6, 47, 24, says: *dáśa rátham prásṭimataḥ śatám gā átharvebhyaḥ aśvatháḥ pāyávé dāt//* "Aśvatha gave to the Atharvans ten chariots with the foremost horse, and a hundred cows, so also to Pāyu".[106] Velankar[107] takes the Atharvans here as the followers of Pāyu. If we accept his view, it will only mean that there existed a close relationship among the Bharadvājas (*i.e.*, the Angirases) and the Atharvans.

It is also to be noted that Atharvans are mentioned as *pitṛs* with the groups of the Aṅgirases (RV 10, 14, 6).[108]

The poet Bharadvāja mentions Dadhyañc, the son of Atharvan (RV 6, 16, 14): *tám u tvā dadhyáññṛṣiḥ putrá idhe átharvaṇaḥ/ vṛtrahánam purandarám//* "The seer Dadhyañc, the son of Atharvan, kindled you, the killer of enemies (and) breaker of the forts (which belonged to enemies)'.[109] This seer Dadhyañc is referred to in a number of other verses and is said to have proclaimed to the Aśvins the Madhuvidyā with a horse's head.[110]

7. *Bhṛgu*

Bhṛgu is one of the three ancient seers, who are reverentially mentioned in the RV. His name occurs twentythree times; only twice in singular[110a], at the other places in plural.[111] Besides, its derivative form *bhṛguvát* occurs in the RV once,[112] and *bhṛguvant* thrice.[113] Out of all these occurrences, only one occurrence of the name is noticed in the 6th Maṇḍala (*viz.,* RV 6, 15, 2). Incidentally it is a hymn ascribed to one Vītahavya whom tradition holds as a possible seer of the hymn, Bharadvāja being the other. One Vītahavya had allegiance to the Bhṛgus.[114]

Bhṛgu, like Aṅgiras and Atharvan, was very closely connected with fire-cult, as several Ṛgvedic poets confirm their (*i.e.*, Bhṛgus') relation with Agni. Nodhas of the Gautama family says that the Bhṛgus have kept Agni among men (RV 1, 58, 6).[115] In RV 1, 127, 7, Parucchepa, the son of Divodāsa, affirms that the Bhṛgus recited poems near Agni.[116] Somāhuti, a descendant of the Bhṛgu family, states at RV 2, 4, 2 that the Bhṛgus kept Agni among the people of Āyus.[117] Viśvāmitra also speaks of Agni as the gift of the Bhṛgus at RV, 3, 2, 4[118]. The same poet narrates (RV 3, 5, 10) how god Mātariśvan kindled Agni for Bhṛgus.[119] In RV 4, 7, 1, Vāmadeva (of the Gautama family) informs that the Bhṛgus kindled Agni for the sake of the people.[120] So also, Vītathavya or Bharadvāja (RV 6, 15, 2) says that 'the Bhṛgu placed Agni in the wood like a well established friend.'[121] Dīrghatamas, the half-brother of Bharadvāja, confirms (RV 1, 143, 4) that the Bhṛgus kindled Agni.[122]. At RV 10, 46, 2 Vatsapri Bhālandana reports that the Bhṛgus obtained Agni from the cave.[123] In RV 10, 92, 10 śāryāta Mānava claims that the Bhṛgus created Agni along with the Heaven and Earth, Āpas and Tvaṣṭṛ.[124] Citramahas of the Vāsiṣṭha family also speaks of the Bhṛgus' illuminating Agni with their songs (RV 10, 122, 5).[125]

All these references by various Ṛṣis, point to how much the Bhṛgus were associated with the fire-cult, just like the Aṅgirases and the Atharvans. The Bhṛgus are mentioned in RV 10, 14, 6[126] as the Soma-loving fathers (*somyāsaḥ pitaraḥ*) along with Aṅgiras and Atharvan. It is also said (RV 10, 92, 10)[127] that while Atharvan established the rites with sacrifice, the Bhṛgus showed themselves as gods with special skill.

One of the Bhṛgus, named Uśanas, is named in the RV seventeen times.[128] One such passage occurs in the 6th Maṇḍala (*viz.*, at 6, 20, 11). In RV 1, 51, 11[129] he is referred to as Uśanas *Kāvya* 'the son of Kavi' (cf. also RV 1, 83, 5). Sāyaṇa[130] asserts (RV 1, 83, 5) *Kāvyaḥ kaveḥ putraḥ uśanā bhṛguḥ*, '*Kāvya* (signifies) the son of Kavi, *viz.*, Uśanas of the Bhṛgu family.' (cf. Sāyaṇa in RV 1, 121, 12). In RV 6, 20, 11 Bharadvāja refers to Uśanas thus: *tvám vṛdhá indra purvyó bhur varisyánn uśáne kāvyāya| párā návavāstvam anudéyam mahé pitré dadātha svám nápātam||* Velankar[131] renders this as: "Seeking to give freedom to Uśanā Kāvya, you become his foremost furtherer. You also gave back to the Great father his own child Navavāstva, as a sort of a return gift." Commenting on it Sāyaṇa[132] further takes *Uśáne kāvyāya* to mean *kaviputrāya uśanase bhārgavāya* 'to Uśanas, the son of Kavi and a descendant of Bhṛgu.' In his annotation (to this verse), Velankar[133] maintains that the 2nd hemistich "refers to the story of Navavāstva Bṛhadratha, who once sought to increase the brightness and expanse of the firmament and therefore, was killed by Indra like a Dāsa" (cf. 10, 49, 6). Thus it appears that Uśanas Kāvya was a Bhārgava and a well-known sage in the Ṛgvedic age, and the Sarvā (2, 8, 84 and 2, 9, 87) ascribes the hymns RV 8, 84 and 9, 87-89 to him.[134] His father Kavi Bhārgava is said to have divined other hymns (RV 9, 47-49; 75-79).[135]

Another Bhārgava seer known to the RV is Jamadagni. His name occurs four times[136] and the derivative *jamadagnivát* twice (RV 7, 96, 3 and 9, 97, 15), as also the compound word *jamádagnidatta* (RV 3, 53, 15). Moreover, Cyavāna Bhārgava and Nema Bhārgava are referred to in the RV, but the Bharadvājas do not take note of these seers of the Bhṛgu family.

In the AVŚ the Bhṛgus are mentioned four times only. AVŚ 2, 5, 3[137] says that Indra split Vala asunder as Bhṛgu conquered his enemies under Soma intoxication. In AVŚ 5, 19, 1[138] the Śṛñjayas and the Vītahavyas are supposed to have perished, because, they insulted the Bhṛgus.

The Sarvā ascribes a number of hymns in the RV to quite a few of seers belonging to the family of Bhṛgu, beside the 2nd Maṇḍala as a whole to Gṛtsamada Bhārgava.[138a] These are: Iṭ (of RV 10, 171)[139]; Kavi (of RV 9, 47-49; 75-79)[140]; Kṛtnu (of RV 8, 79)[141]; Cyavāna (of RV 10, 19)[142]; Jamadagni (of RV 3, 62, 16-18; 8. 101; 10, 62; 65; 67, 16-18; 10, 110; 137, 6; 167)[143]; Nema (of RV 8, 100)[144]; Prayoga (of RV 8, 102)[145]; Vena (of RV 9, 85; 10, 123)[146]; Somāhuti (of RV 2, 4-7)[147]; and Syūmaraśmi (of RV 10, 77-78).[148] We have already discussed Gṛtsamada's admission into the Bhṛgu family elsewhere[149].

The Bhṛgus are described in the MBh.[150] This Epic may better be described as a mine of information about the Bhṛgus. From the numerous legends about them, we know that "(a) the Bhṛgus were a clan of warlike Bhrāhmins who had contracted matrimonial relation with the Kṣatriyas; (b) they were brave, arrogant and revengeful in nature; (c) their prowess depended equally on weapons and witchcraft; (d) and they were interested in Dharma and Nīti."[151] Nevertheless, their description in the Epic is always derived from the Vedic literature.

Mutual relationship

It is curious that in some of the Vedic references to the Bhṛgus and the Aṅgirases, they are mentioned together and that indicates their mutual association. It has been pointed out by Karambelkar[152] that, in some of the places the Bhṛgus and the Aṅgirases are mentioned while in some others the Aṅgirases and the Atharvans are mentioned; but nowhere are the Bhṛgus and the Atharvans referred together. In some of the Vedic passages, these three names are noticed as being mutually interchangeable among themselves. The GB 1, 2, 3[153] accounts for the creation of the Atharvan sages; it says that the first Atharvan became Bhṛgu. However, the Cūlikopaniṣad 10[154] holds that the Bhṛgus are foremost among the Atharvans. The three names of the AV (*viz.*, Atharvāṅgiras, Bhṛgvaṅgiras and Atharvaveda) also confirm this. At one stage the AV was called the Atharvāṅgiras, later it came to be known as Bhṛgvaṅgiras and finally it retained only Atharva. A possible conclusion is that the Bhṛgus formed a part of (or were assimilated to) the Atharvans. This explains why the name of any of Atharvan seers is not given in the Pravara list, although those of Bhṛgu and Aṅgiras are conspicuously featured.

As regards their achievements, of the Angirases and the Bhṛgus the latter were associated with the cult of fire (Agni) more than the Aṅgirases who drew nearer to Indra and helped him in his exploits.[155]

Both the seers are mentioned in RV 10, 14, 6:

áṅgiraso naḥ pitátro návagvā átharvāṇo bhṛgavaḥ somyāsaḥ/
téṣām vayám sumataù yajñíyānām ápi bhadre saumanase syāma//

"The Aṅgirases, our fathers the Navagvas, the Bhṛgus (all are) worthy of (drinking) Soma. May we remain in the good auspicious wish of those who (are) worthy of worship."

MBh 12, 69, 11 refers to Bhṛgu and Aṅgiras among the four *mūlagotras:*

catvāri mūlagotrāṇi samutpannāni pārthiva/aṅgirā kaśyapaś caiva vasiṣṭho bhṛgur eva ca// "O king, four original *gotras* have arisen, and they are Aṅgiras, Kaśyapa, Vasiṣṭha and Bhṛgu".

It may also be pointed out that the Aṅgirases had matrimonial relations with the Bhṛgus even earlier. BD 4, 11 cd[156] says that Mamatā, the wife of Ucathya Āṅgirasa, was a daughter of Bhṛgu. The BD, Sarvā and Arṣa report that one Gṛtsamada, the son of Śunahotra Āṅgirasa, was adopted as son by Śunaka of the Bhṛgu family, and he became a Bhārgava seer.[157] The Sarvā 2, 2, 1[158] ascribes the 2nd Maṇḍala of the RV to him. So also AśvŚS 6, 10, 12[159] says that the Mitrayus, who have three *ṛṣi-pravaras* consisting of Bhārgava, Daivodāsa and Vādhryaśva belong to the Bhṛgu-*pakṣas.* We shall elsewhere[160] observe that these Mitrayus along with their *pravara*-seers actually were descendants of Ajamīḍha Sauhotra, who in turn was a remote offspring of Bharadvāja (*i.e.*, also of Aṅgiras).

Thus, all these things point to a full-scale intercourses among the Bhṛgus and the Aṅgirases at different stages of the Indo-Aryan civilization. And we can, therefore, conclude that the RV reveals to us that the Aṅgirases (including the Bharadvājas, the Vāmadevas, the Kāṇvas, the Kakṣīvats and others) played a role more important than that by the progeny of other *Mūlagotras, viz.*, Vasiṣṭha, Kaśyapa and Bhṛgu. The AV bears out the significant contribution of the Bhṛgus and the Aṅgirases to contemporary society. And, in the age of the Epics the Bhṛgus outdid all other families, particularly the Aṅgirases; this is evident from the final redaction of the MBh.

NOTES AND REFERENCES TO CHAPTER I

Section (*i*)

1. (a) In singular: RV 1, 112, 13; 116, 18; 6, 15, 3; 16, 5; 33; 17, 14; 31, 4; 48, 7; 13; 63, 10; 10, 150, 5; 181, 2.
   (b) In plural: RV 1, 59, 7; 6, 10, 6; 23, 10; 25, 9; 35, 4; 47, 25; 50, 15.
2. RV 6, 65, 6.
3. RV 6, 51, 12.
4. The word *Vājineya* has been accepted as a matronymic by commentators and modern scholars. Veṅkaṭa Mādhava explains this matronymic as '*bharadvājaḥ vājinyāḥ putraḥ* and Sāyaṇa also interprets it in the same way, *i.e.*, as *Vājineyaḥ vājinyāḥ putro bharadvājaḥ*. Pradhan appears to have accepted this explanation and without any hesitation applied it to Bharadvāja. According to him, Vājinī was another name of Mamatā Bhārgavī, the mother of Bharadvāja and Dīrghatamas. Also, he identifies this Bharadvāja 'Vājineya', son of Bṛhaspati, with Bharadvāja the priest of Divodāsa Atithigva. Elsewhere, he takes this Divodāsa as a descendant of Tṛkṣa, Mudgala and Vadhryaśva who were themselves the progeny of Vidathin Bharadvāja, a person, some three generations below Bharadvāja Bārhaspatya. Rahurkar (SR), and Mankad, too, (DR pp. 3-4), have taken a similar position, without going into details. Incidentally, we may point out that in RV 6, 61, 6, Sarasvatī is addressed by the same Bharadvāja who is said to be the seer of RV 6, 26, 2, as *vājinī*. Does it mean that Bharadvāja was a son of the river Goddess Sarasvatī? Thus the identification of Vājinī with Mamatā Bhārgavī, without adequate reason (or support) poses a serious problem. We may, therefore, suggest that the word *vājineya* in this verse (*i.e.*, 6, 26, 2) may either signify a person who was born of some woman(?) called Vājinī or serve as an appellative of a Bhāradvāja (whosoever he may be) in the sense of 'one possessing strength'. There is no sound reason, however, for accepting Vājinī as an alternative name of Mamatā. (For details see Pradhan's CAI pp. 7ff. and Rahurkar's SR pp. 90ff.)
5. SR p. 90
6. CAI p. 7ff.
7. SR pp. 90ff.
8. See our section on the Brāhmaṇic references to Bharadvāja.
9. See our Introduction for the broad outline of the method followed in this dissertation.
10. Read: याभिर्विप्रं प्र भरद्वाजमावतं ताभिरुषु ऊतिभिरश्विना गतम् ।
11. See for details the Ch. 5 of Part I below.
12. Keith and Macdonell, VI I p. 543.
13. Read: भरद्वाजाय सप्रथ शर्म यच्छ सहन्त्य । अग्ने वरेण्यं वसु ।
14. VI I p. 542 (Nos. of verses in brackets are mine).
15. Vide for details, Section on Vītahavya below.
16. Sāyaṇa, RVVSM Vol. 3, p. 44 (under 6, 15, 3, cf. also Sāyaṇa's explanation under V. 2: वीतहव्ये एतत् संज्ञ ऋषौ. . . भरद्वाज ऋषिश्चेत् वीतहव्ये दत्तहविष्के भरद्वाज इति योजनीयम् ।) However, an earlier commentator, Veṅkaṭa Mādhava, considers

Vītahavya as qualifying Bhāradvāja or in the sense of a seer belonging to Bhāradvāja family.

17. Velankar, 'Divodāsa Atithigva and other Atithigvas', ABORI, Silver Jubilee Vol. 1942.
18. Velankar, Ibid.
19. 'Indra Hymns by the Bharadvājas', BUJ, 10(2), 1942, p. 88.
20. Velankar: 'Hymns to Indra by the Bharadvājas', BUJ. 11(2), p. 59.
21. Sarvā on 2, 6, 65. Actually Bharadvāja Bārhaspatya is proclaimed as the seer of the 6th book, wherever some other individual poet is found to be the seer of a particular hymn he is personally alluded to, otherwise the authority of Bharadvāja continues to have its application, by way of *adhikāra*-rule given at the Sarvā 2, 6.1.
22. RV 1, 116, 18; 6, 16, 5; 31, 4.
23. Sāyaṇa on RV 1, 116, 18, RVVSM Vol. I p. 723.
24. Chapekar, "Bharadvāja", ABORI, 31 p. 298.
25. Roth, *St. Petersburg Dictionary*, sv. (quoted in VI 2, 98).
26. Velankar, 'Agni Hymns in the Ṛgveda' VI BUJ, XXIV, 30, 2, p. 61.
27. Velankar, *Op cit*.
28. Read: त्वं शतान्यव शम्बरस्य पुरो जघन्याप्रतीनि दस्योः ।
अशिक्षो यत्र शच्या शचीवो दिवोदासाय सुन्वते सुतक्रे ॥
भरद्वाजाय गृणते वसूनि ॥
29. See Ch. 5 below.
30. Sāyaṇa under 6, 50, 15 RVVSM Vol. 3, p. 189. Skandasvāmin understands *napāto mama...bharadvājāḥ* as *mama pautrāḥ bharadvājasya' nvayajātāḥ*. And Veṅkaṭa Mādhava understands the expression as *mama putrāḥ bharadvājakulajāḥ* (RVVIS Vol. 4, p. 2169). Sāyaṇa's interpretation is closer to that of Veṅkaṭa Mādhava.
31. See our section on family hymns, Part II, Ch. 1, Sec. (ii).
32. Read: विद्याम वस्तोरवसा गृणन्तो भरद्वाजा उत त इन्द्र नूनम् ।
33. Read: नू सद्मानं दिव्यं नंशि देवा भारद्वाजः सुमतिं याति होता ।
आसानेभिर्यजमानो मियेधैर्देवानां जन्म वसूयुर्ववन्द ॥
34. See also our comment on the sections on Bharadvāja in Rām, and Divodāsa Vītahavya and Bharadvāja (in MBh.). Cf. RV 1, 116, 18; 6, 16, 5; 3, 1, 4.
35. RV 6, 63, 10.
36. RV 1, 59, 7.
37. RV 6, 63, 9.
38. AIHT, p. 4.
39. Pradhan, S.N., D.R. Mankad, V.G. Rahurkar, P.L. Bhargava.
40. CAI. pp. 7ff.
41. pp. 5 and 7.
42. SR pp. 96-97.
43. For our arguments on these weaknesses, see sections Bharadvāja and Divodāsa (in MBh 13, 31) and Bharadvāja in *Rām*, and see fn. 4 of this section above.
44. See Section on Pāyu Bhāradvāja for details.

Section (ii)

1. Read: अग्निरत्रिं भरद्वाजं गविष्ठिरं प्रावन्नः कण्वं त्रसदस्युमाहवे ।
अग्निं वसिष्ठो हवते पुरोहितो मृकीकाय पुरोहितः ।।
2. Read: यौ भरद्वाजमवथो यौ गविष्ठिरं विश्वामित्रं वरुण मित्र कुत्सम् ।
यौ कक्षीवन्तमवथः प्रोथ कण्वः सो नौ मुंचतमंहसः ।।
3. Read: (Accents are not marked by the ed. in AVP recension).
यौ भरद्वाजमवथो यौ वध्यश्वं विश्वामित्रं वरुण मित्र कुत्सम् ।
यौ कक्षीवन्तमवथः प्रोत कण्वः तौ नौ मुंचतमंहसः ।।
4. Read: विश्वामित्र जमदग्ने वसिष्ठ भरद्वाज गोतम वामदेव ।
शर्दिनौ अत्रिरग्रभीन्नमोभिः सुसंशासः पितेरो मृडता नः ।।
5. Read: जमदग्निः कश्यपः स्वाद्वेतद् भरद्वाजो मध्वन्नं कृणोतु ।
प्रतिग्रहीत्रे गोतमो वसिष्ठो विश्वामित्रो नः प्रतिरन्त्यायुः ।।
6. Read: जमदग्निः कश्यपः स्वाद्वेतद् भरद्वाजो मध्वन्नं कृणोतु ।
प्रतिग्रहीत्रे गोतमो वसिष्ठो विश्वामित्रो ददर्श शर्म यच्छातु ।।

In vv (5) and (6), there is a change in the pāda d only नः प्रतिरन्त्यायुः in (5) is substituted by ददर्श शर्म यच्छातु in (6), evidently the former is better reading.

7. Read: इमाम् अत्रयोऽङ्गिरसो गोतमो वीरुधं विदुः ।
तया भरद्वाजः कण्वो विषं नाशयति ते ।।
8. RV 10, 14, 15cd, ascribed to Yama.

Section (iii)

1. Read: अग्निष्टोमं वै देवा आश्रयन्तोक्थान्यसुरस्ते समावद् वीर्या एवासन्न व्यावर्तन्त तान् भरद्वाज ऋषीणामपश्यद् इमे वा असुरा उक्थेषु श्रितास्तानेषां न कश्चन पश्यतीति सोऽग्निमुदह्वय देहयूषु अवाणि तंऽग्न इत्यतरा गिर इत्यसुर्या ह वा इतरा गिरः सोऽग्निरुपोप्रोतिष्ठन्नब्रवीत् किंस्विदेव मह्यं कृशो दीर्घः पलितो वक्ष्यतीति भरद्वाजो ह वै कृशो दीर्घः पलित आस सोऽब्रवीदिमे वा असुरा उक्थेषु श्रितास्तान्वो न कश्चन पश्यतीति तानग्निरश्वो भूत्वात्भ्यत्यद्रवदयदग्निरश्वो भुत्वाऽभ्यत्यद्रवत्तल् साकमश्वं सामाभवत् तत् साकमश्वस्य साकमश्वं तदाहुः साकमश्वेनोक्थानि प्रणयेद् प्रणीतानि वाव तान्युक्थानि यानि अन्यत्र साकमश्वादिति ।

2. Read: भरद्वाजस्यादारसृद् भवति ।। ७

दिवोदासं वै भरद्वाज पुरोहित ननाजनाः पर्य्ययन्त स उपासीददृषे गातुं मे विन्देति तस्मा एतेन साम्ना गातुम् अविन्दद् गातुविद्घा एतत् सामाऽनेन दारे नासृन्मेति तददारसृतोऽदारसृतोऽदारसृत्त्वं विन्दते गातुं न दारे धावत्यदारसृता तुष्टुवानः ।। ७

3. Read under 15, 3, 6-7:

भरद्वाजः पुरोहितो यस्य तं भरद्वाजपुरोहित दिवोदासं ननाजनाः नानाविधा जनाः शत्रुजनाः पर्य्ययन्त पर्य्यवेष्टयन् । स दिवोदासो भरद्वाजमुपासीदत् विनयपूर्वं मागच्छन्द—हे ऋषे गातुं मार्गं मे मम विन्त् लभेयेति ब्रुवन् । एवमागतस्य तस्मै दिवोदासाय एतेन नाम्ना गातुं मार्गमविन्दत अलभत । अतएतत् साम गातुविद् वै मार्गलम्भकम् एवमस्य भरद्वाज सम्बन्धमुक्त्वा अदासृत्वमपि निर्वक्ति ।

4. See note 2 above.

5. See section on Divodāsa, Vītahavya and Bharadvāja elsewhere and Ch. 5 for further details.

6. Read: भरद्वाजो ह वै ऋषीणामनुचानतम:दीर्घजीवितमस्तपस्वितम आस । (We do not distinguish between an Āraṇyaka and a Brāhmaṇa in respect of a narrative.)

7. भरद्वाजो ह त्रिभिरायुभिः ब्रह्मचर्यमुवास तं ह जीर्णि शयानं इन्द्र उपव्रज्य उवाच । भरद्वाज । यत्ते चतुर्थम् आयु: दद्यां, किमेतेन कुर्या इति । ब्रह्मचर्यमेव एतेन चरेयमिति होवाच । तं ह त्रीन् गिरिरूपान् अविज्ञातान् इंव दर्शयांचकार । तेषां ह एकैकस्मात् मुष्टिमाददे । स होवाच भरद्वाज इति आमन्त्र्य । वेदा वा एते । अनन्ता वै वेदा: । एतद्वा एतैः त्रिभिरायुभिः अन्ववोचथा: । अथ त इतरद् अनुक्तमेव । एहि, इमं विद्धि । अयं ह वै सर्वविद्येति । तस्मै हैतमग्निं सावित्र्यमुवाच । तं स विदित्वा अम्रतो भुत्वा स्वर्गलोकमियाय, आदित्यस्य सायुज्यमिति ।

8. For further information, see sections on Bhāradvājas' contribution to the Science of Language (Grammar), Āyurveda *viz.*, Part II, Chapters 5 and 6. Vide also the section on Bhāradvājas in the Upaniṣads [Part I, Ch. 1, Section (iv), and the legend of Yavakrīt (Part I, Ch. 2, Section (v)].

Section (iv)

1. The date of the early Upaniṣads—like Muṇḍaka and Praśna is said to be between 999-750 B.C.; vide Belvalkar, *Basumallik Lectures on Vedānta*—Poona, 1929, p. 45.

2. The date of the later Upaniṣads ranges between 1st century AD. and the fifteenth century AD. Cf. S.G. Desai: "The Later Upaniṣads—A Study": JUB, 32. Sept. 1963, pp. 130-31.

Cf. Sharma, T.R., *Studies in the Sectarian Upaniṣads*, *Delhi*, 1972, pp. 30-33.

3. Read: ब्रह्मा देवानां प्रथम: संबभूव । विश्वस्य कर्ता भुवनस्य गोप्ता स ब्रह्मविद्यां सर्वविद्या-प्रतिष्ठामथर्वाय ज्येष्ठपुत्राय प्राह । अथर्वणे यां प्रवदेत ब्रह्माथर्वा तां पुरोवाचङ्गिरे ब्रह्मविद्याम् । स भारद्वाजाय सत्यवहाय प्राह भारद्वाजोऽङ्गिरसे परावरम् ॥

4. Read: ओं सुकेशा च भरद्वाज: शैव्यश्च सत्यकाम: सौर्यायणी च गार्ग्य: कौशल्यश्चाश्वलायनो भार्गवो वैदर्भि: कबन्धी कात्यायनस्ते हैते ब्रह्मपरा ब्रह्मनिष्ठा: परं ब्रह्मान्वेषमाणा एषा ह वै ससर्वं वक्षतीति ते ह समित्पाणयो भगवन्तं पिप्पलादमुपसन्ना: ॥

4a. Read: अथ हैन सुकेशा भारद्वाज: पप्रच्छ । भगवन् हिरण्यनाभ: कौशल्यो राजपुत्रो मामुपेत्यैतं प्रश्नमपृच्छत । षोडशकलं भारद्वाज पुरुषं वेत्थ, तमहं कुमारमब्रवं नाप्रमिमं वेद ।

5. Read: अथ भारद्वाज: कुमारं पप्रच्छ कोऽयं भवादृशानां परमशिवभक्तानां सिद्धान्ता: । कुत: सर्वे न विदन्तीति तद्गुह्यमुवाच स्कन्द: ।

6. Read: अथ हैनं भारद्वाज: पप्रच्छ याज्ञवल्कयं किं तारकम् । किं तारयतीति स होवाच याज्ञवल्क्य: ।

7. Read : गारुडब्रह्मविद्यां प्रवक्ष्यामि यां ब्रह्माविद्यां नारदाय प्रोवाच । नारदो बृहत्सेनाय, बृहत्सेनेन इन्द्राय इन्द्रो भरद्वाजाय भरद्वाजो जीवत्कामेभ्य: शिष्येभ्य: प्रायच्छेत् ।

8. For Indra-Bharadvāja relation, see our comment in Section (iii) above and section (v) of Ch. 2 of the Part I.

9. Read: सर्वाण्येवमेवैनं ददामीति होवाच । वृषादर्विस्तदिदं इतिहासो ब्रह्मादित्य: पुरोगाय । पुरोग: काश्यपाय । काश्यपोभारद्वाजाय । भरद्वाज: बहुभि: अनेक महाराजाय त त: . . . . . ।

10. Read: ओं प्रणो देवीत्यस्य मन्त्रस्य भरद्वाज ऋषिः गायत्री छन्दः श्रीसरस्वती देवता।

11. Read: ......पाराशर्यो भारद्वाजाद् भारद्वाजो भारद्वाजाच्च गौतमाच्च गौतमो भारद्वाजाद् भारद्वाजो पाराशर्यात्...... ॥ आसुरि भारद्वाजाद् भारद्वाजो आत्रेयाद्...... ॥

12. Read: आसुरिर्भारद्वाजाद् भारद्वाज आत्रेयादात्रेयो...... ॥

13. Read: ......गौतमीपुत्रो भारद्वाजीपुत्राद् भारद्वाजी पुत्र : पाराशरीपुत्रात्......। गौतमीपुत्रो भारद्वाजी पुत्राद् भारद्वाजीपुत्रः पाराशरीपुत्राद् ...... ॥

Section (v)

1. Rām. 2, 85, 4-23; 90, 1-24; 91, 1-83; 92; 1-40 113, 1-21; 6, 1-22.
2. Rām. 1, 2, 14: मा निषाद प्रतिष्ठां त्वमगमः शाश्वतीः समाः।
   यत् क्रौञ्चमिथुनादेकमवधीः काममोहितम् ॥
3. DRg. p. 5.
4. CAI, p. 7ff.
5. See Ch. 5 of Part I for further details.

Section (vi)

1. RV. 6, 2, 10; 16, 11.
2. RV. 6, 11, 3; 18, 5; 65, 5.
3. RV. 6, 49, 11.
4. We write here *áṅgirasvant* with a view to separating if from the preceding *angirasvát*.
5. RV. 6, 35, 5; 73, 1.
6. RV. 6, 35, 5, and 49, 11—these two are from the hymns ascribed to Nara Bhāradvāja and Ṛjiśvan Bhāradvāja respectively. All other references are from the hymns credited to Bhāradvāja Bārhaspatya.
7. RV. 1, 1, 6 runs thus: यदङ्ग दाशुषे त्वमग्ने भद्रं करिष्यसि।
   तवेत् तत् सत्यमङ्गिरः ॥
   Here *aṅgiras* is in vocative and used as an epithet of *Agni*; cf. also RV 1, 31, 17; 74, 5; 4, 3, 15; 9, 7; 5, 8, 4; 6, 2, 10; 16, 11.
8. Read: समृधो विश्पते कृणु जुषस्व हव्यमङिगरः।
9. Read: तं त्वा समिद्भिरङ्गिरो घृतेन वर्धयामसि।
10. Macdonell, VM p. 97; 143.
11. Raja, C.K., PPOR. p. 165.
    Bergaigne V.R., 1, 47-8.
12. Read: धन्यो चिद्धि त्वे धिषणा वष्टि प्र देवाञ्जन्म गृणते यजध्यै।
    वेपिष्ठो अङ्गिरसां यद्ध विप्रो मधुच्छन्दो भनति रेभ इष्टौ ॥
13. Velankar, BUJ, 24, 30 (part 2) p. 52.
14. Read: तन्नः प्रत्नं सख्यमस्तु युष्मे इत्था वदद्भिर्वलमंगिरोभि :।
    हन्नच्युतच्युद् दस्मेषयन्त मृणोः पुरो वि दुरो अस्य विश्वाः ॥
15. Raja, PPOR p. 170.

16. Read: इदा हि त उषो अद्रिसानो गोत्रा गवामङ्गिरसो गृणन्ति ।
व्यर्श्केण विभिदुर्ब्रह्मणा च सत्या नृणामभवद् देवहूतिः ॥

17. Raja PPOR p. 170.

18. RVVSM, Vol. 3, p. 34: Sāyaṇa says: अङ्गिरसामृषीणां मध्ये वेपिष्ठः अतिशयेन स्तुतेः प्रेरयिता विप्रः मेधावी रेभः स्तोता भरद्वाजः इष्टौ......स्तोत्रं भनति...तदा धिषणा वष्टीति ।

19. cf. RV 2, 15, 8; 4, 16, 18.

20. Read: RV. 2, 11, 20:

अस्य सुवानस्य मन्दिनस्त्रितस्य न्यर्बुदं वावृधाने अस्तः ।
अवर्तयत् सूर्यो न चक्रं भिनदवलमिन्द्रो अङ्गिरसाम् ॥

21. Read for examples: RV 2, 17, 1.

तदस्मै नव्यमङ्गिरस्वदर्चत शुष्मा यदस्य प्रत्नथोदीरते ।
विश्वा यद्गोत्रा सहसा परीवृता मदे सोमस्य दृंहिता न्यैरयत् ॥

22. Read the verse RV 2, 11, 20 quoted in (20) above.

23. Read: तमा नूनं वृजनमन्यथा चिच्छूरो यच्छक्र वि दुरो गृणीषे ।
मा निररं शुक्रदुघस्य धेनोराङ्गिरसान् ब्रह्मणा विप्र जिन्व ॥

24. Velankar, BUJ. 13(2), 1943, p. 59.

25. Read: यो अद्रिभित् प्रथमजा ऋतावा बृहस्पतिराङ्गिरसो हविष्मान् ।
द्विवर्हज्मा प्राघर्मसत् पिता न आ रोदसी वृषभो रोरवीति ॥

26. Read: तव श्रिये व्यजिहीत पर्वतो गवां गोत्रमुदसृजो यदङ्गिरः ।
इन्द्रेण युजा तमसा परीवृतं बृहस्पते निरपामौब्जो अर्णवम् ॥

27. Read: योऽङ्गारेभ्य ऋषिर्जज्ञे तस्य पुत्रो बृहस्पतिः ।
बृहस्पतेर्भरद्वाजो विदथीति य उच्यते ॥
मरुत्स्वासीद् गुरुर्यस्य स एवाङ्गिरसो नपात् ।
सः पुत्रस्य तु तस्यैतन् मण्डलं षष्ठमुच्यते ॥

28. AŚVŚS. 6, 11, 5: भारद्वाजाग्निवेश्यानां आङ्गिरस-बार्हस्पत्य-भारद्वाजेति ।

29. Mt 48, 17ff: Va 99, 139ff. For detailed discussion on the descendants of Bharadvāja, see the Chapter 3 of the Part I.

30. RV 10, 14, 6:

अङ्गिरसो नः पितरो नवग्वा अथर्वाणो भृगवो सोम्यासः ।
तेषां वयं सुमतौ यज्ञियानाम् अपि भद्रे सौमनसे स्याम ॥

31. RV 1, 33, 6; 62, 4; 3, 39, 5; 4, 51, 4; 5, 29, 12; 45, 7; 11; 6, 6, 3; 22, 2; 9, 108, 4; 10, 14, 6; 61, 10; 62, 6; 108, 8.

32. RV 6, 6, 3; 22, 2.

33. RVVSM, Vol. 1, p. 247 under RV. 1, 33, 7.

34. Daśgvas are mentioned in the RV eight times: RV. 1, 62, 4; 2, 34, 12; 3, 39, 5; 4, 51, 4; 5, 29, 12; 8, 12, 2; 10, 62, 6. It is indeed significant that they were mentioned together in RV 1, 62, 4; 4, 51, 4; 5, 29, 12 and 10, 62, 6.

35. Sāyaṇa *op. cit.* He also says: नवग्वाः नवनीयगतयः स्तोतव्य चरित्राः or sometimes, नवग्वाः नवभिः मासै गच्छन्तीति नवग्वाः under 1, 33, 6. Under RV 6, 6, 3 he

says: नवग्वा: नूतनगमनास्ते रश्मय: (RVVSM, 3, 20). Thus, he does not stick to one derivation of the word.

36. Read: तमु न: पूर्वे पितरो नवग्वा: सप्त विप्रासो अभि वाजयन्त ।
नक्षद्दाभं ततुरिं पर्वतेष्ठामद्रोघवाचं मतिभि: शविष्ठम् ॥
37. Velankar: JUB 11(2), 1942, p. 93.
38. Read: *pādas* cd only:

तुविम्रक्षासो दिव्या नवग्वा वना वनन्ति धृषता रुजन्त: ।

39. Velankar: BUJ Vol. 24, No. 30, 1955, p. 40.
40. Vā 99, 36ff. and Mt 49, 17ff. relate a story of Uśija's relation with Bṛhaspati. And he is said to be father of Dīrghatamas, and husband of Mamatā, all belonging to the Aṅgiras family. MT 195, 1ff. gives the names of Āṅgirasa seers, wherein Uśija is also named as one of the sons of Aṅgiras. Mt 195, 11 forbids marriage among the descendants of Aṅgiras, Ucathya and Uśija, who are named as the Pravara-ṛṣis of the *gotras* beginning with Ucathya. AśvŚS 6, 11, 3 says: *kakṣīvatām āṅgirasaucathya-Gautamauśija-kākṣīvateti*—'Āṅgirasa, Aucathya, Gautama, Auśija and Kāksīvat are (the five prominent-seers) of (the *Gotras*) arising of Kakṣīvat (etc.)'
41. VR, Part 1, p. 59.

For further information, see our paper on "Ṛjiśvan" CASS studies series 5, pp. 111-120.

42. RV 1, 18, 1; 112, 11; 10, 99, 11.
43. VR, Part 2, p. 359.
44. *Ṛgveda Saṁhitā* (Tr.) Vol. 4 p. 13.
45. BUJ. vol. 24, No. 30, 1955 p. 43.
46. DRV 2, p. 97.
47. HRV p. 286, fn. 6.
48. AIHT pp. 160-161.
49. Ibid p. 191.
50. Rahurkar and Bhargava support Pargiter in their respective works mentioned in Bibliography.
50a. AśvŚS 6, 11, 3.
51. RV 1, 40; 90; 2, 23; 24; 25; 26; 4, 50; 6, 73; 10, 67; 68; 182.
52. RVVSM, 5, pp. 405-7.
53. RV 6, 73, 1; 10, 67, 2-3; cf. 10, 14, 6.
54. See Pargiter, AIHT, pp. 66; 86-87.
55. 2, 10, 71-72: बृहस्पते बृहस्पतिर्ज्ञानं तुष्टाव नवमी जगती देवानां नव लोक्यो वा बृहस्पति दाक्षायण्य दितिर्वा देवमानुष्टुभम् ।

56. Bali, Sarasvati says in this regard: "Bṛhaspati shares some features with Agni also. Both are three-seated (*triṣadhastha* cf. 4, 50, 1; 5, 4, 8), and were born in the highest heaven (cf. RV 4, 50, 4; 6, 8, 2). Both are identified with *mātariśvan* (RV 3, 26, 2; 29, 11) and *narā-śamsa* (RV 1, 18, 9; 3, 29, 11) and Aṅgiras (3, 23, 18; 1, 1, 6); both are associated with the Aṅgirases (10, 67, 2-3); (4, 3, 11); both are *purohitas* or family priests (2, 49, 9; 1, 2); both offer sacrifice (1, 139, 11; 1, 45, 10) and inspire hymns (1, 18; 7; 6, 1, 1); both dispel darkness (4, 50, 4; 8, 8, 43, 32); both bear the title *sahasas putra i.e.*, son of strength (1, 40, 2; 3, 1, 8)."

57. cf. RV. 2, 24, 3 and 4; 10, 68, 5 and 9; 9, 3, 2.
58. cf. RV. 1, 62, 2,: 3; 4; 5.
59. Read: RV 6, 73, 1 quoted in (25) above.
60. In RV. 10, 67, 1 the poet Ayāsya also called him *naḥ pitā* 'our father', and in verse 10, 67, 10 he has referred to Bṛhaspati's soaring to heaven. Incidentally, it may be mentioned that this poet Ayāsya belongs to the Āṅgirasa family.

61. Read: येना नः पूर्वे पितरेः पदज्ञा
अर्चन्तो अङ्गिरसो गा अविन्दत् ॥

62. Read: इन्द्रस्याङ्गिरसां चेष्टौ विदत् सरमा तनयाय धासिम् ।
बृहस्पतिर्भिनदद्रिं विदद्गा समुस्त्रियाभि र्वावशन्त नर ॥

63. Read: स सुष्टुभा स स्तुभा सप्त विप्रैः स्वरेणाद्रिं स्वर्यो३ नवग्वैः ।
सरण्युभिः फलिगामिन्द्र शक्र वलं रवेण दरयो दशग्वैः ॥

64. Read in (30) above.
65. Read the verse quoted in (26) above.
66. Velankar, *Ṛgveda Maṇḍala II.* (tr.) p. 64.
67. Bṛhaspati can be called an Aṅgiras (this Sāyaṇa interprets appropriately). This should not lead one to equate him with Agni Aṅgiras. Agni is called Aṅgiras, because of his *association* with the latter. Agni associated with the Bharatas is called 'Bhārata' also. But Bṛhaspati was a descendant of Aṅgiras. Just as a descendant of Bharadvāja is, sometimes, called by his family name Bharadvāja, so is Bṛhaspati by his family name Aṅgiras.
68. Sāyaṇa: under 2, 23, 18, RVVSM 2, p. 96.
69. RVVIS 3, p. 1218.

70. Read: मातली कव्यै र्यमो अङ्गिरोभि र्बृहस्पतिर्ऋक्वेभिर्वावृधानः ।
यांश्च देवा वावृधुर्ये च देवान् स्वाहान्ये स्वधयान्ये मदन्ति ॥

71. Read: देवेभ्यः कमवृणीत मृत्युं प्रजायै कममृतं नावृणीत ।
बृहस्पतिं यज्ञमकृण्वत ऋषिं प्रियं यमस्तन्वर प्रारिरेचीत् ॥

The verse is repeated in AV 18, 3, 41 with slight change *i.e. Bṛhaspatiḥ* and *ṛsiḥ* replace *bṛhaspatim* and *ṛṣim.*

72. It is significant that Bṛhaspati, the seer, was sacrificed. Does this indicate a *puruṣamedha* sacrifice? If so, can one god be sacrificed at the altar of another? Absurd it is to answer the latter question in the affirmative. This should affirm that Bṛhaspati was a primeval seer, who might have been sacrificed for the betterment of the people!

73. MBh (12, 29, 16-21) describes a quarrel between Bṛhaspati and his brother Saṁvarta relating to the priestly office held by the latter. The Purāṇas also give us the tale of Bṛhaspati's approaching Mamatā, the wife of Ucathya (which we have treated in ch. 2, Section earlier). Ucathya is said to be Bṛhaspati's elder brother and definitely a mortal. Bharadvāja is reported to have been born as a result of Bṛhaspati's union with Mamatā. There are some of the references wherein Bṛhaspati's connection with the mortal is clear.
74. Read note (55) above.
75. Williams, M. *Sanskrit-English Dictionary,* S.V. Laukya.
76. RV 18, 13; 20, 5; 26, 3; 31, 3.
77. RV 1, 33, 14; 51, 6; 53, 10; 63, 3; 106, 6; 112, 9; 23; 121, 9; 174, 5; 175,

4; 2, 14, 7; 19, 6; 4, 16, 10; 11; 12; 26, 1; 30, 4; 5, 29, 9; 10; 31, 8; 6, 18, 13; 20, 5; 26, 3; 31, 3; 7, 19; 2; 25, 5; 8, 1, 11; 24, 25; 53, 2; 10, 29, 2; 38, 5; 40, 6; 49, 3; 4; 99, 9; 105, 11; 138, 1.

78. Read: शतं वा यदसुर्य प्रति त्वा सुमित्र इत्थास्तौद्दुर्मित्र इत्यास्तौद ।
श्रावो यद्दस्युहत्ये कुत्सपुत्रं प्रावो यद्दस्युहत्ये कुत्सवत्सम् ॥

79. Read: श्रहं कुत्समार्जुनेयं न्यृञ्जेजऽहं कविरुशना पश्यत मा ॥

80. Read: त्वं कुत्सेनाभि शुष्णमिन्द्राशुषं युध्यं कुयवं गविष्ठौ ।
दश प्रपित्वे श्रध सूर्यस्य मुषायश्चक्रमविवे रपांसि ॥

81. Velankar: BUJ. Vol. 13(2), 1943, p. 55.

82. Read: महो द्रुहो श्रप विश्वायु धायि वज्रस्य यत् पतने पादि शुष्णः ।
उरु ष सरथ सारथये करिन्द्रः कुत्साय सूर्यस्य सातौ ॥

83. Velankar: BUJ, 11(2) 1942, p. 92.

84. Read: त्वं कविं चोदयोऽर्कसातौ त्वं कुत्साय शुष्णं दाशुषे वर्क् ।
त्वं शिरो श्रमर्मणः पराहन्नतिथिग्वाय शंस्यं करिष्यन् ॥

85. Velankar: BUJ, 11(2), 1942, p. 96.

86. Read: प्र तत्ते श्रद्या करणं कृतं भूत् कुत्सं यदायुमतिथिग्वमस्मै ।
पुरु सहस्रा निशिशा श्रभिक्षाभूत् तूर्वयाणं घृषता निनेथ ॥

87. Velankar: BUJ, 11, (2), 1942, p. 90.

88. Read: त्वमाविथ सुश्रवसं तवोतिभिस्तव त्रामभिरिन्द्र तुर्वयाणम् ।
त्वमस्मै कुत्समतिथिग्वमायुं महे राज्ञे यूने श्ररन्धनायः ।

89. SR. p. 191.

90. Ibid.

91. Read: प्रमन्दिने पितुमदर्चता वचो य कृष्णगर्भा निरहन्नृजिश्वना ।
श्रवस्यवो वृषणं वज्रदक्षिणं मरुत्वन्तं सख्याय हवामहे ॥

92. See Ch. 3, Section V for details on Rajiśvan.

93. Sarvā 2, 10, 105 ascribes RV 10, 105 to Sumitra and Durmitra Kautsas: कदा कौत्सो दुर्मित्रो नाम्ना सुमित्रो गृणतः सुमित्रो वा नाम्ना दुर्मित्रो गृणत औष्णिहं हरी वज्रं पिपीलिकमध्ये त्रिष्टुबन्त्याद्या गायत्री वा ।

94. RV 1, 80, 16; 83, 5; 6, 16, 13; 14; 47, 24; 8, 9, 7; 9, 11, 2; 10, 14, 6; 21, 5; 48, 2; 92, 10; 120, 9.

95. RV 6, 16, 13; 14; 47, 24.

96. Sarvā 2, 10, 97: या ओषधीस्त्रयधिकाथर्वणो भिषगोषधिस्तुतिरानुष्टुबन्तम् ।

97. Sarvā 2, 10, 120: तदिन्नवाथर्वणो बृहद्दिवः ।

98. These three seers and their descendants are mainly responsible for compiling the AV. Very few seers of other families, (*viz.*, of Vasiṣṭha, Viśvāmitra, etc.) have made some contribution to it. *Vide:* Karambelkar; *The Atharvaṇic Civilization,* Chapter VI, The sages of the Atharva Veda, pp. 248-266.

99. Most of MSS of the AVŚ mention Atharvāṅgirasaḥ as the name of this Veda (AV) and it is also mentioned in AVŚ 10, 7, 20. Besides, it is referred to in Baud DS 3, 5; 9; 14; MS 9, 33; YS 1, 312; MBH. 3, 305, 20; 8, 30, 33. The name Bhṛgavaṅgirasaḥ is found in the Atharvaṇic works, such as GB 1, 3, 3; 1, 2, 22. vide Karambelkar, AVC pp. 1-3.

100. The Atharvaveda Pariśiṣṭas hint at the growing popularity of the Athar-

vans. The following few citations will lend support to it. In Rājaprathamā-bhiṣeka—AVPari 3 reads:

यस्य राज्ञो जनपदेऽथर्वशान्तिपारगः ।
निवसत्यपि तद्राष्ट्रं वर्धते निरुपद्रवम् ॥
यस्य राज्ञो जनपदे स नास्ति विविधर्भयः ।
पीडयन्ते तस्य तद्राष्ट्रं पङ्के गौरिव मज्जलति ॥
तस्माद्राजा विशेषेण अथर्वाणं जितेन्द्रियम् ।
दानसन्मानसत्कारैर्नित्यं समभिपूजयेत् ॥

In Rāṣṭrasaṁvarga, AV Pari 2: says

न हविः प्रतिगृह्णन्ति देवताः पितरो द्विजाः ।
तस्य भूमिपतेर्यस्य गृहे नाथर्वविद् गुरुः ॥

also:

बह्वृचो हन्ति वै राष्ट्रं अध्वर्युर्नाशयेत् सुतान् ।
छन्दोगा धनं नाशयेत् तस्मादाथर्वणो गुरुः ॥

Outside the Atharvaṇic texts, Kauṭilya also says:

पुरोहितमुदितोदितकुलशीलं षड्ङ्गेलो वेदे दैवे
निमित्ते दण्डनीत्यां चाभिविनीतमापदां दैवमानुषी-
णामथर्वभिरुपायैश्च प्रतिकर्तारं कुर्वीत ॥

Kālidāsa, in the Raghu (1, 59) says that Vasiṣṭha, the *purohita* of the Raghus was a treasure-house of Atharvan.

101. Karambelkar AVC pp. 1-2; 13ff; Bloomfield, M., AVGB, pp. 7-9.
102. Bloomfield, M. AVGB, pp. 9-10; Karambelkar, AVC p. 2; also pp. 260-264.
103. Bloomfield, AVGB, pp. 7-10; Karambelkar, AVC, pp. 248-264.
104. Velankar, BUJ, 24, No. 30, 1955, p. 61.
105. Ibid, p. 60.
106. Velankar, BUJ, 13(2), 1943, p. 72.
107. Ibid.
108. Read: the verse in (30) above.
109. Velankar, BUJ 24, No. 30, 1955 p. 61. As regards the content of the verse Macdonell says (in his VM p. 142): "It is noteworthy that in the only older passage (6, 16, 14) in which name of Dadhyañc occurs, he is the son of the ancient fire-priest Atharvan and is himself a kindler of fire. Otherwise he is chiefly connected with the secret above of Soma and with Indra in the release of the cows."
110. RV 1, 80, 16; 84, 13; 116, 12; 117, 22; 139, 9; 119, 9; 6, 16, 14; 9, 108, 4; & 10, 48, 2.
110a. RV 1, 60, 1; 8, 3, 9.
111. RV 1, 58, 6; 127, 7 (twice); 143, 4; 2, 4, 2; 3, 2, 4; 5, 10; 4, 7, 1 :16, 20, 6, 15, 2; 7, 18, 6; 8, 3, 9; 16; 6, 18; 35, 3; 43, 13; 9, 101, 13; 10, 14, 6; 39, 14; 46, 2; 9; 92, 10; 122, 5.
112. RV 8, 43, 13.
113. RV 1, 71, 4; 120, 5; 4, 7, 4.
114. For detailed information see Ch. 4 Section 2 on Vītahavya.

115. Read: दधुष्ट्वा भृगवो मानुषेष्वा रयिं न चारुं सुहवं जनेभ्यः ।
होतारमग्ने अतिथिं वरेण्यं मित्रं न शेवं दिव्याय जन्मने ॥
116. Read (*pāda b* only): उपवोचन्त भृगवो मन्थन्तो दाशा भृगवः ।
117. Read: (ab only): इमं विधन्तो अपां सधस्थे द्वितादधुर्भृगवो विश्वाइयोः ॥
118. Read (*cd* only): रातिं भृगूणामुशिजं कविक्रतुम् अग्निं राजन्तं दिव्येन शोचिषा ॥
119. Read (*cd* only): यदी भृगुभ्यः परि मातरिश्वा गुहा सन्तं हव्यवाहं समीधे ॥
120. Read: (*cb* only) यमप्नवानो भृगवो विरुरुचु वनेषु चित्रं विभ्व विशेविशे ॥
121. Read: (*ab* only). मित्रं न यं सुधितं भृगवो दधुर्वनस्पता वीडयमूधवशोचिषम् ॥
122. Read (*ab* only). यमेरिरे भृगवो विश्ववेदसं नाभा पृथिवी भुवनस्य मज्मना ।
123. Read (*cd* only). गुहा चतन्तमुशिजो नमोभिर इच्छन्तो धीरा भृगवोऽविन्दन् ॥
124. Read (*cd* only). यज्ञैरथर्वा प्रथमो वि धारयद् देवा दक्षैर्भृगवः सं चिकित्रिरे ॥
125. Read (*cd* only). त्वां मर्जयन् मरुतो दाशुषो गृहे त्वां स्तोमेभिर्भृगवो वि रुरुचुः ॥
126. Read note 30 above.
127. Read the verse, note No. 124 above.
128. RV. 1, 51, 10; 11; 83, 5; 121, 12; 130, 9; 4, 16, 2; 26, 1; 5, 29, 9; 31, 8; 34, 2; 6, 20, 11; 8, 7, 26; 23, 17; 9, 87, 3; 9, 97, 7; 10, 22, 6; 40, 7.
129. Read (*ab* only): मन्दिष्ट यदुशने काव्ये सचौं इन्द्रो वङ्कू वङ्कुतराधि तिष्ठति ।
130. RVVSM, Vol. 1, p. 516.
131. BUJ 11(2), 1942, p. 92.
132. RVVSM Vol. 3, p. 82.
133. op. cit.
134. Sarvā 2, 8, 84 reads: प्रेष्ठमुशना काव्य आग्नेयम् and 2, 9, 87 reads: प्रते नवोशना ।
135. Ibid. 2, 9, 47: अया सोमः पञ्च कविभार्गवः । also 2, 9, 75. अभि प्रियाणि पञ्च कविः ।
136. RV 3, 62, 18; 8, 101, 8; 9, 62, 24; 65, 25.
137. Read: इन्द्रस्तुराषाण्मित्रो वृत्रं यो जघान यतीर्न । बिभेद वलं भृगुर्न ससहे शत्रून् मदे सोमस्य ॥
138. Read: अतिमात्रमवर्धन्त नोदिव । दिवमस्पृशन् भृगुं हिंसिता सृञ्जया वैतहव्यो पराभवन् ॥
138a. Sarvā 2.2.1.
139. Ibid. 2, 10, 171.
140. Ibid. 2, 9, 47; 75.
141. Ibid. 2, 8, 79.
142. Ibid. 2, 10, 19.
143. Ibid. 2, 3, 62; 8, 101; 10, 62.
144. Ibid. 2, 8, 100.
145. Ibid. 2, 8, 102.
146. Ibid. 2, 10, 123.
147. Ibid. 2, 2, 4.
148. Ibid. 2, 10, 77.
149. See Ch. 3, Sec. 2 on Śunahotra Bhāradvāja for details.
150. Sukthankar, V.S., "The Bhṛgus and the Bhārata: a Text-Historical Study" ABORI, 18, pp. 1-76. Goldman, Robert P. *Gods, Priests, and Warriors*, Introduction, pp. 1-8.
151. Karambelkar, AVC, p. 259.
152. Ibid p. 260.
153. See GB. ed. R.L. Mitra, Delhi, 1972, pp. 1-3; also at p. 39 read—अथर्वाणश्च ह वा आङ्गिरसश्च भृगुचक्षुषी तद् ब्रह्माभिव्यपश्यंस्तदजानन्वयं वा सर्वं यद् भृग्वाङ्गिरस इति ।

154. Read अथर्वाणो भृगुन्तमाः।

155. Karambelkar: AVC, p. 261. 155a. cf. MBh, 12, 265, 17.

156. Read: आसीदुचथ्यभार्या तु ममता नाम भार्गवी।

157. BD 4, 78; तस्माद् गृत्समदो नाम शौनहोत्र भविष्यसि। Sarvā: 2, 2, 1: य आङ्गिरसः शौनहोत्र भूत्वा भार्गवः शौनकोऽभवत् स गृत्समदो द्वितीयं मण्डलमपश्यत्।

cf. Ārṣa: ऋषिगृत्समदो नाम विज्ञेयः स च शौनकः।
औरसः शौनहोत्रस्य शुनकस्य च कृत्रिमः।
तस्मादाङ्गिरसः पूर्वं पश्चात् स भृगुतां गतः।

158. Read: य आङ्गिरसः शौनहोत्रो भूत्वा भार्गवः शौनकोऽ
भवत् स गृत्समदो द्वितीयं मण्डलमपश्यत्।

159. AŚVŚS 6, 10, 12: मित्रयुवां वाध्य्रश्वेति त्रिप्रवरं वा भार्गवदैवोदास वाध्य्रश्वेति।

160. See part I, Ch. 3, Section VII on Ajamīḍha and appendix 1.

Chapter Two

BHARADVĀJA BĀRHASPATYA AND OTHER BHARADVĀJAS

(i) *Bharadvāja Bārhaspatya: The Seer of the Sixth Maṇḍala of the Ṛgveda*

The Sarvā[1] of Kātyāyana ascribes the sixth Maṇḍala of the RV to the family of Bharadvāja. The sixth Maṇḍala is, therefore, called the Bharadvāja Maṇḍala. According to the Sarvā (2, 6,1)[2] Bharadvāja is the son of Bṛhaspati. The BD (5, 102-3)[3] also states that Bharadvāja was the son of Bṛhaspati and the grandson of Aṅgiras who was one among several sons of Brahmā. The Ārṣa[4] of Śaunaka, too, corroborates the Sarvā's statement. Although the Sarvā ascribes the 6th Maṇḍala to Bharadvāja, he alone is not the seer of all the hymns contained therein. There are, altogether, seventyfive hymns in the 6th Book. Out of these, the Sarvā ascribes all the Agni hymns (1-16, excepting the 15th)[5] to Bharadvāja. He is also said to be the seer of majority of the Indra hymns (17-30 and 37-43). The hymns addressed to all other individual gods or dual divinities (except the hymns to Viśvedevāḥ and the Ode to War, i.e. 75th) are ascribed to Bharadvāja Bārhaspatya. The remaining hymns are ascribed to other members of his family. In the Sarvā, hymns 31 and 32 are ascribed to Suhotra Bharadvāja[6], 33 and 34 to Śunahotra,[7] 35-36 to Nara[8], 47 to Garga,[9] 49-52 to Ṛjiśvan[10] and the 75th i.e. the last hymn to Pāyu.[11] All of them are called the *Bhāradvājāḥ* 'the sons' or 'descendants' of Bharadvāja Bārhaspatya[12] Hymns 44-46 and 48 are ascribed to Śaṁyu Bārhaspatya[13] who is said to be the brother of Bharadvāja. The hymn 15 is ascribed either to Bharadvāja Bārhaspatya or to Vītahavya.[14] Also, the majority of the hymns of the sixth Maṇḍala of the RV being ascribed to Bharadvāja, he is named as the visionary of RV (9, 67, 1-3,[15] and 10, 137, 1)[16]. Thus, as Bharadvāja is the seer of the majority of the hymns (i.e. 59 out of the total 75 hymns) in the sixth Maṇḍala, he, in keeping with the maxim *prādhānyena vyapadeśāḥ bhavanti*, is known as 'the seer of the sixth Maṇḍala'.

The NA[17] ascribes a fairly large number of verses[18] including the *pratīka mantra* ('initial verse')[19] of the SV to Bharadvāja Bārhaspatya.[20] The Vās[21] also ascribes quite a large number of verses in the VS[22] of the white YV to Bharadvāja. So also ABS[23] ascribes a good number of hymns (viz. 2, 12; 19, 49; 20, 36; 58, 3-4; 63, 3 and 90) to Bharadvāja and a verse (viz. 20, 81, 1)[24] to Bhāradvāja.[25] However, all the verses ascribed to Bharadvāja in the SV and VS are mere repetition of the verses from the hymns in the RV ascribed to him. But AVŚ 2, 12; 19, 49 and 20, 58, 3-4 appear to be his original contribution, while AVŚ 8, 1; 20, 36; 63, 3; and 90, 1-2 are the same as those from the RV 6, 22; 6, 17, 3; 6, 17, 15 and 6, 73, 1-2 respectively. Curiously, a number of verses ascribed to him in the RV are found in the AVŚ repeated and ascribed to Brahmā, Atharvan, Praṣkaṇva, Kaurupathin and Uparivabhrava.[26] A large number of verses ascribed to Bharadvāja in RV are repeated in the TS.[27]

Now various questions arise. Who was this Bharadvāja? What was his parentage? Whether *Bharadvāja* is a personal name or a nickname or surname? Whether there was one Bharadvāja or there were more than one? If there were more than one persons bearing that name, what was the reason behind their 'having the same name'? To which period did 'he' or 'they' belong? These queries show how complex the problem is. No direct answer is possible. A thorough investigation is required for these issues to be settled.

(*ii*) *Bharadvāja Bārhaspatya: Birth and Parentage*

The legends of the birth of Bharadvāja and that of Dīrghatamas run parallel. The birth of Dīrghatamas has, however, been much talked about in the Epics and Purāṇas,[1] while that of Bharadvāja is given in details in only two of the Purāṇas, viz., Va (99, 141-151) and Mt (49, 16-26). It is alluded to in Vis (4, 19, 5-7) and Bh (9, 20, 36-38) also, but only briefly. However, the legends of the births of these two seers are so very intimately knit together that, for our purpose, it is convenient to separate that of Bharadvāja from that of Dīrghatamas.[2] The account, below, of birth of Bharadvāja follows those given in Va and Mt.

Once Bṛhaspati, while staying on the Earth, saw Mamatā, the wife of his elder brother Uśija[2a] and addressed her, "O fair Lady, please wait upon me". Thus addressed, she said to him, "(O

Bṛhaspati,) there is already a child in my womb and it is matured. Further, it is reciting Veda *mantras*. As such it is not proper to unite with you—a person having a seed which is not fruitless. Besides, your overture will encroach upon virtue." Yet Bṛhaspati said to her, "O Beautiful one, you need not teach me discipline". When he forcibly tried to unite with her, the child in her womb told him: "O Bṛhaspati, I am already here in the womb. Also there is no room for two." When Bṛhaspati was thus told by the child-in-womb (of Mamatā), he became enraged and retorted to the child thus, "As you, in such a time so dear to a man, speak thus, you will certainly enter into long darkness".[3]

At this, the child-in-womb closed the genital organ of his mother with his feet and therefore the seed of Bṛhaspati fell on the ground. And lo! instantly a child was born.[4]

Thereupon, Mamatā said: "O Bṛhaspati, I am going home, please take care of the boy born of two (fathers)". While she was about to leave the place, Bṛhaspati said to her, "Please, you take care of it that is born of two (fathers)". It is because of these reciprocal utterances of the parents that the child became known as Bharadvāja. Eventually, they abandoned the baby. When the Maruts saw the new born baby, deserted by the parents in such a pitiable condition, they took it under their care through their kindness.[5]

This legend is found in Mt and Va in identical words. Va adds only a minor detail: the prevention of the entry of Bṛhaspati's seed into Mamatā's womb by the child already there.

Vis and Bh give the legend in brief. Vis 4, 19, 5 refers to it and gives the background story of Bharadvāja's adoption by Bharata and repeats the false etymology of the word *bharadvāja* as suggested in the two early Purāṇas. Bharadvāja is said to have been born of Mamatā as a result of the kick inflicted by Dīrghatamas (who was already in Mamatā's womb and incurred Bṛhaspati's wrath by preventing him) at the time of his getting orgasm.[6] Bh (9, 20, 37-38) gives the legend with a little innovation that the gods were responsible for naming the child Bharadvāja.[7]

BD (4,11-14)[8] also gives the background of Dīrghatamas' having been born blind as a result of Bṛhaspati's curse leading to the birth of Bharadvāja. It fully agrees with the one given in the MBh and Bd. In BD (5, 102-103)[9], it is said that Bṛhaspati was a son of Aṅgiras, and his son was Bharadvāja. The Sarvā,[10] confirms that Bṛhaspati was the father of Bharadvāja, and states that Bharadvāja, the son of Bṛhaspati, saw the 6th Maṇḍala and it further states that Suhotra and others were 'sons' of Bharadvāja and 'grandsons' of Bṛhaspati or Bharata Dauṣyanti. In RV (6, 73, 1), the seer Bharadvāja actually claims Bṛhaspati Āṅgirasa as 'our father'.[10a]

From the legend relating to the birth of Bharadvāja described in Va, Mt, Vis, Bh and that of Dīrghatamas described in MBh, Bd and Mt, it appears to us that both the legends intimately overlapped. The circumstances leading to the instantaneous birth of Bharadvāja is nothing but the background story of Dīrghatamas' having been born blind. It now follows from the above that: (i) Bharadvāja and Dīrghatamas had a common mother, (ii) they had, however, two fathers, Bṛhaspati and Uśija (or Ucathya in RV), (iii) it is also possible that they were born as twins, and (iv) they were contemporaries.

Now let us resolve the controversy over the different names given in different texts, of the husband of Mamatā. BD (4, 11-14)[11] says that the name of Mamatā's husband was Ucathya and also he was the elder brother of Bṛhaspati and he also was the father of Dīrghatamas. Ucathya himself was a Ṛgvedic seer and the Sarvā (2, 9, 50)[12] ascribes RV 9, 50-52 to him. Also the Sarvā (2, 1, 140)[13] ascribes RV 1, 140-64 to Dīrghatamas Aucathya, sometimes also called as Dīrghatamas Māmateya, 'the son of Mamatā'. RV (8, 46, 28)[14] mentions Ucathya (the father of Dīrghatamas) and RV (1, 158, 1 and 4) mentions Dīrghatamas by his patronymic, viz. as Aucathya 'the son of Ucathya'.[15]

We have already mentioned that the MBh also gives detailed information about Dīrghatamas' birth and his parentage. However, for Ucathya it has the variant 'Utathya'[16] who is "husband" of Mamatā and brother of Bṛhaspati and father of Dīrghatamas. Among the Purāṇas, Vis (4, 19, 5)[17] alone gives Utathya as the husband of Mamatā. It would not, therefore, be wrong to accept Utathya of MBh and Vis as identical with Ucathya of the RV, BD and Sarvā.

Mt and Bd give the name of Mamatā's husband as Uśija,[18] while Va gives as Aśija.[19] Uśija may be correct, and Aśija a misreading for Uśija.[20] It is a fact that Ucathya and Uśija were two distinct Āṅgirasa seers. The patronymic Aucathya occurs in RV (1, 158, 1 and 4), and Auśija in RV (1, 18, 1 and 10, 99, 11). In spite of Auśija conveying a patronymical sense, Bergaigne[21] once said that "Uśijs are mythical clan, of which the head is none other than Agni. The word *auśija* itself must denote a mythical being". On another occasion, the French savant after a long discussion on the significance of *Uśija* and *auśija*, observed that "the word *Uśij* must have been already used as a proper name"[22], and that he understood it in the sense of a Soma-presser or sacrificer. Happily, our historical tradition sustains enough evidence to show that Uśija was a seer belonging to the Āṅgirasas and the patronymic Auśija significantly denoted his descendants, even in the RV as noted above. Now it may be seen that Auśija in RV (1, 18, 1)[23] is Kakṣīvat who is said to be the son of Dīrghatamas, and in RV (10, 99, 11)[24] he is Ṛjiśvan who is said to be a descendant of Bharadvāja Vidathin. Kakṣīvat is called 'born of Uśij' by the Sarvā (2, 1, 116),[25] and by VD. They probably relied for their statements on *Kakṣīvantam ya Auśijaḥ* in RV (1, 18, 1). It is also suggested that this Auśija might be a matronymic, if the Śūdrā woman whom Dīrghatamas married was named Uśij.[26] Such a suggestion would be wrong, when Kakṣīvat could have this patronymic Auśija.[27] Besides, the acceptance of Auśija as a matronymic applied to Kakṣīvat could not explain why it was used in case of Ṛjiśvan. But a patronymic form 'Auśija' applicable to Ṛjiśvan would also hold good for him, because, (1) Ṛjiśvan, is said to be a descendant of Vidathin Bharadvāja[28] in RV (4, 16, 13 and 5, 29, 11), and (2) he is said to be a 'son' of Bharadvāja and a descendant of Bṛhaspati or Bharata in the Sarvā (2, 6, 52). Thus it is established that Ṛjiśvan has Bharadvāja Bārhaspatya as his ancestor and not Dīrghatamas. Hence his appellation Auśija cannot be accepted as a matronymic derived from Uśij, the Śūdrā, married to Dīrghatamas. This goes to prove that his forefather Vidathin Bharadvāja had his lineage from one Uśija. As Kakṣīvat did receive this appellation and his father and grandfather were named Dīrghatamas and Ucathya, Uśija appears to be their ancestor, perhaps, the father of Ucathya and (his brother) Bṛhaspati.[29] In Va[30] it is said that Ucathya, Uśija and Bṛhaspati all were sons born of Surūpā married to Aṅgiras. And Bṛhaspati is said to be an Āṅgirasa in BD (5, 102) and in RV (6, 73, 1) Bṛhaspati Āṅgirasa is called 'our father'[31] by the poet Bharadvāja Bārhaspatya himself. But in many cases, traditional sources are prone to abridge the genealogy, particularly, of the seers.[32] Thus the names of a person in between Aṅgiras and Bṛhaspati might have been dropped. Moreover, we must notice why and how Mamatā was called the wife of one Uśija or Aśija—due probably to shortening of patronymic form Auśija derived from Uśija,[33] well applicable to Ucathya also. That Uśija was an Āṅgirasa seer is further corroborated by the Mt (195, 11)[34] while giving the *pravararṣis* of the Aṅgirases. The AŚVŚS (6, 10, 3)[35] includes Auśija as one of the five *pravararṣis* of the Kakṣīvats. Some conclusions emerge from the foregoing discussion: (1) Uśija was an ancestor of Dīrghatamas and Bharadvāja, preceding their fathers, Ucathya and Bṛhaspati; (2) all the descendants of Dīrghatamas and Bharadvāja could equally receive the appellation Auśija; (3) Mamatā was the wife of Ucathya; (4) Uśija could be placed between Aṅgiras and Bṛhaspati; and (5) hence, he was the son of Aṅgiras and the father of Ucathya and Bṛhaspati.

Pargiter[36] has already accepted Uśija as the father of Ucathya and Bṛhaspati, and he reconstructed the genealogy of the Bharadvājas (who later coalesced with the Bharatas) and it has been accepted by Rahurkar,[37] Mankad[38] and Bhargava.[39]

The fact is that Mamatā was the wife of Auśija Ucathya. Bṛhaspati was his younger brother. As such, Bṛhaspati as a younger brother-in-law had the right to approach her. She would also have favoured such an approach, had she not been already impregnated by Ucathya. She even told him to approach her at a favourable time. This shows that, in that age, there was no taboo to the union of a woman and a younger brother-in-law.

Again the Purāṇic explanation of Bharadvāja's name indicates that Bharadvāja had two fathers. They say that the name Bharadvāja is a compound of the verbal form *bhara* 'nourish' (Imperative II sg. of root *bhṛ*) and *dvāja* 'born of two (fathers)'.[40] Thus Bharadvāja was so named because he had two fathers, viz. Ucathya, the legitimate husband of Mamatā and Bṛhaspati as the begetter of the son. Thus Bharadvāja could be called an Auśija or Aucathya, or Bārhaspatya or Māmateya.[40a]

From these accounts recorded in different Brāhmaṇical and Epico-Purāṇic sources, it appears that the birth of Bharadvāja is an uncommon happening. He is stated to have been born instantaneously from the semen of Bṛhaspati that dropped on the ground, because the child already existing in the womb of Mamatā prevented the semen from penetrating, for fear of the co-mingling within. The legend, apart from giving the uncommon circumstances of the instantaneous birth of Bharadvāja, throw light on the following details of sociological importance: (i) Bṛhaspati's approach to Mamatā, the wife of Ucathya, the son of Uśija, tells us that there was no taboo that could bar a junior brother from approaching his elder brother's wife. This is clear from Mamatā's own words given in Mt (48, 36): "after the delivery of the son of Auśija (reading Uśija is already amended), you may, O Bṛhaspati, approach me, according to the dictates of your mind".[41] Thus this appears to be a practice prevalent of a polyandrous society. (ii) Mamatā further indicated that Bṛhaspati's approach to her during the period of pregnancy was not only untimely but also improper, i.e. it was against the normal code of conduct, and approaching a woman was considered proper only for begetting a child for race preservation, as in the case of the Raghu princes who approached their wives only for progeny.[42]

Instances of unnatural birth, like the one of Bharadvāja, are frequently noticed in old Indian literature. Some of the similar births may be noted here.

The birth of Vasiṣtha and Agastya (also called Māna) is described in the RV (7, 33, 11 and 13). It is stated there in verse 11 that struck by Urvaśī's 'beauty' Mitra and Varuṇa (who attended a sacrificial feast) dropped their semen and the Viśvedevas took care of it. The 13th verse records that some of the semen fell in a pot, while some fell outside. Vasiṣtha is said to have been born of the semen that fell outside the pitcher while Agastya was born of the semen in the vessel,[43] for which he was called Māna 'measure' or Kumbhayoni 'one whose origin is in the pitcher' or Kumbhasambhava 'one born in a pitcher'.

A similar legend recorded in the MBh (1, 121, 1-5)[44] tells us of the birth of Droṇa Bhāradvāja. It is said that, once when the sage Bharadvāja had been in a sacrificial hall, the nymph Ghṛtācī appeared before him with a bare bosom. The seer, having been excited by the sight of the beautiful nymph, dropped his semen and that was then put in a vessel called *droṇa*, out of which was born a male child who was later known as Droṇa, the *ācārya* of Kurus and the Pāṇḍus and a Brāhmaṇa embracing the life of a warrior.

In still another place in the MBh (i.e. 9, 47, 57-58)[45], one Srucāvatī is reported to have been born of the outflowing seed of one Bharadvāja under similar circumstances.

In still another legend, the birth of the twin Kṛpa and Kṛpī is reported by the MBh (1, 120, 12ff)[46]. It is said there that once when Gautama Śāradvata saw an Apsaras alone, out of exhilaration he dropped his semen, a portion of which was contained in a lotus leaf, while the other portion fell outside. Out of the two portions were born Kṛpa and Kṛpī who were taken under his care by the Kuru prince Śāntanu. Later on Kṛpa became a teacher of the Kuru princes, and Kṛpī was married to Droṇācārya.

Nāmanirvacana

Bharadvāja is the son of Bṛhaspati and Mamatā. While deriving the word and giving its meaning etc., the Vedic texts (followed by various commentators) take a distinct stand that differs from the one taken by the Purāṇas. A *śruti* passage, cited in *Vācaspatyam*,[47] gives the etymological explanation of '*bharadvāja*' as: *prajā vai tā eva bibharti, yad u bibharti tasmād bharadvājaḥ. Vāja* indeed is *prajā* 'people'; since indeed he sustains the people, he is called Bharadvāja.

In ŚB (8, 1, 1, 9), it is again said of Bharadvāja: *bharadvāja ṛṣir iti. mano vai bharadvāja ṛṣir, annaṁ vājo, yo vai mano bibharti so'nnam vājam bharati tasmān mano bharadvājo ṛṣiḥ.* Now about the seer Bharadvāja, *anna*, i.e. the food-stuff is *vāja* which the mind bears; he who bears that food-stuff, (i.e. which is identified with Vāja, 'strength'), is, therefore, verily the seer Bharadvāja.

Sāyaṇa understands the word *bharadvāja* in the sense of 'the one by whom food in the form of offerings is being brought' [*saṁbhriyamāṇa havirlakṣaṇānna* in RV (1, 116, 18) and *saṁbhṛtahavirlakṣaṇānna* in RV (6, 15, 3)].[48] He also derives the word as a compound of two components *bharant* (*√bhṛ+ṣatṛ*) 'bearing', sustaining, and *vāja* 'strength', 'race' or 'food' or 'sacrificial food', 'prize of a race', etc. Mudgala[49] quotes Sāyaṇa *ad verbatim*.

Mahīdhara[50] explains the word under VS (13, 55) as follows: *bharadvāja ṛṣiḥ, bibharti bharan vājam annaṁ ca, sa bharadvājānnadharttā manaḥ manasi svasthe annādānecchotpatteḥ, ṛṣiḥ sacetano manorūpaḥ* "(regarding) the seer Bharadvāja: since he bears, he is bearing the food-stuff (*vāja*), so Bharadvāja means supporter or sustainer of food; this is because, he has a sincere intention of donating food to others; seer means a form of mind that is (ever) conscious".

A passage from the MBh (13, 95, 31) also lends support to the views expressed by the Vedic texts. It says:

bhare' sutān bhare śiṣyān bhare devān bhare dvijān|
bhare bhāryām bharad vājam bharadvājo'smi śobhane||

"I sustain those who are not my sons, I sustain my disciples, I sustain my wife ... Sustaining (thus all these) *Vāja* i.e. people (and food-stuff for them) I am named Bharadvāja, O fair one!" These are given as the words of Bharadvāja himself and bring out the significance of his name.

Grassmann[51] takes it in the sense of '*ursprunglich der Labungbringende*' and Röth[52] and M. Williams[53] specify the meaning as 'bearing speed or strength (of fight)'; they also confirm that it was a name of the son of Bṛhaspati and 'the priest of Divodāsa'.

The Purāṇas[54], however, do not approve of the above etymology and sense of the word '*bharadvāja*' and give another etymology: they split the word into two components, viz. *bhara*+*dvāja*. This is because the Purāṇas trace the birth of Bharadvāja to the 'two fathers' Auśija Ucathya (the legitimate husband of Mamatā) and Bṛhaspati (the brother of Ucathya, who begot Bharadvāja by Mamatā). They also say that while the child was born as a result of Bṛhaspati's cohabiting with Mamatā, each of them urged the other to nourish the new-born baby. The Va (99, 149-150) records it

sadyo jātaṁ kumāraṁ taṁ
dṛṣṭvā'tha mamatā'bravīt|
gamiṣyāmi gṛhaṁ svaṁ vai
bhara dvājaṁ bṛhaspate||
evam uktvā gatāyāṁ sa
putraṁ tyajati tatkṣaṇāt|
bharasva vāḍham ity ukto
bharadvājas tato' bhavat||

"Seeing the new-born baby Mamatā said 'O Bṛhaspati, please sustain the boy born of two, I am going home'. He also, after her departure, left the place immediately saying 'well, you do sustain'. (As they said so), therefore, his name was Bharadvāja."

Mt, Vis and Bh all corroborate this background leading to the naming of the baby born of Bṛhaspati and Mamatā. And Röth and Böhtlingk[55] have considered *dvāja* as a separate word and given its meaning as 'm. *ein Sohn zwei vater*' (and attested it referring to) Bh (9, 20, 38), adding further "*zur erkl. des Namens Bharadvāja, der sich aber in bharant+vāja zerlegt*". Monier Williams[56] also gives the same meaning of the word *dvāja*, as is given by the two Petersburg scholars, but adds to it the following comment in brackets 'wrong explanation of *bharadvāja*'. Hence, this may be considered as the 'folk-etymology' of the name Bharadvāja. The Purāṇas being professedly works meant for the masses, this etymology is quite understandable and suitable to them. This Purāṇic attempt at getting an explanation of a name with a story-element is, however, the legacy of the Brāhmaṇic texts. Both the etymologies have their own importance. The Brāhmaṇic explanation attaches to the name a significance aiming at physical and mental or material and spiritual qualities of the person concerned (on the basis of various meanings of the word *vāja*) while the Purāṇic etymology takes into account the parentage and circumstances leading to his birth. The latter source appears to have exploited the 'words' of the parents as being sufficiently important for naming the child Bharadvāja. Thus both the sources have certain importance of their own, though different, in naming a great sage of yore.

(*iii*) *The alleged adoption of Bharadvāja* (*? Vidathin*) *by Bharata*

In the last section we have discussed the Epico-Purāṇic account of the birth of Bharadvāja and his parentage, etc. The same Epico-Purāṇic sources record, as a sequel to his birth, an account of his (alleged) adoption by Bharata, the son of Duṣyanta and Śakuntalā. It is given in some details in Mt and Va, briefly in Vis and Bh and is also referred to in Br, Hv and Ag Purāṇas.[1] This account is separately treated here, with a view to show that the person adopted by Bharata was not Bharadvāja Bārhaspatya, but probably his descendant.

The Purāṇic account, after describing Bharadvāja's birth, continues to tell us about the circumstances leading to the adoption of the child by Bharata. It says that after a verbal battle that ensued between Bṛhaspati and Mamatā over bringing up the child, both the parents abandoned it. The Maruts saw the nurseling left to his fate and out of pity they took him under their care.[2]

Now it so happened that Bharata, the son of Duṣyanta was in dire need of a child for adoption in order that his line continued. He had three wives and each of them gave birth to three sons, making the total of nine sons. But Bharata did not accept any of these children as none bore resemblance to him. The mothers killed all the children fearing that the king might discard them. Hence Bharata had no progeny that could succeed him. With a view to obtain a son, he then performed a number of sacrifices to the gods. Finally, he performed a Marutsoma sacrifice to the Maruts and the Maruts were pleased with him. To Bharata they brought Bharadvāja whom they had already taken under their care at the very time of his birth and his subsequent desertion by his parents. The king thanked the gods and adopted the child Bharadvāja as his son. As the birth of the children to Bharata and as also the birth of Bharadvāja from his own parents had become futile, Bharata renamed Bharadvāja as Vitatha. This account is given in Va and Mt which agree almost wholly in respect of the details,[3] the only difference being that Mt (49, 14) gives an epidemic of small-pox (*mātṛkākopāt*) as the cause of the children's death.[4]

Now Mt (49, 34-36) further says that, after Bharata's death Vitatha was anointed as the king by Bharadvāja (?) and, thereafter, himself died. Vitatha was later succeeded by his own son Bhuvamanyu. This latter had four sons, Bṛhatkṣatra, Mahāvīrya, Nara and Garga.[5] Va (99, 165)[6] says that Bṛhatkṣatra had a son Suhotra by name and Suhotra's son was Hastin. Mt (49, 42)[7] names Hastin as the son of Bṛhatkṣatra.

Bṛ, Vis, Bh, Hv and Ag all agree with Va and Mt in respect of the adoption of Bharadvāja by Bharata. But Bh (9, 21, 20)[8] agrees with Mt in giving Hastin as the name of the son of Bṛhatkṣatra. Br, Hv and Ag drop Bhuvamanyu and state that Suhotra, Suhotṛ, Garya, Garga and Kapila were the sons of Vitatha.[9] Yet, there is significant difference in that Br (13, 60-61) clearly says: "Vitatha was born 'from' Bharadvāja" (*pūrvaṁ tu vitatho nāma bharadvājāt suto'bhavat*). It also says that, after the birth of Vitatha and also on the death of Bharata, Bharadvāja consecrated Vitatha as the king and himself went away to the forest.[10]

Now we can examine the information contained in the MBh.

which provides us with two versions of the genealogy of the Bharatas. The first version of the Epic, viz. in MBh (1, 89, 17) gives us the background of the sonless state of Bharata (which is in agreement with that of the Purāṇas). Then the Epic says that Bharata received Bhumanyu (whom the Purāṇas call Bhuvamanyu) from Bharadvāja; Vitatha, Suhotra, Suhotṛ, Suhavi and Suyajus were sons of Bhumanyu.[11] In the 2nd version in the Epic, viz. MBh (90, 34-35), Bhumanyu is given as Bharata's own son born of Sunandā, the princess of Kāśī, and he is said to have only one son, viz. Suhotra.[12]

Comparing the above account with that of the Purāṇas, we find certain disagreement between the two. In the MBh, Bharata is said to have received Bhumanyu from Bharadvāja, and Vitatha is said to be Bhumanyu's son and Suhotra's brother. In the Purāṇas—Va, Mt, Vis, Bh—Bharata is said to have adopted Bharadvāja and Vitatha is his other name; of course, Mt further says that Bharadvāja anointed Vitatha as the king. Thus MBh drops Vitatha's name from the succession-list, saying that Bhumanyu succeeded Bharata. In the Purāṇas (Va, Mt, Vis, Bh) Suhotra is given as the son of Bṛhatkṣatra who was son of Bhumanyu. Thus MBh abridges the genealogical list. Only Bṛ, Hv and Ag agree in holding that Suhotṛ, Garya, Garga and Kapila were sons of Vitatha. They also abridge the genealogy, dropping Bhumanyu and Bṛhatkṣatra therefrom.

The Epico-Purāṇic sources discussed so far leave us with certain questions the answers to which are to be sought elsewhere. These questions are: (1) Whether Bharadvāja Bārhaspatya was actually adopted by Bharata Dauṣyanti? (2) Whether Bharadvāja and Vitatha were two names of one and the same person, viz. Bharadvāja Bārhaspatya? (3) If the answers to (1) and (2) are negative, the questions arise: who was the person adopted by Bharata? and what was the relation among the persons involved in these questions?

Let us resolve these:

(1) There is genuine doubt as to Bharata's adopting Bharadvāja as his son. Bharadvāja Bārhaspatya, the progenitor of the family, appears to be anterior to Bharata by two or three generations. In the legend of the birth of Bharadvāja we have already noticed that Bharadvāja Bārhaspatya and Dīrghatamas Aucathya were two uterine brothers, having been born of a common mother

viz. Mamatā, consorted by Bṛhaspati and Ucathya. They were born almost simultaneously and thus twins.[13] AB (8, 23)[14] says that Dīrghatamas presided over the coronation ceremony of Bharata Dauṣyanti. In order to be able to preside over such an august and elaborate function of the Lunar race, Dīrghatamas must have by then attained name, fame, and maturity. RV (1, 158, 6) refers to Dīrghatamas and says that he reached the tenth decade of his life-span.[15] Bharadvāja too lived a long life as is suggested in AB (1, 2, 6).[16] Even if Bharadvāja lived during the reign of Bharata, he must have been older than Bharata who thus could hardly adopt him as a son. And since Bharata had lost all the nine children, he must also have been more aged. Thus the Purāṇic statement that Bharata adopted Bharadvāja is without substance. Rather it leads us to think of a possibility that Bharata adopted a person bearing the patronymic Bhāradvāja.

We have already recognised Bharadvāja Bārhaspatya as the progenitor of the family of the Bharadvājas. Whosoever belonged to or belongs to his *gotra* 'family' was or is called Bhāradvāja. Sometimes, the patronymic Bhāradvāja is substituted by Bharadvāja. Pāṇini (4, 1, 162) says that adoption of a *gotra* involves the persons in descent from grandsons onwards (*apatyam pautraprabhṛti gotram*). However, the application of a *gotra* was not confined to the descendants raised through one's own seed; it was extended also to the *śiṣyas* 'pupils' of a *guru* who established his own *gotra* and school of some *śāstra*. For example, Agniveśya, who is named as a śiṣya of Bharadvāja in MBh (1, 121, 6-7) is said to have belonged to the *gotra* that comes under the three *pravararṣis* Āṅgirasa, Bārhaspatya, and Bhāradvāja.[17]

The probable fact is that after the loss of his sons, Bharata offered sacrifices to the Maruts for a son as his heir apparent. Probably Bharadvāja was also chosen as one of the participating priests in the sacrifice, at the advice of his brother Dīrghatamas, as the latter was born blind. By dint of Bharadvāja's *tapas* 'penance' and *brahman* 'magically potent *mantra*', Bharata could successfully complete his sacrifice. At the same time, through the good offices of Dīrghatamas, Bharata successfully persuaded Bharadvāja to hand over one of his descendants for adoption as a son and heir apparent. Bharadvāja probably took pity upon the sonless Bharata and conceded to his request. This was because, in ancient times, what was achieved by men was almost always ascribed to the god they worshipped.[18]

Another noteworthy suggestion is that the Purāṇas might have confused the Maruts for Marutta. It is said[18a] that Bṛhaspati, the father of Bharadvāja and brother Ucathya and Saṁvarta, lived in the kingdom of Vaiśālī where Marutta, the son of Avīkṣit, ruled. Bṛhaspati was the family chaplain of Marutta. Probably, Bharadvāja also lived with his father. He was of the same age as Dīrghatamas. Dīrghatamas was at that time Bharata's priest. When the latter lost all his *aurasa* sons, Dīrghatamas probably suggested to Bharata that he should adopt a son of high birth. Bharata might have consulted Marutta, the king of Vāiśalī and he, in turn, might have sought opinion of his priest Bṛhaspati and his son Bharadvāja. In the course of these consultations Bharadvāja might have been successfully persuaded to give one of his young descendants to Bharata for adoption. And finally a junior Bhāradvāja was adopted.[19]

Another probability may as well be suggested here: the age-old practice of *niyoga* 'begetting an offspring by a woman by some alternate husband (according to Dharmaśāstra).' When Bharata did not find a son that bore physical resemblance to him, he felt disgusted. And although he resorted to religious means to get a son, he adopted simultaneously *niyoga* as an alternative means of acquiring a son. He probably sought Bharadvāja's help to raise an issue from one of his three wives, and the Brāhmin priest conceded to his request. As a result a son could have been born. Through the same practice, Dīrghatamas is said to have raised sons by Sudeṣṇā at the request of Bali and Kṛṣṇa Dvaipāyana is said to have raised Dhṛtarāṣṭra, Pāṇḍu and Vidura by the wives of Vicitravīrya.[20] Thus *niyoga* was probably practised to save the race of the Moon from extinction; and a son was born, and he was also called Bhāradvāja.

Bharadvāja was, therefore, anterior to Bharata by more than one generation and he could not have been adopted by the latter as his son. In the following paragraphs we shall see that Vitatha and Bharadvāja were two distinct persons. Their being considered as one person points to the abridgment of the genealogy of Bharadvāja and Bharata—this is usual in the Purāṇas. Regarding the identification of Vitatha with Bharadvāja, we notice below a long-standing controversy among the Purāṇas.

Va (99, 156) says: *tataḥ sa vitatho nāma bharadvājas tathā'bhavat* ("then that Bharadvāja became known as Vitatha also"). Mt (49, 32) replaces the word *tathā* of Va (99, 156) by *nṛpaḥ* and it says: *tatas tu vitatho nāma Bharadvājo nṛpo'bhavat* ("then that Bharadvāja, Vitatha by name, became the king"). In both the Purāṇas, the expression *vitatho nāma bharadvājaḥ* ["a Bharadvāja (whose personal) name was Vitatha"] is significant. In another place, i.e. at 99, 158, Va says *tato'tha vitathe jāte bharataḥ,... divaṁ yayau* ("After the birth of Vitatha, (when) Bharata died"). Mt (49, 34) reads the line more clearly as: *tato jāte hi vitathe bharataś ca divam yayau/ bharadvājo divam yāto hy abhiṣicya sutaṁ ṛṣiḥ* ("After the birth of Vitatha and at the death of Bharata, Bharadvāja consecrated his son Vitatha and then went to heaven"). This clearly states Vitatha as the son of Bharadvāja. This is corroborated by Br (13, 60-61) and HV (23, 50-54) when they say: *tato'tha vitatho nāma bharadvājāt suto'bhavat// tato'tha vitathe jāte bharataś ca divaṁ yayau/ vitathaṁ cābhiṣicya bharadvājo vanaṁ yayau//* ("When Vitatha was born from Bharadvāja as his son, Bharata departed to heaven; then Bharadvāja also went to the forest after consecrating Vitatha as the king"). True, Va and Mt thus make contradictory statements (as noted above), but they are found to be aware of the fact that Vitatha was a descendant of Bharadvāja. And Br and Hv appear to be clear and categorical in asserting that Bharadvāja and Vitatha were two persons, i.e. father and son. Even MBh (1, 89, 18) states that Bharata acquired Bhumanyu 'from' Bharadvāja. Although the Epic substitutes Bhumanyu for Vitatha, still it regards Bhumanyu and Bharadvāja as two distinct persons, thus corroborating what is stated in Br (13, 60-61). The numerous references in the Epic and Purāṇas to a Bharadvāja as the father of another Bharadvāja (i.e. Vitatha) affirm that one Bharadvāja was definitely adopted by Bharata. This Bharadvāja was, in all probability, to be a descendant of Bharadvāja Bārhaspatya and he was father of Vitatha too.

We have already pointed out above that Bharata could not adopt Bharadvāja Bārhaspatya, and further that some one Bharadvāja, other than Vitatha, was connected with Bharata in the matter of adoption. This gives rise to the third question (already raised by us), viz. 'who was the person adopted by Bharata?'

An answer to this may be sought on the basis of evidence supplied by the RV, BD, Sarvā and MBh.

The Sarvā of Kātyāyana, while ascribing hymns to seers, makes sometimes some useful remarks about the individual visionary of a hymn or group of them, and these give us some clue to finding out the origin of a family. While giving the name of the *gotra* of those whose hymns are found in the 6th Maṇḍala, the Sarvā (2, 6, 52) says: *Suhotrādayo' nuktagotrā bhāradvājāḥ pautrā bṛhaspateḥ dauṣyanter vā bharatasya* ("Suhotra and others, whose *gotra* has not been yet stated, are the 'sons' of Bharadvāja; they were grandsons either of Bṛhaspati or Bharata, the son of Duṣyanta"). Commenting upon the word *suhotrādayaḥ*, the commentator Ṣaḍguruśiṣya says: *suhotra-śunahotra-nara-garga-ṛjiśvan ity ete suhotrādayaḥ*. ("*suhotrādayaḥ* means: Suhotra, Śunahotra, Nara, Garga and Ṛjiśvan").

This statement of the Sarvā (2, 6, 52) appears to have abridged a long genealogy of the Bharadvājas and Bharatas. Thus, by the phrase 'the sons of Bharadvāja' (*bhāradvājāḥ*) is meant 'the descendants of Bharadvāja', however distant. This statement adds the names of Śunahotra and Ṛjiśvan to the list of other descendants of Bharadvāja (and Bharata) found in the Epics and the Purāṇas.

Now we have two passages in the RV whereat Ṛjiśvan is called by the patronymic Vaidathina 'descendant of Vidathin'. In RV (4, 16, 13) the patronymic Vaidathina 'descendant of Vidathin' is used as an appellation of Ṛjiśvan, while in RV (5, 29, 11) only the patronymic Vaidathina 'descendant of Vidathin is used'.[21] There is no doubt that in the second place also the patronymic means Ṛjiśvan, because the context in both the verses is one and the same. This Ṛjiśvan is said to be a seer belonging to the family of Bharadvājas, and is mentioned with Suhotra, Śunahotra, Nara and Garga in the Sarvā (2, 6, 52).

Again, MBh (12, 29), i.e. the Ṣoḍaśarājakīya section contains an account of Suhotra who is twice mentioned (vv. 22, 25) as Vaitithina, i.e. 'descendant of Vitithina. This Suhotra Vaitithina is identified with Suhotra Bhārata, who is consequently identified with Suhotra Bharadvāja, son of Bṛhatkṣatra.[22]

The BD (5, 102) states that Bharadvāja, the son of Bṛhaspati, and grandson of Aṅgiras was also Vidathin.[23] Thus, according to the BD Vidathin, an "ancestor" of Ṛjiśvan, is alternate name of Bharadvāja Bārhaspatya.

We have thus seen that the Sarvā (2, 6, 52) categorically and expressely states that Suhotra, Śunahotra, Nara, Garga and Ṛjiśvan were descendants of Bharadvāja Bārhaspatya and they were also grandsons, i.e. descendants, of Bharata Dauṣyanti. Out of these five seers whose hymns are included in the Bharadvāja Maṇḍala, Ṛjiśvan is frequently mentioned in RV[24] and in the two passages (cited above), he is referred to by his patronymic Vaidathina, i.e. descendant of Vidathin. And another seer of the group, Suhotra, is twice mentioned in the MBh (12, 29, 22 and 25) by the patronymic Vaitithina 'the descendant of Vitithin'. Further, the BD (5, 102) says that Bharadvāja Bārhaspatya was also known as Vidathin. Is this mere coincidence? We strongly feel that this is not so. To our mind, Vitithin is a variation of Vidathin. Thus Suhotra and Ṛjiśvan are two descendants of Bharadvāja as well as Vidathin. That Vidathin was a Bharadvāja is clear from the statement of the BD. But Vidathin must have been a person distinct from Bharadvāja Bārhaspatya. In other words, Vidathin was a descendant of Bharadvāja Bārhaspatya. The BD (5, 102) confused Bharadvāja Bārhaspatya for Vidathin Bharadvāja. It overlooked the fact that Bharadvāja was a personal name of Bṛhaspati's son, but a *gotra*-name of Vidathin.

Already we have fully discussed the problem involving Bharadvāja Bārhaspatya and Vitatha Bharadvāja, and pointed out that Bharadvāja Bārhaspatya, Vitatha's father, another Bharadvāja and Vitatha Bharadvāja himself were three different persons. This being so, we wonder if any of these can be identified with Vidathin Bharadvāja, the common ancestor of Ṛjiśvan and Suhotra. Further, the name Vitatha appears to be a form of *Vaitathina*〈*Vaitithina*〈*Vaidathina*. If this be accepted, it may be said that Vitatha was a son or descendant of Vidathin Bharadvāja. This can be adduced from the following contention:

Vidathin is a person, an ancestor of Suhotra and Ṛjiśvan. The Purāṇas have given consistent and continuous genealogy from Vitatha to Suhotra without a gap. Thus Vidathin cannot be placed between Vitatha and Suhotra, but somewhere above Vitatha. We know that Vidathin was a descendant of Bharadvāja Bārhaspatya. If Vidathin is to lend patronymic Vaidathina to Bharata's descendants, viz. Suhotra and Ṛjiśvan, a gap left out by Bharata must be accounted for. This gap occurred when Bharata had lost all his issues and had to adopt a descendant of Bharadvāja. Most probably, Bharata actually did adopt Vidathin

Bharadvāja. This is why the Purāṇas confused Vidathin for Vitatha and vice-versa, because of the similarity of the two names and they tried to identify one with the other, contending that Vitatha implies the futility of the birth of issues to Bharata, etc.

Now it seems probable to us that this Vidathin Bharadvāja was a Brāhmin by birth, and he became a Kṣatriya through adoption by a Kṣatriya king Bharata. In this regard Va and Mt have preserved some information:

Va (99, 157) says:
Tasmād divyo bharadvājo
brāhmaṇāt kṣatriyo' bhavat/
dvyāmūṣyāyaṇa nāma
sa smṛto dvipitarastu vā//

"From that divine Bharadvāja who was earlier (born as) a Brāhmaṇa, became a Kṣatriya and (therefore) became known as the son of two persons of such and such names (or simply, 'a son of two fathers')." This is verily said of Bharadvāja, the son of Bṛhaspati, who, according to the Purāṇas, was an adoptee. The same fact appears in a slightly modified form in Mt (49, 33) also as:

tasmād api bharadvājād
brāhmaṇāḥ kṣatriyā bhuvi/
dvyāmūṣyāyaṇakaulināḥ
smṛtās te dvividhena vai//

"From that Bharadvāja, also, were born Brāhmaṇas and Kṣatriyas who were known as persons born in the family of one who was a *dvyāmūṣyāyaṇa* 'son of two persons of such and such names'."

These Purāṇic statements go well with what we have noticed above. The MBh (1, 69, 50) also lends support to this by saying that in the race of Bharata there ruled many high-souled kings, some of whom were likened to gods and others to the brāhmaṇas.[25] These statements in the Purāṇas and the Epic point to an important aspect of social life in the history of ancient Aryans.

(*iv*) *Bharadvāja, Divodāsa and Vītahavya*

The MBh (13, 31, 7-54) gives an account of the perpetual struggle between the princes of the Haihaya and the Kāśī dynasty. It is said that Śaryāti, the son of Manu Vaivasvata, had two sons: Tālajaṅgha and Haihaya. They ruled in the country of Vatsa (13, 31, 7). The sons of Haihaya became very powerful and were equally learned in the Vedas and Dhanurveda (13, 31, 8-9). At the same time, king Haryaśva ruled in the kingdom of Kāśī. He also was famous for his prowess. The sons of Vītahavya, who were descendants of Haihaya, marched against Haryaśva and defeated the latter in a war fought in the region between the Gaṅgā and the Yamunā (vv. 10-11). After killing Haryaśva in that battle the Haihayas returned to their kingdom. Sudeva, the son of Haryaśva now assumed the kingship of Kāśī. He was very virtuous. While he was ruling his kingdom, the Vītahavyas invaded Kāśī again and killed king Sudeva in that fight (vv. 12-14). Now Sudeva's son Divodāsa was installed as the king of Kāśī. Divodāsa, being aware of the aggressive might of the Vītahavyas, built a city called Vārāṇasī at the instance of Indra (vv. 15-16). While he lived in peace in the city of Vārāṇasī the Haihayas attacked the Kāśī kingdom once more. Divodāsa came out of his capital and gave a valiant fight to his enemies. But he lost the battle and ultimately had to flee for his life. He straightaway went to the hermitage of Bharadvāja and sought refuge (vv. 19-22). Divodāsa related to the sage all about his miserable plight due to the aggression committed by the Vītahavyas. Then he requested the sage, "O Bhagavan, kindly protect me with the same kindness as one shows to one's disciple. These Vītahavyas have viciously annihilated my race" (vv. 23-25). At this Bharadvāja assured him of his help and advised him not to be afraid of his enemies. Also he promised that he would do everything so as to enable the king to endure the onslaughts of the Vītahavyas (vv. 26-27). Bharadvāja performed a sacrifice with a view to procuring a heroic son for the king Divodāsa; consequently, a son named Pratardana was born to Divodāsa. It is said that as soon as the child was born, he appeared to be a boy of thirteen years and he possessed the knowledge of all the Vedas and had mastery over Dhanurveda. And Bharadvāja by dint of yoga endowed him with all the powers of the world. At this Pratardana became exalted with a coat of mail, a bow and arrows and exhibited the glow of the Fire god (vv. 28-31). Seeing that such an extraordinary son was born to him, Divodāsa was very pleased and dreamt of burning the Vītahavyas. Pratardana was soon installed by the king Divodāsa as the crown prince and sent to annihilate the Vītahavyas (vv. 32-34). At his father's command, he quickly crossed the river Gaṅgā and invaded the capital of the Vītahavyas. As soon as the Vītahavyas heard the war-cry of the foes, they accepted the challenge and resisted the attack. But they could not withstand the assault inflicted by Kāśī prince Pratardana and soon all the sons of Vītahavya fell in the battle (vv. 35-40). The king Vītahavya had to flee his capital and he took refuge in the hermitage of Bhṛgu. Bhṛgu granted asylum assuring him protection, while his disciples offered him hospitality (vv. 41-42). But Pratardana chased him to Bhṛgu's *āśrama* (hermitage), and demanded an early audience with the head of the hermitage who came out to receive the incoming young prince. Pratardana was offered due honour by Bhṛgu. Pratardana thereafter demanded the surrender of Vītahavya as the latter had killed his ancestors (vv. 43-48). At this, Bhṛgu declared that there was no Kṣatriya in his hermitage, but only Brāhmaṇa (v. 49). Having heard these words, Pratardana smiled and then, touching the feet of the sage, expressed his satisfaction at the fact that, at least, he had forced his foes to abandon their own race and that was success enough. Then he took leave and returned to Vārāṇasī like one freed from the clutches of a snake (vv. 50-52). By mere words uttered by Bhṛgu, now Vītahavya became a *Brahmarṣi* and attained *brahmavāditva*. And his descendants are also classed as Brāhmaṇas (v. 54).

From this legend, the following points emerge: (1) Bharadvāja, Divodāsa and Pratardana of Kāśī, Bhṛgu, and Vītahavya of Vatsa—all were contemporaries. The contemporaneity of Bhṛgu, the son of Brahmā, and others is not tenable. Bhṛgu probably was anterior to Bharadvāja, Divodāsa, Vītahavya and Pratardana, because Bhṛgu is considered to be one of the four *mūlagotras*[1] and belongs to a hoary past. Possibly a junior Bhṛgu (i.e. descendant of Bhṛgu) granted asylum to Vītahavya; and (2) Divodāsa and Pratardana of Kāśī had Bharadvāja as their priest (*Purohita*). Pargiter[2] says that this Bharadvāja was Bṛhaspati's son and he was a young contemporary of Divodāsa II of the Kāśī dynasty. He further points out that the PB (15, 3, 7) and KS (11, 10) also refer to this Divodāsa II and not to the Ṛgvedic Divodāsa of North Pāñcāla.[3]

Pradhan[4] identifies the Ṛgvedic Bharadvāja who was priest of

Divodāsa Atithigva, with Bharadvāja in the Rām. Then he turns to identify Divodāsa of Kāśī dynasty with the one in the RV, and Bharadvāja (the priest of the Kāśī king) with the priest of Divodāsa Atithigva and with one in the Rām who received Rāma and Bharata. Appreciating these, Mankad[5] says: "Pradhan has admirably shown that Divodāsa, who was often called Atithigva in the Ṛgveda was the same person as Divodāsa, the king of Kāśī. He has shown how the Kāśī king Divodāsa is described in the Purāṇas as the son of Vadhryaśva and how even in the Ṛgveda this Divodāsa is called the son of Vadhryaśva." And subsequently he (Mankad)[6] has tried to show how "Divodāsa, Sudās and Prastoka were Daśaratha's contemporaries. So also, Bharadvāja who received gifts from these, was Daśaratha's contemporary." Rahurkar[7] also alludes to the story of Vītahavya and Divodāsa and then tries to identify two Bharadvājas described in RV and MBh as one and the same person. In these arguments, we detect the following weaknesses: (1) Divodāsa of Kāśī dynasty is not, anywhere in the traditional sources, called an offspring of the Bharatas. (2) Then Pratardana and his son Kṣatraśrī are never mentioned as the princes of the Bharatas. (3) Divodāsa who was defeated by the Haihaya Vītahavyas could not have defeated the mighty Śaṁbara, as stated in RV. (4) The loci of both the Divodāsas are clearly mentioned. (5) The Haihaya Vītahavyas are nowhere described in the RV as Divodāsa's enemy, as Śaṁbara's name is missing from the MBh legend. (6) So also Divodāsa's name is not mentioned in the Rām, but Ahalyā is.[8] (7) Allusion to Pratardana in the Uttarakāṇḍa of the Rām is doubtful, because this sixth part is considered as a later work. Thus untenable is the identification of the two kings, postulated irrespective of their age, time and race. It is equally wrong to accept Bharadvājas—said to be associated with the two Divodāsas on the one hand, and that mentioned in the Rām, on the other—as one and the same Bharadvāja. It would be better to consider each of these Divodāsas and Bharadvājas as distinct personalities.

Incidentally, the legend of the strife between the Vītahavyas and the Kāśī kings throws light on the Bharadvājas' role in it. This fully demonstrates that Bharadvāja, the priest of Divodāsa was one of the best of the ascetics—due to his yogic attainments he could give Pratardana to Divodāsa. And this Bharadvāja helped Pratardana to recover the Kāśī kingdom from the Vītahavyas.

This episode thus bears striking similarity with the one in the BD (5, 124-42) as the background of the RV (6, 27; 6, 47, 22-25 and 6, 75), where a battle between Cāyamāna and Vṛcīvats is described.

(*v*) *Bharadvāja and his son Yavakrīta*

Another interesting legend recorded in the MBh[1] is that of Yavakrīta, the son of Bharadvāja. The story goes that a Bharadvāja and one Raibhya were friends. They lived in the forest in all cordiality (establishing their own Āśramas side by side).[2] Bharadvāja had Yavakrīta as his only son and Raibhya had two, Parāvasu and Arvāvasu.[3] Raibhya himself was learned (in the Vedas) but Bharadvāja was given to penance. Yet between them there was incomparable love. Raibhya and his sons were highly honoured (by the people) whereas Bharadvāja was not. On this, Yavakrīta was overpowered by such mental affliction that he began to perform severe penance with the intention of acquiring the knowledge of the Vedas.[4] He tormented his own body, sitting by the side of a blazing fire during the course of his penance and thereby caused great anxiety in the mind of Indra.[5] Indra personally came to Yavakrīta and asked him why he had resorted to such supreme penance.[6] Yavakrīta replied that he wanted to acquire the knowledge of the Vedic lore through penance, since one is required to spend a lot of time in learning the same from a Guru.[7] Even after hearing this, Indra advised him to go to a Guru to learn the Vedas.[8] But Yavakrīta continued his penance for securing his objects. Once again, he caused great anxiety to Indra who called on Yavakrīta for a second time and asked him to desist. Indra told Yavakrīta that the purpose for which he had set himself upon severe penance, was impossible of achievement by this method; therefore, his was not an act of wisdom. Further, he added, if Yavakrīta and his father made an attempt to learn the Vedas, the Vedic lores would dawn on them in course of time.[9] Thereupon, Yavakrīta told Indra that he would continue his penance with yet greater austerity; if his wish were not granted, he would offer sacrifice to him (Indra) by throwing himself into the fire.[10] Indra understood his firm resolve and thought of a trick for preventing him from continuing the penance. He disguised himself as an old Brāhmin of several hundred years suffering, as if, from consumption (*yakṣman*) and appeared near the Gaṅgā where Yavakrīta used to take his bath, etc. He appeared busy in building a bridge of sand over the (mighty) river.[11] When Yavakrīta saw this unusual activity of the old Brāhmin afflicted with an acute disease, he could not help laughing at it and asked him why he was exerting himself so much at such an advanced age.[12] Being thus questioned, the Brāhmin (really Indra) told Yavakrīta that he wanted to build a bridge, in the absence of which people were facing great difficulties when crossing the river.[13] Yavakrīta then told the Brāhmin that the task as undertaken by him was impossible to achieve and, therefore, he should desist from it.[14] The Brāhmin thereupon, got an opportunity and observed that this act (of his bridging the river) was similar to the one that Yavakrīta had undertaken.[15] Having recognised him as Indra, Yavakrīta addressed him: "O Pākaśāsana, if you deem my work as an impossible one and compare it with that of yours, I urge you to do what is just possible for me, and, pray, grant me a boon so that I may attain the object of my desire.[16] Being thus requested by Yavakrīta, Indra granted him a boon that the Vedas would reveal themselves unto him and to his father. Having thus achieved his cherished object, Yavakrīta went back home and reported to his father all that had happened,[17] and that on account of Indra's blessing the Vedas would reveal to both of them and they would supersede others.[18] Hearing his son's statement, Bharadvāja told him that this boon would make him conceited and ultimately prove fatal. He drew his son's attention to the plight of one called Bāladhī who was a person of similar state of mind. Bharadvāja further warned his son Yavakrīta not to visit Raibhya and his two sons lest that might annoy them; they were very strong and could even harm him.[19] Yavakrīta assured his father that he would act according to his advice, and that he would respect Raibhya as his own father.[20]

One day, however, in the month of *Caitra*, i.e. in spring season, Yavakrīta went to the hermitage of Raibhya. There he saw the daughter-in-law of Raibhya and asked her to wait upon him. Out of fear of being cursed, she agreed.[21] Thereafter, when alone, she wept bitterly over the bygone incident. At that moment, Raibhya came to know all about Yavakrīta's misconduct. His wrath knew no bound. He drew a portion of his matted lock and burnt it in the fire (probably reciting some magically potent mantras): a Rākṣasa was born and was directed to kill Yavakrīta.[22]

The Rākṣasa chased him and Yavakrīta ran towards a pond but was shocked to see it drying up. The river along which he ran also dried up.[23] Then he dashed to his father's Agnihotraśālā ('Daily-sacrificial Hall') where his entry was blocked by the blind Śūdra gate-keeper. Yavakrīta could not get a safe refuge, his heart was pierced by the Rākṣasa's trident (*triśūla*) and he died instantly. After Yavakrīta's end, the Rākṣasa returned to the sage Raibhya.[24]

Meanwhile Bharadvāja, Yavakrīta's father, performed all his daily duties (like the *svādhyāya, āhnika* etc.), gathered the required sacrificial fuel and then came to the sacrificial hall. Daily, all the fires led the sage to the sacrificial hall. But, that day, because of the sudden death of his son, the fires did not wait upon him. Noticing this unusual happening and the Agnihotra in a disorderly state, Bharadvāja was bewildered and inquired from the Śūdra door-keeper: "O Śūdra, why do the fires not grace my sight today? You are also found in an unusual state? Did not my son go to Raibhya? Tell me all about it; my heart has many a misgiving".[25] The Śūdra, thereupon, described to him all that had happened to Yavakrīta.[26] "On hearing the plight that befell Yavakrīta, Bharadvāja was so overhelmed by grief that he began to lament,[27] and cursed Raibhya that he would also be killed by his elder son.[28] Then after a long wail, he cremated his son's body and entered into the funeral fire.[29]

In the meantime, king Bṛhaddyumna had instituted a sacrificial session (*satram āsta*), with Raibhya as his priest. King Bṛhaddyumna invited Arvāvasu and Parāvasu, the two sons of Raibhya, also, as assistants. With their father's permission both the brothers attended the sacrifices, while their father Raibhya and Parāvasu's wife stayed in the hermitage.[30]

One evening Parāvasu stealthily went home and he saw a deer (i.e. actually it was his father covered with a hide of *kṛṣṇasāra* 'deer'). Parāvasu (under illusion) killed him (i.e. his own father) in that dark night. Later, seeing his father killed by him, he performed all his funeral rites. Back to the sacrifices he addressed his younger brother Arvāvasu: "This work (of a priest in the sacrifice) cannot be borne by you alone. I have killed our father, thinking him to be a deer. So you please perform the act of atonement on my behalf as prescribed for a killer of a Brāhmaṇa. I would be able to carry out the work of the sacrifice alone.[31]

Arvāvasu assented to his brother's proposal and undertook to perform the act of atonement prescribed for a killer of a Brāhmaṇa relentlessly. Having successfully removed the sins (*lit*. having crossed the sins) of the killing of a Brāhmaṇa, Arvāvasu arrived in the sacrificial session again. When Parāvasu saw his brother there, he said to the king in the assembly of the learned: "This killer of a Brāhmaṇa should not be seen in the sacrificial hall. Because, the sight of a killer of a Brāhmaṇa would afflict you doubtlessly." On hearing this, Arvāvasu repeatedly denied the charge of killing a Brāhmaṇa brought against him by his elder brother. And he told the king that really the murder was committed by his brother and he had undertaken to perform the act of atonement on behalf of his brother.[32] At this, the gods were pleased with him, supported Arvāvasu, discarded Parāvasu and offered to grant him a boon of his choice. Thereupon, Arvāvasu asked for, (1) the revival of his father (from death), (2) the removal of his brother's sin, (3) and revival of Bharadvāja and his son Yavakrīta. And (as a result of it) all of them rose alive.[33] Having gained a new lease of life, Yavakrīta asked the gods, led by Agni: "I read the '*brahman*', observed vows according to prescribed rules. How could then Raibhya do harm to me, a scholar in the (Vedic) lore; pray, say about it, O best of immortals".[34] The gods replied: "O Yavakrīta, do not repeat what you have just now said. You have studied the Vedas (easily) without the help of a Guru. Because of this, you have undergone a great unhappiness. It is best to get the knowledge of the *brahman* 'magically potent *mantra*' in due course, with great effort."[35] Thus saying to Yavakrīta, the gods, with Agni as their chief, left the place.[36]

We cannot say anything regarding the real identity of this Bharadvāja, the father of Yavakrīta. But he appears to be a descendant of Bharadvāja Bārhaspatya.

(*vi*) *Bharadvāja and his son Droṇa Bhāradvāja*

The MBh lists a number of persons frequently mentioned as the 'son'(s) or descendant(s) of Bharadvāja. Among those two were famous and known for their valour uncommon among Brāhmaṇas. They were Droṇācārya Bhāradvāja and his son Aśvatthāman

Bhāradvāja. The Epic devotes chapter after chapter eulogising the father and the son. This section describes Droṇa's parentage, birth, career and descent very briefly. Droṇācārya was the precepter of the Kaurava and the Pāṇḍava princes. The *ācārya* lived a righteous life and died a glorious death as the Commander-in-chief of the Kaurava army in the great Mahābhārata war, fought at Kurukṣetra.

The legend of Droṇa's birth is repeated at least four times in different contexts, particularly in the Ādiparvan of the Epic.[1] In two slightly different versions, he is said to be the son of Bharadvāja. Details are given of Droṇa's learning archery (*Dhanurveda*) from Agniveśa who in turn happened to be a disciple of Droṇa's father Bharadvāja. One of these versions says about Bharadvāja's friendship with Pṛṣata, the king of the North Pāñcāla dynasty and father of Drupada Yajñasena.[2] The first version runs as follows:

Once Bharadvāja, while staying inside *havirdhāna* ('sacrificial hall'), saw Ghṛtācī, a nymph of extraordinary beauty. It so happened that Ghṛtācī's clothes were blown away by the wind, leaving her nude beauty fully exposed to Bharadvāja. At this sight, he was excited and dropped his semen, later preserved in a *droṇakalaśa* (a vessel used in sacrifice). From that wooden vessel (*droṇa*) was born the intelligent Droṇa.[3]

Now the second version: Bharadvāja the great seer lived at Gaṅgādvāra, observed vows and did penance. One day he went, as usual, to the sacred Gaṅgā for a holy bath. There had also come a nymph called Ghṛtācī, in her daily routine, but a bit before he reached there. It so chanced that the wind blew away her garments fully uncovering her and presenting her physical beauty to him. On this sight his passions were roused. Enamoured of her, the seer who had so long maintained his celebacy, dropped his semen which he preserved in a *droṇa* ('wooden vessel' used in sacrifice). From that was born his son Droṇa.[1] He was very intelligent and studied all the Vedas with all their Vedāṅgas.[4]

The legend continues to tell us that Bharadvāja had friendship with Pṛṣata, the king of the North Pāñcāla dynasty.[5] In the boyhood, Pṛṣata's son Drupada developed intimate friendship with Bharadvāja's son Droṇa, while they studied the ancient lore together in the seer's hermitage.[6] However, this friendship did not last. Once it so happened that when Droṇa Bhāradvāja reminded

Drupada of his boyhood promise, viz. that he would give half of the kingdom to him at the time of his assumption of kingship after Pṛṣata's death, Drupada went back on his word and ridiculed Droṇa. Droṇa already having acquired mastery of archery at the feet of Paraśurāma undertook the honourable job of teaching the sons of Pāṇḍu and Dhṛtarāṣṭra. On a later date when his pupils had attained full expertise in archery, Droṇa asked them to conquer Pāñcāla country where Drupada ruled. Under the able leadership of young prince Arjuna, Droṇa's pupils conquered Pāñcāla and brought Drupada as captive. Drupada then conceded half of the kingdom to Droṇa. After his release, he lived to wreak vengeance upon Bhāradvāja Droṇa. The war of Kurukṣetra saw Droṇa and Drupada on opposite sides on that account.

In the same context, we may refer to the handing over of the Āgneyāstra, ('a fire missile') recorded in the MBh (1, 158, 26-27).[7] Tradition holds that Bṛhaspati gave the Āgneyāstra to Bharadvāja (Droṇa's father?) and Bharadvāja gave it to Agniveśya who then handed it down to Droṇa and Droṇa to Arjuna.

Another one is in respect of handing of a coat of mail (*varma*) (MBh 7, 69, 65-67).[8] Droṇa informed Duryodhana, in the wake of the fierce battle fought (the Droṇa-parvan) after Abhimanyu's death, that the coat of mail had its divine origin. In the hoary antiquity, it is stated, Indra having been clad in that particular coat of mail fought Vṛtra and won the battle. Then that coat of mail was given to Aṅgiras who gave it to his son Bṛhaspati; from the latter it came to Agniveśya and finally to Droṇa. Droṇa gave the same to Duryodhana (with the muttering of the potent *mantras*) so that Arjuna's shaft would not cleave Duryodhana's heart.

Here Bṛhaspati is mentioned as the preceptor of Agniveśya while on an earlier occasion Bharadvāja was. However, on both the occasions, the preceptor-pupil relationship between Agniveśya and Droṇa on the one hand, and between Droṇa and Arjuna or Duryodhana on the other, is found in conformity with the spirit of MBh legend as a whole.

Now we can examine the relationship among the personalities mentioned in these legends. (1) First of all, Indra's relationship with Aṅgiras in respect of his handing over the coat of mail does not go beyond a giver-god and a recipient of god's gift. (2) But the relationship between Aṅgiras and Bṛhaspati is not confined to that of the donor and the recipient, but appears to be more intimate. Elsewhere, we have noted the genealogy of the Bhāradvāja family that Aṅgiras is the son of Brahmā and the father of Bṛhaspati. Besides, a father could act as a preceptor to his son and instruct him in *śastras* and *śāstras*. Thus Bṛhaspati might have learnt Dhanurveda (inclusive of the knowledge of the coat of mail, etc.) from his father Aṅgiras. (3) Agniveśya is said to be the recipient of this armour from Bṛhaspati and Āgneyāstra from Bharadvāja. On the other hand, Agniveśya had Droṇa as his pupil. There appears to be an unbridgeable gap of time between the age of Bṛhaspati and that of Agniveśya. Either Bṛhaspati must have lived nearer to Agniveśya's time or Agniveśya should have been closer to Bṛhaspati's. Otherwise, there should be two Agniveśyas to live in both the periods, one getting that coat from Bṛhaspati in hoary antiquity and passing the same through his descendants until another Agniveśya received it and later handed it over to Droṇa before the MBh war. However, Agniveśya's living in an age nearer to that of Droṇa and of his father Bharadvāja is probable. It is likely that Agniveśya learnt Dhanurveda directly from Bharadvāja. This Agniveśya is said to be the son of Agniṣṭut.[9] Probably the same Agniveśya is also included in the list of 32 Aṅgirases[10] who gave rise to the *gotras* under the three-*ṛṣi-pravaras* of Āṅgirasa, Bārhaspatya and Bhāradvāja, and persons belonging to this Agniveśya *gotra* cannot marry with those of Bharadvāja and others coming under the same *ṛṣi-pravaras*. This establishes a relationship among Aṅgiras, Bṛhaspati, Bharadvāja and Agniveśya. (4) On the identity of Bharadvāja, Droṇa's father, we have pointed out above that there was a vast time-gap between the ages of Bṛhaspati and of Droṇa who died on the 15th day of the Kurukṣetra war and at the age of 85 (*aśītipañcaka*).[11] Bharadvāja, the father of Droṇa is said to have expired before Droṇa married Kṛpī,[12] the twin-sister of Kṛpācārya, another *guru* of the Pāṇḍavas and Kauravas. Thus this Bharadvāja cannot be son of Bṛhaspati. Bṛhaspati's son Bharadvāja lived three or four generations before Bharata; Yudhiṣṭhira, Droṇa's pupil and a scion of the Bharatas, lived about 30 generations after Bharata. So Bharadvāja, the father of Droṇa was separated from Bharadvāja Bārhaspatya by some 33 generations; and therefore, they were two distinct personalities. This Bharadvāja, his son Droṇa and grandson Aśvatthāman all belonged to the *gotra* of Bharadvāja and were called by the surname

Bhāradvāja. Tradition has lost the personal name of Droṇa's father.

Most important for us is the fact that the members of the family of Bharadvājas were constant adherents to Vedic sacrifices etc., were always well-versed in the Vedas and *Śāstras*, and maintained a long tradition of Dhanurveda. In sum, the Bharadvājas excelled in both *śāpa* 'curse' (which was often hurled upon others) and *śastra* (i.e. playing of a martial role in war) (cf. the adage *śāpād api śarād api*).

As regards his time, (1) the Epic tells us that Droṇācārya, the son of this Bharadvāja and preceptor of the princes had a glorious death in the Kurukṣetra war on its 15th day at the age of 85. Bharadvāja, Droṇa's father must have been at least 30 years (one generation = 30 years) older than his son. So he lived in the pre-MBh age and died before Droṇa married Kṛpī Śāradvatī. The same conclusion can be arrived at on the basis of some other facts. The Epic says that Bharadvāja died before Droṇa's marriage, i.e. before the birth of Aśvatthāman. Aśvatthāman was a fellow-student, i.e. class-mate, of Arjuna. Arjuna's son was Abhimanyu. The latter died gloriously on the 14th day of the MBh war at the age of sixteen. Taking the span of a generation as thirty years we can say that Arjuna's age at that time was forty-six. Aśvatthāman would also be almost as old, i.e. 45 years, adding 30 years to it. Droṇa's age was 76 years, which is just 9 years less than 85 years given in the Epic. Adding 30 years to 76 we get the age of Bharadvāja, i.e. the sage was born at least 106 years before the war and lived up to 46 years before it started. All these calculations are, however, tentative.

(3) Now we may say that this Bharadvāja was a senior contemporary of Devavrata Bhīṣma and Kṛṣṇa-Dvaipāyana Vedavyāsa. The facts may be clarified as under: Kṛpācārya and his sister Kṛpī were born of the seed of Gautama Sāradvata and they were under the fostering-care of Śāntanu, Devavrata's father. Supposing Kṛpa and Droṇa were of the same age and Droṇa married Kṛpī, all of them were almost contemporaries of Bhīṣma Devavrata. All of them lived during the last part of the rule of Śāntanu. Although Droṇa's father Bharadvāja died before Droṇa married Kṛpī, he probably thrived in the early part of Śāntanu's rule. Kṛṣṇa Dvaipāyana who was born of Satyavatī through Parāśara, was of the age of Bhīṣma and had been a junior con-

temporary of Bharadvāja. This Bharadvāja may be dated some 33 generations after the son of Bṛhaspati Āṅgirasa. He was a scion of the same family.

This Bharadvāja is said to have lived at Gaṅgādvāra, i.e. on the bank of the Gaṅgā. B.C. Law,[13] identifies Gaṅgādvāra with Haridvār where the Gaṅgā has descended to the plains.

(*vii*) *Bharadvāja, father of Srucāvatī*

The MBh (9, 47) contains a legend of one Srucāvatī who is said to be the daughter of Bharadvāja. The legend of her birth appears to be similar to that of Droṇa and further the same nymph, viz. Ghṛtācī, is responsible for her birth too.

Bharadvāja once saw the nymph Ghṛtācī of wide eyes, and at once he dropped his semen, which he collected in his hand and put into a leafy-cup (*parṇapūṭa*) wherefrom, later on, was born a beautiful girl.[1] In due course of time, the sage Bharadvāja performed her *jātakarman* ('ceremony pertaining to birth') and gave her the name Srucāvatī ('one possessing the ladle that can be used in sacrifice'). Thereafter (when she came of age), she was put incharge of the Āśrama of the sage during the time whenever the sage went to the Himālayas.[2] Srucāvatī was a very dedicated soul. Also, she was very beautiful. She desired to get Indra as her husband and, for that purpose, she began to perform severe penance.[3] Her penance shook Indra. The lord of the gods taking the guise of the sage Vasiṣṭha came to her. He gave her a handful of *badara* fruits and asked her to cook these.[4] Respectfully, she undertook to cook those fuits. While doing so, she exhausted all the fuel that was available, but she could not get the *badaras* boiled. She then burnt her hands and feet in order to cook the fruit on the fire, thus keeping it burning. At this devotion of Srucāvatī, Indra (disguised as Vasiṣṭha) was highly pleased with her[5] and granted her the desired boon.[6] The place where Bharadvāja's daughter Srucāvatī cooked *badara* fruits for Indra and thereby had him as her husband in her next birth, thus acquired celebrity; that is, it became known as a place of pilgrimage called Badarapācana; it was visited by Balarāma while the Kurukṣetra war was in progress.[7]

It is difficult to identify this Bharadvāja, the father of Srucāvatī. The association of Bharadvāja with Ghṛtācī is however an important clue. The legend of Droṇa's birth which is reported several times in the MBh tells us also of the similar association of Bharadvāja with Ghṛtācī.[8] As such, probably this Bharadvāja was the father of Droṇācārya also. If we accept this identification we can further say that this Bharadvāja was a junior contemporary of Śāntanu. Bharadvāja, the father of Droṇa, was a friend of king Pṛṣata of the North Pāñcāla dynasty and thus a senior to both Bhīṣma and Kṛṣṇa Dvaipāyana.[9]

We have been told that Bharadvāja, the father of Droṇa, lived at Gaṅgādvāra which might not be too far from the Pāñcāla capital at Ahicchatra and the capital of the Kurus at Hastināpura. Now Badarapācana is given as the place of residence of Bharadvāja, Srucāvatī's father. It is difficult to say that Gaṅgādvāra and Badarapācana were two names of the same place. Even if these are taken as two distinct places, it is possible to say that the same Bharadvāja could have two Āśramas or hermitages at two different places. Badarapācana must have been nearer the Himālayas. Whether it was also known as Badarikāśrama associated with seers, is not known. Because of the existence of Badara, the second place was so named. The legend behind Badarapācana also indicates the same reality. Thus it is possible that one and the same place was thus known as Badarīkāśrama[10] or Badarapācana.

(*viii*) *Bharadvāja and Origin of Śuklatīrtha*

Beside the story of the birth of Bharadvāja Bārhaspatya and adoption of Bharadvāja (Vidathin), as given in Va and Mt and corroborated by a number of other Purāṇas, some of them supply additional material pertaining to the other Bharadvājas, identification of which, however, is not easy. However, one thing is certain that these legends are also narrated in the same strain, i.e. stressing piety, religious observances and asceticism, etc. The following legend recorded in Br 133, tells us about the origin of a place of pilgrimage (*tīrtha*) called Śuklatīrtha: a Bharadvāja is responsible for its origin. It runs as follows:

There was a sage, Bharadvāja by name. He was virtuous by nature. His wife Paiṭhinasī adorned the family by her virtues and good conduct. They lived on the bank of the river Gomatī. Paiṭhinasī was very much devoted to her husband and helped him in his ritual observances. One day it so happened that while Paiṭhinasī kept herself busy in preparing sacrificial cakes for Agni and Soma (*agnisomīya puroḍāśa*) and for Indra and Agni (*aindrāgna purodāśa*), a dark being came out of the smoke from the hearth and began to consume the cakes she had prepared. Bharadvāja, who was nearby, saw the creature eating the cakes meant for the sacrifice, and was angry with that being. The sage asked the dark-skinned one as to who he was. The dark-skinned replied that he was the eldest son of Prācīnabarhis, Havyaghna by name, born of Saṁdhyā. He further informed Bharadvāja that Lord Brahmā had granted him a boon, viz. that he could consume the sacrificial offerings, and that his brother Kali by name is very strong and hideous in looks and monstrous by nature. "I am black, my father is black, my mother is black, so is my brother." "So I destroy the sacrificial poles and also the eternal religion", he added. At this, Bharadvāja politely requested him: "Please protect my sacrifice. The eternal religion is dear (to us). I know you are a destroyer of sacrifice, but you are a good twice-born. So save my sacrifice". Thereupon, the dark-skinned addressed the sage: "O Bharadvāja, listen to me in brief. In the days of old, I was cursed by Brahmā at the meeting of gods and Dānavas. Being propitiated by me Brahmā said to me, "When a great sage will, in course of time, sprinkle you with ambrosia, then only you will be redeemed from my curse, not otherwise. Sir, if you please agree to do this, then Brahmā's words will come true." Further he added, "Whatever I have told you is true". Bharadvāja then addressed him, "O great one, you are my friend. Tell me by what means I can protect this sacrifice (from destruction). I shall do it. And you probably know that gods and demons churned the ocean and obtained ambrosia: how will it be available to me? If you are pleased with me, tell me an easy method to get it." Hearing these words, the dark-skinned was happy and said: "The water of the river Gomatī is considered to be ambrosia and ambrosia is gold; it is said, the product of cow, (viz. *ājya*' 'ghee') is also ambrosia, so is Soma. You may sprinkle me with all these, or with three of them. You may sprinkle me with the water of the Gaṅgā, with *ājya* and gold. Above all, the water of Gomatī is considered to be divine ambrosia." The seer was very much pleased at these words. And thereupon, he took in his hand the water of the Gaṅgā, with all reverence, sprinkled it over that dark-skinned one. All the ingredients of the sacrifice also were sprinkled over him with the same water by the sage, and lo! all of a sudden everything turned white. And even the dark being became white as he had desired. Thereafter, Bharadvāja having performed his sacrifice bid adieu to all the *ṛtvijs* and threw away the sacrificial pole (*yūpa*) in the water of the Gaṅgā. That pole continued to exist there even after that incident. And now the black one who was sprinkled over with ambrosia in that *tīrtha* 'place of pilgrimage' said to Bharadvāja: "I am going, O Bharadvāja, as you have made me white again. But since this happening whosoever takes bath or performs worship (of gods and forefathers) in this *tīrtha*, would attain his desired fruit or acquire merit of the sacrifice. Even by remembering this *tīrtha*, one would be able to remove one's sins". It is said that, since then, that place was known as Śuklatīrtha, and this *tīrtha*, on the bank of Gomatī, thus opened the gate of heaven.

The legend brings out the following points of interest:

(1) Bharadvāja was a virtuous man and devoted to eternal religion. He was anxious to safeguard the sacrifice, etc., and to perform the daily and occasional sacrifices regularly. He was probably committed to daily Agnihotra, besides periodical Darśa and Paurṇamāsa, as the mention of the preparation of the cakes indicates.

(2) Also the legend brings out the efficacy of the sacrifice and of the holy water of the Gaṅgā and the Gomatī. So also the products of the cow and gold and soma used in sacrifice are considered equally effective and therefore on par with ambrosia. It points to popular belief in the efficacy of sacrifices and materials used in them.

(3) Removal of blackness of one and turning into white through sprinkling water of a holy river in the wake of a sacrifice, hints at magical practices and their use. This shows a harmony of the two aspects of religion, viz. popular and hieratic, centring round the sacrifice.

(4) Releasing the son of Prajāpati, Prācīnabarhis, from a curse pronounced on him by Brahmā for specific reason is miraculous. As for the curse imposed upon the eldest son of Prācīnabarhis, it is nowhere mentioned except in this legend.

Prācīnabarhis was a king of yore. He was son of Havirdhāna and Dhiṣaṇā. He became a Prajāpati, and married Samudrā, the daughter of Samudra, and had ten sons known as Prācetas. He is said to have made Kuśa-grass bend eastward and earned thereby his name, Prācīnabarhis. He performed many a sacrifice.[1] It is said that the fire coming out of the mouth of Prācetas, the sons of Prācīnabarhis, plunged the whole world into a conflagration. They were, however, well-versed in Dhanurveda.[2] No personal name of any of the Prācetas is ever given. B.C. Law says that Gomatī is identical with the Ṛgvedic Gomatī (RV 10, 75, 6) and is probably the modern Gomel, a western tributary of the Indus. He further says, "it has also been sought to be identified with the modern Gumtī which joins the Gaṅgā below Benares and which is described in the Rāmāyaṇa as situated in Ayodhyā and as being crowded with cattle (Ayodhyākāṇḍa, Ch. 49)."[3] Gomatī in our story may be identified with the latter.

(*ix*) *Bharadvāja, Revatī's brother*

Another legend in the Br (121, 1-20) tells us about the origin of another *tīrtha* ('a place of pilgrimage') called Revatītīrtha. Its background is that Revatī was none other than a sister of one Bharadvāja. This Bharadvāja was the preceptor of Kaṭha, probably the author of the school of the Kaṭhas of the Black YV. He married Revatī at the advice of Bharadvāja. The legend leading to their marriage and the origin of this place of pilgrimage is as follows:

On the southern bank of the holy river Gaṅgā there lived one Bharadvāja in a hermitage. He had a sister of marriageable age, Revatī by name. She was very ugly, and had a hoarse voice. Even in her youth she failed miserably to attract the attention of young men around her. She being in this miserable condition, Bharadvāja had to think as to how this sister could get a suitable match. He wondered if any one with good sense would of his own accord come forward to marry her at all. While Bharadvāja was still pondering over this, there came, one day, a sage to see him in his hermitage. This visitor was a young man, sixteen years old and possessed all good qualities. His name was Kaṭha. After receiving the young visitor with due respect, Bharadvāja asked him about the purpose of his visit. Kaṭha said in reply that he had come there to learn something more (*vidyārtham*) and urged Bharadvāja to impart learning to him. At this Bharadvāja asked Kaṭha to undertake the study of the Vedas, Purāṇas, Smṛtis and all those works which were considered as the fountain of virtues. Also, he exhorted Kaṭha to develop and maintain good conduct, resort only to virtues and devote himself to the service of the preceptor, because a disciple endowed with knowledge of his own self and memory is rarely attained. Kaṭha in turn requested his *Guru* 'preceptor' to guide him in study and assured him that he would ever remain devoted, truthful and maintain good conduct. Bharadvāja blessed him saying 'Be it so' and he taught Kaṭha whatever he wanted to learn. Having soon mastered the lore, Kaṭha was very much pleased. He implored Bharadvāja, "Revered Sir, I want to pay your fees, as agreeable to you. Kindly tell me whatever you like, be it even something rare. I would like to worship you at any cost, because after getting the cherished knowledge whosoever hesitates to give his *guru* the required honorarium certainly goes to hell." Thereupon, Bharadvāja proposed that Kaṭha should agree to marry Revatī, his sister, that could be as much as a *dakṣiṇā* 'fee' or 'honorarium' paid to him (Bharadvāja). Having heard this from his *Guru*, Kaṭha said that a *śiṣya* 'pupil' generally remains as a brother or a son of the *Guru*. Under this circumstance, it would not be proper for him to enter into such a relation with his *Guru*. However, Bharadvāja told Kaṭha to marry Revatī and fulfil his command. Kaṭha had then no option but to marry Revatī according to the prescribed rituals.

After the marriage was solemnised, Kaṭha worshipped Śaṅkara. And through the grace of god Śaṅkara, Revatī attained incomparable beauty. The water with which Revatī was sprinkled over fell from her body and flowed as river Revatī which joined the Gaṅgā. Thereafter, another river called Vidarbhā also flowed from *darbhas* ('bent grass') tinged in the water with which Revatī was sprinkled over her deformed physique. These two rivers met the holy river Gaṅgā. At the confluence of all these rivers, there originated a *tīrtha* 'place of pilgrimage' which became known as Revatītīrtha.

A man who takes bath in the confluence of the Revatī and the Gaṅgā, becomes free from all sins and is eligible for the world of Viṣṇu. So also, one who bathes in the confluence of the Vidarbhā and Gotamī attains all enjoyments here and salvation after death. Thus these two *tīrthas* originated on the bank of these rivers.

The legend stresses the relation of *guru* and *śiṣya* 'preceptor and pupil' where the words of *guru* are considered as untransgressable. It also attaches importance and efficacy to the worship of Śaṅkara, through which one could acquire even physical beauty. In similar circumstances, we saw earlier how a dark-skinned person turned fair through magical rites, i.e. sprinkling water of holy river. However, here sprinkling of waters is described to have originated rivers and holy places. In both the legends, efficacy of sprinkling after some sort of sacrifice or worship is given prime importance. Probably there is involved some popular magic and belief in these religious activities.

It is not possible to assign a date or exact locale to this Bharadvāja. The legend must have been a popular one about the *tīrthas* and remained current in society until it was included in the chain of legends in the Br. If at all we attach to it historicity, we must date it back to the time of the collection and arrangement of the Vedic *Śākhās* ('recensions').

Gotamī is identified by B.C. Law[1] as the modern Godāvarī. Also, he says that the river Revatī is a 'small river flowing by the side of the Pārśvanātha temple at Bijholi. It is named after Revatī *kuṇḍa*'.[2] Further, the same scholar confirms that Vidarbhā *tīrtha* referred to at Br 121 is situated on the bank of the river Godāvarī.[3]

On the basis of the above facts we can say that this Bharadvāja had his Āśrama somewhere near the river Godāvarī in the South.

(*x*) *Vāmanāvatāra and Bharadvāja*

Vām (62-63) has preserved the story of the birth of Vāmana who is said to be an *avatāra* ('incarnation', *lit*. 'person who has descended') of Lord Viṣṇu, and informs us how one Bharadvāja was connected with Vāmana. As we are interested only in that part which that Bharadvāja played, we summarise the relevant passages as follows:

This incident relates to the time during which Bali, the Daitya king, had instituted an Aśvamedha sacrifice (63, 1-32). This was in progress and the horse was let loose for conquest. Three months' time had already passed, during which period Agni was always worshipped, and the prominent Daityas were duly honoured. When the Sun was in Mithunarāśi, the mother of the gods (i.e. Aditi) gave birth to Mādhava in the form of a Vāmana 'dwarf' (62, 33-34).[1]

Immediately after his birth, Bharadvāja, the son of Bṛhaspati, who was a repository of penance and of great prowess, performed all the necessary ceremonies of the god incarnate. The sage who knew all the Śāstras also performed the *vratabandha* of the god. Thereafter, gods and sages gave him choice gifts. Bharadvāja, the scion of Aṅgirases, presented to him the high sounding Sāmaveda. The sage taught Vāmana all the Śāstras, within a single month (62, 43-50).[2] Thereafter, the god requested Bharadvāja, the foremost among the Brāhmaṇas: "O Brāhmaṇa, kindly permit me to go to Kurukṣetra where Bali, the lord of the Daityas, is performing the Aśvamedha sacrifice" (62, 53).[3] Bharadvāja replied: "Of your own accord, go or stay, I should not permit. However, if you do not mind, may I also accompany you to the sacrifice arranged by Bali (62, 54).[3a] But I like to ask you certain questions. In which places, O Best of the Puruṣas, you are accessible, I would like to know (62, 55)".[4] In his reply to this question, Vāmana declared his omnipotence and omnipresence. Then he gave the names of the places where he was accessible to the devotees. Also he related to Bharadvāja the legend of his previous incarnations such as *Matsya* 'fish', *Kūrma* 'turtle' etc. ... (Ch. 63).

Vāmana and Bharadvāja arrived at the gate of the sacrificial hall at Kurukṣetra. And Bali paid due respect to the god and ushered him into the sacrificial hall together with Bharadvāja (65, 4).[5] As soon as the god entered the Hall, Bali worshipped him in accordance with the procedures and asked him, "O Bhagavan, what shall I offer you, please tell me" (65-5).[6] Thereupon the best of the gods, having laughed for a long while and looked at his guru Bharadvāja addressed the lord of the Daityas: "My *Guru's Guru* is an Agnihotrin. He does not like to establish fire on other's land. So, O Lord of Dānavas, for him I beg of your land measuring only three steps of a man" (65, 6-8).[7]

That what followed next is well known. We are concerned here with the Bharadvāja's role. We have already analysed it from that angle. In fact, Vāmana played an active role while Bharadvāja played a passive one. However, Bharadvāja as the *guru* of Lord Vāmana is not at all a minor. He being Vāmana's preceptor raises not only his personal status but also that of his family. In the legend he is once mentioned as the scion of the Aṅgirases from whom Vāmana learnt the great music of the SV[8] and on another occasion he is referred to as the son of Bṛhaspati.[9] Because of his being one of the best ascetics he was assigned place of honour, viz. of the preceptor of Vāmana. Although there is reference to Vāmana's *guru's guru*, i.e. the *guru* of Bharadvāja, we are not told who he was. All these references, however, point to Bharadvāja without any historical sense of time and place. However, this Bharadvāja appears to be the founder of his family, and was Bṛhaspati's son.

(*xi*) *Bhāradvāja, son of Śāntā*

Va (111, 58-63)[1] records yet another legend relating to one Bharadvāja whose mother's name was Śāntā and who had two fathers (!). The legend is as follows:

In the past a sage Bharadvāja by (sur-)name performed *śrāddha* ceremony in a place (deriving its name from Kaśyapa). When he was about to offer *piṇḍa* offering to the deceased he saw that two hands—one black and the other white, came up to receive the offering. Seeing those strange claims of two, Bharadvāja was puzzled and, approaching his mother, asked as to which of the two—black and white—he should offer the *piṇḍa*. His mother *Śāntā* advised him to give the *piṇḍa* to the black one. Bharadvāja returning to the place of Kaśyapa was about to offer the *piṇḍa* in the hand of the black one, when the white one raised his voice (remaining himself unseen) and said that Bharadvāja was his son born from his seed. At this the black one said that he was born in his legitimate wife (*kṣetra*) and claims his share of the *piṇḍa*.[2] He accused his wife as a whore, who asked him to offer the *piṇḍa* to the black one first and then to the white one. Thereupon, Bharadvāja offered the *piṇḍa* to both of them at Kaśyapa's place and soared to heaven (*brahmaloka*) mounting on a plane carried by swans.

This strange story speaks of a Bhāradvāja 'one belonging to the family of Bharadvāja', who had Śāntā as his mother. Śāntā is said to be the wife of one who was of black complexion, but a white person impregnated in her this Bhāradvāja. Thus the black one is called *kṣetrin* 'possessor of the *kṣetra* in the form of his wife', while the white one was signified as the *bījin* 'possessor of seed', i.e. 'the begetter of the child with his own seed'.[3] Strangely enough, such a situation arose at the birth of Bharadvāja Bārhaspatya also. There Mamatā appeared to be the mother of Bharadvāja, Uśija or Ucathya, the *kṣetrin* and Bṛhaspati, the *bījin*. While we discussed about him, we held the view that it was possible polyandry. In the present case, it is incest or an illegal love affair.

NOTES AND REFERENCES TO CHAPTER II

Section (i)

1. Sarvā 2, 6, 1: बार्हस्पत्यो भारद्वाजः षष्ठं मण्डलमपश्यत् ।
2. Cf. 2, 6, 52.
3. Read: योऽङ्गारेभ्य ऋषिर्जज्ञे तस्य पुत्रो बृहस्पतिः ।
   बृहस्पतेर्भरद्वाजो विदथीति य उच्यते ॥
4. Published with BD edited by R. Mitra in the Bibliotheca Indica Series. On page 253 Śaunaka says:
   त्वं ह्यग्न इत्युपक्रम्य षष्ठाख्यं मण्डलं प्रति ।
   बार्हस्पत्यो भरद्वाज ऋषिरित्यवगम्यताम् ॥
5. RV 2, 6, 15 is ascribed to Vītahavya (optionally) with Bharadvāja in Sarvā 2, 6, 15.
6. Sarvā 2, 6, 31.
7. Ibid., 2, 6, 33.
8. Ibid., 2, 6, 35.
9. Ibid., 2, 6, 47.
10. Ibid., 2, 6, 49.
11. Ibid., 2, 6, 75.
12. Read 2, 6, 52. सुहोत्रादयोऽनुक्तगोत्रा भारद्वाजाःपौत्राबृं हस्पतेर्दौं ष्यन्तेर्वा भरतस्य ।
13. Ibid., 2, 6, 44.
14. Cf. note 5 above.
15. Sarvā 2, 9, 67.
16. Read 2, 10, 137: उत देवाः सप्त ऋषय एकर्चा वैश्वदेवम् । Vide Sāyaṇa on the point: उत देवा इति सप्तर्षं नवमं सूक्तमानुष्टुभं वैश्वदेवं भरद्वाजकश्यपगोतमात्रिविश्वामित्रजमदग्निवसिष्ठा इति क्रमेण प्रत्यृचमृषयः ।
17. NA. 1, 1; 3; 7; 8, 9; 2, 1; 6; 3, 1; 5; 4, 3; 7; 8; 9; 5, 1; 7; 6, 3; 7, 3; 2, 1, 4; 6; 8; 10; 13; 16.
18. NA with numerous references (we have dropped the nos. of ch.) ascribes the following verses to Bharadvāja. The Ṛgvedic references are shown within brackets: 1, 1, (6, 16, 10); 2 (6, 16, 1); 4 (6, 16, 34); 7 (6, 16, 16); 9 (6, 16, 13); 23 (6, 16, 28); 25 (6, 16, 43); 67 (6, 7, 1); 68 (6, 24, 6); 75 (6, 58, 1); 83 (6, 2, 6); 84 (6, 2, 1); 148 (6, 57, 4); 201 (6, 45, 28-ascribed to Śaṁyu); 202 (6, 57, 1); 234 (6, 46, 1-ascribed to Śaṁyu); 281 (6, 59, 6); 286 (6, 46, 3-ascribed to Śaṁyu); 333 (6, 47, 11-ascribed to Garga); 352 (6, 42, 1); 365 (6, 2, 4); 378 (6, 70, 1); 392 (6, 43, 1); 554 (6, 17, 15); 511 (9, 107, 4-seven seers including Bharadvāja); 609 (6, 8, 1); 660 (6, 16, 10); 661 (6, 16, 11); 662 (6, 16, 12); 705-707 (6, 16-18); 853-855 (6, 60, 4-6); 991-993 (6, 60, 7-9); 1140-1142 (6, 7, 1-3); 1149-1151 (6, 60, 10-12); 1323-1325 (9, 67, 1-3); 1383-1385 (6, 16, 43-45); 1396-1398 (6, 16, 34-36); 1434-1436 (6, 16, 1-3); 1567-1569 (6, 15, 7-9-ascribed also to Vītahavya Āṅgirasa; 1593 (6, 53, 10); 1705-7 (6, 16, 7-9); the numbers of verses are given following Satavalekar's edn. of SV.

19. SV 1, 1: अग्न आ याहि वीतय गृणानो हव्यदातये ।
नि होता सत्सि बर्हिषि ॥

20. NA sometimes drops the patronymic Bārhaspatya. Yet, we have taken Bharadvāja and Bharadvāja Bārhaspatya as one and the same seer.

21. 1, 10; 12; 28; 29; 30; 2, 3; 14; 25; 33; 3, 6; 21; 23; 4, 3.

22. The following verses are ascribed to Bharadvāja in the VS of White YV: Bharadvāja, composer of the RV VI.

VS 3, 3 (6, 16, 11); 13 (6, 60, 13); 7, 24 (6, 7, 1); 39 (6 19, 1); 8, 6 (6, 71, 6); 1, 32 (ascribed to Bhāradvāja in VS, 6, 16, 13); 13, 36, (6, 16, 43) ; 17, 10 (6, 15, 5); 17, 16 (6, 16, 28); 18, 74 (6, 5, 7); 19, 2 (not traced in RV); 26, 13 (6, 16, 16); 33, 8 (6, 7, 1); 33, 13 (6, 4, 7); 61 (6, 60, 5); 69 and 84 (6, 71, 3); 35, 45 (6, 70, 1).

23. ABS 1, 18; 10, 28; 11, 5; 7; 9.

24. Ibid., 11, 1.

25. Read: (भ) भारद्वाजकुत्सविश्वामित्राः प्रत्यृचम् ।

26. Ascribed to Brahmā AV 4, 21, 1-7 (RV 6, 28, 1-7); AV 9, 4, 23 (RV 6, 28, 8); to Atharvan AV 18, 4, 59 (RV 6, 2, 6); 3, 3, 1 (RV 6, 11, 4); to Praskaṇva AV 7, 42, 1-2 (RV 6, 73, 2-3); 44, 1 (RV 6, 69, 8); Kaurupathin AV 7, 58, 1-2 (RV 6, 68, 10-11); Uparivabhrava AV 7, 9, 3; (RV 6, 54, 9-10).

27. Bracketed verses are quoted from RV.

TS 1, 1, 14, 1 (1, 5, 5, 1) (RV 6, 60, 13); 2 (6, 15, 19); 3, 14, 2(6, 5, 2); 3 (6, 5, 7); 7 (6, 4, 4); 8 (6, 4, 2); 4, 13, 1 (6, 7, 1); 17, 1 (6, 19, 11); 21, 1 (6, 19, 1); 23 (6, 71, 6); 5, 11, 2 (6, 8, 6); 6, 12, 1 (6, 25, 8); 24, 1 (6, 71, 3); 8, 22, 1 (6, 61, 4; 74, 2-3); 2, 2, 12, 1 (6, 16, 21); 2, (6, 71, 6); 5, 7, 3 (6, 16, 10); 8, 1 (6, 16, 11); 12, 5 (6, 15, 10); 6, 11, 4 (6, 16, 39); 3, 2 11, 2, (6, 69, 1; 8); 3, 11, 1 (6, 6, 3); 5, 11, 2 (6, 15, 16); 3 (6, 16, 13-14); 4 (6, 16, 40-42); 4, 1, 3, 2 (6, 16, 13); 3 (6, 16, 14); 11, 1, (6, 60, 1); 2 (6, 54, 5); 3 (6, 66, 9); 22 (6, 58, 1); 2, 11, 1 (6, 60, 1); 9, 5 (6, 16, 43); 3, 13, 1 (6, 16, 34); 2 (6, 4, 1); 4 (6, 15, 14); 5 (6, 16, 28).

Section (ii)

1. MBh 1, 98, 6-16; Mt 48, 32-42; 49, 17-23; Va 99, 36-46; Bd 2, 3, 74, 36-46; BD 4, 11-14.

2. The legend of the birth of Dīrghatamas is summarised from Mt as follows:

There was a very learned seer named Uśija and he had a wife Mamatā by name. Bṛhaspati was his younger brother. Once Bṛhaspati approached Mamatā for sexual intercourse. At this Mamatā told him that she was already in an advanced state of pregnancy and the child in the womb was reciting Veda *mantras*. However, Bṛhaspati did not pay heed to her words and forcibly secured fulfilment of his desire. At the time of emitting his seed, the child in womb addressed Bṛhaspati and asked him not to deposit his seed as there would not be, in the womb, any room for two. At this, Bṛhaspati was angry with it and cursed the child in womb for his interference in such an affair, and said that the child would be born blind. As a result of the curse, the child was born blind and as he was born blind, he was named Dīrghatamas.

Except the name of Mamatā's husband who is given as Ucathya, other details in the MBh, Mt, Va, Bd and BD are common.

2a. Va gives a variant of it, viz. Aśija. We shall discuss problem relating to Uśija in subsequent paragraphs.

3. Mt. 49, 17-23; cf. Va 99, 141-151:

पत्न्यामापन्नसत्वायामुशिजः स स्थितो भुवि।
भ्रातुर्भार्यां स दृष्ट्वा तु बृहस्पतिरुवाच ह॥
उपतिष्ठ स्वलंकृत्य मैथुनाय च मां शुभे।
एवमुक्त्वाऽब्रवीत् एनं स्वयमेव बृहस्पतिम्॥
गर्भः परिणतश्चायं ब्रह्म व्याहरते गिरा।
अमोघरेतास्त्वञ्चापि धर्मश्चैवं विगर्हितम्॥
एवमुक्तोऽब्रवीदेनां स्वयमेव बृहस्पतिः।
नोपदेष्टव्यो विनयस्त्वया मे वरवर्णिनि॥
धर्षमाणः प्रहस्यैनां मैथुनायोपचक्रमे।
ततो बृहस्पतिं गर्भो धर्षमाणमुवाच ह॥
सन्निविष्टो ह्यहं पूर्वमिह नाम बृहस्पते।
अमोघरेताश्च भवान् नावकाश इह द्वयोः॥
एवमुक्तः स गर्भेण कुपितः प्रत्युवाच ह।
यस्मात्त्वमीदृशे काले सर्वभूतेप्सिते सति।
अभिषेधसि तस्मात्त्वं तमो दीर्घं प्रवेक्ष्यसि॥

4. Va 99, 148:

पादाभ्यां तेन तच्छन्नं मातुर्द्वारं बृहस्पतेः।
तद्रेतस्तु तयोर्मध्येऽनिवार्यः शिशुकोऽभवत्॥

Cf. Mt 49, 24:

ततः कामं सन्निवृत्य तस्यानन्दाद् बृहस्पतेः।
तद्रेतस्त्वपतद् भूमौ निवृत्तं शिशुकोऽभवत्॥

5. Va 99, 149-151:

सद्योजातं कुमारं तं दृष्ट्वाऽथ ममताऽब्रवीत्।
गमिष्यामि गृहं स्वं वै भर द्वाजं बृहस्पते॥
एवमुक्ता गतायां स पुत्रं त्यजति तत्क्षणात्।
भरस्व वाढमित्युक्त्वा भरद्वाजो ततोऽभवत्॥
मातापितृभ्यां सन् त्यक्तं दृष्ट्वाऽथ मरुतः शिशुम्।
गृहीत्वैनं भरद्वाजं जग्मुस्तत् कृपया ततः॥

6. Read: ततोऽस्य पुत्रजन्मनि वितथे पुत्रार्थिनो मरुत्स्तोमयाजिनो दीर्घतमसा पार्ष्ण्य-पास्तबृहस्पतिवीर्याद् उतथ्यपत्नीममतासमुत्पन्न भरद्वाजाख्या नाम पुत्रो मरुद्भिः दत्तः।

7. Read: तां त्यक्तुकामां ममतां भर्तृत्यागविशङ्किताम्।
नामनिर्वचनं तस्य श्लोकमेनं सुरा जगुः॥
मूढे भर द्वाजमिमं भर द्वाजं बृहस्पते।
यातो यदुक्तो पितरौ भरद्वाजस्ततस्त्वयम्॥

8. Read: द्वावुचथ्यबृहस्पती ऋषिपुत्रो बभूवतुः।
आसीदुचथ्यभार्या तु ममता नाम भार्गवी॥
स व्याजहार तं गर्भं तमस्ते दीर्घमस्त्विति।
स च दीर्घतमा नाम बभूवर्षिरुचथ्यजः॥

9. Read: योऽङ्गारेभ्य ऋषिर्जज्ञे तस्य पुत्रो बृहस्पतिः।
बृहस्पतेर्भरद्वाजो विदथीति य उच्यते॥
मरुतस्त्वासीद् गुरुर्यश्च स एवाङ्गिरसो नपात्।
स पुत्रस्य तु तस्यैतन् मण्डलं षष्ठमुच्यते॥

10. 2, 6, 1; 6, 52:
बार्हस्पत्यो भरद्वाजः षष्ठं मण्डलमपश्यत्।
सुहोत्रादयोऽनुक्तगोत्रा भारद्वाजाः पौत्रा बृहस्पतेर्दौःष्यन्तेर्वा भरतस्य।

10a. Read: यो अद्रिभित् प्रथमजा ऋतावा
बृहस्पतिराङ्गिरसो हविष्मान्।
द्विबर्हज्मा प्राधर्मसत् पिता न
आ रोदसी वृषभो रोरवीति॥

11. Read: द्वावुचथ्यबृहस्पती ऋषिपुत्रो बभूवतुः।
आसीदुचथ्यभार्या तु ममता नाम भार्गवी॥
x x x x x x
स व्याजहार तं गर्भं तमस्ते दीर्घमस्त्विति।
स च दीर्घतमा नाम बभूवर्षिरुचथ्यजः॥

12. Read: उत्तेशुष्मास उच्चथ्यः।

13. Read: वेदिषदे सप्तोना दीर्घतमा औचथ्य आग्नेयम्।
तु द्वित्रिष्टुबन्तं तु त्रिष्टुब् दशमी वा।

14. Read: उचथ्ये३ वपुषि यः स्वरलुत वायो घृतस्वाः॥

However, Sāyaṇa takes the word Ucathya to mean *vaktavye, stutye.*

15. Sāyaṇa takes it in the sense of Dīrghatamas.
उचथ्यस्य पुत्रो दीर्घतमः।

16. MBh 1, 98, 6:
अथोतथ्य इतिख्यातं आसीद् धीमानृषिः पुरा।
ममता नाम तस्यासीद् भार्या परमसंमता॥

17. Vis 4, 19, 5: उतथ्यपत्नी ममता समुत्पन्नो etc. follows the MBh. 1, 98, 6.

18. Mt 48, 32: अथोशिजः इति ख्यात आसीद्विद्वानृषिः पुरा।

Cf. 49, 17: पत्न्यामापन्नसत्वायामुशिजः स स्थितो भुवि।

Bd. 2, 4, 74, 36:
उशिजो नाम विख्यात आसीद्धीमान्नृषिः पुरा।
भार्या वै ममता बभूवास्य महात्मनः॥

19. Va 99, 36-37:
अशिजो नाम विख्यात आसीद्धीमानृषिः पुरा।
भार्या वै ममता नाम बभूवास्य महात्मनः॥
अशिजस्य कनीयांस्तु पुरोधा यो दिवौकसाम्।
बृहस्पतिर्बृहत्तेजा ममतां सोऽभ्यपदत॥

20. Pargiter, AIHT, p. 158, 'Aśija is a mistake for Uśija.' Mankad, D Rg. p. 2, also holds the same view.
21. VR 2, 359.
22. Ibid., 1, 59.
23. Read: सोमानं स्वरणं कृणुहि ब्रह्मणस्पते।
कक्षीवन्तं यं औशिजः ॥
24. Read: अस्य स्तोमेभिरौशिज ऋजिश्वा
व्रज दरयद्वृषभेण विप्रोः।
सुत्वा यद्यजतो दीदयद्गीः पुर
इयानो अभि वर्पसा भूत् ॥
25. Read: नासत्याभ्यां पञ्चाधिका कक्षीवान्
दैर्घतमस उशिक्पुत्र अश्विनं वै।

Cf. BD 4, 24-25; ŚB 2, 3, 4, 35.

26. Sharma, U.C. "The Legend of Kakṣīvān" SP, AIOC, Poona, 1978, p. 36.
27. MBh 13, 151, 31—reads Auśijaḥ:
यवक्रीतोऽथ रैभ्यश्च कक्षीवानौशिजस्तथा।
भृग्वङ्गिरास्तथा कण्वो मेधातिथिरथ प्रभुः।
बर्हीं च गुणसम्पन्नः प्राची दिशमुपाश्रिताः ॥

Here also Auśija is identified with Kakṣīvat.

28. See Sections on Vidathin Bharadvāja and Ṛjiśvan Bhāradvāja for details.
29. Pargiter, AIHT, pp. 160-61.
30. Read: सुरूपा जनयामास ऋषीन् सर्वेश्वरानिमान्।
बृहस्पतिं गौतमं च संवर्तं तु महाऋषिम्।
अयास्यं वामदेवं च उचथ्यमुशिजं तथा ॥

Cf: Mt. 195, 3-4. The verse appears to be concocted, because it enumerates names of some junior Aṅgirases with the seniors as the sons of Surūpā.

31. Read: यो अद्रिभित् प्रथमजा ऋतावा
बृहस्पतिराङ्गिरसो हविष्मान्।
द्विबर्हज्मा प्राधर्मसन् पिता व
आ रोदसी वृषभो रोरवीति ॥
32. Pargiter, AIHT, p. 5; and see our sections on Suhotra Bhāradvāja and Ajamīḍha for similar inference.
33. For similar inference see our section on Vidathin Bharadvāja (Ch. 2, Section (iii)), where Vitatha is considered as the short form of Vaitatha ⟩ Vaidatha ⟩ Vaidathina.
34. Read: अङ्गिराः सुवचोचथ्य उशिजश्च महानृषिः
परस्परमवैवाह्या ऋषयः परिकीर्तिताः ॥
35. Read: कक्षीवतां अङ्गिरसोचथ्यगौतमौशिजकाक्षीवतेति।
ĀpŚS Pravarakāṇḍa, sūtra 9.
36. Op. cit. pp. 161, 163, 191 (Chronological table).
37. SR, pp. 100-101.
38. DRg. pp. 2-3.

39. IVA p. 181.
40. For details see below about the naming of Bharadvāja.

40a. However Bharadvāja was known as Bārhaspatya, as Budha as Soumya 'son of Soma'.

41. Read: अस्मिन्नेव गते काले तथा वा मन्यते प्रभो ।

42. Mt 49, 19: अमोघरेतास्त्वं चापि धर्मंचैव विर्गर्हितम् ॥

Cf. Raghuvaṁśam: 1, 7:

त्यागाय संभृतार्थानां सत्याय मितभाषिणाम् ।
यशसे विजिगीषूणां प्रजायै गृहमेधिनाम् ॥

Commenting on प्रजायै गृहमेधिनाम् Mallinātha says: प्रजायै संतानाय गृहमेधिनां दारपरिग्रहाणाम् । न तु कामोपभोगाय ।

Raghuvaṁśam, Cantos I-V, Ed. M.R. Kale, Delhi, 1972.

43. Read: उतासि मैत्रावरुणो वसिष्ठोर्वश्या ब्रह्मन् मनसोऽधि जातः ।
द्रप्सं स्कन्नं ब्रह्मणा दैव्येन विश्वेदेवाः पुष्करे त्वाददन्त ॥
सत्रे ह जातविषिता नमोभिः कुम्भे रेतः सिषिचतुः समानम् ।
ततो ह मान उदियाय मध्यात् ततो जातमृषिराहुर्वसिष्ठम् ॥

Cf. 1, 19, 10; Bd 4, 15, 32; 39, 58.

44. Read: महर्षिस्तु भरद्वाजो हविर्धाने चरन् पुरा ।
ददर्शाप्सरसं साक्षाद् घृताचीमाप्लुतामृषिः ॥
तस्याः वायुः समुद्धतो वसनं व्यपकर्षत ।
ततोऽस्य रेतश्चस्कन्द तदृषिर्द्रोण आदधे ।
तस्मिन् समभवद्द्रोण कलशे तस्य धीमतः ॥

45. Read: भारद्वाजस्य विप्रर्षेः स्कन्नं रेतो महात्मनः ।
दृष्ट्वाप्सरसमायान्तीं घृताचीं पृथुलोचनाम् ॥
स तु जग्राह तद्रेतः करेण जपतां वरः ।
तदावपत् पर्णापूटे तत्र सा समभवच्छुभा ॥

Cf. MBh 1, 121, 3-5.

46. Read in particular verses 12-14.

स विहायाश्रमं तं च तां चैवाप्सरसं मुनिः ।
जगाम रेतस्तत तस्य शरस्तम्बे पपात ह ॥
शरस्तम्बं च पतितं द्विधा तदभवन्नृप ।
तस्याथ मिथुनं जज्ञे गौतमस्य शरद्वतः ॥
मृगयां चरतो राज्ञः शंतनोस्तु यदृच्छया ।
कश्चित् सेनाचराऽरण्य मिथुनं तदपश्यत ॥

Also Cf: MBh 1, 57, 90.

47. Vol. VI p. 4643. The quotation could not be traced to any of the Vedic texts.
48. RVVSM Vol. 1, p. 723 and Vol. 3, p. 44.
49. RVVIS, Vol. 2, p. 876.
50. Mahīdhara comments upon *bharadvāja*, referred to in the passage: *bharadvāja ṛṣiḥ/ prajāpatigṛhītayā tváyā máno gṛhṇāmi prajābhyaḥ//*

51. *Der Wörterbuch zum der Ṛgveda*, p. 928.
52. PW Fünfter Teil p. 214.
53. *Sanskrit-English Dictionary*, Delhi, 1963, p. 747.
54. Va 99, 149-150; Mt 49, 25.
55. Op. cit, p. Dritter Teil, p. 822.
56. Op. cit. p. 503.

Section (iii)

1. Mt 49, 26-35; Va 99, 151-158; Vis 4, 19, 4-9; Bh 9, 20, 34-35; 39; Br 13, 58-63; Hv 23, 50, 53; Ag 278, 1, ff;

2. Mt 49, 26: मातापितृभ्यां त्यक्तं तु दृष्ट्वा तं मारुतः शिशुम् ।
जगृहुस्तं भरद्वाजं मरुतः कृपया स्थिताः ॥

Cf: Va 99, 151:

मातापितृभ्यां सन्त्यक्तं दृष्ट्वाऽथ मरुतः शिशुम् ।
गृहीत्वैनं भरद्वाजं जग्मुस्ते कृपया ततः ॥

3. Va 99, 137-139; 141; 152-156:

भरतस्त्रिसृषु स्त्रीषु नव पुत्रानजीजनत् ।
नाभ्यनन्दच्च तान् राजा नानुरूपान् ममेत्युत ॥
ततस्त्वा मातरः क्रुध्वा पुत्रान्निन्युर्यमक्षयम् ।
ततस्तस्य नरेन्द्रस्य वितथं पुत्रजन्म तत् ॥

ततो मरुद्भिरानीय पुत्रस्तु स बृहस्पतेः । संक्रामितो भरद्वाजो मरुद्भिः क्रतुभिर्विभुः ॥ तत्रैवोदाहरन्तीदं भरद्वाजस्य धीमतः । जन्म संक्रमणं चैव मरुद्भिर्भरताय वै ॥ १४१ ॥ ... तस्मिन् काले तु भरतो मरुद्भिः काम्यनैमित्तिकैर्यज्ञैर्यजते पुत्रलिप्सया ॥ १५२; यदा स यतमानो वै पुत्रान्नऽसादयत् प्रभुः । यज्ञं ततो मरुत्सोमं पुत्रार्थे पुनराहरेत् ॥ १५३ तेन ते मरुतस्तस्य मरुत् सोमेन तोषिताः । भरद्वाजं ततः पुत्रं बार्हस्पत्यं मनीषिणम् ॥ भरतस्तु सहृदायां वै कृतार्थोऽहं तया विभो ॥ पूर्वं तु वितथं तस्य कृतः वै पुत्रजन्म हि । ततः स वितथो नाम भरद्वाजस्तथाऽभवत् ॥

Cf. Mt 49, 14-15; 26-32.

4. Read: भरतस्य विनष्टषु तनयेषु पुरा किल ।
पुत्राणां मातृकात् कोपात् सुमहान् संक्षयः कृतः ॥

Cf. Va 99, 138, quoted above.

5. Read: ततो जाते हि वितथे भरतश्च दिवं ययौ ।
भरद्वाजो दिवं यातो ह्यभिषिच्य सुतं ऋषिः ॥
दायादो वितथस्यासीद् भुवमन्यु महायशाः ।
महाभूतोपमाः पुत्राश्चत्वारो भुवमन्यवः ॥
बृहत्क्षत्रो महावीर्यः नरो गर्गश्च वीर्यवान् ।

Cf. Va 99, 158-159.

6. Read: बृहत्क्षत्रस्य दायादः सुहोत्रो नाम धार्मिकः ।
सुहोत्रस्याऽपि दायादो हस्ती नाम बभूव ह ॥

7. Read: बृहत्क्षत्रस्य दायादो हस्तिर्नाम बभूव ह ।
तेनेदं निर्मितं पूर्वं पुरन्तु गजसाह्वयम् ॥

8. Read: बृहत्क्षत्रस्य पुत्रोऽभूद्धस्ती यद्धस्तिनापुरम् ।

9. Br 13, 62-63:

स चापि वितथः पुत्राञ्जनयामास पञ्च वै ।

सुहोत्रं च सुहोतारं गयं गर्गं तथैव च कपिलं च महात्मानम् ॥

Cf. Hv 1, 23, 53-54; Ag 278, 9-10.

10. Read: पूर्वं तु वितथे तस्य कृते वै पुत्रजन्मनि ।

ततोऽथ वितथो नाम भरद्वाजात् सुतोऽभवत् ॥

ततोऽथ वितथे जाते भरतस्य दिवं ययौ ।

वितथं चाभिषिच्याऽथ भरद्वाजो वनं ययौ ॥

11. MBh 89, 18-21:

ततो महद्भिः क्रतुभिरीजानो भरतस्तदा ।

लेभे पुत्रं भरद्वाजाद् भुमन्युं नाम भारत ॥

ततः पुत्रिणमात्मानं ज्ञात्वा पौरवनन्दन ।

भुमन्युं भरतश्रेष्ठ यौवराज्येऽभ्यषेचयत् ॥

12. Read: भरतः खलु काशेयीमुपयेमे सार्वसेनीं सुनन्दां नाम ।

तस्यामस्य जज्ञे भुमन्युः ॥ ३४

भुमन्युः खलु दाशार्हीमुपयेमे जयां नाम ।

तस्यामस्य जज्ञे सुहोत्रः ॥ ३५

13. For further information on this point, see our section (ii) of Ch. 2 on Bharadvāja Bārhaspatya.

14. Read: एतेन ह वा ऐन्द्रेण महाभिषेकेण

दीर्घतमा मामतेयो भरतं दौषन्तिमभिषिषेच ।

15. Read: दीर्घतमा मामतेयो जजुर्वान्दशमे युगे ।

अपामर्थं यतीनां ब्रह्मा भवति सारथिः ॥

16. Read: भरद्वाजो ह वै ऋषीणामनूचानतमो दीर्घजीवितमस्तपस्वितम आस ।

17. That the persons belonging to the *Gotra* of Agniveśya have three-*ṛṣi pravara* consisting of Āṅgirasa, Bārhaspatya and Bhāradvāja is referred to in Mt 195, 12, and in Sūtras. Although this does not mean that the Agniveśyas were the Bharadvājas, yet it is a fact that the *gotra* is included in Bharadvāja group (*gaṇa*), that speaks of their mutual and close relationship.

18. Pradhan in his CAI pp. 13ff. has ably pointed out how the devotees ascribe their own achievement to the gods they worship.

18a. MBh 12, 29, 16-20.

19. Pargiter, AIHT, p. 163 and Rahurkar SR, p. 98. We have, however, modified the suggestion of the two scholars.

20. For further information, see Pargiter, AIHT, p. 158-159 (fn. at p. 159).

21. Read: त्वं पिप्रुं मृगयं शूशुवांसमृजिश्वने वैदथिनाय रन्धीः ।

सोमासस्त्वा गौरिवीतेरवर्धन्नरन्धयो वैदथिनाय पिप्रुम् ।

आ त्वामृजिश्वा सख्याय चक्रे पचन् पक्तीरपिबः सोममस्य ॥

For further information see our article: "Ṛjiśvan", CASS Studies, No. 5, 1980, pp. 111-118.

22. We shall discuss it later in a separate section on Suhotra Bhāradvāja (vide Ch. 3, sec. (i)).

23. Read: योऽङ्गारेभ्य ऋषिर्जज्ञे तस्य पुत्रो बृहस्पतिः।
बृहस्पतेर्भरद्वाजो विदथीति य उच्यते ॥

24. He is mentioned in the RV nine times: RV 1, 51, 5; 53, 8; 101, 1; 4, 16, 13; 5, 29, 11; 6, 20, 7; 8, 49, 10; 10, 99, 11 and 138, 3.

25. Read: भरतस्यान्ववाये हि देवकल्पा महौजसः।
बभूवुर्ब्रह्मकल्पाश्च बहवो राजसत्तमाः ॥

Cf.: Bh 9, 20, 1:

पुरुवंशं प्रवक्ष्यामि यत्र जातोऽसि भारत।
यत्र राजर्षयो वंश्या ब्रह्मवंश्याश्च जज्ञिरे ॥

Section (iv)

1. MBh 12, 265, 17:

मूलगोत्राणि चत्वारि समुत्पन्नानि पार्थिव।
अङ्गिराः कश्यपश्चैव वसिष्ठो भृगुरेव च ॥

2. Pargiter has rightly pointed out that there were two Divodāsas born in the Kāśī dynasty, viz. the first one was the son of Bhīmaratha and the second one was the son of Sudeva, and between them reigned at least three kings, Aṣṭaratha, Haryaśva and Sudeva. Divodāsa II was the father of Pratardana (AIHT, p. 154) and contemporary of Bharadvāja Bārhaspatya (AIHT. p. 164).

3. AIHT. p. 154, fn. 5.

4. CAI, pp. 16-17.

5. DRg, p. 5.

6. Ibid., p. 7.

7. SR. pp. 96-97.

8. See our Section (vii) of Ch. 3, on Ajamīḍha for Divodāsa and Ahalyā.

Section (v)

1. MBh 3, 135-139.

2. MBh 3, 135, 12:

भरद्वाजश्च रैभ्यश्च सखायौ संबभूवतुः।
तावूषतुरिहात्यन्तं प्रीयमाणौ वनान्तरे ॥

3. MBh 3, 135, 13:

रैभ्यस्य तु सुतावास्तामर्वावसुपरावसू।
आसीद् यवक्रीः पुत्रस्तु भरद्वाजस्य भारत ॥

(Yavakrī and Yavakrīta are two variants of the same word.)

4. MBh 3, 135, 14-16.

5. MBh 3, 135, 17:

सुसमिद्ध महत्यग्नौ शरीरमुपतापयन्।
जरयामास संतापमिन्द्रस्य सुमहातपाः ॥

6. MBh 3, 135, 18:

तत इन्द्रो यवक्रीतमुपगम्य युधिष्ठिर।
अब्रवीत् कस्य हेतोस्त्वमास्थितस्तप उत्तमम् ॥

7. MBh 3, 135, 91-21:

द्विजानामधीता वै वेदाः सुरगणार्चित।
प्रतिभान्त्विति तप्येऽहमिदं परमकं तपः॥
स्वाध्यायार्थे समारम्भो ममायं पाकशासन।
तपसा ज्ञातुमिच्छामि सर्वज्ञानानि कौशिक॥
कालेन महता वेदाः शक्या गुरुमुखाद्विभो।
प्राप्तुं तस्मादयं यत्नः परमो मे समास्थितः॥

8. MBh, 3, 135, 22:

अमार्ग एष विप्रर्षे येन त्वं यातुमिच्छसि।
किं विघातेन ते विप्र गच्छाधीहि गुरोर्मुखात् ॥

9. MBh 3, 135, 23-26. Indra's words are:

अशक्योऽर्थः समारब्धो नैतद्बुद्धिकृतं तव।
प्रतिभास्यन्ति वै वेदास्तव चैव पितुश्च ते॥

10. MBh, 3, 135, 27-28:

न चैतदेवं क्रियते देवराज ममेप्सितम्।
महता नियमेनाहं तप्स्ये घोरतरं तपः॥
समिद्धेऽग्नावुपकृत्याङ्गमङ्गं
होष्यामि वा मघवंस्तन्निबोध।
यद्येतदेवं न करोषि कामं
ममेप्सितं देवराजेह सर्वम् ॥

11. MBh, 3, 135, 29-33:

निश्चयं तमभिज्ञाय मुनिस्तस्य महात्मनः।
प्रतिवारणहेत्वर्थं बुद्ध्या संचिन्त्य बुद्धिमान् ॥
तत इन्द्रोऽकरोद्रूपं ब्राह्मणस्य तपस्विनः।
अनेकशतवर्षस्य दुर्बलस्य सयक्ष्मणः॥
यवक्रीतस्य यत्तीर्थमुचितं शौचकर्मणि।
भागीरथ्यां तत्र सेतुं वालुकाभिश्चकार सः॥

x x x x x

वालुकामुष्टिमनिशं भागीरथ्यां व्यसर्जयत्।
सेतुमभ्यारभच्छक्रो यवक्रीतं निदर्शयन् ॥

12. MBh 3, 135, 34-35:

तं ददर्श यवक्रीस्तु यत्नवन्तं निबन्धने।
प्रहसंश्चाब्रवीद्वाक्यमिदं स मुनिपुंगवः॥
किमिदं वर्तते ब्रह्मन् किं च ते ह चिकीर्षितम्।
अतीव हि महायत्नः क्रियतेऽयं निरर्थकः॥

13. MBh 3, 135, 36:

बन्धिष्ये सेतुना गङ्गां सुखः पन्था भविष्यति।
क्लिश्यते हि जनस्तात तरमाणः पुनः पुनः॥

14. MBh 3, 135, 37:

नायं शक्यस्त्वया बद्धुं महानोघः कथंचन।
अशक्याद्विनिवर्तस्व शक्यमर्थं समारभ॥

15. MBh 3, 135, 38:

यथैव भवता चेदं तपो वेदार्थमुद्यतम्।
अशक्यं तद्वदस्माभिरयं भारः समुद्यतः॥

16. MBh 3, 135, 39-40:

यथा तव निरर्थोऽयमारम्भस्त्रिदशेश्वर।
तथा यदि ममापीदं मन्यसे पाकशासने॥
क्रियतां यद्भवेच्छक्यं मया सुरगणेश्वर।
वरांश्च मे प्रयच्छान्यान्यैरन्यान् भवितास्म्यति॥

17. MBh 3, 135, 41-42:

तस्मै प्रादाद्वरान् इन्द्र उक्तवान् यान् महातपाः।
प्रतिभास्यन्ति ते वेदाः पित्रा सह यथेप्सिताः॥
यच्चान्यत् काङ्क्षसे कामं यवक्रीर्गम्यतामिति।
स लब्धकामः पितरमुपेत्याथ ततोऽब्रवीत्॥

18. MBh 3, 136, 1:

प्रतिभास्यन्ति वै वेदा मम तातस्य चोभयोः।
अति चान्यान् भविष्यावो वरान् लब्धास्तथा मया॥

19. MBh 3, 136, 2-16.

20. MBh 3, 136, 17:

एवं करिष्ये मा तापं तात कार्षीः कथंचन।
यथा हि मे भवान् मान्यस्तथा रैभ्यः पिता मम॥

21. MBh 3, 137, 1-4:

चङ्क्रम्यमाणः स तदा यवक्रीरकुतोभयः।
जगाम माधवे मासि रैभ्याश्रमपदं प्रति॥
स ददर्शाश्रमे पुण्ये पुष्पितद्रुमभूषिते।
विचरन्तीं स्नुषां तस्य किंनरीमिव भारत॥
यवक्रीस्तामुवाचेदमुपतिष्ठस्व मामिति।
निर्लज्जो लज्जया युक्तां कामेन हृतचेतनः॥
सा तस्य शीलमाज्ञाय तस्माच्छापाच्च बिभ्यती।
तेजस्वितां च रैभ्यस्य तथेत्युक्त्वा जगाम सा॥

22. MBh 3, 137, 5-13:

23. MBh 3, 137, 14-16:

तत उद्यतशूलः स राक्षसः समुपाद्रवत्॥
तमापतन्तं संप्रेक्ष्य शूलहस्तं जिघांसया।
यवक्रीः सहसोत्थाय प्राद्रवद्येन वै सरः॥
जलहीनं सरो दृष्ट्वा यवक्रीस्त्वरितः पुनः।
जगाम सरितः सर्वास्ताश्चाप्यासन्विशोषिताः॥

24. MBh 3, 137, 17-20:

स काल्यमानो घोरेण शूलहस्तेन रक्षसा।
अग्निहोत्रं पितुर्भीतः सहसा समुपाद्रवत् ॥
स वै प्रविशमानास्तु शूद्रेणान्धेन रक्षिणा।
निगृहीतो बलाद्द्वारि सोऽवातिष्ठत पार्थिव ॥
निगृहीतं तु शूद्रेण यवक्रीतं स राक्षसः।
ताडयामास शूलेन स भिन्नहृदयोऽपतत् ॥
यवक्रीतं स हत्वा तु राक्षसो रैभ्यमागमत्।

25. MBh 3, 138, 1-5:

भरद्वाजस्तु कौन्तेय कृत्वा स्वाध्यायमाह्निकम्।
समित्कलापमादाय प्रविवेश स्वमाश्रमम् ॥
तं स्म दृष्ट्वा पुरा सर्वे प्रत्युत्तिष्ठन्ति पावकाः।
न त्वेनमुपतिष्ठन्ति हतपुत्रं तदाग्नयः ॥
वैकृतं त्वग्निहोत्रे स लक्षयित्वा महातपाः।
तमन्धं शूद्रमासीनं गृहपालमथाब्रवीत् ॥
किं नु मे नाग्नयः शूद्र प्रतिनन्दन्ति दर्शनम्।
त्वं चापि न यथापूर्वं कच्चित्क्षेममिहाश्रमे ॥
कच्चिन्न रैभ्यं पुत्रो मे गतवानल्पचेतनः।
एतदाचक्ष्व मे शीघ्रं न हि मे शुध्यते मनः ॥

26. MBh 3, 138, 6-8.
27. MBh 3, 138, 9-14.
28. MBh 3, 138, 15:

यथाहं पुत्रशोकेन देहं त्यक्ष्यामि किल्विषी।
तथा ज्येष्ठः सुतो रैभ्यं हिंस्याच्छीघ्रमनागसम् ॥

29. MBh 3, 138, 16-19.
30. MBh 3, 139, 1-3:

एतस्मिन्नेव काले तु बृहद्युम्नो महीपतिः।
सत्रमास्ते महाभागो रैभ्ययाज्यः प्रतापवान् ॥
तेन रैभ्यस्य वै पुत्रावर्वावसुपरावसू।
वृतौ सहायौ सत्रार्थे बृहद्युम्नेन धीमता ॥
तत्र तौ समनुज्ञातौ पित्रा कौन्तेय जग्मतुः।
आश्रमे त्वभवद्रैभ्यो भार्या चैव परावसोः ॥

31. MBh 3, 139, 4-9.
32. MBh 3, 139, 10-15.
33. MBh 3, 139, 16-19ab.
34. MBh 3, 139, 19cd-20:

अथाब्रवीद्यवक्रीतो देवानग्निपुरोगमान् ॥
समधीतं मया ब्रह्म व्रतानि चरितानि च।
कथं नु रैभ्यः शक्तो मामधीयानं तपस्विनम्।
तथायुक्तेन विधिना निहन्तुममरोत्तमाः ॥

35. MBh 3, 139, 21-22:

मैवं कृथा यवक्रीत यथा वदसि वै मुने।
ऋते गुरुमधीता हि सुखं वेदास्त्वया पुरा॥
अनेन तु गुरून् दुःखात्तोषयित्वा स्वकर्मणा।
कालेन महता क्लेशाद् ब्रह्माधिगतमुत्तमम्॥

36. MBh 3, 139, 23-24.

Section (vi)

1. MBh 1, 57, 89; 61, 63; 121, 3-5; 154, 1-5.
2. MBh 1, 121, 8.
3. MBh 1, 121, 3-5:

महर्षिस्तु भरद्वाजो हविर्धाने चरन् पुरा।
ददर्शाप्सरसं साक्षाद् घृताचीमाप्लुतामृषिः॥
तस्या वायुः समुद्धूतो वसनं व्यपकर्षत।
ततोऽस्य रेतश्चस्कन्द तदृषिर्द्रोण आदधे॥
तस्मिन्समभवद्द्रोणः कलशे तस्य धीमतः।
अध्यगीष्ट स वेदांश्च वेदाङ्गानि च सर्वशः॥

4. MBh 1, 154, 1-5:

गङ्गाद्वारं प्रति महान् बभूवर्षिर्महातपाः।
भरद्वाजो महाप्राज्ञः सततं संशितव्रतः॥
सोऽभिषेक्तुं गतो गङ्गां पूर्वमेवागतां सतीम्।
ददर्शाप्सरसं तत्र घृताचीमाप्लुतामृषिः॥
तस्या वायुर्नदीतीरे वसनं व्यहरत्तदा।
अपकृष्टाम्बरां दृष्ट्वा तामृषिश्चकमे ततः॥
तस्यां संसक्तमनसः कौमारब्रह्मचारिणः।
हृष्टस्य रेतश्चस्कन्द तदृषिर्द्रोण आदधे॥
ततः समभवद्द्रोणः कुमारस्तस्य धीमतः।
अध्यगीष्ट स वेदांश्च वेदाङ्गानि च सर्वशः॥

5. MBh 1, 154, 6:

भरद्वाजस्य तु सखा पृषतो नाम पार्थिवः।
तस्यापि द्रुपदो नाम तदा समभवत् सुतः॥

Cf. MBh. 1, 121, 8 also.

6. MBh 1, 154, 7:

स नित्यमाश्रमं गत्वा द्रोणेन स पार्षतः।
चिक्रीडाध्ययनं चैव चकार क्षत्रियर्षभः॥

Cf. 1. 121. 9.

7. Read: पुरास्त्रम् इदमाग्नेयं प्रादात् किल बृहस्पतिः।
भरद्वाजस्य गन्धर्व गुरुपुत्रः शतक्रतोः॥
भरद्वाजादग्निवेश्यो अग्निवेश्याद्गुरुर्मम।
स त्विदं मह्यमददाद्द्रोणो ब्राह्मणसत्तमः॥

Cf. MBh 1, 121, 6-7:

अग्निवेश्यं महाभागं भरद्वाजः प्रतापवान् ।
प्रत्यपादयद् आग्नेयमस्त्रं धर्मभृतां वरः ॥
अग्निष्टुज्जातः स मुनिस्ततो भरतसत्तमः ।
भारद्वाजं तदाग्नेयं महास्त्रं प्रत्यपादयत् ॥

8. Read: ततो जघान समरे वृत्रं देवपतिः स्वयम् ।
तं च मन्त्रमयं बन्धं वर्म चाङ्गिरसे ददौ ॥
अङ्गिराः प्राह पुत्रस्य मन्त्रज्ञस्य बृहस्पतेः ।
बृहस्पतिरथोवाच अग्निवेश्याय धीमते ॥
अग्निवेश्यो मम प्रादात्तेन बन्धामि वर्म ते ।
तवाद्य देहरक्षार्थं मन्त्रेण नृपसत्तम ॥

9. See verse MBh 1, 121, 7 quoted above.

10. Mt 195, 12; 19-20:

. . .एषां त्यार्षेयः प्रवरो नृप ।
अङ्गिराः प्रथमस्तेषां द्वितीयश्च बृहस्पतिः ॥
तृतीयश्च भरद्वाजः प्रवराः परिकीर्त्तिताः ।
परस्परमवैवाह्या इत्येते परिकीर्त्तिताः ॥

11. MBh 1, 121, 11:

ततः पितृनियुक्तात्मा पुत्रलोभान्महायशाः ।
शारद्वतीं ततो द्रोणः कृपीं भार्यामविन्दत ॥

12. RV 6, 75, which is called Saṁgrāmāśīrṣa, is seen by Pāyu Bhāradvāja, indicates that at the Ṛgvedic time even Bharadvājas were participating in war.

13. HGAI, pp. 31, 81.

Section (vii)

1. MBh 9, 47, 57-58:

भरद्वाजस्य विप्रर्षेः स्कन्नं रेतो महात्मनः ।
दृष्ट्वाप्सरसमायान्तीं घृताचीं पृथुलोचनां ॥
स तु जग्राह तद्रेतः करेण जपतां वरः ।
तदावपत् पर्णपूटे तत्र सा संभवच्छुभा ॥

2. MBh 9, 47, 59:

तस्यास्तु जातकर्मादि कृत्वा सर्वं तपोधनः ।
नाम चास्याः स कृतवान् भारद्वाजो महामुनिः ॥

3. MBh 9, 47, 3:

तपश्चचार सात्युग्रं नियमैर्बहुभिर्नृप ।
भर्ता मे देवराजः स्यादिति निश्चित्य भामिनी ॥

4. MBh 9, 47, 6-18.
5. MBh 9, 47, 19-23.
6. MBh 9, 47, 24-27.
7. MBh 9, 47, 1; 27.

8. MBh 1, 57, 89; 61, 63 etc.
9. See our section on Droṇa (Ch. 2, Section *vi*)
10. Law, B.C., HGAI, p. 69.

Section (viii)

1. Va 63, 23-25; Mt 4, 46-47; Bd 2, 13, 39, 69; Vis 1, 14, 4-7; Bh 4, 4, 4.
2. Va 30, 36.
3. Law, B.C. HGAI p. 80.

Section (ix)

1. Law, B.C., HGAI, p. 152.
2. Ibid., p. 328.
3. Ibid., p. 152.

Section (x)

1. Read: एवमश्वे समुत्सृष्टे वितते यज्ञकर्मणि।
गते च मासत्रितये हूयमाने च पावके ॥
पूज्यमानेषु दैत्येषु मिथुनस्थे दिवाकरे।
सुषुवे देवजननी माधवं वामनाकृतिम् ॥
2. Read: ततश्चकार देवस्य जातकर्मादिकाः क्रियाः।
भरद्वाजो महातेजा बार्हस्पत्यस्तपोधनः ॥
व्रतबन्धं तथेशस्य कृतवान् सर्वशास्त्रवित्।
ततो ददुः प्रीतियुक्ताः सर्व एव वरान् क्रमात् ॥
3. Read: ब्रह्मन् व्रजामि देव्याज्ञां कुरुक्षेत्रं महोदयम्।
तत्र दैत्यपतेः पुण्यो हयमेधः प्रवर्तते ॥
3a. Read: स्वेच्छया तिष्ठ वा गच्छ नाहमाज्ञापयामि ते।
गमिष्यामो वयं विष्णो बलेरध्वरं मा खिद ॥
4. Read: यद्भवन्तमहं परिपृच्छामि तद् वद।
केषु केषु विभो नित्यं स्थानेषु पुरुषोत्तम।
सान्निध्यं भवतो ब्रूहि ज्ञातुमिच्छामि तत्त्वतः ॥
5. Read: ततोऽर्घ्यं देवदेवेशमर्च्यमर्घादिनासुरः।
भरद्वाजर्षिणा सार्धं यज्ञवाटं प्रवेशयत् ॥
6. Read: प्रविष्टमात्रं देवेशं प्रतिपूज्य विधानतः।
प्रोवाच भगवन् ब्रूहि किं दद्मि तव मानद ॥
7. Read: ततोऽब्रवीत् सुरश्रेष्ठो दैत्यराजानमव्ययः।
विहस्य सुचिरं कालं भरद्वाजमवेक्ष्य च ॥

गुरोर्मदीयस्य गुरुस्तस्यास्त्यग्निपरिग्रहः ।
न स धारयते भूम्यां पारक्यां जातवेदसम् ॥
तदर्थमभियाचेऽहम् मम दानवपार्थिव ।
मच्छरीरप्रमाणेन देहि राजन् पदत्रयम् ॥

8. Vām 62, 49:

भरद्वाजादाङ्गिरसात् सामवेदं महाध्वनिम् ।
महदाख्यानसंयुक्तं गन्धर्वसहितं मुने ॥

9. Vām 62, 43:

भरद्वाजो महातेजा बार्हस्पत्यस्तपोधनः ॥

Section (xi)

1. Read: कश्यपस्य पदे दिव्ये भरद्वाजो मुनिः पुरा ।
श्राद्धं कृत्वोद्यतो दातुं पित्रादिभ्यश्च पिण्डम् ॥
शुक्लकृष्णौ ततो हस्तौ पदमुद्भिद्य निर्गतौ ।
दृष्ट्वा हस्तद्वयं तत्र मुनिः संशयमागतः ॥
ततः स्वमातरं शान्तां पप्रच्छ महामुनिः ।
कश्यपस्य पदे दिव्ये शुक्ले कृष्णेऽथवा करे ॥
पिण्डो देयो मया मातर्जानासि पितरं वद ॥
शान्तोवाच । भारद्वाज महाप्राज्ञ देहि कृष्णाय पिण्डम् ।
भरद्वाजस्ततः पिण्डं दातुं कृष्णाय चोद्यतः ॥
श्वेतोऽदृश्यो ब्रवीत्तत्र पुत्रस्त्वं हि ममौरसः ।
कृष्णोऽब्रवीन् मम क्षेत्रं ततो मे देहि पिण्डम् ॥
स्वैरिण्यथब्रवीद् दातुं क्षेत्रिणे बीजिने ततः ।
भारद्वाजस्ततः पिण्डं कश्यपस्य पदे ददौ ।
हंसयुक्तविमानेन ब्रह्मलोकमुभौ गतौ ॥

2. As regards the claim and counter-claim of *bījin* and *kṣetrin* see the concluding remarks, where the point is discussed again.

CHAPTER THREE

DESCENDANTS OF BHARADVĀJA BĀRHASPATYA: SEERS OF THE ṚGVEDA

(*i*) *Suhotra Bhāradvāja*

The Sarvā (2, 6, 31) of Kātyāyana ascribes two hymns of the RV (6, 31-32) to Suhotra Bhāradvāja.[1] Both these hymns are addressed to god Indra. The verse (6, 32, 1) is repeated in the SV.[2] Four verses of VS (33, 53, 77, 93), and (34, 41) are also credited to him.[3]

It is unfortunate that the ancient Indian traditional sources have preserved scanty information about Suhotra Bhāradvāja. The Vedic texts are conspicuously silent about him. Only two Anukramaṇīs of Kātyāyana (Sarvā of (i) RV and (ii) VS) mention him as a seer belonging to the Bhāradvāja family. The Epics and Purāṇas also do not say anything about Suhotra as a seer. In fact, they mention at least four Suhotras belonging to the same Lunar race, and yet one more is presented as a Brāhmaṇa and still another is called a Daitya; and this means utter confusion in attempting to identify one of them as the seer Suhotra Bhāradvāja of RV.

In the previous chapter[4] we have discussed the statement of the Sarvā (2, 6, 52), wherein Suhotra and others were called 'sons' of Bharadvāja and grandsons of either Bṛhaspati or Bharata, the son of Duṣyanta. We have also looked into Ṣaḍaguruśiṣya's comment on Sarvā (2, 6, 52) which gives additional information of Bharadvāja's adoption by Bharata Dauṣyanti and then came to the conclusion that Bharata adopted a descendant of Bharadvāja but Suhotra and others were remote descendants of that adoptee (Bharadvāja). It was also suggested that the adoptee was Vidathin Bharadvāja, a probable grandson or great-grandson of Bharadvāja Bārhaspatya. Thus the statement at the Sarvā (2, 6, 52) appears to be an abridgment of the genealogy of the Bharadvājas.

Now we are to examine further the line of the Bharatas with a view to finding details about Suhotra Bhāradvāja and other Suhotras.

Before examining the facts about various Suhotras let us consider the hymns the Sarvā has ascribed to Suhotra Bhāradvāja. It is already stated that Suhotra's name is mentioned nowhere in the Vedic texts. Generally the Sarvā considers a hymn to be revealed to a seer when his name is mentioned in the compositions ascribed to him. (Of course, this may not always hold good.) But Suhotra's name does not occur in any of the hymns ascribed to him.

Suhotra has mentioned a few persons in his hymns. At RV (6, 31, 3)[5] the poet says: "Befriended by Kutsa, do you fight the weak Śuṣṇa and Kuyava and ten more demons in a battle, at the time of sunset; you stole away the sun's wheel (i.e. the orb from the heaven) and drove away the revilers."[6] Kutsa appears to be the seer of RV (94-98; 101-115; 9, 97, 45-58). He is frequently mentioned in the RV and thrice in the 6th Maṇḍala.[7] Śuṣṇa and Kuyava are two non-Aryan antagonists of the Aryan folk—particularly of Kutsa. Thus Indra is asked to put them down. In RV (6, 31, 4)[8], the poet mentions an important feud between the Aryan hero Divodāsa and non-Aryan chieftain Śaṁbara as follows: "You battered down the hundred matchless forts of the Dasyu Śaṁbara, when you sought to give rich treasures to the sacrificer Divodāsa and the singer Bharadvāja, by your power, O powerful god bought by soma".[9] Śaṁbara-Divodāsa fight is a popular theme in the RV. It appears, here that Divodāsa and Bharadvāja were closely related to each other, when Indra conquered the hundred forts of their enemy Śaṁbara and gave them away in booty. The mention of Divodāsa-Śaṁbara together with Bharadvāja in a verse is indeed significant. The praise of some good deed of an ancient person by a a seer normally points to him as a descendant of the former. There is, however, some problem as regards the identification of Divodāsa mentioned above, whether he was Divodāsa Pāñcāla or someone else. It will be shown (vide Ch. 5) that Divodāsa Pāñcāla was a distant descendant of Suhotra Bhāradvāja. If we identify Divodāsa mentioned in Suhotra's composition with Pāñcāla Divodāsa, wc shall find ourselves in an awkward position as regards the very authorship of the hymn, viz. we will have to admit that a remote ancestor has named a remote descendant of his. That would raise the doubt as to the genuineness of the Sarvā's ascription of the hymns to Suhotra Bhāradvāja. In other words, the question is: Who is the real author of RV 6, 31-32?

We have already mentioned above that there were more than

one Suhotra known to Indian tradition; at least four of them are interwoven in the thread of the Lunar race (*Candravaṁśa*). We shall first note down the information about each of them, in their chronological order, and then see if any one of them was the seer of RV 6, 31-32, and/or a descendant of Bharadvāja.

(a) One Suhotra was an immediate descendant of Purūravas Aila who had several sons: Āyus, Dhīmat, Amāvasu, Viśvāyu, Śatāyu and Gatāyu.[10] Amāvasu's son Bhīma had a son named Kāñcana; this Kāñcana's son was known as Suhotra.[11] We may refer to him as Suhotra I as it appears that he is the first of all the Suhotras in the line of descent from chronological point of view.[12] The son of this Suhotra was the famous Jahnu who adopted Gaṅgā as his daughter Jāhnavī.[13] This may be shown in the following genealogical tree:

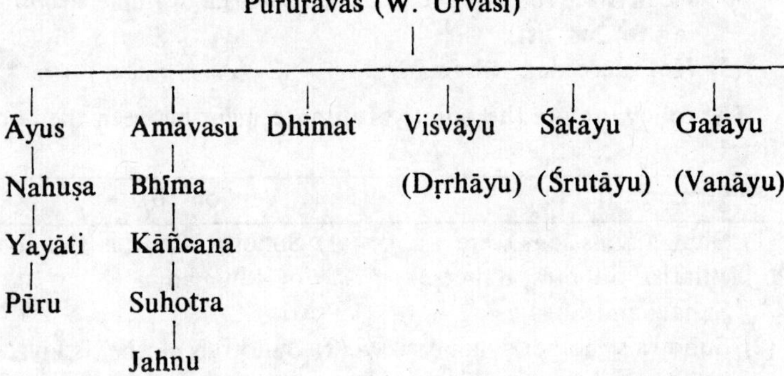

We have purposefully shown above the descendants of Āyus (who was the eldest son of Purūravas, too) and those of Amāvasu. Now it appears that Kāñcana's father Bhīma and Kāñcana himself could have been contemporaries respectively of Nahuṣa and Yayāti. Probably, all of them were junior contemporaries of Uśanā Kāvya (who is known also as Śukrācārya), and of Bṛhaspati (called Devaguru, the son of Aṅgiras). Yayāti's youngest son Pūru, born of Śarmiṣṭhā, the daughter of the Daitya king Vṛṣaparvan, patron of Śukrācārya, was contemporary of Suhotra I. Nahuṣa, Yayāti and Pūru—all were famous kings of the line of Āyus; their contemporaries Bhīma, Kāñcana and Suhotra I respectively do not appear to be so well-known.[14] But Suhotra's son Jahnu has come to be renowned.

(b) The next Suhotra is among the immediate descendants of

Bharata, the illustrious son of Duṣyanta and Śakuntalā. This Suhotra figures in both the genealogical lists of the Bharatas furnished in the MBh Ādiparvan.[15] In the first list (i.e. in MBh 1, 89, 17-26), Suhotra, Suhotṛ, Suhavi and Suyajus are said to have been born in Puṣkariṇī as the sons of Bhumanyu. Suhotra, who was the eldest among these princes, inherited the kingdom.[16] And Suhotra, the Lord of the Earth, begot Ajamīḍha, Sumīḍha and Purumīḍha by the princess of Ikṣvāku family.[17] In the second version of the Epic (MBh 1, 90, 34-38), Suhotra is stated to have been born of Jayā, the Dāśarhī princess married to Bhumanyu. Suhotra married the Ikṣvāku princess Suvarṇā who gave birth to Hastin who built the city of Hastināpura.[18]

The following are the points of agreement between the two lists:

(1) Suhotra was the son of Bhumanyu.
(2) He married the Ikṣvāku princess (Suvarṇā by name, according to 2nd list).
(3) He succeeded Bhumanyu.

The following are the points of disagreement between the two lists:

Version (i)	Version (ii)
(1) Bhumanyu's sons were Vitatha, Suhotra, Suhotṛ, Suhavi and Suyajus.	(1) Suhotra alone is the son of Bhumanyu.
(2) Suhotra's mother's name is Puṣkariṇī.	(2) Suhotra's mother is Jayā.
(3) Suhotra had three sons—Ajamīḍha, Sumīḍha and Purumīḍha.	(3) Suhotra's only son is Hastin. Ajamīḍha is Hastin's son.

Besides, the two genealogical tables where Suhotra figures, the MBh has preserved more detailed information about him. The MBh (1, 89) bears somc biographical data in addition to the dynastic.[19] Moreover, there are two Ṣoḍaśarājīya sections—one in the Droṇaparvan and the other in the Śāntiparvan—of the MBh.[20] The Ṣoḍaśarājīya section of the Droṇaparvan is, however, considered as an interpolation by the editor (of the critical edition) and is placed in the appendix of the Second Volume of the Droṇaparvan. The contents of the two Ṣoḍaśarājīyas have striking similarity in description; and Suhotra figures there as Vaitithana.

They also bear close resemblance to the account of Suhotra in the Ādiparvan (89) where Suhotra is considered as a Bharata king and a descendant of Bharadvāja.

MBh (1, 89, 22-25)[21] says that Suhotra, being the eldest among his brothers, ascended the throne. Now in the Droṇaparvan[22] it is said that Suhotra was invincible, and a destroyer of groups of enemies. As soon as he ascended the throne (as right successor), he invited the learned *ṛtviks* and *purohitas* ('priests') and sought their opinion on good action. The priests' advice he followed. When he learnt that the duty of a king was to protect his subjects, to offer charity to the needy, to offer sacrifices to gods and to vanquish enemies, he undertook to amass wealth only through virtuous means. Through righteous means (i.e. rites) he worshipped gods, conquered his enemies by means of sharp arrows, and won over all through his own merits. He brought under his sovereign rule the entire Earth extending up to the seashore, excepting the lands of the Mlecchas and the forests. During his virtuous rule there was substantial increase in animals and vegetation. The Earth was over-burdened by multiplication of men, elephants, horses, (chariots,) cows, etc., as if the Earth was about to *sink*.[23]

It is further stated in MBh (12, 20, 22ff)[24] that during his virtuous rule, once it so happened that Maghavat showered gold on Earth throughout the year. Consequently, the rivers flowed with golden tortoises, crabs, alligators, porpoises and sharks. Having beheld all those golden animate objects, Suhotra, the son of Vitithin, was wonder-struck. Having gathered that vast quantity of wealth (gold) that had covered the surface of the Earth, Suhotra performed a thousand Aśvamedha and hundred Rājasūya sacrifices at the site of Kurujāṅgala followed by a good number of *kāmya* and *naimittika iṣṭis*. He gave to the Brāhmaṇas enormous wealth in gold by way of Dakṣiṇā. Further, during his virtuous rule the surface of the whole earth was dotted all over with a hundred thousand sacrificial poles.[25] Having Suhotra as her Lord, it is said, "the Earth became truly worthy of the name Vasumatī ('possessed of treasures')".[26]

We have already seen above how far the two genealogical lists of the Bharatas agree and disagree with each other. Both the lists agree to hold Suhotra as the son and successor of Bhumanyu. Now let us see how far the Purāṇas corroborate these facts (of the MBh).

The Purāṇas[27] (Mt, Va and Vis) say that Bhuvamanyu was the son of Vitatha. Bh (9,21,1)[28] gives his name as only Manyu. Br, Hv and Ag drop his name. So Bhumanyu (MBh), Bhuvamanyu (Mt, Va, Vis) and Manyu (Bh) were all the names of one and the same person. Now Bhuvamanyu (in the Purāṇas) is said to have four sons, viz., Bṛhatkṣatra, Mahāvīrya,Nara and Garga.[29] Vis (4, 19, 9) adds '&c' (*ādayaḥ*)[30] to these four while Bh (9, 21, 1) adds the name of Jaya to the four (i.e. Bṛhatkṣatra etc.)[31]

Br, Hv and Ag say that Suhotra, Suhotṛ, Garya, Garga and Kapila were sons of Vitatha.[32] It agrees with neither the MBh nor the other Purāṇas in minute details.

Va (99, 165) and Vis (4, 19, 10) say that Bṛhatkṣatra had a son named Suhotra; his son was called Hastin or Hastinara,[33] while Br (13, 80-81) holds that Suhotra had a son whose name was Bṛhat.[34] The MBh confirms that Hastin was Suhotra's son. Probably, Hastin and Bṛhat were two names of one and the same person. Mt and Bh drop the name of Suhotra from their lists.

In one version of MBh (1, 89, 26)[34a] Ajamīḍha, Sumīḍha and Purumīḍha are said to be sons of Suhotra and his wife, a princess of Ikṣvāku and in the other (1, 90, 36) *Hastin* is named as the son of Suhotra born of Suvarṇā.[35] Now in the Purāṇas—Mt, Va, Vis and Bh—Ajamīḍha, Dvimīḍha (or Dvijamīḍha) and Purumīḍha are given as the three sons of Hastin, while in Br, Hv and Ag they are named as the three sons of Bṛhat. Hastin, Hastinara, and Bṛhat may be identified as one and the same person. So also Dvimīḍha and Dvijamīḍha appear to be the same individual. Sumīḍha may be considered as the fourth son of Hastin. Sumīḍha, Purumīḍha and the descendants of Ajamīḍha (*Ajamīḍhāḥ*) are met in the RV. According to the Sarvā (2, 4, 43) Ajamīḍha and Purumīḍha are joint seers of the RV (4, 43-44), and they are called the 'sons' or descendants of Suhotra (*Purumīḍhājamīḍhau sauhotrau*) which is only abridging the genealogy.

At this stage we may assess comparatively the evidences in the Epic and Purāṇas. We have already seen that Suhotra, the descendant of Vaitithina is mentioned in the *Śāntiparvan* (=Droṇa parvan) twice. We have also found that there was a Suhotra among the immediate descendants of Bharata Dauṣyanti. Now the question arises whether one can be identified with the other? The following common points are already there in the Ādiparvan (1, 89, 21-26) and Śāntiparvan (12, 29, 22-26).

(1) Suhotra was a great sacrificer;

(2) He was a very prosperous king—particularly having large quantities of gold;

(3) Kurujāṅgala was the sacrificial ground of Suhotra Vaitithina, in the vicinity of Hastināpura where the Bharatas ruled, and was under Suhotra.

Thus it may be possible to identify Suhotra, a descendant of Bharata and Bharadvāja (as stated in Ādiparvan) with Suhotra, the descendant of Vaitithina of the MBh (Śāntiparvan).

We have seen above that the list of kings of the Bharatas (as in the two versions of MBh) more or less agrees with that of the Purāṇas. In the MBh (in both the versions) Bṛhatkṣatra was dropped, while in the Purāṇas he is the father of Suhotra. So there remains no doubt that Suhotra, son of Bṛhatkṣatra, was mistaken as son of Bhumanyu in the MBh (Ādiparvan) and he is none other than the descendant of Vitithin of the Bharatas. We have seen in the last chapter that this Vitithin is the ancestor of Ṛjiśvan (Bharadvāja), a seer of RV (6, 48-52). Suhotra and Ṛjiśvan are sons or descendants of Bharadvāja. Thus Vitithin or Vidathin is a common ancestor of Suhotra and Ṛjiśvan, but he was a descendant of Bharadvāja. BD (5, 102) has mistaken Bharadvāja as Vidathin. The Purāṇas also wrongly state that Bharadvāja was adopted as a son by Bharata and the former was renamed as Vitatha. Already our investigation has proved that Vitatha was a son of a Bharadvāja (probably Vidathin) who was adopted by Bharata. Thus Ṛjiśvan and Suhotra can rightly be called Vaitithina or Vaidathina.[35a]

In the foregoing pages the life sketch of Suhotra is drawn particularly from the Epico-Purāṇic evidence more as a *kṣatriya* and a king, and less as a *brāhmaṇa* and a seer. In the section on Vidathin Bhāradvāja (in the second chapter), we said that Vidathin, a descendant of Bharadvāja, after his adoption by Bharata, became a *kṣatriya* and he gave rise to both the *brāhmaṇas* and *kṣatriyas*. His descendants—Suhotra, Garga, Nara, Śunahotra and Ṛjiśvan—all were seers and brāhmaṇas. Particularly, descendants of Garga and Nara were brāhmaṇas.[36]

Although some of the descendants of Vidathin Bhāradvāja became kings and remained *kṣatriyas*, they composed hymns of the RV and they were known as Royal-seers (*rājarṣis*). Suhotra is an example. In a passage in the MBh, it is stated that the race of Bharata saw many noble kings, some of whom were godly and others like brāhmaṇas.[37] Thus, in pursuit of intuitive knowledge and wisdom, caste was relegated to the background.

(c) Let us now pass to the next Suhotra. The MBh (3, 27, 24-25) mentions this Suhotra among a host of brāhmaṇas who met Yudhiṣṭhira while he lived with his brothers and wife in Dvaitavana. The relevant passage is:

Ṛcavāk ca suvāk caiva bṛhadaśca ṛcāvasuḥ|
ūrddhvaretā vṛṣāmitraḥ suhotro hotravāhanaḥ|
ete cānye ca bahavo brāhmaṇāḥ saṁśitavratāḥ|
ajātaśatrum ānarcuḥ purandaram iva ṛṣayaḥ|

"Ṛcavāk, Suvāk, Bṛhad, Ṛcāvasu, celibate Vṛṣāmitra, Suhotra, Hotravāhana were among many other brāhmaṇas who resorted to strict observances, honoured (Yudhiṣṭhira), to whom no enemy was ever born, as the seers honoured Purandara." The names of the seers in the above verses are similar in form and, to my mind, they are a homogeneous group by themselves, for which they were mentioned together as coming to greet the Pāṇḍavas in exile. And Suhotra is mentioned here as a brāhmaṇa and a contemporary of Yudhiṣṭhira.

(d) There was still another Suhotra in the race of the Bharatas (whom we can signify as Suhotra III, as he belongs to the same line). He was the son of Sudhanu[38] who was the son of Kuru and grandson of Ṛkṣa and great-grandson of Ajamīḍha. We have seen above that this Ajamīḍha was the eldest son and successor of Suhotra II whom we have identified above as Bhāradvāja. Between the periods of Suhotra II and Suhotra III there were at least five kings; they were: Hastin, Ajamīḍha, Ṛkṣa, Kuru and Sudhanu. All of them ruled in the main line at Hastināpura. Sudhanu and Jahnu II (Jahnu I is noticed above as a son of Suhotra I) were brothers. Suratha, the son of Jahnu II was a contemporary of Suhotra III. The son of Suhotra III was Cyavāna[39] whose son was Krimi.

(e) The great line of the Bharatas saw yet another Suhotra who was known to be son of Sahadeva.[40] Sahadeva was one of the five illustrious sons of Pāṇḍu. Pāṇḍu's second wife Mādrī, the daughter of Madra king, gave birth to twins by the grace of the Aśvins.[41] They were Sahadeva and Nakula. Sahadeva (probably) was the youngest of the Pāṇḍavas. He once attended the *Svayaṁvara-sabhā* ('an assembly of suitors, where the bride chose a groom of her own accord'), on invitation by king Dyutimat of the Madra country.[42] This Dyutimat was, in all probability, a king of a principality in Madra where Śalya, the brother of Mādrī, ruled in all prosperity; or he might be a brother of Śalya who ruled a part of the kingdom. However, Sahadeva attended the *Svayaṁvara Sabhā* and won the hand of Vijayā, the daughter of Madra king. Sahadeva begot from her a son named Suhotra (who being in the race of the Bharatas, may be signified as Suhotra IV). This Suhotra IV was a contemporary of the sons of Draupadī, who were, besides having their personal names, known as Draupadeyas (or also called Pāṇḍaveyas). Other two famous contemporaries of Suhotra IV were Abhimanyu, the son of Arjuna and Subhadrā, and Ghaṭotkaca, the son of Bhīmasena and the demoness Hiḍimbā. Abhimanyu and Ghaṭotkaca caused havoc in the Kurukṣetra war before meeting their glorious death. The five Draupadeyas and other sons of the Pāṇḍavas were among the remaining two thousand warriors mostly Pāñcālas, who were recklessly killed by Droṇa's revengeful son Aśvatthāman in the fateful night of the final and 18th day of the MBh war. It may be presumed that this Suhotra, a minor son of Sahadeva also must have met his death at the hand of Droṇa's infamous son who incidentally was called Bhāradvāja. From the genealogies supplied by tradition it appears that this Suhotra was 30 generations below Bharata Dauṣyanti.

(f) Another Suhotra described in traditional texts is a Daitya.[43] He is said to have been the ruler of the *Bhūtala* (Earth) in the hoary past. It is no use investigating the details of his bio-data as, by class, he differs from our Suhotra Bhāradvāja.

After considering all the Suhotras one by one we can now decide which of them can be identified with Suhotra Bhāradvāja of the Sarvā. We have noted above that Kāñcana's son Suhotra I was just four generations below Purūravas Aila and some 12 generations anterior to Bharata, the son of Duṣyanta, who adopted Bharadvāja (of course, Vidathin). Thus it is improbable to identify Suhotra I as Suhotra Bhāradvāja.

Suhotra III, the son of Sudhanu, was some 11 generations posterior to Bharata Dauṣyanti. Thus he could hardly have any contact with Bharata. These remote descendants of Bharata did not adopt the *gotra* of Bharadvāja and thus his career does not fulfil the requirements for his identification with Suhotra Bhāradvāja. The same consideration is emphatically applicable to Suhotra IV who was 30 generations below Bharata.

So also Suhotra who appears to be a brāhmaṇa and a contemporary of Pāṇḍu's eldest son Yudhiṣṭhira, cannot be identified with Suhotra Bhāradvāja. Suhotra Daitya's case is in every way beyond consideration for our purpose.

Thus we come to Suhotra II. We have fully considered all details about him and found him to be nearer to Bharata, as well as Bhāradvāja. He was a king four generations posterior to Bharata. An excellent sacrificer, he was one of the illustrious descendents of Bharata, who were as good as brāhmaṇas and could be called royal seers (*rājarṣayaḥ*). This Suhotra is also a descendant of Vitithin (=Vidathin), the adopted son of Bharata. The Sarvā lends support to the thesis that Suhotra could claim descent from Bharadvāja and therefore from Bharata Dauṣyanti. The Sarvā thus shows its acquaintance with the Epico-Purāṇic background of Suhotra's lineage and the fact that he was a king and a seer. Thus its ascription of the two hymns to Suhotra Bhāradvāja is justifiable.

On the basis of these conclusions we may reconstruct the genealogy of the Bharadvājas (which of course, overlaps that of the Bharatas as well), beginning from Bṛhaspati Āṅgirasa to Ajamīḍha Hāstina. In the genealogy thus reconstructed Suhotra's place among the Bharadvājas (coalesced with Bharatas) is pinpointed. Hereunder we furnish three genealogical trees, one according to Vedic ancillaries, and the other two reconstructed and modified in the light of our findings from the Vedic and Epico-Purāṇic sources.

Table 1

Genealogy of the Bharadvāja family according to BD and Sarvā.

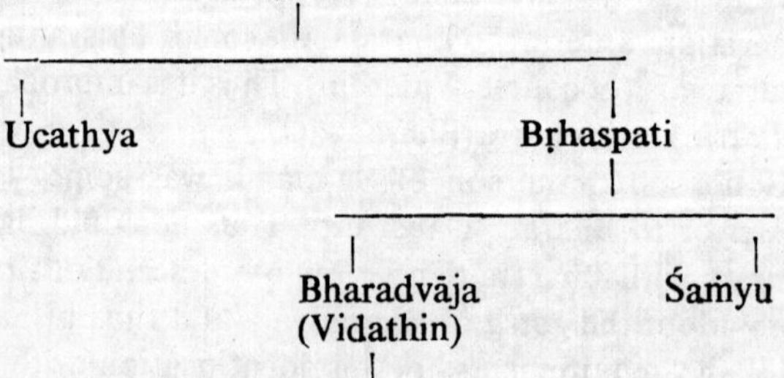

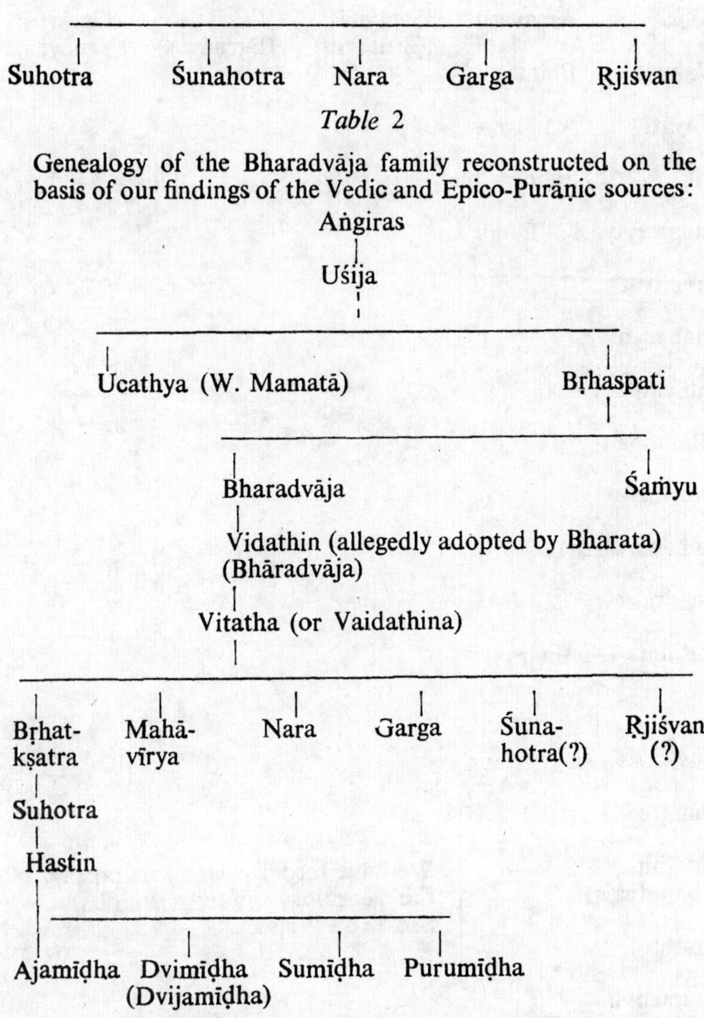

Table 2

Genealogy of the Bharadvāja family reconstructed on the basis of our findings of the Vedic and Epico-Purāṇic sources:

Table 3

Geneaology of the Bharadvāja family, coalesced with the Bharata line based on the data from Mt and Va. It presents the positions of four Suhotras described earlier in the Lunar race (*Candravaṁśa*).

Purūravas (W. Urvaśī)

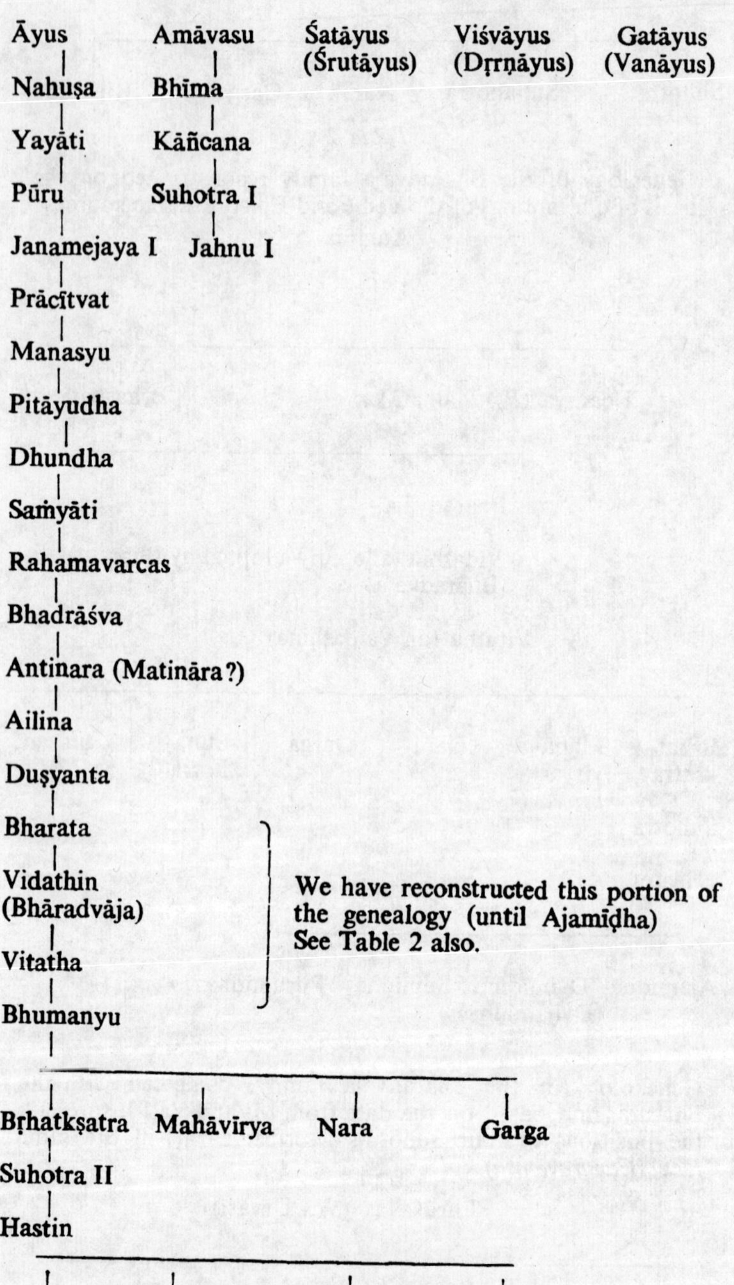
Āyus
Amāvasu
Śatāyus (Śrutāyus)
Viśvāyus (Dṛṛṇāyus)
Gatāyus (Vanāyus)
Nahuṣa
Bhīma
Yayāti
Kāñcana
Pūru
Suhotra I
Janamejaya I
Jahnu I
Prācītvat
Manasyu
Pitāyudha
Dhundha
Saṁyāti
Rahamavarcas
Bhadrāśva
Antinara (Matināra?)
Ailina
Duṣyanta
Bharata
Vidathin (Bhāradvāja)
Vitatha
Bhumanyu
We have reconstructed this portion of the genealogy (until Ajamīḍha) See Table 2 also.
Bṛhatkṣatra
Mahāvīrya
Nara
Garga
Suhotra II
Hastin

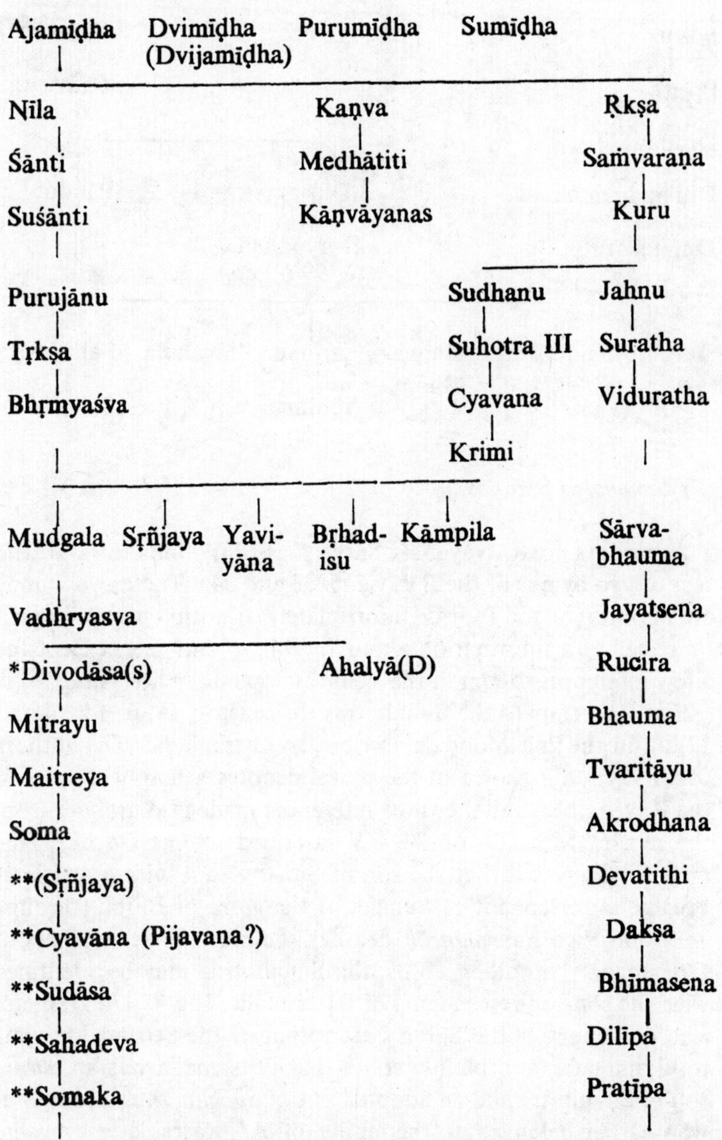

* This Divodāsa is identified as Divodāsa Atithigva of the RV and Ch. 5 is devoted to deal with the problem of his identity. This table indicates that Divodāsa was a remote descendant of Bharata and Vidathin (Bhāradvāja) and that helps reconstruct chronology.

** S.N. Pradhan (CAI) has touched the problem relating to them.

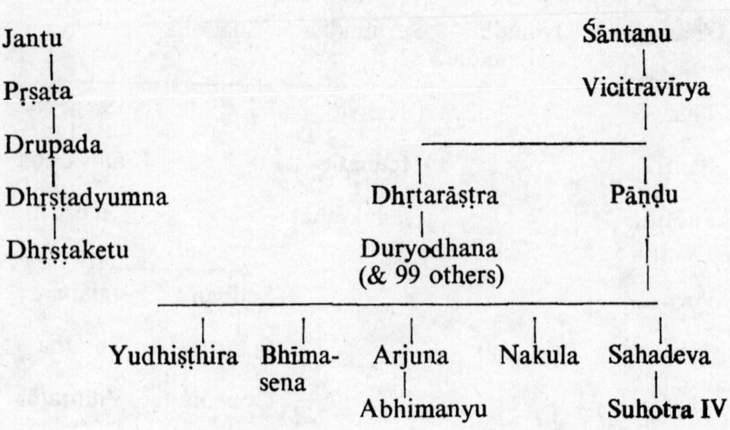

(*ii*) *Śunahotra Bhāradvāja*

According to Kātyāyana's Sarvā (2, 6, 33)[1] Śunahotra is the seer of two hymns of the RV, viz. 6, 33 and 34. These two hymns are in praise of god Indra. Unfortunately, tradition has preserved practically no information about the life of this seer, except for a few references to him in the Vedic and ancillary literature.

The RV refers to the Śunahotras thrice (in 2, 18, 6; 14, 14 and 17) all in the 2nd Maṇḍala ascribed to Gṛtsamada. The authors of VI say: "Śunahotra in the plural denotes a family of seers in the Ṛgveda".[2] As all the three references made in plural are from the second Maṇḍala of the RV (ascribed to Gṛtsamada) 'the person who was earlier the son of Śunahotra Āṅgirasa and later became a descendant of Śunaka of the *gotra* of Bhṛgu (through adoption)'[3] so *Śaunahotrāḥ* denotes the sons or descendants of Gṛtsamada. In other words, the Śunahotras may be identified with the sons or descendants of Gṛtsamada. The Ārṣānukramaṇī[4] also corroborates the Sarvā's ascription of the Second Maṇḍala to Gṛtsamada, and plainly states that Gṛtsamada was an *aurasa* son of Śunahotra and an adopted one of *Śunaka*, thus a composer who earlier belonged to the family of Aṅgirases later on went over to that of the Bhṛgus. The Anukramaṇīs are clear that Gṛtsamada was son of Śunahotra who was a son of the Aṅgirases.

It is significant, that both Gṛtsamada and Śunahotra (in plural), occur in the 2nd Maṇḍala.[5] Gṛtsamada is referred to in RV (2, 4, 9; 19, 8; 39, 8 and 41, 18) while Śunahotra (in pl.) in RV (2,

18, 6; 41, 14 and 17). However, both the names occur prominently in a single hymn, (viz. 2, 41). In this hymn, Gṛtsamada is mentioned in verse 18 and the Śunahotras in verses 14 and 17—this indicates the affiliation of the former with the family of the latter.[6] 'Śunahotra' in plural always stands for the family of that eponymous seer, and probably connotes his descendants, too. Doubtless, Gṛtsamada was one of the descendants of Śunahotra; in all probability, he was his son. This is corroborated by the fact that the AśvŚS (6, 10, 13) has mentioned these names in the *pravara* list.[7] BD (2, 40; 4, 78)[8] further refers to the patronymic Śaunahotra ('the son or descendant of Śunahotra') twice; (in 4, 78) he is identified with Gṛtsamada, affirming the views of the Sarvā (2, 2, 1)[9] and (Ārṣa)[10] that Gṛtsamada was the son of Śunahotra.

We have already mentioned above that Śunahotra, the father of Gṛtsamada, was a descendant of Aṅgiras. Gṛtsamada is also said to have been adopted by Śunaka of the Bhṛgus. Now the MBh (13, 30) says that there was one Vītahavya, a Haihaya king. He was rescued by a Bhārgava sage from Pratardana's hand.[11] Vītahavya later became a brāhmaṇa and adopted the Bhārgava *gotra*; his name is included in the *pravara* list of the Bhṛgus.[12] The Epic[13] gives a long genealogy of his descendants extending up to the fifteenth generation. His son was the Gṛtsamada whose eleventh descendant was Pramati. Pramati's son was Ruru. Ruru's son was Śaunaka whose descendants were known as Śaunaka Bhārgavas. Thus it appears that there were one Gṛtsamada and one Śunaka among the Bhṛgus. But the Śaunakas appear to be remote progeny of Gṛtsamada. This list of the Vītahavyas neither names Śunahotra as the father of Gṛtsamada nor does it mention the adoption of Gṛtsamada by a Bhārgava sage.

However, the Purāṇas say elsewhere that a Śunaka and the Śaunakas were progeny of a Gṛtsamada, who was a son of Śunahotra, the son of Kṣatravṛddha who founded the Kāśī dynasty.[14] These Epico-Purāṇic legends make a Gṛtsamada an ancestor of the Śaunakas. But Gṛtsamada, the seer of the 2nd Maṇḍala, is clearly stated to be an adopted son of a Śunaka—his father being Śunahotra Āṅgirasa. Thus we may safely affirm that there were two Śunahotras—one was a king of the Kāśī dynasty and a son of Kṣatravṛddha, and the other an Āṅgirasa sage. There were three Gṛtsamadas: (i) son of Vītahaya; (ii) a king, son of Śunahotra of Kāśī; (iii) the seer of the 2nd Maṇḍala of the RV, and son of

Śunahotra Āṅgirasa who was adopted by one Śunaka of the Bhārgava family. And thus there were more than one Śunaka also—(i) a descendant of Kāśī king Gṛtsamada; (ii) an offspring of Gṛtsamada Vaitahavya. The sūtras clearly mention in their *pravara* list Vītahavya, Gṛtsamada and Śunaka who belonged to the Bhṛgus.[15] This Gṛtsamada appears to be the son of Vītahavya only, thus he is to be distinguished from Gṛtsamada Śunahotra, the seer of the 2nd Maṇḍala.

Now the issue is about the actual identification of Śunahotra Āṅgirasa and Śunahotra Bhāradvāja, the seer of RV (6, 33-34).

The Sarvā (2, 6, 52) informs that Suhotra, Śunahotra, Nara, Garga and Ṛjiśvan were sons of Bharadvāja, grandsons of Bṛhaspati or Bharata Dauṣyanti. (We have discussed the issue involved here in details in the sections on Suhotra Bharadvāja and on the adoption of Bharadvāja.[16])

The BD (5, 102) points out that the same Bharadvāja was the son of Bṛhaspati, the son of Aṅgiras. Thus Bharadvāja, the ancestor of Śunahotra appears to be a descendant of Aṅgiras.[17]

Elsewhere, we have pointed out how Nara calls himself a descendant of Bharadvāja as well as of Aṅgiras.[18] Nara and Śunahotra were from the lineage of Aṅgiras, Bṛhaspati and Bharadvāja. Thus Gṛtsamada's father Śunahotra Āṅgirasa appears to be none other than Śunahotra Bhāradvāja. However, Gṛtsamada's adoption by a Śunaka of the Bhṛgu family shows some relationship between the Bhṛgus and the Aṅgirases.[19]

(*iii*) *Nara Bhāradvāja*

The Sarvā of Kātyāyana ascribes two hymns, viz. 35-36,[1] in the 6th Maṇḍala of RV to Nara Bhāradvāja. Both the hymns are addressed to god Indra. In comparison to other members of the family of Bharadvāja Nara appears to have a less significant profile in that he suffers obscurity; tradition has preserved scanty information about him.

As regards the sources, the Vedic texts do not contain a single passage where Nara's name occurs. Among the ancillaries, it is only the Sarvā of Kātyāyana that ascribes two hymns of RV to him and gives some facts as to his parentage and family.[2] The Purāṇas however give us definite details of his ancestry and lineage.[3]

In the hymns ascribed to Nara, there are two references that may be pertinent to and helpful in reconstructing his biography.

In RV (6, 35, 4)[4] the poet asks Indra thus:

"Such as you are, bestow on your singer foods which are accompanied by gifts of cows, which are lively with horses, and famous for their strength. Fatten our nourishments and also our easily milked milch-cow. Make them shine so as to be glorious among the Bharadvājas."[5]

This reference to 'the Bharadvājas' indicates that the poet belonged to the family of Bharadvāja. Again, in the next verse, (RV 6, 35, 5)[6] the poet addresses the same deity:

"Today and for ever in future I (choose) him (i.e. Indra) as a great power (Vṛjanam) since, O Śakra, being brave you are praised in spite of the strong gates (of Vala's cave). May I not sleep away from the cow of the bright-milked (Indra). Inspire the descendants of the Aṅgirases owing to their prayer, O singer."[7]

Here, reference is made to the descendants of the Aṅgirases who, according to Velankar,[8] 'are of course the Bharadvājas'. This passage rather brings the Aṅgirases and the Bharadvājas so close that one may be identified with the other; this is already done by Velankar and poet's having the *pravaras* of Aṅgiras, (Bārhaspatya) and Bharadvāja becomes almost certain. Bṛhaspati is to be included among the *pravaras* for he is said to be son of Aṅgiras and father of Bharadvāja. It will be clear from the following paragraph based on the Sarvā (2, 6, 52) and the BD (5, 102).

According to the Sarvā (2, 6, 52)[9], Nara was one of the five sons of Bharadvāja, the son of Bṛhaspati. Nara and other four Bhāradvājas, Suhotra, Śunahotra, Garga and Ṛjiśvan are said to be *pautras* ('grandsons') of either Bṛhaspati or Bharata Dauṣyanti. According to the BD 5, 102,[10] Bharadvāja was son of Bṛhaspati and grandson of Aṅgiras. This relation is indicated by the two references made in RV (6, 35, 4 and 5) noted above.

We have already discussed in full all about Bharadvāja's birth, his alleged adoption by Bharata Dauṣyanti and the genealogy of the Bharata dynasty *vis-a-vis* that of the Bharadvājas. Also, we have said elsewhere that the Sarvā's statement (at 2, 6, 52) is an abridgement of the genealogy of the Bharadvājas. Our findings from those discussions were that (1) Suhotra, Śunahotra, Nara, Garga and Ṛjiśvan were not the sons of Bharadvāja, but they were his descendants; (2) Bharata adopted Vidathin

Bharadvāja and Suhotra, Nara and others also were his progeny; (3) and consequently Suhotra and others including Nara were scions of Bharata as well; (4) they enjoyed the option of being brāhmaṇa and kṣatriya; (5) Bṛhatkṣatra, Mahāvīrya, Nara and Garga were sons of Bhuvamanyu, the great-grandson of Bharata.[11]

Now, according to the Purāṇas, Nara had a son named Saṁkṛti[12] who had two sons. One of them was Rantideva.[13] He was a famous king, a devout Vaiṣṇava and well-known for his liberality and hospitality.[14] His kingdom was on the bank of the river Carmaṇvatī (modern Chambal) and its capital was Daśapura.[15]

The name of the second son of Saṁkṛti is given differently in the Purāṇas,[16] Guruvīrya (Va), Gurudhī (Mt), Guru (Bh) and Ruciradhī (Vis).

Now Guruvīta (Mt 144, 102)[17] or Gauravīti (Mt 195, 30)[18] is named as a seer (*Mantrakṛt*) among the Aṅgirases. The correct name, however, appears to be Gaurīvīti. Making a mention of two seers of the same name, the Sarvā, (2, 5, 29)[19] ascribes a hymn (viz. the RV 5, 29) in the Atri Maṇḍala to Gaurīvīti Śāktya; while the Sarvā (2, 10, 73)[20] ascribes two hymns (RV 10, 73-74) to one Gaurīvīti (wihout appellation). This gives rise to a doubt whether the seer (of RV 5, 29) and the other (of RV 10, 73-74) was one and the same person or two different persons.

There were two Śaktis also, one was the son of Vasiṣṭha, while the other is from the Aṅgirases.[21] Some of the Sūtras also confuse when talking of *pravararṣis*. BaudhŚS (p. 23) says that Saṅkṛtis have three-ṛṣi-*pravaras*, viz. Āṅgirasa, Sāṁkṛtya and Gaurīvīti.[22] The Bhāradvāja Gotrakāṇḍa[23] by Kātyāyana and Laugakṣi also gives three *ṛṣi pravaras* of the Saṁkṛtis. Baudhāyana[24] treats Saṁkṛtis under the Bharadvāja family among the larger group of the Aṅgirases in his Śrauta Sūtra. Āśvalāyana[25] also places the Saṁkṛtis among the Bharadvājas and Aṅgirases, but points out that Saṁkṛtis have option to adopt three *ṛṣi-pravaras*: Āṅgirasa, Gaurīvīta and Saṁkṛti or of Śāktya, Gaurīvīta and Saṁkṛti. We have already stated that there was a Śakti and also a Gaurīvīti among the Vasiṣṭhas. Taking this into consideration perhaps Āpastamba[25a] puts the Saṁkṛtis among the Vasiṣṭhas and he gives three-*ṛṣi pravaras* of Saṁkṛtis: Śāktya, Saṁkṛti and Gaurīvīti. This gives rise to the controversy whether Gaurīvīti was a descendant of Saṁkṛti or Śakti. As majority of the Sūtras drop the name of Śakti and relate the Saṁkṛtis to the Bhāradvāja group, it will be more reasonable to accept Gaurīvīti as a descendant of Saṁkṛti. Kātyāyana and Laugakṣi[26] regard Saṁkṛtis as *dvyāmuṣyāyaṇas* together with Śuṅga-Śaiśiris. And Saṁkṛtis avoided matrimonial relation not only with the Aṅgirases under the aforesaid three-*ṛṣi-pravaras*, but also with the Vasiṣṭhas.[27]

From the foregoing discussion it follows that the Saṁkṛtis including Gaurīvīti were remote descendants of Bharadvāja. They, however, did not add Bharadvāja and Bṛhaspati to their *pravara ṛṣis*, because new seers like Saṁkṛtis and Gaurīvīti had to be accommodated in the place of the former. However, they rightly claimed to be the Aṅgirases. Their inclusion among the Vasiṣṭhas appears to be due to a wrong notion that Śakti could not be other than the son of Vasiṣṭha. Under such a wrong notion Saṁkṛtis were treated among the Vasiṣṭhas in the ĀpŚS; and the Saṁkṛtis were also termed *dvyāmuṣyāyaṇa* by Kātyāyana. It also emerges from the discussion that there were two Śaktis, one among the Vasiṣṭhas. So also there were two Gaurīvītis, one was the son of Saṁkṛti (among the Aṅgirases) and the other of Śakti (among the Vasiṣṭhas). Both Gaurīvītis were seers. Under such circumstances, one can claim that Gaurīvīti Śāktya, the composer of RV (5, 29), was Gaurīvīti, the son of Saṁkṛti of the Aṅgirases. Also he probably authored RV (10, 73-74).

(*iv*) *Garga Bhāradvāja*

The Sarvā (2, 6, 47)[1] of Kātyāyana ascribes a hymn (RV 6, 47) to Garga Bhāradvāja, found at the end of a few, addressed to Indra in the 6th Maṇḍala. It is the family prayer of the Bharadvājas as it fulfils certain conditions of being so.[2] Thus Garga appears to be the composer of a very important hymn that gives valuable information about the relation of the Bhāradvāja family with that of the Bharatas. Indra hymn being traced to Garga he may be considered his devotee.

Indian traditional sources are replete with numerous references to Gargas and Gārgyas. From a perusal of the relevant passages it appears that Garga or Gārgya was not a single person, rather, there were quite a few bearing the same surname but belonging to different epochs of history.

The numerous references to Gargas and Gārgyas point also to another fact, that in all probability they had an ancestor

Garga in the hoary past. From him originated the family of Gargas, Gārgyas. Gārgis, or Gārgāyanas—all derived from a single substantive *Garga*. Thus different Gargas, Gārgyas, Gārgis and Gārgyāyanas are to be considered as the progeny of only one Garga, depending upon different circumstances of place and time.

It is, however, worth noting that Garga or Gargas were not ordinary persons. They appear to have contributed to the Indian culture in various fields of arts and sciences. Their contribution to Vedic literature and rituals is equally outstanding. And, they contributed to Vedic exegesis, etymology and grammar, astrology, *dharmaśāstra* or politics, philosophy and religion.[3]

Garga's name does not occur in the Vedic Saṁhitās except in the AVP 8, 15, 2[4] where they are mentioned together with Āgastya, Kāṇva, Mudgalas (*Mudgalāḥ*), Ayaskāḥ (probably misreading for Ayāsyāḥ), Śaunakas, Saṁkṛtis as brāhmaṇas. Most of these brāhmaṇas might have been the *kṣatropeta brāhmaṇas*, as stated by the Purāṇas.[5] The Gargas are also said to be the *kṣatropeta brāhmaṇas*. All of them except the Śaunakas come from the stock of the Aṅgirases.

Some of the descendants of Garga are mentioned by their proper names in various traditional texts. A few of them are enumerated below:

The BU (2, 1-14; 16)[6] reproduces a dialogue between Bālākī Gārgya and Ajātaśatru by way of an example. Thus Bālākī Gārgya and Ajātaśatru, the king, appear to be anterior to Janaka Videha and Yājñavalkya.

Gārgī Vācaknavī[7] figures in the BU (3, 6, 12[8] and 3, 8 and 1-5; 7-12) very prominently. She actually participated in a debate on the enquiry into the Brahman and her queries perplexed even Yājñavalkya who had withstood the test in an assembly of the learned. She appears to be a very intelligent *brahmaviduṣī* of her time. Vācaknavī is probably her personal name or an appellation received after her successful debate in Janaka's assembly. The Śānkh GS (4, 10, 3)[9] has quoted her as Gārgī Vācaknavī.

In the BU (4, 6, 2)[10] some other Gārgyas ('descendants of Garga') and Gārgyāyanas' (remotely related to Garga) are mentioned while describing the succession of preceptors and pupils. *Garga, Gārgi, Gārgya* and *Gārgyāyanas* require some explanation. Garga is generally accepted as the progenitor of the family.

So, *Gārgi* denotes his son, just as Droṇa's son was Aśvatthāman *Drauṇi*, or Daśaratha's son was Rāma *Dāśarathi*. Gārgya however appears to have Garga as his ancestor. In the Garga family, Gārgya presides as the *gṛhapati* or as the *vṛddha*; and others in that circle would be *Gārgyāyanas*. Gārgyāyanas are termed *yuvans* ('young') in relation with Gārgya who is *vṛddha* ('matured' or 'old one'). They may be described as 'seniors' and 'juniors' of the same family. When the *vṛddha* dies, the senior-most *junior* succeeds him, i.e. to *vṛddhatva*.

The Praśnopaniṣad (1.1)[11] mentions Sūryāyaṇi Gārgya who, accompanied by Sukeśa Bhāradvāja, Śaibya Satyakāma, Kausalya Āśvalāyana, Bhārgava Vaidarbhi, and Kabandhī Kātyāyana, called on Pippalāda to know about the nature of Brahman. Here this Gārgya appears to be son of one Sūryāyaṇa of Garga *gotra*.

In the Vaṁśa Brāhmaṇa of the Sāmaveda, a few Gārgyas are mentioned by personal names; they are: Śarvadatta (1, 2), Maśaka (2, 8), and Sthiraka (2, 9). All of them might have been the heads of their own sub-families.

Again, the MBh (9, 51, 3-4)[12] mention one Kuṇi Gārgya, and another Kroṣṭuki Gārgya in the Va (34, 63)[13] while Kālāyani Gārgya is stated to be a pupil of Bāṣkali Bhāradvāja in the Vis (3, 4, 26).[14] The ĀśvŚS (10, 2), ŚānkhŚS (16, 22, 2) and KātŚS (23, 2, 8) speak of a three-day (or three-night) feast of Garga (*Garga-trirātra*). And the Atharvapariśiṣṭas frequently speak of Garga or Gārgya.[15]

The Sarvā (2, 6, 52)[16] groups Garga with Suhotra, Śunahotra, Nara and Ṛjiśvan—as the sons of Bharadvāja and grandsons of Bṛhaspati or Bharata Dauṣyanti. This, when compared with the Epico-Purāṇic list of the Bharatas, indicates that the Sarvā (2, 6, 52) has only abridged the genealogy, and that Kātyāyana was aware of the relation between the Bharadvājas and the Bharatas. We have, however, fully discussed the passage of the Sarvā (2, 6, 52), in the light of the Epico-Purāṇic evidences, and came to the conclusion that Suhotra, Śunahotra, Nara, Garga and Ṛjiśvan were distant descendants of Bharadvāja Bārhaspatya.[17] Also, they were scions of Bharata, because of his having adopted Vidathin Bhāradvāja as his son. Thus Garga was also one of the *dvyāmuṣyāyaṇakaulina*.

Bṛhatkṣatra, Mahāvīrya, Nara and Garga are stated to be sons of Bhumanyu and great grandsons of Vidathin Bhāradvāja who was adopted by Bharata Dauṣyanti. Now, Purāṇas say that Garga's son was Śini[18] who was also a seer, a *pravorarṣi*.[19] Śini's progeny are *Śainyas*. The Gargas and Śainyas are signified as *kṣatropeta brāhmaṇas*.[20]

Āśvalāyana was, however, doubtful about the origin of Garga; he wondered whether Garga was a son of Bharadvāja.[21] Kātyāyana asserts that Garga was a son of Bharadvāja.[22] We think that while Āśvalāyana doubted the parentage of Garga, he probably thought that: (1) Garga was born in a kṣatriya family and could not be a brāhmaṇa, and (2) as Garga was far removed from Bharadvāja in lineage he could not be his son. Kātyāyana, himself a Bhāradvāja, is regarded an important authority. While affirming that Garga was Bharadvāja's son, Kātyāyana probably did not give due weightage to the Purāṇic legend of Bharata adopting a Bharadvāja; or perhaps he interpreted *suta* ('son') in the sense of issues as Pargiter[23] has also argued. The fact that Garga's descendants also cannot marry to the Bharadvājas[24] was noticed by him.

However, the Śrauta Sūtras[25] notice Gargas under Bhāradvāja *gaṇa*. They have two sets of *pravaras* one with five *pravara-ṛṣis* and the other with three:

(i) Āṅgirasa, Bārhaspatya, Bhāradvāja, Gārgya and Śainya.
(ii) Āṅgirasa, Bārhaspatya, Bhāradvāja, Śainya and Gārgya.
(iii) Āṅgirasa, Gārgya and Śainya.
(iv) Āṅgirasa, Śainya and Gārgya.

The *pravaras* (i) and (iii) are in accordance with genealogical list of the family; at the same time, the *pravaras* (ii) and (iv) violate that order by putting Śainya before Gārgya. However, importance attaches to the number of *ṛṣis* in the *pravaras*. It is said that the Gargas with five *pravara-ṛṣis* cannot inter-marry with the Bharadvājas. Apart from the Gargas being the descendants of Bharadvāja the reason for this restriction is the overlapping of the three *ṛṣi-pravaras* of the Bharadvājas and the five *ṛṣi-pravaras* of the Gargas. The Bharadvājas have a three *ṛṣi-pravara* comprising Āṅgirasa, Bārhaspatya and Bhāradvāja—repeated in the five *ṛṣi-pravaras* of the Gargas. This means, three of the five *pravara-ṛṣis* of the Gargas are in common with those of the Bharadvājas. This fact means that the *gotra* (*samānagotra*) of the Gargas and Bharadvājas is the same; hence inter-marriage among them was prohibited. Thus close relations of the Gargas with the Bharadvājas are established: the former are a part of the large Bharadvāja family. Coming from the Bharadvājas, they are not allowed to marry with them. But this is not applicable to the Gargas with three-*ṛṣi-pravaras* [i.e. those having the *pravaras* (iii) and (iv)].[26] Because, here two out of three *ṛṣi-pravaras* of the Bharadvājas are not common and thus they are not considered an offshoot of the Bharadvājas, but as the Kevalāṅgirases, hence, these Gargas can marry with the former, as also the other groups of the Kevalāṅgirases.[27]

Moreover, the Śrautasūtras and the Purāṇas describe Garga as one of the 33 seers or *mantrakāras* of the Vedas and as one of the Aṅgirases.[28] Further, Mt (195, 24)[29] confirms that he was a scion of *pravara-ṛṣis*.

The Epic and the Purāṇas often mention Gargas or Gārgyas.

According to MBh (9, 51, 3-4),[30] there was a Gārgya whose personal name was Kuṇi. He was very famous as a strong seer. He practised severe penance and through his mental power he produced a daughter named Subhrū. He was very much pleased to see his daughter thus born, and then left the terrestrial world for heaven.

In the MBh (12, 59, 117)[31] one Garga is described to have some connection with Pṛthu Vainya. The MBh (9, 36, 14-17)[32] describes one Vṛddhagarga who was a prominent astrologer. He is said to have possessed the knowledge of time, of the planets and luminaries and their exceptional movements. Also, he knew about the calamities and good omen also. He is said to have lived on the bank of Sarasvatī; this place was known as *Gargasrota*, and was considered to be a place of pilgrimage. The AP[33] contains certain works on astrology that corroborate the MBh evidence. The Vis (2, 5, 26)[34] also states that Garga practised astrology. It is said that one Garga pleased Śeṣa, the chief of the Nāgas, through his prayer and learnt from him astrology in its entirety, and became capable of predicting the future events at the sight of the signs thereof.

The Purāṇas have preserved a few legends relating to one or the other Garga. We may assess their value from socio-historical point of view.

The Mt (20, 1-10)[35] describes one Garga who happened to be the preceptor of seven sons of the seer Kauśika. After the death of Kauśika, a famine starved all the seven brothers. Garga took pity upon them and appointed them to herd his milch-cow. One day the brothers were very hungry and proposed to eat beef. They offered the beef to their father in a Śrāddha and then ate up the left-over. However, they brought back the calf to their preceptor Garga and said that the cow had fallen a prey to the tiger. This legend stresses the merits of Śrāddha; the personality of Garga is pushed into background. However, this Garga appears to be a kind man and follower of Vedic *āhnika kriyās*, and the cow appears to be a *homadhenu*. Yet we cannot fix chronology, because 'Kauśika', related to the story, does not provide a clue. Kauśika might have been a *gotra*—his name indicating the family.

The Vis (5, 6, 8-9)[36] says that Vasudeva sent Garga from Mathurā to Gokula to perform secretly the *nāmakaraṇa* ceremony of his two sons. Garga went to Gokula and performed that *saṁskāra* secretly; he gave the names Rāma and Kṛṣṇa respectively to the elder and the younger sons of Vasudeva.

The Br (12, 6-11)[37] mentions yet another Garga, who was a contemporary of Janamejaya, the son of Parikṣit. The story is that Janamejaya killed the son of this Garga and incurred his wrath. Through the curse pronounced by the sage, a chariot that was handed down from Yayāti to Janamejaya for several generations as family loom, was instantly destroyed.

The Br (14, 46ff)[38] describes an incident relating to one Gārgya, a descendant of Garga, and gives the origin of the Mleccha king Kālayavana, as follows:

Once a woman named Vṛkadevī, the wife of Śiśirāyaṇi, who gave birth to Agāvaha, wanted to test the virility of a Gārgya. As no ejaculation was effected, the twice-born people insulted him while they were in an assembly in front of the Yādavas. Being thus outraged, and his anger aroused, he went to the South and resorted to severe penance with a desire to get a son that would cause havoc among the Yādavas. He worshipped Mahādeva feeding himself upon iron-filings; his complexion became iron-black. At the end of twelve years Mahādeva was pleased with him and granted him a boon that he would beget a son according to his desire. He then came back (to Mathurā) and tried to satisfy his carnal desire when he met a cowherd's daughter. This Gopī was none other than a nymph in the guise of cowherdess. With his seed, she bore him a child. As a result of the boon granted by

Śūlapāṇi, the wife of Garga bore a son who was in human form. This son was known as Kālayavana. Afterwards Garga crowned him king and left for the forest.

The Mārk (18, 1-25)[39] also preserves a legend relating to one Garga who was a minister of Arjuna, the son of Kṛtavīrya. When Arjuna succeeded his father as king, he resolved to be worthy of his office. He sought his minister Garga's advice and was told to worship Datta, the son of Atri. Garga also narrated to him how the Daityas were earlier destroyed by Dattātreya. He said that once the Daityas and Dānavas invaded the kingdom of gods who propitiated Dattātreya at the advice of their *Guru* Bṛhaspati. Datta, the son of Atri, was in fact an incarnation of Lord Viṣṇu. He was at that time enjoying the company of the goddess Lakṣmī. But at the same time the Daityas abducted Lakṣmī from his hermitage; and his wrath meant their instant death.

Acting on the advice of Garga, Arjuna worshipped Dattātreya who granted him a boon that he should reign righteously, prosperously and gloriously.

The legend speaks of a Garga's relation with Arjuna Kṛtavīrya of the Haihayas, but it is difficult to decide who this Garga was. Also, the story belonged to a later date in that he propagated the cult of Dattātreya.

(*v*) *Ṛjiśvan Bhāradvāja*

Ṛjiśvan Bhāradvāja is said to be the composer of five hymns of the RV (6, 49-52 and 9, 98) and a part of another (9, 108, 6-7)[1]; four of these (6, 49-52) are in praise of All-Gods (*Viśvedevāḥ*), while the rest of Soma Pavamāna. Again, some verses from these hymns are fully or partly repeated in SV, VS, TS, MS and KS.[2] The AVŚ (2, 12, 6) (= RV 6, 52, 2) is also ascribed to him.[3] Counting the number of hymns in the RV (about six) credited to him one may assign to him the third important place among the Bharadvājas, Bharadvāja and Śaṁyu, the two sons of Bṛhaspati, occupying the 1st and 2nd places respectively. As many as eight seers belonging to different families of the Ṛgvedic sages have mentioned Ṛjiśvan in nine passages of the RV. Besides, he is referred to in three passages of the JB (2, 160; 161; 414).

The seers who have mentioned Ṛjiśvan, have referred also to some other persons along with him—some of them appear to be

Aryans but others Dāsas or Dasyus. The Aryan personalities mentioned together with Ṛjiśvan, do not appear to be his contemporaries. They are: Kaṇva,[4] Trasadasyu,[5] Paktha,[6] Daśavraja[7] and Gośarya[8] who could not have been related to him; the first two belong to the stock of Aṅgirases of which Ṛjiśvan himself came. In the RV or elsewhere at least there is no evidence which might lend support to their being his contemporaries. Possibly, they might have belonged to different epochs of the Ṛgvedic age; the poets regrouped them together with Ṛjiśvanas favourites of some particular god. Even Atithigva who is mentioned in RV (1, 53, 8)[9], might not have been related to Ṛjiśvan, although he is identified with Divodāsa, a patron of the Bharadvājas.[10] So also, it cannot be proved that Gaurīvīti was Ṛjiśvan's *purohita* ('domestic chaplain') as suggested by Geldner.[11] It is, however, noticed that there was one Gaurīvīti who was a descendant of Nara Bhāradvāja; his name is listed among prominent Aṅgirases as a *pravararṣi* together with Aṅgiras and Saṁkṛti.[12]

In some Ṛgvedic passages are mentioned persons hostile to Ṛjiśvan, and for his sake Indra killed them. Among them Pipru[13] is the foremost and is repeatedly struck down by Indra for Ṛjiśvan's sake. Pipru had strong forts[14] and was a Dāsa or Asura,[15] i.e. a non-Aryan hero. RV (1, 101, 1) describes him as having a dusky brood, and again RV (6, 20, 7) as an *ahimāya* (one who has the magical powers of Ahi).[16] RV (10, 99, 11) says, Indra released the cattle after opening Pipru's *vraja* ('stall of cattle')[17].

Others hostile to Ṛjiśvan and killed by Indra are: Karañja,[18] Parṇaya,[19] Mṛgaya[20] and Vaṅgṛda[21]—the last was the master of a hundred forts—indicating his chieftainship.

In the hymns mentioned above Ṛjiśvan has not named any individual, either a predecessor or a contemporary. Only once, (RV 6, 50, 15)[22] he has referred to 'the children of Bharadvāja' who sings songs to please the gods. According to the commentator Sāyaṇa,[23] Ṛjiśvan had pronounced a curse on a rival Ṛṣi (seer) Atiyāja (*lit.* one who has offered sacrifices more than necessary) in RV (6, 52, 1). However, modern scholars do not hold Sāyaṇa's interpretation as correct.[24]

Three out of nine passages of the RV wherein the name of Ṛjiśvan occurs appear to be important insofar as they contain two patronymic terms indicating Ṛjiśvan's parentage; these are: (1) Vaidathina (a descendant of Vidathin) in RV (4, 16, 13 and

5, 29, 11)[25] and (ii) Auśija 'a descendant of Uśija' in RV (10, 99, 11).[26] Besides, there is his own composition in RV (6, 50, 15)[27] where Ṛjiśvan claimed descent from Bharadvāja—as alluded to above.

We have already discussed the problem of Vidathin Bharadvāja in great details[28] and come to the conclusion that he was the very person whom, in all probability, Bharata Dauṣyanti did adopt as his son for the purpose of race preservation. Also we stated above that Suhotra, Nara, Garga and Ṛjiśvan were all descendants of this Vidathin Bharadvāja, among whose progeny were several groups of *kṣatropeta* brāhmaṇas. Thus there should not be any doubt as to Ṛjiśvan's descent from Vidathin.

As regards the second patronymic i.e. Auśija (descendant of Uśija),[29] we have already seen in the account of Bharadvāja's birth that the former was an ancestor of Bharadvāja Bārhaspatya. He was, probably, the son of Aṅgiras, and the father of Ucathya and Bṛhaspati. Thus, whosoever descended from Ucathya and Bṛhaspati have lineage from Uśija too. Hence the descendants of Ucathya and Bṛhaspati may be called Auśija (descendant of Uśija). That is why Ṛjiśvan is called by the patronymic Auśija. Another person claiming descent from Uśija was Kakṣīvat Dairaghatamasa.

That Ṛjiśvan was a descendant of Bharadvāja is clearly stated in the Sarvā (2, 6, 52)[30]: "Suhotra, Śunahotra, Nara, Garga, Ṛjiśvan were sons of Bharadvāja, grandsons of Bṛhaspati or Bharata Dauṣyanti." This statement is very precise and, therefore, we have discussed its significance elsewhere. There we have shown that, as a matter of fact, Suhotra, Śunahotra, Nara, Garga and Ṛjiśvan were not sons but remote descendants of Bharadvāja, Bṛhaspati and Bharata. In that analysis, we had to depend upon evidence supplied by the Epico-Purāṇic sources—these were:

(1) Three passages from the MBh,[31] where Suhotra is described as a descendant of Vitithin;
(2) Accounts of Suhotra given in that Epic[32];
(3) Accounts of Bharadvāja's birth given in the Purāṇas;[33]
(4) Accounts of the adoption of (Vidathin) Bharadvāja and of his descendants given in (i) two versions of the MBh and (ii) the Purāṇas.
(5) And statements of the BD[34] and the Sarvā (2, 6, 52).

After comparing the material noticed in the above-mentioned sources with the one in the Sarvā (2, 6, 52) we held that Ṛjiśvan was one of the remote descendants of Vidathin, Uśija and Bharadvāja and so he could optionally claim to be a brāhmaṇa or kṣatriya. We also suggested that, even if the name of Ṛjiśvan occurs nowhere in the Epico-Purāṇic sources, he could be assigned a place among the sons of Bhuvamanyu on the clear evidence of the Sarvā (2, 6, 52).

(*vi*) *Pāyu Bhāradvāja*

Pāyu Bhāradvāja is said to be the seer of RV (6, 75) which is traditionally known as the lone Saṁgrāma Sūkta or Saṁgrāmāśiṣaḥ ('Battle hymn' or 'Blessings in the Battle').[1] He is regarded as the composer of VS (29, 38-60) and of ŚYV also; the first fourteen stanzas of this hymn are a repetition of RV (6, 75, 1-14) *ad verbatim* and the rest of VS (29, 52-57) are a repetition of RV (6, 47, 26-31) which are addressed to Dundubhi ('War drum').[2] Verses in RV (6, 47, 26-31) are ascribed to Garga Bhāradvāja. So also are verses 1, 80, 95, 2, 12, 13 and 1220 of the SV[3]. All of the verses of the RV (6, 75, except verse 15) are repeated in TS, MS and KS.[4]

Most of the Vedic and Epico-Purāṇic texts do not offer any bio-data of Pāyu and any information about his works. There is a lone reference in one verse of the RV (6, 47, 24). Yet the BD (5, 124-142) and the Sarvā (2, 6, 75) offer some information which is helpful in reconstructing an account of his life.

Pāyu Bhāradvāja is referred to in the RV (6, 47, 24)—a verse in a hymn ascribed to Garga Bhāradvāja. Its translation[5] runs as follows:

"Aśvatha gave Pāyu and followers of the Atharvans, ten chariots with the foremost horse and a hundred cows."[6]

Sāyaṇa has identified Aśvatha with Prastoka, the son of Sṛñjaya (*aśvathaḥ aśvavān etatsaṁjñaḥ Prastokaḥ*).[7] Griffith[8] identifies him with Divodāsa and takes the Atharvan as the persons of the Atharvagotra[9] who are considered as the Aṅgirases, to which *gotra* Pāyu Bhāradvāja belongs. In this verse Velankar[10] considers Atharvans as the followers of Pāyu.

BD (5, 124-142)[11] states that Pāyu under orders of his father Bharadvāja helped Prastoka (the son of Sṛñjaya) and Abhyāvartin (the son of Cayamāna) to secure victory over the Varaśikhas on the bank of Hariyūpīyā. At the instance of his father Pāyu is said to have consecrated all the war materials and weapons reciting the verses of the hymn (6, 75). Further, having emerged victorious, the two princes gave manifold gifts to their family priest Bharadvāja whose *brahma* ('priestly power') had boosted their morale in the battle. Again, while returning home with gifts from the palace of the princes Bharadvāja and his 'son' Garga met Indra. The two seers informed him about the gifts of Prastoka and Abhyāvartin (verses *dvayān*: 6, 27, 8 and *Prastoka*: 6, 47, 22).[12] It may be pointed out that in the second verses attributed to Garga mention is made of the gifts of Prastoka and Divodāsa, while in RV (6, 27, 8,[13] ascribed to Bharadvāja), Cāyamāna and Prastoka are praised for their gifts.

It appears, therefore, Bharadvāja, Pāyu, Garga, Divodāsa, Abhyāvartin and Prastoka were contemporaries. In our discussion of the history of the Gargas,[14] we said that Garga was not the son but a remote descendant of Bharadvāja Bārhaspatya, to whom 6, 27 is ascribed. We shall see below[15] that Bharadvāja, the *purohita* ('priest') of Divodāsa was a person different from Bharadvāja Bārhaspatya. But above discussion points out that Pāyu and his father belonged to the family of the Bharadvājas and in all probability they were intimately connected with the Bharatas, particularly with Divodāsa, Sṛñjaya and his son Prastoka and Abhyāvartin. Probably these two Bharadvājas and their descendants were responsible for composing a number of hymns in the 6th book.[16] And the Sarvā ascribing some hymns to the early Bharadvājas may be considered only as traditional practice that lacks historicity in the strict sense.[17]

(*vii*) *Ajamīḍha*

Kātyāyana's Sarvā (2, 4, 43) ascribes two hymns of the RV (4, 43-44) to Ajamīḍha and Purumīḍha, the two 'sons' of Suhotra (Sauhotrau).[1] They are also said to be the seers of AVŚ (20, 143, 1-7).[2] Both of them were joint authors of a few verses of the VS.[3] To Purumīḍha alone were revealed hymn in SV (1, 6; 2, 904).[4]

Suhotra is accepted as a Bhāradvāja in the Sarvā (2, 6, 52)[5] and the seer of RV (6, 31-32).[6] Now in the Sarvā (2, 4, 43) he is described as 'the father' of Ajamīḍha and Purumīḍha.[7] If this be true, Ajamīḍha and Purumīḍha may be considered as the two descendants of Bharadvāja. Whether they were 'sons' or 'descendants' of Suhotra Bhāradvāja is to be examined below.

One cannot but be surprised at the hymns by Ajamīḍha and Purumīḍha being included in the Vāmadeva Maṇḍala and not in the Bhāradvāja Maṇḍala. However, it should not be overlooked that the RV is not free from an unusual placement of hymns, in a particular Maṇḍala—a family Maṇḍala, credited to a person or persons belonging to another family.[8] Probably, the Saṁhitākāras either overlooked the family affiliation of some sages, or they adopted a flexible approach in the arrangement of hymns into Maṇḍalas. A similar anomaly may be noticed in regard to Gaurīvīti, the composer of RV (5, 29).[9]

The patronymic term Ājamīḍha occurs only once in RV (4, 44, 6)[10], which is also repeated in AVŚ (20, 143, 6). And while noticing this occurrence in the Vedas, the two authors of VI[11] observe: "The Ājamīḍhas or descendants of Ajamīḍha are referred to in a hymn of the RV."[12] Ludwig[13] and Oldenberg[14] deduce from the use of this patronymic Ājamīḍha ('the descendants of Ajamīḍha,) that probably a later descendant of Ajamīḍha was the seer of the hymns (RV 4, 43-44).

The two hymns ascribed to Ajamīḍha and Purumīḍha are addressed to the twin-gods, the Aśvins. This indicates that both the seers were their devotees. In their hymns the sages have not referred to any person other than the descendants of Ajamīḍha. If we believe in the joint authorship of these two hymns, RV (4, 43-44), the question arises as to why only the descendans of Ajamīḍha were mentioned in their hymns. The answer may be that either the two hymns were authored by a later descendant of Ajamīḍha (as suggested earlier) or even that Ajamīḍha and Purumīḍha composed those hymns and Purumīḍha might have died sonless.[15]

Already, we have discussed the Epico-Purāṇic sources extending up to Suhotra while dealing with Suhotra. Now, we may take up the sources (where we discontinued) up to the immediate descendants of Ajamīḍha.[16] According to the MBh, Ādiparvan (89, 26)[17], Ajamīḍha, Sumīḍha and Purumīḍha were regarded as sons of Suhotra, begotten of Ikṣvāku princess. The second account in the Epic (MBh 1, 90, 36-38)[18] records that Suhotra got a son named Hastin from Suvarṇā, the daughter of Ikṣvāku king. Hastin married Yaśodharā, a princess of Trigarta country, and she gave birth to Vikunthina. This Vikunthina married Sudevā, the daughter of the Daśārhas. From Sudevā was born only Ajamīḍha. Thus at one place the Epic notes that Ajamīḍha was the son of Suhotra, as the Sarvā (2, 4, 43) holds (as seen above), while at another it reports that Ajamīḍha was the great-grandson of Suhotra. The story in the MBh (1, 89) appears to be an abridgement of the second one in the MBh (1, 90) as also those of the Purāṇas.

Now, the Mt and Bh omit Suhotra and hold Hastin as the son of Bṛhatkṣatra[19] whom the Va (99, 165) and Vis(4, 19, 10) regard to be the father of Suhotra.[20] (It may be pointed out that the MBh does not mention Bṛhatkṣatra as the father of Suhotra.) Yet, all these Purāṇas unanimously claim that Ajamīḍha, Dvimīḍha (or Dvijamīḍha) and Purumīḍha were the sons of Hastin.[21] The Br, Hv and Ag say that Suhotra's son was Bṛhat who had three sons, Ajamīḍha, Dvimīḍha and Purumīḍha.[22] Nevertheless, none of the Purāṇas mentions Vikunthina, the "son" of Hastin and "father" of Ajamīḍha in the MBh (1, 90, 37). Thus, in all these Purāṇas, Ajamīḍha, Dvimīḍha and Purumīḍha are reported to be grandsons of Suhotra. So, the Sarvā's statement (at 2, 4, 43) *Purumīḍha ajamīḍha sauhotrau* is interpreted in the sense of 'Purumīḍha and Ajamīḍha were two descendants of Suhotra'.

Another issue is the number and the names of Hastin's sons. Excepting MBh (1, 90), all other accounts in the Epic and the Purāṇas name three sons of Hastin. The MBh (1, 90, 38) mentions Ajamīḍha (as the son of Suhotra). Sumīḍha is described in the RV (6, 63, 9) as a patron of the Bharadvājas: it confirms that a king called Sumīḍha lived in the Ṛgvedic age. All the Purāṇas point to Dvimīḍha as the third son of Hastin. Dvijamīḍha may be identified with Dvimīḍha, but it is difficult to do so in the case of Sumīḍha whose name occurs in the RV (6, 63, 9) and the MBh (1, 89, 26). It would be plausible to maintain that Ajamīḍha, Sumīḍha, Dvimīḍha and Purumīḍha were (all four) sons of Hastin (identified with Bṛhat).

From the order of the enumeration of the names of the brothers, it appears that Ajamīḍha was the eldest of all and thus naturally he succeeded to the throne of his father Hastin. He appears to have been a celebrated king just as Bharata and Suhotra were, because of which Yudhiṣṭhira, a remote descendant of him, was often addressed as 'Ājamīḍha' 'a scion or descendant of Ajamīḍha',[23] as he was addressed elsewhere as Bhārata a bit more frequently. This signifies that Bharata and Ajamīḍha were two of his ancestors and both were celebrated kings of the Lunar race (*Candravaṁśa*).

The MBh (1, 89, 27)[24] reports that Ajamīḍha had six sons born from his three wives. The MBh (1, 90, 39)[25] however, says that he had twenty-four hundred sons (*caturviṁśam putraśatāni*) (i) born to the princesses Kekayā, Nāgā, Gāndhārī, Vimalā and Ṛkṣā, and that all of them (princes) established different lines. This is an extremely exaggerated statement.

The Purāṇas say that Ajamīḍha had three queens, viz. Nīlinī, Keśinī and Dhūminī and on them he begot a number of sons who were endowed with divine lustre.[26]

Ajamīḍha and Nīlinī begot Nīla[27]; he was the originator of a very important line of the North Pāñcālas; many kings of this dynasty are mentioned in the RV. The account of this dynasty is available to some extent. Nīla's son was Suśānti.[28] His son was Purujānu[29] whose son is variously named in the Purāṇas: Ṛkṣa in Va, Pṛthu in Mt, Cakṣu in Vis and Arka in Bh.[30] But the AśvŚS (6, 12, 1)[31] names him Tṛkṣa. This is accepted as correct by S.N. Pradhan.[32] Similarly, Tṛkṣa's son is named variously in the Purāṇas: as Bhadrāśva in the Mt, Bhārmyaśva in Bh, Bāhyaśva in Br, Hv and Ag, Haryāśva in Vis; Va, however, omits him.[33] One of his sons, according to the Purāṇas,[34] was Mudgala who is called by a patronymic Bhārmyaśva in the Sarvā (2, 10, 102)[35] and is said to be an author of RV (10, 102). Thus the correct name of Tṛkṣa's son appears to be Bhṛmyaśva that gives a derivative-patronymic Bhārmyaśva ('the son or descendant of Bhṛmyaśva), an appellative of Mudgala.[36] This Bhṛmyaśva fathered five sons: Mudgala, Sṛñjaya, Bṛhadiṣu, Yavīyāna and Kāṁpilya. And the Purāṇas state that, as all these five sons were equally capable of protecting themselves, the father (Bhṛmyaśva) called them Pāñcālas wherefore the country ruled by them was named Pāñcāla.[37]

Among these five, Mudgala is twice mentioned in the RV (10, 102, 5; 9) and his wife Mudgalānī Indrasenā in RV (10, 102 and 6) as only Mudgalānī ('wife of Mudgala'). In the MBh (3, 113, 24)[38] her name is given as Indrasenā Nāḍāyaṇī. According to Pradhan, Naḍāyaṇī is a patronymic meaning 'the daughter of Nala'[39] and thus Indrasenā was the daughter of Nala and Damayantī of the Niṣadha country. The Purāṇas further inform that Mudgala's progeny were Maudgalyas also known as *kṣatropeta dvijātayaḥ* (the twice-born or *brāhmaṇas* born of the kṣatriya); they were called (*Kevala*) Aṅgirases.[40] The son of Mudgala and Indrasenā is variously named in the Purāṇas: Badhyaśva in the Va (99, 199-200)[41], Vindhyaśva in the Mt (50, 6)[42], Vadhryaśva in the Vis (4, 19, 16)[43]. One Vadhryaśva is mentioned in RV (6, 61, 1): he received Divodāsa from the goddess Sarasvatī.[44] Again according to the Purāṇas Vadhryaśva's wife gave birth to twins Divodāsa and Ahalyā.[45] Thus the identification of Mudgala's son Vadhryaśva is established (in RV) as a king in the line of the North Pāñcāla dynasty. Vadhryaśva's *fire* is mentioned in RV (10, 69, 1; 2; 4-5; 9; 11-12). His name is read, however, in the *Pravara* list of the Bhṛgus; this confirms some relationship between the Aṅgirases and the Bhṛgus.[46] His son Divodāsa is more frequently referred to in the Ṛgvedic hymns[47] as the most famous patron of the Bharadvājas. Divodāsa, a scion of the North Pāñcāla dynasty, happened to be a remote descendant of Vidathin Bhāradvāja, allegedly adopted by Bharata Dauṣyanti. Also Divodāsa,[48] Pijavana,[49] Sudās,[50] Sṛñjaya's descendant,[51] Prastoka,[52] Cāyamāna Abhyāvartin,[53] Sahadeva,[54] and his son Somaka[55] are mentioned in the RV. Among them the Sṛñjayas and Cāyamāna are closely connected with the Bharadvājas, while Sudās with Vasiṣṭhas and Viśvāmitras and Sahadeva Somaka with Vāmadevas. After Somaka a gap might have remained until Pṛṣata's rise. Pṛṣata was a contemporary of Bhīṣma; his son Drupada had developed a rivalry with Droṇa, the preceptor of the Kuru-Pāṇḍava princes.[56] Later on, owing to matrimonial relations the Pāñcālas under the leadership of Drupada and his able sons helped the Pāṇḍavas to win the Kurukṣetra war. The destruction of the Pāñcālas in the war appears to have been total.

Another wife of Ajamīḍha was Dhūminī by name. To her was born Bṛhadvasu.[57] He founded a very long dynasty of kings right up to Janamejaya. As one of his descendants was called Nīpa, this line was also known as the Nīpas who met their destruction at the hand of Ugrāyudha of the Solar race (*Sūryavaṁśa*).[58]

Dhūminī had another son Ṛkṣa[59] from whom originated very illustrious kings later known as Kurus. Kuru was the grandson of Ṛkṣa.[60] Kuru's line was again bifurcated into two—the main offspring ruled in Hastināpura, and its branch in Magadha.[61] In the principal line were born Śāntanu and his brother Devāpi.[62] Devāpi was probably Ārṣṭisena, 'a descendant of Ṛṣṭisena' who happened to be his ancestor. Devāpi Ārṣṭisena is said to be the composer of RV (10, 98).[63] Devāpi is mentioned in RV (10, 98, 2; 4-8) and Śāntanu in RV (10, 98, 3 and 7). Śāntanu's sons were Devavrata Bhīṣma, Vicitravīrya and Citrāṅgada.[64] Vicitravīrya's sons were Dhṛtarāṣṭra and Pāṇḍu who gave rise to the lines of Kauravas and Pāṇḍavas respectively and these Kauravas and Pāṇḍavas were locked in the great fratricidal Kurukṣetra war.[65] Incidentally, it may be mentioned that the Sṛñjayas, the Somakas and the Pāñcālas who participated in that war as Pāṇḍavas' allies were scions of the great Bharatas. This line of the Pāṇḍavas continued to rule in Hastināpura even after the great war.[66]

Another wife of Ajamīḍha, Keśinī, gave birth to Kaṇva whose son is Medhātithi; from this Medhātithi were born the Kāṇvāyana brāhmaṇas.[67] They form an important class within the larger stock of the Aṅgirases. One version is that Kaṇva was son of Apratiratha, one of the sons of king Matināra;[68] yet another that he was a son of Ajamīḍha, a remote descendant of Matināra 32 generations below the latter.[69] A *gotra* called Kāṇvas is traced among the Vasiṣṭhas.[70] But this does not explain why the Kāṇvas were prominently mentioned among the Aṅgirases.

The existence of the Kāṇvas was not noticed prior to Ajamīḍha. A Kaṇva is said to have adopted Śakuntalā who was married by Duṣyanta. He is said to be a Kāśyapa and Kaṇva was his personal name only. He did not marry and hence a celibate could not give rise to the Kāṇvas. This Kaṇva is anterior to Ajamīḍha. All other Kāṇvas are found to be posterior to Ajamīḍha. There were several Kāṇvas, who were also called Aṅgirases. Many of them composed some Ṛgvedic hymns. Medhātithi Kāṇva is given as the seer of the RV (1, 12-23; 8, 1, 3-39; 2, 32 and 9, 2).[71] So also is one Medhātithi[72] of several hymns in 8th and 9th Maṇḍalas.[73] Āyu Kāṇva is author of RV (8, 52);[74] Kuruśruti Kāṇva that of the RV (8, 76-78);[75] Kusīda Kāṇva is creator of RV (8, 81-83)[76]; Kṛśa Kāṇva of RV (8, 55);[77] Triśoka Kāṇva of RV (8, 45);[78] Devātithi Kāṇva of RV (8, 4-21);[79] Nābhāka Kāṇva of RV (8, 39-42);[80] Nārada Kāṇva of RV (8, 13; and 9, 104-10);[81] Nīpātithi Kāṇva of RV (8, 34, 1-15);[82] and Parvata Kāṇva of RV (8, 12; 10, 104-105)[83]—to mention a few Kāṇva seers named in the Sarvā. A few Kāṇvāyanas (young or junior Kāṇvas) are also referred to, e.g. Aśvasūkti and Gosūkti. They are joint seers of RV (8, 14-15).[84] Pargiter[85] has tried to establish that some of them were living at the same time as other persons: Pragātha Kāṇva (author of RV 8, 1-2; 10; 48; 62-65) was a contemporary of Durgaha's grandsons (RV 8, 65, 12); Pṛṣadhra of Dasyavevṛka (RV 8, 65, 1-2), and so on. Beside these Devātithi, Vatsa, Sadhvaṁśa, Medhātithi—"all are later than Ajamīḍha."[86]

Thus it is clear that the Kāṇvas descended from Ajamīḍha (whose ancestor was Bharata's adopted son Vidathin Bhāradvāja) and related to the Bharadvājas and Aṅgirases. It also points to "the fact that just before and just after Ajamīḍha the Paurava line spread branches who later became brāhamaṇas."[87] The Kāṇvas probably belonged to the age of the North Pāñcāla dynasty.[88]

Now we may conclude that Ajamīḍha was really a distant descendant of Bharadvāja. He and his brother Purumīḍha were also seers. He fathered a number of important families of sages: Kāṇvas, Mudgalas, Mitrayus, etc. His descendants also ruled in several Janapadas, e.g. Hastināpura and North and South Pāñcālas; they were known as the Kuru-Pāñcālas for several centuries until the fatal conflict in the Kurukṣetra war. They played vital role in various fields of Indian culture as princes and seers. The above findings may lead one to fix a tentative chronology of the hymns of the Bharadvājas and others: (the Gṛtsamadas, the Kāṇvas and the Aṅgirases) composers of different Maṇḍalas in the RV. The hymns included in the 6th Maṇḍala were probably older than those by the Gṛtsamadas.[89] The hymns revealed to the Aṅgirases and the Kāṇvas included in the first, eighth, ninth and tenth Maṇḍalas may be considered of a later date.

(*viii*) *Purumīḍha*

It was earlier said that Purumīḍha composed conjointly with Ajamīḍha the two hymns 4, 43-44 of the RV.[1] Besides, one Purumīḍha is said to be a joint seer of RV 8, 71 with Suditi.[2] Probably, this second Purumīḍha is different from the first. We have already noticed that Purumīḍha and Ajamīḍha were two brothers and the sons of Hastin, the son of Suhotra Bhāradvāja. The Vedic and the Epic sources inform that he had another brother Sumīḍha (RV 6, 63, 9 and MBh 1, 89, 26); while the Purāṇas add Dvijamīḍha or Dvimīḍha as his third brother. Among the Purāṇas Mt, Bh, Br, Hv and Ag name him Dvimīḍha while Va and Vis name him Dvijamīḍha.[3] Ajamīḍha secured the kingdom of Hastināpura.

Dvimīḍha probably ruled in the South Pāñcāla, but it is not clear where Sumīḍha ruled. That he was a king and patronised the Bharadvājas is clear (RV 6, 63, 9). There is, however, no clue as to whether Purumīḍha was also a king. Pargiter, in a footnote at page 316 of his work AIHT,[4] says, "Rigv. iv, 43 and 44 are attributed to Purumīḍha and Ajamīḍha, Sauhotras, who were no doubt king Ajamīḍha and his brother Purumīḍha". But, he, too, could not say whether Purumīḍha was a king. Bh (9, 21, 20) says: *Purumīḍho' prajo'bhavat* ("Purumīḍha was issueless"). That is why his progeny is not mentioned anywhere, while that of Ajamīḍha (Ājamīḍha) is in a hymn (RV 4, 44, 6) composed by Ajamīḍha and Purumīḍha.

Probably, Purumīḍha remained a celibate because of his indifference to the world; he became famous as a seer even in the Ṛgvedic age. Thus among all the brothers he figures mostly in Vedic literature. His name occurs four times in the RV.[5] There is, of course, difference of opinion in accepting Purumīḍha mentioned in RV 1, 151, 2; 183, 5 and 8, 71, 14 as one and the same person. But "Purumīḍha" (RV 5, 61, 9) is a person different from the one referred to in other passages. In RV (1, 151, 2)[6] a descendant of Dīrghatamas (*Dairghatamasa*) talks of Purumīḍha as a *Somin* 'a soma offerer'. A poet belonging to the family of Agastya says (RV 1, 183, 5)[7] that Gotama, Purumīḍha and Atri invoked the Aśvins for protection. RV (8, 71, 14)[8] asks Purumīḍha to worship Agni with the *gāthās* for protection of Suditi. Incidentally it may be pointed out that one Suditi and a Purumīḍha are said to be joint authors of the hymn RV 8, 71. From these it appears that this Purumīḍha was definitely a worshipper of Agni and the Aśvins and a singer-poet as well.

Purumīḍha is called a *vipra* 'wise' and a *dīrghayaśas* 'one of lofty fame' (RV 5, 61, 9).[9] As regards this Purumīḍha, the BD (5, 49ff)[10] narrates a legend of Śyāvāśva's attaining the seer-hood and marrying the daughter of Rathavīti Dārbhya: Śyāvāśva went to Taranta and Purumīḍha, the princes and sons of Vidadāśva, who gave several gifts to Śyāvāśva. JB (1, 161)[11] also says that Taranta and Purumīḍha were two sons of Vitadāśva (identical with Vidadāśva in BD 5, 62). It also connects Purumīḍha of RV 8, 71, 14 with Purumīḍha 'Vaitadāśva'. As suoh, it is difficult to identify Purumīḍha Sauhotra (the son of Suhotra) with Purumīḍha Vaidadāśva.

Purumīḍha is grouped with Śyāvāśva, Vadhryaśva, Atri, Vimada and Saptavadhrī (AVŚ 4, 29, 4)[12] as being the proteges of Mitra and Varuṇa. Again, an Atharvan poet prays for extending his protection to Purumīḍha together with Kāṇva, Kakṣīvat, Agastya, Śyāvāśva, Saubhari, Arcanānas, Viśvāmitra, Jamadagni, Atri, Kaśyapa and Vāmadeva (AVŚ 18, 3, 15).[13] Though these references do not indicate his contemporaneity with any of these seers, yet they show the eminence he attained as a seer: he was one of a few to be reckoned. However, one may infer that Purumīḍha who gave presents to Śyāvāśva, was son of Vidadāśva. He must be different from Ajamīḍha's brother Purumīḍha. And Purumīḍha mentioned in RV 5, 61, 9 and 8, 71, 14, AVŚ 4, 29, 4 and 18, 3, 15 may be Vidadāśva's son. We attach significance to Śyāvāśva and Arcanānas being named along with Purumīḍha; this leads one to differentiate Purumīḍha Vidadāśva from Purumīḍha Sauhotra, to whom the RV refers in other passages.

(*ix*) *Vasu Bhāradvāja*

The Sarvā (2, 9, 80[1]) ascribes three hymns of the RV (9, 80-82) to Vasu Bhāradvāja. All these are addressed to Soma Pavamāna. Vasu is also said to be the seer of SV (1, 562).[2] The other two Vedas (AV and YV) do not contain any verse by him. He is called a Bharadvāja, the 'son' or 'descendant' of Bharadvāja. But traditional sources do not yield any evidence as regards a Vasu being a son or a descendant of Bharadvāja.

(*x*) *Śirimbiṭha Bhāradvāja*

According to the Sarvā (2, 10, 155) one Śirimbiṭha Bhāradvāja is the seer of RV (10, 155).[1] He is also said to be the seer of AV (20, 137,1)[2] and VS (36, 18).[3]

Śirimbiṭha occurs in the first stanza of the hymn RV 10, 155.[4] Yāska in his Nir (6, 30)[5] interprets the word to mean 'cloud which is shattered in atmosphere.' He suggests that it is 'a name of a seer, viz. Bhāradvāja, who endowed with black ears destroyed evil fortunes.'[6]

The commentators[7] follow the interpretation offered by Yāska and offer the same meaning. Sāyaṇa[8] specifically calls him a son of Bharadvāja. The lexicographers[9] also accept it as the name of a person. In this context, Macdonell and Keith[10] say that "name of a man may possibly be meant". There is not, therefore, sufficient ground to dispute this; hence we concede that Śiriṁbiṭha Bhāradvāja was the seer of these Vedic hymns. However, his name does not occur in any list of *gotras*, *pravaras*, or in the genealogy of the Sūtras and Epico-Purāṇic sources.

(*xi*) *Śāsa Bhāradvāja*

The Sarvā (2, 10, 152)[1] ascribes a verse in RV (10, 152) to the seer Śāsa Bhāradvāja. He is also said to be the composer of hymns in SV (2, 1215)[2] and VS (9, 44-46; 18, 70).[3] But none in the AV is credited to him.

The word *śāsa* occurs in the initial verse of a hymn (RV 10, 152).[4] The commentator Veṅkaṭa Mādhava[5] takes it in the sense of 'ruler', 'commander' (*śāsitṛ*). And Sāyaṇa[6] takes it in the sense of a name of a person.[7] The authors of VI[8] say that the word *Śāsa* means a 'sword' or 'knife' which is used to slay a victim. However, the meaning given by Veṅkaṭa Mādhava appears correct; and, in all probability there was a descendant of Bharadvāja by that name. But his name is not found in the list of *gotras* and *pravaras* in any work of the *Sūtra* literature and in genealogy furnished in the Purāṇas.

(*xii*) *Sapratha Bhāradvāja*

The Sarvā (2, 10, 181)[1] ascribes a hymn (RV 10, 181-2) to Sapratha Bhāradvāja. It consists of only three verses: the first and the third are composed by one Pratha, a 'descendant' of Vasiṣṭha, and a Gharma, the 'son' of Sūrya, respectively.[2]

The words *pratha* and *sapratha* occur in the first stanza[3] and the word *gharma* in the third.[4] As regards the significance of *sapratha* and *pratha*, Griffith[5] says in a note under his translation of the verse that the meanings of these words are 'far extending' and 'extending' respectively. The former refers to the Rathantara Sāman while the latter to the Bṛhat Sāman. According to him, *Gharma* in the third verse means 'warm oblation of milk'. Although the meaning of the verse is not clear, *prathas* and *saprathas* appear to imply oblations and may not signify any person. So also *Gharma*. But tradition holds with the Sarvā (2, 10, 181) that Sapratha is a seer and he belonged to the family of Bharadvāja and Pratha is another seer belonging to the family of Vasiṣṭha. In spite of the etymological meaning of the two words having not been favourable to the Sarvā's ascription of verses to the seers called Pratha and Sapratha, we need not throw off Sapratha Bhāradvāja as the seer of the RV 10, 181, 2. It is also not impossible that a sage of his name may have played a pun in the word in the verse, which is not rare in our literature. So also regarding the other two.[6]

The first two verses of the hymn give us important information that Vasiṣṭha brought the Rathantara from Dhātṛ, Savitṛ and Viṣṇu,[7] while Bharadvāja brought Bṛhat from Dhātṛ, Savitṛ, Viṣṇu and Agni.[8] Further, Vasiṣṭha and Bharadvāja envisioned the earliest *Yajus* that formed a pathway to gods and they also brought *Gharma* from Dhātṛ, Savitṛ, Viṣṇu and the Sun (Sūrya) (v.3).[9] Of prime importance from ritualistic point of view, the hymn traces the growth of Vedic rituals.

(*xiii*) *Rātrī Bhāradvājī*

Rātrī Bhāradvājī composed a hymn (RV 10, 127)[1] jointly with one Kuśika, the son of Sobhari. Incidentally, Rātrī is also the deity of the hymn. That is why, Rahurkar,[2] pointing out some of the female seers observes: "Some of them are merely natural phenomena, etc., personified, such as Rātrī, singing a hymn of poetic beauty to herself (10, 127), Sūryā (10, 85), Śraddhā (10, 151), Dakṣiṇā (10, 107), etc., all singing hymns to themselves." But Rahurkar avoids discussing why the patronymic Bhāradvājī was attached to 'a natural phenomenon' and not elsewhere. The ancient Indian traditional sources do not have more information about Rātrī Bhāradvājī, but merely mention the hymn (RV 10, 127) as revealed to her.

However, we may here draw attention to another similar instance: one Kaśipā Bhāradvājī is also stated to be the Ṛṣikā 'female seer' of a verse in the VS (34, 32).[3] She is the 'daughter' of Bharadvāja (*bharadvājaduhitā*); her verse, too, is addressed to Rātrī. We see no ground for doubting the statement of VāŚ[4] as regards the identity of the female seer who was probably a female scion of the Bharadvāja family and her personal name was Kaśipā. These circumstances would tempt one to identify Rātrī Bhāradvājī with

Kaśipā Bhāradvājī, but in the absence of any other evidence we refrain from this conclusion. Also we do not reject Rātrī's claim to the authorship of the hymn (RV 10, 127). And since she is called by a patronymic Bhāradvājī, that would give her a place among the seers belonging to the Bharadvāja family.

Notes and References to Chapter III

Section (i)

1. Read: 'अभूरेक' इति पञ्चर्चमष्टमं सूक्तं भरद्वाजस्य सुहोत्रस्य आर्षम् ।
2. SV 1, 322.
3. Vas 3, 213; 239; 253; 4, 15.
4. For details see Ch. 2, Section (iii) on Vidathin Bharadvāja.
5. Read: त्वं कुत्सेनाभि शुष्णमिन्द्राऽशुषं युध्य कुयवं गविष्ठौ ।
   दश प्रपित्वे अध सूर्यस्य मुषायश्चक्रमविवे रपांसि ॥
6. Velankar, BUJ. 11(2) p. 56.
7. RV 6, 18, 13; 20, 5; 31, 3.
8. Read: त्वं शतान्यव शम्बरस्य पुरो जघन्थाप्रतीनि दस्योः
   अशिक्षो यत्र शच्या शचीवो दिवोदासाय सुन्वते सुतक्रे भरद्वाजाय गृणते वसूनि ॥
9. Velankar, BUJ 11(2) p. 56.
10. Va 91, 51-52:

    तस्य पुत्रा बभूवुर्हि षडिन्द्रोपमतेजसः ।
    गन्धर्वलोके विदिता आयुर्धीमानमावसुः ॥
    विश्वायुश्च शतायुश्च गतायुश्चोर्वशीसुताः ।

MBh 1, 10, 22 reads last line: दृढायुश्च वनायुश्च श्रुतायुश्चोर्वशीसुताः which replaces Viśvāyu, Śatāyu and Gatāyu.

11. Va 91, 52-53:

    अमावसोस्तुवै जातो भीमो राजाथ विश्वजित् ॥
    श्रीमान् भीमस्य दायादो राजाऽऽसीत् काञ्चनप्रभः ।
    विद्वांस्तु काञ्चनस्याऽपि सुहोत्रोऽभून्महाबलः ॥

12. See the genealogical tree given at the end of this section.
13. Va 91, 54; 58:

    सुहोत्रस्याभवज्जह्नुः कौशिकागर्भसंभवः ।
    प्रज्यागत्य ततो गङ्गां वितते यज्ञकर्मणि ॥ ५४ ॥
    x x x x x
    उपनिन्युर्महाभागा दुहितृत्वेन जाह्नवीम् ॥ ५८ ॥

14. Pargiter, AIHT, p. 114: (he has shown Kāñcana and Suhotra I as the contemporaries of Svāhi and Citraratha respectively of Āyus descendants.)
15. MBH 1, 89, 17-26; 90, 34-36.

16. Read particularly vv. 21-22:

सुहोत्रश्च सुहोता च सुहविः सुयजुस्तथा ।
पुष्करिण्यामृचीकस्य भुमन्योरभवन् सुताः ॥
तेषां ज्येष्ठः सुहोत्रस्तु राज्यमाप महीक्षिताम् ।
राजसूयाश्वमेधाद्यैः सोऽयजद्बहुभिः सवैः ॥

17. MBh 1, 89, 26:

ऐक्ष्वाकी जनयामास सुहोत्रात् पृथिवीपतेः ।
अजमीढं सुमीढं च पुरुमीढं च भारत ॥

18. Read the relevant passage at 1, 90, 35-36:

भुमन्युः खलु दाशार्हीमुपयेमे जयां नाम ।
तस्यामस्य जज्ञे सुहोत्रः ॥ ३५
सुहोत्रः खल्विक्ष्वाकुकन्यामुपयेमे सुवर्णां नाम ।
तस्यामस्य जज्ञ हस्ती । य इदं हास्तिनपुरं
मापयामास । एतदस्य हास्तिनपुरत्वम् ॥36

19. MBh 1, 89, 22-25.
20. MBh 12, 29, 22-26; Droṇaparvan, Appendix 1, No. 8, vv. 360-84.
21. Read: तेषां ज्येष्ठः सुहोत्रस्तु राज्यमाप महीक्षिताम् ॥
22. Appendix 1, No. 8, *vv.* 361*ft.*

यः प्राप्य राज्यं धर्मेण ऋत्विग्ब्रह्मपुरोहितान् ।
अपृच्छदात्मनः श्रेयः पृष्ट्वा तेषां मते स्थितः ।
प्रजानां पालनं धर्मो दानमिज्या द्विषज्जयः ।
एतान् सुहोत्रो विज्ञाय धर्मेणैच्छद्धनागमम् ।365
धर्मेणाराध्य यद्देवान् बाणैः शत्रूञ्जयंस्तथा ।
सर्वाण्यपि च भूतानि स्वगुणैरप्यरञ्जयत् ।
योऽभुङ्क्तेमां वसुमतीं म्लेच्छाटविविवर्जिताम् ।

23. MBh 1, 89, 23-24:

सुहोत्रः पृथिवीं सर्वां बुभुजे सागराम्बराम् ।
पूर्णां हस्तिगवाश्वस्य बहुरत्नसमाकुलाम् ॥
ममज्जेव मही तस्य भूरिभारावपीडिता ।
हस्त्यश्वरथसंपूर्णा मनुष्यकलिला भृशम् ॥

24. Read: सुहोत्रं चेद् वैतिथिनं मृतं सृञ्जय शुश्रुम ।
यस्मै हिरण्यं ववृषे मघवा परिवत्सरम् ॥
सत्यनामा वसुमती यं प्राप्यासीज्जनाधिप ।
हिरण्यमवहन्नद्यस्तस्मिञ्जनपदेश्वरे ॥
कुर्मान् कर्कटकान्नक्रान् मकरान् शिशुकानपि ।
नदीष्वपातयन् राजन् मघवा लोकपूजितः ॥
हैरण्यान् पतितान् दृष्ट्वा मत्स्यान् मकरान् कच्छपान् ॥
सहस्रशोऽथ शतशस्ततोऽस्मयन् वैतिथिः ॥
तद्धिरण्यमपर्याप्तमावृतं कुरुजाङ्गले ।
इजानो वितते यज्ञे ब्राह्मणेभ्यः समाहितः ॥

cf. Droṇaparvan, Appendix 1, No. 8, vv. 369-ff.

यस्मै ववर्ष पर्जन्यो हिरण्यं परिवत्सरम् ।
हिरण्योदास्तथा नद्यः सुहोत्रस्य महात्मनः ।370
यस्मिन् कूर्मान् कर्कटकान् मत्स्यांश्च विविधान् बहून् ।
कामान् वर्षति पर्जन्यो रूपाणि विविधानि च ।
सौवर्णान्यप्रमेयानि वाप्यश्च क्रोशसंमिताः ।
स तत्र शतसाहस्रान्नक्रान् मकरकच्छपान् ।
सौवर्णान् पतितान् दृष्ट्वा ततोऽस्मयत वैऽतिथिः ।375
तत् सुवर्णमपर्यन्तं राजर्षिः कुरुजाङ्गले ।
ईजानो वितते यज्ञे ब्राह्मणेभ्यो ह्यमन्यत ।
सोऽश्वमेधसहस्रेण राजसूयशतेन च ।
पुण्यैः क्षत्रिययज्ञैश्च प्रभूतवरदक्षिणैः ।
काम्यनैमित्तिकाजस्रैरिष्टां गतिमवाप्तवान् ।

25. MBh 1, 89, 25:

सुहोत्रे राजनि तदा धर्मतः शासति प्रजाः ।
चैत्ययूपाङ्किता चासीद् भूमिः शतसहस्रशः ।
प्रवृद्धजनसस्या च सहदेवा व्यरोचत ॥

26. Read: MBh 12, 29, 23 only above.

27. Va 99, 158:

वितथस्य तु दायादो भुवमन्युर्बभूव ह ॥

cf. Mt 49, 35; Vis 4, 19, 8.

28. Read: वितथस्य सूतो मन्युः . . . . ॥

29. Va 99, 159

महाभूतोपमाश्चाऽस चत्वारो भुवमन्युजाः ।
बृहत्क्षत्रो महावीर्यः नरो गर्गश्च वीर्यवान् ॥

cf. Mt 49, 35-36:

महाभूतोपमाः पुत्राश्चत्वारो भुवमन्यवः ॥
बृहत्क्षत्रो महावीर्यः नरो गर्गश्च वीर्यवान् ।

30. Read: बृहत्क्षत्रमहावीर्यनरगर्गाद्या भुवमन्युपुत्राः ।

31. Read: वितथस्य सुतो मन्युर्बृहत्क्षत्रो जयस्ततः ।
महावीर्यो नरो गर्गः संकृतिस्तु नरात्मजः ॥

32. Br 13, 62-63:

स चापि वितथः पुत्रान् जनयामास पञ्च वै ।
सुहोत्रं च सुहोतारं गयं गर्गं तथैव च ॥

cf. Hv 1, 23, 53-54; Ag 278, 9-10.

33. Read: बृहत्क्षत्रस्य दायादः सुहोत्रो नाम धार्मिकः ।
सुहोत्रस्याऽपि दायादो हस्ती नाम बभूव ह ॥

cf. Vis 4, 19, 10:

बृहत्क्षत्रस्य सुहोत्रः, सुहोत्राद्धस्तिनरो. . . . . ।

34. Read: सुहोत्रस्य बृहत् पुत्रो बृहतस्तनयास्त्रयः।
अजमीढो द्विमीढश्च पुरुमीढश्च वीर्यवान् ॥

34*a*. Read: ऐक्ष्वाकी जनयामास सुहोत्रात् पृथिवीपतेः।
अजमीढं सुमीढं च पुरुमीढं च भारत ॥

35. Read: सुहोत्रः खल्विक्ष्वाकुकन्यामुपयेमे सुवर्णां नाम।
तस्याम् जज्ञे हस्ती ॥

35*a*. For details see ch. 2, Section (iii) and Ch. 3, Section (v) on Vidathin Bharadvāja and Ṛjiśvan respectively.

36. For detailed information on Nara and Garga see the two sections (iii) and (iv) below of this chapter.

37. MBh 1, 69, 50:

भरतस्यान्ववाये हि देवकल्पा महौजसः।
बभूवुर्ब्रह्मकल्पाश्च बहवो राजसत्तमाः ॥

cf. Bh 9, 20, 1:

पुरुवंशं प्रवक्ष्यामि यत्र जातोऽसि भारत।
यत्र राजर्षयो वंश्या ब्रह्मवंश्याश्च जज्ञिरे ॥

38. Va 99 218. सुधन्वनस्तु दायादः सुहोत्रो महिमान् स्मृतः।

39. Va 99, 219. च्यवनस्तस्य पुत्रस्तु राजा धर्मार्थकोविदः।

cf. Vis 4, 19, 19:

सुधनुषः सुहोत्रस्तस्मात् च्यवनश्चवनात् कृतक. . . ॥

40. Va 99, 248:

सुहोत्रं विजया माद्री सहदेवादजायत।

cf. Mt 50, 55:

सुहोत्रं तनयं माद्री सहदेवादजायत।

Vis 4, 20, 11: सहदेवाद् विजया सुहोत्रं नाम पुत्रं प्राप्तवती।

41. Va 99, 244: अश्विभ्यां सहदेवश्च नकुलश्च माद्रिजौ।

cf. Mt 50, 50: नकुलं सहदेवं च माद्र्यश्विभ्यामजीजनत्।

42. MBh 1, 90, 87:

सहदेवोऽपि माद्रीमेव स्वयंवरे विजयां नामोपयेमे।
तस्यां पुत्रमजनयत् सुहोत्रं नाम।

43. MBh 12, 220, 50.

Section (ii)

1. Read: 'य ओजिष्ठ' शुनहोत्रस्तु।'

2. Macdonell and Keith, VI, 2, 386.

3. Sarvā 2, 2, 1.

4. Ed. by R.L. Mitra, published with the Bṛhaddevatā in *Bibliotheca Indica*, Calcutta, 1892; at page 245, it reads:

ऋषिर्गृत्समदो नाम विज्ञेयः स य शौनकः।
औरसः शुनहोत्रस्य शुनकस्य तु कृत्रिमः ॥
तस्मादाङ्गिरसः पूर्वं पश्चात् स भृगुतां गतः।

5. On the basis of all these occurrences in the 2nd Maṇḍala, once, Weber in a paper entitled "Double authorship of the Second Mandala" (published in Sitzungsherischte der Preussischen Akademie der Wissenschaften, Berlin, 1900) is reported to have argued that the 2nd Maṇḍala can be divided into two Maṇḍalas, viz. Śunahotra Maṇḍala and Gṛtsamada Maṇḍala. However, V.G. Rahukar in his '*The Seers of the Ṛgveda*' has made certain observations and refuted the contention of Weber. However, we abstain from entering into this discussion as the paper by Weber could not be procured for our detailed study. We only make a mention of it and hope to express our opinion in future, when the said paper will be available to us.

6. Read: RV 2, 41, 18:

इमा ब्रह्म सरस्वति जुषस्वे वाजिनीवति ।
या ते मन्म गृत्समदा ऋतावरि प्रिया देवेषु जुह्वति ॥

RV 2, 41, 14: तीव्रो वो मधुमाँ अयं शुनहोत्रेषु मत्सरः ।
एतं पिबतं काम्यम् ।

RV 2, 41, 17: त्वे विश्वा सरस्वति श्रितायूंषि देव्याम् ।
शुनहोत्रेषु मत्स्व प्रजां देवि दिदिड्ढि नः ॥

7. Read: शुनकानां गृत्समदेति त्रिप्रवरं वा भार्गव शौनहोत्र गार्त्समदेति ।

8. Read: ब्रह्म वाग् ब्रह्म सत्यं च ब्रह्म सर्वमिदं जगत् ।
पातारं ब्रह्मणस्तेन शौनहोत्र स्तुवञ्जगौ ॥ 2; 40॥
गृणन्मादयसे यस्मात् त्वमस्मानृषिसत्तम ।
तस्माद् गृत्समदो नाम शौनहोत्रो भविष्यति ॥ 4, 78॥

9. Read: य आङ्गिरसः शौनहोत्रो भूत्वा भार्गवः शौनकोऽ
भवत् स गृत्समदो द्वितीयं मण्डलमपश्यत् ।

10. Read the passage at note 4 above.

11. See Ch. 2, Section (iv) on Bharadvāja, Divodāsa and Vītahavya in the MBh for details.

12. AśvŚSP 6, 10, 10: यस्कादीनां भार्गव-वैतहव्य सावेतसेति ।
cf. ĀpŚSP 2, 3.

13. MBh 12, 30.

14. Va 92, 2-4: Bd 3, 67, 2-4; Br 11, 31-33.

15. AśvŚSP 6, 10, 10; 13; ĀpŚS 2, 3; 4.

16. For detailed discussion the Sarvā 2, 6, 52. See Ch. 2 Section (iii) on Vidathin Bharadvāja and Ch. 3, Sec. (i) on Suhotra Bhāradvāja.

17. Ibid; and read also: BD 5.102:

योऽङ्गारेभ्य ऋषिर्जज्ञे तस्य पुत्रो बृहस्पतिः ।
बृहस्पतेर्भरद्वाजो विदथीति य उच्यते ॥

18. For details see our sections on persons referred to by Bharadvāja in RV and Nara Bhāradvāja Ch. 3, Sec. (iii).

19. The Mitrayus, the remote descendents of Ajamīḍha, adopted the Bhārgava *gotra*. Cf. our ch. 3, Section (vii) on Ajamīḍha for further information.

Section (iii)

1. Read: 'कदा' नरस्तु ।'
2. Sarvā 2, 6, 52. सुहोत्रादयोऽनुक्तगोत्रा भारद्वाजाः पौत्रा बृहस्पतेर्दौःषन्तेर्वा भरतस्य ।
3. Va 99, 159-60; Mt 49, 36-37; Vis 4, 19, 9; Bh 9, 21, 1; Ga 1, 140, 6.
4. Read: स गोमघा जरित्रे अश्वश्चन्द्राः
वाजश्रवसो अधि धेहि पृक्षः ।
पीपिहीषः सुदुघामिन्द्र धेनुं
भरद्वाजषु सुरुचो रुरुच्याः ॥
5. Velankar, BUJ 11(2) p. 59.
6. Read: तमा नूनं वृजनमन्यथा चिच्छूरो यच्छक्र विदूरो गृणीषे ।
मा निररं शुक्रदुघस्य धेनोराङ्गिरसान् ब्रह्मणा विप्र जिन्व ॥
7. Velankar, BUJ 11(2) p. 59.
8. Ibid.
9. The same has been fully noticed in the section on Bharadvāja (Vidathin)'s adoption and Suhotra Bhāradvāja.
10. This was also discussed earlier. Vide Ch. 2, Section (iii) on Vidathin Bharadvāja's adoption. Read the passage under note No. 3, Section (i) of Chapter 3.
11. See for details Section on Suhotra Bhāradvāja (Ch. 3, Section (i)).
12. Mt 49, 36:

बृहत्क्षत्रो महावीर्यः नरो गर्गश्च वीर्यवान् ।
नरस्य संकृतिः पुत्रस्तस्य पुत्रो महायशाः ॥

cf. Va 99, 59-60, Vis 4, 19, 9.

13. Mt 49, 37: गुरुधी-रन्तिदेवश्च संकृत्यान्तावुभौ स्मृतौ ।
14. Bh 9, 21, 2-18; MBh 12, 29, 113-31.
15. MBh 12, 29, 116:

महानदी चर्मराशेरुत्क्लेदात् सुस्रुवे यतः ।
ततश्चर्मण्वतीत्येवं विख्याता सा महानदी ॥

cf. Pad 1, 24, 3.

16. Mt 49, 37: Read at 13 above.

Va 99, 159: गुरुवीर्यस्त्रिदेवश्च सांकृत्याववरौ स्मृतौ ।
Vis 4, 19, 9: संकृतेरुचिरधीरन्तिदेवौ ।

17. Read: गुरुवीतश्च मान्धाता अम्बरीषस्तथैव च ।
युवनाश्वः पुरुकुत्सः
18. Read: He is named as one of the three *ṛṣi pravaras:*
अङ्गिराः संकृतिश्चैव गौरवीतिस्तथैव च ।
19. Read: त्र्ययंमा पञ्चोना गौरिवीतिः
शाक्त्य ऐन्द्रमुशना यदौशनसो वा पादः ।
20. Read: जनिष्ठा एकादश गौरिवीतिः ।
21. Mt 195, 32: कपीतरः स्वस्तितरो दाक्षिः शक्तिः पतञ्जलिः ।

22. Read: संकृतयो लमकाः पौत्यस्तण्डिः शम्भुः शवगवः परिभवस्तारकाद्या हारिग्रीवा वैतलेयाः श्रौतायनाश्चारायणा श्राग्रायणा श्रार्षयश्चान्द्रयणा श्रापघ्रापयः पूतिमाषा इत्येते संकृतयः। तेषां त्र्यार्षेयः प्रवरो भवति। श्राङ्गिरस सांकृत्य गौरिवीतेति होता। गौरिवीतवत् संकृतिवदङ्गिरोवदित्यध्वर्युः ॥

23. Chentsalrao, ed. GPM p. 61.

24. BaudhŚSP. 23.

25. AśvŚS 6, 12, 5-6:

संकृतिपूतिमाषतण्डिशम्बुशैवगवानाङ्गिरसगौरिवीतसांकृत्येति ॥५॥
शाक्त्यो वा मूलं शाक्त्यगौरिवीत सांकृत्येति।

ApŚSP. 3, 12. श्रथ संकृतिपूतिमाषाणां त्र्यार्षेयशशक्त्यसांकृत्यगौरिवीतेति।

Actual name of Vasiṣṭha's son was Śaktri. He is often called so in the Purāṇas.

26. GPM p. 74: संकृत्यादीनामिहाङ्गिरसां गणेषूक्तानां उत्तरत्र श्रापस्तम्बादिभिः वसिष्ठगणान्ते वक्ष्यमाणत्वात् वासिष्ठस्यापि शक्तेरङ्गिरसां प्रवरेषूपदेशाच्च किं वासिष्ठास्संकृतयः। किं वाऽङ्गिरसः? इत्यत्रसंदेहेऽन्यतरपक्षनिश्चयहेतोरभावात्द्व्यामुष्यायणास्संकृतय इत्यवसातव्यम्, कात्यायनेनोत्तरत्र द्व्यामुष्याणागणमध्ये प्रसिद्धद्व्यामुष्यायणैः शुङ्गशैशिरिभिस्सह वक्ष्यमाणत्वात् ॥

27. Ibid. cf. also read Puruṣottama under Aśv ŚS 6, 12, 6.

Section (iv)

1. Read: स्वादुरेकत्रिंशद् गर्गः।
2. Velankar, JBBRAS, 42, pp. 8, 12.
3. See note 33 below.
4. Read: श्रागस्त्यो यः काण्वः कुत्सप्रस्रवणा
विश्वरूपा गार्गा मुद्गला श्रयस्काः।(?)
शौनकाः संकृतयो ब्राह्मणा ये न
द्रग्धास् तेभ्यः प्रब्रूम इह किल्विषाणि ॥
5. Mt 49, 38: स्मृताः शैव्यास्ततो गर्गाः क्षत्रोपेता द्विजातयः।

Mt 40, 5: मुद्गलस्यापि मौद्गल्याः क्षत्रोपेता द्विजातयः।

6. Read: दृप्तबालाकिर्हानूचानो गार्ग्यो श्रास स होवाचाजातशत्रुं
काश्यं ब्रह्म ते ब्रवाणीति स होवाचाजातशत्रुः सहस्रमेतस्यां
वाचि दद्मो जनको जनक इति वै जना धावन्तीति ॥

The discourse continues further.

7. It is also possible that she was daughter of one Vacaknu who belonged to the *gotra* of Garga.

8. Read: श्रथ हैनं गार्गी वाचक्नवी पप्रच्छ याज्ञवल्क्येति होवाच
यदिदं सर्वमप्स्वोतं च प्रोतं च कस्मिन्नु स्वल्वाप ओताश्च
प्रोताश्चेति वायौ गार्गीति कस्मिन्न्नु खलु वायुरोतश्च प्रोतश्चेति ॥

and so on.

9. At Śāṅkh GS 4, 10, 3, Gārgyas are mentioned twice and Gārgī once among hosts of other seers and sages. See ŚāṅkhGS, ed. Sehgal, p. 52.

10. Read: आग्निवेश्यादाग्निवेश्यो गार्ग्याद्गार्ग्यो गार्ग्याद् गार्ग्यो गोतमाद् गोतमः सैतवात् सैतवः पाराशर्यायणात् पाराशर्यायणो गार्ग्यायणात् गार्ग्यायण उद्दालकायनात् उद्दालकायनो जावालायनाज्जाबालायनो माध्यन्दिनायनान्माध्यन्दिनायनः . . कौशिकायनिः ।

11. Read: शुकेशा च भारद्वाजः शैव्यश्च सत्यकामः सौर्यायणी च गार्ग्यः कौसल्यश्चाश्वलायनो भार्गवो वैदर्भिः कबन्धी कात्यायनस्ते हैते ब्रह्मपुरा ब्रह्मनिष्ठाः परं ब्रह्मान्वेषमाणा एष ह वै तत्सर्वं वक्ष्यतीति तेह समित्पाणयो भगवन्तं पिप्पलादमुपसन्नाः ।

12. See below at (30).

13. Read: वार्षायणिस्तु सामुद्रं शरावं चैव गालवः ।
ऊर्ध्ववेणीकृतं गार्ग्यः क्रोष्टुकिः परिमण्डलम् ॥

14. Read: शिष्याः कालायनिगार्ग्यस्तृतियश्च कथाजवः ।

15. AP 51, 1, 2; 62, 1, 1; 50, 4, 4; 51, 5, 6.

16. Read: सुहोत्रादयोऽनुक्तगोत्रा भारद्वाजाः पौत्रा बृहस्पतेर्दौःषन्तेर्वा भरतस्य ।

17. See Ch. 2, Section (iii) on Vidathin Bhāradvāja and Ch. 3, Section (i) Suhotra Bhāradvāja elsewhere for details.

18. Mt. 49, 37-38.

गर्गस्य चैव दायादः शिवि विद्वान् अजायत ।
स्मृताः शैव्यास्ततो गर्गाः क्षत्रोपेता द्विजातयः ॥

cf. Va 99, 161; which offers a corrupt form viz. गाग्र

19. ĀpSSP 2, 14: आङ्गिरस गार्ग्यसैन्येति ।

śini and *sini* are freely used as two variants of one name. So also, Śainya and Sainya.

20. See note 18.

21. AśvŚS Pariśiṣta 3.

भरद्वाजाग्निवेश्यर्क्षाश्शुङ्गश्शैशिरयः कताः ।
एते समानगोत्रास्सुगर्गानिके वदन्ति वै ।।३

22. GPM p. 60.

23. AIHT p. 221 'where the word 'son' obviously does not mean immediate *sonship*'.

24. GPM p. VIII, fn.

25. AśvŚS 6, 12: गर्गाणां आङ्गिरसबार्हस्पत्यभारद्वाजगार्ग्यशैन्येति ।
आङ्गिरसशैन्यगार्ग्येति वा ॥

cf. BaudhŚSP 19. गर्गाः . . .पौलय इत्येते गर्गाः । तेषां पञ्चार्षेयस्त्र्यार्षेयो वा प्रवरो भवति । आङ्गिरस बार्हस्पत्य भारद्वाज शन्य गार्ग्येति होता ।
आङ्गिरस शैन्य गार्ग्येति वा ।

26. AśvŚS Pariśiṣṭa: द्व्यार्षेयाणां त्र्यार्षेय सन्निपाते अविवाहः ।

27. The *Pravaras* (iii) and (iv) are not considered as the *samāna pravara* with (i) and (ii).

28. Read notes 19, 25 above and 29 below.

29. Read: अङ्गिराश्च महातेजा देवाचार्यो बृहस्पतिः ।
भरद्वाजस्तथा गर्गः सैन्यश्च भगवानृषिः ॥

30\. Read: ऋषिरासीन्महावीर्यः कुणिर्गार्ग्यो महायशाः।
स तप्त्वा विपुलं राजंस्तपो वै तपतां वरः॥
मानसीं स सुतां सुभ्रूं समुत्पादितवान् विभुः॥
तां स दृष्ट्वा भृशं प्रीतः कुणिर्गार्ग्यो महायशाः।
जगाम त्रिदिवं राजन् संत्यज्येह कलेवरम्॥

31\. Read: मन्त्रिणो वालखिल्यास्तु सारस्वतो गणो ह्यभूत्।
महर्षिर्भगवान् गर्गस्तस्य सांवत्सरोऽभवत्॥

32\. Read: तस्माद् गन्धर्वतीर्थाच्च महाबाहुररिंदमः।
गर्गस्त्रोतो महातीर्थमाजगामैककुण्डली॥
यत्र गर्गेण वृद्धेन तपसा भावितात्मना।
कालज्ञानगतिश्चैव ज्योतिषां च व्यतिक्रमः॥
उत्पाता दारुणाश्चैव शुभाश्च जनमेजय।
सरस्वत्याः शुभे तीर्थे विहिता वै महात्मना।
तस्य नाम्ना च तत्तीर्थं गर्गस्त्रोत इति स्मृतम्॥
तत्र गर्गं महाभागमृषयः सुव्रता नृप।
उपासांचक्रिरे नित्यं कालज्ञानं प्रति प्रभो॥

33\. Works like Candraprātipadikam, Grahayuddham, Grahasaṁgraha, Bhūmikampalakṣaṇam, Utpātalakṣaṇam, etc., are ascribed to Garga.

34\. Read: यमाराध्य पुरार्णषिर्गर्गो ज्योतींषि तत्वतः।
ज्ञातवान् सकलञ्चैव निमित्तपठितं फलम्॥

cf. Br 21, 26-27.

35\. Read the relevant passages only:

कौशिको नाम धर्मात्मा कुरुक्षेत्रे महान् ऋषिः।
नामतः कर्मतस्तस्य सूतान् सप्त निबोधत॥2
स्वसृपः क्रोधनो हिंस्रः पिशुनः कविरेव च।
वारदुष्टः पितृवर्ती च गर्गशिष्यास्तदाभवत्॥3
पितर्य्युपरते तेषामभूद् दुर्भिक्षमुल्वणम्।
अनावृष्टिश्च महती सर्वलोकभयङ्करी॥4
गर्गादेशाद् वने दोग्ध्रीं रक्षन् ते तपोधनाः।
खादामः कपिलामेतां वयं क्षुत्पीडिता भृशम्॥5
× × ×
तथैकमतिथिं कृत्वा श्राद्धदः स्वयमेव तु।
चकार मन्त्रवच्छ्राद्धं स्मरन् पितृपरायणः॥
विना गवा वत्सकोऽपि गुरवे विनिवेदितः।
व्याघ्रेण विहता धेनुर्वत्सोऽयं प्रतिगृह्यताम्॥

36\. Read: गर्गश्च गोकुले तत्र वसुदेवप्रचोदितः।
प्रच्छन्नस्तत्र गोपानां संस्कारमकरोत्तयोः॥
ज्येष्ठं च राममित्याह कृष्णं चैव तथापरम्।
गर्गो मतिमतां श्रेष्ठो नाम कुर्वन् महामतिः॥9

cf. Bh 9, 8, 1-6; Br 184, 29-30.

37. Read, particularly v. 11.

गर्गस्य हि सुतं बालं स राजा जनमेजयः।
कालेन हिंसयामास ब्रह्महत्यामवाप सः॥

38. Read: अगावहं महात्मानं वृकदेवी व्यजायत।
कन्या त्रिगर्तराजस्य भार्या वै शिशिरायणेः॥
जिज्ञासां पौरुषं चक्रे न चस्कन्दे च पौरुषम्।
कृष्णायससमप्रख्यो वर्षे द्वादशमे तथा॥
मिथ्याभिशस्तो गार्ग्यस्तु मन्युनाऽतिसमीरितः।
घोषकन्यामुपादाय मैथुनाय प्रचक्रमे॥
गोपाली चाप्सरास्तस्य गोपस्त्रीवेषधारिणी।
धारयामास गार्ग्यस्य गर्भं दुर्धरमच्युतम्॥
मानुष्यां गर्गभार्यायां नियोगाच्छूलपाणिनः।
स कालयवनो नाम जज्ञे राजा महाबलः॥

cf. Bṛ 197, 1-5.

39. Mārk P tr. by F.E. Pargiter, pp. 101-03.

Section (v)

1. Cf. Sarvā 2, 6, 49: स्तुषे पञ्चोन ऋजिश्वा ह वैश्वदेवं ह शक्वर्यन्तम्।
Sarvā 2, 9, 98: अभि नो द्वादशाम्बरीष ऋजिश्वा चानुष्टुभं ह बृहन्त्या।
9, 108: पवस्व षोलश गौरिवीतिर्द्धचं शक्तिरेकामूरुऋजिश्वोर्ध्वसद्मा कृतयशा ऋणञ्जय
इत्यृषयो द्वृचास्तिस्त्रः शक्तिः काकुभाः प्रगाथाः स सुन्वे गायत्री यवमध्या।

2. RV 6, 48, 1 (=SV 35; 706; VS 27, 42); 2(=SV 704 VS 27, 44); 7 (=SV 37); 9=(SV 41; 1623); 49, 4(=VS 33, 55; KS 4, 10); 7(=TS 4, 1, 11, 12); MS 4, 14, 3; 219, 3; KS 17, 18); 8(=VS 34, 42; 1, 1, 14, 2); 50, 14(=VS 34, 53; MS 1, 6, 2; 88, 12); 51, 13(=SV 105); 16(=VS 4, 29; TS 1, 2, 1; MS 1, 2, 5; 14, 1; KS 2, 6; 24, 6); 52, 7(=RV 2, 41, 13; VS 7, 34); 9(=SV 1595; VS 33, 77; TS 2, 4, 14, 5; 10; 13; KS 26, 11); 10(=TS 2, 4, 14, 5; MS 4, 10, 3: 150, 10; KS 13, 15); 13(=VS 33, 53; MS 4, 12, 1: 179, 7; TS 2, 4, 14, 5); 9, 98, 1, (SV 1, 549; 2, 288); 3(=SV 2, 590); 6(=SV 2, 680); 7(=SV 1, 552; 2, 279; 2, 1031); 10 (=SV 2, 681; 798; 1029).

For SV we have used Satavalekar's edition of SV.

3. RV 1, 51, 5; 53, 8 (=AVŚ 20, 21, 8); 101, 1 (=SV 1, 380); 4, 16, 13; 5, 29, 11; 6, 20, 7; 8, 49, 10; 10, 99, 11; 138, 3.

4. Kaṇva is very frequently mentioned in the RV. He is referred to in RV. 1, 36, 8; 11; 17; 19; 39, 7; 45, 5; 47, 45; 48, 4; 112, 5; 117, 8; 118, 7; 139, 9; 5, 41, 4; 8, 2, 22; 5, 23; 25; 6, 11; 7, 18; 8, 4; 20; 34, 1; 49, 10; 50, 10; .52, 8; 10, 31, 11; 115, 5; 150, 5.

5. Trasadasyu is mentioned in RV 1, 112, 14; 4, 38, 1; 42, 8; 9; 5, 27, 3; 33, 8; 7, 19, 3; 8, 8, 21; 8, 19, 36; 36, 7; 37, 7; 49, 10; 10, 150, 5.

6. RV 8, 22, 10; 49, 10; 10, 61, 1.

7. RV 8, 8, 20; 49, 1; 10; 50, 9.

8. RV 8, 8, 20; 49, 1; 10; 50, 9.

9. Read : त्वं करञ्जमुत पर्णयं वधीस्तेजिष्ठयातिथिग्वस्य वर्तनी ।
त्वं शता वङ्गृदस्याभिनत् पुरोऽनानुदः परिषूता ऋजिश्वना ।

10. Divodāsa and Bharadvāja are mentioned together in RV 1, 112, 13; 14; 116, 18; 6, 16, 5; 31, 4; 47, 22.

11. *Der Rigveda*, Cambridge, II, 26.

12. According to the Sarvā 2, 5, 29; 9, 108 Gaurivīti Śāktya is the seer of RV 5, 29, and 9, 108, 1-2; and according to the Sarvā 2, 10, 73 one Gaurivīti (without surname) is the seer of RV 10, 73-74. Gaurivīti is found in the Pravara list viz. Mt 195, 30:

अङ्गिराः संकृतिश्चैव गौरिवीतिस्तथैव च ।

For further information, see our Ch. 3 Section (iii) on Nara Bhāradvāja.

13. Pipru is referred to eleven times in the RV. In RV 1, 51, 5; 4, 16, 13; 5, 29, 11; 6, 20, 7; 10, 99, 11 and 138, 3 he is mentioned as being killed by Indra for Ṛjiśvan, while in RV 1, 101, 2; 103, 8; 2, 14, 5 and 6, 18, 8 he is spoken of without reference to Ṛjiśvan. Strikingly enough, all the eleven passages are from Indra hymns.

14. RV 1, 51, 5; 4, 16, 13; 6, 20, 7; 10, 108, 3.

15. RV 10, 138, 3.

16. Read : वि पिप्रोरहिमायस्य दृल्हाः पुरो वज्रिञ्छवसा न दर्दः ।
सुदामन् तद् रेकणो अप्रमृष्यमृजिश्वने दात्रं दाशुषे दाः ।।

17. Read : अस्य स्तोमेभिरौशिज ऋजिश्वा
व्रजं दरयद्वृषभेण पिप्रोः ।
सुत्वा यद्यजतो दीदयद्गीः
पुर इयानो अभि वर्पसा भूत् ।।

18. RV 1, 53, 8: Read in note (9) above.

19. RV 1, 53, 8. Ibid.

20. Geldner in his *Der Rigveda*, 1, 437 takes Mṛgaya as an adjunct of Pipru, while Velankar in his "Indra Hymns by the Vāmadevas", BUJ, Vol. 6, p. 31, takes Mṛgaya as a person different from Pipru. Mṛgaya is further mentioned in RV 8, 3, 19 and 10, 49, 5.

21. Vaṅgṛda is mentioned only once in RV i.e. in 1, 53, 8.

22. Read : एवा नपातो मम तस्य धीभिर्
भरद्वाजा अभ्यर्चन्त्यर्कैः ।
ग्ना हुतासो वसवोऽधृष्टा
विश्वे स्तुतासो भूता यजत्राः ।।

23. Read : 'मम ऋजिश्वनः नपातः पुत्राः भरद्वाजाः
भरद्वाजगोत्रजाः सुहोत्रादयः . . .।'

RVVSM, 3, 189.

24. Geldner in his *Der Rigveda* Vol. 2 p. 155 writes: "*atiyājá bedeutet spáter (einen Gott) im Opfer ubergehen*, TS 2, 5, 4, 4; *Ṣadv. Br.* 1, 6, 1. *Hier paBt nur: einen anderen durch Opfer uberbieten, atiyājá* also *das Uberopfer oder der Opferuberbietes*". Griffith in his *Hymns of the Ṛgveda*, Delhi, reprint 1973, p. 318 says : "but the name Atiyāja (from *ati* and *yaj*) seems to be employed expressedly to signify one who over-sacrifices."

25. Read : त्वं पिप्रुं मृगयं शुशुवांस मृजिश्वने वेदथिनाय रन्धीः।
स्तोमासस्त्वा गौरिवीतेरवर्धन्नरन्धयो वैदथिनाय पिप्रुम् ॥ (RV 4-16, 13)
आ त्वामृजिश्वा सख्याय चक्रे पचन् पक्तीरपिबः सोमस्य ॥ (RV 5,92, 11)

26. Read the verse in fn. (17)

27. Read the verse in note (22) above.

28. See our Ch. 2, Section (iii) on adoption of Vidathin Bharadvāja.

29. Bergaigne in his *Vedic Religion* (Translated by Paranjape, Poona, 1972, Vol 2, p. 359) says that "*uśijs* are mythical clan, of which, the head is none other than Agni. The word *auśija* itself must denote a mythical being". Earlier (in Vol 1, at p. 59), the same scholar after a long discussion on the significance of 'uśij' and *auśijá*, very hesitatingly says that "the word *uśij* must have been already used as a proper name" and he understands that in the sense of a soma-presser or sacrificer. For further discussion, see our paper on Ṛjiśvan, CASS Studies, No. 5, pp. 111-18.

30. It has been fully discussed in Ch. 2, Section (iii) on adoption of Vidathin Bharadvāja.

31. MBh Droṇaparvan, Appendix 1, No. 8. Verse 375 and Śāntiparvan App.1 Ch. 29, 22, 25.

32. MBh 1, 89, 16-26; 90, 36-38; 12, 29, 22-25 and Droṇaparvan App. 1 No. 8.

33. Va 99, 151-66; Mt 49, 14-43; Vis 4, 19, 5ff.; Bh 9, 20, 34-39.

34. 5, 102-03.

Section (vi)

1. Sarvā 2, 6, 75 : जीमूतस्येवैकोना पायुर्भारद्वाजः संग्रामाङ्गान्यृक्शोऽभितुष्टाव वर्म . . .संग्रामाशिषोऽन्त्यानुष्टुब्जीत आलाक्तेतिच द्वे द्वे ॥

2. VaS 3, 12: जीमूतस्येव पायुर्भारद्वाजः संग्रामाङ्गान्यृकशोऽस्तौषीत्।

3. NA 1, 1, 8; 10; 2, 1, 22 (This last one ascribes 2, 1220 to Śāsa optionally).

4. RV 6, 75, 1-14 (= VS 29, 38-51; TS 4, 6, 6, 1-5; MS 3, 16, 3; KSA 6, 1); 16 (= SV 2, 1213; VS 17, 45; 17 (= SV 2, 1216; TS 4, 6, 4, 5); 19 (= 2, 1222; AV 1, 19, 4). On examination, it is found that Vv 6, 75, 16-18, repeated in VS 17, 45; 48; 49 are ascribed to one Apratiratha and V 6, 75, 18, repeated in AV 7, 118, 1 is ascribed to Atharvāṅgirasa. This development may be considered only as an afterthought.

5. Velankar, H. D. BUJ, 11(2) p. 72.

6. Read : दश रथान् प्रष्टिमतः शतं गा अथर्वभ्यः।
अश्वथः पायवेऽदात् ॥ (RV 6, 47, 24)

7. Sāyaṇa under RV 6, 47, 24; RVVSM Vol. 3, p. 167.

8. Griffith in a fn. says: "Prastoka, Divodāsa and Atithigva are the name of one and the same prince, who is called also Aśvatha and Sārñjaya or son of Sṛñjaya". HR (1973 reprint) p. 313.

9. While doing so Griffith probably relies on Sāyaṇa's statement viz.,
अथर्वभ्यः अथर्वगोत्रेभ्यः ऋषिभ्यः पायवे भरद्वाजपुत्राय एतत् संज्ञायास्मद्भ्रात्रे चाश्वथोऽश्ववानेतत्संज्ञः प्रस्तोकोऽदात्।

10. See his translation of the verse above and Note (5).

11. Read : the relevant passages only :

अभ्यावर्ती चायमानः प्रस्तोकश्चैव साञ्जंयः ।
आजग्मतुर्भरद्वाजं जितौ वारशिखैर्युधि ॥
अभिगम्योचतुस्तौ तं प्रसाद्याख्याय नामनी ।
युधि वारशिखैर्ब्रह्मन्न आवां विद्ध विनिर्जितौ ॥
भवत्पुरोहितावावां क्षत्रबन्धूञ्जयेवहि ।
क्षत्रं तदपि विज्ञेयं ब्रह्म यत्पाति शाश्वतम् ॥ 126
ऋषिस्तौ तु तथेत्युक्त्वा पायुं पुत्रमभाषत ।
अधर्षणीयौ शत्रूणां कुरुष्वैतौ नृपाविति ॥ 127
पितरं स तथेत्युक्त्वा युद्धोपकरणं तयोः ।
जीमूतस्येति सूक्तेन पृथक्त्वेनान्वमन्त्रयत् ॥ 128
प्रथमा त्वस्य सूक्तस्य योद्धारं स्तौति वर्मिणम् ।
धनुषश्च द्वितीया तु तृतीया ज्याभिमन्त्रिणो ॥ 129
सूक्तेनानेन तु स्तुत्वा संग्रामाङ्गान्यृषिस्तयोः ।
ततः प्रस्थापयामास पुनर्वारशिखान् प्रति ॥ 136
एतत्त्यत्ते चतसृभी राज्ञो साहाय्यकाम्यया ।
भरद्वाजोऽभितुष्टाव प्रीतस्तेन पुरंदरः ॥ 137
अभ्यावर्तिनमभ्येत्य हर्युपीयानदीतटे ।
सहितश्चायमानेन जघानैनाञ्छचीपतिः ॥138
तौ तु वारशिखान् जित्वा ततोऽभ्यावर्तिसाञ्जयौ ।
भरद्वाजाय गुरवे ददतुर्विविधं वसु ॥ 139॥
भरद्वाजश्च गर्गश्च दृष्टाविन्द्रेण वै पथि ।
द्वयान् प्रस्तोक इत्याभिर्दानं तद्वै शशंसतुः ॥ 140

12. Read : प्रस्तोक इन्नु राधसस्त इन्द्र
दश कोशयीर्दश वाजिनोऽदात् ।
दिवोदासादतिथिग्वस्य राधः
शाम्बरं वसु प्रत्यग्रभीष्म ॥

13. Read : द्वयाँ अग्ने रथिनो विंशति गा
वधूमतो मघवा मह्यं सम्राट् ।
अभ्यावर्ती चायमानो ददाति
दूणाशेयं दक्षिणा पार्थवानाम् ॥

14. For details see Ch. 3, Section (iv) on Garga Bhāradvāja.

15. See Ch. 5 of Part I, on Divodāsa.

16. See Introduction, Section on Bharadvāja in Ṛgveda Ch. 1 Section (i) and Rāmāyaṇa Ch. 1, Section (v).

17. Pargiter has already expressed his doubts as regards these Brāhmaṇic sources, in his AIHT p. 9.

Section (*vii*)

1. Read : क उ श्रवत् सप्त पुरुमील्हाजमील्हो सौहोत्रो त्वाश्विनं हि । Purumīḍha and Ajamīḍha are given as variants of Purumīlha and Ajamīlha respectively.

2. cf. Bṛh. S. 11, 11: त्वं वाम नव । पुरुमील्हाजमील्हो आश्विनम् ।

3. Vas. 3, 18; 4, 22.

4. cf. NA 1, 1: सौहोत्रः पुरुमीढो वा ।

5. Read : सुहोत्रादयोऽनुक्तप्रोत्रा भारद्वाजाः ।

6. cf. Sarvā 2, 6, 31 : अभूरेकः सुहोत्रस्तु ।

7. cf. note 1 above.

8. For example, the hymn 6, 15 seen by Vītahavya is included in 6th Maṇḍala; hymn 4, 29 seen by Gaurivīti Śāktya is included in the Atri Maṇḍala.

9. For details, see our Ch. 3, Section (iii) on Nara Bhāradvāja.

10. Read :
नू नो रयिं पुरुवीरं बृहन्तं
दस्रा मिमाथामुभयेष्वस्मे ।
नरो यद् वामश्विना स्तोममावन्
त्सधस्तुतिमाजमील्हासो अग्मन् ॥

11. VI, 1, 13.

12. Read the verse at note 10 above.

13. *Der Rigveda*, Band III, pp. 123, 135.

14. "Zeitschrift der Deutschen Morgen landischan Geselschaft", 42, p. 215.

15. Bh 9, 21, 30: Says: पुरुमीढोऽप्रजोऽभवत् ।

16. See Ch. 3, Section (i) on Suhotra Bhāradvāja for details.

17. Read :
ऐक्ष्वाकी जनयामास सुहोत्रात् पृथिवीपतेः ।
अजमीढं सुमीढं च पुरुमीढं च भारत ॥

18. Read : सुहोत्रः खल्विक्ष्वाकुकन्यामुपयेमे सुवर्णां नाम । तस्यामस्य जज्ञे हस्ती । य इदं हास्तिनपुरं मापयामास । एतदस्य हास्तिनपुरत्वम् ॥36॥ हस्ती खलु त्रैगर्तीमुपयेमे यशोधरां नाम । तस्यामस्य जज्ञे विकुण्ठिनः ॥37॥ विकुण्ठिनः खलु दाशार्हीमुपयेमे सुदेवां नाम । तस्यामस्य जज्ञे अजमीढः ॥३८

19. Mt. 49 42 : बृहत्क्षत्रस्य दायादो हस्तिनामा बभूव ह ॥
Aslo cf. Bh 9, 21, 20-21.

20. Read :
बृहत्क्षत्रस्य दायाद सुहोत्रो नाम धार्मिकः ।
सुहोत्रस्यापि दायादो हस्ती नाम बभूव ह ।
येनेयं निर्मितं पूर्वं नाम्ना वै हस्तिनापुरम् ॥
Aslo cf. Vis 4, 19, 10.

21. Va 99, 166: सुहोत्रस्यापि दायादास्त्रयः परमधार्मिकाः ।
अजमीढो द्विजामीढः पुरुमीढस्तथैव च ॥
cf. Mt 49, 43; Vis 4, 19, 10; Bh 9, 21, 2.

22. Br 13, 80-81 : सुहोत्रस्य बृहत्पुत्रो बृहतः तनयस्त्रयः ।
अजमीढो द्विमीढश्च पुरुमीढश्च वीर्यवान् ॥
cf. Hv. 1, 23, 82; Ag 278, 15.

23. MBh 1, 50, 6 : यज्ञः श्रुतो नो दिवि देवसूनो–
युधिष्ठिरस्याजमीढस्य राज्ञः ।

Cf. *Mahābhārata Kośa* by R.K. Roy, Part I, p. 96, where it has been shown that the patronymic Ājamīḍha was used to denote Yudhiṣṭhira, Nakula, Dhṛtarāṣṭra, Duryodhana, Arjuna, etc.

24. Read: षट् पुत्रान् सोऽप्यजनयत्तिसृषु स्त्रीषु भारत ॥ and verses 28-55 in this section describe the line of Hāstinapura dynasty.

25. Read: अजमीढस्य चतुर्विंशं पुत्रशतं बभूव कैकेयां नागायां गान्धार्यां विमलायामृक्षायां चेति । पृथक् पृथग्वंशकरा नृपतयः ।

The passages which follow this statement describe the Hāstinapura line.

26. Va 99, 167:

अजमीढस्य पत्न्यस्तु शुभाः कुरुसुतोद्वहाः ।
नीलिनी केशिनी चैव धूमिनी च वराङ्गनाः ।
अजमीढस्य पुत्रास्तु तासु जाताः कुलोद्वहाः ।
तपसोऽन्ते सुमहतो राज्ञो वृद्धस्य धार्मिकाः ॥

cf. Mt 49, 44-45.

27. Va 99, 194: अजमीढस्य नीलिन्यां नीलः समभवन् नृपः ।

cf Mt. 50, 1; Vis 4, 19, 15.

28. Va 99, 194: नीलस्य तपसोग्रेण सुशान्त्यभ्यजायत ॥

cf Mt 50, 1; Vis 4, 19, 15.

29. Va 99, 195: पुरुजानुः सुशान्तेः . . . ।

cf. Mt 50. 2.

30. Va 99, 195... ऋक्षस्तु पुरुजानुतः ।

cf. Mt 50, 1: reads: पुरुजानुः सुशान्तेस्तु पृथुस्तु पुरुजानुतः ।

Vis 4, 19, 15: पुरुजानुस्ततश्चक्षुः . . . ।

Bh 9, 21, 31.

31. Read: तार्क्ष्यं हैके ब्रुवतेऽतीत्याङ्गिरसं तार्क्ष्यंभार्म्यंश्वमौदगल्येति ।

32. CAI, p. 1.

33. Mt50, 2: भद्राश्वः पृथुदायादो भद्राश्वतनयान् शृणु ॥

Cf. Bh 9, 21, 31; Ag 278, 19; Hv 1, 32, 64; Br 13, 93: Vis 4, 19, 15.

34. Va 99, 196-197: मुद्गलेः सृञ्जयश्चैव राजा बृहदिषुस्तथा ।
यवीयांश्चापि विक्रान्तः काम्पिल्यश्चैव पञ्चमः ॥

Cf. Vis 4, 19, 15; Mt 50, 3; Bh 9, 21, 31-32.

35. Sarvā 2, 10, 102: प्र ते मुद्गलो भाम्यश्वो द्रुघणेन..... ।

36. CAI, p. 2.

37. See note 34 above, and read also:

Va 99, 197-98:

पञ्चानां विद्धि पंचैतान् स्फीतजनपदायुताः ।
अलं संरक्षणे तेषां पञ्चाला इति विश्रुताः ।

38. Read: नाडायनी चेन्द्रसेना यथैव ।
वश्या नित्यं मुद्गलस्याजमीढः ॥

Cf. MBh 3, 57, 21:

हयांस्तत्र विनिक्षिप्य सूतो रथवरं च तम् ।
इन्द्रसेनां च तां कन्यामिन्द्रसेनं च बालकम् ॥

39. *Naḷa* is variant of Naḷa, from which patronymic Nāḍāyanī or Nāḷāyanī is derived.

40. Va 99, 198-99:

मुद्गलस्याऽपि मौद्गल्याः क्षत्रोपेता द्विजातयः ।
एते ह्याङ्गिरसः पक्षे संश्रिताः कण्वमुद्गलाः ॥

cf. Mt 50, 4-5; Vis 4, 19, 14.

41. Read: मुद्गलस्य सुतो ज्येष्ठो ब्रह्मिष्ठः सुमहायशाः ।
इन्द्रसेना यतो गर्भं बध्यश्वं प्रत्यपद्यत ॥

42. Read: मुद्गलस्य सुतो जज्ञे ब्रह्मिष्ठः सुमहायशाः ।
इन्द्रसेनः सुतस्तस्य विन्ध्याश्वस्तस्य चात्मजः ॥

(Mt reads Indrasena for Indrasenā which leads one to take Indrasena as the son of Mudgala.)

43. Read: मुद्गलाद् वध्र्यश्वः. . . ।

Vis gives the correct name as at RV 6, 61, 1.

44. Read: इयमददाद्रभसमृणच्युतं दिवोदासं वध्र्यश्वाय दाशुषे ।

45. Va 99, 200-201:

वध्र्यश्वान्मिथुनं जज्ञे मेनका इति नः श्रुति : ।
दिवोदासश्च राजर्षिरहल्या च यशस्विनी ॥

cf. Mt 50, 6; Vis 4, 19, 16.

46. AŚVŚSP 6, 10, 12:

मित्रयुवां वाध्र्यश्वेति त्रिप्रवरं वा भार्गवदैवोदासवाध्र्यश्वेति ।

Cf. also section on Śunahotra, for the relationship between the Bhṛgus and Aṅgirases.

47. He is mentioned in the RV 18 times. For details see Ch. 5 below.

48. Patronymic Paijavana derived from Pijavana is referred in RV 7, 18, 22; 23; 25.

49. Sudās is mentioned 28 times in the RV. Detailed information of his activities is recorded in RV 7, 18, and also in 7, 83 and 3, 53.

50. RV 4, 15, 4; 6, 27, 7; Patronymic Sārñjaya in 6, 47, 25.

51. RV 6, 47, 22; he is referred to by the patronymic Sārñjaya at RV 6, 47, 25.

52. RV 6, 27, 5; 8; also with the patronymic Cāyamāna in RV 7, 18, 8; 10, 94, 14.

53. Patronymic Sāhadevya with reference to Somaka is mentioned in RV 4, 15, 7-10.

54. RV 4, 15, 9.

55. See our Ch. 2, Section (vi) on Bharadvāja, Droṇa's father for other information.

56. Va 99, 170: अजमीढस्य धूमिन्यां जज्ञे बृहद्वसुर्नृपः ।

57. Va 99, 182: भल्लाटस्य तु दायाद आसीज्जनमेजयः ।
उग्रायुधेन तस्याऽर्थे सर्वे नीपाः प्रणाशिताः ॥

58. Va 99, 214: ऋक्षं सा जनयामास धूम्रवर्णं सिताग्रजम् ।

59. Va 99, 214: ऋक्षात् सम्वरणो जज्ञे कुरु सम्वरणादभूत् ।

60. Va 99, 217ff.
61. Va 99, 234: दिलीपसूनुः प्रतीपस्तस्य पुत्रास्त्रयः स्मृताः ।
देवापिः शन्तनुश्चैव वाल्हीकश्चैव ते त्रयः ॥
62. Sarvā: 2, 10, 98
63. Va 99, 239-241
64. Va 99, 242ff.
65. Va 99, 250ff.
66. Va 99, 169-170: अजमीढस्य केशिन्यां कण्वः समभवत् किल ।
मेधातिथिः सुतस्तस्य तस्मात्कण्ठा (कण्वा)-यणद्विजाः ॥

In the second line the word Kaṇṭhāyaṇa is nothing but a misreading of Kāṇvāyana.

67. Vis 4, 19, 4; 5; 8; Bh 9, 20, 6.
68. AIHT p. 225.
69. Mt 200, 9.
70. Sarvā 2, 1, 12; 8, 1.
71. Medhyātithi is probably a variant of Medhātithi. In the RV Medhātithi occurs once while Medhyātithi 9 times.
72. RV 8, 1, 3-29; 8, 3; 33; 9, 41-43. Sarvā 2, 8.
73. Sarvā 2, 8, 52.
74. Ibid. 2, 8, 76.
75. Ibid. 2, 8, 81.
76. Ibid. 2, 8, 55.
77. Ibid. 2, 8, 45.
78. Ibid. 2, 8, 4.
79. Ibid. 2, 8, 39.
80. Ibid. 2, 8, 13.
81. Ibid. 2, 8, 34.
82. Ibid. 2, 8, 12.
83. Ibid, 2, 8, 14.
84. AIHT p. 227.
85. Ibid.
86. Ibid.
87. Ibid.
88. See concluding remarks.

Section (viii)

1. Sarvā 2, 4, 43: क उ श्रवत्सप्त पुरुमील्हाजमील्हौ सोहोत्रौ त्वाश्विनं हि ।
2. Sarvā 2, 8, 71.
3. The problem is discussed fully in Ch. 3, Section (vii) on Ajamīḍha.
4. p. 316, fn. 1.
5. RV 1, 151, 2; 183, 5; 5, 61, 9; 8, 71, 14
6. Read: यद्ध त्यद् वां पुरुमील्हस्य सोमिनः
प्र मित्रासो न दधिरे स्वाभुवः ।
अध क्रतुं विदतं गातुमर्चत
उत श्रुतं वृषणा पस्त्यावतः ॥

7. Read: युवां गोतमः पुरुमीळ्हो अत्रि-
दंस्रा हवतेऽवसे हविष्मान् ।
दिशं न दिष्टामृजूयेव यन्ता
मे हवं नासत्योप यातम् ॥

8. Read: अग्निमीळिष्वावसे गाथाभिः शीरशोचिषम् ।
अग्निं राये पुरुमीळ्ह श्रुतं नरोऽग्निं सुदीतये छर्दिः ॥

The verse is repeated in AVŚ 20, 103, 1.

9. Read: उत मेऽरपद् युवतिर्ममन्दुषी
प्रति श्यावाय वर्तनिम् ।
वि रोहिता पुरुमीळ्हाय
येमतुर्विप्राय दीर्घयशसे ॥

10. The relevant passage, where Śyāvaśva is said to have attained ample gifts is the following: ततस्तौ तु निवर्तेताम् उभावेवाभिजग्मतुः ।
शशीयसीं तरन्तं च पुरुमीळ्हं च पार्थिवम् ।
तरन्तपुरुमीळ्हौ तु राजानौ वैददश्वयो ।
ताभ्यां तौ चक्रतुः पूजामृषिभ्यां नृपती स्वयम् ।
ऋषिपुत्रं महिष्याश्च दर्शयामास तं नृपः ।
तरन्तानुमता चैव प्रादाद्बहुविधं वसु ॥
B.D. 5, 61ff.

11. Read: तरन्तपुरुमीळ्हौ वै वैतदश्वी माहेयौ
मह्या आर्चनानस्यैव पुत्रौ & so on

12. Read: यौ श्यावाश्वमवथो बध्र्यश्वं
मित्रावरुणा पुरुमीळ्हमत्रिम् ।
यौ विमदमवथ सप्तवध्रिं
तौ नो मुञ्चतमंहसः ॥

The verse except the Ist pada is repeated in AVP 4, 38, 5 verbatim.

13. Read: कण्वः कक्षीवान् पुरुमीळ्हो अगस्त्यः ।
श्यावाश्वः सोभर्यर्चनानाः ।
विश्वामित्रोऽयं जमदग्निरत्रि
रवन्तु नः कश्यपो वामदेवः ॥

Section (ix)

1. Read: सोमस्य वसु र्भरद्वाजः ।
2. NA 1, 6, 7: असावि भारद्वाजो वसुः ।

Section (x)

1. Read: अरायि शिरिम्बिठो भारद्वाजोऽलक्ष्मीघ्नं द्वितीया
तृतीया ब्राह्मणस्पत्ये अन्त्या वैश्वदेवी ।
2. ABS 11, 11.
3. Vas 4, 4.

4. Read: अरायि काणे विकटे गिरिं गच्छ सदान्वे ।
शिरिम्बिठस्य सत्वेभिस्तेभिष्ट्वा चानयामसि ॥

5. Read: शिरिम्बिठो मेघः । शीर्यते बिठे (बिठमन्तरिक्षम्) ॥

6. Nir 6, 30: अपि वा शिरिम्बिठो भरद्वाजः कालकर्णेपितः । of Nigh 4, 3.

7. Veṅkaṭa Mādhava, AVVIS Vol. 8, p. 385. Sāyaṇa; RVVSM, Vol. 4, pp. 840-41.

8. Read under RV 10, 155, 1: शिरिम्बिठस्य एतत्संज्ञकस्य भरद्वाजपुत्रस्य तेभिस्तैः अनुष्ठितैः सत्वेभिः कर्मभिर्हे अलक्षि त्वा विनाशयामः ।

9. Roth and Böhtlingkt: PW. VII, pp. 192-93: '*Nach RV Anukar. N. pr. des Verfasser des angebenen liedes mit dem patron, Bharadvāja*'. Grassmann, *Wörterbuchzum Ṛgveda*, p. 1395: m. *wol-Eigenname eines Mannes.*

10. VI 2, 381.

Section (*xi*)

1. Read: शासः शासो भारद्वाजः ।

2. NA 2, 2.

3. Vas 1, 33; 2, 32.

4. Read: शास इत्था महां अस्यमित्रखादो अद्भुतः ।
न यस्य हन्यते सखा न जीयते कदाचन ॥

5. RVVIS Vol. 4, p. 3851: शासिता त्वं सत्यमेव महान् . . . ।

6. RVVSM Vol. 4, p. 836: शास एतत्संज्ञोऽहम् इत्था वक्ष्यमाणप्रकारेणेन्द्र स्तौमीति शेषः ।

7. Macdonell and Keith, VI. Vol 2, p. 376.

Section (*xii*)

1. Read: प्रथश्चैकर्चा प्रथो वासिष्ठः सप्रथो भारद्वाजो घर्मः सौर्यो वैश्वदेवम् ।

2. Ibid.

3. RV 10, 181, *lab*: प्रथश्च यस्य सप्रथश्च नामानुष्टुभस्य हविषो हविर्यत् ।

4. RV 10, 181, 3d: सूर्यादभरन् घर्ममेते ।

5. HR, pp. 659-60, *fn*. 1.

6. In general the Sarvā always ascribes a hymn or verse to a seer whose name occurs in any of the verses of the hymn, preferably in the Ist verse. This holds true for a number of cases. For relevant information see Sections (x) (xi) and (xiii) of the Chapter 3 above.

7. Read: प्रथश्च यस्य सप्रथस्य नामा-
नुष्टुभस्य हविषो हविर्यत् ।
धातुर्द्युतामात् सवितुश्च विष्णो
रथन्तरमा जभारा वसिष्ठः ॥

8. Read: अविन्दन् त अतिहितं यदा-
सीद् यज्ञस्य धाम परमं गुहा यत् ।
धातुर्द्युतानात् सवितुश्च विष्णो-
र्भरद्वाजो बृहदा चक्रे अग्नेः ॥

9. Read: तेऽविन्दन् मनसा दीध्याना
यजुः स्कन्नं प्रथम देवयानम् ।
धातुद्युतानात् सवितुश्च विष्णो-
रा सूर्यादाभरन् घर्ममेते ॥

Section (xiii)

1. Sarvā: 2, 10, 127: रात्री कुशिकः सौभरी रात्रिर्वा भारद्वाजी रात्रिस्तवं गायत्रम् ।
2. "The Ṛṣikās (female Seers) of the Ṛgveda", *Indian Antiquary* (Third Series) Vol. III, 1-4, 1969, p. 42.
3. Vas 4, 2: आ रात्रि पथ्याबृहतीं रात्रिदेवत्यां
कशिपां भरद्वाजदुहिता . . . ।
4. Ibid.

Chapter Four

OTHER SEERS OF THE ṚGVEDA, MAṆḌALA VI

(i) *Śaṁyu Bārhaspatya*

The Sarvā (2, 6, 44) has ascribed four hymns of the RV (viz. 6, 44 to 46 and 48) to the seer Śaṁyu Bārhaspatya ('the son of Bṛhaspati')[1]. The first three are in praise of Indra, while the fourth is addressed to All-Gods (*Viśvedevāḥ*). Śaṁyu is further said to be the 'seer' of four hymns of the AV (20, 78; 80; 83 and 98)[2]. Further, SV (1, 42; 115; 127; 146; 201; 262; 286; 351 and 586)[3]; and VS (3, 42; 43; 27, 36-38; 42; 44-45)[4] are also ascribed to him. However, most of these hymns and verses are repetition of the Ṛgvedic hymns and verses. Also, a few verses from his composition in the RV are repeated in other three Vedas.[5] Although the traditional sources present very scanty information about Śaṁyu Bārhaspatya that might be useful for constructing his biography.

Śaṁyu is said to be the son of Bṛhaspati[6]. We have already found that Bharadvāja was also a son of the same Bṛhaspati[7]. They thus appear to be brothers. However, the name of Śaṁyu's mother is not given anywhere, while Bharadvāja's mother was one Mamatā, the wife of Ucathya[8]. Śaṁyu appears to be one of the distinguished composers of the Vedic hymns. His compositions are included in all the four Vedas, and if we consider the extent of his literary contribution as found in the Bhāradvāja Maṇḍala of the RV, Śaṁyu may be assigned a place next only to Bharadvāja Bārhaspatya. His four hymns comprise 93 verses, while Ṛjiśvan's four hymns comprise only 63 verses; as such the latter can be assigned the third place among the seers of the family of Bharadvāja. All this accounts for the importance of Śaṁyu Bārhaspatya and the distinguished position he occupies in the sixth Maṇḍala of the RV.

We have said earlier that three out of the four hymns ascribed to Śaṁyu are addressed to god Indra, indicating his devotion to that god. The remaining hymn (6, 48) is in praise of the *Viśvedevāḥ* ('all-gods') and it shows his inclination to the faith in the plurality of god-head.

In the hymns (RV 6, 44-46 and 48) attributed to him, Śaṁyu has mentioned Bharadvāja twice.[9] In RV (6, 48, 7) he has referred to Agni kindled by Bharadvāja. Pṛśṇi (RV 6, 48, 13) is said to have milked the cows for Bharadvāja and given him food and nourishment. These may be references to Bharadvāja, the son of Bṛhaspati.

Besides, Śaṁyu has celebrated the gifts made to Bharadvāja by one Bṛbu, a Paṇi-chief, in the three verses[10] of his compositions as follows :

31. Bṛbu has stood at the highest head (*i.e.* peak) among the Paṇis, being spacious (i.e. generous) like the (fertile) (i.e. the banks) of the Ganges.
32. Bṛbu whose auspicious bounty, like that of Vāyu himself, consists of a thousand gifts and quickly desires for an immediate donation.
22. Hence all bards as well as the nobles always very well praise Bṛbu, the best among the givers of a thousand and the best among the winners of a thousand.[11]

Sāyaṇa, the commentator, has referred to a legend recorded in the Manusmṛti (10, 107).[12] The legend is given in the Nītimañjarī[13] as well. According to this legend, once Bharadvāja, while travelling through a thick forest, was afflicted with severe hunger and thirst. He was accompanied by his son. Somewhere in that forest the seer saw Bṛbu. The sage asked him to wait upon him. Bṛbu, at once, stood before him with folded hands and introduced himself to be a carpenter by profession. He addressed the seer, "O Brāhmaṇa, it is learnt that the Brāhmaṇas do not accept anything from carpenters and out-castes (*cāṇḍālas*), etc. If your virtues do not come into conflict, please tell me." Thereupon, Bharadvāja assured him, "I shall not reject your donation anyway". Then saying, 'well' Bṛbu attended to him in accordance with the norm for one's attending to the guest. After some time Bṛbu again addressed Bharadvāja thus: "I am a Śūdra by caste and possessed of a great number of cows, but I cannot perform any sacrifice. But your honour told me earlier that 'your gift will not be rejected'. So, to elevate yourself (i.e. to recover yourself from hunger physically) and to make me a sharer of the heaven, please accept these cows offered by me." Saying thus, Bṛbu gave the seer a thousand cows. Bharadvāja accepted those cows from him and conveyed it to his son and then to his brother Śaṁyu. Thus Śaṁyu, the son of Bṛhaspati, praised Bṛbu's gift in the three verses cited above.

It appears from the RV passages that Bṛbu belonged to the Paṇis who probably were a tribe of non-Aryan origin. The Paṇis are described in the RV as miserly. But Bṛbu is found to be extremely generous to Bharadvāja in giving a thousand cows, for which Śaṁyu celebrates him as *sahasradātama sūrī* ('thousand-giving noble). MS (10, 107) however, calls this Bṛbu as *takṣan* (i.e. a carpenter by trade). The commentator Sāyaṇa[14] while giving the above legend, says that Bṛbu was a *takṣan* equal to *cāṇḍālas* in social rank and, on another occasion, a Śūdra who cannot perform sacrifice. All these statements complicate the problem. The authors of VI[15] say that Bṛbu was a merchant prince, while Velankar says: "The adjectives *sahasradātama* and *sūrī* rather indicate that he was a fighter and warrior".[16]

Moreover, the above information as regards Bharadvāja Śaṁyu has also spoken in one passage (6, 45, 1) of Turvaśa and Yadu, being led by Indra.[17] In another passage (6, 46, 8), he mentions a king named Tṛkṣi together with Druhyu and Puru.[18] He is again referred to in RV (8, 22, 7) wherein he is called by a patronymic *Trāsadasyava* ('a descendant of Trasadasyu')[19]. However, Sāyaṇa paraphrases the patronymic as *trāsadasyavam trasadasyoḥ putram* ('To Trāsadasyava, i.e. to the son of Trasadasyu')[20]; the authors of VI appear to have accepted it when they say: "Tṛkṣi is, in the Ṛigveda, the name of a prince who was a Trāsadasyava ('descendant of Trasadasyu')".[21]

Śaṁyu refers also to the tribes of Nahuṣas and the 'Five tribes' (*Pañca Janāḥ*) in RV (6, 46, 7)[22]. Frequently talking about them, the RV is uncertain who they five are[23]. Zimmer's[24] view is that by Pañcajanāḥ 'Aryans' are meant, but in particular five tribes of the Anus, Druhyus, Yadus, Turvaśas and Purus. Excepting the Anus, the other four are referred to by Śaṁyu (in RV 6, 46, 8; and 6, 45, 1) as noted above.

In TS (3, 3, 8, 11)[25] Śaṁyu is spoken of as the son of Bṛhaspati. So also a number of Brāhmaṇas mention Śaṁyu. Giving the background of the Śaṁyorvāk pronounced at the end of a sacrifice ŚB (1, 9, 1, 24-26) says: "It was Śaṁyu, the son of Bṛhaspati, who perceived in its true nature the successful completion of the sacrifice, and visited the world of gods. By pronouncing the

Śaṁyorvāk the Ṛṣis then attained the knowledge of the successful completion of the sacrifice, which Śaṁyu, the son of Bṛhaspati had perceived; so does the Hotṛ attain that by pronouncing the Śaṁyorvāk. For this reason, he pronounces the 'All hail and blessing mantra'[26].

This account is repeated in the AB and Śāṅkh B also. Śāṅkh B (3, 8)[27] says: "That he recites speech (i.e. formula) of Śaṁyu. Stability indeed is the Speech of Śaṁyu. Verily Śaṁyu Bārhaspatya brought to (safe) conclusion (a number of) sacrifices (by his speech). Therefore, he recites the speech of Śaṁyu. (Now) that he touches water. Since water (indeed) is pacification, it is employed (lit. made) in the medicine at the end of sacrifice." Thus, it appears to us that Śaṁyorvāk is nothing but a benedictory speech (which is a composition of Śaṁyu) recited by the Hotṛ at the time when the *prastara* and *paridhi*, etc., are thrown in the fire at the end of the New-Moon and the Full-Moon sacrifices.[28]

Vā (71, 36-80)[29] contains a long discourse on the Pitṛsarga, Śrāddha, Tarpaṇa and *tīrtha māhātmya*, etc. This is really a discourse introduced by Bṛhaspati when he was questioned by his son Śaṁyu. In the opening stanza, the Sūta says "Śaṁyu, the son of Bṛhaspati with all his modesty, makes queries from his father (who was the embodiment of knowledge), about ancestors". Bṛhaspati gives him the information.

Pargiter[30] places Śaṁyu among the Aṅgirases two generations below Bharadvāja Bārhaspatya in the 'Chronological table of the Ṛishis' (AIHT p. 191) and says, "Śaṁyu, son of 'Bṛhaspati', must be placed before Vidathin and after Bṛhaspati..." (AIHT, p. 221). Following him P.L. Bhargava[31] goes a step further to say that Śaṁyu was a son or a descendant of Bharadvāja. But the evidence from the traditional sources does not lend any support to the views of the two scholars. Bhargava based his contention, it appears, on Pargiter's observations, and the latter on the wrong interpretation of the passage in the VD on the Sarvā (2, 6, 52)[32]. However, we may caution against a conclusion that is in conflict with the tradition, especially when there is no obscurity or absurdity. Thus, we see no reason why one should place Śaṁyu two generations after Bharadvāja. Nor can he be included among the descendants of Bharadvāja. We concur with the traditional view and regard Śaṁyu as a son of Bṛhaspati and a brother of

Bharadvāja. And, therefore, he was a contemporary of Bharadvāja.

One may raise a question: "If Śaṁyu was not a descendant of Bharadvāja, why were his hymns included in the Bharadvāja Maṇḍala?" To this we answer that although Śaṁyu was not a son or a descendant of Bharadvāja, he found a place for his hymns in the family book of Bharadvāja. It was not necessary that one must have been only in the lineage of a seer after whom a Maṇḍala was named; it was sufficient that one was his relative.[33] Śaṁyu, in all probability, perhaps lived with the family of Bharadvāja. Thus, Śaṁyu's hymns were collected and placed along with those by the other Bharadvājas.

(*ii*) *Vītahavya*

The Sarvā (2, 6, 15)[1] ascribes RV 6, 15 optionally to Vītahavya and Bharadvāja Bārhaspatya. One Vītahavya appears to be the seer of AVŚ 6, 136-137, also[2]. And one Vītahavya Āṅgirasa is said to have composed SV 2, 917, again *optionally* with Bharadvāja. And a few verses from RV 6, 15 are repeated in other Saṁhitās of the Vedas (SV, VS, and TS)[4]. Now arises the question as to who this or these Vītahavya(s) were and what again was his/theirs' relation to the Bharadvājas, if he (they) did not belong to this family.

In the RV, Vītahavya is referred to twice, once alone in RV 6, 15, 2[5], and once with Bharadvāja in RV 6, 15, 3[6]. On both the occasions, Sāyaṇa[7] gives a tentative interpretation. Under RV 6, 15, 2 he takes Vītahavya as the name of a seer (*Vītahavya etat saṁjña ṛṣau*) and then offers an alternative meaning to it as *bharadvāja ṛṣiś cet vītahavye dattahaviṣke bharadvāja iti yojanīyam* ("in the case of the seer Bharadvāja it is to be understood as Bharadvāja who offers oblation"). Under, V.3, while interpreting the *pādas* 'd' and 'e' first he says: *bharadvājāya saṁbhṛtahavirlakṣaṇānnāya vītahavyāya* "to a Vītahavya who has collected food in the form of offerings" and then gives an alternative interpretation of the same as: *vītam gamītam havyam havir yena tādṛśāya bharadvājāya iti vā yojyam* ("a person by whom offering of *havis* has been made, i.e. to such a Bharadvāja—this may be added alternatively here"). While interpreting these verses and giving them different meanings, Sāyaṇa probably followed one of his predecessors, viz. Veṅkaṭa Mādhava[8] who is precise in saying: *dattahaviṣkāya bharadvājāya, bharadvājakulajāya vā vītahavyāya* "to Bharadvāja who offered oblation of *havis*, or to Vītahavya who was born in the family of Bharadvāja". Difference in their approaches lies in the fact that Veṅkaṭa Mādhava says a bit more definitely that the person mentioned in the verse was one Vītahavya born in the family of Bharadvāja, while Sāyaṇa was not certain. Still, they must have had the Sarvā's statement regarding the seers of the hymn before them. But Veṅkaṭa Mādhava appears to have gone a little further and comprehended the v.3 in a definite way, that steered clear of the problem about the seer. However, it is also true that the two words can be used either as adjectives or as proper nouns. But most of the modern scholars and translators have preferred to take Vītahavya as the name of a seer, following the alternative interpretations of the commentators. Even *Chapekar*[9] has also taken *bharadvāja* in a attributive sense viz., 'one who is full of valour' qualifying *Vītahavya*. Hence, both the words may be treated as proper nouns in the absence of contrary evidence. And, since some other sources, too, confirm the existence of at least one Vītahavya or more than one, it is necessary to examine these traditional sources and find out whether any of them can be identified as the seer of RV 6, 15.

Vītahavya's name occurs twice in the AVŚ (at vv. 6, 137, 1, and 20, 37, 3). At AVŚ 6, 137, 1[10] a story is recorded that Jamadagni dug out for his daughter a medicine called *Keśavardhinī* which was carried away from Asita's house by Vītahavya. The authors of VI dismiss this legend saying that 'there is no substance' in it.[11] This legend may not have been important as such, but for the light that it throws on Vītahavya's association with Bhṛgu's family. At AVŚ 20, 37, 3[12] Vītahavya is mentioned together with Sudās and Purukutsa who enjoy Indra's favour. Here again, Sāyaṇa gives a different interpretation of the word *vītahavya* as qualifying Sudās (*dattahaviṣkaṁ sudāsaṁ*) and then regards *Vītahavya* as a personal name (*athavā vītahavyaṁ sudāsam ca* etc.)[13]

The Vītahavyas, i.e. the descendants of Vītahavya (*vaītahavyāḥ*) are also referred to in the AVŚ thrice.[14] AVŚ (5, 18, 10)[15] says: "They who ruled over a thousand and were themselves ten hundred, the Vītahavyas, when they devoured the cow of the

Brāhmaṇa perished".[16] In the next verse (AVŚ 5, 18, 11)[17], it is further stated: "The cow herself when slaughtered, came down upon the Vītahavyas, who had roasted for themselves the last she-goat of Keśaraprabandha."[18] Thus we are told in the two verses that the Vītahavyas probably thus insulted the Bhṛgus and incurred their wrath. Consequently, they perished. It even said that they killed the cow of the Brāhmaṇas and the last cow (she-goat?) of some Brāhmaṇa woman known by the name Keśaraprabandha[19]. Now the issue is: Who were these Brāhmaṇas, whose cows the Vītahavyas snatched away? Probably they were the Bhṛgus. AVŚ (5, 19, 1)[20] observes: "Beyond measure they waxed strong, just fell short of touching the heavens. When they infringed upon Bhṛgu they perished, the Sṛñjaya Vītahavyas".[21] This Sṛñjaya probably belonged to the Vītahavyas. MBh[22] reports that the Haihaya-Kārtavīryas had a long feud with the Bhṛgus. The feud started, when the Haihaya king demanded from Jamadagni a cow that gave milk for sacrifice. When the latter refused, there started a quarrel between the Bhṛgus and the Haihayas. Jamadagni was killed, and was avenged by his youngest son Rāma, better known as Paraśurāma[22a] who cleared the world of kṣatriyas. To our mind this is probably referred to in the verses. The Vītahavyas are identified with the Haihayas. Thus a feud between the Bhṛgus and Vītahavyas means a feud between the Bhṛgus and the Haihayas.[23]

TS (5, 6, 5, 3)[24] talks of Vītahavya Śrāyasa, son of Śrayas. He appears to be a king. The authors of VI think that 'he may be identified with the Vītahavya of the Ṛgveda' or he may 'belong to the same line.'[25] Among the Sāmavedic Brāhmaṇas, the JB names him four times[26]. Only JB 1, 214[27] attributes a Sāman called *okanidhanam* to Vītahavya, the son of Śrayas. With the help of this Sāman the gods killed the demons. PB also refers to him four times.[28] PB (9, 1, 9)[29] regards Vītahavya as the author of Sāman called *Jyogniruddha*, etc. Also, PB (25, 16, 3)[30] informs that Vītahavya (the son of Śrayas) together with Trasadasyu, (the son of Purukutsa), and Kakṣīvat (the desendant of Uśija), went to one Satrāyaṇa, desiring thousands of sons. The name of Purukutsa and his son Paurukutsi Trasadasyu occur frequently in the RV. They are the "son" and "grandson" of Māndhātṛ of the Solar race (*Sūrya-vaṁśa*). Purukutsa and Trasadasyu were great kings, as per Vedic, Purāṇic and Epic evidence.[31].

Kakṣīvat was probably an Āṅgirasa seer, as indicated by his appellation Auśija ('a descendant of Uśija'). Uśija is considered to be the son of Aṅgiras (grandfather of Dīrghatamas). Kakṣīvat is the son of Dīrghatamas. Identification of Satrāyaṇa is, however, not possible. He might have been one endowed with yogic powers, with which he could grant children to a person desiring to have them. JAB[32] also mentions him (Vītahavya) thrice as an author of some Sāmans.

One Aruṇa Vaitahavya, the son of Vītahavya, composed Ṛgvedic hymn 10, 91[33].

Also, the Va (89, 22)[34] describes another king Vītahavya ruling in Mithilā. He was the son of one Sunaya and the grandson of Ṛta. He had a son named Dhṛti.

The MBh (13, 31,7-54)[35] describes another Vītahavya, who belonged to the Haihaya dynasty of Vatsa country. After a long feud with the kings of Kāśī Vītahavya was defeated by Pratardana, the son of Divodāsa and grandson of Sudeva. Bharadvāja is said to have helped Divodāsa and his son to take revenge on the Vītahavya. In the last battle Pratardana inflicted a total defeat on Vītahavyas. Vītahavya then took refuge in the hermitage of Bhṛgu. When Pratardana approached Bhṛgu and demanded the surrender of the fugitive king, the sage denied that there was a kṣatriya under his protection; thus by virtue of these words Vītahavya became a brāhmin.

The above explains how a kṣatriya king, Vītahavya, turned a brāhmaṇa. Vītahavya's relations with Bhṛgus are emphasized. Elsewhere, we have noted the connection of one Vītahavya with Jamadagni of the Bhṛgus. In v. 2 (hymn 15, of the 6th Maṇḍala) ascribed to Vītahavya, Bhṛgus are mentioned to have placed Agni in the wood like a well-established friend.[36] We have already noted above that in this verse and in the next the name of Vītahavya occurs. Incidentally, Bhṛgus are mentioned only here and Uśanākāvya in RV 6, 20, 8. And it was noticed earlier that in v.3 of hymn 15, Bharadvāja is grouped with Vītahavya. Should we conclude that Vītahavya first joined the Brāhmaṇic fold of the Bhṛgus and then the Aṅgirases, and that is why his hymn was accommodated in the 6th Maṇḍala?

All the Sūtrakāras[37] include Vītahavya in the list of *pravararṣis* of the Bhṛgus. The Vītahavyas who are regarded as a part of the Bhṛgus, have the three *ṛṣi-pravaras*: Bhārgava, Vaitahavya and Sāvedāsa. Mt (194, 39)[38] names Vītahavya among the Bhārgava seers and the *gotra-pravaras*.

There is, therefore, no doubt that one Vītahavya was a Bhārgava seer. But this does not explain why a hymn revealed to a Bhārgava seer Vītahavya should be included in the Bharadvāja Maṇḍala.

As noted earlier, the commentators gave alternative explanations about Vītahavya; and yet, they believed in Sarvā's ascription of RV 6, 15 to Vītahavya as correct. Still, they have left few clues to identify the seer.

SV 2, 917 is also ascribed to one Vītahavya Āṅgirasa.[39] This reference goes to point out that there was a Vītahavya among the Aṅgirases. Now Veṅkaṭa Mādhava, a pre-Sāyaṇa commentator of the RV, while explaining the passage *vītahavyāya sapratha bharadvājāya sprathaḥ* (RV 6, 15, 3) ['grant ample riches and protection to Vītahavya and also to Bharadvāja'], says: *dattahaviṣkāya bharadvājāya bharadvājakulajāya vā vītahavyāya* ['to Bharadvāja who offers oblation or to Vītahavya, a descendant of the family of Bharadvāja].[40] Another interpretation offered by the commentator Veṅkaṭa Mādhava may be based on the authority of the Anukramaṇīs and affirms that tradition was accepted for the identity of the seer up to the 10th century AD, which is Veṅkaṭa Mādhava's age[41]. Thus this Vītahavya need not be identified with any of those Vītahavyas referred to above. The author of the NA insists that he was an Āṅgirasa, a composer of RV 6, 15, and a member of the Bharadvāja family. We discussed elsewhere that the Bharadvājas came from three ṛṣi pravaras: Āṅgirasa, Bārhaspatya and Bhāradvāja'[42]. Hence, any member of this family was entitled to be called an Āṅgirasa. Secondly, a large number of distant descendants of Bharadvāja assumed that they were "only Aṅgirases" (*kevala Āṅgirasa*)[43]. Ajamīḍha and his descendants Kāṇvas adopted this surname. Not surprising that Vītahavya, being one of them, was addressed as Āṅgirasa.

The following points emerge from the above discussion :

1. According to the Sarvā and the commentator Sāyaṇa, Vītahavya is an *optional* seer of the RV 6, 15.
2. The commentators give two interpretations of the word *Vītahavya* taking it as an attribute and as a surname.

3. There were traditionally at least four or five persons named Vītahavya.
4. One of those Vītahavyas was a Bhārgava, whose hymns are lost to us.
5. One of those Vītahavyas was a member of the Bhāradvāja family and composer of RV 6, 15. Thus, in RV 6, 15, 3 the word Vītahavya is to be taken as a personal name and Bharadvāja as the surname of that Vītahavya. Like Śunahotra Āṅgirasa, this Vītahavya was known as Vītahavya Āṅgirasa.

NOTES AND REFERENCES TO CHAPTER IV

Section (i)

1. Sarvā 6, 44: यो रयिवश्चतुर्विशतिः शंयुर्बार्हस्पत्यो ह्यादौ षलनुष्टुभस्तिस्रश्च विराजो मध्यमैव वासाम् ।

2. ABS 11, 9; 11 (Most of the Atharvaṇic hymns ascribed to Śaṁyu are repetitions of his RV verses).

3. NA 1, 4; 2, 3; 4; 6; 3, 1; 7; 10; 4, 6; 7, 1.

4. YVS 1, 14; 3,9.

5. 4 (=1, 357); 45, 1 (=SV 1, 127); 10 (SV 2; 1036; AV 20, 64, 6); 22 (=SV 1016); 23(=SV 2, 1017); 24 (=SV 2, 1018); 25 (=SV 1, 46); 28 (=SV 1, 201), 46, 1(=SV 1, 234; 2, 159; TS, 2, 4, 14, 3; MS 2, 13, 9; 158, 18; KS 12, 15; 39, 11; 12, 2 (=SV 2, 160; MS 2, 13, 9: 159, 2; KS 39, 12); 9 (=SV 1, 266; KS 9, 19): 48, 1 (=SV 1, 35; 2, 53); MS 2, 12, 9: 159, 10; KS 39, 12); 2 (=SV 2, 54; MS 2, 13, 9; 159, 12; KS 39, 12) 5 (=SV 2, 1024; 1050); 7 (=SV 1, 37); 9 (=SV 2, 973): 10 (=SV 2, 974).

6. Sarvā 6, 44: read at note 1.

7. Sarvā 6, 1. बार्हस्पत्यो भरद्वाजः षष्ठं मण्डलमपश्यत् ।

8. For detailed information see our Ch. 2, Section (ii) on Bharadvāja Bārhaspatya's birth.

9. For detailed information see our Ch. 1 Section (i) on Bharadvāja in the Ṛgveda—where these passages come under close scrutiny.

10. RV 6, 45, 31-33: अधि बृबुः पणीनां वर्षिष्ठे मूर्धन्नस्थात् ।
उरुः कक्षोः न गाङ्ग्यः ॥
यस्य वायोरिव द्रवत् भद्रा रातिः सहस्रिणी ।
सद्यो दानाय मंहते ॥
तत् सु नो विश्वे अर्य आ सदा गृणन्ति कारवः ।
बृबुं सहस्रदातमं सूरि सहस्रसातमं ।

11. Velankar, BUJ 9(2) p. 68.

12. MS 10, 107: भरद्वाजः क्षुधार्तस्तु सपुत्रो निर्जने वने ।
बह्वी गाः प्रतिजग्राह न स पापेन लिप्यते ॥

cf. NM 94 असाधोरपि गृह्णीयात् सीदत प्रतिग्रहं द्विजः ।
भरद्वाजो हि तक्ष्णः क्षुत्पीडितो जगृहे बृवोः ।

13. NM 94ff.
The legend has been treated at length by the commentators, Sāyaṇa, RVVSM Vol. 3, p. 152, Veṅkṭamādhava, RVVIS Vol. 4, p. 2105.

14. Sāyaṇa on RV (6, 45, 31ff.) and RVVSM 3, p. 152.

15. Macdonell and Keith, VI 2, 70.

16. Velanker, JBBRAS 42, p. 8.

17. RV 6, 45, 1: य आनयत् परावतः सुनीती तुर्वशं यदुम् ।
इन्द्रः स नो युवा सखा ।

18. RV (6, 46, 8): यद्वा तृक्षौ मघवन् द्रुह्यावा जनेयत् पूरौ कच्च वृष्ण्यम् ।
अस्मभ्यं तद् रिरीहि सं नृषाह्येऽमित्रान् पृत्सु तुर्वणे ॥

19. RV (8, 22, 7): उप नो वाजिनीवसु यातमृतस्य पथिभिः ।
येभिस्तृक्षि वृषणा त्रासदस्यवं महेक्षेत्राय जिन्वथः ॥

20. Sāyaṇa, under RV 8, 22, 7:
त्रासदस्यवं त्रसदस्योः पुत्रं तृक्षिम् । etc.

21. Macdonell and Keith, VI 1, 319;
Cf. Pargiter, AIHT pp. 169-70.

22. RV (6, 46, 8):
यदिन्द्र नाहुषीष्वाँ ओजो नृम्णं च कृष्टिषु ।
यद्वा पञ्च क्षितीनां द्युम्नमा भर सत्रा विश्वानि पौंस्या ।

23. Macdonell and Keith, VI 1, 466-468.

24. *Alitindische Leben*. pp. 119-23.

25. Read: शंयोरा वृणीमहे इत्याह शंयुमेव बार्हस्पत्यं भागधेयेन समर्धयति ।

26. Read: अथ शंयुर्हं वै बार्हस्पत्योऽञ्जसा यज्ञस्य संस्था विदाञ्चकार । स देवलोकमपीयाय । तत्तदन्तर्हितमिव मनुष्येभ्य आस ॥ तद्वा ऋषीणामनुश्रुतमास । शंयुर्हं वै बार्हस्पत्योऽञ्जसा यज्ञस्य संस्थां विदाञ्चकार स देवलोकमपीयायेति ते तामेव यज्ञस्य संस्थामुवायन्यां शंयुर्बार्हस्पत्योऽवेद्यच्छंयोर-ब्रुवंस्ताम्वेवैष एतद्यज्ञस्य संस्थामुपेति याँ शंयु बार्हस्पत्योऽवेद्यच्छंयोराह तस्माद्वै शंयोराह ॥ स प्रति-पद्यते । तच्छंयोरावृणीमह इति तां यज्ञस्य संस्थामावृणीमहे यां शंयु बार्हस्पत्योऽवेदित्येवैतदाह ॥

27. Read: यच्छंयोर्वाकिमाह । प्रतिष्ठा वै शंयोर्वाक प्रतिष्ठित्या एव अथो शंयुर्हं वै बार्हस्पत्यः सर्वान् यज्ञाञ्छमयांचकार । तस्माच्छंयोवाकमाह । यदव उपस्पृशति शान्तिर्वै भेषजमापः शान्तिरेवैषा भेषजमन्ततो यज्ञे क्रियते ॥

28. L. Renou in his *Vocabulaire du Ritual Vedique*, Paris, 1954, at page 145, gives the significance of Śaṁyorvāk:

> "A benedictory recitation by the *hotṛ* at the time when the *prastara* and *paridhi* are thrown in the fire at the end of the new-moon and full-moon offerings. cf. ĀpŚS 3.7.10."

29. Read: एतद्वोऽहं प्रवक्षामि पितृसर्गमनुत्तमम् । शंयुः पप्रच्छ यत् पूर्वं पितरं वै बृहस्पतिम् ॥ बृहस्पतिमुपासीनं सर्वज्ञानार्थकोविदं । पुत्रः शंयुरिमं प्रश्नं पप्रच्छ विनयान्वितः ॥ क एते पितरो नाम कियन्तः के च नामतः । समुद्भूताः कथं चैते पितृत्वं समुपागताः ॥

30. AIHT p. 191.

31. IVA p. 176.

32. AIHT p. 221 Particularly his statement: "The Vedārthadipikā also says they belonged to the Bārhaspatya *gotra* of Śaṁyu, etc." is wholly erroneous and misinterpretation of VD's exposition on the Sarvā 2, 6, 52.

33. The arrangement of the RV does not always reveal uninformity of the principle. Thus, though a Family Book should, ordinarily, comprise the hymns revealed to the seers of that particular family, we notice that the Vāma-deva Maṇḍala contains the hymns (43-44) composed by Ajamīḍha and Purumīḍha Aṅgirases who are sons or descendants of Suhotra Bhāradvāja. So also, the Atri Maṇḍala contains a hymn (29) by Gaurivīti who belongs, probably, to the Aṅgirases, if not to the Vasiṣṭhas. Even the seer Vītahavya who authored the hymn 6, 15 is not a mere descendant of Bharadvāja, but he may be called an Āṅgirasa, i.e. a Kevalāṅgirasa.

Section (ii)

1. Sarvā 2, 6, 15: इममूष्वेकोना वीतहव्य ऋषिर्वा।
2. ABS 4, 25: पूर्वे द्वे केशवर्धनकामो वीतहव्यः।
3. NA 2, 1, 15: समिद्ध भरद्वाजो वीतहव्यो वा आङ्गिरसः।
4. RV 6, 15, 5 (=VS 17, 10; TS 4, 5, 1, 2); 7 (=SV 1567); 8(SV=1568); 9 (=SV 1569); 10 (=TS 2, 5, 12, 5); 14(=TS 4, 3, 13, 4); 16(=TS 3, 15, 11, 2).
5. Read: मित्रं न यं सुधितं भृगवो
दधुर्वनस्पतावीड्यमूर्ध्वशोचिषम्।
स त्वं सुप्रीतो वीतहव्ये अद्भुत
प्रशस्तिभिर्महयसे दिवेदिवे॥
6. Read: स त्वं दक्षस्यावृको वृधो
भूरर्यः परस्यान्तरस्य तरुषः।
रायः सूनो सहसो मर्त्येष्वा
छर्दिर्यच्छ वीतहव्याय सप्रथो
भरद्वाजाय सप्रथः॥
7. RVVSM. Vol. 3, 43-44.
8. RVVIS. Vol. 4, 1990.
9. ABORI Vol. XXXI, 1950, p. 292.
10. Read: यां जमदग्निरखनद् दुहित्रे केशवर्धनीम्।
तां वीतहव्य आभरदसितस्य गृहेभ्यः॥
11. Macdonell and Keith, VI, 2, 317.
12. Read: त्वं धृष्णो धृषता वीतहव्यं प्रावो विश्वाभिरूतिभिः सुदासम्।
प्र पौरुकुत्सिं त्रसदस्युमावः क्षेत्रसाता वृत्रहत्येषु पूरुम्॥

    This verse is repeated from RV (7, 19, 3).
13. Sāyaṇa, under AVŚ 20. 37, 3.
14. AVŚ 5, 18, 10; and 11, 19, 1.
15. Read: ये सहस्रमराजन्नासन दशशता उत।
ते ब्राह्मणस्य गां जग्ध्वा वैतहव्याः पराभवन्॥
16. Bloomfield: Hymns of the Atharvaveda, SBE Vol. XLII, p. 170.
17. Read: गौरेव तान् हन्यमाना वैतहव्याँ अवातिरत्।
ये केसरप्राबन्धायाश्चरमाजामपेचिरन्॥
18. Bloomfield : *op. cit.*
19. *Ibid.*, p. 433.
20. Read: अतिमात्रमवर्धन्त नोदिव दिवमस्पृशन्।
भृगुं हिंसित्वा सृञ्जया वैतहव्याः पराभवन्॥
21. Bloomfield: *op. cit.*, p. 171.
22. MBh 3, 115-17.

22*a*. None of Vedic texts however mention Paraśurāma in any context. Our inference is based on the MBh.

23. Pargiter, AIHT, pp. 151-156.

24. Read: कक्षीवाँ औशिजो वीतहव्यः श्रायसस्त्रसदस्युः
पौरुकुत्स्यः प्रजाकामा अचिन्वत . . . ।

25. Macdonell and Keith, VI 2, p. 317.

26. 1, 214; 323; 2, 110; and 3, 196.

27. Read: तास्व् ओकोनिधनं वैतहव्यं। ओकोनिधनेन वै वैतहव्येन देवा असुरान् ओकस-ओकसोऽनुदन्त।

28. 9, 1, 8; 9, 1, 9; 2, 1; and 25, 16, 3.

29. Read: 'वीतहव्यः श्रायसो ज्योग्निरुद्ध एतत् सामाऽपश्यत् सोऽवगच्छत् प्रत्यतिष्ठदवगच्छति प्रतितिष्ठत्येतेन तुष्टुवानः।'

30. Read: पर आह्णारत्रसदस्युः पौरुकुत्सो वीतहव्यः श्रायसः कक्षीवानौशिजस्त एतत् प्रजापतिकामाः सत्रायणमुपायंस्ते सहस्रं सहस्रं पुत्रान् पुष्यन्ति यं एतदुपयन्ति।

31. IVA, p. 118.

Cf. RV 1, 63, 7; 112, 7; 1 74, 2; 4, 42, 9; 6, 20, 10. for Purukutsa and RV 1, 112, 14; 4, 38, 1; 42, 8; 9; 5, 27, 3; 33, 8; 7, 19, 3; 8, 8, 21; 19, 36; 36, 7; 37, 7; 49, 10; 10, 150, 5 for Trasadasyu.

32. 1, 155; 188; 214.

33. Sarvā 2, 10, 91: संजागृवद्भिः पञ्चोनारुणो वैतहव्य आग्नेयम्।

34. Read: विजयस्य ऋतः पुत्र ऋतस्य सुनयस्मृतः।
सुनयाद्वीतहव्यस्तु वीतहव्यात्मजो धृतिः॥

35. For details see Chapter 2, Section on Bharadvāja, Divodāsa and Vītahavya. Here we reproduce a few details only for argument's sake.

36. Read at note no. 5 above.

37. ĀśvŚS, 6, 10, 10: भार्गववैतहव्य सावेतसेति॥

Cf: ĀpŚSP3. तेषां त्र्यार्षेयो भार्गववैतहव्यसावेतसेति॥

38. Read: ग्रामदश्च तथैषामार्षेयाः प्रवर मताः।
भृगुश्च वीतहव्यश्च तथा रैवसवैनसौ।॥ 194, 39

39. NA. 2, 1, 15: समिद्ध भरद्वाजो वीतहव्यो वाऽङ्गिरसः।

40. RVVIS Vol. 4. p. 1990.

41. Raja, C.K., Introduction to the Ṛgvedānukramaṇī, p. xiii.

42. ĀśvŚS 6, 10, 5. See Chapter 1, Section (i) on Bharadvāja in the RV; and Ch. 2, Sec. (ii) on Bharadvāja Bārhaspatya's birth, etc.

43. Baudh ŚS: 20-26.

Chapter Five

THE BHARADVĀJAS VIS-A-VIS *DIVODĀSA ATITHIGVA AND OTHER DIVODĀSAS*

In the galaxy of the princes, whose names occur in the Śākala Saṁhitā of RV, Divodāsa stands the foremost.[1] The MBh contains quite a few legends about him.[2] The Purāṇas[3] place him in the genealogy of the Bharatas. The Śrauta Sūtras[4] show him as belonging to the Bhārgavas.

The Ṛgvedic Divodāsa, who fought perpetual wars against Śaṁbara, the demon, is said to have been Bharadvājas' patron.[5] Divodāsas of PB[6] and MBh[7] had some relation with the Bharadvājas. Some of the evidences in this has already been noticed and certain observations on them made in the course of our discussion thereon.[8] But since the problem of identification of different Divodāsas still awaits a detailed study, we propose to append this section here in order to deal with the problem exclusively.

The name Divodāsa occurs in the RV eighteen times including once in plural;[9] eight of these are in the hymns of the Sixth Maṇḍala,[10] i.e. the hymns ascribed to the Bharadvājas themsleves. And most of the remaining ten references are in the hymns ascribed to the Aṅgirases who are closely connected with the Bharadvājas.[11] As Divodāsa is mostly referred to by the Bharadvājas and Āṅgarasas, it may be presumed that he had some affinity with them or their families.[12] Also, the epithet Atithigva (identical with Divodāsa)[13] occurs in the RV thirteen times[14]—most of these are in the hymns ascribed to Aṅgirases and Bharadvājas. This cannot in any way be a coincidence; it significantly reveals Divodāsa Atithigva's relation with the Bharadvājas in particular and the Aṅgirases in general.

In Ṛgveda, there is a verse in the Sixth Maṇḍala (6, 61, 1) which hints at Divodāsa's parentage. It says that Sarasvatī gave to Vadhryaśva, the sacrificer, Divodāsa who was impetuous and could release him (Vadhryaśva) from debt (*iyám adadāt rebhasám ṛṇacyútam dívodāsam vadhryaśváya dāśúṣe*). This may mean that Vadhryaśva, who ruled the kingdom on the bank of the river Sarasvatī, had a child, Divodāsa, by the grace of the river-goddess Sarasvatī. Velankar,[15] however, thinks that Divodāsa was not Vadhryaśva's (aurasa) son, but he was brought to him by the (river) goddess Sarasvatī—Vadhryaśva adopted him as his own. In RV (6, 61, 1c and 3ab) it is said that Sarasvatī helped Vadhryaśva to destroy his Dāsa foes, the chief of whom was Bṛsaya. Agni Vaiśvānara also aided Vadhryaśva in the same mission. This means that the Dāsa chieftain Bṛsaya and his followers lived somewhere on the bank of the river Sarasvatī and their fortresses were burnt down by Vadhryaśva and his army; those which remained were washed away by the floods of the Sarasvatī. Also, might have been swept the young prince of Bṛsaya, the king of the Dāsas; the child fell into the hands of the Aryan king Vadhryaśva and was adopted and named Divodāsa (*divaḥ+dāsaḥ*)—'the servant of the Heaven', not of any human being, even an Aryan. Or[16] Divodāsa was actually an Aryan prince, who had very unluckily fallen into the hands of the Dāsa chieftain Bṛsaya, who instead of putting him to death, brought him up carefully till the Aryans, led by Vadhryaśva vanquished him, completely destroying him together with his *Dāsa* followers and secured the release of the captive Prince. As a reminiscence of his erstwhile captive state he was named as Divodāsa. This account appears to be highly probable and may be preferred to the former. Yet another story is still more likely that this Divodāsa was actually a Bharata prince, may be an *aurasa* son of Vadhryaśva himself. He might have been taken as a captive by the Dāsa chieftain Bṛsaya in an earlier encounter with Vadhryaśva and his people, wherein the Aryans were defeated and Bṛsaya lifted the prince and adopted him. Later, the Aryan king Vadhryaśva avenged the earlier defeat and secured the release of the young prince after putting Bṛsaya and his Dāsa followers to death. (This version might be preferred to the two earlier ones because no Vedic or Purāṇic text gives an instance when an Aryan king ever adopted a Dāsa Prince as his son.) However, as the sages always saw God's hand in every affair of their life, so also the regaining of the young prince was attributed to the goddess incarnate of the river Sarasvatī, on whose bank the Aryans performed sacrifices in order to please the gods. It is not, thus, absurd to name the child as Divodāsa, as he was got by the grace of a god or goddess. The legends of being blessed with sons and daughters by the grace of gods abound in our literature, and Divodāsa's birth or release from captivity is one of them.

However, among the modern scholars Hillebrandt[17] considered Divodāsa to be a king of the Dāsa people, like Bṛbu. He inferred this from RV (6, 61, 1 and 3ab). He thought that Divodāsa was engaged in conflicts with the tribes of Arachosia. Macdonell and Keith[18] disagree with Hillebrandt's suggestion. For, the river Sarasvatī on which the battle in question took place can hardly be Haraquity of Arachosia. To our mind it appears that Hillebrandt's view neglects the Purāṇic sources, wherein the genealogy of the Bharatas consistently names Divodāsa as the son of Vadhryaśva. It is needless to repeat that these Bharatas were of the Aryan origin and their locale was the Doab the of Gaṅgā and the Yamunā while Sarasvatī might have joined these two at Prayāga.

Divodāsa and Atithigva

At one time, Bergaigne[19] took Divodāsa and Atithigva as two different individuals. Macdonell and Keith[20] rightly differed from him "in view of the complete parallelism in the acts of the *two* persons." And thus Divodāsa and Atithigva were identified as one and the same person. In a later date, Velankar[21] found that the view of the authors of VI "is not still very accurate." In his opinion, there is 'one king called Divodāsa' while "there are not less than four different kings of the name Atithigva mentioned in the Ṛgveda." In the RV, there are at least four verses that refer to Divodāsa and Atithigva in the same breath.[22] The poet Kutsa Āṅgirasa says (RV 1, 112, 14): 'With whatever help you protected great Atithigva Divodāsa, who rushed to the waters,[22a] for the killing of Śaṁbara; with whatever help you protected Trasadasyu at the time of destroying the castles, with those, You, O Asvins, come to us' (*yā́bhir mahā́m atithigvám Kaśojùvam dívodāsam śaṁbarahátye ā́vatam/ yā́bhiḥ purbhídye trasádasyu, ā́vatam tā́bhir ū ṣú ūtíbhir aśvinā́ gatam//*) Atithigva here appears in apposition to Divodāsa. In RV (4, 26, 3 ascribed to Vāmadeva) Indra himself is reported to have said: "I have overthrown the ninetynine castles of Śaṁbara at one stroke as I was filled with wild delight, while I favoured Divodāsa Atithigva" (*ahám púro mandasānó vyáiram náva sakám navatī́ḥ śaṁbarasya/... dívodāsam atithigvám yád ā́vatam//*). In this passage also, Divodāsa and Atithigva appear to be one and the same person. In both the extracts, cited above, Divodāsa and Atithigva are (grammatically) in the same case and number. But in the following verse (*i.e.* RV 6, 47, 22) the two names have different cases, when Garga Bharadvāja reports to Indra: 'We have received from Divodāsa a gift which is worthy of Atithigva and consists in treasures that once belonged to Śaṁbara, (the vanquished)', (*Divodāsād atithigvásya rā́dhas śā́mbaraṁ vásu práty agrabhīṣma*). Again, the poet Parucchepa Aindra says (RV 1, 130, 7) that Indra battered down ninetynine forts (of Śaṁbara) for Divodāsa, to help Atithigva and he hurled the demon Śaṁbara from the mountain. While recounting Indra's exploits of destroying the fortifications (that belonged to Śaṁbara) and the killing of Śaṁbara, the poet made two statements to affirm Indra's support for Divodāsa and Atithigva. But we need not lose sight of the fact that the action against the demon must have been in sequence; instead of repeating Divodāsa's name in the second stanza, he denoted his epithet, may be for metrical reasons or poetic licence. Thus all those four quotations point to the fact that Divodāsa and Atithigva were one and the same person. Even while commenting upon these verses where only the epithet *Atithigva* occurs, Sāyaṇa[23] takes it to mean Divodāsa (cf. Sāyaṇa under RV 1, 51, 6; 6, 18, 13; 26, 3; 7, 19, 8). And Sāyaṇa is right to hold that Atithigva mentioned in RV (1, 51, 6) is none but Devodāsa, for, Śaṁbara was killed to serve former's interest. Śaṁbara is elsewhere[23a] spoken of as Divodāsa Atithigva's enemy. However, it is difficult to decide whether Atithigva mentioned together with Kutsa and Āyu can be identified with Divodāsa. Probably that Atithigva was different from Divodāsa Atithigva.

Divodāsa and Śaṁbara

Now we turn to the Divodāsa-Śaṁbara episode. There are 24 passages in the RV in which Śaṁbara is referred to.[24] Out of these 6 references occur in the Sixth Maṇḍala, mostly in the hymns addressed to Indra, who killed Śaṁbara, for the sake of Divodāsa. Whether Indra himself killed Śaṁbara and destroyed his hundred castles [and therefore he (Indra) was called Purandara, is an open issue] or did Divodāsa, a prince of the Bharatas, kill the demon, who happened to be his contemporary from some non-Aryan race but antagonised the Aryan hero and his people, is doubtful.

Abel Bergaigne[25] thinks that the Śaṁbara-Divodāsa episode is a myth. But in recent time Bhat[26] has refuted his contention and has brought out the human aspects of Divodāsa-Śaṁbara conflict. We assess the problem afresh.

Śaṁbara is said to be the son of Kulitāra (Kaulitāra) in RV (4, 30, 14). He figures in RV (1, 101, 2) with Vyaṁsa, Pipru and Śuṣṇa, in RV (1, 103, 8 with Śuṣṇa and Pipru), in RV (2, 19, 6 with Śuṣṇa), in RV (6, 18, 8 with Cumuri, Dhuni, Pipru and Śuṣṇa), and in RV (2, 14, 6 and 6, 47, 21 with Varcin). Sometimes, he is called a *dasyu* (as in RV 1, 59, 6; 6, 31, 4). He is reported to have been killed in a slaughter of *dasyus* (*dasyuhátye* of RV 1, 51, 6; 112, 14). Occasionally, he is described as a *dāsa* (dāsam kaulítāram, etc., RV 4, 3, 14; 6, 26, 5). Probably, he lived in the hilly region and was thrown to death from the mountain peak (RV 1, 130, 7; 2, 24, 2; 4, 30, 14; 6, 26, 5). He had a hundred castles, out of which Indra destroyed all but one. In certain texts, Indra is described to have battered down ninety castles (RV 1, 130, 7) but in others all ninetynine (RV 2, 19, 6; 4, 26, 3; 6, 47, 2; 7, 99, 5; 9, 61, 1). After destroying all those fortresses, Indra killed Śaṁbara. After a long search for forty years, Indra tracked him to a mountainous region (*yaḥ śámbaram párvateṣu kṣiyántam catvārimsyám śarády anvávindat*; RV 2, 12, 11). Indra killed Śaṁbara for the sake of Divodāsa (RV 1, 112, 14; 130, 7; 2, 19, 6; 4, 26, 3; 6, 26, 5; 43, 1; 47, 22; 9, 61, 2). And it is said that Indra acquired the 100th castle (of Śaṁbara) for Divodāsa Atithigva (RV 4, 26, 3: *Śatatamam veśyàm sarvátātā dívodāsam atithigvám yád ávam*). RV(6, 47, 22)[27] states that Divodāsa gifted to Bharadvāja treasures acquired from the vanquished Śaṁbara. All these point to the battle fought by Indra *for the sake of* Divodāsa Atithigva. As a matter of fact, Divodāsa himself was involved in the war against Śaṁbara and his people. Indra was Divodāsa's favourable god, with whose grace, the poets believed, the Aryan hero vanquished the non-Aryan enemy. Whatever brought victory to Divodāsa was attributed to Indra. From this narrative, it appears to have been actually a human action. There were two sides, one the Aryan invader and the other native non-Aryan people. Due to the pressure and large-scale destruction of human habitations, the non-Aryans probably took to the hills but were pursued by Divodāsa and his army; after a long protracted and bloody war Śaṁbara was killed in his mountainous abode. Thus Divodāsa was an Aryan hero, who extended the Aryan habitation further towards Indian midland.

Divodāsa and Bharadvāja

Bharadvāja and Divodāsa are frequently mentioned together.[28] Their juxtaposition in those references hints they were related to each other. And we would see what sort of alliance is indicated.

In the Sixth Maṇḍala itself we come across a passage ascribed to Bharadvāja (6, 16, 5), where the poet addresses Agni: 'Do you bring these ample boons to Divodāsa, the presser (of soma) (and) to Bharadvāja who offers oblations to you.' (*tvám imā́ vā́ryā purú dívodāsāya sunvaté/ bharádvājāya dāśúṣe//*). Here the two persons pose as if they were involved in a sacrificial session, where one was a soma presser (may be sacrificer), while the other, the tenderer of offerings into fire (*i.e.* the priest). Similar inference is drawn from RV (6, 31, 4) which is addressed to Indra: "You battered down the hundred matchless forts of Dasyu Śaṁbara, when you sought to give rich treasure to the sacrificer Divodāsa and the singer Bharadvāja, by your power, O powerful god brought by Soma" (*tvám śatány áva sáṁbarasya púro jaghanthā-pratī́ni dásyoḥ/áśikṣo yátra śacyā śacīvo dívodāsasya sunvaté sutakre bharádvājasya gṛṇaté vásūni//*). In this particular verse, Divodāsa acts as a soma-presser and Bharadvāja, a singer-poet. The hymn (RV 6, 47, 22)[29] ascribed to Garga Bhāradvāja and addressed to Indra, states, 'We received from Divodāsa gift which is worthy of Atithigva; the gift consists in the treasures of Śaṁbara, conquered from him.' In the verse (RV 6, 47, 23) the poet reports receiving from Divodāsa ten horses, ten treasure-boxes, ten highly valuable garments and ten lumps of gold with prominent horse and a hundred cows' (*dáśáśvān dáśa kóśān dáśa vástrádhibhojana/dáśo hiraṇyapiṇḍán dívodāsādasāniṣam//*). The next verse (6, 47, 24)[30] indicates that Aśvatha made a gift to Pāyu and his followers, the Atharvan. The following verse (6, 47, 25)[31] states that the son of Sṛñjaya (Prastoka) honoured the Bharadvājas. Thus Pāyu Bharadvāja (who composed, RV 5, 75) and his father Bharadvāja (as stated in BD 5, 125-142) lived in the same period as Divodāsa Atithigva, and Sṛñjaya's son

Pratoka.[32] Elsewhere[33], we have seen that former (two) and Abhyāvartin were contemporaries, descendants of the Bharatas, and linked with the Bharadvājas. Bharadvājas helped Prastoka and Abhyāvartin against the Varaśikhas, and probably, Divodāsa against Śaṁbara. That is why all the princes made gifts to the Bharadvājas. The Bharadvājas were the priests of the Bharatas, particularly of Divodāsa—reference to their names with the same breath confirms this. This conclusion is further strengthened by the other three verses, outside the Sixth Maṇḍala. In two passages of the hymn (RV 1, 112) Bharadvāja and Divodāsa are together described as the proteges of the Aśvins, (cf. vv. 13-14)[34]. RV hymn (1, 116, 18) speaks of Bharadvāja and Divodāsa in the same *pāda*: "when with great speed you, O the Aśvins, went to Divodāsa, to Bharadvāja, on your usual round your car brought splendid riches: a porpoise and a bull were yoked together." (*yád áyātam dívodāsāya vartír bharádvājāyaśvinā háyantā revádu vāha sacanó rátho vāṁ vṛṣabhásya śiṁśumárasya yuktá*). These point to the intimate relationship between Bharadvāja and Divodāsa as the proteges of the Aśvins. But Divodāsa was a prince of the Bharata family and the patron and liberal donor, who made gifts to that Bhāradvāja, who was a descendant of Bharadvāja Bārhaspatya and the father of Pāyu Bharadvāja. He probably composed most of the hymns of Sixth Maṇḍala—and that cannot be earlier than Divodāsa's time.

Divodāsas of Epics and Purāṇas

After discussion all about the Ṛgvedic Divodāsa Atithigva, his priest and enemies we may now examine Epics and Purāṇas, which mention more than one Divodāsa, each of distinct parentage, locale and time.

The Kāśī kingdom saw probably two Divodāsas. The first was the son of Bhīmaratha; he established the city of Vārāṇasī[35] (Va 92, 23). For certain reasons, the city was cursed by Nikuṁbha; and Divodāsa had to vacate it. And a Rākṣasa, Kṣemaka, took the city.[36] Divodāsa built another one on the banks of the Gomatī and settled there. After the period of curse lapsed, Bhadraśreṇya, a king of the Haihaya dynasty, occupied the city.[37] Divodāsa recovered the kingdom from Bhadraśreṇya's sons. But Bhadraśreṇya's son Durdama re-captured it.[38] Aṣṭaratha succeeded

Divodāsa. According to the Purāṇas, Pratardana was the son of Divodāsa and he put an end to the feud.[39]

The MBh (13, 30)[40] says that there was perpetual strife between the Haihayas and the princes of Kāśī. The Haihayas, under the leadership of Vītahavya attacked the Kāśī kingdom and defeated the king Haryaśva. Subsequently, his son Sudeva was killed in action by the Haihayas. Sudeva's son Divodāsa, apprehending danger from the Haihayas, built a city called Vārāṇasī at the confluence of the Gomatī and the Gaṅgā. The Haihayas again attacked. Divodāsa gave them a valiant fight before he was defeated and driven out of his capital. He took refuge with his Purohita Bharadvāja, who assured him help. The sage performed a sacrifice, desiring for Divodāsa a son, powerful enough to defeat the Haihayas. As a result of the sacrifice, it is said, a son called Pratardana was born. Pratardana was sent to attack the Haihayas. Pratardana not only inflicted a defeat on the Haihayas led by Vītahavya, but also routed them. Vītahavya then fled and sought protection of a Bhārgava sage. When Pratardana demanded the surrender of Vītahavya, the Bhārgava sage announced that there was no Kṣatriya in his Āśrama. Having heard this, Pratardana was satisfied with the fact that he had at least compelled Vītahavya to be a Brāhmaṇa leaving his Kṣatriyahood.

Pargiter,[41] who analysed these legends, is of the opinion that there were two Divodāsas in the Kāśī dynasty, one the son of Bhīmaratha, who was succeeded by his brother Aṣṭaratha. This Divodāsa probably established his capital in Vārāṇasī. He was a contemporary of Bhadraśreṇya of the Haihayas. The other was son of Sudeva and father of Pratardana. He was a contemporary of Vītahavya of the Haihayas and also of Bharadvāja. Thus, there were at least three generations between Divodāsa I and Divodāsa II viz., Aṣṭaratha, Haryaśva and Sudeva. Pratardana, who recovered the Kāśī kingdom, was the son of Divodāsa II. Even the KS (21, 10)[42] and PB (15, 5, 7)[43] state that the priest Bharadvāja helped Pratardana and restored to him the kingdom of Kāśī.

The third Divodāsa was son of Vadhryaśva of the North Pāñcāla dynasty that branched forth from the Bharatas. The Purāṇas[44] give us a genealogical tree of the Bharatas after Ajamīḍha, the grandson of Suhotra Bhāradvāja. According to the Purāṇas,[45] Ṛkṣa (probably Tṛkṣa as suggested by Pradhan) was

Ajamīḍha's son. Tṛkṣa's son was Bhṛmyaśva, who had five sons: Mudgala, Sṛñjaya, Bṛhadiṣu, Yaviyān and Kāmpilya. As each of them was capable of defending himself and the kingdom, they were called the Pāñcālas (from *Pāñca* + *alaṁ*—an instance of popular etymology!). The eldest of them Mudgala is said to have married Indrasenā Nāḷyāyanī, the daugher of Nāḷa (or Naḍa).[46] She is sometimes called Mudgalānī. Mudgala is referred to in the RV(10, 102, 5 and 9) and Mudgalānī Indrasenā in RV (10, 102, 2 and 6). Their son was Vadhryaśva, who is referred to in the RV (6, 61, 1; 10, 69, 1; 2; 4; 10; 11 and 12). Vadhryaśva's wife Menakā gave birth to twins: Divodāsa and Ahalyā. This Ahalyā was given in marriage to Gotama, the son of Śaradvat and they are said to have had a son named Śatānanda who was the priest of Sīradhvaja Janaka of Mithilā.

We have already seen above that in RV(6, 61, 1) Sarasvatī is said to have brought Divodāsa to Vadhryaśva. We have also identified Divodāsa with Atithigva. And now we find that this Divodāsa and his father Vadhryaśva were descendants of Bharata and princes of the North Pāñcāla dynasty.

Pradhan,[47] Pargiter,[48] Rahurkar,[49] and Mankad[50] all agree that Divodāsa Atithigva of the RV and king Divodāsa of North Pāñcāla dynasty was one and the same person. Pradhan[51] further identifies this Divodāsa (of RV) with Divodāsa of Kāśī, mentioned in the Epic. His argument is that Bharadvāja was the priest of both Divodāsas; and Bharadvāja occurs in the Rām, a contemporary of Rāma. Rāma redeemed Ahalyā from a curse. In the Purāṇas, Ahalyā is stated as the sister of Divodāsa of North Pāñcāla. So also is Śatānanda the son of Ahalyā. Besides, Pratardana of Kāśī visited Ayodhyā at the time of Rāma's coronation. And thus Pradhan[51a] proves Bharadvāja, Rāma, Pratardana, Ahalyā, Śatānanda as contemporaries. He contends that as Pratardana is mentioned in the Rām he was Rāma's contemporary, and therefore, Divodāsa, Pratardana's father, was a contemporary of Daśaratha. As Ahalyā is mentioned in the Rām, her brother Divodāsa was identified with Pratardana's father Divodāsa. And thus, according to Pradhan, Divodāsa Atithigva of the RV, Divodasa of Kāśī, and Divodāsa of the North Pāñcāla dynasty, were one and the same person. Rahurkar[52] and Mankad[52a] appear to have accepted Pradhan's thesis. However, Pargiter holds that Divodāsa Atithigva and Divodāsa of Pāñcāla were identical,[53] but Divodāsa of the Kāśī dynasty was different from Divodāsa Atithigva who is identified with Divodāsa of the North Pāñcāla dynasty.[54] Further, he says that Divodāsa II of Kāśī was a contemporary of Bharadvāja Bārhaspatya; the latter was the priest of the former. They flourished before Bharata Dauṣyanti. Divodāsa I was still anterior to Divodāsa II. They cannot be identified with Divodāsa Atithigva. We fully uphold Pargiter's contentions in preference to those of Pradhan, because Divodāsa I, Divodāsa II and Pratardana were princes of the Kāśī dynasty and their parentage etc., are clearly stated in the Epic and Purāṇas. The first Divodāsa was a contemporary of Bhadraśreṇya, and the second of Vītahavya of the Haihayas; Pratardana, the son of the Divodāsa II, was contemporary of Sagara of Ayodhyā. All of them lived before Bharata. On the other hand, Divodāsa Pāñcāla was a remote descendant of Vidathin Bhāradvāja, adopted by Bharata. His parents are distinctly stated in the text as Vadhryaśva and Menakā. The question is : Where can we place all these in a series? That would involve location of places. Nowhere in Vedic and post-Vedic texts Kāśī princes are described as the scions of the Bharatas. The Kāśī dynasty is always a separate entity. Thus Divodāsa and Pratardana (of Kāśī) cannot be regarded as Bharata princes; consequently, to consider Divodāsa of Kāśī as Divodāsa of the Pāñcāla dynasty is untenable. Redemption of Ahalyā by Rāma from her curse is mythical and the genealogy from Gotama Śāradvata to Kṛpa is too discontinuous to be credible. Even if Ahalyā were the sister of Divodāsa (Atithigva) of Pāñcāla, Pratardana's father, Divodāsa, would be her brother. Pratardana's exploits are given in the Uttarakāṇḍa—which is deemed as a later addition to Rām—and he is described as prince of Kāśī, not as a Pāñcāla prince. Nothing is recorded in the text to prove that Kāśī and Ahicchatra were administered by the same Bharata prince.

It has been also argued by S.N. Pradhan[55] that Timidhvaja Śaṁbara was a contemporary of Daśaratha; the latter fought with the former, in accompaniment of Rājarṣis ('royal seers'), who probably included Divodāsa. Yet, we fail to understand why Vālmīki should have refrained from giving Divodāsa's name. On the other hand, Timidhvaja might have been a descendant of Śaṁbara or any other person. One Śaṁbara lived in the times of Pradyumna, the son of Kṛṣṇa.[56] Should we, therefore, hold that he was the Ṛgvedic Śaṁbara? Even Pratardana of Kāśī mentioned in the Rām might have been a descendant of Pratar dana, the son of Divodāsa Saudeva. Divodāsa Atithigva was a king powerful enough to kill Śaṁbara with the grace of Indra. He could not have been a vassal of Daśaratha. So also Divodāsa of Kāśī, who was overwhelmed by Vītahavyas, cannot be considered as the overthrower of Śaṁbara. On the whole, Divodāsas of Kāśī and of Pāñcāla cannot be the same person in the face of several discrepancies. And we conclude, they are different persons.

H.C. Seth[57] has tried to identify Divodāsa and others with the scions of Median Princes. He sums up his findings in the following table :

	Median kings
Ṛgveda	*Herodotus and other Greek Sources*
Divodāsa	Deioces
Pratardana	Phraortes (Fravartis)
Atithigva	Astyages (Ishtuvegu)

The above line of Ṛgvedic kings is based on a wrong contention. We have already seen that Divodāsa of the Kāśī line and his son Pratardana were not Bharata princes. And we said that Atithigva and Divodāsa of Pāñcāla dynasty were identical, but Divodāsa of Kāśī was another person. But Seth has sought to establish that (1) Divodāsa and Pratardana were ancestors of Atithigva and (2) Divodāsa, Pratardana and Atithigva belonged to the same line—Median royal family. Thus Seth's contention is erroneous and untenable.

Further, Seth has sought to establish a chronology of certain hymns (viz. RV 6, 26 and 31), through the above thesis. In his view, these hymns were composed in the 6th century B.C. He has thus ignored the basis of Indian chronology. Everyone knows it well that between the age of the RV and that of Gautama, the Buddha, one or two millennia might have lapsed. None can date the Ṛgvedic hymns so as to place them nearer Gautama, the Buddha. Hence Seth's thesis is not tenable.

The date of Divodāsa Atithigva depends upon that of the Mahābhārata war.[58] Divodāsa was a contemporary of Jayatsena or his son Rucīra of the Hastināpura line and lived 13 or 14 generations prior to the Pāṇḍavas and the Kauravas who were later locked in the fatricidal war of MBh. If we assume that a generation span is thirty (30) years, the period between the

Kurukṣetra War and Divodāsa's time would be at least $(14 \times 30) = 420$ years. If Mahābhārata war was fought in 3100 B.C., Divodāsa would have lived around $(3100+420)=3520$ B.C.[59] This date, however, may depend on duration of a generation and the time of the great war of the MBh.

We may now outline our views as follows:

(i) There were at least three Divodāsas known to traditional sources; two belonged to the Kāśī dynasty while the third to the Pāñcāla line of the Bharatas.

(ii) There were more than one Atithigva known to the Ṛgvedic poets. One of them could be identified with Divodāsa of the RV, and he in turn with Divodāsa of the North Pāñcāla dynasty.

(iii) Divodāsa II of Kāśī, who was father of Pratardana, cannot be Divodāsa Atithigva because of the differences in parentage, time and locale.

(iv) Divodāsa II of Kāśī had probably Bharadvāja Bārhaspatya as his priest and lived before Bharata Dauṣyanti.

(v) Divodāsa Atithigva was a contemporary of Sṛñjaya, and his sons Prastoka, and Abhyāvartin Cāyamāna—all of them had Bharadvāja, the father of Pāyu (seer of RV 6, 75), as their common priest.

(vi) Bharadvāja, the priest of Divodāsa Atithigva, was probably a remote descendant of Bharadvāja Bārhaspatya, the priest of the Kāśī princes.

(vii) Most of the hymns of the Sixth and some other Maṇḍalas may not be assigned a date earlier than 3520 B.C., *i.e.* that of Divodāsa Atithigva.

(viii) The Bharadvājas were first aligned with the Kāśī princes and then with the Bharatas.

(ix) Timidhvaja Śaṁbara of the Rām could not have been Śaṁbara of RV; they are two different persons.

NOTES AND REFERENCES TO CHAPTER V

1. A number of princes are mentioned in the Ṛgveda; some of them are already taken into consideration in a separate paper (to be published) on the family hymns of the Bharadvājas. Besides these, some of the princes are also encountered when the biographical sketch of Ajamīḍha was analysed (Part I, Ch. 3, Section viii) above. Vadhryaśva, and Sudās are noted here. Besides, there are yet some other princes who belong to dynasties other than the Bharatas—they cannot be treated here for want of place.

2. See our section on Divodāsa in Part I, Ch. 2, Section (iv).
3. Read notes 36-39 and 45 below.
4. AśvŚSP 6, 10, 12; BaudhŚS p. 6.
5. See the section on the Bharadvājas in the RV. (Ch. 1, Section i) above.
6. PB 15, 3, 6-7.
7. Read note (2) above.
8. See Part I, Ch. 1, Sec. (i); Ch. 2, Sec. (iv) especially; also see Ch. 3, Sec. (vii) on Ajamiḍha.
9. RV 1, 112; 116, 18; 119, 4; 130, 7; 10 (in plural); 2, 19, 6; 4, 26, 3; 30, 20; 6, 16, 5; 19; 26, 5; 31, 4; 43, 1; 47, 22; 23; 61, 1; 7, 18, 25; 9, 61, 2.
10. Ibid.
11. Only two occurrences, *viz.* RV 7, 18, 25 and 9, 61, 2 found in the hymns composed by the seers other than those from the Aṅgirases.
12. Divodāsa himself was a descendant of Aṅgiras. See Part I, Ch. 3, Section (vii) for details.
13. Identify of Divodāsa and Atithigva is established in subsequent paragraphs.
14. RV 1, 51, 6; 53, 8; 10; 112, 14; 130, 7; 2, 14, 7; 4, 26, 3; 6, 18, 13; 26, 3; 47, 22; 7, 19, 8; 8, 53, 2; 10, 48, 8.
15. ABORI, Silver Jubilee Vol. 1942, p. 659 ff.
16. Velankar, Ibid.
17. Hillebrandt, VM, I, 96, fn. 2.
18. VI Vol. 1, p. 363.
19. VRII, pp. 352, 354-356.
20. op. cit. 1, 364.
21. op. cit. p. 657.
22. RV 1, 112, 14; 130, 7; 4, 26, 26, 3; 6, 47, 22.

22a. The meaning of the word *kaśoju* is not clear. The commentator Skandasvāmin (RVVIS 2, 818) suggests that *kaśoju* is singer of praise (*stotṛ*) (?) Sāyaṇa takes it as an epithet of Divodāsa (*asurabhītyā Udakam praveṣṭum gantāram*, RVVSM 1, 681). Velankar translates it "who has the speed of a whip" (ABORT, 23, 661) and (Griffith HRV p. 73) treats it as a proper noun. Following Sāyaṇa, K.P. Jog, translates it as 'who rushed to the waters' (cf. his unpublished Thesis "The Aśvins in the Ṛgveda and their traces in the later literature", submitted to Bombay University, 1964, p. 306).

23. RVVSM 1, 346; 3, 73; 103; 314.

23a. See the paragraphs that follow.

24. RV 1, 51, 6; 54, 4; 59, 6; 101, 2; 103, 8; 112, 14; 130, 7; 2, 12, 11; 14, 6; 19, 6; 24, 2; 3, 47, 4; 4, 26, 3; 6, 18, 8; 26, 5; 31, 4; 43, 1; 47, 2; 21; 7, 18, 20; 99, 5; 9, 61, 2. It is surprising that the Śambara episode finds no mention in the 5th, 8th and 10th Maṇḍalas of RV.

25. VR 2, 352-56.
26. *Vedic Themes*, p. 72.
27. Read: प्रस्तोक इन्नु राधसस्त इन्द्र दश कोशयीर्दश वाजिनोऽदात् ।
दिवोदासादतिथिग्वस्य राधः शाम्बरं वसु प्रत्यग्रभीष्म ॥
28. RV 1, 112, 13-14; 116, 18; 6, 16, 5; 31, 5; 47, 22.
29. Read note 27 above.

30. Read: दश रथान् प्रष्टिमतः
शतं गा अथर्वभ्यः ।
अश्वथः पायवेऽदात् ॥

31. Read: महि राधो विश्वजन्यं दधानान्
भरद्वाजान्त् साञ्जयो अभ्ययष्ट ॥

32. See Part II, Ch. 3 Sections (iv) on Garga and (vi) on Pāyu Bharadvājas respectively for further information.

33. Ibid.

34. Read: याभिः सूर्यं परियाथः परावति
मान्धातारं क्षैत्रपत्येष्वावनम् ।
याभिर्विप्रं प्र भरद्वाजमावतं
ताभिरू षु ऊतिभिरश्विना गतम् ॥
याभिर्महामतिथिग्वं कशोजुवं
दिवोदासं शम्बरहत्य आवतम्
याभिः पूर्भिद्ये त्रसदस्युमावनं
ताभिरू षु ऊतिभिरश्विना गतम् ॥

35. Read: अथ केतुमतः पुत्रो विभो भीमरथो नृपः ।
दिवोदास इति ख्यातो वाराणस्याधिपोऽभवत् ॥

36. Va 92, 24 ff.

37. Ibid. 92, 63.

38. Ibid. 92, 63.

39. Ibid. 92, 64. The subsequent verses give the genealogy further.

40. We have already discussed the whole legend in Part I, Ch. 2, Section (iv).

41. AIHT, pp. 154-155.

42. Read: एतेन ह स्म वै भरद्वाजः प्रतर्दनं संनयह्यन्नेति ततो वै स राष्ट्रमभवत् ।

43. Read: दिवोदासं वै भरद्वाजपुरोहितं ननाजनाः पर्ययन्त स उपासीद्रदृशे गातुं मे विन्देति ।
तस्मा एतेन साम्ना गातुमविन्दत् । . . . . . .

44. Some parts of this genealogy have been already discussed in Part I, Ch. 3, Section (vii), while referring to Ajamiḍha.

45. Va 99, 194-211; Mt 50, 1-16.

46. The identification of Indrasenā as the daughter of Nala, the king of the Niṣadha country has been ably established by S.N. Pradhan, CAI, p. 5, fn. 3. And Pradhan's discussion on the genealogy of the North Pāñcāla dynasty is commendable; vide CAI pp. 1-19, also 83ff ... cf. Pargiter, AIHT pp. 115-117.

47. op. cit. pp. 1-19.

48. AIHT pp. 115-117; 168-170.

49. SR. pp. 96-97.

50. DRg. pp. 5-7.

51. op. cit.

51a. op. cit.

52. op. cit. p. 97.

52a. op. cit. 5-7.

53. op. cit. pp. 115-117 and 168-170

54. op. cit. pp. 153-155 nd fn. 5 at page 154.
55. op. cit. pp. 16-18.
56. Vis. 5, 27, 1-31.
57. ABORI 23, 1942, pp. 451-64. *Histories of Herodotus*, Book I, Ch. 96-130.
58. The date of the Mahābhārata has been the bone of contention for a long time. Many an eminent scholar has tried vigorously to give a definite or near-definite date of the war. S.B. Roy, in his recently published work, the *Date of the Māhabhārata Battle*, (Delhi, 1976) pp. 101-164 has given the summary of the previous researches on the date of the Māhabhārata War. Roy has pointed out four views of the date given by scholars:

Group A	circa 3100 B.C.
Group B	circa 2500 B.C.
Group C	circa 1450 B.C.
Group D	circa 950 B.C.

Mankad (*Puranic Chronology*, p. 107), Krishnamacari (*History of Classical Literature* pp. xli-lxxvii), C.V. Vaidya (*History of Sanskrit Literature*) (Vedic period pp. 4-8 and *Mahābhārata, A Criticism* pp. 65-92) belong to group A.P.C. Sengupta (*Indian Chronology*) represents the Group B. Cunningham (*Archaeological Survey—first report*, 1864), A.D. Pusalkar, (*History and Culture of Indian People* Vol. I, pp. 300 and 269), B.G. Tilak (*Gitā Rahasya* (Hindi) pp. 548-552), Pradhan, (CAI pp. 269)—among many others represent the group C. Pargiter (AIHT pp. 175-183) and Roy Chaudhury (*Political History of Ancient India*, 5th Ed, pp. 35-36) represent the last group.

After a great deal of argument, Roy (p. 146) has come to the conclusion that 1424 B.C. is the date of the war: this actually falls in his group C. The author(s) of the Vedic Age (*History and Culture of Indian People*) also hold the same view. We are, however, inclined to accept the date given by the scholars who belong to the Group A (*i.e.* circa 3100 B.C.) as the probable date of the Mahābhārata War. And on the basis of this date, our calculation of the Age of the Vedas, particularly the date of Bharadvāja and Divodāsa Atithigva of Ṛgvedic fame is made.

59. See also concluding remarks on this date.

PART TWO

SELECTED CONTRIBUTIONS OF THE BHĀRADVĀJA FAMILY

CHAPTER SIX

VEDIC THEMES

Section (i)

Pūṣan: Myth and Cult

The contribution of the Bharadvājas to ancient India's culture, religion and mythology can be gleaned from the Pūṣan hymns of the Sixth Maṇḍala; these not only throw light upon myth-making and the specially-preserved Pūṣan-cult of the family, but also reveal a pastoral-nomadic character of the people in and around the Bhāradvāja clan. To note their significant contribution is relevant here.

In this Maṇḍala of the RV, god Pūṣan occupies the third important place, *i.e.* just after Indra and Agni; Indra has the first position with 30 hymns addressed to him, and Agni the second with 16. Pūṣan is praised in five hymns in RV (6, 53-56 and 58) alone and in another place (RV 6, 57) conjointly with Indra. All these hymns are ascribed to Bharadvāja Bārhaspatya.[1] Besides, Śaṁyu Bārhaspatya praises him in six stanzas of a long hymns, (viz. RV 48, 14-19). Moreover, Pūṣan is referred to and praised in RV (6, 17, 11; 21; 9; 24, 5; 49, 8; 50, 5 and 51, 11) with other gods. However the portion of the Sixth Maṇḍala which is dedicated solely to Pūṣan is so striking that the German Vedist Hillebrandt preferred to call it *eine kleine Pūṣansaṁhitā* ('a small Pūṣan saṁhitā').[2]

It is noteworthy that in the whole of the RV Pūṣan is celebrated in altogether eight hymns and in two other hymns he forms a dual divinity with Indra (RV 6, 57) and Soma (RV 2, 40). Thus it is indeed remarkable that six out of ten hymns should be in the sixth Maṇḍala alone.

Another noticeable fact is that Pūṣan's name occurs in the whole of the RV 120 times; in the Sixth Maṇḍala alone 36 times, in the 2nd 3 times, in the 3rd 5 times, in the 4th thrice, in the 5th 8 times, in the 7th 6 times, and in the 8th 6 times. In the First Maṇḍala he is mentioned twenty-eight times and in the Tenth twenty-six times. The Ninth Maṇḍala contains only four references to Pūṣan.

It may be noted that out of the four hymns (addressed to Pūṣan alone or jointly with some other gods) that occur outside the Sixth Maṇḍala, two are in the First Maṇḍala, one each in the Second and the Tenth. The hymn in RV (1, 42 and 138) are ascribed to Kaṇva Ghora and Parucchepa Daivodāsi respectively.[3] Kaṇva is an Āṅgirasa seer. Parucchepa Daivodāsi probably belonged to the family of Divodāsa, who claimed his descent from Bharata. As pointed out elsewhere, they are connected with the Bharadvājas. As regards Gṛtsamada (the author of RV 2, 40 addressed to Soma and Pūṣan), we have stated that he was a son of Śunahotra Bharadvāja and was adopted by Śaunaka of the Bhṛgus.[4] We are, however, not sure of Vimada or Vasukra (a seer of RV, 10, 26)[5] —whether both or either of the two were related to the Bharadvājas. However, we have noticed that most of the sages who praise Pūṣan either in well-knit hymn or in stray verses, belong to the Aṅgirases. This indicates that Pūṣan was probably a household deity of the Aṅgirases, specially of the Bharadvājas. Elsewhere[6], we have seen that the Aṅgirases were cow-worshippers. Pūṣan being a god connected with the cattle—cows, it is but natural that they should be his devotees.

There are different theories, regarding one or the other aspect of the god, put forward by scholars, about his real character; someone emphasizing his pastoral nature,[7] some other his path finding aspect,[8] still another describing him as the Moon-god,[9] yet someone else taking him for the Sun-god[10] and so on. Among these theorists Dandekar[11] appears to have correctly stressed the original character of Pūṣan as pastoral.

Pūṣan appears to be a curious and enigmatic deity for a Vedic student. His anthropomorphic traits are very scanty but distinct from those of other gods. Pūṣan is portrayed with braided hair (6, 55, 2 *kapardín*) and a beard (10, 26, 7). In his right hand (6, 54, 10), he holds typical weapons *ārā* ('awl') and *áṣṭrā* ('goad'). The fellies and the wheel of his chariot also are mentioned (6, 54, 3). His car is drawn not by the horses but by the goats (*ajā́śva*). He eats gruel of grains (*karambhá*). His popular epithet is the glowing one (*ā́ghṛṇi*). Most of these traits are exclusively distinguishing him from other Vedic gods. It would appear that the Pūṣan mythology was independent of that of other well-known gods and his cult was probably developed among the Aṅgirases, with Bharadvājas being prominent. This sect ran concurrently with those of Indra, Agni and Soma for some time, until at a later period some assimilation was achieved among them, through hymns to dual divinities such as Indra and Pūṣan, and Soma and Pūṣan etc.

To our mind Pūṣan's primary character as a pastoral god is stressed in the hymns seen by Bharadvāja. The hymn (RV 6, 54) describes Pūṣan as such. At RV 6, 54, 5 he is asked to look after the cows (as a shepherd?) and protect the horses (*pūṣā́ gā́ ánvetu naḥ| pūṣā́ rakṣatu árvataḥ||*). Also, in the next verse he is urged to tend the cattle of the sacrificer, who presses soma for him and those of the poet himself (*pū́ṣann ánu prá gā́ ihi yájamānasya sunvatā́ḥ| asmā́kam stuvatā́m utá ||*). He is asked to keep vigilance on cows so that none be lost, none be injured, none fell into a pit; he is asked to come back (home) with them unharmed (*mā́kir neśan mā́kīṁ riṣan mā́kīṁ saṁ śāri kévaṭe|áthā́riṣṭābhir ā́ gahi||*). Then the poet exhorts his people: "We come as suppliants to Pūṣan who listens to us, who is (ever) watchful, whose property (*i.e.* cattle) is never lost, who is Lord of wealth (*śṛṇvántaṁ pūṣáṇaṁ vayám íryam ánaṣṭavedasam|ī́śānaṁ rāyá īmahe* || RV 6, 54, 8). Here the epithet *ánaṣṭavedasam* (whose property is never lost) is significant, and comparable to *ánaṣṭapaśu* (at 10, 17, 3 : *ánaṣṭapaśur bhúvanasya gopā́ḥ*), which clearly says that Pūṣan is a deity whose cattle are never lost and then cattle (in sense of property) is used earlier also. Thus our poet further hopes that whatever be lost (*i.e.* whichsoever cattle be lost) let Pūṣan drive the same home (*púnar no naṣṭám ā́jatu*). These activities attributed to Pūṣan are primarily related to a herdsman who rears cattle in a grassy field. And, if Pūṣan was primarily a Sun-god or Moon-god, these activities could not have been expected from him. In this connection we may notice some more epithets here. One such is *paśupā́* (the cattle-protector) (RV 6, 58, 2). This is significant because a god related to a pastoral tribe is described as a protector of their cattle. He is also *ajā́śva* 'whose carriers (horses) are goats.'[12] Goats are sure-footed and climb up mountainous slopes. Thus as a god herding cattle, Pūṣan is expected to ride a goat, a cart drawn by goats. Our poet remarks "let the two sure-footed goats convey Pūṣan on his chariot, drawing the god who brings a good fortune." Besides, in connection with the Aśvamedha sacrifice, a goat is said to be Pūṣan's share that is suitable for All-gods and that is led ahead with a mighty steed (*eṣá chāgah puró áśvena vājínā pūṣṇó bhāgó niyate viśvádevāḥ* RV 1, 162, 3). This indicates that the goat which is Pūṣan's share leads the sacrificial horse—something significant.

Pūṣan's weapons are typical of a shepherd. Pūṣan is asked (RV 6, 53, 5): "Pierce the (hard) heart of the Paṇis with thy goad, O poet" (*pári tṛndhi páṇīnām árayā hṛdayā kave*/). Árā (√*ar*) refers to a weapon having sharp points (as indicated by the verb pári tṛndhi). Sāyaṇa[13] explains it as: *sūkṣmalohāgro daṇḍaḥ pratodaḥ* 'a goad with sharp-pointed iron pins'. Thus it appears to be an awl or a goad with a sharp needle or a pin at its end used for punishing the hated enemies (like the Paṇis).[14] It is also called *brahmacódanī* as it secured riches and thereby inspires hymns.[15] Another interpretation of *brahmacódanī* is that which is invested with or consecrated by muttering *bráhma* 'magically potent formula' (in accompaniment of certain practices). The weapons were, in time of war, always hurled at the enemies after they were consecrated with magically potent *mantra* (vide *bráhma várma mámántaram* RV 6, 75, 19).

The other typical weapon held by Pūṣan is *aṣṭrā*; it is described as: "made of leather thongs" (góopaśā) and "means for increasing cattle or driving the cattle forward" (*paśusádhanī*).[16] The form *opaśá* has been explained as *ava+paś*> 'to *bind*' *avapāśa*>*opaśā* means 'tuft or cresy or thong'.[17] Thus *go-opaśā* appears to mean that which has a tuft or cresy of cows (hide). Áṣṭrā is called *paśusádhanī* (6, 53, 9) that helps increase the cattle or that drives the cattle to field and back to stall. Thus these two weapons served for Pūṣan two distinct purposes: *árā* for punishing the enemies who (probably) lift the cows, (*i.e.* the Paṇis) while *aṣṭrā* was used to guard the cattle who, it was believed, would multiply by its use.[18] All these emphasize the pastoral chatacter of Pūṣan.

Pūṣan is called *karaṁbhád*, one who eats *karaṁbhá* ('gruel', 'ground food'). The pastoral tribes habitually take gruel instead of cooked food, particularly when they are tending the cattle in a field or a forest. The cowherd often goes out with his animals early in the morning. He has to carry some food for mid-day meal. It is not possible for him to carry cooked food. But he can easily take the gruel with him anywhere. It is worth noting that even in a sacrifice Pūṣan is offered *karaṁbhá* (in pots) instead of Soma. The sage Viśvāmitra says (RV 3, 52, 7): "For you, (Indra) accompanied by Pūṣan, we have prepared gruel" (*Pūṣan-*

váte te cakṛmā karaṁbhám). In RV (6, 57, 2), Pūṣan is said to have desired gruel (*karaṁbhám anyā icchati*). Because, earlier the cowherd offered *karaṁbhá* to Pūṣan before he ate. The cowherd was never ashamed of being called *karaṁbhā́d*; so also he did not consider it food for a weakling. Thus their god who was offered *karaṁbhá* was not a weakling. The poet puts it as "whosoever aims at Pūṣan saying malignantly that he is merely a gruel-eater and can never strike him successfully" (*yá enam ādīdeśati karaṁbhā́d iti pūṣáṇam ná téna devá ādíśe* // RV 6, 56, 1). Thus the poet Bharadvāja and the fold do not consider *karaṁbhā́d* as derogatory in sense. This means that *karaṁbhá* was a time-honoured food among the seers.

Why does Pūṣan take *karaṁbhá*? To answer such question, SB[19] preserves a passage which states that Pūṣan was toothless. The Purāṇas[20] also preserve a myth about Pūṣan's being toothless.

As a pastoral god, Pūṣan is involed to lead the singer to a pasture. The poet's concern over the cows' being lost while going to the pasture is expressed (in RV 8, 4, 18): "The cows often go to the pasture; may that wealth be sure to us O Immortal one" (*párā gā́vo yávasam káccid āghṛṇe nítyam rékṇo amartya*).

The word *pastoral* is used in a wider context that includes agriculture also. Thus we find (RV 4, 57, 7) the poet Vāmadeva[21] saying: "Let Indra press down the furrow, let Pūṣan direct it. Rich in milk may it yield milk for us year after year" (*indraḥ sī́tām ní gṛhṇātu tā́m pūṣānu yacchatu/ sā́ naḥ páyasvatī duāhm úttarām-ūttarām sámām*). Pūṣan is mentioned in two agricultural hymns of the AVŚ.[22] In AVŚ (3, 17)—which contains much material from RV 10, 101 and 4, 57—the poet prays for success in ploughing, Indra is called upon to press down the plough-share (the furrow) and Pūṣan to protect it (AVŚ 3, 17, 4=RV 4, 57, 7).[23] Another hymn (AVP 12, 6, 6) seeks success in agriculture: this bears close resemblance to AVŚ 3, 17: it says "Dhātṛ, Pūṣan and Bṛhaspati have effected *samajim* of the earth; the gods who are dispensers of light have effected Kṛṣi (*i.e.* the personification of the cultivated soil)."[24] A question may be asked, if Pūṣan is called pastoral for his association with agriculture why are not Indra, Bṛhaspati and Dhātṛ so called? We have already seen Pūṣan's connection with cattle; other gods (Dhātṛ, Indra, Bṛhaspati) are not so connected with cattle. They are mentioned in the company of Pūṣan.

While discussing Pūṣan as a pastoral god, we may point to other two aspects of Pūṣan which very well fit in the context. We have seen that an epithet *'rathī́tamaḥ'* is thrice repeated (RV 6, 55, 2; 56, 2; 3) in connection with Pūṣan. Besides, at RV 10, 26, 5 he is called driver of chariot-steeds (*aśvahayó ráthānām*), at RV 10, 26, 1 he is described as possessing a chariot equipped with a team (*niyútrathaḥ*). The poet invokes (RV 10, 26, 8[25]): "O Pūṣan, may thy goats turn hither thy chariot's pole. (You are) the friend of every suppliant, born of old, steadfast." So also he says (RV 10, 26, 9): "Let mighty Pūṣan advance our chariot (*i.e.* the hymn) by his might."[26] In RV (6, 57, 6) poet Bharadvāja says: "We draw Pūṣan and Indra up, close to ourselves for our broad well-being as the charioteer (does) his reins."[27] Thus there remains no doubt that the poet considered Pūṣan as an excellent charioteer, who needs to be an expert in the *Aśvavidyā*. Kṛṣṇa and Śalya are mentioned in the MBh as excellent charioteers, because they were experts in the horse-rearing.[28] Kṛṣṇa's connection with the pastoral tribe of Gokula is well-known. Thus, Pūṣan's being an excellent charioteer points to the same fact. As Pūṣan was an expert charioteer, the wheel of his chariot does not get damaged, the cabin of the chariot does not fall off, nor does the felly of the chariot wheel become loose (RV 6, 54, 3).[29]

Pūṣan's character is emphasized as the lord of Paths (*Pathas pati*). The seer asks Pūṣan to bless him with wealth and a brave and loveable household (RV 6, 53, 2), to the person who knows (the path) to the lost property (RV 6, 54, 1). He is regarded as the best leader. He clears off the obstructions on the paths, and kills the enemies. Above all, Pūṣan leads his band of people to success, while they are seeking for their cows. His authority is emphasized by such epithets as *pathás pathás pāripatiḥ* 'the guardian of every path-way' (RV 6, 49, 8). RV (1, 42) composed by Kāṇva Ghora affords further evidence of this role. This is confirmed in RV (10, 17, 5).[30] This hymn, ascribed to Devaśravas Yāmāyaṇa (vide the Sarvā 2, 10, 17) says: 'Pūṣan knows all these regions thoroughly. May he conduct us by the safest (path). Bestowing well being, glowing, keeping (our) descendants undiminished, alert, let him go ahead (of us) (*i.e.* lead our way) knowing (the way)."[31] And "On the forward (leading) path of paths was Pūṣan born, on the forward (leading) path of heaven on the forward (leading) path of Earth. To both the regions, dearly loved (by him), he goes (travelling) to and fro (*i.e.* between Heaven and

Earth) knowing (the way)."[32] Thus, Pūṣan's knowledge of path is praised and he is asked to lead the dead. In the funeral hymn AVŚ (18, 2, 53)[33], the poet says: "Send Pūṣan to (us) that he may lead us on straight forward leading paths, him, who goes there (to heaven)". And in the marriage procession also, Pūṣan is invoked: "Let Pūṣan taking thy hand, lead thee hence; let the Aśvins convey thee forth on their chariot" (RV 10. 85, 26).[34] Even Pūṣan's goat leads the horse of the Aśvamedha because of its master's knowledge of the paths.[35]

To our mind, Pūṣan's knowledge of paths was primarily needed for guiding the cowherd and shepherd. At times, a shepherd or a cowherd had to face trouble while leading the cattle in far off grazing fields, forests, hills and dales. They always prayed Pūṣan for guiding them in the right direction. This invocation, later, became so popular that it was solicited for a bridal procession, Aśvamedha excursion and even for the journey of the dead—all in the late hymns. This aspect originated in the traditions, which emphasized only the pastoral aspect of the god.

As a god of the pastoral tribe Pūṣan was invoked to put down the enemies of the tribe, *viz.* the Paṇis. The hymn (6, 53) appears to be a sort of magic formula directed towards them. In RV (6, 53, 3-10) Pūṣan is asked either to soften the heart of the Paṇis or to kill them. At v. 3 the poet invokes Pūṣan to motivate him who is not so inclined to give; soften the heart even of a Paṇi.[36] In vv. 5-7[37] the god is repeatedly requested to pierce the hearts of the Paṇis, or prick them with the awl of the god or tear open and rend the hearts of the Paṇis. In v. 8, the poet asks the god to tear and rend the heart of everyone (of the Paṇis) with his awl, that is stimulated by the magically potent *mantras.*[38] This hymn (6, 53) thus expresses bitterness of the Aryan poet-priest towards the Paṇis, about whom nothing definite can be said. But the author leaves an impression that these Paṇis were non-Aryan, anti-religious persons and lacked generosity.

The Paṇis prominently figure in RV (10, 108)[39] where Saramā, a messenger of Indra asks the Paṇis to release the cows and wealth of Indra, who, otherwise, could inflict punishment upon the erring ones. From this hymn it appears that they were dwellers of rocky regions where they could hide their cows. They probably had worn some arrow-proof garments (v. 6), and their words offended others. Depending probably upon this information,

Dandekar[40] says, "The Paṇis represent a distinct community belonging to a religion different from the official Vedic. They always wandered with the Vedic cattle breeding tribes and often used to harass them. References to their riches and thefts are quite common in the Veda. The Paṇis were notorious cattle-lifters, and therefore, particularly antagonistic to the Bharadvājas. Thus, there was, in the early Vedic times, a continuous conflict between the Bharadvājas and the Paṇis; and the former often invoked their patron-god, Pūṣan, to punish these mischievous cattle-lifters".

It is noteworthy that Bṛsaya, Vala and Bṛbu are considered as representing the Paṇis. Bṛsaya's forces were washed away by Sarasvatī and referred to in RV (6, 61, 1-3); Vala's conflict with Bṛhaspati and Indra is mentioned in many passages of RV; while Bṛbu is the only person described as a generous patron of Bharadvāja in RV (6, 45, 31-33)[40a]. The Vala myth relates to Bṛhaspati, the father of Bharadvāja. Bṛsaya is referred to by Bharadvāja in relation to Vadhryaśva, Divodāsa's father, the latter's patron probably Pāyu's father. And Bṛbu was generous patron (*sūri*) to Bharadvāja, probably the same as the son of Bṛhaspati. Thus it appears that Paṇis were connected with the Bharadvājas, either as their friends or their foes. But the hymn (RV 6, 53) mainly treats them as foes and prays to Pūṣan to punish them.

It will be worthwhile to see Pūṣan's relation with other gods. We have already mentioned that Pūṣan is praised conjointly with Indra in RV (6, 57) and with Soma in RV (2, 40). In RV (6, 57) a contrast between the character of Indra with that of Pūṣan is brought out. Indra is described sitting near the pressed out Soma, and Pūṣan longing for gruel (v. 2);[41] while Indra has bay-steeds as his carriers, Pūṣan has only goats (v. 3).[42] Yet, the poet yearns for their friendship to ensure his well-being (v. 1) and says that, while Indra achieved great deeds, Pūṣan was his ally (v. 4). This hymn attempts to bring the two gods together. Dandekar[43] sees in it an attempt at assimilation of two distinct Indra and Pūṣan-cults, which, according to him, ran parallel for some time. It was Bharadvāja who successfully achieved their integration. Originally, there was a marked difference between Indra and Pūṣan, so far as their food (RV 6, 57, 2) and vehicles were concerned. But subsequently Pūṣan came to be regarded as his associate in action (RV 6, 56, 2; 57, 4) and later on he was called brother of Indra (RV 6, 55, 5). This development could be artificial.

In RV (2, 40) also, this assimilation is suggested.[44] This hymn seeks to secure for Pūṣan a share in the sacrifice. It is ascribed to Gṛtsamada whom we have already considered as a descendant of Śunahotra Bhāradvāja.[45] It praises Soma and Pūṣan as creators of riches, Heaven and Earth and protectors of all the world, and gods made them the navel of the immortal (v. 1).[46] Pūṣan resides in Heaven while Soma on Earth: both are asked to release wealth (v. 2).[47] Pūṣan is called all-pervading, and Soma the grantor of wealth (v. 6).[48] In spite of their distinct character, two gods are sought to be brought together.

Thus, the two hymns attempt at depicting connections between Indra and Pūṣan, and Soma and Pūṣan.

"Pūṣan's relations with Sūryā, the Sun-maiden, certainly speak for some sort of connection with Sun, although the part that he plays in her marriage is extremely obscure and almost impossible of satisfactory interpretation."[49] Impelled by desire, Pūṣan goes on Sūryā's embassy with his golden ships which glide in the atmosphere (RV 6, 58, 3). Gods gave him Sūryā (RV 6, 58, 4). But when the Aśvins were recommended by the gods, as the suitors of Sūryā, Pūṣan agreed to be their son (RV 10, 85, 14). Then Pūṣan is asked to lead the Aśvins to the marriage (RV 1, 184, 3). Yet, Pūṣan is called the lover of his sister and suitor of his mother in RV (6, 55, 4 and 5). Atkins[50] thinks that the mother and the daughter referred to above are one and the same, namely Sūryā. In addition to Pūṣan being connected with Sūryā and the Aśvins, he is said to have set off on a travel at Savitṛ's inspiration (10, 139, 1) with his divine might, he oversees all forms and is of constant *ordinance* like Savitṛ (RV 10, 139, 3) and Savitṛ becomes Pūṣan by his paths (RV 10, 17, 4). All this goes to show Pūṣan's relation with solar divinities.

It may also be pointed out that there is some faint similarity between Pūṣan and Rudra. Pūṣan is called *kapardin* (RV 6, 55, 2 and 9, 67, 11) which Atkins[51] takes to mean "one who wears strings of cowry-shell" or "who has his hair adorned with cowry-shells". RV (1, 114, 1) describes Rudra as *karpardin* (*imā́ rudrā́ya tavā́se kapardíne* (cf. RV 1, 114, 5 also). Macdonell[52] takes it in the sense of 'one who wears braided hair'. Both the gods are connected with animals. Pūṣan is *paśupā́* 'protector of the cows, or animals' (*ajā́śvaḥ paśupā́ vā́japastyaḥ*, etc., RV 6, 58, 2). And elsewhere, particularly in the VS[52a], AV[52b] and Brāhmaṇas[53] epithet *paśupati* 'lord of beasts' is assigned to Rudra "because unhoused cattle are peculiarly exposed to his attacks and are, therefore, especially consigned to his care"[54]. Thus Pūṣan is connected with the domestic animals, cattle, cows, horses, goats, etc., and he is "the protector" of the cattle (*paśupā́*) while Rudra lords over all the untamed animals and is, therefore, *paśupati*. It is noteworthy that both the gods are invoked in the ritual of *Vṛṣabhotsarga*. The *Vṛṣabhotsarga* is held on a full-moon day which falls on Revatī *nakṣatra,* the presiding deity of which is Pūṣan himself.

There are a few epithets which hint at the solar aspect of Pūṣan, the most frequent being *āghṛṇi,* which occurs fifteen times in the RV.[55] It means 'glowing with heat' (derived from *ghṛ* 'to boil'). Another one in lesser usage, is *agohya* 'unconcealable' (10, 64, 3), which is given to Savitṛ as well. Pūṣan is also called *Ī́śānam jágatas tasthúṣas páti* '(to) the lord of the animate and inanimate objects' (1, 89, 5), *víśvam...abhicákṣāṇa* 'beholding all beings' (2, 40, 5); *saṁcákṣāṇo bhúvanā*: 'beholding all creatures' (6, 58, 2), *saṁpáśyan víśvā bhúvanāni* gopā́ḥ: 'the protector surveying all creatures' (10, 139, 1); *bhúvanasya gopā́ḥ*: 'the protector of creatures' (10, 17, 3); *viśvaminváḥ*: 'all impelling' (2, 40, 6); *nṛcákṣā*: 'looking on men' (10, 139, 2); and *subándhur divá ā́ pṛthivyā́*: 'close relative to heaven and earth' (6, 58, 4). Pointing out at all these give his distinctive traits. Atkins[56] says that "he was a sun god with distinct characteristics and functions, a deity differing markedly from Sūrya, Savitṛ, Viṣṇu and Mitra. He was, surely, a rural divinity, the deity of the herdsmen, of the shepherds, and of the countrymen".

Pūṣan is often invoked by the Vedic seers as a benevolent god. From a pastoral deity who protected the cattle and herds of the worshippers, prevented them from being lost, guarded them from the way-layers and thieves, and caused them to multiply. Pūṣan, in course of time, developed into the lord of riches, and a dispenser of wealth and welfare among men in general. "As Pūṣan was a herdsman-god, so the gifts and property that he bestowed were measured at first in terms of cattle wealth as noted above. From his concrete and specific aspect as a dispenser of cattle he advances to the position of a lord of nurture and god of general affluence."[57] Thus the Vedic seers considered him as *rāyó dhā́rā*: 'a stream of wealth' and *vásu rāsír* 'an abundance of riches' (6, 55, 3); and *ī́śānam rā́dhaso maháḥ* 'lord of great munificence' (6, 55, 2; 1, 138, 3). So also he is called *vā́jānāmvṛdháḥ* 'increaser of wealth' (10, 26, 9). Thus, as a god of affluence, he is requested to shower riches upon seers and their people. Two other peculiar epithets of importance are *vimócana* 'liberator' (8, 4, 15; 16) and *vimúco nápāt* 'son of liberation' (1, 42, 1; 6, 55, 1). In this respect, attention is drawn to some passages in the AV where he is once asked to help the delivery of a woman at parturition[58] and another time, from sin incurred by a man marrying when his elder remains a bachelor.[59] It is easy to understand that the Atharvaṇic poet considers him a god presiding over marriage, who can grant a husband to even a widow.[60]

From the above discussion, it may be inferred that Pūṣan was primarily a deity of a pastoral tribe with certain distinct features. Pūṣan, probably emerged as a god through a process of elevation from a human hero[61] who was credited with protection of the cattle, guiding them on safe path, securing increase in cattle and granting liberally wealth to the people around, etc. This type of a hero was particularly required to inflict punishment upon the notorious enemies of the nomadic (Aryan) pastoral tribe, *viz.*, the Paṇis. This hero, Pūṣan, who successfully protected the cows, etc., from the Paṇis and other evils was elevated to godhead and a Pūṣan-cult came into existence among the Bharadvājas and Aṅgirases. Steadily, the deeds of the hero (*i.e.* the historical facts) passed through the process of mythologization[62] and reality was obscured because of the mythological dust that enveloped it. Yet the worship continued to persist among the Bharadvājas and other Āṅgirasa sub-clans like the Kāṅvas, Daivodāsas etc. This Pūṣan religion continued for a long time, as distinct from other well-known Indra-cult, Agni-cult and Soma-cult. Probably the Bharadvājas and Gṛtsamadas made a conscious attempt to bring Pūṣan nearer to Indra and Soma. Consequently all families later on accepted Pūṣan as one of the gods of the Vedic pantheon and some *ṛcas* were addressed to him in the hymns addressed to the Viśvedevas. This is borne out by the fact that none of the family Maṇḍalas except those of Bharadvāja and Gṛtsamada contain Pūṣan hymn(s); it is only in the hymns to the Viśvedevas that he is met with, but rarely.

Atkins[63] tried his best to show that Pūṣan was primarily a solar divinity of 'a pastoral tribe' or 'a sun-god pastorally conceived'. His approach is contested by Dandekar[64] who contends that Pūṣan is primarily a pastoral god, upon whom a halo was imposed at a later date. We have no hesitation in accepting Dandekar's viewpoint. We agree with him that the Bharadvājas were the custodians of the Pūṣan-cult and shaped the Pūṣan mythology on the basis of the pastoral phenomenon and left it as their legacy. To be a god, association of light is needed, for the word *deva* means 'bright-one'. Thus Pūṣan mythology was caused to be connected with light—the sun and Heaven, and Pūṣan, a tribal hero of a pastoral community, became a full-fledged god and claimed his share with Indra and Soma. But some of the tribal traits and cultural elements remained to speak of the background of the godhead of Pūṣan. Two cultural words *karaṁbhā́d* and *kapardín* probably hint at this development. Besides, the two distinct weapons of Pūṣan—*brahmacódanī ā́rā* ānd *gó-opaśā paśusā́dhanī áṣṭrā* are two other material remnants of that tribal culture. To our mind the two expression *mātúr didhiṣú* and *svásuḥ jāráḥ* may be considered as the legacy of the non-material elements of the same culture, that speak of a distinct custom prevailing in the society of a pastoral community, wherein Pūṣan-cult and Pūṣan-mythology took its primary shape.

Section (ii)

The Family Hymn(s) and the Battle Charms

Each of the so-called family Maṇḍalas of RV contains some traces of the uncommon activities of early ancestors or the forefathers. Their uncommon acts are generally recorded in some hymn(s), ascribed usually to a junior member of the family. Important from socio-historical point of view these are designated "the family hymns".[1] Thus RV 3, 53; 5, 40; 6, 47 and 7, 33 are family hymns respectively of Viśvāmitra, Atri, Bharadvāja and Vasiṣṭha. Each of these seeks to glorify some important event or an achievement by its founder or its prominent ancestor in connection with their patron king.

Generally, a "family hymn" always comes at the end of a group addressed to Indra.[2] Beside the description of the eploits of the ancestor concerned, it always contains a *dānastuti* or an Atharvaṇic charm or the both.[3]

The hymn RV 6, 47, ascribed to Garga Bharadvāja[4] also, comes at the close of the Indra-hymns in that Maṇḍala and contains a *dānastuti* and a charm. However this *dānastuti* cannot be treated in isolation; for, according to BD,[5] it relates to another *dānastuti*, occurring in RV 6, 27, 5-8 and also to the *Saṁgrāma Sūkta* (RV 6, 75), which is considered as an Atharvaṇic charm used at the time of the war. Under this uniformity (of contexts) we may treat these hymns serially, *i.e.* (i) RV 6, 47 (ii) RV 6, 27 and (iii) RV 6, 75.

The hymn RV 6, 47 can be divided into five component parts[6]: (1) vv. 1-5 in praise of Soma; (2) vv. 6-13 in praise of Indra, where the poet requests the deity for his help in the impending battle against the foes; (3) vv. 14-21 : description of Indra's readiness to help even a weakling; (4) vv. 22-25 : a *dānastuti* referring to the princes Prastoka (the son of Sṛñjaya) and to Divodāsa Atithigva who bestowed gift on Pāyu Bhāradvāja and his men; (5) vv. 26-31 : in praise of *dundubhi*; this may be related to hymn RV 6, 75, which is normally known as a battle charm. Vv. 26-28 and 29-31 are repeated in the AVŚ forming two separate hymns (viz., 6, 125 and 126).

It will be seen that the fourth and the fifth parts of the hymn (RV 6, 47) are far more important than others inasmuch as they contain some data of socio-historical importance, and also a charm usable in a battle.

V.22[7] says that Prastoka, the son of Sṛñjaya, gave to Bharadvāja ten treasure boxes and ten horses from the booty gained in a just-then-concluded-war. The poet (and his people) also received from Divodāsa, the wealth previously possessed by Śaṁbara, which now belonged to Atithigva. As per v. 23[8] the poet has obtained from Divodāsa ten horses, ten treasure-boxes, ten highly valuable garments and ten lumps of gold. V. 24[9] adds that Aśvatha gave to Pāyu and his followers, the Atharvans, ten chariots with best horses and a hundred cows. V. 25[10] records that the son of Sṛñjaya, *i.e.* Prastoka, has honoured the Bharadvājas and conferred on them such a great gift as is helpful to people. These verses clearly constitute a *dānastuti* and describe, thus, how and with what the princes Prastoka, Divodāsa (and Aśvatha) honoured the Bharadvājas, particularly Pāyu and his Atharvan's followers.

These princes acquired the booty in the war where they emerged victorious and probably against Śambara and Varcin (verse 21). In verse 22, the booty is termed as *Śāmbarám vásu* "the wealth belonging to Śambara". Śambara was a sworn enemy of the Aryan hero Divodāsa for whom Indra killed him in the fortieth autumn,[11] at a place called Udavraja. Definitely, the Bharadvājas played a great role in that war as the priests of these princes. Though their role is not explicit from the hymn, it is yet apparent from their receiving the gifts for more than one reason.

The background of the war and the Bharadvāja's role therein are given in the account of the BD.[12] The BD traces the background of these three compositions (RV 6, 27; 47, 22-25 and 75). It clearly shows that they are interconnected in that they speak of a chain of events. Describing what is behind hymn 6, 75, Śaunaka[13] says that once two princes, Abhyāvartin (the son of Cayamāna), and Prastoka (the son of Sṛñjaya), were badly beaten in a battle with the Varaśikhas. The Aryan heroes then approached Bharadvāja seeking his advice and help against the Varaśikhas. Bharadvāja, who was their priest readily assured them of his help and called his son Pāyu to consecrate the war materials of the two princes. And Pāyu carried out his father's command, reciting the verses of the hymn (RV 6, 75). In a subsequent battle, the two princes defeated the Vṛcivats, the descendants of Varaśikhas and acquired a large booty, out of which they made a great gift to Bharadvāja. Bharadvāja, while returning home (from the battlefield) with those gifts met on the way Indra; and Garga who accompanied his father Bharadvāja, praised Indra with 6, 47, 22-25 and 27, 5-8[14], describing how he helped the princes to succeed in their encounter with their foes and how on the occasion of the celebration of their victory, they gave them (Bharadvāja and Garga) costly gifts.

On the basis of the account given in the BD, RV 6, 27, 5-8[15] it is said that seeking to help Abhyāvartin Cāyamāna, Indra slew the descendants of Varaśikha, when he killed the Vṛcivats in the vanguard of his army on the bank of the Hariyūpīyā and then the rear-guard fled away in terror. Longing for fame (*i.e.* victory), the three thousand Vṛcivats went to the wrong goal, i.e. all were put to death, as they became the target of Indra's weapon. Also, they broke into pieces like an earthen pot, *i.e.* they ran away helter-skelter, leaving their belongings—utensils, etc., in great disorder, on the bank of the river Yavyāvatī. Seeking to help him (Sṛñjaya), Indra subjugated Turvaśa and the Vṛcivats to Sṛñjaya, who was the son of Devavāta and Abhyāvartin, the son of Cāyamāna (the liberal sovereign), who also presented the poet with two yoking bulls plus twenty more together with their harness. This gift of the Pārthavas is regarded as difficult to reach (or emulate).

Verses 5 and 6 give a vivid description of the war, which is rarely met with in the RV (except in RV 7, 18 about the Dāśarājña war). The poet must have been a witness to the war, as the priest of the victors, Abhyāvartin Cāyamāna and Sṛñjaya Daivavāta and himself saw the action and immediately thereafter, he recorded celebration of the victory or the occasion of sacrifice, in this hymn (RV 6, 27). Subsequently, he received gifts from the princes, as detailed in verses 7 and 8. The two allies, Abhyāvartin, the son of Cāyamāna, and Sṛñjaya, the son of Devavāta had one Bharadvāja as their priest; they had been defeated by Vṛcīvats and, therefore, they later approached Bharadvāja, whose son Pāyu consecrated their war-weapons with magically potent *mantras* (of RV 6, 47, 26-31 and 75, 1-19). As a result of his excercise by Pāyu (who descended from Aṅgiras) the two princes came out victorious in the subsequent action with the Vṛcīvats. RV (6, 47, 25) says that Prastoka was a contemporary of Divodāsa. It appears to us that Sṛñjaya was probably a senior contemporary of Abhyāvartin Cāyamāna, while Divodāsa and Sṛñjaya's son Prastoka were his junior contemporaries. The events described in the hymn (RV 6, 27) might have been taken place relatively earlier than the war that Divodāsa fought against Śambara and his ally Varcin. Abhyāvartin and Sṛñjaya are called Pārthavas, (RV 6, 27, 8), *i.e.* the descendants of Pṛthu.[16] This means that they had a common ancestor in Pṛthu and might have belonged to the same family, ruling in two contiguous principalities or states. So also, Divodāsa was their close ally. Again, since Divodāsa is alluded to as a Bharata, all of them probably belonged to the clan of Bharata.[16a]

As regards the location of the scene of action we are not sure whether Hariyūpīyā and Yavyāvatī were names of places or rivers. Sāyaṇa[17] says that Hariyūpīyā was the name either of a river or of a township (*hariyūpīyā nāma kācin nadī kācin nagarī vā*) and, by Yavyāvatī, he means Hariyūpīyā (*Yavyāvatyām pūrvoktāyām hariyūpīyāyām*). Veṅkaṭa Mādhava[18] says that Hariyūpīyā was a township (*hariyūpīyākhyāyām nagaryām*). So also he takes Yavyāvatī as a township (*yavyāvatyām nagaryām*).

Röth and Böhtlingkt also take a similar stand when they state that Yavyāvatī is '*eines flusses oder einer Oertlichkeit*'[19], and Hariyūpīyā is 'einer *Oertlichkeit*'[20]. However, they do not say that Hariyūpīyā may signify a river. In the same view Grassmann says about Yavyāvatī : '*Bezeichung einer Gegend Oder Flusses*'[21] and about Hariyūpīyā : *Bezeichung einer Oertlichkeit*'[22]. Ludwig[23] takes Hariyūpīyā as the name of a town on the bank of the river Yavyāvatī, and thus Grassmann and Ludwig agree with the authors of PW. Hillebrandt[24] identifies Yavyāvatī with Djob (Zhobe) near Iryab (Haliab) a tributary of the Kurum (Krumu). Macdonell and Keith[25] do not accept Hillebrandt's theory, and opine "(Yavyāvatī) may denote either a place or a river, since many battles seem to have been fought on the banks of the rivers". Wheeler[26], at one time, tried to connect Hariyūpīyā with Harappa and said: "It is not indeed impossible that the name Harappa itself is concealed in the Hari-yūpīyā which is mentioned in the *Ṛgveda* as the scene of a battle about this time. But these are mere conjectures; picutresque, perhaps probable, but not proven." Thus the identifications of Hari-yūpīyā and Yavyāvatī is not final. However, the greater likelihood is that these were rivers, because most of the battles referred to in the RV were fought on the banks of rivers. For example, the battle of the ten kings was fought on the bank of the Puruṣṇī and another on the bank of the Yamunā. This battle took place probably on the confluence of the Śutudrī and the Vipāśā. As the Bharadvājas lived in a region around the North Pāñcāla, and were patronised by the Bharata kings—of the North Pāñcāla dynasty—it is probable that this battle took place at some place not very far from Ahicchatra, the capital of North Pāñcāla. Unfortunately the Vedic names of rivers are no longer extant.

We have mentioned above that verses RV 6, 47, 26-31 are addressed to *dundubhi* and hymn RV 6, 75 addressed to various weapons of war and these are charms Atharvaṇic in character. And, according to BD,[27] Pāyu employed the *mantras* contained in them when consecrating the war materials of Abhyāvartin Cāyamāna and Prastoka Sṛñjaya. These *mantras* can be claimed as the singular and unique contribution of the Bharadvājas to the Vedic literature in general and RV in particular.

Moreover, these two hymns (RV 6, 75 and RV 6, 47, 26-31) may be ascribed to one common seer despite the account in the Sarvā. Our argument can be stated as follows:

(i) RV hymns 6, 47, 26-31 and 6, 75 are repeated in the TS,[28] VS,[29] MS[30] and KS[31] also. An examination of the texts of TS and VS reveals that these (RV 6, 75 and 47, 26-31) are treated as a single unit without any break in between. (ii) There is no denial of the fact that there is continuity of thought. (iii) Both are Atharvaṇic in character. (iv) The AśvGS (3, 12) uses them for a single purpose in succession and thus these are complementary to each other; (v) the Sarvā[22] ascribes the hymn to Pāyu, and the other hymn (RV 6, 47) to Garga ignoring the fact that it was Pāyu who is named in the latters' 24th[33] verse. Usually the Sarvā ascribes a hymn to one whose name is mentioned therein. All these create a genuine doubt as regards the Sarvā's ascription (of RV 6, 47) to Garga, though, of course, this is supported by BD.

The hymns RV 6, 47, 26-31 and 6, 75 are thus Atharvaṇic in character and Pāyu Bhāradvāja did actually employ these *mantras* along with some Atharvaṇic practices for promoting the prospect of victory in the battle of Hariyūpīyā in favour of Abhyāvartin Cāyamāna and his ally. According to BD 5, 129ff. Pāyu employed these *mantras* at his father's command, after a request by the princes.

The AśvGS 3, 12 describes the usage of the *mantras* (RV 6, 47, 26-31 and of the hymn 6, 75); the unity therein confirms the identity of their composer.

AśvGS 3, 12[34] says that, when hostilities break out, royal priest conventionally robed the king in his armour. Then himself standing to the west of king's chariot he should first recite the verse RV 10, 173 and then with another *jīmū́tasya iva bhavati prátīkcm*—'like a thunder cloud is his countenance'—(RV 6, 75, 1) he tendered the coat of mail (*varma*) to the king.[35] With *dhánvanā gā́ dhánvanā ājím*—'with bow the cow, with bow the race'—(RV 6, 75, 2) he gave the bow to him and then he requested the king to repeat another (*i.e.* RV 6, 75, 3).[36] The *purohita* ('the priest') should recite the fourth verse (RV 6, 75, 4).[37] The fifth verse *bahvī́nām pitā́ bahúr asya putrā́* ('one, father of many daughters, whose son(s) are many') the priest presented the quiver to him.[38] When the king started off to the battle he recited the *mantra* (RV 6, 75, 6), *ráthe tíṣṭhan nayati*, etc. ('standing on the chariot who leads etc. ...')[39]; and the verse (RV 6, 75, 7) *tīvrấn ghóṣān kṛṇvate*, etc., —"neighing loudly" over the horses.[40] And at his instance the king repeated the verse (RV 6, 75, 8) *rathavấhanam havír asya nấma*, etc.,—"car-bearer is the name of his oblation", etc.—when the latter looks at the arrows.[41] When he binds the leather for protecting the arms, he recites the verse (RV 6, 75, 14), "*áhir iva bhogái páry etibāhúm*" :[6] it compasses the arms with serpents fangs' etc.[42] Then the priest mounts on the chariot and getting closer to the king makes him repeat the Abhivarta hymn (RV 10, 174, seen by Abhivarta Āṅgirasa) and the two stanzas, (RV 8, 101, 3 and 4) composed by Bhārgava Jamadagni.[43] Thereafter, the priest recites three hymns: *viz*. Apratiratha (RV 10, 103 by Apratiratha Aindra), Śāsa (RV 10, 152, by Śāsa Bhāradvāja), and Suparṇa hymn (not traced in the Śākala Saṁhitā).[44] The king is advised to drive his chariot in all directions and then start the fight; in the line of battle he should take up his position in the direction of the Sun (Āditya) or the Venus (Uśanas).[45] Then he should touch the drum with the three verses, *viz*., *úpa śvāsaya pṛthivī́m utá dyấm*, etc.; "Make the earth and the heaven breath loudly" etc. (RV 6, 47, 29-31)[46]. Next the king shoots an arrow with *ávasṛṣṭā párā páta* etc. (RV 6, 75, 16)—'Loosed from (the bowstring) fly away', etc.[47] At the time of fighting he utters v. 17: *yátra bāṇấḥ sampátanti*—'where the arrows fly, etc.'[48] The AśvGS 3, 12, 20[49] alternatively prescribes that either the priest recites the texts of the *mantra* or he instructs the king how to repeat them.

The hymns RV 6, 47, 26-28 are an independent entity in the AVŚ (viz. 6, 125, 1-3) and constitute a charm of the battle-drum. Kauśika GS 15, 11[50] prescribes offerings to the forces of waters and of the thunderbolt of Indra, to bring force and success to the chariot. RV 6, 47, 29-31 being repeated in the AVŚ 6, 126, 1-3 constitutes the charm of the battle-drum.

'The battle drum is sounded to encourage and to infuse vigour among the fighting men. It is made of wood. It resounds in the enemies' camps.'[51] The Kauśika (GS 16, 1)[52] ordains that all the musical instruments are to be washed and dipped in the mixtures of the powders of *tagara* and *uśīra*. Then these instruments are to be annointed with ghee. Thereafter, the priest sounds each of them thrice and hands them one by one to the warriors when they march to the battlefield.

Thus, the three hymns RV 6, 27; 47 and 75 ascribed to the Bharadvājas appear to be significant from socio-cultural point of view. These hymns bring out the warlike character of the Bharadvājas. They also reveal that the Bharadvājas did possess knowledge of the battle charms that formed the parts of Atharvaṇic magic. The three hymns point to the historical role played by the Bharadvājas in times of warfare. They were, thus, connected with the Bharatas. The Dānastutis (in RV 6, 27 and 47) speak volumes of the patronage of the Bharatas to the Bharadvājas. The unity of the authorship of the hymns RV 6, 47, 26-31 and 75, 1-19 is an established fact, despite claim of the Sarvā.

Section (iii)

The Go-sūkta

Although the RV bears frequent references to the cow (*gauḥ*) and the word *gauḥ* is met with in numerous forms and compounds,[1] only two or three hymns are devoted exclusively to her description and praise. The hymn (RV 10, 169) ascribed to Śabara (a descendant of Kakṣīvat), is in her praise.[2] So also is another (RV 4, 58) composed by Vāmadeva Gautama and addressed (alternatively) to Agni or Sūrya or Waters or Ghṛta or the Cows.[3] And the third one RV 6, 28 glorifying cows along with Indra occurs in the midst of these addressed to Indra and is authored by Bharadvāja Bārhaspatya.[4]

This last hymn, under study, consists of 8 verses; the first seven are repeated in AVŚ (4, 21, 1-7) and form an independent hymn. Verse 8 also occurs in AVŚ (9, 4, 23). Both the hymns are ascribed to Brahmā.[5] But this situation need not lead one to suppose that our hymn is composite, for, as in this case, so also in that of others, we notice that the AVŚ uses their verses in different hymns of its different books. The problem of the unity of this hymn is already discussed by Velankar[6] in his annotation to RV 6, 28. He says that "the imperative and potential forms of these stanzas show their unity and through them also that of the entire hymn. The AV separates the last stanza (AV IX, 4, 23) from the first seven stanzas (AV, 4, 21, 1-7) and seems to suggest that the two parts were originally separate hymns." He also points out that "the Atharvaṇic tradition about the employment of the first part (*i.e.* vv. 1-7) for a purpose (which is suggested in v. 8), as recorded in the Kauśika G. Sūtra (19, 1-2), evidently supports the unity which we have assumed."[7]

The purpose of the hymn is given by the Kauśika GS (19, 1-2).[8] It says that, after muttering this as a spell, the cows which are suffering from disease, or barrenness, or defective pregnancy are to be given water mixed with salt for their drink. It is believed that this sanctified salt-water cures illness or rectifies the defect of the unborn calf, and that of milch cow. However, Sāyaṇa[9] says that the water mixed with salt alone is given to the cows for drinking and the grains of corn (or cooked rice) are to be offered to Indra.

The AśvGS (2, 10, 6)[10] and the Śānkh GS (3, 9, 3)[11] prescribe the hymn for blessing the cows when they return after grazing. Also, Āśvalāyana designates another one (RV 6, 28) as the Āgāvīya hymn,[12] following its initial words (viz., *ā́ gā́vo agman* "come hither the cows").

The Vaitāna Sūtra (21, 24)[13] says that the Sūkta is to be used at the time of a Yajamāna's receiving back a cow that is set aside as *dakṣiṇā* (fee) to be given to the priest.

Its special features[14] may be noted: In verse 1, the poet claims that the cows are meant for the good of the people and he expects that they may prosper in the cow-pen and give milk for Indra (probably for daily rituals). V.2 praises Indra exclusively, as a liberal donor. V.3 asserts that no thief can injure cows and no enemy can threaten their movement and a true worshipper (of Indra) could always keep them for good. V.4 says that the dust raised by the movement of horse does not touch the cows, nor are the cows slaughtered. And thus cows can move about freely without fear. V.5 identifies cows with Bhaga and Indra, and they are the food of Soma. The poet emphatically says that these cows are but Indra himself (*imā́ yā́ gā́vaḥ sá janāsa Indra*) and in his heart and mind the poet longs for this Indra (*icchā́míd hṛdā́ mánasā cid Īndram*). In v.6 cows are so potent that they make a slender man fat and endorse a gloomy-looking person with bright appearance. Cows make houses auspicious, as their lowing itself is auspicious. In v.7 the cows are expected to drink pure water and raise abundant progeny and the poet hopes that neither a robber nor a wicked person may harm them; even Rudra's weapon avoids them(?). In v.8, the poet says: "May this (medical) mixture rest closely in these cows; may it rest in the seed of the bull (which is in their womb) and also in your power (*i.e.* milk in their udders), O Indra."[15]

Thus the last stanza appears to be a proper Atharvaṇic charm, while the first and the seventh benedictory in nature. In verses 1-7, the cows appear to be Indra's special gifts to the worshipper. They are the means of worshipping Indra and securing own well-being. They are fearless. They were worshipped and praised on par with Indra. "The hymn, though chiefly glorifying the cows, has nevertheless steadily kept Indra in the background (cf. vv. 1; 2ab; 3cd; 5; 8d); this explains its place in the mist of the Indra hymns."[16]

This hymn (to the cows) elevates the domestic animals, and cows, to the status of (a worship-deserving) deity. The poet's assertion that "the cows are Bhaga and Indra; they are none else than Indra and he looks upon them as Indra,"[17] goes to point to their complete deification. And Indra is pushed into the background. Incidentally it can be pointed out that the Bharadvājas were at one time, worshippers of Pūṣan, a pastoral deity. While dealing with the cult of Pūṣan above,[18] we discussed how this god was closely connected with cattle. As such it should not be surprising that the Bharadvājas were inclined to cow-worship also, for that was already a part of Pūṣan worship. In a hymn (RV 6, 57), the Bharadvājas addressed the dual divinity Indra and Pūṣan and that probably marks Pūṣan's elevation to a status equal to that of Indra. So, also, the Gṛtsamadas[19] tried (in RV 2, 42) to elevate Pūṣan to the status of Soma. Now we have seen a similar tendency in another hymn (RV 6, 28), where the cows are acquiring the position of Indra (cf. vv. 1; 2ab; 5; 8d).[20]

We have already noted that the hymns (RV 4, 58; 6, 27 and 10, 169) were divined by Vāmadeva Gautama, Bharadvāja Bārhaspatya and Śabara Āṅgirasa respectively. These were all descendants of, or related to, the Aṅgirases.[21] This shows that the worship of the cows developed among the Aṅgirases and this ultimately hints at the uniformity of thought and belief among the clans and sub-clans of the Aṅgirases. This identity of approach to Pūṣan among the Aṅgirases is already made elsewhere.[22]

Veneration to the cow did not appear among the Bharadvājas and other clans of the Aṅgirases suddenly. It might have been a natural consequence of Bṛhaspati's release of the cows from the clutches of Vala and other Paṇis. We have already seen that Bṛhaspati played a significant role in the Vala-myth while he helped Indra to secure release of cows and he was accompanied by the Aṅgirases. These cows were not taken by them only as booty or property, but also as a sacred possession that enabled them (Bṛhaspati and the Aṅgirases) to wage a war against Vala. To our mind Bṛhaspati's release of the cows was not an isolated incident but it might have had a bearing upon veneration to the cow culminating in a cult.

Section (iv)

The Sāmans

The Bharadvājas are intimately connected with the Sāmaveda. A tradition preserved in the CV (4, 23)[1] says that SV's Gotra is Bharadvāja. (It appears to be an arbitrary statement based on no specific ground.) Another noteworthy fact is that the first verse of the SV '*ágna ấ yāhi vītáye*' (etc.) ascribed to Bharadvāja[2] is a repetition of RV 6, 16, 10 with which the Sarvā (2, 6, 1) credits him. Also, a good number of verses composed by the seers of the Bharadvāja family are repeated in the SV.[3] More specifically the Ṛgvedic and the Sāmavedic Brāhmaṇas *viz.*, AB, JB (TMB and JAB) ascribe a good number of Sāmans to them.[3a] Among these Brāhmaṇa-texts, the JAB contains a long list[4] of the Sāmans (credited to them); to this other texts also agree. (See the list of the Sāmans on the following pages.)

If we look at the making of the Sāmans ascribed to Bharadvāja and their original *ṛcs* (*yoni-mantras*) in the Ṛgvedic hymns, it would become clear that most of these Ṛgvedic *ṛcs* are ascribed to other seers. Only a few are credited to Bharadvāja, Śaṁyu Bārhaspatya and Ṛjiśvan Bhāradvāja. There are a number of *ṛcs* taken from the hymns divined by Śaṁyu Bārhaspatya. We have elsewhere[5] talked about Śaṁyu as the brother of Bharadvāja Bārhaspatya. His hymns are included in the Sixth Maṇḍala. A number of *ṛcs* derived from these hymns ascribed to Śaṁyu are the basis for composing some Sāmans, ascribed to Bharadvāja. This shows the close relationship between the two seers, who happened to be brothers. Ṛjiśvan is another sage, whose *ṛcs* form the basis for a Sāman identically authored. Ṛjiśvan is a distant descendant of Bharadvāja Bārhaspatya. Regarding Gaurivīti also.

List of the Sāmans

No.	Name of the Sāman	Seer of the Sāman	The Ṛc contained in it	Seers of the Ṛc according to Sarvā
1.	Bṛhat	Bharadvāja (Agni or Sūrya)	RV 1, 12, 1; SV 3	Medhātithi
2.	Bṛhat	Pertaining to Agni	SV 81/1	—
3.	Bṛhat (Bharadvāja)	Bharadvāja	RV 6, 46, 1; SV 234	Śaṁyu Bārhaspatya
4.	Upahava	Bharadvāja	RV 6, 8, 1; SV 35/4	Bharadvāja Bārhaspatya
5.	Snauṣṭigava	Vaiśvānarāgni	RV 6, 8, 1; SV 35/3	,,
		from Snuṣṭigu	RV 6, 46, 7; SV 262/1	Śaṁyu Bārhaspatya
6.	Yajñayajñīya	Use of Yajñayajñīya	RV 6, 48, 1; SV 35/4	,,
7.	Bharadvāja-Pṛśni	Bharadvāja	RV 6, 48, 7; SV 35/4	,,
	(Acchāvāka)	,,	RV 6, 48, 7; SV 37/1, 2	,,
8.	Bharadvāja Gadhā	,,	RV 6, 48, 1; SV 41/1	,,
9.	Bharadvāja Maukṣa (Dakṣanidhana)	,,	RV 6, 82, 4; SV 141/1, 2	Śyāvāśva
10.	Bharadvāja Arka	,,	RV 7, 32, 2; SV 233/1, 2	Vasiṣṭha
11.	Bharadvāja Loma	,,	RV 9, 108, 13; SV 582/1, 2	Gaurivīti, Ṛjiśvan, and others
12.	Bharadvāja Bṛhat	,,	RV 6, 46, 1; SV 24/1, 2	Śaṁyu Bārhaspatya
13.	Bharadvāja Bṛhata	Bharadvāja	RV 9, 100, 1; SV 550, AG 31/1	Rebhasūnu

No.	Name of the Sāman	Seer of the Sāman	The Ṛc contained in it	Seers of the Ṛc according to Sarvā
14.	Bharadvāja	,,	RV 1, 3, 10; SV 189/1	Hiraṇyastūpa
15.	Bharadvāja	,,	RV 8, 32, 10; SV 217/1	Medhātithi
16.	,,	,,	RV 3, 46, 1; SV 234/1, 2	Viśvāmitra
17.	,,	,,	RV 8, 1, 24; SV 345/1-4	Pragātha Kāṇva
18.	,,	,,	RV 3, 30, 22; SV 329/1	Viśvāmitra
19.	,,	,,	RV 6, 44, 4; SV 257/1	Śaṁyu Bārhaspatya
20.	,, (Śuṅdhyu)	,,	RV 8, 24, 24; SV 396/1	Viśvāmitra
21.	,,	,,	RV 10, 157, 1; SV 452/1	Bhuvana or Sādhana
22.	,,	,,	RV 6, 17, 15; SV 454/1	Bharadvāja
23.	,,	,,	RV 9, 111, 1; 463/1-3	Anānata
24.	,,	,,	RV 1, 127, 1; SV 465/1-2	Parucchepa
25.	,,	,,	RV 9, 52, 1; SV 496/1	Pragātha
26.	,,	,,	RV 9, 61, 25; SV 510/1	Nābhānediṣṭha
27.	,,	,,	RV 9, 107, 1; SV 512/3, 4	Seven seers
28.	,,	,,	RV 9, 103, 3; SV 577/1	Dvita Āptya
29.	,,	,,	RV 8, 1, 14; SV 245/2, 3	Pragātha Kāṇva

we opined that Saṁkṛti, the son of Nara Bharadvāja, not Vasiṣṭha, might have been his ancestors.[6] Some of the Sāmans were made up of the *ṛcs* from the hymns composed by Pragātha Kāṇva, Medhātithi, Hiraṇyastūpa, Parucchepa and Anānata. We have noted[7] that the Kāṇvas descended from Ajamīḍha, who was an offspring of Suhotra Bhāradvāja; they profess intimate relationship with Bharadvāja. Parucchepa is from the line of Divodāsa. There are differences of opinion as regards this Divodāsa. Velankar[8] thinks that Divodāsa, the seer of some Ṛgvedic hymns, was different from Divodāsa Atithigva, while Pradhan[9] identifies him as Divodāsa of Pāñcāla, the father of Parucchepa. Anānata is regarded as Parucchepa's son. But Rahurkar[10] has no definite opinion about him. Parucchepa and Anānata may be kinsmen of the Bharadvājas, if we accept Pradhan's[11] argument. These seers came under the Bhārgava-*pakṣa* and had kinship with Aṅgirases and Bharadvājas.[12] Hiraṇyastūpa is another seer whose *ṛcs* were treated as the base of the Sāmans ascribed to Bharadvāja. As he was an Āṅgirasa, it is but natural that his *ṛcs* should come under Bharadvāja's authorship. Strangely enough, we find a number of *ṛcs* of the RV credited to Vasiṣṭha, Viśvāmitra and Śyāvāśva as forming the basis of the Sāmans ascribed to Bharadvāja. Some relationship probably existed among these seers of various Ṛgvedic families as reflected by their hymns or *ṛcs*. The fact remains that for ritual purposes the hymns by any of the seers belonging even to some different families could be utilized by the seers belonging to another family. Due to this flexibility, the *ṛcs* of Viśvāmitra and others were used by the Bharadvājas for compiling the Sāmans.

The Vedic texts, particularly the Sāmavedic Brāhmaṇas, state the special characteristics of and information about the Sāmans. Sometimes, they give a mythical background[13] of a Sāman and also its mystic explanation. In a few cases, the Ṛgvedic Brāhmaṇa AB[14] also speaks of the Sāmans. Even the RV talks about some of these.

Amongst all the Sāmans, traced to Bharadvāja, Bṛhat is the most important. In RV 10, 181, 2[15] Sapratha Bharadvāja says that 'from the radiant Dhātṛ, Savitṛ, Viṣṇu and Agni, Bharadvāja brought the Bṛhat (Sāman)'. AB[16] corroborates the Ṛgvedic statement: "Bharadvāja has brought the Bṛhat from Agni and he possessed of it." AB, however, does not refer to other gods (*viz.*

Dhātṛ, Savitṛ, and Viṣṇu) who, together with Agni, granted the Bṛhat to Bharadvāja.

As regards the origin of Bṛhat (and Rathantara ascribed to Vasiṣṭha) JB 1, 129[17] recalls that once gods and demons contested for supremacy. The gods created a thunderbolt in the shape of a man. This reached the demons who turned it back to the gods. The gods could finally achieve a victory over the demons by virtue of Bṛhat and Rathantara. And, therefore, it is said, one who desires to conquer his foes should render the enemies' missiles powerless through the two Sāmans—Bṛhat and Rathantara. In JB 1, 136[18] the significance of Bṛhat is further stated in a myth, *viz.*, that the gods were cherishing high hope to conquer the heaven with the metre Bṛhatī but they could not succeed. So they uttered '*Svargaṁ lokam gatvā Bṛhat vāvedam abhūd yena svargaṁ lokaṁ vyāpāma* ('Having gone to the heaven let Bṛhat be so and so, through which we shall spread over Heaven.') In TS (4, 4, 2, 1)[19] the Bṛhat Sāman is prescribed for stability. It represents the western direction. This world is termed as Rathantara and the other world Bṛhat. At AB (5, 30)[20] Agni is identified with Rathantara and Āditya with Bṛhat. In AB 8, 1[21] Bṛhat is described as a lordly power while Rathantara a holy one. AB 8, 12[22] further states in connection with the Mahābhiṣeka of Indra that Bṛhat and Rathantara are the two front pedestals of the throne.

Another important one is the Yajñayajñīya Sāman. The name is borrowed from *Yajñayajña* in the verse RV 6, 48, 1. Two myths explain its origin. According to TMB 8, 6, 3[23] this Sāman is so named because, with it as the womb, Prajāpati created sacrifice. Another TMB (8, 6, 5)[24] myth describes how gods saw Yajñayajñīya as the means of getting credit for the sacrifices of the demons. Each part of this particular Sāman was applied in a particular type of sacrifice. JB 1, 169-170[25] bring out its significance thus: Once the Vaiśvānara Agni burnt everything. At this, the gods were terribly frightened and apprehended danger to their existence and actively thought of averting such a catastrophe. At last, they decided to collect the lustre of Vaiśvānara Agni, pondering about a place where they should deposit the same; they finally said '*yajñe yajñe no bhaviṣyati*' (in every sacrifice it will be with us). Thus, the Sāman was called Yajñayajñīya.

The TMB 8, 6, 9[26] states the rules required for chanting the Yajñayajñīya.

The manifold praise of this Sāman is found in a number of Vedic texts. AB 3, 14[27] equates Yajñayajñīya with the thunderbolt. ŚB 9, 1, 2, 39[28] advises that the Sāman be chanted by the Adhvaryu after he completes the erection of an altar. ŚB 9, 4, 4, 10[29] identifies it with the heavenly world. MS 4, 4, 9[30] points out that it is the very essence of the Yajus and the Sāmans (created by Brahman), and of speech. And the Ch. U. 2, 19, 1[31] says that the Yajñayajñīya spread over the body.

Another Sāman called *Bharadvājasya Adārasṛt* is also prescrībed for conquering enemies. Bharadvāja composed this Sāman for saving Divodāsa from his enemies (TMB 15, 3, 7).[32] And in the same Brāhmaṇa (*i.e.* TMB 15, 3, 7)[33] this Sāman is explained as: *dare na prāpayati.*

According to TMB 13, 11, 11-13[34] the Sāman called Bharadvājasya Loma is used for obtaining cattle as also for attaining long life.

Bharadvājasya Pṛśni is said to be an Acchāvāka Sāman which enables one to obtain food. JB 3, 75[35] narrates that once when Bharadvāja desired to have progeny, he divined it and could get innumerable progeny. The seer asks Pṛśni to obtain progeny for him. Therefore, the significance of this Sāman lies in its capability of securing food and progeny. Being ascribed to Bharadvāja himself it is called Bharadvājasya Pṛśni.

Another important Sāman is the Śākamaśva Sāman. Its title is derived from *śāka* meaning *śārdha* (*i.e.* 'with') and *aśva* (horse). TMB 8, 8, 4[36] traces its origin from the fact that the gods achieved victory over their enemies (*viz.*, the Asuras) with the help of Agni in the form of a horse as their leader. JB 1, 182[37] reports that when the gods resorted to penance for the attainment of heaven, this Sāman was revealed and transformed into a horse and took them to heaven. Thus it is called Śākamaśva. We have noted how AB 3, 49[38] has given a semi-mythical account of its origin implicating the seer Bharadvāja, who helped Agni in the form of a horse to chase the Asuras. This gave this Sāman, its name.

Section (v)

The Bhāradvāja Kalpasūtras

The Kalpasūtras are considered as one of the six Vedāṅgas[1];

and comprise four classes; *viz.,* the Śrauta, Gṛhya, Śulba and Dharma Sūtras.[2] The Śrautasūtras[3] describe the major sacrifices—*iṣṭis, yāgas* and *homas,* etc. They give details of the complex sacrifices, *e.g.* of Aśvamedha, Vājapeya, Rājasūya and the Sattras ('sessional sacrifices'). The Gṛyhasūtras[4] spell out all domestic rites and ceremonies, *viz. pañcamahāyajñas, śrāddhas,* ten *saṁskāras* pertaining to every twice-born, etc. The Śulbasūtras[5] are known as works on Vedic Geometry in that they deal with the graphic structure of the sacrificial places, etc. The Dharmasūtras[6] lay down the day-to-day duties of a man in society, manner and custom, etc. They share some topics with other three sūtras.[7]

In the past, when the Vedas were sub-divided into many recensions—*Śākhās,* probably a few distinct schools of thought came up.[8] Further, out of these schools, sub-schools of the Vedāṅgas, and of other scriptures, took shape. Thus there arose a good number of schools reflecting the śākhās of each of the Vedas.[9] That is why we have so many ancillary texts attached to each of the recensions of the Vedic texts. Somehow, there flourished several schools each based on a recension of the Kṛṣṇa YV also.[10] Of all these, the Taittiriya is one of great importance for its wealth of auxiliaries.[11] Particularly, many Śrauta texts are attached to it.[12] Originally, it might have had only one recension, but later on sub-divided into many. Thus we have as many as six different schools in the Sūtra literature of the Taittirīyas, *viz.,* Baudhāyana, Bharadvāja, Āpastaṁba, Satyaṣāḍha Hiraṇyakeśin, Vaikhānasa and Vādhūla.[13] Further, there is reason to believe that each of them had full four-fold sūtra texts, forming a Kalpasūtra. Some of them have completely survived even to this day,[14] while most of them have lost one part or the other *e.g.* the Kalpasūtra of the Bharadvājas also. The Śrauta and Gṛhya texts (including Pitṛmedha and Pariśiṣṭa Sūtras) of Bharadvājas[15] have been retrieved. The text of Śrauta Sūtra appears to be incomplete. There are traces of Dharmasūtras of Bhāradvājas,[16] but not those of the Śulbasūtras. Since we have definite knowledge of the other three sub-divisions, we see no reason why we should doubt the fact that some time in the past, the Śulba text of the Bharadvājas did exist but now it is lost to us. This is confirmed by evidence in some other schools, still extant in their entirety.[17]

The Bharadvāja Śrauta Sūtra is linked to the Taittirīya recension of the Black YV.[17a] The CV[18] of Śaunaka which gives details about various recensions of the four Vedas, informs that the Taitt. recension of the Black YV is divided into two schools, namely, Aukheya and Khāṇḍikeya. The latter further branches off into five schools (or sections)—viz., Kāletā, Śāṭyāyanī, Hairaṇyakeśī, Bhāradvājī and Āpastambī.[19] The commentator, Mahīdāsa has examined the enumeration of the different recensions belonging to the Khāṇḍikeya school differently. He says that Āpastambī, Baudhāyanī, Satyāṣāḍhī, Hiraṇyakeśī and Bhāradvājī are five recensions of the Khāṇḍikeya school.[19a] He does not refer to Kāletā and Śāṭyāyanī schools, mentioned by Śaunaka. He replaces these two by Baudhāyani and Hiraṇyakeśī. (This is all about the Chowkhamba edition of the CV.) But the commentary in the Ayacit edition does not give the name of Bhāradvājī school. It says that Āpastambī, Baudhāyanī Satyāṣāḍhī, Hiraṇyakeśī and Audheyī are five recensions of the Khāṇḍikeya school.[20] The two editions of the CV name Kāletā and Śāṭyāyanī, but they are replaced by the two recensions, namely Baudhāyanī and Audheyī. The names of the five recensions would, therefore, be: Baudhāyanī, Audheyī, Hiraṇyakeśī, Bhāradvājī and Āpastambī. But the Chowkhamba edition reads Satyāṣāḍhī recension in place of Audheyī, while the Ayacit edition gives Satyāṣāḍhī in the place of Bhāradvājī. Now it has been ascertained that the schools Satyāṣāḍhī and Hiraṇyakeśī are identical.[21] It is possible that in the Ayacit edition the scribe dropped the name of Bhāradvājī, which is found in the list of Mahādeva, who commented on the SatyHirŚS. The existence of the Śrauta, Gṛhāya-, Pitṛmedha- and Pariśeṣa-Sūtras prove beyond doubt that there was a distinct Bhāradvājī recension of the Taitt. School as a sub-branch of the Khāṇḍikeyas in existence. This is further affirmed by the existence of the Śikṣā of the Bharadvāja school,[22] that gives correct readings of the Taitt. texts.

The Bhāradvāja Śrauta Sūtra: According to Mahādeva, the commentator of the SatyHirŚS, the Bhāradvāja Śrauta Sūtra (BhārŚS) is one of the six Śrauta schools of the Kṛṣṇa YV, the other five are those of Baudhāyana, Āpastamba, Satyāṣāḍha Hiraṇyakeśin, Vaikhānasa and Vādhūla.[23] Generally, while listing these, the Bhāradvāja Sūtra ranks next to the Baudhāyāna Sūtra and before the Āpstamba Sūtra. This probably indicates the relative importance and chronology of the schools concerned.[24] That is why Baudhāyana Sūtra is considered as the oldest among the six

Sūtras. But Bharadvāja's Sūtra is dated as relatively later than the Baudhāyana. (We shall discuss chronology later.)

The BhārŚS consists of fifteen Praśnas, each of which comprises a number of Kaṇḍikās which in turn are groups of Sūtras. There are altogether 4649 Sūtras distributed in 318 Kaṇḍikās forming 15 Praśnas. The contents of the BhārŚS may be detailed thus:

Praśnas	*Titles*	*Relation to ṛtviks, etc.*
I	Darśapaurṇamāsa	Ādhvaryava
II	-do-	-do-
III, 1-13	-do-	-do-
III, 14-18	-do-	Brahmatva
IV	-do-	Yājamāna
V	Agnyādheya, Punarādheya	—
VI, 1-6	Agnyupasthāna	—
VI, 7-14	Agnihotra	—
VI, 15-18	Āgrāyana	—
VII	Nirūḍhapaśubadha	—
VIII	Cāturmāsyas	—
IX	Prāyaścittas relating to Iṣṭi and Agnihotra	—
X	Jyotiṣṭoma	Ādhvaryava
XI	Pravargya	-do-
XII-XIV	Jyotiṣṭoma	Ādhvaryava
XV, 1-4	-do-	Brahmatva

The above arrangement of the contents in the BhārŚS strikingly agrees with that of the ĀpŚS up to Praśna XV, 1-5.

The large number of citations[25] gathered from various commentaries on different Sūtras testify to the authenticity of the extant text of the BhārŚS and further prove that, in addition the Sūtra had dealt with Dākṣāyaṇa sacrifice, the optional animal sacrifice and its expiation rites, and the Soma sacrifice. Paśvaikādaśini and Aśvamedha are not traced as yet; it may be presumed that those portions are lost to us.[26] This is indicated by the fact that Praśna IX of the BhārŚS dwells on the expiatory rites pertaining to the Agnihotra sacrifice and the Iṣṭiyāgas, and this Praśna is called Pūrvaprāyaścitta. This implies that there might have probably been another Praśna in the Sūtra which dealt with the expiation rites pertaining to the animal and the Soma sacrifices. This Praśna, probably called Uttaraprāyaścitta, is also lost to us.

BaudhŚS and BhārŚS.[27] We have already noted that the Śrautasūtras of Bodhāyana and Bharadvāja belong to the Taitt. recension of Kṛṣṇa YV. However, the BaudhŚS is considered to be the oldest of all the five sūtras (viz. BaudhŚS, BhārŚS, ĀpŚS, SatyHirŚS and VaikhŚS). Mahādeva, the commentator of SatyHirŚS, in his homage to the *ṣūtrakāras*, places Bodhāyana at the head of the group. Next he mentions Bharadvāja followed by others. So also BaudhŚS (2, 5, 9, 14), in prescribing the rite of *tarpaṇa*, ranks Kāṇva, Bodhāyana, Āpastaṁba, the Sūtrakāra, and Satyāṣāḍha Hiraṇyakeśin, one after the other. Again, BaudhGS 4, 8 lists these *sūtrakāras* in the same order. That BaudhŚS is the oldest can be substantiated from textual evidence, too; the Sūtra is a *pravacana* ('an exposition'), *i.e.* a ritual fixed by oral tradition. Its style and language are closer to those of the Brāhmaṇa texts. The sūtra narrates the rituals in an extensive manner, and fully quotes the *mantras*. It frequently quotes passage from the Saṁhitā, Brāhmaṇa and Āraṇyaka of the Taittirīya school, introducing them with *atha vai bhavati*. The BaudhŚS consists of the sections on the main sūtra texts, Dvaidha, Karmānta, Prāyaścitta, Śulba and Pravara.

Although the BhārŚS has not laid down the rituals in the manner so extensively as in the BaudhŚS, they have some common features. The BhārŚS does not quote the *mantras* in full. It introduces a number of Brāhmaṇa passages, of course less frequently than by Bodhāyana, with the word *vijñāyate*. The topics of the BhārŚS do not correspond to those treated in the BaudhŚS entirely. The placement of the sections on the Brahmatva and Yājamāna in the Iṣṭi is distinct. In the BhārŚS, the Prāyaścitta section precedes the Jyotiṣṭoma, while the same section is found as supplementary portions in the BaudhŚS. So also the Pravargya rite that follows the Agniṣṭoma in the BaudhŚS has been kept in the BhārŚS within the Jyotiṣṭoma sacrifice, *i.e.* in a proper sequence of the ritual.

As regards the manner of reference to *mantra* ('formula') and *vidhi* ('injunction') in the BaudhŚS, the former precedes the latter, while in the BhārŚS, the order is reversed. The BaudhŚS has no separate section on Paribhāṣā, although a small portion in Praśna 2, may be so designated. In the BhārŚS also, there is no separate section that can be called exclusively as Paribhāṣā section. In the BhārŚS (1, 1; 6, 15-16 and 9, 1) we meet groups of sūtras, which dwell upon the Paribhāṣā. The BhārŚS does not quote any Brāhmaṇa which does not belong to the Taitt. School. But the BaudhŚS quotes some Brahmaṇa texts other than its own school. The names of some teachers referred to in the BaudhŚS are not there in the BhārŚS. So also, the names of some teachers mentioned in the BhārŚS are not referred to in the BaudhŚS. This was done by the two authors, probably deliberately. Particularly, the BaudhŚS does not mention the names of Āśmarathya and Ālekhana (except in the Pravarakāṇḍa 3, 46), while the BhārŚS does twenty-eight times. Although the BhārŚS cannot, like the BaudhŚS, be claimed as a *pravacana,* it betrays signs of ritual fixed by oral tradition. The use of the demonstrative pronoun *idam* in both the works indicates that.

The BhārŚS and ĀpŚS[28] : Among all the Sūtras belonging to the Taitt. recension, the ĀpŚS bears the closest resemblances to the BhārŚS. The contents, the construction and even the expressions, in both the Sūtras, are found to be identical. In construction, Praśna I-V, in both the Sūtras are in the same order. In Praśna VI, the BhārŚS treats the Agnyupasthāna before Agnihotra, while the ĀpŚS reverses this order. The next two Praśnas (VII, VIII) again reveal the same pattern and order in both the sūtras. But unlike the ĀpŚS, the BhārŚS does not treat the *Paśuprāyaścittas* in the Praśna IX after those of Iṣṭi and Agnihotra. In fact, the BhārŚS has dropped the *Prāyaścittas* relating to the Paśuyāga and Soma sacrifice. As regards the treatment of the Jyotiṣṭoma, the BhārŚS differs from the ĀpŚS in a significant way. The BhārŚS deals with the Jyotiṣṭoma sacrifice and its modifications in Praśnas X-XIV The Jyotiṣṭoma involves the chanting of the Sāmans characterised by the specific number of Stomas, viz., *trivṛt*, *pañcadaśa*, *saptadaśa* and *ekaviṁśa*, (which are called *jyotis* in TS 6, 1, 1-3). The Jyotiṣṭoma consists of five Soma sacrifices; the Agniṣṭoma, the Ukthya, the Ṣoḍaśin, the Atirātra and Āptoryāma. Among these five sacrifices, the Agniṣṭoma constitutes the norm for the remaining four, therefore, called modifications of the Agniṣṭoma. The Ukthya, the Ṣoḍaśin, the Atirātra and the Āptoryāma also provide norms for Gauḥ, Vājapeya, Viśvajit and other Āptoryāmas (*i.e.* the secondary modifications) respectively. Of course, there are many such minor changes in the above sacrifices. The Agniṣṭoma and the other four constitute Jyotiṣṭoma. In other words, *jyotiṣṭoma* is a wider term than *agniṣṭoma*. However, the ĀpŚS treats the Agniṣṭoma in Praśnas X-XIII first and then gives the modifications, *i.e.* the Ukthya, the Ṣoḍaśin, the Atirātra and the Āptoryāma in the Praśna XIV. The BhārŚS has aptly used the title Jyotiṣṭoma for Praśnas X-XIV because, in all these Praśnas, it describes all the (primary and secondary) norms of the Soma sacrifices. The commentator Rudradatta has rightly noted the propriety of the designation of the sacrifice as found in the BhārŚS.

Unlike other sūtras of the YV, the BhārŚS treats the Pravargya in one Praśna and includes the same within the Agniṣṭoma after the Ātithyeṣṭi. The other Sūtras, including the ĀpŚS, describe the Pravargya in a separate Praśna (*i.e.* XV), after having described the Agniṣṭoma and its modifications. Kashikar[29] expresses his doubts about the authenticity of the present position of the Pravargya in the BhārŚS for it is an independent rite having its own *mantra*, and Brāhmaṇa portions in the TA. He thinks that to be the reason why the sūtras treat it independently. But the BhārŚS treats it in the midst of the Jyotiṣṭoma sacrifices.

Again, as regards style, the ĀpŚS follows the BaudhŚS in giving the *mantra* followed by *vidhi* (unlike the BhārŚS).

The ĀpŚS quotes the Brāhmaṇa passages more frequently than the BhārŚS. It quotes Vājasaneyin's views also. But the BhārŚS never does that. However, both the sūtras have often referred to the views of Āśmarathya and Ālekhana.

The BhārŚS and SatyHirŚS[30]: The SatyHirŚS is closely connected with the ĀpŚS. Many sūtras in the former are literally identical with those of the latter. On the other hand, the BhārŚS and the ĀpŚS are closely connected with each other. Thus it is only natural that the SatyHirŚS should bear some relation to the BhārŚS through the ĀpŚS. Sometimes, some injunctions in the SatyHirŚS agree more closely with those in the BhārŚS than those of the ĀpŚS.

The Bharadvāja Pitṛmedha Sūtra[31]: The Pitṛmedha Sūtras form an important part of the Vedic Sūtra literature. Some of the schools have Pitṛmedha sūtras independent of the Śrauta or Gṛhya sūtra. Some other schools, however, deal with the Pitṛmedha rites in their Gṛhya texts. The Pitṛmedha sūtras of Bharadvāja, Āpastaṁba and Satyāṣāḍha hold a peculiar position among the Pitṛmedha sūtras in the Kṛṣṇa YV. All the three sūtras show close affinities among themselves as regards their arrangement summarised in the following table:

BhārPitṛS	*ĀpPitṛS*	*SatyHirPitṛS*
I, 1-12	I, 1-12	XXVIII, 1-12
II, 1	II, 1	XXIX, 7
II, 2-5	II, 2-5	XXIX, 1-4
II, 6-7	Supplementary Sections 1-2	XXIX, 5-6
II, 8	Section 3, & Part of 4	XXIX, 8-9
II, 9-11	Part of 4 & Section 5	XXIX, 9-11
II, 11	Section 6	XXIX, 11
II, 12	Section 7	XXIX, 11

Thus in arrangement, the three sūtras have very little differences. The notable variation is the Brahmamedha, that forms section 1 of Praśna II in the BhārPitṛS and ĀpPitṛS, but section 7 of Praśna XXIX in the SatyHirPitṛS.

The extant PitṛS of Bharadvāja and that of Āpastaṁba exhibit much similarity. Probably, the Kalpasūtras of Āpastaṁba did not originally contain the PitṛS, and his school followed the PitṛS of Bharadvāja and in course of time, began to regard the PitṛS of Bharadvāja as their own. This may be why the MSS of the Āpastaṁba Sūtra are of a later date.

From Kapardinsvāmin's commentary on the BhārPitṛS, it appears that the sūtra was divided into Paṭalas. This Paṭala division in the BhārPitṛS is also exactly identical with the Paṭala division of the ĀpPitṛS. It may be outlined below:

Paṭala	*BhārPitṛS*	*ĀpPitṛS*
I	I, 1-8	I, 1-8
II	I, 9-10	I, 9-10
III	I, 11-12	I, 11-12
IV	II, 1-4	II, 1-4
V	II, 5	II, 5

In addition to these Paṭalas, there are seven more sections added to II, 5; *i.e.* II, 6-12 in both the works. These seven sections are considered to be later interpolations. But since Kapardinsvāmin is found to have commented upon the whole sūtra including these new seven sections, it can be presumed that the texts took the present form before the commentator had it.

The quotations exclusively from the BhārPitṛS which are met

with in the commentaries of Sāyaṇa, Rudradatta and others[32] also support the view that, in their time, the ĀpPitṛS was not independently in existence and probably the followers of Āpastaṁba school used the BhārPitṛS.

Moreover, the Kalpasūtras of Satyāṣāḍha-Hiraṇyakeśin did not originally contain the Praśnas XXVIII and XXIX, which form the PitṛS. According to Kashikar[33] the followers of Satyāṣāḍha-Hiraṇyakeśin school borrowed the PitṛS from Bharadvāja, which Caland[34] holds to be identical, inasmuch as the two Praśnas are found to be of the nature of appendices. Mahādeva who, commented upon some parts of the SatyHir Sūtra, details the contents of SatyHir Kalpa Sūtra while commenting on the opening sūtra. He says: *idam hi saptaviṁśatipraśnātmakaṁ satyāṣāḍha-hiraṇyakeśī sūtram*[35]; he concludes his commentary with the statement that the last two Praśnas (XXIV-XXVII) form the Dharmasūtra. And, he says that the PitṛS, which consists of the two Praśnas (XXVIII-XXIX), was composed by Bharadvāja and later adopted by the venerable sage (Satyāsāḍha Hiraṇyakeśin): *Pitṛmedhas tu bhāradvājīyo, muninā parigṛhito dvau praśnau.*[36] Thus it is clear that the SatyHir Kalpasūtra did not originally comprise the PitṛS, but later borrowed it from the BhārPitṛS, just as the Āpastaṁbīyas did. In course of time, the adapted text incorporated certain changes. We have already pointed to the displacement of the Brahmamedha section, as a change in the arrangement. "As a matter of fact", says Kashikar, "however, there is no difference at all between the BhārPitṛS on the one hand, and the ĀpPitṛS and SatyPitṛS on the other, as regards ritualistic details, and the use of formulas and verses. Therefore, the conclusion is that the ĀpPitṛS and the SatyPitṛS were not independently compiled texts, but that the followers of the Āpastaṁba and Satyāṣāḍha schools adopted the BhārPitṛS itself and regarded it as a component part of their own Sūtras."[37]

The Bharadvāja Pariśeṣa Sūtra: The Pariśiṣṭa texts constitute an important part of the sūtra literature. "Sometimes these supplements are independent works, sometimes they are integrated with the original texts in such a way that it becomes difficult to spot out their real character."[38] We have Pariśeṣasūtra of Bharadvāja school[39] that pre-supposes the BhārŚS. The aim of the BhārPariS is mainly twofold: (1) it seeks to supplement the injunction already made in the BhārŚS, and (2) it gives a set of Paribhāṣā where BhārŚS shows a lack of it. Out of a total number of 222 Pariśeṣa sūtras, 102 pertain to Paribhāṣās, and 9 to Anugrahas, while the rest (*i.e.* 111) are of the nature of a supplement to the main BhārŚS. The Paribhāṣā sūtras, however, agree with the Paribhāṣā sūtras in the ĀpŚS and BaudhŚS, and a few of them with those of the Vārāha Pariśiṣṭa.

The BhārPariS also refers to the views of Āśmarathya, Ālekhana, Bādarāyaṇa and Audolomi. The Brāhmaṇa-like passages are quoted fifteen times.

There is an indication that this sūtra was earlier divided into Kaṇḍikās.

It is a collection of miscellaneous sūtras and has no specific order or ritual. The sūtras dealing with a specific ritual are scattered here and there. Thus it lacks proper arrangement.

The BhārPariS gives "something...which can be regarded as new."[40] It prescribes an Atipavitreṣṭi for one desirous of *brahmavarcas*. This *iṣṭi* follows the pattern of the Pavitreṣṭi with some modification. So also, it says of the Cāturmāsya that it takes twelve to fifteen days to complete as the ceremony is held on alternate days in between the two *iṣṭis*.

One-third of the Pariśeṣa sūtras deal with ritual topics, not described in the BhārŚS. This affirms the hypothesis that the original texts of the BhārŚS dealt with Dākṣāyaṇa, Kāmyāh paśavah, Paśuprāyaścittas, Paśvaikādaśini and Aśvamedha—none available in the current text.

The BhārPariS was quoted in different commentaries on the Śrauta or Gṛhya-texts.

It has been postulated that this BhārPariS was not the work of the author of BhārŚS but was compiled at a later date even after ĀpŚS was.[41]

The Ritual Teachers: Āśmarathya and Ālekhana: The authors of the sūtras, while describing the Vedic sacrifices, draw upon the Brāhmaṇa texts and authorities anterior to them. In doing so, they leave a clue to their compilation date and sometimes locale. Moreover, by their selection of opinions, they betray their attitude (*i.e.* conservative or reformist). It is, therefore, always rewarding to examine the authorities they quote and find out the rationale behind that.

The author(s) of the sūtras (ascribed to Bharadvājas) has (have) not only quoted the Brāhmaṇas, particularly the TB, but also the views of two earlier authors of ritual manuals. Preference has been for one who prescribed a simple and convenient ritual—this points to Bharadvājas' catholic attitude towards the growth and advancement of rituals.

The two oft-quoted ritual-teachers are Āśmarathya and Ālekhana. They are mentioned 28 times in the BhārŚS, 9 times in the Pariśeṣa sūtra, and only once in the BhārGS.[42] Only Āśmarathya occurs in the BhārPitṛS (1, 10, 12). Kashikar[43] who has collected the citations and made an extensive study of these two teachers, discovered that these two teachers were spoken of not less than 65 times in the Śrauta and other sūtras and commentaries. But the largest number of references (*i.e.* 39 times) are met with in the sūtras ascribed to the Bharadvājas.

It is noteworthy that the works which have quoted or referred to the two teachers, Āśmarathya and Ālekhana (*i.e.* the BhārŚS, BhārGS, BhārPitṛS, BhārPariśeṣasūtra, ĀpŚS, commentaries of Mahādeva and Rudradatta on SatyHirŚS and ĀpŚS respectively) belong to the Ādhvaryava school.[44] Even the occurrences in the ĀśvŚS and Atharvaprāyaścittāni deal with the Ādhvaryava ritual. "It is, therefore, clear that the two teachers, Āśmarathya and Ālekhana, belonged to the Ādhvaryava school,"[45] *i.e.* to the YV, a book of the Adhvaryu priest.

A comparison of their views shows that Āśmarathya 'represents what may be regarded as strictly traditional ritual', while Ālekhana 'prescribes a form of ritual which is less complicated and more convenient'.[46] This means, in other words: Āśmarthya represents a more orthodox school which was based on convention, while Ālekhana tried to introduce novelty by suggesting simpler ways of performing sacrifice. In a word, he was a reformist. Thus it will be plausible to hold that Āśmarathya preceded Ālekhana. While quoting their views, Bharadvāja and others paid due regard to these two *pūrvācāryas*, and leaving the choice open. This can be inferred from the manner of quoting the two teachers' opinions. The authors of the sūtras always quote Āśmarathya first and Ālekhana later, which points not only to their relative chronology but also to their comparatively modern views.

In fact, these two were ancient teachers on Kalpasūtras. "From the commentary on Pāṇini 4, 3, 105: *purāṇaprokteṣu brāhmaṇakalpeṣu*,[47] it is evident that Āśmaratha Kalpa was considered recent in Pāṇini's time in comparison with the more ancient Kalpas like the Paiṅgīkalpa". Pāṇini mentions Aśmaratha (Pāṇini Gaṇa 4.1.105), Aśmaratha (Pā 4, 2, 111) and Aśmarathi (Pā 4, 1, 73) and Ālekhanā (Pā 6, 1, 142).

The BaudhPS[48] groups Aśmarathas with the Kuṇḍinas(from the Vasiṣṭhas), but Kāt. PS[49] with Viśvāmitras. The BaudhPS[50] consider Ālekhana to be one of the Vatsas of the Bhṛgus. This means that Āśmarathya was a descendant of or a student belonging to the school of Aśmaratha (that originated from Vasiṣṭha or Viśvāmitra), while Ālekhana probably to one set up by Ālekhana of the Bhṛgus. These two teachers represented two distinct schools of thought that prevailed prior to that of Bharadvājas who composed the sūtras on rituals. But, in course of time, their schools became extinct, while new schools of rituals replaced them.

We have already said that the views of Ālekhana are simple and convenient and that he was a reformist. We have also seen that he belonged to the Bhṛgus. Kashikar[51] draws our attention to a possible Bhṛguisation in rituals also. The thesis of Bhṛguisation was enunciated first by Sukthankar[52] who, in his exhaustive study, has ably shown the Bhṛgus' influence in the MBh. So also, Kashikar[53] has pointed out that the Bhṛgus affected the rituals as well. We have also noted that Ālekhana (belonging to the Bhṛgus) probably sought to bring some reform in conventional rites and sacrifices, and Bharadvāja and Āpastaṁba could not but appreciate his views.

The Date and Locale of Bharadvāja, the Sūtrakāra: It is difficult to give an exact date of Bharadvāja(s) who composed the Śrauta and Gṛhya sūtras. But a comparative chronology may be suggested on the basis of available internal and external evidence.

We have already mentioned that Mahādeva in his commentary, Vaijayantī on the SatyHirŚS has mentioned the Sūtrakāras of the Taitt. School in the following order:

(1) Baudhāyana, (2) Bharadvāja, (3) Āpastaṁba, (4) Satyāṣāḍha Hiraṇyakeśin, (5) Vaikhānasa, and (6) Vādhūla,[54] and several scholars—Garbe,[55] Winternitz,[56] Bühler,[57] Caland,[58] Kashikar[59] and Ramgopal[60] have attached great significance to this order of the Sūtrakāras in the list.[61] Some of these scholars[62] have successfully tried to substantiate this sequence of Sūtrakāras in Mahādeva's list by adducing textual evidence therefrom. It is pointed out that among the sūtras of the Taitt. School, the Kalpasūtra of Baudhāyana is the oldest.[63] This *pravacana* is nearer in style to the

Brāhmaṇas; it quotes the *mantras* in full, and lacks in the sūtra-style of brevity, unlike the later sūtras. According to the BaudhŚS, the ritual of the Piṇḍapitṛyajña is to be performed by a sacrificer. But Bharadvāja and other sūtra writers assign the preliminary duties in this connection to Adhvaryu. This deputisation trend is of a later date. The interrogatives have been frequently used in the Karmānta portion of the BaudhŚS; generally, this usage is indicative of *pravacana* text and of the antiquity of the work. Bharadvāja has rarely used it, while Āpastaṁba has never.

In the Gṛhya text also Baudhāyana reveals its antiquity relatively. In connection with the *Upanayana* rite Baudhāyana talks of the Rathakāras. Bharadvāja also reports similarly about the Rathakāra, while Āpastaṁba does not. This means that, at the time of Baudhāyana, the Rathakāras were allowed to perform *Upanayana,* and continued to do so till Bharadvāja's time, but the custom was discontinued in Āpastaṁba age. This confirms Bharadvāja's nearness to Baudhāyana.

In connection with the Śulagava ceremony, Baudhāyana prescribes immolation of a cow. But Bharadvāja and Āpastṁba suggest cooked food-grains instead. Ramgopal[64] thinks it to be "a change in social custom". To us, absence of cow immolation and prescription of cooked rice instead need not indicate a social change. It shows a peculiar practice prevalant among certain families. This means that Bharadvāja and Āpastaṁbīyas did not immolate a cow in the Śulagava rite but preferred to make an offering of cooked rice. The cow slaughter was very much prevalant prior to Pāṇini and continued to be so in the time of Bhavabhūti (7th Century A.D.) who implicitly referred to it. There can be no contention about a change of ritual in regard to cow slaughter prior to Pāṇini. However, we agree with Ramgopal[65] who on the basis of textual evidence suggests that Bharadvāja, the Sūtrakāra, must have lived at an intermediary period between Baudhāyana and Āpastaṁba. This is borne out also by the well-knit texts of the Āpastaṁba School, which recorded a comparative progress in scientific arrangement in their texts in relation to Baudhāyana and Bharadvāja Sūtras.

While the scholars accept the chronological order suggested by Mahādeva, they do not agree on dating the Sūtrakāras—in that scholars[66] have depended upon the date of Pāṇini. True that in the *vidādigaṇa* (Pā 4, 1, 104)[67] the names of Bharadvāja and

Āpastamba are given, but the Gaṇapāṭha cannot be said to be free from interpolations,[68] and therefore not reliable. The language and style of the sūtras of three schools is such as to date them earlier than Pāṇini. Further, there is no consensus on timing Pāṇini. R.G. Bhandarkar (JBRAS 16, p. 340ff) and Goldstücker[69] place Pāṇini in the 8th century B.C. In the opinion of S.K. Belvalkar[70] Pāṇini flourished in the 7th century B.C. According to Winternitz,[71] he could probably have lived in the 5th century B.C. Agrawal[72] also places him in the 5th century B.C. Ramgopal[73] and Kashikar[74] range the Pāṇini era between 600-550 B.C. Thus, the date of our sūtras may vary accordingly if it is based on Pāṇini. However, Ramgopal[75] and Kashikar[75a] fixed the period of the sūtras between 800-500 B.C.; this is acceptable.

The Home of Bharadvāja: It is difficult to decide the locale where the Sūtrakāra Bharadvāja lived. The problem was once discussed by Kashikar[76] who located Sūtrakāra Bharadvāja along the bank of the Yamunā in Northern India. Against this opinion, there is evidence to show that the Taittirīya schools, including that of Bharadvāja, had for long flourished in South India. Bühler,[77] therefore, concluded that the home of Āpstamba was in the South; same about Baudhāyana.[78] The three Sūtrakāras, Baudhāyana, Bharadvāja and Āpastamba are closely related to one another. This could not sustain if one lived in the South and the other in the North. The problem of the home of Baudhāyana and Āpastamba has been re-examined by Ramgopal[79] whose conclusion is that irrespective of the overwhelming majority of the followers of these schools living in the South, the home of Baudhāyana and Āpastamba was somewhere in or around Kurupāñcāla country. If this is true, Bharadvāja's homeland must also be in the neighbourhood of Baudhāyana and Āpastamba. Probably, during foreign rule and under alien pressures and threats of persecution, a large number of the followers of the Taitt. School migrated to the South leaving the Āryāvarta which they considered their sacred land. They could preserve the sūtra MSS of those as well. In the North, several Sanskrit MSS were destroyed by foreign invaders and temples were levelled to the ground. Not surprising, if MSS of the sacrificial manuals were not traceable in the North.

That Bharadvāja lived on the North bank of the Yamunā is borne out by the fact that this river is mentioned in BhārGS (1, 21) in the description of *Sīmantonnayana: soma eva no rāje'ty āhur brāhmaṇīḥ prajāḥ/ vivṛttacakrā āsīnās tīreṇa yamune tava.*[80] The sūtra says that the word Yamunā is to be replaced by the name of the river on whose bank the person reciting the *mantra* lives: *yathā tireṇa vegavatī tava, tireṇa kāverī.*[81] The commentator has cited this example, giving the name of the Kāverī, probably because his residence was on the bank of the river Kāverī. So also, has Bharadvāja mentioned the name of the Yamunā, because he lived along its bank.

Besides, the two teachers who are frequently quoted by Bharadvāja also lived probably somewhere in Āryāvarta. Āśvalāyana who names Sarasvatī, Plakṣaprasravaṇa, Kārapacana, etc. also refers to Āśmarathya and Ālekhana.[82] Āśvalāyana seems to have been a resident of Āryāvarta. Baudhāyana who defines Āryāvarta and prescribes expiational recourse to one who travels outside must have been a native. Bharadvāja who flourished sometime later than Baudhāyana and had composed a sūtra that has affinity with the former's work must have hailed from the same region.

Further, we have elsewhere come across a number of Bharadvājas who lived in Gaṅgādvāra or Prayāga, or Badaripācana or on the bank of the Godāvarī. Prayāga and Gaṅgādvāra were the home of the Bharadvāja described in the Rām and the MBh respectively; each of them being an *āhitāgni.* The Bharadvājas living on the bank of the Revatī—a tributory of the Godāvarī flourished later than those of the Epics. It is thus probable that Bharadvāja, the Sūtrakāra, belonged to the early groups who lived in the North. In other words, he might have been a descendant of a Bharadvāja living at Prayāga or Gaṅgādvāra; and recited a *mantra* in which the Yamunā is referred to. As one Bharadvāja was living on the bank of the Revatī, the tributary of Godāvarī, in the South—and since he also appears to be an *āhitāgni*, he might have been a follower of the Bharadvāja school only. This shows a gradual migration of the Bharadvājas Southwards.

Section (vii)

The Bhāradvāja Gṛhya Sūtra

The Bhāradvāja Gṛhya Sūtra (BhārGS)[1] forms a part of the Kalpasūtras of the same school. Already, in our discussion of the

Śrauta sūtra of Bharadvāja, we noted that the Kalpasūtras of Baudhāyana, Bharadvāja, Āpastaṁba, Satyāsāḍha Hiraṇyakeśin and Vaikhānasa belong to the Kṛṣṇa YV.[2] We observed that the school of Bharadvāja forms a *śākhā* ('branch') of the Khāṇḍikeyas who belonged to the Taitt. recension of the Kṛṣṇa YV.[3]

The contents of the BhārGS are more or less the same as those of the other Gṛhyasūtras.[4] However, the description of the materials varies only in minute details—and that too, in a minor way. Striking in the BhārGS is its arrangement of the topics. Most of the Gṛhyasūtras begin with the description of the seven *Pākayajñas* followed by the *Haviryajñas* and the so called *Śarīrakarmans*—beginning with *Garbhādhāna*, etc., and ending with *Vivāha* and the five *Mahāyajñas*, and finally the funeral rituals. Strangely enough, the BhārGS starts with a description of the *upanayana* ceremony. *Vivāha*, other *Śarīrakarmans* and *Cauḍakarman* are followed by other minor Gṛhya rituals such as *Śravaṇakarman*, etc. Mrs. Salomons who edited the texts of the BhārGS remarks: "The contents of our sūtra are rather extensive. The succession of the different subjects is not very logical; I cannot find any system in it."[5] However, we furnish the contents in three Praśnas, subdivided into a number of Kaṇḍikās as under:

Contents	*Chapter & Sections*
Upanayanam (Medhājananam, Godānam)	1, 1-10
Vivāhaḥ	1, 11-20
Sīmantonnayanam	1, 21
Puṁsavanam	1, 22
Kṣipraṁsuvanam	1, 22
Vijātārakṣaṇam	1, 23
Jātakarmāṇi (Medhājananam, Āgāra-Śaucam, Mātāputrayoḥ Snānam)	1, 24-26
Nāmakaraṇam	1, 26
Viproṣyakarman	1, 27
Annaprāśanam	1, 27
Cauḍam (Godānam)	1, 28
Śravaṇakarman	2, 1
Āgrahāyaṇi	2, 2
Hemantapratyavarohaṇam	2, 2
Śālākarman	2, 3

Contents	*Chapter & Sections*
Āgārapraveśah (Vāstuśamanam)	2, 4-6
Śvagrahaprāyaścittam	2, 7
Śulagavam	2, 8-10
Māsi-śrāddham	2, 11-14
Aṣṭakā	2, 15-17
Snānam	2, 18-22
Arghyam	2, 23-26
Saṁvādajayanam	2, 26
Subhṛtyaguptiḥ	2, 27
Bhāryāguptiḥ	2, 28
Rathārohaṇam	2, 29
Hastyārohaṇam	2, 29
Prāyaścittāni	2, 29-31
Adbhutaprāyaścittāni	2, 32
Aupāsanakalpaḥ	3, 1-3
Vratādeśavisarjanam	3, 4-5
Avāntaradīkṣā	3, 6-7
Upākaraṇavisarjane	3, 8-11
Vaiśvadevam	3, 12-14
Nāndiśrāddham	3, 16
Sapiṇḍīkaraṇam	3, 17
Gṛhyaprāyaścittāni	3, 18-21

The above arrangement of the topics agrees to some extent with that of the SatyHirGS.

Some of the uncommon factors and special features of the rites are:

Much attention has been paid to the *prāyaścittāni* 'expiation rites'. One can distinguish four kinds of these rites:

(1) The first are to beapplied out of door, *i.e.* when one passes a crossing or cremation ground, or when the sacrificial fire enkindles of its own or when one happens to see an uncommon tree, etc. (BhārGS, 2, 29-31).

(2) The second, specifically called *adbhuta-prāyaścittāni*, are applied in the case of abnormal occurrences in the house, such as the budding of a door-post, the presence of a honey-comb inside the house, etc. (BhārGS 2, 32).

(3) The third *prāyaścittas,* called *gṛhyaprāyaścittāni*, are described at the end of the BharGS. These are meant for the atonement

of neglect in the domestic sacrifice, *e.g.* when sacrificial vessels are broken or *havis* is burnt or when the routine for the sacrifice is not properly observed, etc. This last *prāyaścitta* is treated elaborately (BhārGS 3, 18-21).

(4) Moreover, our texts describe a specific *prāyaścitta* called *śvagrahaprāyaścitta*. It is prescribed for one who touches or catches a dog on any occasion (BhārGS 2, 7). Such an elaborate atonement for a minor 'sin' committed by one is rare in other Gṛhya texts.

Some other new topics discussed in the text are *Saṁvāda-jayanam* (2, 26), *Subhṛtyaguptiḥ* (2, 27), *Bhāryāguptiḥ* (2, 28), *Avāntaradīkṣā* (3, 6-7), and *Māsiśrāddham* (2, 11-14). The first three topics appear to be Atharvaṇic in essence and character.

Some notable features of a Gṛhyasūtra crystallised from our text are: the general description of the *pākayajñas*, the Darśa and the Paurṇamāsa sacrifices. The funeral rites were not treated here, for these are detailed in the PitṛS,[6] which is closer to the Śrautasūtra than to the Gṛhayasūtra.

We have already discussed the comparative chronology of the Śrautasūtras of Baudhāyana, Bharadvāja, Āpastaṁba, Satyāṣāḍha Hiraṇyakeśin, and come to the conclusion that the Śrautasūtra of Bharadvāja was authored later than that of Baudhāyana but earlier than those of Āpastaṁba and Satyāṣāḍha Hiraṇyakeśin.[7]

Now as regards the authorship and chronology of the Gṛhyasūtras of the above mentioned schools, Kashikar[8] and Ramgopal[9] share the same view, *viz.*, that the timing of the Śrautasūtras applies to the Gṛhyasūtras also. Kashikar[10] has ably clarified the relation of the Śrauta, Gṛhya and Pitṛmedha-texts of the Bharadvājas and opines that these were the works of the same author. Kashikar further agrees with Ramgopal that there is close relationship among the texts and the materials of the schools of Bharadvāja, Āpastaṁba and Satyāṣāḍha Hiraṇyakeśin.[11] But these scholars have outright ignored the passage in the BhārGS (3, 11[12]), where the names of three sūtrakāras (*viz.*, Baudhāyana, Bharadvāja and Āpastaṁba) are mentioned, among many other seers, *ācāryas*, sūtrakaras, etc. If the name of Āpastaṁba, the sūtrakāra, occurs in the BhārGS, how can one say that the latter preceded the former?

We have verified the three Gṛhya texts of Bharadvāja, Āpastaṁba and Satyāṣāḍha and found that BhārGS[13] and SatyHirGS[14] provide two lists of seers, *ācāryas, sūtrakāras*, etc., to whom oblations are offered in the *Utsarjana* rite, but the ĀpGS does not. These are compared below:

BhārGS	*SatyHirGS*
Seven seers:	
Viśvāmitra	Viśvāmitra
Jamadagni	Jamadagni
Bharadvāja	Bharadvāja
Gautama	Gautama
Atri	Atri
Vasiṣṭha	Vasiṣṭha
Kaśyapa	
Arundhatī (Vasiṣṭha's wife)	
Sages:	
Kṛṣṇa Dvaipāyana	Kṛṣṇa Dvaipāyana
Jātukarṇa	Jātukarṇa
Tarukṣa	Tarukṣa
Bṛhaduktha	—
Tṛṇabindu	Tṛṇabindu
Somaśravas	Varmin
Somaśuṣmin	Varuthin
—	Vājin
Vājaśravas	Vājaśravas
Vājaratna	Satyaśravas
Varmin	Suśravas
Varuthin	Somasuśmayana
Satvavat	Satvavat
Haryajvan	Bṛhaduktha
Vāmadeva	Vāmadevya
Udamaya	Vājiratna
Ṛṇañjaya	Haryajvāyana
Ṛtañjaya	Udamaya
Dhanañjaya	Gautama
Babhru	Ṛṇañjaya
Tryaruṇa	Ṛtañjaya
Trivarpa	Kṛtañjaya
Tridhātu	Dhanañjaya
Aśvayajña	Babhru
Parāśara	Tryaruṇa
Vasiṣṭha	Trivarṣa

BhārGS	*SatyHirGS*
Indra	Tridhātu
Mṛtyu	Sibinta
Kartṛ	Parāśara
Tvaṣṭṛ	Viṣṇu
Dhātṛ	Rudra
Vidhātṛ	Skanda
Savitṛ	Kāśīśvara
Suśravas	Jvara
Satyaśravas	Dharma
Sāvitrī, etc.	Artha
	Kāma
	Krodha
	Vasiṣṭha
	Indra
	Tvaṣṭṛ
	Kartṛ
	Dhātṛ
	Mṛtyu
	Savitṛ
Pitṛs, etc.	Sāvitrī
Vaiśampāyana	Vaiśampāyana
Phaliṅga	Paliṅga (*sic*)
Tittira	Tittira
Ukha	Ukha
Ātreya (the author of the *Padapāṭha*)	Ātreya
Kauṇḍinya (Vṛttikāra)	Kauṇḍinya
Bodhāyana	—
Bharadvāja (Sūtrakāra)	Satyāṣāḍha
Āpastaṁba	—

These two lists broadly agree. Particularly, the names of the Pitṛs are identical. In the BhārGS, Kāṇva, Baudhāyana, Bharadvāja and Āpastaṁba are mentioned, but in the SatyHirGS these are not—instead the name of Satyāṣāḍha is included. Thus, it appears that these two sūtras mention the names of the authors(?) as the persons to whom an initiated Brāhmaṇa should pay his due regards. Probably, these works are the product of schools established by the teachers, Bharadvāja and Satyāṣāḍha, and their pupils gave credit to their teachers by way of homage. But this does resolve the issue why a later Sūtra-writer Āpastaṁba finds a place in the BhārGS. Kashikar[15] maintains that the Āpastaṁba and Satyāṣāḍha schools used the Pitṛs of Bhāradvāja prior to their own collection and that this has been proved beyond doubt. Alternatively the schools of Āpastaṁba and Satyāṣāḍha used BhārGS some time prior to its adoption in their own. The list of the teachers supports this presumption. The Gṛhya texts of the three schools are remarkably similar. Perhaps the followers of the Āpastaṁba School were interested in and responsible for entering the name of Āpastaṁba in the BhārGS. As such, we are constrained to observe that the section where the *upakaraṇavisarjana* rites are treated, is a later addition or interpolation, by the followers of Āpastaṁba in collusion with those of Bhāradvāja. The latter did not raise an objection because all were attached to the Taitt. recension of the Kṛṣṇa YV.

In view of the foregoing discussion we accept the date suggested for the Śrauta Sūtra. But the interpolated portion might have been incorporated later.

Notes and References

Section (i)

1. cf. Sarvā 2, 6, 1; 53.
2. *Vedische Mythologie*, II, 330.
3. cf. Sarvā 2, 1, 36 and 42; also, 2, 1, 127 and 138.
4. cf. Sarvā 2, 2, 1: य आङ्गिरस शौनहोत्रो भूत्वा भार्गवः शौनकोऽभवत् स गृत्समदो द्वितीयं मण्डलमपश्यत् ।

   Also see Part I, Ch. 3, Section (ii) above.
5. Sarvā: 2, 10, 20.
6. See the next section on the Go-sūkta for details.
7. Dandekar, VMT, pp. 91-117.
8. Oldenberg, *Die Religion des Veda*, pp. 73; 234-237.
9. Guntert, *Der Arische Weltkonig und Heiland* pp. 41-44; Siecke, *Pushan, Studien zur Idee des Hirtengottes im Anschluss an die studien uber "Hermes den Mondgott,"* Leipzig, 1914. Siecke thinks in Pūṣan there lies an ancient latent Moon-God.
10. Atkins, *Pūṣan in the Ṛgveda*, pp. 9-16; also Introduction pp. 2 ff. Before Atkins, other scholars were also busy in speculation and discussion, taking Pūṣan as a Sun-god from different points of view. For example, Grassmann (*Rig Veda, Ubersetzung*, 1876-77) makes Pūṣan a god of prosperity and

growth related to the Sun; Schroeder (*Arische Religion* II, p. 11) took Pūṣan as an original Sun-god bestowing bounty; De Gubernatis (*Letture sopra la mitologia vedica*, Florence, 1874, p. 82) and Grill (*Hundert Lieder des Atharvaveda*, Ubersetzung, Tubingen, 1879) consider Pūṣan as the setting sun; Flensburg (*Bidrag till Ṛgvedas mythologi.* Om guden Pūṣani Ṛgveda Lund, 1909) takes Pūṣan as the Sun of the mid-day, when he is nearer to earth; Hillebrandt (VM II, 332-333) takes Pūṣan primarily as Sun-god with pastoral functions.

11. op. cit. pp. 104 ff.
12. RV 6, 55, 3: रायो धारास्याघृणे वसो राशिरजाश्व । धीवतो धीवतः सखा ।
cf. RV 1, 138, 4; 6, 55, 4; 58, 2; 9, 67, 10.
13. Sāyaṇa under 6, 53, 5; RVVSM 3, 201.
14. Atkins, op. cit. p. 59; Upādhyāya S.A., "Hymns to Pūṣan", BV 25, 1-2 p. 43.
15. Upādhyāya, S.A. Ibid-p. 43.
16. Read: RV 6, 53, 9: या ते अष्ट्रा गोओपशाऽऽघृणे पशुसाधनी । तस्यास्ते सुम्नमीमहे ॥
17. See Atkins, op. cit. p. 60. Dandekar, op. cit. p. 108.
18. Dandekar, op. cit.
19. 1, 7, 4, 7: तस्मादाहुरदन्तकः पूषा पिष्टभाजन इति ।
cf. GB 2, 1.2; KB. 6, 13; TS 2, 6, 8, 5.
20. SP 3, 42, 8.
21. The poet is Vāmadeva Gotama, an Āṅgirasa seer. The Bharadvājas also are the Āṅgirasas. Thus we think it fair to consider some passages from other Āṅgirasas too.
22. AV passages are treated here by way of analogy only, to support Pūṣan's pastoral character.
23. Read: इन्द्रः सीतां नि गृह्णातु तां पूषाभि रक्षतु ।
सा नः पयस्वती दुहाम् उत्तरामुत्तरां समाम् ॥
24. Read: धाता पूषा बृहस्पतिर्भुम्यास्समजीमकन् ।
कृषिं देवास्स्वर्विदः कल्याणी सुभगेव या ॥
25. Read: आ ते रथस्य पूषन् अजा धुरं ववृत्युः ।
विश्वस्यार्थिनः सखा सनोजा अनपच्युतः ॥
26. Read: अस्माकमूर्जा रथं पूषा अविष्टु माहिनः ।
27. Read: उत् पूषणं युवामहे ऽभीशूंन्र इव सारथिः ।
मह्या इन्द्रं स्वस्तये ॥
28. The traits of Kṛṣṇa and Śalya as the charioteers have been praised in many places of the MBh. Cf. MBh 8, 22-23 specially, and read the following verses where Karṇa compares the two:

Read: MBh 8, 22, 54 and 56

यथाश्वहृदयं वेद दाशार्हः परवीरहा ।
तथा शल्यऽपि जानीते हययानां वै महारथः ॥ 54

x x x x x

तथा शल्यसमो नास्ति हयाने ह कश्चन ।
सोऽयमभ्यधिकः पार्थाद् भविष्यतिं रथो मम ॥56/1

29. Read: पूष्णश्चक्रं न रिष्यति न कोशोऽव पद्यते।
नो अस्य व्यथते पविः॥

30. Read: पूषेमा आशा अनुवेद सर्वाः सो अस्माँ अभयतमेन नेषेषत्।
स्वस्तिदा आघृणिः सर्ववीरःऽप्रयुच्छन् पुर एतु प्रजानन्॥

31. Translation by Atkins, op. cit. p. 86.

32. Read: RV 10, 17, 6: प्रपथे पथामजनिष्ट पूषा प्रपथे दिवः प्रपथे पृथिव्याः।
उभे अभि प्रियतमे सधस्थे आ च परा च चरति प्रजानन्॥

And we have adopted Atkins' translation (op. cit.) here also.

33. Read: उप प्रेष्यन्तं पूषणं यो वहात्यञ्जोयानैः पथिभिस्तत्र गच्छतम्।

34. Read: पूषा त्वेतो नयतु हस्तगृह्याऽश्विना त्वा प्रवहतां रथेन।

35. Read: एष छागः पुरो अश्वेन वाजिना
पूष्णो भागो नीयते विश्वदेव्यः॥

36. Read: अदित्सन्तं चिदाघृणे पूषन् दानाय चोदय।

37. The refrain अथेमस्मभ्यं रन्धय is repeated in these verses besides such expressions, namely* *pari*

*परि तृन्धि पणीनामारया हृदया कवे। (v.5), or
वि पूषन् आरया तुद पणेरिच्छ हृदि प्रियम्। (v.6), or
आ रिख किकिरा कृणु पणीनां हृदया कवे। (v.7) etc.

38. Read: यां पूषन् ब्रह्मचोदनी-मारां विभर्ष्याघृणे।
तयो समस्य हृदयम् आ रिख किकिरा कृणु॥

39. Bergaigne has fully discussed the hymn (RV 10, 108) from mythological point of view in his *Vedic Religion* (English Translation by Paranjape) pp. 317ff. He says at p. 324: "And in fact the whole of the hymn X. 108 is only a dialogue between the demons who had robbed the cows, called Paṇis here, and our Saramā, who comes on the part of Indra to demand back the cows which they had stolen."

40. VMT, p. 111. See also the fn. 68 at the same page.

40a. See on this point Section on Śaṁyu Bārhaspatya, Part I, Ch. 4, Section (i) above.

41. Read: सोमम् अन्य उपासदत् पातवे चम्वोः सुतम्।
करम्भमन्य इच्छति॥

42. Read: अजा अन्यस्य वह्नयः हरी अन्यस्य संभृता।

43. VMT, pp. 92, 115ff.

44. Ibid.

45. Read note in 4 above.

46. Read: सोमापूषणा जनना रयीणां
जनना दिवो जनना पृथिव्याः।
जातौ विश्वस्य भुवनस्य गोपौ
देवा अकृण्वन्नमृतस्य नाभिम्॥

47. Read: इमौ देवौ जायमानौ जुषन्ता
इमौ तमांसि गूहतामजुष्टा

ग्राभ्यामिन्द्रः पक्वमामास्वन्तः
सोमापूषभ्यां जनदुस्त्रियासु ।।

48. Read: धीयं पूषा जिन्वतु विश्वमिन्वः रयिं सोमो रयिपतिर्दधातु ।
49. Atkins, op. cit., p. 9.
50. Ibid., p. 11.
51. Ibid., p. 65.
52. VM p. 74.
52a. VS 16, 28; 40; 24, 3; 39, 9.
52b. AVŚ 2, 34, 1; 11, 2.29.
53. ŚB 6, 1, 3, 7; 1, 7, 3, 8, where Agni is called Rudra, Paśupati etc.
54. Macdonell, VM p. 75.
55. RV 1, 23, 13; 14; 138, 4; 3, 62; 7; 6, 48, 16; 53, 3; 8, 9; 55, 1; 3; 7, 40, 6; 8, 4, 17; 18; 9, 67, 12; 10, 17, 5.
56. op. cit., p. 14.
57. op. cit., p. 19.
58. AVŚ 1, 11. 1.
59. AVŚ 6, 12, 3.
60. AVP 2, 61, 5.
61. For a similar treatment of Indra as a human hero, vide Dandekar, VMT p. 162ff. A similar treatment may be applicable to Pūṣan also, in spite of the scanty anthropomorphic traits of the gods available in RV.
62. For the case of mythologisation of history relating to Indra, see Dandekar, ibid., pp. 186ff, where he exemplifies how history transforms into mythology.
63. op. cit., pp. 9ff.
64. op. cit., pp. 111ff.

Section (ii)

1. Geldner, DR. 2, 143-144; Velankar, JBBRAS, 18, 1942, p. 8ff. Rahurkar, S.R. Introduction, pp. XVII; 91ff.
2. Velankar, op. cit., p. 8ff; "Indra-Hymns" JUB 13, p. 70. Rahurkar, op. cit. p. 91ff.
3. Velankar, op. cit.
3a. Rahurkar, op. cit.
4. Sarvā 2, 6, 47.
4a. See our section on Garga, Part I, Ch. 2, (iv).
5. BD 6, 125-142.
6. For this division, see Geldner, DR, 2, 143-144 and Velankar, BUJ 13(2), 1943, p. 70.
7. Read: प्रस्तोक इन्नु राधसस्त इन्द्र दश कोशयीर्दश वाजिनोऽदात् ।
दिवोदासादतिथिग्वस्य राधः शाम्बरं वसु प्रत्यग्रभीष्म ।।
8. Read: दशाश्वान् दश कोशान् दश वस्त्राधिभोजना ।
दशो हिरण्यपिण्डान् दिवोदासादसानिषम् ।।
9. Read: दश रथान् प्रष्टिमतः शतं गा अथर्वभ्यः ।
अश्वथः पायवेऽदात् ।।

10. Read: महि राधो विश्वजन्यं दधानान् ।
भरद्वाजान्त् साञ्र्जयो अभ्ययष्ट ॥

11. Read: RV 2, 12, 11 यः शम्बरं पर्वतेषु क्षियन्तं चत्वारिंश्यां शरद्यन्वविन्दत् ।

12. BD 5, 124-142.

13. Read: अभ्यावर्ती चायमानः प्रस्तोकश्चैव साञ्र्जयः ।
आजग्मतुर्भरद्वाजं जितौ वारशिखैर्युधि ॥ 124
अभिगम्योचतुस्तौ तं प्रसाद्याख्याय नामनी ।
युधि वारशिखैर्ब्रह्मन् आवां विद्धि विनिर्जितौ ॥ 125
भवत् पुरोहितावावां क्षत्रबन्धूञ्जयेवहि ।
क्षत्रं तदपि विज्ञेयं ब्रह्म यत् पाति शाश्वतम् ॥ 126
ऋषिस्तौ तु तथेत्युक्त्वा पायुं पुत्रमभाषत ।
अधर्षणीयौ शत्रूणां कुरुष्वैतौ नृपाविति ॥ 127
पितरं स तथेत्युक्त्वा युद्धोपकरणं तयोः ।
जीमूतस्येति सूक्तेन पृथक्त्वेनान्वमन्त्रयत् ॥ 128
× × × ×
अभ्यावर्तिनमभ्येत्य हर्युपीया नदीतटे ।
सहितश्चायमानेन जघानैनाञ्छचीपतिः ॥ 138
तौ तु वारशिखाञ्जित्वा ततोऽभ्यावर्तिसाञ्जयौ ।
भरद्वाजाय गुरवे ददतुर्विविधं वसु ॥ 139

BD 5, 124-128; 138-9.

14. Read: भरद्वाजश्च गर्गश्च दृष्टाविन्द्रेण वै पथि ।
द्वयान् प्रस्तोक इत्याभिर् दानं तद्वै शशंसतुः॥

BD 5, 140.

15. Read: वधीदिन्द्रो वरशिखस्य शेषोऽभ्यावर्तिने चायमानाय शिक्षन् ।
वृचीवतो यद्धरियूपीयायां हन् पूर्वे अर्धे भियसापरो दर्त् ॥
त्रिंशच्छतं वर्मिण इन्द्र साकं यव्यावत्यां पुरुहूत श्रवस्या ।
वृचीवन्तः शरवे पत्यमानाः पात्रा भिन्दाना न्यर्थान्यायन् ॥
यस्य गावावरुषा सूयवस्यू अन्तरूषु चरतो रेरिहाणा ।
स सृञ्जयाय तुर्वशं परादाद् वृचीवतो दैववाताय शिक्षन् ॥
द्वयाँ अग्ने रथिनो विंशतिं गा वधूमतो मघवा मह्यं सम्राट् ।
अभ्यावर्ती चायमानो ददाति दूणशेयं दक्षिणा पार्थवानाम् ॥

16. On the word *pārthavānām* Velankar (BUJ 11(2), 1942 p. 109) comments: "This refers to Abhyāvartin and his followers, descendants of Pṛthu."

16a. For details on this point see chapter 5 of the Part I.

17. RVVSM 3, 106 under verses RV 6, 27, 5 and 6 respectively.

18. RVVIS 4, 2037 under RV 6, 27, 5 and 6 respectively.

19. P.W. 6, p. 90.

20. Ibid. 7, p. 1555.

21. WR p. 1099.

22. Ibid. p. 1649.

23. Der Rigveda (Tr.) 3, 158.

24. VM 3, 268, n. 1.
25. VI 2, 188.
26. *Early India and Pakistan*, London, 1968, p. 113.
27. 5, 129-136.
28. TS 4, 6, 6, 1-7 (=RV 6, 75, 1-14+6, 47, 26-31).
29. VS 29, 38-57 (RV 6, 75, 1-14+6, 47, 26-31).
30. MS 3, 16, 3; 185, 10-13.
31. KSA 6, 1.
32. 2, 6, 15: जीमूतस्यैवैकोना पायुर्भारद्वाजः ....।
33. Read the verse at (9).
34. Read: संग्रामे समुपह्ले राजानं संनाहयेत् । 1
35. Read: आ त्वाऽहार्षमन्तरेधीति पश्चाद्रथस्यावस्थाय । 2
    जीमूतस्येव भवति प्रतीकमिति कवचं प्रयच्छेत् ।। 3
36. Read: उत्तरया धनुः । उत्तरां वाचयेत् ।। 4-5
37. Read: स्वयं चतुर्थीं जपेत् ।। 6
38. Read: पञ्चम्येषुधिं प्रयच्छेत् ।। 7
39. Read: अभिप्रवर्तमाने षष्ठीम् ।। 8
40. Read: सप्तम्याऽश्वान् ।। 9
41. Read: अष्टमीमिषूनवेक्षमाणं वाचयति ।। 10
42. Read: अहिरिव भोगैः पर्येति बाहुमिति तलं नह्यमानम् ।। 11
43. Read: अथैनं सारयमानमुपारुह्यामीवतं वाचयति प्र यो वां मित्रावरुणेति च द्वे ।। 12
44. Read: अथैनमन्वीक्षेता प्रतिरथशाससौपर्णैः ।। 13
    प्रधारयन्तु मधुनो धृतस्येत्येतत् सौपर्णम् ।। 14
45. Read: सर्वा दिशोऽनुपरियायात् ।। आदित्यमौशनसं वाऽवस्थाय प्रयोधयेत् ।। 15-16
46. Read: उपश्वासय पृथिवीमुत द्यामिति तृचेन दुन्दुभिमभिमृशेत् ।। 17
47. Read: अवसृष्टा परापतेतीषून् विसर्जयेत् ।। 18
48. Read: यत्र वाणाः संपतन्तीति युध्यमानेषु जपेत् ।। 19
49. Read: संशिष्याद्वा मंशिष्याद्वा ।। 20
50. Read: यं राजा न पश्येत् उदपात्रं तयोस्ततो न युध्येत राजा ।। नि तद्दधिषे वनस्पते अया विष्ठा अग्न इन्द्रो दिशश्चतस्र इति नवं रथे राजानं ससारथिमास्थापयति इति दारिलः ।
51. Shende, N.J. *Religion and Philosophy of Atharvaveda*, p. 89.
52. Read: भेर्यादीनि सर्वाणि वादित्राणि प्रक्षाल्य तगरोशीरेण प्रलिप्य। समुच्य च एकवद्भावात् । उशीरं जीर्णं प्रमन्दोशीरेति वचनात् । संपातवत् करणम् । त्रिस्त्रिरेवैकं वादित्रं वादयित्वा पुरोधा वादयितृभ्यः प्रयच्छेत् । सर्वग्रहणादत्यत्रनियमः । प्रक्षालनादिषु मन्त्राभावः । संपातवत्वात् ।

Section (iii)

1. See RVVSM, Vol. V, pp. 192, 193, 194-5; 200-202.
2. Sarvā 2, 10, 169: मयोभूः शवरः काक्षीवतो गव्यम् ।

3. Ibid: 2, 4, 58: समुद्रादेकादशाग्नेयं जगत्यन्तं सौर्यं वापं वा गव्यं वा धृतस्तुवितर्वा ।।
4. Ibid: 2, 6, 1: बार्हस्पत्यो भरद्वाजः षष्ठं मण्डलमपश्यत् ।
   and Sarvā 2, 6, 28 reads: आ गावो गव्यं द्वितीयैन्द्री वान्तस्य पादोऽन्त्यानुष्टुब्जागतस्तृचो द्वितीयादिः ।।
5. ABS 2, 19: आ गाव इति ब्रह्मा ABS 6, 15 reads: साहस्रत्वेष । इति चतुर्विंशतिकम् । ब्रह्मा । आ ऋषभम् ।

The hymn AVŚ 9, 4 is alternatively ascribed to one Ṛṣabha, but is of doubtful identity.

6. JUB 11(2), 1942, p. 109.
7. Ibid.
8. Read: अम्बयो यन्ति शम्भुमयोभुम्यां ब्रह्म जज्ञानमा गाव एका च म इति गा लवणं पाययत्युपतापिनीः । प्रजननकामाः ।।
9. AVVIS, Vol. 1, p. 485: तत्र आगावः इति प्रथमेन सूक्तेन गवां रोगापशमनपुष्टिप्रजननकर्मसु सलवणं केवलं वा उदकम् अभिमन्त्र्य पाययेत् ।
10. Read: आयतीः यासामूधश्चतर्बिलं मधोः पूर्णं घृतस्य च । ता नः सन्तु पयस्वतीर्बहवो गोष्ठे घृताच्यः । उपमैतु मयोभुव ऊर्जं शौचश्च विभ्रतीः । दुहाना अक्षितं पयो मयि गोष्ठे निविशध्वं यथा भवाम्युत्तमो या देवेषु तन्ममैरयन्तेति च सूक्तशेषम् ।।
11. Read: यासामूधच्छतुर्लि मधोः पूर्णं घृतस्य च । ता नः सन्तु पयस्वतीर्बहवोगोष्ठे घृताच्य च इति । आ गावो अग्मनिति च प्रत्यागतासु । उत्तमामा कुर्वन् । मयोभूर्वाति इति सूक्तेन गोष्ठे गताः ।।
12. Aśv 2, 10, 7: आ गावीयमेके । आयतीनामनुमन्त्रणे 'आ गावो अग्मन्' इत्येतत् सूक्तमेक इच्छन्ति । इति नारायणः ।
13. Read: हिरण्यहस्तो यजमानो बर्हिर्वेदि दक्षिणा आयतीः आ गावः (AV 4. 21.1) इति प्रत्युत्तिष्ठति । Commentator says: दक्षिणा गावः । वा बर्हिर्वेद्यागच्छन्तीः हिरण्यहस्तो यजमानः प्रत्युत्तिष्ठति ।
14. Read: आ गावो अग्मन्नुत भद्रमक्रन् त्सीदन्तु गोष्ठे रणयन्त्वस्मे ।
    प्रजावतीः पुरुरूपा इह स्युरिन्द्राय पूर्वीरूषसो दुहानाः ।।
    इन्द्रो यज्वने पृणते च शिक्षत्युपेद् ददाति न स्व मुषायति ।
    भूयोभूयो रयिमिदस्य वर्धयन्नभिन्ने खिल्ये नि दधाति देवयुम् ।।
    न ता नशन्ति न दभाति तस्करो नासामामित्रो व्यथिरा दधर्षति ।
    देवाँश्च याभिर्यजते ददाति च ज्योगित् ताभिः सचते गोपति. सह ।।
    न ता अर्वा रेणुककाटो अश्नुते न संस्कृतत्रमुप यन्ति ता अभि ।
    उरुगायमभयं तस्य ता अनु गावो मर्तस्य वि चरन्ति यज्वनः ।।
    गावो भगो गाव इन्द्रो मे अच्छान् गावः सोमस्य प्रथमस्य भक्षः ।
    इमा या गावः स जनास इन्द्र इच्छमीद्हृदा मनसा चिदिन्द्रम् ।।
    यूयं गावो मेदयथा कृशं चिदश्रीरं चित् कृणुथा सुप्रतीकम् ।
    भद्रं गृह कृणुथ भद्रवाच वृहद् वो वय उच्यत सभासु ।।
    प्रजावतीः सूयवसं रिशन्तीः शुद्धा अप सुप्रपाणे पिबन्तीः ।
    मा वः स्तेन ईशत माघशंसः परि वो हेती रुद्रस्य वृज्याः ।।
    उपेदमुपपर्चनमासु गोषूप पृच्यताम् ।
    उप ऋषभस्य रेतस्युपेन्द्र तव वीर्ये ।।

15. Velankar, H.D. BUJ 11(2) 1942, 98.
16. Ibid p. 110.
17. Read v. 5 in (17) above.
18. See the Section on Pūṣan above for detailed information.
19. For identity of Gṛtsamada, see Part I, Ch. 3, Sec. (ii) above.
20. Read the verses in (17) above. Also cf: RV 8, 101, 15 where cow is identified with Aditi, who is said to be mother of the Rudras, daughter of the Vasus, sister of Ādityas and navel of immortality.

माता रुद्राणां दुहिता वसूनां स्वसादित्यानाममृतस्य नाभिः ।
प्र नु वोचं चिकितुषे जनाय मा गामनागामदितिं वधिष्ट ॥

The composer is Jamadagni.

21. Read notes (2) to (4) above.
22. See the Section on Pūṣan above.

Section (iv)

1. Read: ऋग्वेदस्यात्रिगोत्रं सोमदैवत्यं गायत्री छन्दो, यजुर्वेदस्य काश्यपगोत्रं इन्द्रदैवत्यं त्रिष्टुप् छन्दः। सामवेदस्य भारद्वाजगोत्रं रुद्रदैवत्यं जगती छन्दोऽथर्ववेदस्य बैजानगोत्रं ब्रह्मदैवत्यम् अनुष्टुप् छन्दः।
2. N.A: 1, 1 अथ आर्षम् आर्चिकस्य अग्ने... भरद्वाजो बार्हस्पत्यः।
3. For details, see Ch. 2, Section (i) in the Part I on Bharadvāja Bārhaspatya, the seer of the RV VI and Notes No. 17 and 18.

3a. See also Chapter 1, Section (iii) in the Part I above, on the Bharadvājas in the Brāhmaṇas, for information.

4. This list has been re-produced by Sakuntala A. Iyer in JUB, Vol. 31, No. 37, 1962, pp. 46-61.
5. See Part I, Ch. 4, Sec. (ii) for details about Śaṁyu.
6. See Part I, Ch. 3, Section (iii) on Nara Bhāradvāja for details.
7. See Part I, Ch. 3, section (vii) on Ajamīḍha.
8. ABORI, Vol. XXIII p. 660.
9. CAI pp. 9, 38.
10. SR p. 201.
11. op. cit.
12. See Part I, Ch. 1, Section (vi) about the interrelation of the seers.
13. See also our Part I, Ch. 1, Section (iii) on the Bharadvājas in the Brāhmaṇas for such information.
14. Ibid.
15. Read: अविन्दन् ते अतिहितं यदासीद्
यज्ञस्य धाम परमं गुहा यत्।
धातुर्द्युतानात् सवितुश्च विष्णो-
र्भरद्वाजो बृहदा चक्रे अग्नेः॥
16. Read: भरद्वाजो बृहदा चक्रे अग्नेरिति।
17. Read: देवासुरा अस्पर्धन्त। ते देवा वज्रं क्षुरपविम् असृजन्त पुरुषमेव। तम् असुरान् अभ्यवृंजन्। सोऽसुरान् अपोप्य देवान् अभ्यवर्तत तस्माद्देवा अबिभयुः। तमभिपद्य बृहद्रथन्तरयोः प्रौहन्। स एव वज्रः क्षुरप्रविबृहद्रथन्तरयोः पुरुष एव। स यं द्विष्याद् बृहद्रथन्तरयोरेनम् मुखेऽपिध्यात्।

18. Read: बृहता वै देवाः स्वर्गं लोकमजिगांसन्। तेन न व्याप्नुवन्। तस्मिन्न उष्णिकुक्कुभा उपादधुः। तेन व्याप्नुवन्। ते ब्रुवन्. . . ।

19. Read: . . .बृहत्साम् प्रतिष्ठित्यै सम्राडसि प्रतीची दिक्।

20. Read: राथन्तरी वै रात्र्यबार्हतमन्विर्वै रथन्तरमादित्ये।
बृहदन्ते ह वा एनं देवते बध्नस्य विष्टपं स्वर्गं
लोकं गमयतो य एवं विद्वादनुदिते जुहोति ॥

21. Read: ब्रह्म वै रथन्तरं क्षत्रं बृहद् ब्रह्म खलु वै प्रतिष्ठा क्षत्रात् पूर्वम्।

22. Read: अथात रोन्द्री महाभिषेकस्ते देवा अब्रुवन् प्रजापतिका, अयं वै देवानमोजिष्ठो बलिष्ठः सहिष्ठः सत्तमः पारयिष्णुतम इममेवाभिषिञ्चामहा इति तथेति तद्वैत-दिन्द्रमेव तस्मा एतामासंदीं समभरन्नृचं नाम तस्यै बृहच्च रथन्तरञ्च पूर्वौ पादाव-कुर्वन् वैरग्रं च वैराजं चापरौ शाक्वररैवते शीर्षण्ये. . . ।

23. Read: योनिर्व्वै यज्ञायज्ञीयमेतस्माद्वै योनेः प्रजापतिर्य्यज्ञमसृजत तस्माद् यज्ञायज्ञीयम्।

24. Read: असुरेषु वै सर्वो यज्ञ आसीत्ते देवा यज्ञायज्ञीयमपश्यंस्तेषां यज्ञायज्ञा वो अग्नय इत्यग्निहोत्रमवृंजत. . . ।

25. Read: अग्निर्वैश्वानरः प्रजा अभ्युदतिष्ठत्। स इदं सर्वं प्रातपत् तस्य देवाः प्रदाहाद् अबिभयुः। तेऽब्रुवन् सर्वं वायम् इदं प्रधक्ष्यति। एतस्य हरो पैरयामेति। तस्य हरोऽपैरयन्। तद् यत् प्रथमम् अपैरंस्तस्मिन् व्यवदन्त क्वेदं भविष्यंतीति। यज्ञेयज्ञे नो भविष्यतीत्यब्रुवन्। तद् यज्ञायज्ञीयमभवत्। तद् यज्ञायज्ञीयस्य यज्ञायज्ञीयत्वम्।

26. Read: एषा वै शिशुमारी यज्ञपथेऽप्यस्ता यज्ञायज्ञीयं यद्गिरागिरेत्याहात्मानं तदुद्गाता गिरति।

27. Read: प्रतिष्ठा यज्ञायज्ञीयं वज्रेणैव तत् प्रतिष्ठाया मृत्युं नुदते।

28. Read: यज्ञायज्ञीयं पुच्छम्। चन्द्रमा वै यज्ञायज्ञीयं यो हि कश्च यज्ञः संतिष्ठतएवमेव तस्याहुतीनां रसोऽप्येति तद्यदेतं यज्ञो यज्ञोऽप्येति तस्माच्चन्द्रमा यज्ञायज्ञियं चन्द्र-मसमेवस्यैतत् पुच्छं करोत्यथो पुच्छमेवास्यैतदनस्थिकममृतं करोति।
(In SB यज्ञिय is written with short इ)

29. Read: आप्त्वा तं कामं यस्मै कामायैनं युंक्त यज्ञायज्ञियं स्तोत्रमुपाकरिष्यन्त् स्वर्गो वै लोको यज्ञायज्ञियमेतस्य वै गत्वाएनं युंक्ते तदाप्त्वा न कामं यस्मै कामायैनं युंक्ते ॥

30. Read: . . .ब्रह्म यदग्रे व्यभंबदृक्साम यजुस्तस्य वा एव रसो यद्यज्ञायज्ञीयं गायते ब्रह्मण्येव रसं दधाति. . . ।

31. Read: लोम हिङ्कारस्त्वक प्रस्तावो मांसमुद्गोथोऽस्थि प्रतिहारो मज्जा निधनमेतद्-यज्ञायज्ञीयमङ्गेषु प्रोतम्।

32. Read: दिवोदासं वै भरद्वाज पुरोहितं ननाजनाः पर्ययन्त स उपासीददृषे गातुं मे विन्देति तस्मा एतेन साम्ना गातुमविन्दद् गातुविद्वा एतत् सामाऽनेन दारे नासृन्मेति तददारसृतोऽदारसृत्त्वं विन्दते गातुं न दारे धावत्यदारसृता तुष्ठुवानः।

33. Ibid

34. Read: भरद्वाजस्य लोम भवति। पशवो वै लोम पशूनामवरुध्यै। तदु दीर्घमित्याहुरायुर्वै दीर्घमायुषो वरुध्यै।

35. Read: भरद्वाजो वाऽकामयत बहुः प्रजया पशुभिः प्रजायेयेति। स एतत् सामापश्यत्। तेनास्तुत। ततो वै स बहुः प्रजया पशुभिः प्रजायत। सोऽब्रवीत् प्रश्निर्वै बहुः प्रजया

पशुभिः प्राजनिषीति तत् पृश्निनः पृश्नित्वम् । तदेतत् प्रजननं साम यद् उ भरद्वाजोऽपश्यत् तस्माद् भरद्वाजस्य पृश्नीत्याख्यायते ।

36. Read: तेऽग्निम्मुखं कृत्वा साकमश्वेनाभ्यक्रामन् यत् साकमश्वेनाभ्यक्रामंस्तस्मात् साकमाश्वन् । cf. TMB 8. 8. 5 also.

37. Read: तासु साकमश्वम् । देवा वै स्वर्गकामास्तपोऽतप्यन्त । त एतत् सामापश्यत् । तेनास्तुवत । तदेनानश्व एव भूत्वा स्वर्गं लोकमवहत । तेऽब्रुवन् स्वर्गं लोकं गत्वा साकं वाश्वेन स्वर्गं लोकमगन्मेति । तदेव साकमश्वस्य साकमश्वत्वम् ।

38. Read: अग्निष्टोमं वै देवा आश्रयन्तोक्थान्यसुरास्ते समावद्वीर्या एवाऽऽसन्न व्यावर्तन्त तान् भरद्वाज ऋषीणामपश्यदिमे वासुरा उक्थेषु श्रितास्तानेषां न कश्चन पश्यतीति सोऽग्निमुदव्यह्वयद् राह्यूषु ब्रवाणि तेऽअग्न इत्येतरागिर इत्यसुर्याह वा इतरा गिरः, सो ग्निरूपोत्तिष्ठन्नवब्रवीत् किंस्विदेव महयं कृशो दीर्घः पलितो वक्ष्यतीति भरद्वाज ह वै कृशो दीर्घः पलित आस सोऽब्रवीदिमे वा असुरा उक्थेषु श्रितास्तान्वो न कश्चन पश्यतीति तानग्निरश्वोभूत्वाऽभ्यद्रवद्यदग्निरश्वो भूत्वाऽभ्यत्यद्रवत्तत्साकमश्व सामाभवत्तत्साकमश्वस्य साकमश्वत्वं. तदाहुः साकमश्वेनोक्थानि प्रणयेदप्रणीतानि वाव तान्युक्थानि यान्यन्यत्र साकमश्वादिति प्रमंहिष्टीयेन प्रणयेदित्याहुः प्रमंहिष्ठीयेन वै देवा असुरानुकथेभ्यः प्राणुदन्त तत् प्राहैव प्रमंहिष्ठीयेन नयेत्प्र साकमश्वेन ॥

Section (v)

1. For a detailed discussion on the six Vedāṅgas see MaxMüller's HASL p. 56ff. He discusses the Kalpas, cf. pp. 88-103. Also Ramgopal analyses the internal relationship of various Kalpasūtras in his "India of Vedic Kalpasūtras" pp. 1-10.

2. NA, 1. 1.

3. For nature and scope of the Śrauta-sūtras, see Kashikar: "Survey of Śrautasūtras" BUJ, Vol. 35, (New Series) Part 2, Arts No. 41, 1966 pp. 1-3. Gonda, J. HIL, Vol. 1, Fasc. 2, pp. 489ff.

4. For discussion on the subject matter of the Gṛhyasūtras see Ramgopal: IVK, pp. 11ff; also Gonda J. HIL, Vol. 1, fasc. 2, pp. 546ff.

5. For detailed discussion on the Śulbasūtras see Kātyāyana Śulba Sūtra Text with English tr. by S.D. Khadilkar, Introduction pp. VIII-XI.

6. For detailed information on the Dharmasūtras see Kane, P.V. I, 1, 19-149.

7. For a relationship between the Gṛhya and Dharmasūtras see Ramgopal op. cit., p. 7-13; also Gonda J. HIL, Vol. I, Fasc. 2, pp. 469ff.

8. For detailed information about the Śākhās see Bhagavaddatta, *Vaidik Vāṅmaya kā Itihāsa*, Vol. I, Chapter V, pp. 900ff; also MaxMüller, op. cit. p. 65 and 92ff. Gonda J HIL, Vol. 1, Fasc. 1, pp. 323ff.

9. Some of the Śākhās claim a good number of works on each of the six Vedāṅgas, for example, the Taitt. school claims as many as sixteen Śikhās in addition to the Taitt. Prātiśākhya.

10. For example, the Taitt. recension has six Śrautasūtras and other allied

texts (some of them) forming complete Kalpasūtras. Besides these, Agniveśya, Mānava, Kāṭhaka and Vārāha Gṛhyasūtras are also found.

11. See notes (9) and (10) above.

12. Six Śrautasūtras are extant. Moreover, there is reason to believe that the Śrauta texts of Āśmarathya and Ālekhana, whose opinions are frequently quoted by Bhāradvāja and Āpastaṁba, were then current. We cannot say, however, whether the Gṛhya sūtras of Mānava, Vārāha, Agniveśya and Kāṭhaka presuppose the Śrauta texts.

13. The order of the names of the Sūtras and Sūtrakāras is given by Mahādeva, the commentator of SatyaHirŚS.

14. The Kalpas (consisting of a fourfold division) along with Pravarādhyāya and Pariśiṣṭas (found intact) are those of Āpastaṁba and Baudhāyana, while others are incomplete.

15. Pitṛmedhasūtra and Pariśiṣṭas are also attached to the Kalpas for its completion or removal of deficiency.

16. We have collected a few prose sūtras of Bharadvāja relating to Dharmasūtra and a good number of smṛti verses, which pre-suppose a Dharmasūtra.

17. Only the following Śulbasūtras are available:
(i) Baudhāyana (ii) Āpastaṁba (iii) Satyāṣāḍha (iv) Mānava (v) Maitrāyaṇiya (vi) Vārāha (vii) Vādhūla and (viii) Kātyāyana. The Śulba Sūtras I-VII belong to the Kṛṣṇa YV, and VIII belongs to the Śukla YV.

17a. The Bhāradvāja Śrautasūtra was first edited and published by Raghuvira in the Journal of Vedic Studies, Lahore, Vols. I and II, 1934-35. It covers text only up to 9th Sūtra of the 6th Kaṇḍikā of Praśna 12.

17b. The Śrauta, Pitṛmedha and Pariśeṣa Sūtras of Bharadvāja (Texts, Translation, Introduction) in two vols. were edited by C.G. Kashikar and published by VSM, Pune, in 1964.

18. Read: तत्र तैत्तिरीयक नाम द्विभेदा भवन्त्यौखेयः खाण्डिकेयश्चेति। तत्र खाण्डिकेय नाम पञ्चभेदा भवन्ति कालेता शात्यायनी। हैरण्यकेशी भारद्वाज्यापस्तम्बी चेति।

19. Read: खाण्डिकेयानां पञ्च भेदा भवन्ति—आपस्तम्बी, बौधायणी, सत्याषाढी, हिरण्यकेशी भारद्वाजी; कालेता शात्यायणीति द्वे मूलोक्ते तयोः स्थाने बौधायणी औधेया इति बोध्ये।

19a. Mahidāsa comments on the passage quoted in (19) above.

20. Read: खाण्डिकेयानां पञ्च भेदा भवन्ति—आपस्तम्बी, बौधायणी, सत्याषाढी, हिरण्यकेशी, औधेयी चेति।

21. See V.V. Bhide, *The Cāturmāsya Sacrifices*, University of Poona, Pune, 1979, Introduction, pp. 1-3.

22. See Part II, Chapter 5, Section (i) on the Bhārśikṣā.

23. See note (13) above.

24. The chronological importance of ranking the six Śrauta Sūtras is discussed below. Garbe, Winternitz, Bühler, Kashikar, and Ramgopal have accepted the order signifying their chronology, while Gonda has reservations.

25. Kashikar, SBh, pp. 271-279; his Introduction, pp. iv. ff.

26. Ibid. pp. Lv.

27. Kashikar, SBh 1, Introduction, pp. Lxxvi—Lxxviii.

28. Ibid. pp. Lxxix—Lxxxiv.

29. Ibid.
30. Ibid. pp. Lxxxiv-Lxxxv.
31. Published with the Śrauta and Pariśeṣa Sūtras of Bharadvāja from VSM, Poona, in 1964. Ed. C.G. Kashikar.
32. Kashikar op.cit., p. xLviii, also pp. 228, 230, 240 etc., footnotes under text.
33. Kashikar, op.cit., p. xLx.
34. Pitṛmedhasūtrāṇi, Preface, p. xiv.
35. Ānandāśrama edn. Vol. I, Poona, 1907, p. 8.
36. Ibid.
37. Kashikar, op.cit.
38. Kashikar, op.cit., p. Lxxxv.
39. Edited by Kashikar and published by VSM, Poona, 1964 (with the texts of Śauta and Pitṛmedha Sūtras and their translation).
40. Kashikar, ibid., p. Lxxxix.
41. Ibid., p. xci.
42. For details see Kashikar, SBh I, Intr. pp. Lxviii-Lxx.
43. Ibid., p. Lxix.
44. The three of the four Vedas viz. RV, SV and YV are generally attached to the three *ṛtviks*, viz. Hotṛ, Udgātṛ and Adhvaryu respectively. But some assign the AV to Brahmā, and others hold that Brahmā should have knowledge of all the three (early) Vedas (RV, SV, YV). So Ādhvaryava signifies office of Adhvaryu and his associate priests. Their school relates to the YV only.
45. Kashikar, op. cit., p. Lxx.
46. Ibid., p. Lxxii.
47. Under the Sūtra No. 1485 Bālamanoramā has given examples as *Kalpe paiṅgikalpāḥ*. Patañjali and Vāmana Jaydityamgive no such instance in their respective works.
48. GPM p. 106.
49. GPM p. 90.
50. BaudhŚS p. 3: (GPM p. 29).
51. op. cit., p. Lxxv.
52. "Epic Studies" ABORI Vol. XVIII, Part, 1, 1936, pp. 1-76,
53. op. cit., p. Lxxvi.
54. Introductory verses 7-9 in Mahādeva's commentary on the SatyHirŚS, Ānandāśrama Sanskrit Series, Poona, Vol. 1, pp. 1-2.
55. ĀpŚS Vol. 3, preace, p. xvii.
56. "Das altindischef Hochzeitsrituell-nach dem Āpastambīya Grihyasūtra and einigen anderen ve rwandeten Werken," Denkschriften der Kais. Akademie der Wissenschaften in Wien, Vol. XL, Vienna, 1892, pp. 5ff.
57. SBE Vol. 2, pp.xviii ff.
58. *Uber das Rituelle Sūtra des Baudhāyana*, pp. 2-11.
59. SBh I, Introduction, pp. Lxxvii and XCV.
60. IVK, p. 73. ff.
61. Recently J. Gonda has expressed doubts about the chronological significance of the order of the names in Mahādeva's list. See Gonda J. HIL, Vol. 1, Fasc. 2, pp. 476, 482.
62. See Kashikar, op. cit., pp. xci-xcv, for detailed study; and Ramgopal, op. cit. pp. 73-77.
63. Caland, op. cit; Kashikar, op. cit., p. xcv.

64. IVK. p. 76.
65. Ibid. pp. 73-77.
66. Keith, Introduction to the TS, p. xLv.
67. Ramgopal op. cit., 73-77.
    Kashikar BhS. Intr., p. xcv.
    बिद । उर्व । कश्यप । कुशिक । भरद्वाज । उपमन्यु । किलालप । किदर्भ । विश्वानर । ऋष्टिषेण । ऋतभाग । हर्यश्व । प्रियक । आपस्तम्ब । कूचवार । इत्यादयः, काशिकावृत्तिः, तृतीयभागः । पृ. 445-446
68. Kapiladeva Sastri, *Saṁskrita Vyākaraṇa men gaṇapāṭha kī paramparā aur ācārya Pāṇini*, p. 153ff.
69. *Pāṇini: His Place in Sanskrit Literature*, London, 1861.
70. SSG, p. 15.
71. HIL, Vol. 3, part 2, pp. 423-424.
72. *India as known to Pāṇini*, p. 475.
73. IVK, p. 88.
74. SBh, Intr. p. xcv.
75. op. cit., p. 88
75a. op. cit., p. xcv.
76. op. cit., pp. xcv-xcvi.
77. SBE Vol. II, pp. xxxiii ff.
78. Ibid. Vol. XIV pp. xLiii ff.
79. op. cit., pp. 94-100.
80. *The Bharadvāja Gṛhyasūtra*, ed. Solomons, p. 21.
81. As quoted by Kashikar, op. cit., p. xcv.
82. See Part I, Chapter I, Section (v) and Chapter 2, Sections (vi)-(ix).

Section (vi)

1. It was edited by Henriette Johanna Wilhelmina Salomons of Rotterdam, and published with Introduction, list of *Mantras*, Index of Words from Leiden in 1913.
2. See the Introduction to the Śrauta Sūtra of Bharadvāja in the preceding section.
3. Ibid.
4. For details of the contents of the Gṛhyasūtras See SBE Vol. XXX, pp. 299-307.
5. BhārGS Introduction, p. xiv.
6. Treated separately, with the Śrautasūtra.
7. See the section on Śrautasūtra.
8. SBh, Introduction, p. xcv.
9. IVK pp. 74, 77.
10. op. cit., pp. Li ff.
11. IVK pp. 74ff; BhS pp. Lxxvi-Lxxxv.
12. Read: बोधायनाय भरद्वाजाय सूत्रकारायापस्तम्बाय . . . कल्पायामीति ।
13. 3, 11-12.
14. 2, 8, 19-20.
15. op. cit.

CHAPTER SEVEN

POST-VEDIC SURVEY

Section (i)

The Bhāradvāja Rājaśāstra

"The history of ancient Indian political thought is the story of great minds that evolved political institutions and guided Hindu society for nearly three milleniums."[1] That in the process of the evolution of the ancient Indian political thought, a large number of thinkers played a vital role, each one contributing his own bit, is evident from the very first passage of the KA: *pṛthivyāḥ lābhe pālane ca yāvanty arthaśāstrāṇi pūrvācāryaiḥ prasthāpitāni prāyaśas tāni samāhṛtyaikam idam arthaśāstraṁ kṛtam.* "This single (treatise on the) science of politics has been prepared mostly by bringing together (the teachings of) as many treatises on the science of Politics as have been composed by ancient teachers for the acquisition and protection of the earth."[2] And Kauṭilya has mentioned as many as nineteen ancient teachers (*pūrvācāryāḥ*) including himself in the body of his Arth. and they are: Manu, Bṛhaspati, Uśanas, Bhāradvāja, Viśālākṣa, Parāśara, Piśuna, Kaunapadanta, Vatavyādhi, Bahudantiputra, Kātyāyana, Kaṇiṅka Bhāradvāja, Cārāyaṇa, Gotamukha, Kiñjalka, the descendant of Piśuna (Paiśuna), Aṁbhiyas, the unnamed teacher of Kauṭilya and lastly Kauṭilya himself.[3] This long list of the ancient teachers of the science of Politics suffers from two major deficiencies: (i) it does not have unity of thought among the teachers, as reflected in their quotations, cited in the Arth.; they have sharply different opinions on even a single point, and (ii) chronology of these teachers is so fluid that none of them can be assigned a definite date. Although we have presented the whole list of the ancient teachers from the age of Manu to that of Kauṭilya, we are interested only in Bhāradvāja who is no exception to these statements.

That some of these teachers belong to the Mahābhārata or pre-Mahābhārata age can be gleaned from a passage in the MBh (*i.e.* 12, 58, 2-3)[4] which says that Bṛhaspati, Viśālākṣa, Kāvya (*i.e.* Uśanas), Prācetas, Manu, Bhāradvāja (known here as *bhagavān*) and Gauraśiras were *rājaśāstra praṇetāraḥ* ("the authors of the science of politics") and *brahmavādinaḥ* ("knowers of the *brahman*"). That Bhāradvāja was a teacher of politics is further supported by facts in MBh (12, 138, 7-9).[5] "A king should always have his *daṇḍa* 'rod of punishment' ready. He should always show his prowess and have no weak point visible to others; rather he should seek the weak points of others and pursue his foes taking the thread of those weak points. People are kept dreaded of the king, who holds his *daṇḍa* always ready. Therefore, *daṇḍa* is the principal among the four *upāyas* ('means')." Elsewhere (MBh 5, 34, 3 repeated in the MBh 12, 67, 11)[6] it is said that "he who bows to a stronger (foe) really bows to Indra." The text of the MBh does not mention whose opinion this is. The KA cites the same as a quotation from Bhāradvāja. The MBh (12, 138) summed up the teachings of one Kaṇiṅka Bhāradvāja imparted to the king Śatruntāpa of the Sauvira kingdom.[7]

The Pañcatantra (3, 30) by Viṣṇuśarman (A.D. 4th Cen. ?)[8] quotes Bhāradvāja: "an insignificant (person) possessed of might and valour may kill (or fight) a big one, as a lion of small size would fight with a large-size elephant."[9] The Kāmandaka (9, 56) also echoes a view similar to that of Bhāradvāja: "Having observed the valour and might of one as of a lion shown to an elephant, a man should accept only the mightier (of the two)."[10]

We have already said that Kauṭilya in his AŚ has quoted a number of his predecessors including Bṛhaspati and Bhāradvāja. Elsewhere, we have fully discussed their relationship.[11] Besides these two authorities, Kauṭilya has cited the views of Uśanas, Manu and Viśālākṣa. He has on seven occasions quoted Bhāradvāja's opinion followed by that of Viśālākṣa. These are:

(1) In the first instance, Bhāradvāja's opinion is referred to when framing suitability criteria for the post of *amātyas* ('ministers'), in the AŚ. Bhāradvāja is reported to have laid down: "He (the king) should make his fellow-students his ministers, their integrity and capability being known (to him, the king)". For, they (the fellow-students) enjoy his confidence (KA 1, 8, 1-2).[12] Kauṭilya then quotes Viśālākṣa, who criticises this opinion and points out that these fellow-students, who might have been a

king's playmates earlier, might not pay due respect to him (KA 1, 8, 3-4).[13]

(2) Kauṭilya, while discussing the importance of the maintenance of secrecy of *mantra* ("king's consultations on statecraft",) has also taken into consideration various contemporary views on how it be ensured and expert opinion ascertained. Here also, the discussion starts with Bhāradvāja: "The divulgence of secret counsel is fatal to the security and well-being of the king and the officers appointed by him. Therefore, he should deliberate alone over confidential matter. For, even councillors have (other) councillors and these also have yet others. Thus, the series of councillors lead to the divulgence of secret counsel" (KA 1, 15, 13-16).[14] "Therefore, others should not know about the work sought to be done by him. Only those who undertake it should know (about it) when it is begun or even when it is actually completed" (KA 1, 15, 17).[15]

This advice is questioned by Viśālākṣa who opines that "effective deliberation is possible only when one consults someone else." (KA 1, 15, 18ff).[16]

(3) On proper security of the king, he gives Bhāradvāja's counsel: "He should guard against the princes right from their birth. For, the princes devour their begetters, being of the same nature as of crabs. Before love (for them) is produced in the father, silent punishment for them is best" (KA 1, 17, 4-6).[17]

Bhāradvāja again evokes strong censure from Viśālākṣa : he terms this policy as wicked, since it means murdering innocent children or princes; this may destroy the Kṣatriyas race ultimately (KA 1, 17, 7-8).[18]

(4) Kauṭilya discusses the duties of the chief minister, in the event of the death of the ruling monarch. The chief minister is broadly advised to adopt a number of measures to ensure the continuous suzerainty of the ruling family. After enumerating these measures, Kauṭilya quotes Bhāradvāja with whom the author of the AŚ disagrees. Bhāradvāja advises: "No. When the king is dying, the ministers should make members of the family, the princes and the principal officers fight against one another or against (other) principal officers. When anyone fights, he should get him slain by a rising of the subjects, or getting rid of the members of the family, the princes and principal officers by a silent punishment; he should seize the kingdom himself, since,

for the sake of the kingdom, the father fights with the sons, and the sons with the father; what to do then of the constituent, namely the minister, the one support of the kingdom. He should not disdain that when it has come to him of its own accord. A woman approaching one, of her own accord curses if discarded—such is a saying among the people" (KA 5, 6, 24-30).[19]

'Time comes but once to a man waiting for an opportunity; that time it is difficult for that man to get again when he wants to do his work' (KA 5, 6, 31).[20]

Here Kauṭilya discards Bhāradvāja's view on the ground that it is immoral to usurp the kingdom of a king under whom the minister served. Besides, it is dangerous to play such a game which may, as well, cause a popular rising (KA, 5, 6, 32ff).[21]

(5) Kauṭilya while discussing the crises for the seven *prakṛtis* (primary or basic constituent elements of the state) viz., *svāmin* (the king) (lit. 'master'), *amātya* (minister), *janapada* (kingdom), *durga* (castle), *kośa* (treasury), *daṇḍa* (punishment), and *mitra* (friend), says that the calamity befalling each is, in the opinion of the *ācāryas* (ancient authorities) of the *śāstras* (political science)[22], more serious than the successive one. This statement is contested by Bhāradvāja, who states: 'No. Of the calamities befalling the king and the minister, that of the minister is more serious. Deliberation in counsel, securing the fruits of deliberation, carrying out an undertaking, managing income and expenditure, infliction of punishment, warding off the enemies and forest tribes, protection of the kingdom, taking steps against calamities, guarding of princes, are (all) dependent on the minister. In the absence of these, those (activities) are *lacking*, and there would be a loss of all activity on the part of the king, as of a (bird) with clipped wings, if the minister were in calamity. And in the calamities (of these), secret instigation and other actions by the enemy, are close at hand. And if these are hostile, there is danger to (the king's) life, since they move near the person of the king" (KA 8, 1, 6-11).[23]

However, Kauṭilya does not accept this view and points out how the king's calamities are more serious and how his position is supreme among all the constituents (KA 8, 1, 12ff).[24]

(6) Kauṭilya further discusses the bad consequences from *kopa* (anger) and *kāma* (passion) and says that the former are more harmful than the latter. But in this respect, also, Bhārad-

vāja differs and considers these (*kopa* and *kāma*) as necessary for a king.[25] He says: "No. Anger is behaviour proper for a good man, (a means of) acquiring enmity, extirpation of insults and keeping a man in dread. And resort to anger is ever needed for putting down evil. Lust is (a means of) attainment of success, conciliation, generosity of nature and of being loveable. And resort to lust is ever needed for enjoyment of the fruits of works done" (KA 8, 3, 8-12).[26]

Kauṭilya does not agree with the above, and re-establishes his viewpoint.[27]

(7) While extending a piece of advice to a weak king, Bhāradvāja says: "A weak king attacked by a stronger king should everywhere remain submissive showing the characteristics of a reed. For, he submits to Indra who submits to a stronger king" (KA 12, 1, 1-2).[28]

Again (as ever) Viśālākṣa disputes Bhāradvāja's view. He advises that the weak king should fight to the last, as a Kṣatriya; his duty is to fight his foes irrespective of victory or defeat (KA 12, 1, 3-5).[29]

While judging the views of Bhāradvāja stated above R.P. Kangle says: "In most cases he appears to advocate extremely one-sided views, ignoring all moral considerations, sometimes even practical considerations. He feels no scruples whatsoever in recommending the murder of princes at birth or advising to seize the kingdom if an opportunity were to come his way."[30]

Question has been asked as to who was this Bhāradvāja whose views are quoted by Kauṭilya in his AŚ. One must first admit that 'Bhāradvāja' is not a personal name here, it is a *gotra* name. The personal name of the teacher of the political science, who is here called Bhāradvāja is not known. Thus the opinions of some persons are quoted as of one who belonged to the Bhāradvāja *gotra*. A passage in the MBh (12, 58, 2-3) says that Bṛhaspati, Viśālākṣa, Kāvya (Uśanas), Prācetasa, Manu, Bhāradvāja (who is qualified here by the epithet *bhagavān*) and Gauraśiras were *rājaśāstrapraṇetāraḥ* (authors of political science) and were *brahmavādinaḥ* (knowers of *brahman*).[31] However, it is not clear as to who this Bhāradvāja was. Elsewhere in the epic, (MBh 12, 138, 3-4) mention is made of a Bhāradvāja, whose personal name is given as Kaṇiṅka the minister of one Śatruntāpa of the Sauviras.[32] Kauṭilya also refers to one Kaṇiṅka Bhāradvāja in his AŚ.[33]

This Kaṇiṅka was appointed as a minister by a king; but, seeing an evil omen indicated by the flying of a *krauñca* to his left, he fled away from the kingdom.

J. Jolly and R. Schmidt in their edition of the AŚ in the Punjab Sanskrit Series have suggested Bhāradvāja's identification with Kaṇiṅka Bhāradvāja.[34] The views of Kaṇiṅka Bhāradvāja appear at the Śāntiparvan of the MBh (12, 138). Kangle examines the MBh passages and finds that "there is hardly anything common between the teaching of Kaṇiṅka Bhāradvāja in the MBh and the views attributed to Bhāradvāja in the Arthaśāstra. On one or two points, in fact, the former is not in consonance with the latter."[35] Kangle appears to have rejected the suggestion of Jolly and Schmidt identifying Kaṇiṅka Bhāradvāja of MBh with Bhāradvāja of AŚ.[36]

In the face of the disagreement of the opinions of Kaṇiṅka with those of Bhāradvāja in the AŚ, we think that the latter cannot be identified with the former. The Epic itself quoted two different Bhāradvājas. So also does the AŚ. On which ground can we then identify one with the other? Therefore, we treat them as two persons, one's personal name is given as Kaṇiṅka, while the personal name of the other is lost to us. The latter probably established a school of politics and his students probably introduced themselves as Bhāradvājas.

Section (ii)

The Bhāradvāja Śikṣā

A treatise, Bhāradvāja Śikṣā[1] is handed down to us. A work called the *Veda-lakṣaṇānukramaṇikā*[2] mentions nine primary and three secondary Śikṣās. The nine primaries are: "Bhāradvāja, Vyāsa, Śaṁbhu, Pāṇini, Kauhalīya, Bodhāyana, Vālmīki and Hārita Śikṣās; the three secondaries are: the Sarvasaṁmata, the Āraṇya and the Siddhānta Śikṣās. These nine are mentioned in the commentary on Siddhānta Śikṣā.[3]

The Bhār Śikṣā belongs to the Taitt. Śākhā of the Kṛṣṇa Yajurveda, which has a large number of Śikṣās. The Bhār Śikṣā has been examined by Varma among at least sixteen Śikṣās of the Taitt. school.[4]

The Śikṣās form one of the six Vedāṅgas[5] (ancillaries attached to the Vedic Studies). The other five Vedāṅgas are, *Kalpa* (*sūtra*) (manuals of liturgy and secular topics such as ethics etc.), *Nirukta* (etymology), *Vyākaraṇa* (Grammar), *Chandas* (metre), and *Jyotiṣa* (Astrology). One can realise the importance of the Vedāṅgas from the fact that even in Vedic literature, there is evidence of their existence in the hoary past and that these were studied along with the Vedic texts. The aim and purpose of these ancillaries was evidently to preserve the Vedic texts in utmost accuracy, and teach, spread and propagate the Vedas among the Aryan and the non-Aryan people.[6] Thus the Vedāṅgas partly grew and took shape according to the need of the people of the later Vedic Age. If the Kalpasūtras and Jyotiṣa mainly aimed at the propagation of the Vedic Culture in general and religion in particular, the other four Vedāṅgas *viz*., Śikṣā, Nirukta, Vyākaraṇa and Chandas—aimed at the learning and teaching of the Vedic texts and their preservation. As regards the probable date of the Vedāṅgas M. Ghosh[7] says "that treatises on different Vedāṅgas might have been in existence between 1000-600 B.C."

According to Pāṇini (7, 4, 54),[8] the word *śikṣā* is a desiderative noun derived from the root *śak* (intransitive and transitive) meaning (respectively) 'to be able' and 'to enable'. Hence the literal meaning of the term *Śikṣā* would be (i) 'a desire to be able' and (ii) 'a desire to enable'. It is probably the second meaning that points to what the term Śikṣā should denote. Phonetics enables the reciters of the Veda to acquire correct pronunciation of the Vedic texts. Nevertheless, it appears that this second derivation perhaps did not strike some earlier scholars who found an anomaly in the derivation from the root and its meaning. Therefore, Weber and Max Müller assumed that the word *śikṣā* is derived from the root *śikṣ* which originally meant 'a desire to know' (*zu konnen suchen*).[9] But even then the difficulty remains as to how one could equate 'knowing' to 'pronunciation'. M. Ghosh,[10] however, seems to have guessed a proper derivation, since he suggests that as the learners of the Vedic lore 'had to have indeed a very strong desire to be able to recite the Vedic hymns', the original meaning of 'to desire to be able' came to be narrowed to, 'to desire to be able to recite the Vedas correctly'.

While discussing the term *śikṣa* and the scope of a Śikṣā work, Varma[11] says: "Originally, the term (śikṣā)[12] seems to have been restricted to a rudimentary instruction in pronunciation, as the literal meaning of the word implies". This scope is first hinted at in the Taitt. U. 1, 2[13]. "In the next stage, the scope of '*Śikṣā*' further developed into "general phonetics."[14] The term '*Śikṣā*' has been used in this sense in the VP (1, 29) *atha śikṣā vihitāḥ* 'now *śikṣās* (i.e. general phonetics) are enunciated'.[15] "In the second stage, then, Śikṣā emerged from a schoolmaster's vocation to these general principles of phonetics which were further applied by the Prātiśākhyas, to the various Vedic texts with which they were concerned," adds Varma.[16]

In the third stage, after the advent of the Prātiśākhyas, the Śikṣās dwelt on minute details regarding the general conditions of correct pronunciation, of relation of vowels and consonants, of the nature of accentuation, of prosodical length or quantity, of *Svarabhakti* as an independent syllable after the *svarita* accent, of nature and quantity of *anusvāra* and *raṅga*, and of observations on Abhinidhāna, consonant groups and doubling, etc.[17]

In its fourth and the final stage, the scope of the Śikṣā "was its identification with the treatises on 'applied phonetics'—*viz.*, the Prātiśākhyas"[18]; like the authors of the Śikṣās, the authors of the Prātiśākhyas were also authorities on phonetics, and significantly contributed to observations on syllabication, accentuation, etc. "There was, therefore, a close interaction between Śikṣā and Prātiśākhya, leading to the advancement of both. But when the term śikṣā was applied to the Prātiśākhya, it was done so in a secondary sense."[19]

In the light of the nature and scope of śikṣās—and also relatively, those of the Prātiśākhyas, we may now consider in brief the text of the Bhār Śikṣā.

We have already said that the Bhār Śikṣā is one of the numerous Śikṣās belonging to the Taitt. School; some of these are considered to have made very important contribution to general and applied phonetics. But many a Śikṣā is mere catalogue of certain sounds in the Vedas, and contains very little matter of any general interest for linguistics. "Even more famous Śikṣā like those of Bhāradvāja and of Siddhānta are on the whole mere catalogues of words containing different sounds in alphabetical order and were presumably prepared to insure accuracy in Vedic pronunciation or to facilitate research work."[19a] These Śikṣās resemble the Prātiśākhyas and show how the edifice of the Prātiśākhyas was built up.

It may be pointed out that the Bhār Śikṣā heads at least two lists of the nine Śikṣās incorporated in different works on Śikṣā or their commentaries, which we have already mentioned.[20] All the nine Śikṣās listed there belong to the Taitt. School. The Bhār Śikṣā is further mentioned in the preface to the Taitt. Prātiśākhya.[21]

This Bhār Śikṣā is named as the Sāṁhitika-Śikṣā in the *Vedataijasa* commentary on the Vyāsa Śikṣā.[22] The importance of the Bhār Śikṣā lies "in the fact that it is the only authoritative ancient work which enables us to fix the proper reading of the texts of the Taittirīya,"[23] which comprise not only the Saṁhitā of that śākhā but also the Brāhmaṇa including the Kāṭhaka Brāhmaṇa, Āraṇyaka and the Ekāgnikāṇḍa of the Āpastaṁba School. Thus the Bhār Śikṣā is a monograph on a certain number of words of the Taitt. texts. These words were either liable to be mispronounced or confused with those of slightly different construction. However, bulk of the vocabulary of those texts has been kept out of its treatment. While treating those words, the Śikṣā has arranged them in an alphabetical order and has consistently pursued its avowed task of guiding as to their correct reading. Thus the treatment of the Bhār Śikṣā having been one of empirical nature, 'it contains very few observations of general interest to linguistics'.[24]

One of the notable observations made in the Bhār Śikṣā at v.25[25] relates to *ḷ*. It is said here that *ḷ* was never a vowel at the beginning and at the end of a word, but it was vocalic only in the medial position in a word, as is noticeable in the word *kḷpta*.

However, most parts of the work dwell on the words with their correct reading and enable a student to recite the Taitt. texts accurately.

In a verse (2[26]), for example, the Śikṣā points out where *vṛjana* with an *udātta a* in *ja* is to be read (TS 1, 4, 9 *vṛjanam dohase*; TB 2, 8, 4 *vṛjanam jīradānum* etc.), and where a similar form like *vṛjinā* is to be read (TS 5, 5, 4 *vṛjinā ca martān*; TB 3, 3, 7 *vṛjinam anṛtam duscaritam*). So also, in the same verse it is taught where *suṣṭutā* is to be read (TS 1, 4, 46) and where *suṣṭuti* is to be read (TS 1, 3, 14). Through these two words *vṛjana* and *suṣṭuta* the pronunciation of sound *a* is taught. This approach pervades the whole text.

It can now be pointed out how the Bhār Śikṣā differs from another one (*e.g.* of Pāṇini). In the first two verses of PS, Pāṇini enumerates the sixtythree or sixtyfour sounds (*varṇas*); vowels and consonants being separately given. The verses 3-6 give a theory of the speech-sounds. It is followed by the fivefold division of the sounds mentioned above according to their pitch, quantity, place of articulation, the primary effort (*prayatna*) and the secondary effort (*anupradāna*) (7-18).[27] This being the content of the PS, we can justifiably say that it is the subject matter of general phonetics. And the same theory applies more or less to the Vedic language as a whole. But the contents of the Bhār Śikṣā, as has been indicated above, are only a certain number of variant readings drawn from the Taitt. texts, set in accurate spelling or combination of sounds, meant for correct recitation. It is more or less the domain of a Prātiśākhya, the scope of which, as we have indicated earlier is that of applied phonetics. Thus the term śikṣā here, in the Bhār Śikṣā, is applied in a secondary sense,[28] while the same is used in the case of the PS in its primary sense.

The Bhār Śikṣā contains 130 verses of *śloka* metre. These *ślokas* are, however, arranged topic-wise. Sometimes, the device of *anuvṛtti* is also introduced, here and there, to avoid the repetition of the same rule, or word(s).

At the beginning of the work, (*i.e.* in verse 1)[29], the author has clearly stated that the Śikṣā is the basis of the Vedas and its aim is to remove doubts about text interpretation. And at the end of the work (in verse 130)[30], it is stated that (whosoever acquires the knowledge of this (work), viz., the Bhār Śikṣā attains the domain of Brahmā just as a *Gṛhamedhin* acquires a *gṛha* ('a wife' lit. house). From the last verse, also it becomes clear that this was named as the Bhāradvāja Śikṣā.

It is noticed that most of the works on Śikṣā are ascribed to some notable and famous seers of ancient time; thus we find the Śikṣā ascribed to Bharadvāja, Vasiṣṭha, Parāśara, Vyāsa, Nārada, Yājñavalkya, etc. There is no doubt that the surviving works cannot claim an age higher than the middle centuries; at the most, they may belong to tenth or twelfth century A.D. But they might have been written or composed by those who followed some oral tradition of their different *śākhās* that existed before them. Thus the kernal of every such work can be taken to represent the thought from some old traditional work.

As regards the date of the Bhār Śikṣā, it is said to be "comparatively old" perhaps contemporary of the Vyāsa Śikṣā, [31] for, it has been named at the head of nine Śikṣās mentioned in the commentary of the Siddhānta Śikṣā and also in the Vedalakṣaṇānukramaṇikā. And the commentator of the Pāri Śikṣā too has given at the beginning of the work a list containing the names of the authors of the Śikṣās, while describing the purpose of that Śikṣā[32] (*i.e.* Pāri Śikṣā) as follows: "The author follows the works on phonetics, etc., composed by the sages Bhāradvāja, Vyāsa, Pāri. Śaṁbhu, Kauhala, Hārita, Bodhāyana, Vāsiṣṭha, Vālmīki, etc.. incomprehensible to the people of modern times". If the author and the commentator may be considered as one and the same person, as is indicated by the above statement, it appears that Bhāradvāja Śikṣā may be anterior to many in the list, including one of Pāri. Now this Pāri preceded the Siddhānta Śikṣā also, 'for it is quoted both by the Tribhāṣyaratna and the Vaidikābharaṇa, which are mentioned in the Siddhānta Śikṣā.[33] Now the probable date of the Siddhānta Śikṣā is the fifteenth century A.D. The date of the author of the Vaidikābharaṇa, Gārgya Gopala Yajvan, is said to be "circa fourteenth to fifteenth century A.D."[34] As the Pāri Śikṣā is still anterior to the Vaidikābharaṇa we may consider that 14th century A.D. is the probable lower limit of the extant work of Bhār Śikṣā. It is already noted that the Bhār Śikṣā is considered as contemporaneous with the Vyāsa Śikṣā and it is mentioned in the *Vedataijasa,* the commentary on the Vyāsa Śikṣā.[35]

H. Lüders, while discussing the date of the Vyāsa Śikṣā is of the opinion that the compilation of the Vyāsa Śikṣā cannot be later than the middle of the 13th century A.D.[36] This he said having considered the materials before him in that Śikṣā. The Bhār Śikṣā may be comparatively older than the Vyāsa Śikṣā[37] and so the lower limit of the Bhār Śikṣā cannot be later than the middle of the 13th century A.D.

As regards the higher limit of the Bhār Śikṣā, it may be somewhere after the Taitt. School of the YVK was fixed, because, the present Bhār Śikṣā closely follows the current redaction of the Taitt.[38] Veda and its classification into *Kāṇḍas, Praśnas* and *Anuvākas.* It can thus be tentatively said that Śikṣā was composed sometime after this Veda assumed the present form, which leaves the question open yet. However, we think that at such a high age nearer to the Saṁhitākaraṇa, there might have existed or arisen an oral tradition of the Bhār Śikṣā only. The present work does not betray any archaic sign that could assign it a high age. The language and the metre also go against such a presumption. Already, we have stated that the date of the Bhār Śikṣā is comparatively earlier than that of the Vyāsa Śikṣā. If the Vyāsa Śikṣā is assigned (a date as is suggested by Lüders), (*viz.*, the 13th century A.D.), the date of the Bhār Śikṣā may be one century *prior* to it (*i.e.* the 12th century A.D.).

Section (iii)

(*A*) *Bharadvāja: a grammarian*

The contribution of the Bharadvājas was not limited to the Vedic lore alone; they contributed to the diverse fields of traditional Śāstras, including the Vedāṅgas also. We have already noticed their contribution to Vedic phonetics, in the form of the Bhāradvāja Śikṣā.[1] Here we will see what they contributed to another Vedāṅga, *viz.* Grammar.

Pāṇini[2] and other Grammarians[3] have referred to Bharadvāja as a Grammarian; he has mentioned the opinion of the School of Bharadvāja. Once at 7, 2, 63, *ṛto Bhāradvājasya*, "In the opinion of Bhāradvāja, (it is only) after a root which ends in short *ṛ* after which the Periphrastic furture *tās* is always devoid of the augment *iṭ*, that *thal* also, like *tās*, does not take the augment *iṭ*".[4]

The patronymic form 'Bhāradvāja (which is evolved out of a secondary suffix) is taken to mean *bharadvājasyāpatyaṁ pumān* ('a male descendant of Bharadvāja') by the specific Pāṇini rule *tasyāpatyam*—the suffix *aṇ* mentioned in Pā 4, 1, 83 and those which follow it denote: 'the descendant of someone' (Pā 4, 1, 92).[5] Otherwise, the same patronymic term Bhāradvāja may also be obtained by applying the general rule *tasyedam* (Pā 4, 3, 120).[6] This rule means that: After a word in the sixth case in construction, an affix (Pā 4, 1, 13 &c.) comes in the sense of 'this is his'. This rule (viz. Pā 4, 3, 120) would have also included the particular case of *tasyāpatyaṁ* (Pā 4, 1, 92), asmuch as the word *idam* may be applicable to things like *apatya*, *samūha*, *vikāra*, etc., with a few exceptions. Thus "it may be reasonably maintained that Bhāradvāja was one who used to regularly read and understand the subject of Grammar taught by Bhāradvāja."[7] It was probably a school of Grammar, established by Bharadvāja, which was similar to that of Indra. The Grammatical school of Bharadvāja, however, is not included in the list of the nine schools enumerated in a verse current among grammarians.[8] The name of Bharadvāja does not occur in the other well-known couplet where mention is made of eight other *śābdikas.*[9] But this school was so famous in the age of Pāṇini that even Patañjali did not fail to notice its speciality, at least twice. Thus Patañjali in his MBh under *uṣavidajagṛbhyo'nyatarasyām* ("The suffix *ās* is optionally employed after these, viz., *uṣ* 'to burn', *vid* 'to know', and *jāgṛ* 'to wake', when *liṭ* follows")[10] (Pā 3, 1, 38), draws his students' attention to how the Bhāradvājīyas differ from Pāṇini as *bhāradvājiyāḥ paṭhanti viderāṁ kim/ nipātād vā aguṇatvam iti// uṣarvida//* "The Bhāradvājīyas read 'why *ām* is suffixed to *vid*?' After a *nipāta* 'particle' there can be absence of *guṇa* optionally". So also under Pāṇini's rule (3, 1, 89)[11] *na duhasnunamām yakcinau* "The affixes *yak* (taught by Pā 3, 1, 67) and *cin* (taught by Pā 3, 1, 62) are not employed in the reflexive voice of the verbs *duh* 'to milk' *snu* 'to fall in drops' and *nam* 'to bow'." Paṭañjali says: *bhāradvājīyāḥ paṭhanti yakcinoḥ pratiṣedhe*, "The Bhāradvājīyas read: where there is bar of *yak* and *cin.*"

These are two of the *vārtikas* quoted from texts on Grammar by Bharadvāja, probably current at the time of Patañjali.

In the RP, which is generally accepted as a pre-Pāṇinian work,[12] Bharadvāja's opinion is quoted.[13] Puṣparṣi in his PS,[14] which also is a Prātiśākhya pertaining to the SV, has quoted an opinion of Bharadvāja. In the Sāmavedic verse *brahmayujo haraye iti*[15] (so may the long-maned Bays yoked by devotion), Bharadvāja has prescribed the analytical way of singing (*padagīta*) instead of the combined chanting (*saṁdhigīta*) while reciting an *udgītha* of the SV. Bharadvāja further prescribes that the syllabic divisions of *pyā* in the *pada sepyā* (the skin, which covers the tail) occurring in *marāye sepyā bhāradvāje* and *bhyaḥ* in that of *Putrebhyaḥ* are to be contracted (*saṁkṛṣṭa*) instead of becoming extended (*vikṛṣṭa*). This sort of *saṁkarṣaṇa* (extraction) and *vikarṣaṇa* (removal) does not relate to the *svaras* (accents); they relate the *padas*: 'analytical texts'. It may be presumed that these prescriptions of chanting in a peculiar way must have been connected with some grammatical notions.[16]

That Bharadvāja was a grammarian is corroborated by a tradition recorded in the Rt,[17] a Prātiśākhya of the SV. It says that Brahmā taught Grammar to Bṛhaspati (father of Bharadvāja?). Bṛhaspati taught the same Grammar to Indra, and Indra in his turn to Bharadvāja (the son of Bṛhaspati?). Bharadvāja taught Grammar to sages who handed down the same to the Brāhmaṇas.[18] V.S. Agrawal[19] comments upon this as follows: 'Brahmā is the originator of all sciences. Indra is the symbol of divinity. In the stage of human progress, Bharadvāja is held responsible for the spread of grammatical science.' This mythical account confers authority of an ancient grammatical school on Bharadvāja long before the other schools arose. A tradition of this type is not found even in relation to other well-known grammarians, Śākaṭāyana, Gārgya, Gālava or even Pāṇini. Pāṇini's receiving the Śivasūtras cannot be compared to this tradition. This myth speaks of the existence of a very old school of Grammar, that became foremost among all. The relationship of that of a teacher and the taught, referred to, between Indra and Bharadvāja is evidenced on a number of other occasions also.[20] If we believe that Indra received the Grammatical science from Bṛhaspati and the latter transmitted the same to Bharadvāja, we may assume that the Grammar of the school of Bharadvāja was probably that of Indra.

The school of Grammar founded by Bharadvāja, was one of the many schools of Grammar which existed long before Pāṇini. Belvalkar[21] has suggested 700 B.C. as the date of Pāṇini. As such the school of Grammar of Bharadvāja must have existed prior to the former's era.

In the previous section[22], we noticed that Bhāradvāja Śikṣā is traditionally handed down to us. Although the present work in *śloka* metre might not be of high antiquity, we hold that it might have represented an older school of phonetics. The upper limit of the date of the Śikṣā (of oral transmission, if any) must have been of a date nearer the Taitt. texts.[23] This thesis of ours will be further substantiated by the fact that the school of Grammar followed by the Bhāradvājas was of a high antiquity, much prior to Pāṇini. Grammar and Phonetics are twin brothers, and may be born of the same parents, at the same date, too. Let us not overlook the fact that Pāṇini also gave rise to Śikṣā and Vyākaraṇa.

Section (iii)

(*B*) *Gārgya: a Grammarian*

In the previous two sections we have taken note of the contribution of the Bharadvājas to *Śikṣā* and *Vyākaraṇa*. Here we dwell upon another school of Grammar (*i.e.* the one ascribed to Gārgya). As noted earlier, Gārgya is a descendant of Garga who himself is a remote descendant of Bharadvāja.[1] Thus the Gargas are intimately connected with the Bharadvājas. As such, it should be quite pertinent to examine this school of Grammar ascribed to Gārgya, in sequence to the one ascribed to Bhāradvāja.

As an authority on Grammar, Gārgya appears to have enjoyed greater celebrity than Bhāradvāja.[2] And he is quoted in the Aṣṭ. of Pāṇini,[3] RP,[4] VP,[5] Nir.[6] of Yāska, and BD.[7] Besides, he authored the Padapāṭha of SV.

Pāṇini in his Aṣṭ quotes Gārgya thrice (*i.e.* in 7, 3, 99; 8, 3, 20 and 4, 67) as under:

(*i*) *aḍ Gārgya-Gālavayoḥ*: 'According to the opinion of Gārgya and Gālava, the augment *aṭ* comes before a Sārvadhātuka affix consisting of a single consonant, after the five roots *rud* &c.'[8] (7, 3, 99).

(*ii*) *Oto Gārgyasya* (8, 3, 20): 'According to the opinion of Gārgya *y* preceded by *o* (*is* elided before an *aś* letter).'[9]

(*iii*) *Nodāttasvaritodayama Gārgyakāśyapa-Gālavānāṁ* (8, 4, 67): '(Except the three) schools of the Ācāryas Gārgya, Kāśyapa and Gālava, all others prohibit the substitution of Svarita (when an Udātta follows an Anudātta).'[10]

This rule debars its preceding rule, viz., *udāttānudāttasya svaritaḥ* (Pā 8, 4, 66) which enjoins that the *svarita* is the substitute of *Anudātta* vowel which follows an *Udātta* vowel.[11]

From the above three citations it appears that there was a distinct Grammatical school of the Gargas that earned name and fame even prior to the age of Pāṇini (c. 700 B.C.). However, this school appears to have had certain affinities with that of Gālava and also that of Kāśyapa, but was distinct from that of Śākaṭāyana.[12]

Gārgya's opinion is quoted thrice in the Nir (1, 3; 12; 3, 13).

(1) In Nir (1, 3) Gārgya's view is specially invoked to counter the opinion of Śākaṭāyana who says that "unconnected preposi-

tions have no meaning", but they only express a subordinate sense of nouns and verbs[13] (*na nirbadhā upasargā arthān nirāhur iti śākaṭāyanaḥ*). To this Gārgya's reaction is that "they (prepositions) have various meanings"[14] (*uccāvacāḥ padārthāḥ bhavantīti Gārgyaḥ*). To this Yāska adds that "whatever be the meaning of the preposition they always express a meaning (which brings about) modification in the sense of noun and verb. Thus *a* is used in the sense of 'hitherwards', *pra* and *parā*, are its antithesis, and so on."[15]

In Nir (1, 12) Gārgya and a group of grammarians are quoted in opposition of Śākaṭāyana's view. Śākaṭāyana holds that "all nouns are derivable from verbs". Sharply reacting to this Gārgya opined that *na sarvāṇīti Gārgyo vaiyākaraṇānāṁ caike*: "All (nouns) are not derivable."[16] "But only those, the accent and grammatical form of which are regular, and which are accompanied by an explanatory radical modification are derivable from verb"[17] (*yatra svarasaṁskārau samarthau prādeśikena guṇenānvitau syātāṁ saṁvijñātāni tāni*).

In the light of Durgācārya's ingenious suggestion, we presume that Gārgya and his fellow grammarians seem to have divided nouns into three groups.[18]

(a) *pratyakṣa-kriyā* (where action is really perceived), e.g., *kāraka, hāraka,* etc.

(b) *prakalpya-kriyā* (where action is to be imagined) e.g. *Gau, aśva*, etc. and,

(c) *avidyamāna-kriyā* (where the very idea of an action is totally absent), e.g. *ḍitthaḥ, ḍavitthaḥ*, etc. The etymologists are concerned with the last two groups, while the grammarians with the first. Gārgya most probably was an etymologist and a grammarian. As such, he could clearly point to the difficulty in deriving a noun. But Śākaṭāyana appears to be a mere grammarian. He is mentioned in the Mbh as *vaiyākaraṇānāṁ ca śākaṭāyanaḥ*.[19] They however had separate schools of grammar.

In Nir (3, 13), referring to the general characteristics (*sāmānya lakṣaṇa*) of a simile (*upamā*), Gārgya is quoted: "when an object bears (some) resemblance to another which is otherwise dissimilar, it is denoted by a simile"[20] (*athāta upamā yad atat tatsadṛśam iti gārgyaḥ*). In connection with this definition, it is further stated that the function of an *Upamā* is to compare an inferior quality or an unknown object with a superior quality or a famous object.

Further, it compares the higher with the lower (*tad āsām karma jyāyasā vā guṇena prakhyātatamena vā kanīyāṁsam vāprakhyātam vopamimīte| athāpi kanīyasā jyāyaṁsam*).[21]

From the above observations of Gārgya, it appears that he was an etymologist and a grammarian of first rank, and also casually discussed the function of *upamā* (simile), as Yāska did, purely from grammatical and etymological angles.

Gārgya was an author of the *Pada-pāṭha* of the SV.[22] Yāska in Nir (4, 4) while commenting upon the expression *mehanā* occurring in *yad indra citra mehanāsti* (RV 5, 39, 1; SV 1, 345), gives the meaning of the expression, as a whole, to be *maṁhanīya* following Śākalya's lead. Later, he splits up that expression into three intermediate words (*padas*) *me, iha, na* (cp. *atra tat iti prathamaṁ padam| ataḥ paraṁ me, iha, na ity etāni trīṇi madhyamāni padāni|*), upon the authority of Gārgya, in the Pp. of the SV. Yāska, however, omits the names of the two authors of the Pp (*viz.* Śākalya and Gārgya), and it is Durgācārya who explicitly assigns the two views to the respective *padakāras.* Through a further discussion on the matter, Durga explains the standpoints of the two Padakāras, Śākalya and Gārgya.

In Uvaṭa's commentary[23] on VP 4, 177, *avasānārthaṁ punar grahaṇam* a rule about the Pp. of Gārgya is quoted as:

punar uktāni lupyante padānīty āha śākalaḥ:|
alopa iti gārgyasya kāṇvasya arthavaśād iti||

According to this verse, in the Pp. of Gārgya, the words of the mantras when repeated are not dropped. But, in the Pp. of Śākala (and Mādhyandina Śākhā), the repetitions are dropped. Kāṇva's Pp., also, does the same—the meaning of the words being kept in view. If the Pp. of the SV is examined in the light of this statement, it would be seen that the repeated words of the Saṁhitā are met everywhere. So, on the testimony of the VP, one can accept that Gārgya is the author of the Pp. of the SV.

Gārgya has been quoted in the RP five-times (1, 15; 6, 36; 19, 17; 26 and 13, 31).

In RP (1, 15)[24], Gārgya is said to have taken a contact consonant in the pause, apart from that (*i.e.* apart from the final consonant of each class), as the third (of its respective class), while Śākaṭāyana is said to have taken it as the first (of the class).

Again, according to Gārgya (RP 6, 10),[25] there is a nasal

vowel-part after a twin, and a (nasal) breathing is inserted after an aspirate (twin or after a twin arising from an aspirate).

RP (11, 10)[26] speaks of *krama*; Gārgya is quoted: "If two words, each of which is cause of a *krama*-group of three words, occur immediately, Gārgya (proceeds) with three words and again with three words." Also, at RP 11, 14,[27] Gārgya's opinion is: "But (with regard to the *krama* of three words), according to Gārgya (cp. 11, 17, one should show the Pada form) after one has recited the second *krama*-group of three words. In RP (13, 12),[28] Śaunaka quotes Gārgya's opinion together with that of two others as: "The teachers Vyāḷi, Śākalya and Gārgya give the name *samāpādya* (*i.e.* requiring restoration in the Pada-text) to (the changes into) *ṣ, ṇ,* the so-called *sāmavaśa* combinations and sibilation of *Visarjanīya* supported by a rule".

In the VP (4, 165) Gārgya is referred to once. He says that '*kh* and *y* in the root *khya* become *k* and *s* respectively with the exception of the words *sakhya, ukhya* and *mukhya*' (*khyāteḥ khyau kaśau Gārgyaḥ sakhyokhya-mukhyavarjam*).

Śaunaka names Gārgya only once in the BD at 1, 26 in connection with the origin of the appellations:

caturbhya iti tatrāhur yāska-gārgya-rathītarāḥ|
āśiṣo'thārthavairūpyād vācaḥ karmaṇa eva ca||:

"With regard to that (question), Yāska, Gārgya and Rathītara say from four, *i.e.* from prayer, from diversity or objects, from speech and from action." In other words, appellations are derived from prayer, from diversity of objects, from speech and from action.

From the above, it appears to us that Gārgya was an ancient Grammarian, etymologist and a phonetician. He lived before Pāṇini (700 B.C.), Śaunaka, Kātyāyana and Yāska (800 B.C.). At the time of these authorities of grammar, etymology, etc. Gārgya had earned fame as an authority of all those Śāstras; so Pāṇini and others could not but help mentioning his name and opinion. This being accepted as a fact, Gārgya's authority on the Pada-text of the SV is confirmed. It would be justifiable if we assign him a date one or two centuries before Yāska and Pāṇini and place him circa 1000 B.C.

Section (*iv*)

Āyurveda

The Caraka Saṁhitā[1] which represents the Āyurvedic tradition together with the Suśruta Saṁhitā tells us of a legend where Bharadvāja is described to have propagated the science of Ayv among the mortals on the earth.[2]

A team of great seers (*ṛṣayaḥ*) and thinkers (*munayaḥ*) gathered on the holy Himālayas. Among them were Aṅgiras, Jamadagni, Vasiṣṭha, Kaśyapa, Bhṛgu, Ātreya, Gautama, Gārgya, Bādarāyaṇa, Śāṅkhya, Pulastya, Nārada, Asita, Agastya, Vāmadeva, Cyavana, Bharadvāja and other eminent sages. They discussed the theme: "Good health is said to be at the root of Dharma, Artha, Kāma and Mokṣa. Disease steals away the bliss of life. What will be the way out from this? Let us resolve this." They meditated on it, and it appeared to their intuitive vision that "Indra is the only refuge for us. He alone will be able to reveal the remedy of the diseases."

Now the question arose 'who will go to Indra's place to ask about it?' Then Bharadvāja stood and told them: 'Well, I shall go to him'. He then went to Indra's place and saw him sitting in all splendour among the divine sages. He hailed Indra: 'Victory to thee', and then reported to him the discussion that took place among the mortal sages. Also, he said, 'The diseases have broken out and threaten the life of all the animate world. Please let me know the remedies thereof, if any.' Thus requested, Indra, told Bharadvāja, whom he deemed very clever and intelligent, about the science of Avy in a few suggestive words. Bharadvāja, on his part, very soon acquired the knowledge of the three fundamental doctrines of Ayv, *viz*., the cause, sign and remedies. Then by knowledge and practice of Ayv, Bharadvāja acquired a very long life of bliss. And he acquainted all the sages with what he had learnt from Indra, and communicated to them the knowledge of the Veda, which aims at long life. One of them, Ātreya Punarvasu taught it to his six pupils named Agniveśa, Bhela, Jātukarṇa, Parāśara, Hārita and Kṣarapāṇi. Agniveśa proved to be the most intelligent and he first compiled a Śāstra.

Another Āyurvedic text, BP of Bhāvamiśra,[3] contains several legends about the origin of Ayv, in two recensions. Of these one[4] is similar to that of the CS, which might have been derived from the same source. The other,[5] as usual names Brahmā as the originator of Ayv. He is held responsible for the origin of the Śāstras including that of Ayv. Here the traditional account of the descent in learning from Brahmā to Dakṣa Prajāpati, from him to the Aśvins (Dasra and Nāsatya), and, in turn, from the Aśvins to Indra is described. Among the mortals, Ātreya is said to have received it from Indra.[6] Agniveśa, Bheda, Jātukarṇa, Parāśara, Kṣirapāṇi and Hārita were Ātreya's pupils.[7] According to this legend, Brahmā was the first who penned an Āyurveda Saṁhitā consisting of a hundred thousand (*lakṣa*) ślokas.[8] The Aśvins authored another Saṁhitā. Agniveśa wrote the third work (*tantra*) in the series.[9]

The two legends described above may be considered as complementary. In the first legend Brahmā, Dakṣa, and the Aśvins do not appear, while in the second Bharadvāja does not come into the picture. Yet Indra, Ātreya, Agniveśa, Parāśara and Hārita are common to both. Bhela and Kṣarapāṇi in CS may be the same as in BP. In the second legend, Ātreya, instead of Bharadvāja, studied the śāstra with Indra. But Indra's relation with Bharadvāja, as the latter's preceptor is frequently mentioned in the TB (3, 10, 11), Rt (1, 4) and Garuḍopaniṣad.[10] Again, one Agniveśa appears to have learnt Dhanurveda from a Bharadvāja, "the father of Droṇa" in the MBh[11]; he is one of the *mantrakṛts*.[12] However, it is difficult to identify Droṇa's father with Bharadvāja, who received instruction on Ayv from Indra. Besides, many a name found in the list of seers and sages in CS may be an interpolation. Particularly Aṅgiras, Bharadvāja and Gārgya could not be contemporaries. However, the kernel of the legend that Bharadvāja was the pioneer in popularising the doctrines of Ayv among mortals cannot be dismissed as a mere myth.

An older tradition recorded in Va 92, 22 also says that Bharadvāja first composed the Ayv and having divided the same into eight sections taught it to eight of his pupils.[13]

Section (*v*)

Purāṇic Narration: Garga Saṁhitā

The Garga Saṁhitā (GS)[1] is a Vaiṣṇava work dealing with the

Kṛṣṇa legends in a vivid manner. The work is ascribed to one Garga,[2] the family priest of the Yādavas, who lived in the Āśrama (hermitage) Gargācala.[3] The same Garga performed the marriage of Devakī and Vasudeva.[4] Also, he was secretly deputed by Vasudeva to Gokula for Jātakarman and Nāmakaraṇa (the rites relating to the birth and naming) ceremonies of Kṛṣṇa and Balarāma.[5] The same Garga gave the two Lords their names viz., Kṛṣṇa and Balarāma, that have ever remained enshrined in the hearts of crores of their devotees over the generations. Garga also, presided over the Rājasūya and Aśvamedha sacrifices (detailed in GS) performed by Ugrasena after his restoration as king of Mathurā and later of Dvāravatī.[6]

The ascription of the work under study to Garga is very significant; this is based on very sound reasons. That one Garga was the domestic chaplain of the Yādavas at the time of the Epic is undeniable. Attached to the Yādavas, Garga had full knowledge of the Lord's activities. As he is shown to have outlived the Lord, he was acquainted with the Lord's immediate descendants, down to Vajranābha, Kṛṣṇa's great grandson. Thus Garga was Yādavas' priest for at least five generations. Hence, Garga would have been the most authentic author of a Saṁhitā describing the life and deeds of the Lord, his ancestors and descendants. We examine later the question of his being veracious.

Before tackling such problems as date and actual authorship of the Saṁhitā, etc., it may be worthwhile to notice its text and contents.

The GS is broadly divided into *Khaṇḍas* (parts), which are further sub-divided into *adhyāyas* (chapters). These ten *khaṇḍas* are:

(i) Golakakhaṇḍa containing 20 chapters
(ii) Vṛndāvanakhaṇḍa containing 26 chapters
(iii) Girirājakhaṇḍa containing 10 chapters
(iv) Mādhuryakhaṇḍa divided into 24 chapters
(v) Mathurākhaṇḍa divided into 26 chapters
(vi) Dvārakākhaṇḍa in 22 chapters
(vii) Viśvajitkhaṇḍa in 50 chapters
(viii) Balarāmakhaṇḍa in 13 chapters
(ix) Vijñānakhaṇḍa in 10 chapters, and
(x) Aśvamedhakhaṇḍa in 62 chapters.

There is clear evidence, within the text itself, to indicate that our work initially contained only first nine *khaṇḍas* and the tenth—*i.e.* the Aśvamedhakhaṇḍa was added at a later date. For example, there is the following statement which names the first nine parts:

गर्गाचार्येण कथिता नाम्नेयं गर्गसंहिता।
सर्वदोषहरा पुण्या चतुर्वर्गफलप्रदा॥
गोलोकवृन्दावनयोर्गिरीश्वरमाधुर्ययोः श्रीमथुरापुरस्य च।
द्वारावती विश्वजिता हलायुधाविज्ञानयोः खण्डाः पृथङ्नव॥

These passages name the first nine *khaṇḍas* but not that there is another *khaṇḍa.* Further, the following statement suggests that the work was completed in the nine *khaṇḍas* and sealed against any addition:

इत्युक्त्वा तान् मुनीन् सर्वान् गर्गाचार्यो महामुनिः।
अनुज्ञाप्य प्रसन्नात्मा गन्तुमभ्युद्यतोऽभवत्॥
नवसर्गविसर्गाद् यां स्वर्गभूद् गर्गसंहिताम्।
चतुर्वर्गप्रदामुक्त्वा गर्गो गर्गाचलं ययौ॥

Again, the first nine *khaṇḍas* were referred to in an assembly of sages (attended by Śaunaka and others); the tenth was first discoursed in the court of Vajranābha, who summoned the sage for that special purpose and also listened to an account of the Aśvamedha sacrifice by Ugrasena. All these facts point to the comparative lateness of the tenth *khaṇḍa* and its character as an appendix. However, the text of tenth *khaṇḍa* does not betray that in language and style. Probably it was composed by another author and added to the bulk after some time.

The work also shows more than one redaction just as MBh does. In the first one, a Vaiṣṇava king of Mithilā, Bahulāśva, questions Nārada on Kṛṣṇa's life and deeds, and the sage described to him a number of legends of Kṛṣṇāvatāra. In the second one, Garga narrates the legends of Kṛṣṇāvatāra to an assembly of sages headed by Śaunaka. Thus the style of narration is similar to that of the MBh, which unfolds three layers of a similar type.

The work is based on the legends described in Bh, Hv and Bv. The GS can, in other words, be looked upon as a better and improved version of the fourth part, *i.e.* the Śrīkṛṣṇajanmakhaṇḍa of the Bv and the tenth chapter of Bh. Rather, it may be described as a sort of a commentary upon Kṛṣṇa legends of Bh and Bv. But it has surpassed these two works at least in its innovation of contents, if not of style.

Bh gives the legends of Kṛṣṇa, even of Rāsa (dalliance) without naming Rādhā. Kṛṣṇa might have shown some inclination towards a particular *gopī* (a cowherdess). It is Gāthāsaptaśatī, (circa 8th century A.D.) which for the first time names Rādhā as the beloved of Kṛṣṇa. Bv however, abounds in the Rādhākṛṣṇa legends which have a deep erotic tinge, in the wake of Vātsāyana, as also of Kumārasaṁbhavaṁ (Canto VIII) of Kālidāsa and Naiṣadhacaritam (Canto IX of Śrīharṣa). But GS delineates these in all serenity, bliss and peace. The youth and its manifestation in Rāsa dalliance described in Bv is unbridled and uninhibited while GS has restraint and maturity.

The work is composed in the Paurāṇic style, with an invocation to Lords Nara and Nārāyaṇa, to Sarasvatī and Vyāsa. This verse, which marks the beginning of the MBh and of most of the Purāṇas, is followed by a series of Kṛṣṇa legends in our GS also. This very fact groups the GS with the Purāṇas. Secondly, the sage Garga, the narrator, is ranked with the Purāṇic sages, Śaunaka, Nārada, Sauti, etc.

The GS begins with Kṛṣṇa's descent (*avataraṇa*) from Goloka (his heavenly dwelling and the highest abode of the Lord), with a view to relieving Vasumatī (the Earth) of the burden of over-population and of the sins committed by the masses. Also, various gods took it as their solemn duty to be born as helpmates of the Lord in this mission. Similarly, Rādhā the "beloved" of the Lord, was reborn, and so were Nandas and Upanandas as cowherds. Part I of GS named as the Golokakhaṇḍa explains the birth of Lord Kṛṣṇa. It describes his early boyhood adventures, *viz.* the killing of Pūtanā, and Tṛṇāvarta (against the background of their previous births), uprooting the Yamalārjuna (the twin trees) thus establishing his Godhead.

Part II, the Vṛndāvanakhaṇḍa, lists a number of legends pertaining to various achievements of Lord Kṛṣṇa. It gives an account of His previous births and the present one, of the Govardhana hill and the Yamunā, leading to the Lord's annihilation of Bakāsura, Aghāsura, Dhenuka, Śaṅkha, etc., as a bid for their emancipation. These deeds are credited to the Lord, a humble cowherd (at Nanda's house in Vṛndāvana) in the company of Balarāma and cow-boys. The legends of Kāliya, Tulasī, etc. arouse readers' interest. Still the Rādhā legend rules supreme.

Part III, known as the Girirājakhaṇḍa, describes how the Lord discarded Indra and his worship, and introduced that of Govardhana in view of its merits and role. Here Kṛṣṇa is shown to have established his overlordhip despite Indra's might. Indra was humbled for the first time at the hands of a mere mortal namely Kṛṣṇa (really the Lord in his *avatāra form*).

The fourth part, Mādhuryakhaṇḍa, abounds in legends about the births of *gopikās* (cowherdesses) aspiring for Kṛṣṇa's love. The *gopikās* were, in their previous lives, ladies belonging to different regions. Because of their utmost devotion to the Lord they were reborn as *gopikās* and elevated to be in His company. Some *asuras,* such as Pralaṁba, Ariṣṭa, Vyoman attained salvation on being killed by the Lord.

The Mathurākhaṇḍa (Part V of GS) narrates how the Lord subjugated Kaṁsa, his maternal uncle. Lord Kṛṣṇa and Balarāma were brought to Mathurā by Akrura (at Kaṁsa's command) in order to murder them in cold blood. Akrura, the messenger, however, exhorted the young incarnate Lords to rise to the occasion. The two brothers came up to the expectation of their devotees, *i.e.* the Yādava lay-men. They killed those who failed to pay them (the Lords) tributes. The breaking of the mighty bow, presented by Bhārgava to Kaṁsa as a gift, the killing of the wild elephant (which was incited to charge on the Lord at the very gate of Kaṁsa's palace), gave Kaṁsa an idea of their prowess. Soon a fierce battle was waged on the palatial play-ground between the two young brothers and the accomplices of Kaṁsa, who had usurped his father's kingdom. Cāṇūra, Muṣṭika and other wrestlers (of Kaṁsa's camp) soon courted death at the hands of the two Lords. Kaṁsa realised that the worst was imminent, but it was too late. All of a sudden he was put to death by Kṛṣṇa. In quick succession followed the annihilation of Kaṁsa's younger brothers by Balarāma. GS refers to the previous births of all of them. Next step was restoring the kingdom of Mathurā to the old king Ugrasena, the father of Kaṁsa. Kṛṣṇa, who had so long been a cowherd for Naṅda in Vṛndāvana, now became very much absorbed in the state politics of Mathurā. Still he sent Uddhava to console the *gopīs*, mainly Rādhā (the daughter of Vṛṣabhānu and Lord's beloved consort), and also Nanda and Yaśodā, his foster-parents. Kṛṣṇa returned to Vraja for a short while. The legend of Nārada, and the destruction of Kola demon by Balarāma are some other incidents narrated in this part.

The peace and political harmony restored by the Lord in Mathurā was short-lived. Soon Jarāsandha, the Chieftain of Magadha, the father-in-law of Kaṁsa, imposed a war upon the Yādavas. The Dvārakākhaṇḍa (the sixth part of GS) describes the first encounter that the Magadhas had with the Yādavas. The Magadhas were routed by the Yādava warriors under the leadership of Kṛṣṇa and Balarāma, Jarāsaṅdha had to retreat, with his battered army. Soon followed the second encounter. This time Jarāsaṅdha consulted his Brāhmaṇa advisers, who out of fear blessed him that he would be victorious. Anticipating this, Kṛṣṇa asked the Yādavas to evacuate Mathurā *en masse,* and seek shelter in Dvārakā. Jarāsandha's army set fire to Mathurā, ravaged it badly in revenge, and then returned to Magadha.

Also is delineated the elopement of Rukmiṇī with Lord Kṛṣṇa; this was followed by a fierce battle between the Yādavas and the Kundinas. Victory favoured the Yādavas. Kṛṣṇa married Rukmiṇī and a number of other maidens. A description of the Rāsa, (dalliance) occupies a place here. The Sudāman episode rounds off this part.

The seventh part, Viśvajitkhaṇḍa, is an innovation by the author of the GS as the incidents described in it are untraceable in early literature. Details of the Rājasūya sacrifice performed by Ugrasena, at the instance of Lord Kṛṣṇa, are given. Pradyumna, the eldest son of Kṛṣṇa was entrusted with the difficult job of leading an expedition throughout the Jambudvīpa and collecting tributes and also to extend invitations to all princes to attend the sacrifice. In this expedition, the huge and mighty Yādava army under the leadership of Pradyumna brought a large number of countries under the sway of Ugrasena and established him as the sovereign king. Annexations comprised Kaccha, Kaliṅga, Mālava, Māhiṣmatī, Gurjara, Cedi, Koṅkaṇa, Kutaka, Trigarta, Kerala, Tailaṅga, Mahārāṣṭra, Karṇāṭaka, Karusa, Sālva, Matsara, Laṅkā, Draviḍa, Aṅga, Uddisa, Vaṅga, Kekaya, Mithilā, Magadha, Sūrasena, Hastināpura, Yakṣadeśa, Harivarṣakhaṇḍa, Daśārṇa, Uttarakuru, Hiraṇyamayakhaṇḍa, Mānavadeśa, Manmathadeśa, Iḷāvṛta, Lilāvatīpura, etc. Kṛṣṇa and Balarāma accompanied Pradyumna in this expedition, and humbled a number of mighty demons, viz. Vṛka, Kālanābha, Mahānābha, Hariśmaśru and Śakuni.

The eighth part, Balabhadrakhaṇḍa, is dedicated to the glorification of Balarāma alias Balabhadra, the elder brother of Lord Kṛṣṇa. It describes his marriage with Revatī. Also is given a lucid resume of the activities of Lord Kṛṣṇa and Balabhadra during their stay in Vraja, Mathurā and Dvārakā, along with an account of Rāsalīlā, where Balabhadra was a participant. It has sought to introduce the cult of Balabhadra with all the procedures of his worship and, moreover, furnished a *Balabhadrasahasranāma* (a thousand names of Balabhadra). This chapter is author's innovation.

The Vijñānakhaṇḍa is the ninth part of GS, it provides a philosophical introduction to Bhakti. It describes the art of temple construction and the mode of the worship of Kṛṣṇa, which bears similarity with the *sevā* (service), procedures of the Vallabha sect.

The Aśvamedhakhaṇḍa, the tenth and concluding part, deals with the Aśvamedha sacrifice performed by the sovereign monarch Ugrasena of Dvārakā at the advice of divine sage Nārada. The selection of a horse from Kṛṣṇa's stall, the invitation extended to Garga to preside over the sacrifice and Aniruddha's assumption of the leadership of the Yādava army for the difficult task of protecting the sacrificial horse throughout its journey have been ably detailed. In this expedition, Aniruddha subjugated a number of mighty monarchs: of Māhiṣmatī (for the second time), Campāvatīpura, Strīrājya, Upalaṅkāpura, Bhadrāvatīpura, Avantīpura, Rājapura, etc. The victorious army killed a number of demons too during these encounters. The concluding ceremonies of the Aśvamedha sacrifice are vividly described in a separate chapter.

In some initial chapters of this part is narrated the incident of Kṛṣṇa's obtaining *pārijāta* flowers from Nandana-Kānana after vanquishing Indra. The Rāsa (for the third time) in Dvāraka forms a part of the concluding chapter. Lastly, this part lists 'a thousand names of Lord Kṛṣṇa' *Kṛṣṇasahasranāma*. It follows the ascendence to Goloka of Kṛṣṇa and Rādhā and enumerates the merits of the *Ekādaśīvrata*.

The contents, outlined above in brief, suggest that the GS is of the nature of a Purāṇa, but it does not fully conform to all the five Purāṇic characteristics.[7] The sole purpose of the GS is the glorification of Lord Kṛṣṇa. It has preserved the Purāṇic style, as pointed out earlier. In composing this work, the purpose was to elevate to god-head, Balarāma (Kṛṣṇa's brother), Pradyumna (his son) and Aniruddha (his grandson). The process is very simple: (i) The author introduces them as the near relatives of Lord Kṛṣṇa; (ii) then he brings out their valour in battles and establishes their invincibility (being partial *avatāras* of the Lord) and then (iii) the vanquished men rush to take refuge with the conqueror-heroes, *i.e.* the *aṁśāvatāras*.

Curiously, in the Pañcarātra system, Vāsudeva, Saṅkarṣaṇa (Balabhadra), Pradyumna and Aniruddha forms four *vyūhas* (conglomerations). These four so-called *vyūhas*, along with their subsidiaries, are mentioned in a *stuti* 'prayer' of the GS as follows:

ओं विष्णवे मधुसूदनाय वामनाय त्रिविक्रमाया श्रीधराय हृषीकेशाय पद्मनाभाय दामोदराय संकर्षणाय वासुदेवाय प्रद्युम्नाय अनिरुद्धाय अधोक्षयाय पुरुषोत्तमाय श्रीकृष्णाय नमः ।[7a]

The references to the construction of temples, to four *Vyūhas* by name, and consistent admiration for them leads one to think that this work belongs to the Pañcarātra sect. The word 'Saṁhitā' in the sense of 'a systematically arranged collection of texts or verses' after the name of a particular Vaiṣṇavite (of olden days) is utilized in the sect. F. Otto Schrader in his "Introduction to the Pañcarātra and Ahirbudhnya Saṁhitā"[8] furnishes (pp. 6-11) titles of 210 Saṁhitās found in the Kapiñjala, Padma, Viṣṇu, and Hayaśīrṣa Saṁhitās and in the Agni Purāṇa. Surprisingly enough 'Gārgya' Saṁhitā (No. 41) is also included in the list. However, we cannot say anything definitely whether that 'Gārgya' Saṁhitā is represented by our 'Garga' Saṁhitā. One thing, however, appears to be certain that originally a Saṁhitā, expounding the core of Pañcarātra doctrine by Garga, was in existence; the present GS might have been based on that, although quite the bulk of the work deals with the Kṛṣṇa legends. Our work, however, illustrated amply all the six *guṇas*, viz. *jñāna* (knowledge), *aiśvarya* (lordship), *śakti* (ability), *bala* (strength), *vīrya* (virility) and *tejas* (might or splendour) of each of the four *Vyūhas*. Thus there is a possibility that it originated from the Pañcarātra sect. But, with the passage of time, the work might have passed into the hands of the followers of Vallabha.

The GS bears all the Kṛṣṇa legends found in Hv, Bh, Bv and other Purāṇas.[9] It has further incorporated Ugrasena's performance of the Rājasūya and the Aśvamedha sacrifices and the Yādava conquests and supremacy twice over all other countries. The conquests are illustrative of the six *guṇas* of all the four *Vyūhas*, but the narratives suit other sects including the Vallabhas.

Besides, the introduction of the cults of Govardhana and of Yamunā also affirm its affinity to Vallabha sect. Above all, the mode of worship of Lord Kṛṣṇa described in the Vijñāna Khaṇḍa appears to be close to that of the *sevā*, 'service' to God in the Vallabha sect. It is, however, difficult to decide whether the Vallabhites influenced GS, which was originally a Pañcarātra work, or vice-versa.

As regards the date of the work, nothing can be said with certainty. Only an approximate suggestion can be mooted on the basis of some internal and external evidences.

(1) While discussing the contents of GS, we come across a few geographical names of countries conquered by the Yādavas in the wake of the Rājasūya sacrifice (*viz.* Gurjara, Koṅkaṇa, Tailaṅga, Mahārāṣṭra, Karṇāṭaka and Vaṅga), and this betrays its medieval character. These names were prevalant mostly in the middle ages.

(2) The development of the Rādhākṛṣṇa myth is of recent origin. The GS appears to have based them on the Bv the date of which is approximately fixed as the ninth century A.D.[10]

Thus our work is later than the Bv.

(3) The mode of worship of Kṛṣṇa and Rādhā, and also of Govardhana and Yamunā bears nearness to the one in the Vallabha sect. Thus date of our work may be around that of Vallabha's.

(4) Four of the Vaiṣṇava *ācāryas* are mentioned in our text in the following two verses:[11]

विष्णुस्वामी वामनांशस्तथा माध्वस्तु ब्रह्मणः।
रामानुजस्तु शेषांशो निम्बार्कः सनकस्य च॥
एते कलौ युगे भाव्याः सम्प्रदायप्रवर्तकाः।
संवत्सरे विक्रमस्य चत्वारः क्षितिपावनः॥

Thus mention of Viṣṇuśvāmī (12th or 13th century A.D.), Madhva (1199-1278 A.D.), Rāmānuja (1017-1137 A.D.), and Nimbārka (born in 1156 A.D.) confirms that our text, by no means, could be prior to any of these Ācāryas.[12] Dasgupta[13] says that Vallabha followed the *Śuddhādvaitaism* first advocated by Viṣṇusvāmī, and surprisingly, he is mentioned first in the list quoted above. Although we find that the mode of worship contained in GS is similar to the one followed by the Vallabhites, and that they popularised the legends and cult of Rādhā and Kṛṣṇa, the name of Vallabha finds no place in the above verses. Our work may be either contemporaneous with Vallabha or of a little later priod. Vallabha flourished between 1481-1533 A.D.[14] The GS may have been written in the later half of the fifteenth or the sixteenth century.

Once the work is approximately dated, only the question of its authorship remains to be resolved. We have noticed that it is 'ascribed' to one Garga, who was the domestic chaplain of the Yādavas. But we have arrived at a conclusion that the GS is of recent origin; probably the 15th and/or 16th centuries. Garga could not have lived so long. The possibility is that a Gārgya Saṁhitā containing the doctrine of the Pañcarātra sect was previously current. But the work was remodelled on the Kṛṣṇa legends retaining some of the doctrinal ideas of the Pañcarātra system. The later composer(s) might have belonged to the sect of Vallabha. His fondness for certain similes indicates that he (or they) appreciated Sannyāsa and Sannyāsin's utensils.[15] The name of the author is, however, lost to us.

Notes and References

Section (i)

1. Saletore, B.A., *Ancient Indian Political Thought and Institutions*, Bombay, 1963, p. 1.

2. Kangle, R.P., *The Kauṭilya Arthaśāstra*, Part II (Eng. Tr.) Bombay University, Bombay, 1963, p. 1.

3. Saletore, AIPTI, pp. 34-36; Kangle, "Bhāradvāja: An Ancient Teacher of the Political Science", Munshi Comm. Vol. p. 333-39. P.V. Kane: HDS Vol. V; "The Rājaśāstras of Bṛhaspati, Uśanas, Bhāradvāja and Viśālākṣa", BU 13(2), 1943, p. 73ff.

4. Read: एतत्ते राजधर्माणां नवनीतं युधिष्ठिर ।
बृहस्पतिर्हि भगवान् नान्यं धर्मं प्रशंसति ॥
विशालाक्षश्च भगवान् काव्यश्चैव महातपाः ।
सहस्राक्षो महेन्द्रश्च तथा प्राचेतसो मनुः ॥
भरद्वाजश्च भगवांस्तथा गौरशिरा मुनिः ।
राजशास्त्रप्रणेतारो ब्रह्मण्या ब्रह्मवादिनः ॥

5. Read: नित्यमुद्यतदण्डः स्यान्नित्यं विवृतपौरुषः ।
अच्छिद्रश्छिद्रदर्शी च परेषां विवरानुगः ॥
नित्यमुद्यतदण्डस्य भृशमुद्विजते जनः ।
तस्मात् सर्वाणि भूतानि दण्डेनैव प्ररोधयेत् ॥
एवमेव प्रशंसन्ति पण्डितास्तत्वदर्शिनः ।
तस्माच्चतुष्टये तस्मिन् प्रधानो दण्ड उच्यते ॥

6. Read: एतयोपमया धीरः संनमेत बलीयसे।
इन्द्राय च प्रणेते नमते यो बलीयसे॥

7. Read: verses 3-4.
भरद्वाजस्य संवादं राज्ञः शत्रुंतपस्य च॥
राजा शत्रुन्तपो नाम सौवीराणां महारथः।
कणिङ्कमुपसंगम्य प्रपच्छार्थविनिश्चयम्॥

8. Winternitz, HIL. Vol. III Part 2, pp. 365-378. (He has discussed the date extensively in all these pages.)

9. Read: उत्साहशक्तिसम्पन्नो हन्याच्छत्रुं लघुर्गुरुम्।
यथा कण्ठीरवो नागं भारद्वाजः प्रचक्षते॥

10. Read: स्वोत्साहशक्तिमुद्वीक्ष्य निगृह्णेयान् महत्तरम्।
केशरीव द्विपमिति भारद्वाजः प्रभाषते॥

11. See Chapter 2, Section (ii) on Bharadvāja's Birth and Parentage in Part I.

12. Read: सहाध्यायिनोऽमात्यान् कुर्वीत, दृष्टशौचमध्यत्वात्
इति भारद्वाजः। ते ह्यस्य विश्वास्या भवन्ति।

KA 1, 8, 1-2. For Tr. see Kangle, KA II, p. 16.

13. Read: नेति विशालाक्षः। सहक्रीडितत्वात् परिभवन्त्येनम्।

14. Read: मन्त्रभेदो ह्ययोगक्षेमकरो राज्ञस्तदायुक्तपुरुषाणां च। तस्माद् गुह्यमेको मन्त्रयेत इति भारद्वाजः। मन्त्रिणामपि हि मन्त्रिणो भवन्ति, तेषामपि अन्ये। सैषा मन्त्रि-परंपरा मन्त्रं भिनत्ति।

15. Read: तस्मान्नास्य परे विद्युः कर्मकिञ्चित् चिकीर्षितम्।
आरब्धारस्तु जानीयुरारब्धं कृतमेव वा॥

Kangle does not consider this verse to be an opinion of Bhāradvāja. But we think that Bhāradvāja's opinion continues till we come across that of Viśālākṣa. Viśālākṣa's view is preceded by that of Bhāradvāja and thus this verse sums up the opinion of Bhāradvāja. Otherwise, it would have been ascribed to some other authority.

16. Read: नैकस्य मन्त्रसिद्धिरस्ति इति विशालाक्षः। ....तस्माद् बुद्धिवृद्धैः सार्धमासीत मन्त्रम्।

17. Read: जन्मप्रभृति राजपुत्रान् रक्षेत्। कर्कटकसधर्माणो हि जनकभक्षा राजपुत्राः। तेषामजातस्नेहे पित्र्युपांशुदण्डः श्रेयान्। इति भारद्वाजः। Kangle, KA II (tr.) p. 44.

18. Read: नृशंसमदुष्टवधः क्षत्रविनाशश्च इति विशालाक्षः।

19. Read: नैवम् इति भारद्वाजः। प्रम्रियमाणे वा राजन्येऽमात्यः कुल्यकुमारमुख्यान् परस्परं मुख्येषु वा विक्रमयेत्। विक्रान्तं प्रकृतिकोपेन घातयेत्। कुल्यकुमारमुख्यानुपां-शुदण्डेन धातयित्वा स्वयं राज्यं गृह्णीयात्। राज्यकारणाद्धि पिता पुत्रान् पुत्राश्च पितरमुपस्थितं नावमन्येत। स्वयमारूढा हि स्त्री त्यज्यमानाऽभिशपति इति लोकप्रवादः॥ Kangle, KA II (tr.) p. 361.

20. Read: कालश्च सकृदभ्येति यं नरं कालकांक्षिणम्।
दुर्लभः स पुनस्तस्य कालः कर्म चिकीर्षतः॥ Kangle, KA II (tr) p. 361,

We have considered this verse also as forming part of Bhāradvāja's opinion as it supports him and is followed by the counter-argument of his opponent, viz. Kauṭilya (not Viśālākṣa).

21. Read: प्रकृतिकोपकमधर्मिष्ठमनैकान्तिके चैतदिति कौटिल्यः।
22. KA 8, 1, 1-5.
23. Read: नेति भारद्वाजः। स्वाम्यमात्यव्यसनयोरमात्यव्यसनं गरीयः। मन्त्रो मन्त्रफलावाप्तिः कर्मानुष्ठानमायव्ययकर्मदण्डप्रणयनामित्राटवीप्रतिषेधो राज्यरक्षणं व्यसनप्रतीकारः कुमाररक्षणमभिषेकश्च कुमाराणामायत्तममात्येषु। तेषामभावे तदभावः, छिन्नपक्षस्येव राज्ञश्रेष्ठानांशश्च। व्यसनेषु चासन्नः परोपजापः। वैगुण्ये च प्राणाबाधः प्राणान्तिकचरत्वाद्राज्ञः इति।
24. Read: नेति कौटिल्यः।........तत्कूटस्थानीयो हि स्वामीति।
25. KA 8, 3, 1-7.
26. Read: नेति भारद्वाजः। सत् पुरुषाचारः कोपो वैरयातनमवज्ञावधो भीतमनुष्यता च नित्यश्च कोपेन सम्बन्धः पापप्रतिषेधार्थः। कामः सिद्धिलाभः सान्त्वं त्यागशीलता संप्रियभावश्च नित्यश्च कामेन सम्बन्धः कृतकर्मणः फलोपभोगार्थः इति।
Kangle, KA II, (tr.), p. 455.
27. KA 8, 3, 13: नेति कौटिल्यः।
28. Read: बलीयसाऽभियुक्तो दुर्बलः सर्वत्रानुप्रणतो वेतसाधर्मा तिष्ठेत्। इन्द्रस्यहि स प्रणमति यो बलीयसो नमति इति भारद्वाजः।
Kangle, KA II (tr.) p. 532.
29. Read: सर्व संदोहेन बलानां युद्धेत। पराक्रमो दि व्यसनमर्हन्ति। स्वधर्मश्चैव क्षत्रियस्य, युद्धे जय पराजयो वा इति विशालाक्षः।
30. Munshi Comm. Vol. p. 325.
31. Cited above at note No 4.
32. See note No. 7, above.
33. KA. 5, 5, 11: क्रोन्चोऽपसव्यम् इति कणिङ्को भारद्वाजः।
34. pp. 5-6 (of the Introductory notes).
35. op. cit., p. 337.
36. Ibid.

Section (ii)

1. Ed. by (i) Emil Sieg, Berlin (1892); (ii) V. R. Ramachandra Diksitar and P.S. Sundaram Ayyar, BORI, Pune-4, 1938, with the commentary of Nāgeśvara (of unknown date).

2(a) Nine primary Śikṣās:

भारद्वाज-व्यास-शंभु-पाणिनि-कौहलियकम्।
बोधायनो वसिष्ठश्च वाल्मीकिहारितं नव॥5

(b) Three Secondary Śikṣās:

सर्वसंमतमारण्यं तथा सिद्धान्तमेव च।
उपशिक्षा इमे प्रोक्ता लक्षणज्ञानकोविदैः॥

The work is available in MS. No. 967 (Madras) of 1905.

3. On verse 2: (quoted by Varma, POIG p. 38):
भारद्वाज व्यास पाणिनि शंभु कोहलवसिष्ठ वाल्मीकिहारित बोधायनोक्त शिक्षादिकं परामृष्यय . . . ।

4. POIG p. 38.

5. The oldest enumeration of the six Vedāṅgas along with the four Vedas is made in the MU 1, 1, 5: तत्रापराऋग्वेदो यजुर्वेदः सामवेदोऽथर्ववेदः शिक्षा कल्प व्याकरणं निरुक्तं छन्दो ज्योतिषमिति ।

6. Ghosh, M.M., PS pp. 20-21.

7. Ibid. p. 24; Siddheshwar Varma, POIG p. 2, 4.

8. सनि मीमाधुरभलभराकपतपदामच इस् ।

9. Indische Studien, IV, p. 345.

10. PS p. 25.

11. op. cit. p. 5.

12. The bracket is added by us.

13. Read: शीक्षां व्याख्यास्यामः । वर्णः स्वरः । मात्रा बलम् साम सन्तानः । इत्युक्तः शीक्षाध्यायः ॥

Here the word śikṣā is found with long ī; usually it is short. See also note No. 30 below.

14. Varma, op. cit. p. 5.

15. As opposite to the *śikṣā* meaning 'general phonetics' the Prātiśākhya signified 'applied phonetics'.

16. op. cit. p. 5.

17. Ibid. pp. 10-11.

18. Ibid. p. 12.

19. Ibid.

19a. Ibid. p. 29.

20. Vide notes 2 and 3 above.

21. See Introduction to the Mysore ed. of the Prātiśākhya, Bibliotheca Samskrita, as quoted in Intr., BhārŚiksā p. ii.

22. Quoted in Intr. of BhārŚiksā p. ii.

There is a *Grantha* edn. of the Vyāsa Śikṣā with the commentary Vedataijasa by Karupāttur Venkaṭarāma Śāstri.

23. Intr. BhārŚikṣā, p. ii.

24. op. cit. p. 38.

25. Read: ग्रक्षरान्त लृकारो यः स्वरो ज्ञेयो विचक्षणैः ।
उदाहृतः क्लृप्तशब्दे न पदाद्यन्तयोः स्वरः ॥

26. Read: वृजने ज उदात्तश्चेदकारणे सहोच्यते ।
स्तुतं पदं तु वाक्यान्ते प्रचयं परिकीर्तितम् ॥

27. Ghosh, op. cit. p. 40, The editor of PS accepts only 18 verses as original in PS.

28. Varma, op. cit. p. 12.

29. Read: गणेशं प्रणिपत्यहं
सन्देहानां निवृत्तये ।

शीक्षामनुप्रवक्ष्यामि
वेदानां मूलकारणम् ॥

30. Read: यो जानाति भरद्वाजशिक्षाम्
अर्थसमन्विताम् ।
स ब्रह्मलोकमाप्नोति
गृहमेधी गृहं यथा ॥

In the first and last verses quoted above, it is evident that the text shows two variants of the word: '*śikṣā*' (in v. 1) and '*śikṣā*' (v. 130). MaxMüller also noted such anomaly in spelling. See HASL p. 59, fn. 1. See note No. 13 above.

31. Introduction, Bhār Śikṣā, p. iii.
32. MS No. 924. Introductory lines to verse 3:

सांप्रतिकजन दुरवबोध-भारद्वाज-व्यास-पारि-शंभु-कोहल-हारित-बोधायन-वसिष्ठ-वाल्मीकि-प्रभृति मुनिगण विनिर्मित शिक्षादि ग्रन्थानुसारेण. . . प्रतिजानिते ।

For more information, see Varma, POIG, pp. 45ff.

33. Varma, op. cit. p. 47.
34. Ibid.
35. Introduction to Bhār Śikṣā p. (iii).
36. Die Vyāsa Śikṣā, Kiel, (1895) pp. 106-7.
37. Introduction to Bhār Śikṣā, p. iii.
38. Ibid., p. ii.

Section (iiiA)

1. See the section on the Bhāradvāja Śikṣā prior to this section.
2. Pā, 7, 2, 63.
3. MBh 3, 1, 38. 89. RP 7, 22. RT 1, 4.
4. Aṣṭ. ed. and tr. S.C. Vasu, Varanasi, 1962, Vol. 2, p. 1386.
5. Ibid. Vol. 1, p. 658.
6. Ibid. Vol. 1, p. 792.
7. Sastri, K.C., BCSG, Part 1, Calcutta, 1972, p. 98.
8. Read: ऐन्द्रं चान्द्रं काशकृत्स्नं कौमारं शाकटायनम् ।
सारस्वतं चापिशलं शाकल्यं पाणिनीयकम् ॥

Quoted by Yudhiṣṭhira Mīmāṁsaka in his *Saṁskṛta Vyākaraṇaśāstra kā Itihāsa*, Vol. p. 65 from श्रौतत्वविधि: without details.

9. Read: ब्राह्मंममैशानमैन्द्रं च प्राजापत्यं बृहस्पतिम् ।
त्वाष्ट्रमापिशलं चेति पाणिनीयमष्टमम् ॥
हैमचन्द्रं वृत्त्यवचूर्णि ॥ p. 3

10. Aṣṭ. Vol. 1, pp. 364-65.
11. Ibid. Vol. 1, pp. 380-81.
12. Yudhiṣṭhira Mīmāṁsaka, *Saṁskṛta Vyākaraṇaśāstra kā Itihāsa*, Vol. 1, p. 68.
13. RP 7, 22.
14. PS Ch. SS. p. 78(SV 1, 245; 2, 141).
15. SV 1, 245^{c}; 2, 741^{c}; RV 8, 1, 25^{c}.
16. Sastri, K.C. BCSG 1, p. 99.
17. Rt. 1, 4.

18. Read: यथाचार्या ऊचुर्ब्रह्मा बृहस्पतये प्रोवाच बृहस्पतिरिन्द्रायेन्द्रो भरद्वाजाय भरद्वाज ऋषिभ्य ऋषयो ब्राह्मणेभ्यस्तं खल्विममक्षरसमाम्नायमित्याचक्षते।

19. *India as known to Pāṇini*, p. 18.

20. See Part I, Ch. 1, Sec (iii); (iv); Part II, Ch. 7, Section (iv).

21. SSG, pp. 14-15.

22. See our Section of the BhārŚikṣā, (Part II, Ch. 7, Sec. (ii).

23. Elsewhere (Part II, Ch. 6) we have briefly discussed the date of the Sūtras of Baudhāyana, Bhāradvāja and Āpastaṁba as ranging between 800 B.C-500 B.C. (vide R.K. Mukerjee, *Hindu Civilization*, Bombay, 1977, p. 119; Ramgopal, IVK, pp. 88-89). These Sūtras pre-suppose the TS and TB. If we allow a period of two to four centuries for the growth of the Sūtras, it would appear that TS was collected somewhere prior to 1000 B.C. If we believe in the tradition of *Saṁhitīkaraṇa* and Vyāsa as the Saṁhitikāra of the Vedas, it would be reasonable to believe also that the various śākhās of the Vedas came into being after the Mahābhārata War (1400 B.C.) and thus TS cannot be placed prior to the date of that war. (For Mahābhārata War vide: Pusalkar: Vedic Age, p. 300ff.) Thus we differ from Keith's view that TS belonged to 800-700 B.C. (Taittirīya Saṁhitā (Tr.) Introduction, Part I, p. xxiii). Read also note No. 58 under Ch. 5 of the Part I.

Section (iiiB)

1. For detailed information on Garga see Part I, Chapter 3, Sections (i) and (iv) above.

2. Gārgya is referred to by Pāṇini thrice in his Aṣṭ., so also by Yāska. While Pāṇini mentions Bharadvāja only once, Yāska does not mention him at all but his commentator does.

3. Pā 7, 3, 99; 8, 3, 20; 4, 67.

4. RP 1, 15; 4, 36; 9, 17; 26 and 13, 31.

5. VP 4, 167.

6. Nir. 1, 3; 1, 12; 3, 13.

7. BD 1, 26.

8. S. Vasu, Aṣṭ. 2, p. 1449.

9. Ibid. p. 1606.

10. Ibid. p. 1679-80.

11. Ibid. p. 1679

12. In Pā 7, 3, 99 and 8, 4, 67 Gārgya and Gālava are quoted as holding identical views, and in respect of the latter Kāśyapa also agrees. For details on each of these *ācāryas* vide Shastri, K.C. BCSG pp. 67-80; 84-87. Also B. Bhattacharya, YN, pp. 70-72; 73-77.

13. L. Sarup, Nir. tr. p. 7.

14. Ibid.

15. Ibid.

16. Ibid. pp. 13-14.

17. Ibid.

18. Shastri, K.C., BCSG, p. 82.

19. MBh on p. 3, 2, 115.

20. op. cit. p. 47.

21. Nir. 3, 13; vide Nir. tr. p. 47.

22. Shastri, K.C., BCSG p. 84. Bhattacharya, B, YN, pp. 68-69.

23. Uvaṭa under VP 4, 177: *avasānārthaṁ punar grahaṇam* '(The repeated words) are, however, retained for the sake of pause'.—Śuklayajurveda Prātiśākhya, ed. by Indu Rastogi, p. 71.

24. Read: तस्मादन्यवसाने तृतीयं गार्ग्यः स्पर्शं प्रथमं शाकटायनः। cf. VP 4, 177: अवसानार्थं पुनर्ग्रहणम्।

These two rules indicate that Gārgya spoke in his grammatical or phonetic work specifically the behaviour of an *avasāna*.

25. Read: अनन्यस्तु प्रकृतेः (यमाः) प्रत्ययार्थे
न संयोगं स्वरभक्तिर्विहन्ति।
यमान्नासिक्या स्वरभक्तिरुत्तरा
गार्ग्यस्योष्मा सोष्मणो वर्जयेत्तम्॥

26. Read: अनन्तरे त्रिक्रमकारणे यदि
त्रिभिश्च गार्ग्यः पुनरेव च त्रिभिः।
त्रिसंगमे पंचभिरार्ष्यनुग्रह-
श्चतुः क्रमस्त्वाचरितोऽत्र शाकलैः॥

27. Read: अतीत्य तेषां पदतां प्रदर्शयेत्
कृते तु गार्ग्यस्य पुनस्त्यभिक्रमे।
अदृष्टवर्णे प्रथमे प्रदर्शनम्
स्मरन्ति तत्त्वत्र निराह चोदकः॥

28. Read: समासाद्य नाम वदन्ति षत्वं
तथा णत्वं सामवशांश्च सन्धीन्।
उपाचारं लक्षणश्च सिद्धम्
आचार्यव्यालिशाकल्यगार्ग्याः॥

Section (*iv*)

1. ed. G.S. Pandeya, Chowkhamba Sanskrit Series, Varanasi, 1969.

2. CS 1, 1-32.

3. *Bhāvaprakāśa* of Bhāva Miśra, ed. Jivananda Vidyasagara, Calcutta, 1875.

4. BP gives a series of legends, among which this stands second in order.

5. In the series of legends in BP this is the first and has twenty-eight verses.

6. Read: आयुर्वेदं पठिष्यामि नैरुज्याय शरीरिणाम्।
इति निश्चित्य गतवान् आत्रेयस्त्रिदशालयम्॥

7. Read: ततोऽग्निवेशं भेडश्च जातुकर्णं पराशरम्।
क्षीरपाणिं च हारीतम् आयुर्वेदमपाठयत्॥

8. Read: विधाताऽथर्वसर्वस्वम् आयुर्वेदं प्रकाशयन्।
स्वनाम्ना संहितां चक्रे लक्षश्लोकमयीमृजुम्॥

9. Read: तन्त्रस्य कर्ता प्रथममग्निवेशोऽभवत् पुरा।
ततो भेडादयश्लक्ः स्वं स्वं तन्त्रं कृतानि च ।।

10. See for details sections on Grammar, Upaniṣads and Brāhmaṇic references of Bharadvāja in our dissertation.

11. See Section on Bharadvāja, Droṇa's father, for details.

12. Mt. 195, 12.

13. Read: आयुर्वेदं भरद्वाजश्चकार सभिषक्क्रियम्।
तमष्टधा पुनर्व्यस्य शिष्येभ्यः प्रत्यपादयत् ।।

cf. Br. 11.38.

Section (v)

1. The Garga Saṁhitā is edited with a Hindi translation by Ramtej Pandeya Sastri, Pandit Pustakālaya, Kāśi, 1971. A critical edition of the work by Bibhuti Bhattacharya gives the text only upto the *Mathurākhaṇḍa* with good many variant readings brought out as Varanaseya Sanskrit Vidyapitha publication.

2. 'Garga' appears to be a surname or a family-name here. This Garga was a priest of the Yādavas—particularly the family of Kṛṣṇa Vāsudeva, and our Purāṇa says that he was priest for five generations of the family. For details, see our chapter on Garga Bhāradvāja, Part I, Chapter 3, Section (iv).

3. GS 10, 9, 5: तेषामहं वचः श्रुत्वा जग्मिवान् द्वारकां पुरीम्।
गर्गाचलान् नृपश्रेष्ठ यज्ञकौतुकसंयुतः ।।

cf. GS 9, 10, 40: गर्गो गर्गाचलं ययौ।

These passages indicate that the Āśrama was situated on the hillock called Gargācala after the name of the sage.

4. Bv 4, 6, 8: गर्गो युद्धकुलाचार्यः सम्बन्धं वसुना सह।
देवकयाः कारयामास विधिवच्च यथोदितम् ।।

5. Bv 4, 13, 41: गर्गोऽहं यदुवंशानां चिरकालं पुरोहितः।
प्रस्थापितोऽहं वसुना नान्यसाध्ये च कर्मणि ।।

Also, Bv 4, 14, 47: अस्यान्नितप्राशनायाहं नामानुकरणाय च।
गूढेन प्रेषितस्तेन तस्योद्योगं कुरु द्विज ।।

cf. Bv 4, 13, 48-70.

6. GS 7, 50, 7: महा संभृत संभारे राजसूयाध्वरे वरे।
गर्गाचार्यं गुरु कृत्वा यदुराजो हि दीक्षितः ।।

He was specially brought from the Gargācala for conducting the Aśvamedha as a priest: See तेषामहं वचः, etc. quoted at No. 3 above.

7. The five characteristics of a Purāṇa are given in the following verse of Mt which occurs in most of the Purāṇas with some minor changes: (Mt 53, 64):

सर्गश्च प्रतिसर्गश्च वंशो मन्वन्तराणि च।
वंश्यानुचरितं चेति पुराणं पञ्चलक्षणम् ।।

cf. Vis 3, 6, 24; Mar 134, 23: Ag 1, 14; Bd 1, 1, 35; etc.

7a. GS 9, 9, 28.

8. Adyar Library, Adyar, Madras, S. 1916.

9. Bv Part IV Kṛṣṇajanmakhaṇḍa; Bh Part X.

10. In all probability it was the Bv which first mentioned Rādhā. The Bv must have been written before the time of Alberuni (1030 AD), who mentions it in his list of the Purāṇas he knew. "We should like ... to date the Brahma Vaivarta to the 9th century A.D. at least" (S.K. Bhattacharya, *Kṛṣṇa-cult*, p. 188; cf. also p. 83).

11. GS 10, 61, 24-25.

12. R.G. Bhandarkar: *Vaisnavism, Saivism and Minor Religious Systems*, BORI, 1929, pp. 72, 82-83, 88, 109-110. S.N. Dasgupta: *A History of Indian Philosophy*, 1st Indian Edition, Delhi, 1975, Vol. III. pp. 113, 399; Vol. IV-pp. 51, 383.

13. Ibid. Vol. IV p. 382.

14. Ibid. Vol. IV. p. 371.

15. Such similes with the expression *Kamaṇḍalumivārbhakaḥ* are found in good number of verses, e.g.,

गृहीत्वा तं हरिदोर्भ्यां भ्रामयित्वा त्वितस्ततः।
आकाशात् पातयामास कमण्डलुमिवार्भकः॥
शुण्डादंडे संगृहीत्वा भ्रामयित्वा त्वितस्ततः।
पातयामास भूपृष्ठे कमण्डलुमिवार्भकः॥

Also cf. 5, 8, 7; 6, 1, 45; 7, 32, 50; 37, 26; etc. etc.

CHAPTER VIII

CONCLUSION

We have presented above a study of the Bhāradvāja family and attempted (i) to trace a consistent history of the family in Part I and (ii) to highlight the significant contribution the family made to Indian society and its culture in Part II. The results of the study are now placed together with a view to assessing the role of the Bharadvājas in ancient India.

The Bharadvājas originated from an eponymous seer who was the son of Bṛhaspati; the latter was a descendant of Aṅgiras, the son of Brahmā. This family have usually called themselves as Bharadvājas or, sometimes, Aṅgirases. Its family claims a divine origin (read: *tasmād divyād Bharadvājāt*[1], etc. quoted elsewhere) and its descendants form a distinct and distinguished clan within the ambit of the Aṅgirases, and they together with other Aṅgirases contributed to the making of the bulk of the Ṛgvedic poetry, mythology and religion, as also to other areas of Indian culture since early Vedic age.

The early ancestors of the family (i.e. Aṅgiras, Bṛhaspati, Bharadvāja and Ṛjiśvan) claim intimate connection with Lord Indra; and already, even in the Ṛgvedic period, mythological dust started gathering around these historical personages. Among these ancestors, the seers Aṅgiras and Bṛhaspati played a vital role in the Vala myth, assisting Indra to secure the release of the cows from the rocky cave of the Paṇis. Another seer (viz. Ṛjiśvan) came to lime-light on account of the significant role he played against the demon Pipru. Also, one Bharadvāja played a very significant role at the court and sacrificial hall of the Bharatas; he rendered timely help to Divodāsa while the latter had to fight against the demoniac Śaṁbara. This event acquired so much celebrity that it was soon mythologized and repeatedly admired by the poets as the great deed of Indra throughout the RV. Yet the credit for Divodāsa's killing of Śaṁbara to Indra was only natural, since the seers were fervent devotees of god Indra and they could not but ascribe to him great deeds which they themselves accomplished.

From the evidence available in (what may be called) the Pūṣan-Saṁhitā and the Go-sūkta (hymn to the Cows) [RV 6, 28 in Sixth

Maṇḍala], it appears that the Bharadvājas cherished and adhered to a distinct cult of Pūṣan and to the cow-worship, beside attending to the service of the high gods of the Vedic pantheon (viz., Indra, Agni and Soma). Further, the Pūṣan hymns (RV 6, 53-58) point to the conclusion that the family was at one stage connected with a pastoral tribe, may be it was itself so. However, we demur to such a conclusion, since it is only feebly borne out by the evidence from the post-Vedic sources on Indian tradition.

From several hymns and passages of the RV, the Bharadvājas appear to be a warlike clan. The famous Saṁgrāma-sūkta 'Ode to the Battle' (RV 6, 75) and its background supplied by Śaunaka in the BD (5, 12ff) support this assumption. The participation of the Bharadvājas in the wars fought on the bank of the rivers Hariyūpīyā and Yavyāvatī strengthen this presumption. The legends of Droṇa Bhāradvāja and his son Aśvatthāman and that of Divodāsa and his son Pratardana of Kāśī corroborate it. The active roles which Droṇa and his son Aśvatthāman played in the great war of Kurukṣetra forcefully affirms that the Bharadvājas were a martial clan. Bharadvājas' use of aggressive magic in the time of war is but a pointer to their descent from Aṅgiras, the primeval sage who was famous (in the Vedic period) on account of his singularly potent magic. In a similar way, one Bharadvāja "the priest" of Divodāsa of Kāśī, not only provided timely refuge to the patron-king on his defeat (at the hand of the aggressors, the Vītahavyas), but also helped Pratardana (Divodāsa's son) to recover the lost kingdom in a subsequent battle. Thus, the conclusion that the Bharadvājas had military prowess is evident and confirmed by all these references.

In the Brāhmaṇa text (JB), the Epics Rām and MBh, and the Purāṇa (Br), some of the Bharadvājas are engrossed in the practice of *yoga, tapas, adhyayana* (i.e. *svādhyāya*), *adhyāpana* (i.e. *śikṣādāna*) 'learning and teaching or propagating the lores'. TB gives an account of Bharadvājas' effort and perseverance in learning the endless Vedic lores for three lives. The Upaniṣads give names of the Bharadvājas who were busy in acquiring the esoteric knowledge and imparting the same to others. The Rām describes how a Bharadvāja was righteously following the (eternal) Vedic tradition of daily Agnihotra and imparting Vedic knowledge to his disciples. It also says how he could work miracles through *yoga* and *tapas*. In the MBh, Droṇa Bhāradvāja is also said to be a *yogin*.

Further, the MBh depicts Yavakrīta Bhāradvāja as an ardent *tapasvin*. He made an earnest effort to know the Vedic lore through *tapas* and achieved his goal. Yet further Br gives us two legends of the Bharadvājas. In that of Revatī, Bharadvāja is described as a teacher, well-bred in the Vedic traditions, and as one who observed strict discipline. In that of Śuklatīrtha, another Bharadvāja is stated to have been *āhitāgni* and capable of achieving miracles through sacrifices.

The accounts of the birth and the adoption of Bharadvāja are of sociological significance. He was born as a result of Bṛhaspati's consorting Mamatā, the wife of his elder brother Ucathya. Thus Bṛhaspati may be called the *bījin* and Ucathya, the *kṣetrin* in relation to Mamatā, and their son was Bharadvāja. Bharadvāja was *aurasa* son of Bṛhaspati and a *kṣetraja* son of Ucathya. Thus, according to the Purāṇas, Bharadvāja was the son of two fathers.

It is significant that Bṛhaspati, as a younger brother of Ucathya, could approach his brother's wife without any social taboo. This hints at a flexible polyandrous trend acceptable to that society. It may not be out of place here to observe that this presumption about the polyandrous trend and its continuance is supported by numerous instances, the most striking one is Draupadī's marriage to the five Pāṇḍavas. Another one relates to the birth of another Bharadvāja, having two fathers, one *bījin* and another *kṣetrin*[2]; both of them (*i.e.* the begetter and the legal husband) could claim *piṇḍa* from their common son begotten in Śāntā, their common 'wife'. Though these are some of the rare cases, they yet point to the social custom of ancient days and raises, to a certain measure, some sociological issues.

We have noted Bharata adopting a descendant of Bharadvāja, (viz. Vidathin). This legend[2a] is equally significant from sociological and historical points of view: it marks the close interrelation between the Brāhmaṇa Bharadvājas and the Kṣatriya Bharatas. The Purāṇas (Va, Mt, Vis, Bh, Br, Hv, Ag) emphatically tell us that, from Bharadvāja a class of people were born who could claim to be Brāhmaṇas as well as Kṣatriyas. For that reason, they were called *dvyāmuṣyāyaṇas* 'the children of two fathers of such and such names'. The Smṛti texts indicate that *dvyāmuṣyāyaṇas* are born out of *niyoga* 'the practice of begetting of an offspring by some proxy, for the husband'. YS (*Vyavahārādhyāya*, 127) read: *aputreṇa parakṣetre niyogotpāditaḥ sutaḥ*/

ubhayor apy asau rikthī piṇḍadātā ca dharmataḥ ||—'A son' raised in the field (*i.e.* wife) of a sonless person by another, following the religious dictate, becomes the inheritor of the properties of, and the giver of *piṇḍa* to both (i.e. the *bījin* 'the begetter' and the *kṣetrin* 'the legal husband of the woman'). Explaining this, Vijñāneśvara states: *yadā' sau niyukto devarādiḥ svayaṁ apy' aputro'putrasya kṣetre svaparaputrārtham pravṛtto yam janayati, sa dvipitṛko dvyāmuṣyāyaṇo dvayor api rikthahārī piṇḍadātā ca| yadā tu niyuktaḥ putravān kevalam kṣetriṇaḥ putrārtham prayatate, tadā tadutpannaḥ kṣetriṇa eva putro bhavati, na bījinaḥ*|—

'When the employed person, maybe, the brother-in-law, etc., (of the woman), who himself, be sonless, being engaged in raising a son for himself and for another, on the wife of the second, begets a son, that son becomes an heir of and also giver of *piṇḍa* to both the persons. But when the engaged person tries to beget a son for the engager, then the son born thereof becomes the son only of the legal husband of the woman, not of the begetter.'

In the light of the YS and Mitākṣarā thereon, when we consider the incident of so-called adopting of Vidathin Bhāradvāja by Bharata and the fact that the descendants of Vidathin were called *dvyāmuṣyāyaṇāḥ*, or *dvyāmuṣyāyaṇakaulināḥ* or *dvipitaraḥ* we find that Bharata probably did not adopt Vidathin Bhāradvāja; rather Vidathin or Vitatha was begotten by *a* Bharadvāja by any of the wives of Bharata through *niyoga*. The begetter Bharadvāja probably agreed to fulfil Bharata's wish on the condition that the son born of this union would inherit the property of both (*i.e.* of Bharata and of Bharadvāja) and offer *piṇḍa* to the begetter (*bījin*) Bharadvāja and the *kṣetrin* Bharata. And, therefore, their son Vidathin or Vitatha was the king and successor of Bharata and also a Brāhmaṇa. His descendants, therefore, claimed to be Brāhmaṇas, as the scion of Bharadvāja, as well as Kṣatriyas as those of Bharata. That is why Suhotra, Śunhotra, Nara, Garga and Ṛjiśvan, who were born in the line of Bharata, could be regarded as the Bhāradvāja seers—a singular instance of far-reaching sociological significance. We have in the Epic and the Purāṇas instances of *niyoga,* such as Dvaipāyana's raising sons (Pāṇḍu, Dhṛtarāṣṭra, Vidura) through wives of Vicitravīrya (who died sonless),[3] or Dīrghatamas' begetting sons on Sudeṣṇā, the wife of Bali,[4] but none of the begotten sons claimed such double-right to be regarded as Brāhmaṇas and Kṣatriyas at the same time.

Even Viśvāmitra's attaining *brahmatva* 'brahminhood' cannot be cited as an example. Viśvāmitra ceased to be a Ksatriya as soon as he attained *brahmatva*. Thus it would be fair to say that Bharata raised a son through the agency of *a* Bharadvāja and he might not have adopted one. The Purāṇas described the incident in a plain way, and overlooked the circumstances leading to the birth of a *dvyāmuṣyāyaṇa*.

Our explanation holds good in the case of the legend of Bharadvāja, the son of Śāṅtā as given in Va also.

The legend (of Bharadvāja's adoption) clearly states that in the pre-Ṛgvedic and Ṛgvedic age the consideration of caste was not so rigid as later. The flexibility in the caste system then may further be confirmed from another development in the Bhāradvāja family at a later date (viz. the rise of the *Kṣatropeta* Brāhmaṇas).

The Purāṇas, in their version of its genealogy inform about some Kṣatropeta Brāhmaṇas. The descendants of Garga and Saṁkṛti were the first *Kṣatropeta* Brāhmaṇas mentioned by them. These Brāhmaṇas originated from the Kṣatriya clan of the Bharatas. Garga is a descendant of Bharata and Bharadvāja. Saṁkṛti is the son of Nara, who also is a scion of Bharata and Bharadvāja. The Kāṇvas and the Mudgalas are also said to be *Kṣatropeta* Brāhmaṇas. Kāṇva and later Mudgala trace their ancestry from Ajamīḍha. All these are remote descendants of Bharata and Bharadvāja. At a yet later date, the Mitrayus were called the *Kṣatropeta*, all in the line of Divodāsa of the Pāñcāla dynasty. Thus in the Ṛgvedic time, the Brahmins could be Kṣatriyas for some valid cause, and the Kṣatriyas could change over to the Brāhmaṇa caste.

A cursory look at the Sarvā's ascription of the hymns of the RV to the seers fully substantiate our assumption. The Sarvā's statement clarifies that the Brāhmaṇas and the Kṣatriyas could both be the seers of the Vedic hymns. The use of "Brahmarṣi", "Devarṣi", "Rājarṣi", etc., in the Epic sand Purāṇas indicates that caste did not matter for the seers of Vedic hymns. Castes were on the basis of the status the people enjoyed on their own merits, thus Suhotra, Ajamīḍha and Pratardana were Ṛgvedic seers.

Another sociologically important system is that of *gotras* and *pravaras*.[4a] At an early date, the Bharadvājas adopted only a *pravara* of three seer, viz., Āṅgirasa, Bārhaspatya and Bhāradvāja. In the course of time, the Bharadvājas put forth certain branches—such as the Gargas, the Śainyas, the Saṁkṛtis, the Ajamīḍhas, the Kāṇvas, the Mudgalas, the Mitrayus, the Gṛtsamadas, etc. Among these, the Gargas and the Śainyas adopted three or five *ṛṣi-pravaras*. Those three *ṛṣi-pravaras* were Āṅgirasa, Gārgya and Śainya; the five *ṛṣi-pravaras* were Āṅgirasa, Bārhaspatya, Bhāradvāja, Gārgya and Śainya. The distinction between the Garga-Śainyas having the three *ṛṣi-pravaras* and those having five *ṛṣi-pravaras* consists in that the latter could not have matrimonial relations with the Bharadvājas who have three *ṛṣi-pravaras* of Āṅgirasa, Bārhaspatya and Bhāradvāja. But the Gargas and Śainyas having three *ṛṣi-pravaras* retaining only Āṅgirasa from older group of three *ṛṣi-pravaras* (i.e. Āṅgirasa, Bārhaspatya and Bhāradvāja) could marry with the Bharadvājas (because of the absence of the other two *ṛṣis*—Bārhaspatya and Bhāradvāja in their *pravara*, namely Āṅgirasa, Gārgya and Śainya). Thus, the Gargas and the Śainyas having the three *ṛṣi-pravaras* made a departure from their older tradition; this shows an advancement in their adopting two new *pravararṣis*, viz., Gārgya and Śainya in the place of Bārhaspatya and Bhāradvāja. The Ājamīḍhas, the Kāṇvas and the Mudgalas also adopted this custom. They did not have Bārhaspatya and Bhāradvāja in their *pravara* lists; they simply went ahead with absorbing new *ṛṣis* in the place of two old seers and, opted for keeping only Āṅgirasa at the head of the *pravaras*.

The Saṁkṛtis, however, pose a problem. They "adopted" Śāktya, Gaurivīti and Āṅgirasa as their *pravararṣis*. They are described as *dvyāmuṣyāyaṇas* on the presumption that Śakti and Gaurivīti belonged to the Vasiṣṭha clan; nevertheless, we have shown that Śakti and Gaurivīti are named in the Mt among the Āṅgirasas, and we have also ruled out their being included among the *dvigotra* families.

The Mitrayus record another development; they adopted the Bhārgava *pakṣa* and recited either Vādhryaśva alone as the *pravararṣi* or the three *pravararṣis* viz., Bhārgava, Daivodāsa and Vādhryaśva. The adoption of the three *ṛṣi-pravaras* may point to the fact that the Mitrayus had connection with the Bhṛgus. So also, the Gṛtsamadas adopted either a single *pravararṣi* of Gārtsamada or three *ṛṣi-pravaras* (Bhārgava, Śaunaka and Gārtsamada); this shows their affiliation to the Bhṛgus.

Thus the system of Gotras and Pravaras of the Bharadvājas has three-fold sociological impact:

(*i*) The Bharadvājas proper, the Gargas and the Śainyas (with five *ṛṣi-pravaras*) mark the first phase in adopting their first three ancestors as their *pravararṣis*.

(*ii*) The Ajamīḍhas, the Kāṇvas, the Mudgalas and the Saṁkṛtis replaced Bārhaspatya and Bhāradvāja by new seers and called themselves the Kevalāṅgirases.[5]

(*iii*) The Mitrayus and the Gṛtsamadas gave up the Āṅgirasa-*pakṣa* and chose the Bhārgava-*pakṣa* and new seers as their *pravaras*.

The reconstruction of the history of the family of Bharadvāja gives a new dimension to the Ṛgvedic chronology. Our study shows that Bharadvāja was an ancestor not only of Suhotra, Śunahotra, Nara, Garga, Ṛjiśvan and Pāyu, but also of Ajamīḍha, Kāṇva, Medhātithi and some other Āṅgirasas, Mudgala, Divodāsa, Mitrayu and Gṛtsamada. Bharadvāja Bārhaspatya is found to be a contemporary of Dīrghatamas. And Kakṣīvat Dairghatamasa and his daughter Ghoṣā might have been contemporaries of some early descendants of Bharadvāja Bārhaspatya. These generic relations of groups of seers from Bharadvāja Bārhaspatya speak of the comparative chronology of the Ṛgvedic hymns ascribed to those enumerated above. Particularly, the hymns of the second and the eighth Maṇḍalas appear to be later than those of the sixth Maṇḍala.[6] So also the hymns composed by the descendants of Bharadvāja in other Maṇḍalas appear to be of a later date.[7]

In this regard, we should clearly point out that majority of the hymns of the sixth Maṇḍala may be assigned a date later than that of Divodāsa, whose activities are praised in that Maṇḍala. This Divodāsa definitely lived during the period of Pāyu Bhāradvāja (the seer of RV 6, 75), who played a significant role by consecrating the weapons for Abhyāvartin and Sṛñjaya for their great war against the Vṛcīvats on the banks of the rivers Hariyūpīyā and Yavyāvatī. Thus, the three hymns (RV 6, 27; 47 and 75) may be deemed as a contemporary record of the Hariyūpīyā war. Also, Prastoka, Sṛñjaya's son and Divodāsa were contemporaries. Divodāsa is further referred to in the hymns of the 1st, 2nd, 4th, 6th, 7th, 9th and 10th (Maṇḍalas of the RV), which consequently could be dated later than those of the sixth Maṇḍala, (viz. RV 6, 27; 47 and 75).

We have seen in Chapter V of Part I above, that Sudās Paijavana was a near relative of Divodāsa Atithigva. This Sudās is frequently mentioned in the 1st, 3rd, 5th and 7th Maṇḍalas of the RV. These hymns thus cannot claim a date prior to that of the Dāśarājña war which definitely took place sometime after the Hariyūpīyā war; and may be dated later than those of the sixth and other Maṇḍalas wherein Sudās is not mentioned. Thus, a historical study of the Vedic hymns can throw flood of light upon the chronology of the Ṛgvedic hymns.

We can fix a tentative date for the hymns of the RV, calculating backwards from the Mahābhārata War. Without going into a detailed discussion[8] we can accept 3100 B.C. for that, as suggested by scholars. The war was fought when Abhimanyu, the son of Arjuna, was sixteen years old. According to the history of the family of the Bharatas given in the Epic and Purāṇas (partially reconstructed by us), there were thirteen or fourteen generations between Abhimanyu and Rucira, who flourished during the time of Divodāsa, identified by us as the son of Vadhryaśva of the North Pāñcāla dynasty. If we multiply fourteen (generations) by an approximate span of about thirty years we shall have approximately four hundred twenty years. Adding the age of Abhimanyu, i.e. sixteen years to it, we get four hundred thirtysix years. Now we can say that Divodāsa and Rucīra ruled in Ahicchatra and Hastināpura respectively four hundred thirtysix years before the Mahābhārata War (3100 B.C.). That means: Divodāsa flourished about three thousand five hundred thirtysix (=3100+436) B.C. This Divodāsa was a contemporary of Pāyu Bhāradvāja and, may be, a junior one to Sṛñjaya and Abhyāvartin, but a senior one to Prastoka Sārñjaya. Thus the Śaṁbara-Divodāsa war was fought around three thousand five hundred thirtysix B.C. while the battle of Hariyūpīyā took place some years prior to it. Thus the hymns (RV 6, 27, 47 and 75) which can be considered its records were composed around three thousand five hundred thirtysix B.C. Many more hymns of the sixth Maṇḍala, particularly those for Indra and Sarasvatī may be assigned the same date or one approximately nearer to it.

Sudās, who is "a near relative" of Divodāsa can be placed two generations below the latter (*i.e.* Divodāsa). He fought the war of ten kings (*Dāśarājña yuddha*). The date of this war may then be put as (3536–60)=3476 B.C. and the hymns (RV 7, 18, 83), probably its account. As Sudās is mostly praised in the hymns divined by the Vasiṣṭhas and the Viśvāmitras, these were later than those of the sixth Maṇḍala.

With this strictly followed, the dates of almost all the hymns on the Ṛgveda can be ascertained. But it is necessary to reconstruct a properly documented historical account of even other families of seers, before attempting to fix their chronology.

In our assessment of Bharadvājas' contribution, we noted that it was significant to the Vedic hymnody of excellent literary value, with a distinct socio-religious tinge, and narrated mythology of distinction. The hymns to Pūṣan and several pairs of divinities (*e.g.* Soma-Rudra, Indra-Pūṣan, etc.), those to cows and to Sarasvatī and the *Saṁgrāma-Sūkta* can be regarded as of extraordinary nature. The cults of Pūṣan and of cow-worship, adhered to by the family may be taken as their novel gift to Indian culture. So also, a good number of Sāmans are the products of their skill in the making of laudable litanies.

The Bharadvājas made a mark in the growth of the Vedic rituals—through their traditional Kalpasūtras—comprising the Śrauta, Gṛhaya and Pitṛmedhasūtras.

Also, together with the Gargas, they compiled Dharmaśāstra and Rājaśāstra (Arthaśāstra).

In a similar way, this family assisted in the formation and development of Phonetics and the Science of Language.

The Bharadvājas' writings ranged over the Pañcarātra philosophy,[9] the Purāṇic narratives and the Āyurveda.

Thus, the Bharadvājas worked for the development of Indian culture in a remarkable way. Indian people and their great civilizations would always remain indebted to them for that reason, and would pay them solemn homage in the eternal words of the Veda:

idáṁ náma ṛ̀ṣibhyaḥ
pūrvajébhyaḥ pū́rvebhyaḥ pathikṛdbhyaḥ/[10]

Notes and References

1. Va 99, 157, cf. Mt 49, 39.
2. See Part I, Ch. 2, Section (xi) on Bharadvāja, the son of Śāntā.

2a. See Part I, Ch. 2, Section (iii) for details.

3. MBh 1, 99-100.
4. Va 99, 67-92. cf. MBh 1, 98, 21-32.

4a. We have added a list of Gotras and Pravaras to the bulk as Appendix II.

5. The Āṅgirasa *gotras* which are not covered by the *gaṇas* of Gotama and Bharadvāja, the two constituent members of traditional Saptarṣi 'seven seers', are treated as Kevalāṅgirases by the *Sūtrakāras*.

cf. Introduction also.

6. See Part 1, Ch. 3, Section (ii) on Nara Bhāradvāja and Section (vii) on Ajamīḍha for detailed information.

7. See Part 1, Ch. 3, Section (vii).

8. Read note No. 58 under chapter 5 on Divodāsa Part I.

9. The chapter proposed to deal with Bharadvāja Saṁhitā, a Pañcarātra text, had to be dropped as we failed to procure the text in spite of our best efforts. We have added a note based on secondary source at the end of our Introduction.

10. RV 10, 14, 15.

APPENDIX I

Bāṣkala and Bāṣkali Bhāradvājas

We have already made an effort to reconstruct the history of the Bhāradvāja family and the biography of every seer belonging to that family.[1] We have also noted their significant contribution to Indian culture throughout the ages.[2] Yet, there are two more Bhāradvājas, who did a lot in the making of Ṛgvedic *Śākhās* after the hymn-composing came to an end, though the Vedic Saṁhitās were undergoing the process of redaction. The Purāṇas name them as Bāṣkala and Bāṣkali Bhāradvājas. Although the Purāṇas confuse one for the other, it is clear from some traditional account about the divisions of the Vedas that Bāṣkala and Bāṣkali were two different persons but belonged to the same family.

The Purāṇic account[3] says that in the epoch of Manu, the son of Vivasvat, Parāśara's son Kṛṣṇa Dvaipāyana undertook the compilation and the division of the Vedas. Accordingly, he put the entire Vedic lore into four distinct Vedas, viz., Ṛgveda, Sāmaveda, Yajurveda and Atharvaveda, and entrusted each of these texts to four of his *śiṣyas* (disciples): Paila, Jaimini, Vaiśaṁpāyana and Sumantu respectively[3a]. Thereafter, Paila made two sections of the Ṛgveda, and gave one to Indrapramati and the other to Bāṣkala.[4] Now Bāṣkala who was a superior Brāhmaṇa (*dvija sattama*) taught his part to four of his best students, Bodhya, Agnimātṛ, Parāśara and Yājñavalkya—and each of them was given a *śākhā* of the Veda.[5] So also Indrapramati gave the Veda to his pupil Māṇḍūkeya, and the latter, in turn, taught it to his son Satyaśravas.[6] Satyaśravas instructed his son Satyahita in that Veda and the latter his son Satyaśrī.[7] Satyaśrī had three disciples—Śākalya, Rathītara and Bāṣkali Bhāradvāja—all of them established *śākhās* of the RV.[8] Among them Bāṣkali is said to have three pupils—Tvāpanāva, Pannagāri and Ārjava—who established three *śākhās* of their own.[9] According to Vizs Bāṣkali founded three other *śākhās* of the Veda and gave those to his three disciples—Kālāyani, Gārgya and Kaṭhājava.[10] All of them were known to have been the followers of Bahvṛca.[11] Before commenting upon the possible relation between Bāṣkala and Bāṣkali and their place in the Bhāradvāja family, let us show in the table below the position of Bāṣkala and Bāṣkali among numerous *śākhākāras* of the RV.

The *Śākhās* of the Ṛgveda and the places of Bāṣkala and Bāṣkali therein

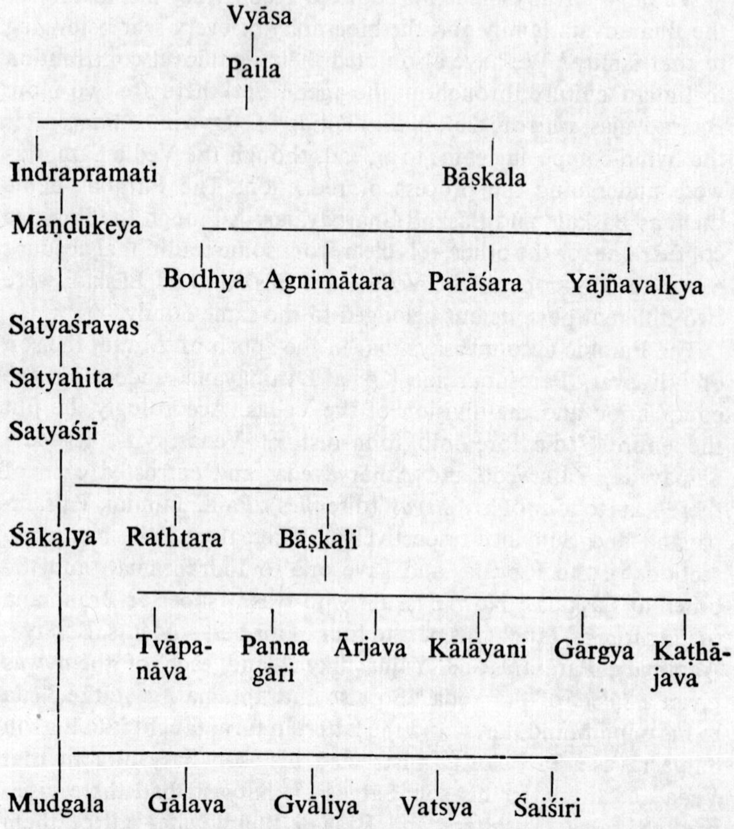

From the above, it is clear that there were two persons: Bāṣkala and Bāṣkali. Although Bd and Va have the same account about the formation of different *śākhās* of the RV, the Bd version appears nevertheless to be clearer than that of the Va which confuses Bāṣkala for Bāṣkali.[12] It appears that Bāṣkala was a disciple and junior contemporary of Paila. Pargiter[13] considers them as contemporaries of the Pāṇḍavas and Abhimanyu respectively. Thus Bāṣkali might have lived in the days of the Mahābhārata War. It is not known whether he was in any way connected with Droṇa and Aśvatthāman who were also scions of the Bhāradvāja *gotra*. But it is possible that they had the same lineage, but sons of different fathers. Again, Bāṣkali appears to be posterior to Bāṣkala by five generations and it would not be wrong to suppose that the former might have been a descendant of the latter. Pargiter[14] considers him to be a contemporary of Adhisīmakṛṣṇa, the great grandson of Janamejaya III (the grandson of Abhimanyu). Thus it would appear that Bāṣkala lived in 3100 B.C. while Bāṣkali lived about [3100—(30×5)]=2950 B.C. Bāṣkali and Śākalya were classmates. Śākalya (? Vedamitra) is a contemporary of Yājñavalkya. This Yājñavalkya was the protagonist of Vājasaneyin *Śākhākāra*, and is different from Yājñavalkya, the pupil of Bāṣkala, who was a Bahvṛca follower. This goes to point to the fact (of course incidentally), that redaction of the white Yajurveda of the Vājasaneyin *śākhā* was made at least one or two centuries later than the great division of the Vedas which was made by Kṛṣṇa Dvaipāyana. Probably the redaction of the extant Śākala *śākhā* also points to the same date. It is, however, difficult to decide whether the Bāṣkala *śākhā*, as described in different texts was related to Bāṣkala or Bāṣkali. We are inclined to hold that it related to Bāṣkali and that would prove its contemporaneity with the Śākala *śākhā*, with which the former differs slightly.

Bāṣkala śākhā

Different lists give us different numbers of the recensions (*śākhās*) of the Vedas and of the RV. Most of the lists contain the name of the Bāṣkala *śākhā* of the RV. Patañjali in his MBh has noted twentyone *śākhās* of the RV—*ekaviṁśatidhā bahvṛcyām.*[15]

The CV[16] of the AV also mentions Bāṣkala as one of the seven *śākhās* of the RV: *tatra ṛgvedasya sapta śākhā bhavanti/ tad yathā āśvalāyanāḥ/ sādhyāyanāḥ/ śākalāḥ bāṣkalāḥ/ auduṁbarāḥ/ māṇḍūkāś ceti/*

Here the name Sādhyāyana may be corrected as Śāṅkhāyana since that appears in the CV of Śaunaka[17]: *eteṣām śākhāḥ pañcavidhā bhavanti/ śākālāḥ/ bāṣkalāḥ/ āśvalāyanāḥ/ śānkhāyanāḥ/ māṇḍukeyāś ceti/*

From the Purāṇic accounts and other texts which enumerate the various recensions of the RV, it is clear that there was a Saṁhitā by Bāṣkala. It can be surmised from different statements recorded in the works that the arrangement and contents of this Saṁhitā are a little different from those of the extant Śākala Saṁhitā of the RV. Some of the distinctive features of the Bāṣkala Saṁhitā may be noted as under:

1. The ĀśvGS (3, 5, 8-9) says:

samānī va ākūtir ity ekā/
tac chaṁyor āvṛṇīmahe ity ekā/

While commenting upon these two sūtras Vedasvāmin says: *yeṣām purvā samāmnāye syāt teṣām nottarā. yeṣām uttarā teṣām na pūrvā/ yat tat pratijñāsūtre upadiṣṭam śākalyasya bāṣkalasya samāmnāyasya ity uktam/*[18]

Haradatta comments: '*samāni va*' *iti śākalyasya samāmnāyasyāntyā tadadhyāyinām eṣā/ tac chaṁyor iti bāṣkalasya tadadhyāyinām eṣā/*[19]

In this *vṛtti* 'gloss' Nārāyaṇa explains the two sūtras (under 3, 5, 9):

Śākalasamāmnāyasya bāṣkalasamāmnāyasya cedam eva sūtram gṛhyam cety adhyetṛprasiddham/ tatra śākalānām samāni va ākūtih ity eṣā bhavati saṁhitānyatvāt bāṣkalānām tu tac chaṁyor āvṛṇīmahe ity eṣā bhavati/ saṁhitānyatvād ity evam viniveśo yuktaḥ/[20]

Thus the ĀśvGS and its commentators assert that *tac chaṁyor āvṛṇīmahe* is the last verse of the Saṁjñāna sūkta in the Bāṣkala Saṁhitā.

2. The Anuvākānukramaṇī[21] also has preserved some information of the Bāṣkala school. It says about the arrangement of the first Maṇḍala:

Gautamād auśijaḥ kutsaḥ parucchepād ṛṣeḥ paraḥ/
kutsād dīrghatamā ityeṣa tu bāṣkalakaḥ kramaḥ//[22]

This verse indicates the difference in the arrangement of the hymns in the Bāṣkala Śaṁhitā from that of the Śākala Saṁhitā. This difference can be shown in the following table of Sūktas and their composers:

Śākala	*Bāṣkala*
(i) Sūktas by Gautama	(i) Sūktas by Gautama
(ii) Sūktas by Kutsa	(ii) Sūktas by Kakṣīvat Auśijaḥ
(iii) Sūktas by Kakṣīvat	(iii) Sūktas by Parucchepa
(iv) Sūktas by Parucchepa	(iv) Sūktas by Kutsa
(v) Sūktas by Dīrghatamas	(v) Sūktas by Dīrghatamas

Thus there is a difference in the placing of the hymns composed by Kutsa Aṅgiras. The Śākala Saṁhitā places the hymns of Kutsa Aṅgiras after the hymns by Gautama, while the Bāṣkala Saṁhitā places the hymns by Kutsa after the hymns seen by Parucchepa Daivodāsi.

3. Again the Anuvākānukramaṇī gives us the number of hymns of the two Saṁhitās:

etat sahasram daśa sapta caivāṣṭavato bāṣkalake' adhikāni|
tān pārane śākale śaiśirīye vadanti śiṣṭā na khileṣu viprāḥ||[23]

The Śākala Saṁhitā, therefore, consists of 1017 *sūktas*, while the Bāṣkala Saṁhitā has eight hymns more—i.e. the Bāṣkala Saṁhitā consists of 1025 *sūktas* altogether. Out of these eight additional hymns, one is the *Saṁjñāna Sūkta*, that appears at the end of the Bāṣkala Saṁhitā, and the remaining seven accord to the first seven *sūktas* of the eleven Vālakhilya hymns which are appended to the Śākala Saṁhitā also, for Mahīdāsa in his commentary on the CV[24] has given the understated order of the seven Khila hymns in the Bāṣkala Saṁhitā:

'svādór abhakṣi' (8, 48) *sūktānte 'abhí prá vah surā́dhasam'* (8, 49), *prá sú śru tám* (8, 50) *iti sūkta dvayam paṭhitvā*: *'ágne ā́ yāhy agnibhiḥ'* (8, 60) *iti paṭhet| tataḥ 'ā́ prá drava'* (8, 52), *'gaúr dhayati'* (8, 94-103) *anuvāko daśasūktātmakaḥ śākalyasya|*
pañcadaśasūktātmako bāṣkalasya|
tatrocyate—
gaúrdhayati (8, 94) *sūktānantaram, yáthā mánau sāṁvaráṇau* (8, 51), *yáthā mánau vivasváti* (8, 52) *upamám tvā* (8, 53)
etát ta' indra (8, 54)
bhū́rī́d indrasya (8, 55) *ity antāni pañca sūktāni paṭhitvā 'á tvā gíro rathī́r iva'* (8, 95) *iti paṭheyuḥ)|*

(The numbers in bracket indicate the serial numbers of the hymns in the Śākala Saṁhitā.) While giving the above order of the hymns in the eighth Maṇḍala of the RV, Bāṣkala Saṁhitā, Mahīdāsa probably had that Saṁhitā before him. It now appears that the 8th Book of the Bāṣkala Saṁhitā had ninety-nine hymns.

It is also worth noting that Ananta commenting on the *Pratijñā Sūtra* (*Pariśiṣṭa*) of the white Yajurveda has indicated that the Bāṣkalas had a separate Brāhmaṇa *bāṣkalādi brāhmaṇānām tānarūpaikasvaryam* (the Brāhmaṇas of the Bāṣkalas and others contain one accent in the form of *tāna* 'monotone').[25] In the

Index by Kavīndrācārya,[26] the Bāṣkala Saṁhitā and Brāhmaṇa are mentioned at entry Nc. 27. In addition to these, there is an Upaniṣad attached to the Bāṣkala school.[27]

Notes and References

1. Part I of the dissertation was devoted to the reconstruction of the history of the family and biographies of individual seers.

2. Part II of the dissertation noted the contribution of the family in general.

3. Bd 1, 2, 34, 11, 12:

अस्मिन् युगे तदा व्यासः पाराशर्यः परन्तपः।
द्वैपायन इति ख्यातो विष्णोरंशः सनातनः॥
ब्रह्मणा चोदितः सोऽस्मिन् वेदं व्यस्तुं प्रचक्रमे।

cf. Va 60, 12; Vis 3, 4, 6-7.

3a. BD 1, 2, 34, 12-15

अथ शिष्यान् स जग्राह चतुरो वेदकारणात्।
जैमिनिं च सुमन्तुं वैशम्पायनमेव च॥
चतुर्थं पैलमेतेषां पञ्चमं लोमहर्षणम्।
ऋग्वेदश्रावकं पैलमग्रहीद विधिवद्द्विजम्॥
यजुर्वेदप्रवक्तारं वैशम्पायनमेव च।
जैमिनिं सामवेदार्थश्रावकं सोऽन्वपद्यत॥
तथैवाथर्ववेदस्य सुमन्तुमृषिसत्तमम्॥

cf. Va 60, 13-15; Vis 3, 4, 8-9.

4. Bd 1, 2, 34, 24-25.

ऋचो गृहीत्वा पैलस्तुव्यभजत्तु द्विधा पुनः।
द्वे कृत्वा संहिते चैव शिष्याभ्यामददाद्विभुः॥
इन्द्रप्रमतये चैकां द्वितीयां बाष्कलाय च।

cf. Va 60, 24-25; Vis 3, 4, 16-17.

5. Bd 1, 2, 34, 26-27:

चतस्रः संहिताः कृत्वा बाष्कलो द्विजसत्तमः।
शिष्यानध्यापयामास शुश्रूषाभिरतान् हितान्॥
बोध्यां तु प्रथमां शाखां द्वितीयमग्निमात ( )रम्।
पाराशरीं तृतीयां तु याज्ञवल्क्यामथापरम्॥

cf. Va 60, 25-26. In the first line Va reads Bāṣkali, which is wrong. Vis 3, 4, 17-18.

6. Bd 1, 2, 34, 28-29:

इन्द्र प्रमतिरेकां तु संहितामृषिसत्तमः।
अध्यापयन् महाभागं माण्डूकेयं यशस्विनम्॥
सत्यश्रवसमग्र्यम् तु पुत्रं स तु महायशाः॥

cf. Va 60, 27-28; Vis 3, 4, 19.

7. Bd 1, 2, 34, 29-30.

सत्यश्रवाः सत्यहितं पुत्रमध्यापयद्विभुः।
सोऽपि सत्यहितः पुत्रं पुनरध्यापयद् द्विजः।

सत्यश्रियं महात्मनं सत्यधर्मपरायणम् ॥

cf. Va 60, 28-29.

8. Bd 1, 2, 34, 31-32.

अभवंस्तस्य शिष्या वै त्रयस्तु सुमहौयसः ।
सत्यश्रियाश्च विद्वांसः शास्त्रग्रहणतत्पराः ॥
शाकल्यः प्रथमस्तेषां तस्मादन्यो रथीतरः ।
बाष्कलिश्च भरद्वाज इति शाखा प्रवर्तकाः ॥

cf. Va 60, 30-31. In the last line Va also read Bāṣkali rightly.

9. Bd 1, 2, 35, 5-6:

बाष्कलिस्तु भरद्वाजस्तिस्रः प्रोवाच संहिताः ।
त्रयस्तस्यामभवञ्छिष्याः महात्मनः गुणान्विताः ॥
धीमांश्च त्वापनापश्च पन्नगारिश्च बुद्धिमान् ।
तृतीयश्चार्जवस्ते च तपसा शंसितव्रताः ॥

cf. Va 61, 2-3.

10. Vis 3, 4, 25-26:

बाष्कलिश्चापरिस्तिस्रः सहिताः कृतवान् द्विज ॥
शिष्यः कालायनिर्गार्ग्यस्तृतीयश्च कथाजवः ॥

It may be possible to identify Kālayani, Gārgya and Kathājava with those three named in Bd and Va: Tvāpanapa, Pannagāri and Ārjava. But in the absence of positive evidence for such identification, we have taken them as distinct persons.

11. Va 61, 4: इत्येते बह्वृचाः प्रोक्ताःसंहितायैः (?) प्रवर्तिताः ।

cf. Vis 3, 4, 26; Bd 1, 2, 35, 7.

12. Read notes 4 and 7 above and cf. Va 60, 25 and 60, 32.
13. AIHT pp. 330-331.
14. Ibid.
15. MBh (Paśpas) Vol. 1, p 9 (under Vārtika 5).
16. AV Pari, 49, 1, 6 (p. 224).
17. CV 1.
18. Quoted by Bhagavaddatta, VVI Vol. I, p. 169.
19. Ibid.
20. AśvGS ed. N.N. Sharma, Delhi, p. 90.
21. Ed. by U.C. Sharma, *with Ṛgveda Sarvānukramaṇī*, Aligarh, 1977.
22. Anuvākānukramaṇi verse 21; cf. BD 3, 125.
23. op. cit. verse 36.
24. Under CV 1.
25. Sūtra 8.
26. Index of Kavīndrācārya S.V. Bāṣkala.
27. Ed. by Schrader, f. Otto, A Descriptive Catalogue of the Sanskrit Manuscripts in the Adyar Library, Vol. 1, Upaniṣads, Madras, 1908.

APPENDIX II

The Gotras and Pravaras of the Bhāradvāja family

The Brāhmaṇic tradition has attached great importance to the institution of the *gotras*[1] and *pravaras*[2] of the twice-born Aryans. Knowledge of one's *gotra* and *pravara* has been made compulsory on the part of a twice-born. While performing a particular ceremony the Hotṛ and the Adhvaryu are assigned with a duty of pronouncing the name of *ṛṣi*-ancestor or ancestors forming the *pravara* of the *yajamāna* (sacrificer). It is said that the Hotṛ (invoker) should address Agni by mentioning the *ṛṣi*-ancestors or the *pravara* of a *yajamāna* from the oldest (or highest) downwards to the youngest one. While the Adhvaryu in choosing the Hotṛ should mention the *ṛṣi*-ancestors forming the *pravara* of the *yajamāna* from the youngest seer backwards to the oldest one.[3] For example, the Hotṛ pronounces: *Āṅgirasa Bārhaspatya-Bhāradvāja iti*; and the Adhvaryu pronounces: *Bharadvājavat-Bṛhaspativat Aṅgirovad iti*—as the *pravara*, if the *Yajamāna* is a Bhāradvāja.

Moreover, the *gotra* and the *pravara* play a vital role in the marriage ceremony of the twice-born, specially among the Brāhmaṇas. It has been prescribed that a twice-born should marry a bride who belongs to a family whose *gotra* and *pravara* bear no similarity with those of his (groom's) own family. This similarity or sameness of the *pravara* lies on the sameness of the name or names, their number and order of the *ṛṣi*-ancestors of the person concerned.[4]

Thus, the institution of the *gotra* and *pravara* does play a prominent role in the *gotra*—and *pravara*—exogamy. It is clearly understood that in the earliest period when population had not much increased, exogamy was not so much practised and thus incestual marriage was not rare. In course of time when the population was growing rapidly the exogamy of the *gotra* and *pravara* was increasingly practised with strict punitive measures. Thus, the institution of *gotra* and *pravara* is of interest for the students of sociology and religion.

Historical outline

The Brāhmaṇas claim their descent from Brahmā, the creator. According to the legends[5] given in scriptures, seven Brahmarṣis arose from sacrifice instituted by Brahmā and they are: 1. Bhṛgu, 2. Aṅgiras, 3. Marīci, 4. Atri, 5. Pulaha, 6. Pulastya, 7. Vasiṣṭha.[5a]

Pulaha and Pulastya became originators of Rākṣasas and Piśācas,[6] while Vasiṣṭha died an early death to re-appear again as a descendant of Marīci.[7]

Bhṛgu, Aṅgiras, Marīci and Atri were responsible for the existence of the seven-seers (*saptarṣi*) and Agastya, as the eighth.[8] They may be shown in following way:

(i)	Jamadagni	Descendant of Bhṛgu.
(ii)	Bharadvāja	Descendants of Aṅgirā
(iii)	Gotama	
(iv)	Kaśyapa	Descendants of Marīci
(v)	Vasiṣṭha	
(vi)	Agastya	
(vii)	Atri	Descendants of Atri (Probably)
(viii)	Viśvāmitra	

The eight seers (i-viii as above) were ancestors of many other seers.[8a] These descendants of each of the above-named *ṛṣis* (i-viii) cannot intermarry among themselves but the progeny of any of these eight seers can intermarry with those of another of the list.[9] This clearly proves that the marriage restriction did not exist prior to the days of the descendants of these eight seers, for, although several of these *gotrakāras* happened to have one and the same ancestor, their issues were allowed to intermarry freely. For example, the descendants of Gotama can intermarry with those of Bharadvāja, though these two seers had descended from Aṅgiras.

In course of time, beside these eight families, ten more families arose. Most of them were known as the *Kṣatropeta Brāhmaṇas*[10], who had once followed the profession of the warrior class (Kṣatriyas) and then took the profession of the Brāhmaṇas, Bhṛgus and Aṅgirases. They are signified as the *Kevala* 'isolated' Bhṛgus or Aṅgirases for, they claimed their descent only from Bhṛgu or Aṅgiras, and ignored all others in between. It is possible also that they were not recognised as Brāhmaṇas for some time by other (genuine) Brāhmaṇas claiming purity of blood, and the *Kṣatropetas* remained 'isolated' from others. Later on, they were welcomed to the Brāhmaṇa fold, and were permitted to marry with all other families. Their names are:

1. Vītahavya 2. Mitrayu 3. Śunaka 4. Vena	Followers of Bhṛgu
5. Rathītara 6. Mudgala 7. Viṣṇuvṛddha 8. Hārita 9. Kaṇva 10. Saṁkṛti	Followers of Aṅgiras

Thus, there are altogether eighteen groups of Brāhmaṇas. The descendants of each of these groups can marry with another group, while intermarriage among the members of one and the same group is strictly prohibited.

A person, who pronounces the name of any one of those groups, is considered as belonging to that group and having that as his *pravara*. A person who pronounces a name other than these, has his descent to be searched out among the ancestors or descendants of these seers.

Among the authors of the PS, Baudh appears to be more reserved in treating the Bharadvājas. He restricts Bharadvājas to the limit of those of the Raukṣāyaṇas and the Gargas, and treats all others under the *Kevala*-Aṅgirases.[11] Āp adds the Śunga-Śaiśiris and the Kapis to those three groups already enumerated by Baudh.[12] Āśv drops the Raukṣāyaṇas from the list of the Bharadvājas.[13] He equates the Mudgalas, Viṣṇuvṛddhas, Hāritas, Saṁkṛtis, Kāṇvas with those of the Gargas, etc.[14] who were already mentioned by Baudh and ĀP in the *Bhāradvāja Kāṇḍa*. Kā goes a step further and brings the Bṛhadukthas from the Gautama fold to the Bharadvājas.[15] Āśv and Kā have no separate section on the 'isolated' Aṅgirases.

Baudh has a larger number of sub-groups under the *Kevalāngirases*. His list includes the Hāritas, the Kāṇvas, the Rathītaras the Mudgalas, the Saṁkṛtis and the Kapis. ĀP shifts the Kapis under the proper Bharadvājas and considers all others as *Kevalāṅgirases*.

These anomalies prevent us from drawing a clear conclusion as to who were loyalists among the Bharadvājas or who were not.

It is clear from our studies that the Bharadvājas form a large part of the Aṅgirases. Elsewhere we have traced broadly the origin and growth of this family.[16] More than once we have discussed the *gotras* and *pravaras* of some sub-groups of the Bharadvājas. We have established that the Garga-Śainyas[17] and Saṁkṛtis[18] formed parts of the Bharadvājas. So also, the Kāṇvas, the Ṛkṣas, the Mudgalas were also included among the Bharadvājas.[19] However, we failed to trace links of the Kapis, the Viṣṇuvṛddhas, the Rathītaras with the orthodox Bharadvājas. But, at the same, we cannot neglect the tradition maintained in the *pravara kāṇḍas* by the authors of the sūtras, who carefully adhered to sacred traditions throughout.

Among those sub-groups, the Śuṅga-Śaiśiris are stated to be *dvyāmuṣyāyaṇas* or *dvigotras.*[20] The Saṁkṛtis also are described to be *dvigotras.*[21] Even, the Mt and Va describe a legend, according to which Bharadvāja himself was a *dvyāmuṣyāṇa* Brāhmaṇa.[22] All the groups included among the *Kevalāṅgirases* are suspected to be the *Kṣatropeta Brāhmaṇas.* We have already stated that even the Garga-Śainyas were also the *Kṣatropeta* Brāhmaṇas. Thus, the Gargas, the Kāṇvas, the Rathītaras, the Mudgalas, the Viṣṇuvṛddhas—all were *Kṣatropetas.* The Ṛkṣas and Kapis, in all probability cannot escape from this stamp. All of them might have descended from a Bhāradvāja adopted by Bharata-Dauṣyanti.[23] Their relation with the Brāhmaṇas and the Kṣatriyas cannot be in doubt at all. Thus the Bharadvājas can be subdivided into three sub-groups: (i) the original orthodox Bharadvājas, (ii) the *dvyāmuṣyāyaṇas* or *dvigotras*, (iii) the *Kṣatropeta* Brāhmaṇas.

The Kevala Bharadvājas

The following is an index of the *gotras* belonging to the *Bhāradvāja gaṇa.* They adopt a *pravara* that consists of three *ṛṣis*-'seers' viz. Āṅgirasa-Bārhaspatya-Bhāradvāja. They cannot intermarry among themselves.

1.	Agniveśa	read	in	Mt
2.	Agniveśas	,,	,,	Baudh
3.	Agniveśya	,,	,,	Mt
4.	Agniveśyas	,,	,,	Āśv, Āp, Baudh, Kā, Mā

5. Agnistaṁbhas	read	in	Baudh, Kā
6. Adhikāragrīva	,,	,,	Kā
7. Āktas	,,	,,	Baudh
8. Ākṣas	,,	,,	,,
9. Āgniveśyas	,,	,,	,,
10. Ātras	,,	,,	,,
11. Ātreyaṇas	,,	,,	,,
12. Ātreyāyani	,,	,,	Kā, Mā, Mt
13. Āpastaṁbi	,,	,,	Kā, Mt
14. Āpastaṁbhas	,,	,,	Baudh
15. Āruṇas	,,	,,	,,
16. Āvikāyana	,,	,,	Mā
17. Āślas	,,	,,	Baudh
18. Āśvalāyani	,,	,,	Kā, Mt
19. Indrastaṁbhas	,,	,,	Baudh, Kā
20. Iṣumatas	,,	,,	,,
21. Uḍupati	,,	,,	Mt.
22. Udvahavyas	,,	,,	Baudh, Kā
23. Urukṣas	,,	,,	Kā, Baudh
24. Uruḍhas	,,	,,	,,
25. Ūrjāyanas	,,	,,	Āp
26. Ṛkṣas	,,	,,	Baudh
27. Okṣas (Aukṣas)	,,	,,	,,
28. Aiṣumati	,,	,,	Mā
29. Aukthas	,,	,,	Baudh
30. Audameghis	,,	,,	Baudh
31. Audamedi	,,	,,	Kā, Mā
32. Audamedis	,,	,,	Baudh
33. Aunteja	,,	,,	Kā
34. Aupaseya	,,	,,	Baudh
35. Aukṣṇas	,,	,,	,,
36. Auseyas (Ausayaḥ)	,,	,,	Baudh
37. Kakka	,,	,,	,,
38. Kakṣalas	,,	,,	,,
39. Karabhīkis	,,	,,	Kā
40. Kalmāśva (ṣas)	,,	,,	,,
41. Kakṣalas	,,	,,	,,
42. Kācaki	,,	,,	Kā, Mt
43. Kāja	,,	,,	,,
44. Kājaki	,,	,,	,,

45. Kātkalas	read	in	Kā, Mt
46. Kātvodaka	,,	,,	Kā
47. Kādalya	,,	,,	,,
48. Kāñcaki	,,	,,	,,
49. Kāṇḍaka	,,	,,	Mā
50. Kāṇḍāyana	,,	,,	Baudh
51. Kāṇḍānya	,,	,,	Kā
52. Kānyavijali	,,	,,	,,
53. Kābalyas	,,	,,	Baudh
54. Kāmakāyana	,,	,,	Kā
55. Kāmbadakas	,,	,,	Baudh
56. Kāyana	,,	,,	Kā
57. Kāraki	,,	,,	Mt
58. Kāragrīvi	,,	,,	Kā
59. Kāriṣāyaṇas	,,	,,	Baudh, Kā
60. Kāruṇāyaṇas	,,	,,	,, ,,
61. Kārupathis	,,	,,	,, ,,
62. Kālakṣalas	,,	,,	,, ,,
63. Kāvalyas	,,	,,	,, ,,
64. Kāsukāyana	,,	,,	Kā
65. Kāṣṭhodakas	,,	,,	Baudh
66. Kāvakika	,,	,,	Mā
67. Kahvodankas	,,	,,	Baudh
68. Kukas	,,	,,	,,
69. Kukṣas	,,	,,	,,
70. Kukṣyas	,,	,,	kā
71. Kukvas	,,	,,	Āpa
72. Kupina	,,	,,	Kā
73. Kulaka	,,	,,	Mā
74. Kulika	,,	,,	Kā
75. Kṛpaṇaparṇa	,,	,,	Mā
76. Keśaravis	,,	,,	Baudh
77. Keśasveyas	,,	,,	,,
78. Kokakṣīya	,,	,,	Mā
79. Kaukvayanas	,,	,,	Baudh
80. Kauṇḍāyana	,,	,,	Kā, Baudh
81. Kauṇḍinyas	,,	,,	Baudh
82. Kauṇḍilyas	,,	,,	Kā
83. Kaumudagandhis	,,	,,	Baudh
84. Kaumudagandhi	,,	,,	Kā, Mā

85. Kaurkakṣa read in Baudh
85a. Kaurukṣetri „ „ Kā, Mt
86. Kaurupati „ „ Mt
87. Kauśivāyanas „ „ Baudh
88. Kroḍāyanas „ „ „
89. Kṣāmyāyaṇas „ „ „ , Kā
90. Khāṅkhālāyana „ „ „
91. Khāraṇāḍi „ „ Kā
92. Khāraṇāḍis „ „ Baudh
93. Khārigrīvis „ „ „
94. Khārigrīvin „ „ Mā
95. Khāriṇāḍi „ „ „
96. Khāruḍā(ṇā) „ „ Baudh, Kā
97. Khāladi „ „ Mt
98. Khelakās „ „ Baudh
99. Gāṅgodaki „ „ Kā
100. Gāṅgodadhi „ „ Mt
101. Gaṇḍaki „ „ Mā
102. Giruṇakarṇi „ „ Kā
103. Godveṣi (ṣī) „ „ „
104. Gomedagandhika „ „ Mt
105. Govāsins „ „ Baudh
106. Gosvapi „ „ Kā
107. Gosvapiṅgali „ „ Mt
108. Gaumṛgandhin „ „ Kā
109. Gaurivāyana „ „ Baudh
110. Calabhāyani „ „ Kā
111. Cavipi „ „ „
112. Cikipi „ „ Mt
113. Cetaka „ „ Baudh
114. Celaka „ „ Baudh, Kā
115. Cauceya „ „ Mā
116. Caupiṣṭa „ „ Kā
117. Jityadroṇi „ „ Kā, Mt
118. Jaikṣalāyaṇi „ „ Mt
119. Jaityadroṇi „ „ Mt
120. Jaitri „ „ Kā
121. Jaitvalāyani „ „ „
122. Jaihmalāyani „ „ Mt
123. Jaihvalāyani „ „ „

124. Jvalayas	read	in	Baudh
125. Turṇakarṇi	,,	,,	Kā, Mt
126. Tṛṇavakarṇi	,,	,,	Mt
127. Taituli (ṇḍi)	,,	,,	Kā
128. Taideha	,,	,,	Baudh, Kā
129. Taulvali	,,	,,	Kā, Mā
130. Daśadaki	,,	,,	Kā
131. Dābhaya	,,	,,	Baudh
132. Dābhava	,,	,,	,,
133. Diṣṭaki	,,	,,	,,
134. Devamata	,,	,,	Mā
135. Devamatis	,,	,,	Baudh
136. Devaya	,,	,,	,,
137. Devarāti(ri)	,,	,,	Mt
138. Devavelas	,,	,,	Baudh
139. Devasthāni	,,	,,	Kā, Mt
140. Devāgāri	,,	,,	Kā
141. Devāgiridhi	,,	,,	,,
142. Devāśvas	,,	,,	Baudh, Kā
143. Daivamatis (Devamatis)	,,	,,	Baudh
144. Drāṅgava	,,	,,	Mā
145. Droṇi	,,	,,	Kā
146. Dvyakhyeya	,,	,,	Mt
147. Dvayaugas	,,	,,	Baudh
148. Dhānā	,,	,,	,,
149. Dhyānyāyana	,,	,,	,,
150. Dhūmagandhas	,,	,,	,,
151. Dhūmita	,,	,,	Mt
152. Dhautaṁbaki	,,	,,	Kā
153. Dhauri	,,	,,	,,
154. Dhrāgavi	,,	,,	,,
155. Dhraugis	,,	,,	Mt
156. Nāyaki	,,	,,	,,
157. Nidrāṅgavadha	,,	,,	Kā
158. Nivincyānauas	,,	,,	Baudh
159. Nṛtyāyanas	,,	,,	Kā
160. Nṛpavarṇi	,,	,,	Mt
161. Naitutaya (ntaya)	,,	,,	Baudh
162. Naitundaya	,,	,,	Mā
163. Pambaki	,,	,,	Kā

164. Parāharis	read	in	Baudh
165. Pariṇaddhedhas	,,	,,	,,
166. Pare(ro)ṣamati	,,	,,	Kā
167. Pāspaci	,,	,,	,,
168. Piṅgali	,,	,,	,,
169. Puṣpaṇveṣi	,,	,,	Mt
170. Paila	,,	,,	,,
171. Pauli	,,	,,	Kā
172. Pauṣuyavaddiśi	,,	,,	Mā
173. Prabhu	,,	,,	Mt
174. Pravāhaneyas	,,	,,	Baudh, Mā
175. Pravāhi	,,	,,	Mt
176. Pragva(vā)śis	,,	,,	Baudh, Kā
177. Prālepi	,,	,,	Mt
178. Prāvahi	,,	,,	Mt
179. Prāvahaneyas	,,	,,	Baudh, Kā
180. Phalāhāra	,,	,,	Mt
181. Barhiṣādi	,,	,,	,,
182. Bājavṛṣṭi	,,	,,	Kā
183. Bādhyogas	,,	,,	Baudh
184. Bāṣkalas	,,	,,	,,
185. Bāṣkali	,,	,,	Mt, Kā
186. Bāhalabas	,,	,,	Baudh
187. Bāhyagacchi	,,	,,	Kā
188. Bahyogitsanti	,,	,,	,,
189. Brahmatanvi	,,	,,	Mt
190. Brahmastaṁbi	,,	,,	Kā
191. Brahmastaṁbhas	,,	,,	Baudh, Kā
192. Bhadradhayas	,,	,,	,,
193. Bharadvāja	,,	,,	,,
194. Bharadvājas	,,	,,	Baudh
195. Bharudeyas	,,	,,	Baudh
196. Bharundeyas	,,	,,	,,
197. Bhāmanyas	,,	,,	,,
198. Bhāradvājas	,,	,,	Āp.
199. Bhūrah	,,	,,	Baudh
200. Bhairava	,,	,,	Kā
201. Bhauvāki	,,	,,	,,
202. Bhrāmaṇyas	,,	,,	,,
203. Magaṇḍas	,,	,,	Baudh

204. Maṅgaṇḍas	read	in	Baudh
205. Matsakāyas	,,	,,	,,
206. Matsakrāthas	,,	,,	Kā
207. Matsakrādhas	,,	,,	Baudh
208. Matsyacchāda(dya)	,,	,,	Mt
209. Manahāla	,,	,,	Mā
210. Mahākapi	,,	,,	Mt
211. Mahāvelas	,,	,,	Baudh
212. Mahāvairilas	,,	,,	,,
213. Mākarṇi	,,	,,	Kā
214. Mākhāyana	,,	,,	,,
215. Mātsyakṣiṣa	,,	,,	,,
216. Mādhukarṇi	,,	,,	,,
217. Mādrapatis	,,	,,	Baudh
218. Mānabidavyas	,,	,,	,,
219. Mānabhidyas	,,	,,	,,
220. Mānabhindavyas	,,	,,	Baudh, Kā
221. Māmandas	,,	,,	Kā
222. Māmanyas	,,	,,	Baudh
223. Mārutas	,,	,,	Mt
224. Mārkaṇḍi	,,	,,	Kā
225. Mārjavṛṣṭi	,,	,,	Mt
226. Mārṣṭapiṅgali	,,	,,	,,
227. Mālāhala	,,	,,	Kā
228. Māhohara	,,	,,	,,
229. Māślaya	,,	,,	Mā
230. Māśvayanti	,,	,,	Kā
231. Mūlahara	,,	,,	Mt
232. Maidhumāti	,,	,,	Kā
233. Maidhu(thu)namati	,,	,,	,,
234. Mauñjavṛṣṭi	,,	,,	Mt
235. Yajñaveśya	,,	,,	Kā
236. Yamastambas	,,	,,	Baudh, Kā
237. Yācarātaki	,,	,,	Mā
238. Yāvarātaki	,,	,,	Kā
239. Rājastaṁbi	,,	,,	Kā, Mā
240. Rājastaṁbha	,,	,,	Baudh
241. Rājastaṁbhas	,,	,,	,,
242. Rāśugas	,,	,,	,,
243. Rudrāṅgapatha	,,	,,	,,

244.	Revāyaṇas	read	in	Kā
244a.	Raukṣayaṇas	,,	,,	Baudh
245.	Raukṣas	,,	,,	,,
246.	Labhāyani	,,	,,	Mt
247.	Lākhāyanas	,,	,,	Kā
248.	Lira	,,	,,	Mā
249.	Lohitaka	,,	,,	Kā
250.	Lauhitaki	,,	,,	Mā
251.	Vayokṣibhedas	,,	,,	Baudh
252.	Valabhikaya	,,	,,	Baudh, Kā
253.	Vatkalas	,,	,,	,,
254.	Vataṅgirathi	,,	,,	Kā
255.	Vāyustaṁbhas	,,	,,	Baudh
256.	Vārāhi	,,	,,	Kā, Mt
257.	Vārāhis	,,	,,	Baudh
258.	Vārkali	,,	,,	Kā
259.	Vālati(hi)	,,	,,	Baudh
260.	Vālabhikaya	,,	,,	Baudh
261.	Vā(Bā)liśāyani	,,	,,	Mt, Kā
262.	Vālkali	,,	,,	Mā
263.	Vāsināyanas	,,	,,	Baudh
264.	Vāsināyani	,,	,,	Kā
265.	Vāhalavas	,,	,,	Baudh
266.	Vāhi	,,	,,	Kā, Mt
267.	Vāhyakgaccha	,,	,,	Mt
268.	Vāhalayas	,,	,,	,,
269.	Vāhyas	,,	,,	Baudh
270.	Vindāyanas	,,	,,	,,
271.	Viṣṇustaṁbhas	,,	,,	,,
272.	Veda	,,	,,	Kā
273.	Vedavelas	,,	,,	Baudh
274.	Vedhas	,,	,,	,,
275.	Velas	,,	,,	,, , Kā
276.	Veśas(-śyas)	,,	,,	,,
277.	Vaidhakika	,,	,,	Mā
278.	Vaidhanki	,,	,,	,,
279.	Vaiyus	,,	,,	Kā
280.	Vailas	,,	,,	Baudh
281.	Vaiṣu	,,	,,	Kā
281a.	Vaudodamedhis	,,	,,	Baudh

282. Vyatāki	read	in	Mt
283. Vyaḍhāki	,,	,,	Mt, Kā
284. Vyayogicchandata	,,	,,	Mā
285. Vyasas	,,	,,	Kā
286. Vyopravāhaneya	,,	,,	Kā
287. Śakti	,,	,,	Baudh
288. Śakra	,,	,,	Kā
289. Śathas	,,	,,	Baudh, Kā
290. Śalālis(śalālis)	,,	,,	,,
291. Śākalas	,,	,,	,,
292. Śādya	,,	,,	Mā
293. Śārdulis	,,	,,	Baudh, Kā
294. Śāla	,,	,,	Mā
295. Śālankāyani	,,	,,	Mt
296. Śālis	,,	,,	Kā
297. Śālāthala	,,	,,	Mā
298. Śālāni	,,	,,	Baudh
299. Śālāhalis	,,	,,	,,
300. Śālāhari	,,	,,	,,
301. Śālohi	,,	,,	Kā
302. Śikṣāyaṇas	,,	,,	Baudh
303. Śikhāgrīvi	,,	,,	,,
304. Śikhāyanas	,,	,,	,,
305. Śilātali	,,	,,	Mt
306. Śilā(ṣ)thali	,,	,,	,,
307. Śuṅgas(śugah)	,,	,,	Baudh
308. Śṛṅgas	,,	,,	,,
309. Śaikeyas	,,	,,	,,
310. Śaikheyas	,,	,,	,,
311. Śailāhalayas	,,	,,	,,
312. Śaivāyatha	,,	,,	Kā
313. Śaiṣis	,,	,,	Mā
314. Śauṅga	,,	,,	Mā
315. Śaudhis	,,	,,	Baudh
316. Śauddhakis	,,	,,	,,
317. Śaudvayas	,,	,,	Kā
318. Śyāmeyas	,,	,,	Baudh, Ka
319. Śrīpatha	,,	,,	Kā
320. Śvaruḍas	,,	,,	Baudh
321. Śviṣṭas	,,	,,	,,

322. Śvelakas read in Baudh
323. Ṣathas ,, ,, ,,
324. Ṣāritaucaki ,, ,, Kā
325. Saghoṣakṛti ,, ,, Baudh
326. Satyakeyas ,, ,, ,,
327. Sadyopakṛtas ,, ,, ,,
328. Saridbhavi ,, ,, Mt
329. Sāṅgi ,, ,, Kā
330. Sājyaṅki ,, ,, ,,
331. Sātyāmugri ,, ,, Kā, Mā
332. Sādyasugrīvi ,, ,, Mt
333. Sāmastaṁbi ,, ,, Kā, Mā
334. Sārāvari ,, ,, ,,
335. Sālaḍi ,, ,, Mt
336. Sālahi ,, ,, Kā
337. Sāluḥ ,, ,, ,,
338. Sāviṣṭa ,, ,, ,,
339. Sāvistya ,, ,, Mt
340. Sāṣṭaṅki ,, ,, Kā
341. Sindus ,, ,, Baudh
342. Sudhupakṛt ,, ,, Baudh
343. Sūryastaṁbhas ,, ,, Kā
344. Sedhyakaithas ,, ,, ,,
345. Somastanvi ,, ,, Mt
346. Somastaṁbi ,, ,, Kā, Mā
347. Somastaṁbhas ,, ,, Baudh, Kā
348. Saihakeyas ,, ,, ,,
349. Saihyakelas ,, ,, ,,
350. Saugeyas ,, ,, Kā
351. Sauṅgi ,, ,, ,,
352. Saujapṛśni ,, ,, ,,
353. Saujvali ,, ,, ,,
354. Sauti ,, ,, Mt
355. Saudhi ,, ,, Kā
356. Sauddhis ,, ,, Baudh
357. Saudhi ,, ,, Kā
358. Saudhvali ,, ,, Kā
359. Saupatha ,, ,, ,,
360. Saupiṣṭya ,, ,, Mā
361. Saurapathi ,, ,, Kā

362. Saurabharāh	read	in	Baudh
363. Saurobhaugas	,,	,,	,,
364. Sauviṣṭa	,,	,,	Kā
365. Sauviṣṭya	,,	,,	Mt
366. Sauvastaṁbi	,,	,,	Mā
367. Sauhakedhas	,,	,,	Kā
368. Stanakarṇas	,,	,,	Baudh, Kā
369. Stomastaṁbhas	,,	,,	,,
370. Staudehas	,,	,,	Baudh, Kā
371. Stojvalis	,,	,,	,,
372. Svajyanki	,,	,,	Kā
373. Svāragrivi	,,	,,	Mt
374. Svojvalis	,,	,,	Baudh
375. Harikarṇa	,,	,,	Mā
376. Harikarṇi	,,	,,	,,
377. Harikīrṇi	,,	,,	Kā
378. Halohara	,,	,,	,,
379. Haritaka	,,	,,	,,

The Gargas

An index of the *gotras* belonging to the Garga-sub-clan (*upagaṇa*) of the Bharadvājas is given. They adopt a *pravara* that consists of five or three seers: *viz*. Āṅgirasa-Bārhaspatya-Bhāradvāja-Gārgya-Śainya or Āṅgirasa-Śainya-Gārgya (according to Baudh and Āśv) or Āṅgirasa-Gārgya-Śainya (according to Āp.P). AP further says that some read Bhāradvāja in place of Āṅgirasa, i.e. Bhāradvāja-Gārgya-Śainya. (The order of names of seers also is noteworthy.)

Kātyāyana says that only Tittiris, Kapibhumis and Khandins do adopt three *ṛṣi-pravara* of Āṅgirasa-Gārgya-Śainya, while all others who belong to the Gārgas, do adopt the five *ṛṣi-pravara* as indicated above.

The Gargas are forbidden to marry with the Bhāradvājas, as the former form a part of the latter.

However, the adoption of three *ṛṣi-pravaras* of Āṅgirasa-Gārgya-Śainya in place of five *ṛṣi-pravara* of Āṅgirasa-Bārhaspatya-Bhāradvāja-Gārgya-Śainya makes some difference. Those who adopt the three *ṛṣi-pravara* consider themselves as *kevalāṅgirasa*, and their *pravara* appears to be unequal to that of the Bhāradvājas. Thus, as a rule, Tittiris, Kapibhumis, Khandins are allowed to forge marriages with the other groups of the Bhāradvājas. But the Gargas having five *ṛṣi-pravara* of Āṅgirasa-Bārhaspatya-Bhāradvāja-Gārgya-Śainya are not free to do so, as the first three *ṛṣis* in the *pravara* are the same as in the case of the Bhāradvājas. Yet a later treatise like the *Garga Bhāradvāja-Kula Vivāhavicāra* of Pattabhirāma Śāstri[24] has not agreed to this.

1.	Upamarkaṭi	read	in	Mā
2.	Aindrāli	,,	,,	Kā
3.	Aupamarkaṭāḥ	,,	,,	Baudh
4.	Aupamarkaṭāyanas	,,	,,	,,
5.	Aupamarkaṭāḥ	,,	,,	Kā
6.	Kapi	,,	,,	,,
7.	Kapibhūmi	,,	,,	,,
8.	Kapibhū	,,	,,	Mt
9.	Kavibhūma	,,	,,	Mā
10.	Kāṇāyanas	,,	,,	Mt, Baudh, Kā
11.	Kāṇvāyanas	,,	,,	Mt, Kā
12.	Kārirātriḥ	,,	,,	Baudh
13.	Kārirauti	,,	,,	,,
14.	Kāri	,,	,,	Kā
15.	Kālakṛt	,,	,,	,,
16.	Kālāyanas	,,	,,	,,
17.	Kevalāyana	,,	,,	Mt
18.	Keśamartha	,,	,,	Kā
19.	Keṣmari	,,	,,	,,
20.	Kaivalis	,,	,,	Mā
21.	Kaivalyas	,,	,,	Baudh
22.	Kaivalāyana	,,	,,	Mā
23.	Kopacayāḥ	,,	,,	Mt
24.	Kośacayās	,,	,,	Mt
25.	Koli	,,	,,	Mt
26.	Kaujapatha	,,	,,	Mt
27.	Kautukis	,,	,,	Baudh
28.	Kaulāstris	,,	,,	Kā
29.	Krindhi	,,	,,	Kā
30.	Kriyāśva	,,	,,	,,
31.	Krīkas	,,	,,	Mā
32.	Krīvas	,,	,,	Kā
33.	Krauṇḍāyanas	,,	,,	,, Mā

34. Kroṣṭakis read in Baudh
35. Kroḍi (Li) „ „ Kā
36. Kroṣṭakṣi „ „ Mt
37. Krauḍi „ „ „
38. Krauṣṭaki „ „ Kā
39. Krauṣṭuki „ „ Baudh
40. Khandita „ „ Kā
41. Khandina „ „ „
42. Gargas „ „ Āśv, Baudh, Kā
43. Gādhi „ „ Mt
44. Gandharāyaṇas „ „ Kā, Baudh
45. Gārgya „ „ Mt
46. Gārgyas „ „ Kā
47. Cakri „ „ Mt
48. Cākrī „ „ „
49. Casmi „ „ Kā
50. Caiṇḍāli „ „ Mā
51. Jānavat „ „ Baudh
52. Jāyāvatas „ „ „
53. Talakrit „ „ Mt
54. Tittiri „ „ Kā, Mt
55. Tetirari „ „ Mā
56. Tulyas „ „ Baudh
57. Dāmi „ „ Mt
58. Niśāntakṛt „ „ Mā
59. Naidrākṣi „ „ Mt
60. Palāśaśākhāvantis „ „ Baudh
61. Paigalāyana „ „ Kā
62. Pailikāyana „ „ „ Mt
63. Paulis „ „ Baudh
64. Paulikāyani „ „ Mt
65. Preṣyaṅgas „ „ Kā
66. Protsaṅgi „ „ Mt
67. Praucikas „ „ Baudh
68. Balāki „ „ Mt
69. Bahuvītī „ „ „
70. Bākṣyās „ „ Baudh
71. Bālāki „ „ Kā, Mt
72. Bāhulaki „ „ Kā
73. Bāhulakis „ „ Baudh

74.	Bhāgī	read	in	Mt
75.	Bhālakṛt	,,	,,	Kā
76.	Bhālavit	,,	,,	Kā, Mt
77.	Bhāluvi	,,	,,	Mā
78.	Bhāllavi	,,	,,	Kā
79.	Bhūmi	,,	,,	,,
80.	Bhṛṣṭavindus	,,	,,	Baudh
81.	Bhraṣṭakas	,,	,,	,,
82.	Bhraṣṭis	,,	,,	,,
83.	Bhraṣṭavindis	,,	,,	,,
84.	Bhraṣṭaviṣṇa	,,	,,	,, Mā
85.	Bhrāstrakṛt	,,	,,	Mt
86.	Bhrājitākṣis	,,	,,	,,
87.	Bhrānākṣi	,,	,,	,,
88.	Bhrājinākṣatreya	,,	,,	,,
89.	Bhrāṣṭuvidus	,,	,,	,,
90.	Bhrāstramiti	,,	,,	Kā
91.	Mathurāvata	,,	,,	,,
92.	Madhurāvahas	,,	,,	Mt
93.	Markaṭi	,,	,,	Mt
94.	Mātuleya	,,	,,	Kā
95.	Mārkaṭi	,,	,,	Mt
96.	Mṛtsaṅga	,,	,,	,,
97.	Yāvakrī	,,	,,	Kā
98.	Yaugandharāyaṇas	,,	,,	Baudh
99.	Rājis	,,	,,	,,
100.	Rāta	,,	,,	Mt
101.	Rāya	,,	,,	Mt
102.	Rāsarāt	,,	,,	Kā
103.	Rāṣṭrapiṇḍi	,,	,,	Mt
104.	Roṣa	,,	,,	,,
105.	Rauti	,,	,,	Baudh
106.	Lātakṛt	,,	,,	Mt
107.	Lāyakṛt	,,	,,	,,
108.	Lāvaki	,,	,,	,,
109.	Lāvakṛt	,,	,,	,,
110.	Lomakṛt	,,	,,	Kā
111.	Laityāli	,,	,,	Mt
112.	Laindrāṇi	,,	,,	,,
113.	Vatsatarāyaṇa(ṇas)	,,	,,	Kā, Mā

114. Vāṭās	read	in	Baudh
115. Vāṅsāyanas	,,	,,	Mā
116. Vātsacatarāyaṇa	,,	,,	Kā, Mt
117. Vārdhanis	,,	,,	Mā
118. Vārdhunis	,,	,,	Kā
119. Vāṣṇi (Varṣṇi ?)	,,	,,	Mt, Kā
120. Vāsāyana	,,	,,	Kā
121. Viśvāyakāyana	,,	,,	,,
122. Vidu	,,	,,	Mt
123. Veṇuhaṇi	,,	,,	Baudh
124. Veṇubhari	,,	,,	,,
125. Vailahāni	,,	,,	Baudh
126. Śankhinas	,,	,,	,,
127. Śākalāyana	,,	,,	Mt
128. Śārayaṇa	,,	,,	Kā
129. Śālaṅkāyana	,,	,,	Kā
130. Śālakāyanī	,,	,,	,,
131. Śikhāyanis	,,	,,	Baudh
132. Śainya	,,	,,	Mā
133. Śyāmāyanas	,,	,,	Kā
134. Śyāmrāyaṇas	,,	,,	Mā
135. Śyāmayani	,,	,,	Mt
136. Śvakrīḍī	,,	,,	,,
137. Sakhīnas	,,	,,	Baudh
138. Sakhīyīs	,,	,,	Kā
139. Satyāpacis	,,	,,	Baudh
140. Satsi	,,	,,	Kā
141. Saṁbhara	,,	,,	,,
142. Saṅkhāyana	,,	,,	Mt
143. Saṅgrāhavān	,,	,,	Baudh
144. Sātyāyani	,,	,,	,,
145. Sāparivaras	,,	,,	Kā
146. Sābhara	,,	,,	Mt
147. Sāṁparivāra	,,	,,	Kā
148. Sāṁparāyaṇas	,,	,,	Kā, Baudh
149. Sāṁbharabhāmat	,,	,,	Mā
150. Sāṁparāvaṇas	,,	,,	Baudh
151. Sāyakāyana	,,	,,	Mā
152. Sāyakāyanī	,,	,,	Mt
153. Sāhani	,,	,,	,, Kā

154. Sāhari	read	in	Mt,
155. Sohartā	,,	,,	Baudh
156. Sauyamuni	,,	,,	,, Kā
157. Skanda	,,	,,	Mt
158. Skandasah	,,	,,	Mt
159. Snāpurāvat	,,	,,	Mā
160. Srohata	,,	,,	Baudh
161. Svanditi(tah)	,,	,,	Kā
162. Svaśva	,,	,,	Mt
163. Hātrāyavi	,,	,,	Baudh
164. Hotrapacis	,,	,,	,,
165. Hotrapacis	,,	,,	,,

The Ṛkṣas

The following is an alphabetical index of the *gotras* belonging to the Ṛkṣas orRaukṣāyaṇas, a sub-clan of the Bhāradvājas. They adopt, according to Baudh. a *pravara* of five *ṛṣis* viz. Āṅgirasa-Bārhaspatya-Bhāradvāja-Vāndana-Mātavacas, or according to ĀP a *pravara* of three *ṛṣis*, also viz. Āṅgirasa-Vāndana-Mātavacas. Āp and Kā place them under *Dvyāmūṣyāyaṇas*.

1. Agnijihvas	read	in	Baudh
2. Agnijihvī	,,	,,	Kā
3. Kaṇvis	,,	,,	Baudh
4. Kapilas	,,	,,	,, Kā
5. Karṇa	,,	,,	Kā
6. Kautumi	,,	,,	Baudh
7. Kauthuma	,,	,,	Kā
8. Bṛhadbhāradvāja	,,	,,	,,
9. Vibhiṇḍa	,,	,,	Baudh, Kā
10. Vaipindi	,,	,,	,,
11. Śapilas	,,	,,	,,
12. Śabaras	,,	,,	,,
13. Suta	,,	,,	Kā
14. Sutis	,,	,,	Baudh

The Kāṇvas

The Kāṇvas appear to have certain link with the Bharadvājas. They are descendants of Ajamīḍha of the line the Bharata-

Bharadvāja combination. They are *kṣatropetas* and belong to the Kevalāṅgirasa. They read a *pravara* of three *ṛṣis*: Āṅgirasa, Ājamīḍha, Kāṇva (according to Āśv, Kā, Baudh, Āp), Āṅgirasa-Ghaura-Kāṇva (Āśv), while replaces Ājamīḍha by Ghora. It is noteworthy that Kā, treats Kāṇvas under the Bhāradvāja-*gaṇa* while all other treat them under the Kevalāṅgirases. The *gotras* are:

1.	Ajamīḍhas	read	in	ĀP; Baudh
2.	Aupamarkaṭāyanas	,,	,,	Baudh
3.	Kāṇvas	,,	,,	Baudh, Kā, Āśv
4.	Kālas	,,	,,	,,
5.	Paulahalins	,,	,,	,,
6.	Mañjimajayus	,,	,,	,,
7.	Matkatis	,,	,,	Kā
8.	Mauñjigandi	,,	,,	Baudh
9.	Ramanas	,,	,,	Kā
10.	Vājaśravas	,,	,,	Baudh
11.	Vijāvajayas	,,	,,	,,
12.	Śānāyanas	,,	,,	Kā

The Kapis

The Kapis are known as the Kevalāṅgiras and they have a *pravara* of three *ṛṣis*: Aṅgirasa-Āmahiyya-Urukṣaya. The following are the *gotras* who used to read this *pravara*.

1.	Āmaukhitaki	read	in	Baudh
2.	Kapis	,,	,,	,,
3.	Karaśikhanda	,,	,,	,,
4.	Kāsavaraṇas	,,	,,	,,
5.	Tarasvins	,,	,,	,,
6.	Tādins	,,	,,	,,
7.	Paṭañjalas	,,	,,	,,
8.	Bhojasin	,,	,,	,,
9.	Vaitālas	,,	,,	,,
10.	Śāyaṇa (Sāyaṇa ?)	,,	,,	,,
11.	Sagasakh	,,	,,	,,

Kā says that those who belong to the *gotras* of Bṛhaduktha and Vāmadeva should pronounce a *pravara* of three *ṛṣis*, viz. Āṅgirasa, Bārhaduktha and Vāmadeva.

The Mudgalas

The sūtras of Baudh and ĀP present the treatment of the Mudgalas under the *Kevalāṅgirases*, while those of Āśv and Kā treat them under the Bhāradvāja *gaṇa* emphasising their relation with the Bharadvājas. They have a *pravara* of three *ṛṣis*: Āṅgirasa, Bhārmyaśva and Maudgalya. All the four authors of the sūtras unanimously present this *pravara*. Beside this, Āśv and ĀP give an alternative *pravara* of three *ṛṣis* also: Tārkṣa, Bhārmyaśva and Maudgalya. The following are *gotras* known to have belonged to the Mudgalas:

1. Ṛṣabhamitras	read	in	Baudh	
2. Gaya	,,	,,	,,	
3. Tārkṣas	,,	,,	,,	
4. Dīrghajaṅghas	,,	,,	,,	
5. (Dīrgha) taraṇa	,,	,,	,,	
6. Dīrghavindus	,,	,,	,,	
7. Mudgalas	,,	,,		Kā
8. Viśvāyanas	,,	,,	,,	
9. Satyamugri	,,	,,	Kā	
10. Hiraṇyākṣas	,,	,,	Baudh	
11. Hiraṇyastambi	,,	,,	Kā	

The Rathītaras

Baudh, Āśv, ĀP place Rathītaras under the Kevalāṅgirasas while Kā under the Bhāradvāja *gaṇa*. However, all the *Sūtrakāras* agree in giving their *pravara* consisting of three *ṛṣis* or seers: Āṅgirasa, Vairupa and Rāthītara.[25] Their link with the Bharadvājas is clear from Kā's treatment. The following are *gotras* belong to the Rathītaras:

1. Aṣṭadraṅgṣṭra	read	in	ĀP
2. Kāhvāyana	,,	,,	Baudh
3. Naitirakṣis	,,	,,	,,

4. Bhairuvāhas	read	in	Baudh
5. Libhāyanas	,,	,,	,,
6. Laibhis	,,	,,	,,
7. Virupas	,,	,,	,,
8. Vairupas	,,	,,	,,
9. Śailalis	,,	,,	,,
10. Sāvahāvas	,,	,,	,,
11. Hastidāsis	,,	,,	,,
12. Haimagus	,,	,,	,,

The Viṣṇuvṛddhas

The sūtras of Baudh and ĀP consider the Viṣṇuvṛddhas as the Kevalāṅgiras, while that of Kā treats them under the Bhāradvājagaṇa, indicating their link with the Bharadvājas. Baudh and ĀP present their *pravara* of three *ṛṣis*-seers: Āṅgirasa, Paurukutsa and Trāsadasyava, while Kā gives instead: Āṅgirasa, Pārṣadaśva and Rathītara—this is doubtful. The following are enumerated as Viṣṇuvṛddhas:

1. Āruṇi	read	in	ĀP
2. Aupagavi	,,	,,	,,
3. Tulyabharaṇyas	,,	,,	Baudh
4. Devasthalis	,,	,,	,,
5. Ṇikatri	,,	,,	Kā
6. Ṇijatri	,,	,,	,,
7. Ṇiputri	,,	,,	,,
8. Nitunda	,,	,,	ĀP
9. Nivadarāyaṇa	,,	,,	Kā
10. Naitunda	,,	,,	Baudh
11. Bhadraṇas	,,	,,	,,
12. Matsaprāyaṇas	,,	,,	,,
13. Madraṇas	,,	,,	,,
14. Vādārayaṇas	,,	,,	,,
15. Viṣṇuvṛddhas	,,	,,	,,
16. Vaimadha	,,	,,	,,
17. Śaṭhamarṣaṇa	,,	,,	,,
18. Śatapatri	,,	,,	,,
19. Satyankāyana	,,	,,	Baudh
20. Sātyaki	,,	,,	Baudh, ĀP

The Śuṅga-Śaiśiris

Only the following few *gotras* belong to the *dvyāmuṣyayaṇas* of the family of the Bharadvājas. They read a *pravara* of five *ṛṣis*: Āṅgirasa, Bārhaspatya, Bhāradvāja, Kātya and Akṣilava (acc. to ĀP), or Āṅgirasa, Bārhaspatya, Bhāradvāja, Śauṅga and Śaiśiris (according to Kā), or Āṅgirasa, Bārhaspatya, Bhāradvāja, Kātya and Ātkila.

1. Kata-Śaiśiris	read	in	ĀP
2. Grādhas	,,	,,	Kā
3. Bharadvājas	,,	,,	,,
4. Bharadvāja-Śuṅgas	,,	,,	ĀP
5. Śuṅga-Śaiśiris	,,	,,	,,
6. Śaiśiris	,,	,,	Kā
7. Śauṅgas	,,	,,	,,

The Saṁkṛtis

It is surprising that the authors of the sūtras should adopt different criteria in dealing with the *Saṁkṛtis*. Baudh treats *Saṁkṛtis* as the Kevalāṅgirasas. ĀP treats them as the Vasiṣṭhas while Kā treats them as the Bharadvājas. We have had a detailed study of the problem elsewhere.[26] Kā gives a *pravara* of three *ṛṣis* as: Āṅgirasa, Sāṅkṛtya and Gaurivīti; Baudh changes the order: Āngirasa, Gaurivīti and Saṁkṛti. And ĀP gives their *pravaras*: Śāktya, Sānkṛtya and Gaurivīti. However, Āśv gives both the *pravaras*: Āṅgirasa, Gaurivīti and Sāṁkṛti; or Śāktya, Gaurivīti and Sāṁkṛti in view of their origin from Śakti. The following *gotras* belong to the Saṁkṛtis:

1. Āgrāyaṇas	read	in	Baudh
2. Āghrāpayas	,,	,,	,,
3. Taṇḍin	,,	,,	,,
4. Jānaki	,,	,,	Kā
5. Tārakādyas	,,	,,	Baudh
6. Tairaghātavya	,,	,,	Kā
7. Paribhāvas	,,	,,	,,
8. Putimāṣas	,,	,,	,,
9. Paiṇayas	,,	,,	,,

10. Paulas	read in	Kā
11. Malakas	,, ,,	,,
12. Laukṣitālagas	,, ,,	,,
13. Vārāyaṇi	,, ,,	,,
14. Śāṁba or Śāṁbu	,, ,,	,, Baudh
15. Śaivagāvas	,, ,,	,,
16. Śaiṁbhavis	,, ,,	,,
17. Śrautāyana	,, ,,	,,
18. Sahigāṅgi	,, ,,	,,
19. Saipathan	,, ,,	Kā
20. Harigrīvis	,, ,,	,,

The Hāritas

Given in this section is an index of the *gotras* belonging to the sub-clan of the Hāritas, forming a part of the Bhāradvāja clan. Kā and Āśv regard them as Bharadvājas while Baudh and ĀP place them under the Kevalāṅgirases. They do pronounce a *pravara* of three *ṛṣis*-seers: Āṅgirasa, Āṁbariṣa and Yauvanāśva (according to Baudh). ĀP gives an alternative *pravara*: Māndhātṛ, Āṁbariṣa and Yauvanāśva—in which Māndhātṛ replaces Āṅgirasa. ĀP further gives a special *pravara* for the only Kautsas or Kutsas: Āṅgirasa-Māndhātṛ-Kautsa. The *gotras* are as under:

1. Ābhilevanas	read in	Kā
2. Kārisis	,, ,,	Baudh
3. Kutsa	,, ,,	Āśv
4. Kautsa	,, ,,	Kā
5. Kautapus	,, ,,	Baudh
6. Kaulis	,, ,,	,,
7. Darbha	,, ,,	Āśv
8. Dālbhya	,, ,,	Kā
9. Piṅga	,, ,,	Āśv
10. Paiṅga	,, ,,	Kā
11. Paulas	,, ,,	Baudh
12. Pauḍalomadhus	,, ,,	,,
13. Bhaimagus	,, ,,	Kā, Āśv
14. Bhairava	,, ,,	Baudh
15. Mamanayu	,, ,,	,,
16. Mandikāris	,, ,,	,,

17. Mahodara	read	in	Baudh
18. Mādrika	,,	,,	Kā
19. Miśrodara	,,	,,	Baudh
20. Māndhātṛs	,,	,,	,,
21. Lavadara	,,	,,	,,
22. Lomāyana	,,	,,	Kā
23. Śaṅkha	,,	,,	Baudh, Āśv, Kā
24. Śāṁkhyodabhya	,,	,,	Baudh
25. Saubhāgas	,,	,,	,,
26. Hārita	,,	,,	Baudh
27. Hāstyadāsi	,,	,,	Baudh
28. Haimagus	,,	,,	,,

Notes and References

1. *Gotra* literally means that which protects (*tra*) cow (*go*) and is used in the RV in the sense of cow-stall, cow-pen, hurdle, etc. Later on, it meant family enclosed by a hurdle. Lastly, it comes to signify the family name. Pāṇini and others used this word in connection with *apatya* vide Pā (4, 1, 162) ग्रपत्यं पौत्रप्रभृतिगोत्रम्. Bodhāyana indicates that the progeny of each of the seven seers, with Agastya as the eighth, is called *gotra* or family (तेषां सप्तर्षीणाम् ग्रगस्त्याष्टमानां यदपत्यं तद्गोत्रमित्युच्यते।)
Baudh Ś S P-54

2. Indicating the significance of *pravara* Paṇḍita Puruṣottama writes in his GPM (p. 8) as follows: 'सर्वेषां ब्राह्मणानां वक्ष्यमाणागस्त्याष्टमसप्तर्षिवंश परंपरा-शाखोपशाखा सहस्त्रप्रयुतार्वुदानेक गोत्राणामाहिताग्नीनां सतां प्रतिपुरुषमाहवनीयस्याग्नेहव्यवाह-नाम्नः सप्रर्षीणामगस्त्याष्टमानामपत्यसम्बन्धेन तत् सादृश्यसंबन्धेन वा प्रकर्षेण वरणानि प्रार्थनानि प्रवराः।'

Thus *Pravara* appears to be one to whom Vedic *mantras* were revealed, and was enumerated among the seven seers, Agastya being the eighth, whose name is chosen to be repeated on religious occasions by his descendants. Thus *ārṣeya* and *pravara* are considered to be synonymous (ग्रार्षेयः प्रवर इति पर्यायौ।)

3. GPM pp. 9-10.

4. Vide Introductory verses 4-5 of GPM Also cf. द्वयार्षेयसन्निपातेऽविवाह-स्त्र्यार्षेयाणां त्र्यार्षेयसन्निपातेऽविवाहः पञ्चार्षेयणामसमानप्रवरैर्विवाहः। एकमेव ऋषिर्यावत् प्रवरेष्वनुवर्तते। तावत् समानगोत्रत्वमन्यत्र भृग्वंगिरसां गणात्।
GPM pp. 14-16.

5. Six of these Brahmarṣis are said to be *mānasaputra* of Brahmā: vide:

ब्रह्मणो मानसाः पुत्रा विदिताः षण्महर्षयः।
x x x x x
मरीचिरङ्गिरा ग्रत्रिः पुलस्त्य पुलहः ऋतुः।
षडेते ब्रह्मणः पुत्रा वीर्यवन्तो महर्षयः॥

(MBh, 1, 60, 1, 4)

And Bhṛgu is said to have been born through Brahmā's heart. Read MBh 1, 61, 40: ब्रह्मणो हृदयं भित्वा निसृतो भगवान् भृगुः।

5a. Vasiṣṭha does not figure in the above list.

6. Read: MBh 1, 60, 7:

राक्षसास्तु पुलस्त्यस्य वानराः किन्नरास्तथा।
पुलहस्य मृगाः सिहा व्याघ्राः किंपुरुषास्तथा॥

Cf. also: Bd 1, 2, 9, 18c.

भृग्वंगिरोमरीचिंश्च पुलस्त्यं पुलहं क्रतुम्।
दक्षमत्रिं वसिष्ठं च निर्ममे मानसान् सुतान्॥

MBh 1.60, 8:

क्रतोः क्रतुसमाः पुत्राः पतंगसहचारिणः।

7. Vasiṣṭha was cursed by Nimi and he regained his body after having been born as a son of Mitra and Varuṇa (Rām 7, 55-56; also RV 7, 33).

8. Read: MBh 12, 284, 17-18:

मूलगोत्राणि चत्वारि समुत्पन्नानि भारत।
अङ्गिरा कश्यपश्चैव वसिष्ठो भृगुरेव च॥
कर्मतोऽन्यानि गोत्राणि समुत्पन्नानि पार्थिव।
नामधेयानि तपसा तानि च ग्रहणं सताम्॥

8a. Seven seers, with Agastya as the eighth, are said to have given rise to numerous *gotras* or families. cf: Aśv.ŚS p. 7-8.

विश्वामित्रो जमदग्निर्भरद्वाजोऽयं गौतमः।
अत्रिर्वसिष्ठ कश्यप इत्येते सप्तऋषयः॥
एतेषां सप्तानां ऋषीणामगस्त्याष्टमानां
यदपत्यं तद् गोत्रमित्याचक्षते।

9. On this point vide Aśv. SS Pariśiṣṭa: 1-10; especially read: S 10:
इत्यसमानप्रवरैर्विवाहो विवाहः।

10. For detailed discussion on the *Kṣatropeta Brāhmaṇas* see Part 1, Ch. 3, Section iv and vi above.

11. *Gotras*, under the Kevala-Aṅgirases are more or less related to the Bhāradvāja family. This trend may reflect some advancement in social outlook of certain sub-clans within the family.

12. Āp. ŚS pp. 2, 12-13.

13. AśvŚS p. 11, 2 considers Ṛkṣas as Kevala-Aṅgirases.

14. AśvŚS pp. 12, 1-5.

15. See KŚSP, Bhāradvāja Gotrakāṇḍa.

16. Part 1 of this dissertation is solely devoted towards that end.

17. See Section on Garga Bhāradvāja, (Part 1, Ch. 3, Section iv) above.

18. See Section on Nara Bhāradvāja, (Part 1, Ch. 3, Section iii).

19. See Part 1, Ch. 3. Section vii on Ajamīḍha Sauhotra.

20. We have discussed the problem in the main body of this work.

21. The problem has been discussed in Part 1, Ch. 3, Section (iii).

22. It is elaborately discussed in Part 1, Ch. 2, Section (iii). Vide Va 99, 157; Mt 49.33.

23. Ibid.

24. This work has been published in the collection of *Gotra Pravara Nibandha Kadambakam* ed. by Chensalrao.

25. Ap reads Aṣṭadraṁṣṭra in place of Āṅgirasa and gives an alternative *pravara* that consists of Aṣṭadraṁṣṭra, Vairupa and Pārṣada.

26. See Nara Bhāradvāja in Part I, Ch. 3.

BIBLIOGRAPHY

(A) *Original Texts and Commentaries*

(Arranged according to Devanāgari alphabet)

Agni Purāṇa ed. Baladeva Upadhyaya, Varanasi, 1966.

Atharva Veda (Paippalāda Saṁhitā) ed. Raghuvira, Lahore, 1936-42.

Atharva Veda (Śaunaka Saṁhitā) (4 vols.) with Sāyaṇa's Commentary ed. Vishva Bandhu, VVRI, Hoshiarpur, 1960-64.

Atharvaveda Pariśiṣṭas, ed. R.K. Ray, Varanasi, 1976.

Atharvavedīya Bṛhat Sarvānukramaṇikā, ed. Vishva Bandhu, VVRI, Hoshiarpur, 1966.

Aṣṭādhyāyī—2 vols. (with Kāśikāvṛtti) text and tr. ed. S.C. Vasu, Varanasi, 1962.

Āpastaṁba Gṛhya Sūtra ed. L.A. Ravi Varma, University of Travancore, Trivandrum, 1940.

Āpastaṁba Śrauta Sūtra, ed. H.R. Rangaswamy Iyenger, Mysore, 1944.

Ārṣānukramaṇī ed. R.L. Mitra, published with the *Bṛhaddevatā* in Bibliotheca Indica, 1892.

Ārṣeya Upaniṣad See Upaniṣad Saṁgrahaḥ below.

Ārṣeya Brāhmaṇa ed. B.R. Sharma, Tirupathi, 1967.

Āśvalāyana Gṛhya Sūtra (Text and Tr. Eng.) by N.N. Sharma, Delhi, 1976.

Āśvalāyana Śrauta Sūtra, ed. (1) Ganesh Shastri, Anandasram Press, Poona, 1917.
(2) With Gārgya Nārāyaṇa's commentary ed. Ramanarayana Vidyaratna, Calcutta, 1874.

Īśādidaśopaniṣadaḥ (with Śaṅkarabhāṣya), Motilal Banarsidass, Delhi, 1964.

Īśādyaṣṭottaraśatopaniṣadaḥ ed. W.L. Shastri Pansikar, Bombay, 1925.

Upaniṣad Saṁgrahaḥ, Ed. Jagdish Shastri, Delhi, 1970.

Ṛktantra with Ṛktantravṛtti and Sāmavedasarvānukramaṇi, ed. Surya Kanta, Delhi, 1970.

Ṛk Prātiśākhya, Vol. I, II ed. and tr. by M.D. Shastri, Varanasi Cantt, 1959.

Eggeling, J., tr. *Śatapatha Brāhmaṇa*, SBE Vols. XII, XXVI, XLI, XLIII, XLIV, Indian reprints, Varanasi.

Geldner, K.F., *Vedische Studien*, Stüttgart, 1889-1901 (in Collaboration with Pischel).

Geldner, K.F., *Der Rig Veda* (aus dem Sanskrit ins Deutsche ubersetzt und mit einem laufenden Kommentar versehen), HOS, Vol. 33-35, Harvard, 1951; Vol. 36, 1957.

Ghosal, U.N., *Studies in Indian History and Culture*, Calcutta, 1965.

Gonda, J., *Stylistic Repetition in the Veda,* Amsterdam, 1959.

The Vision of the Vedic Poets, Moulton : Disputations Rheno-Trajectinae, VIII, The Hague, 1963.

The Dual Deities in the Religion of the Veda, Amsterdam and London, 1974.

Epithets in the Ṛgveda, Mauto. Disp. Rheno-Traj. VI's Gravenhage, 1959.

History of Indian Literature, Fasc. 1-2, Wiesbaden, 1977.

Grassmann, H., *Wörterbuch zum Ṛgveda,* OH, Wiesbaden, 1964.

Griffith, R.T.H., *The Hymns of the Ṛgveda*, Motilal Banarsidass, Delhi, 1973.

Griswold, H.D., *The Religion of the Ṛgveda*, Motilal Banarsidass, Delhi, 1969.

Ghurye, G.S., *Two Brāhmaṇical Institutions, Gotra and Pravara*, Bombay, 1972.

Vedic India, Bombay, 1979.

Hastings, J., *Encyclopaedia of Religion and Ethics* (Fourth Impression), Edinburg, 1959.

Hillebrandt, *Ritualliteratur*, *Vedische opfer and zauber,* Karl, J. Tribner, Strassburg, 1897.

Vedische Mythologie; 2 Bande, verlog Geog Olms, Heidesheim, 1965.

Hopkins, E.W., *The Religions of India*, Boston, 1895.

Epic Mythology, Delhi, 1974.

Great Epic of India, New York, 1901.

Jayaswal, K.P., *Hindu Polity*, Bangalore, 1943.

Jacobi, *Upaniṣadvākyakośah*, Pune, 1891.

Jog, K.P., *The Aśvins in the Ṛgveda and Their Traces in the Later Literature*, Ph.D., Thesis, (unpublished), B.H.U., 1964.

Kaegi, A., *Ṛgveda* (Trans. by R. Arrowsmith) reprint, Delhi, 1950.

Kane, P.V., *History of Dharmaśāstra*, Vols. I-V, BORI, Poona-4, 1930-57.

Kangle, R.P., *Kauṭilīya Arthaśāstra*, Vols. I-III, text tr. and study; Bombay, 1960-63.

Kantawala, S.G., *A Cultural History from the Matsya Purāṇa*; M.S. University, Baroda, 1964.

Kapadia, B.H., *Viśvāmitra*, Sardar Patel University, Vallabh Nagar, Gujarat, 1971.

The Dānastutis of the Ṛgveda (translation of Die *Dānastutis des Ṛgveda* by Manilal Patel), Vallabh Nagar, 1961.

Karambelkar, V.W., *History in the Atharvaveda*, Nagpur, 1974.

Karve, Iravati, *Kinship Organization in India*, Asia Publishing House, London, 1965.

Kashikar, C.G., ed. *Śrautakośa*, Vols. I-II, VSM, Poona, 1970.

The Sūtras of Bharadvāja, Vols. I and II, text, translation and detailed study of the Bharadvāja Śrauta Sūtra, Pitṛmedhasūtra and Pariśesa Sūtra, VSM, Poona, 1964.

Keith, A.B., *The Religion and Philosophy of the Vedas and Upaniṣads*, HOS, Vols. XXI-XXII, (Indian reprint) Motilal Banarsidass, Delhi, 1970.

Ṛgveda Brāhmaṇas (Eng. tr.) HOS, XXV (Indian reprint), Motilal Banarsidass, Delhi, 1970.

Veda of Black Yajus School, (Eng. tr.), HOS, XVIII, XIX (reprint) Delhi, 1967.

Keith and Macdonell (in collaboration). *Vedic Index of Names and Subjects*, (2 Vols. reprint), Delhi, 1967.

Ketkar, S.V., ed. *Mahārāstrīya Jñānakośa*, Vol. III (Vedavidyā), Poona, 1921.

Kosambi, D.D., *An Introduction to the Study of Indian History*, Bombay-7, 1956.

Khadilkar, S.D., Ed. *Kātyāyana Śulba Sūtra*, VSM, Poona, 1974.

Law, B.C., *Pāñcālas and Their Capital Ahicchatra*, Memoirs of the Archaeological Survey of India, No. 67, Delhi, 1942.

Tribes in Ancient India, BORI, Poona, 1943.

Rivers of India, Calcutta, 1944.

Historical Geography of Ancient India, Delhi, 1976.

Law, N.N., *Age of the Ṛgveda*, Firma K.L. Mukhopadhyaya, Calcutta, 1965.

Macdonell, A.A., *History of Sanskrit Literature*, Motilal Banarsidass, Delhi, 1965.

Vedic Mythology, Indological Book House, Delhi, 1963.
Vedic Grammar for Students, Oxford University Press, London, 1971.
Vedic Reader, Oxford University Press, London, 1970.

Macdonell and Keith (in colloboration) *Vedic Index*, 2 Vols. Delhi, 1967.

Mazumdar, R.C., and Pusalkar, A.D., ed. *The Vedic Age*, Bharatiya Vidya Bhavan, Bombay, Fourth Impression, 1965.

Mainkar, T.G., *Mysticism in the Ṛgveda*, Bombay, 1961.
Some Poetical Aspects of the Ṛgvedic Repetitions, University of Poona, 1966.

Mankad, D.R., *Date of the Ṛgveda*, Gangajala Prakashana, Anand, 1952.
Purāṇic Chronology, Gangajala Prakashana, Anand, 1951.

Mani, Vettam, *Purāṇic Encyclopedia*, Motilal Banarsidass, Delhi, 1975.

Max Müller, F., *A History of Ancient Indian Literature*, Revised by S.N. Shastri, Chowkhamba S.S., Varanasi, 1968.
Vedas, Indological Book House, Varanasi, 1969.

Mimamsaka, Yudhisthira, *Saṁskṛta Vyākaraṇa kā Itihāsa*, Vol. I, Sonipat (Haryana), 1952.

Mishra, D.P., *Studies in the Proto-History on India*, Orient Longman, New Delhi, May, 1971.

Monier Williams, M.A., *Sanskrit-English Dictionary*, Motilal Banarsidass, Delhi, 1963.

Mukherji, R.K., *Education in Ancient India*, London, 1947.
Hindu Civilization, Bombay.

Murthy, R.S., Shivagangesha, *A Study of the Important Brāhmaṇas*, Mysore, 1974.

Oldenburg, *Ṛgveda Noten*, Berlin, 1909.
"*Uber die Liedverfasser des Ṛgveda*", Zeitschrift der Deutschen Morgenlandischen Gesselschaft, 42, pp. 199-247.
Die Religion des Veda; Berlin, 1970.
Grihyasūtras SBE, XXIX, XXX, Delhi, 1964.
Ancient India—Its Language and Religions. Calcutta, 1962.

Palsule, G.V., *The Verbal Forms in the Ṛgveda* (*Maṇḍala VI*), Poona University, Poona 7, 1979.

Parab, B.A., *The Miraculous and Mysterious in the Vedic Literature*, Bombay, 1952.

Pargiter, F.E., *Ancient Indian Historical Tradition* (reprint), Delhi, 1962.

Pargiter, F.E., *Dynasties of the Kali Age*, London, 1913.

Patil, D.R., *The Cultural History from the Vāyu Purāṇa*, DCRI, Poona, 1947.

Pillai, G.K., *Vedic History (set in Chronology)*, Kitabistan, Allahabad, 1959.

Traditional History of India, Kitab-Mahal, Delhi, 1960.

Potdar, K.R., *Sacrifice in the Ṛgveda*, Bharatiya Vidya Bhavan, Bombay-7, 1953.

Pradhan, S.N., *Chronology of Ancient India*, University of Calcutta, 1927.

Pusalkar, A.D., *Studies in Epics and Purāṇas of India*, Bombay, 1955.

Radhakrishnan, S., *History of Indian Philosophy*, 2 Vols., London, 1923, 1927.

Rahurkar, V.G., *The Seers of the Ṛgveda*, University of Poona, 1964.

Rai, Ramkumar, *Vālmīki Rāmāyaṇa Kośa*, Chowkhamba SS., Varanasi 1965.

Mahābhārata Kośa, Parts 1-5, Varanasi, 1964; 1966; 1982.

Raja, C. Kunhan, *The Poet-Philosophers of the Ṛgveda: Vedic and Pre-Vedic*, Ganesh & Co., Madras, 1963.

Unpublished Upaniṣads, Adyar Library, Madras, 1933.

The Quintessence of the Ṛgveda, Bombay, 1964.

Ramgopal, *India of the Vedic Kalpasūtras*, Delhi, 1959.

Rangacharya, V., *History of the Pre-Musalman India*, Vol. II, (Vedic India, Pt. I) Indian Publishing House, Madras, 1937.

Rao, N.J., *The Age of the Mahābhārata War*, Varanasi, 1978.

Rapson, E.G., *Cambridge History of India*, Vol. I, Delhi, 1962.

Rawlinson, George, *The Histories of Hirodotus*, Tr. 2 vols, New York, 1964.

Renou, L., *Vedic India*, Delhi, 1971.

Religions of India, London, 1953.

Roy, S.B., *Date of the Mahābhārata Battle*, Gurgaon, 1976.

Roy, S.N., *Historical and Cultural Studies in the Purāṇas*, Purāṇic Publications, Allahabad, 1978.

Sarkar, S.C., *Some Aspects of the Earliest Social History of India*, Oxford, 1928.

Sarma, T. Vedakānanar Ekānjali Phul, (Assamese), Keteki Prakashan, Sarbhog, Assam, 1987.

Sarup, L., *Nighaṇṭu and Nirukta* (Text, tr. and Introduction), Delhi, 1967.

Sanskrityayana, Rahul, *Ṛgveda kā Ārya* (Hindi), Kitab Mahal, Allahabad, 1957.

Satawalekar, *Bhāradvāja Ṛṣi-kā Darśana*, Pardi, 1960.

Saxena, D.P., *Regional Geography of Vedic India*, Kanpur, 1976.

Schmidt, Hanns-Peter, *Bṛhaspati und Indra*, Wiesbaden, 1968.

Schrader, F. Otto, *A Descriptive Catalogue of the Sanskrit Manuscripts in the Adyar Library*, Vol. I Upaniṣads, Madras, 1908.

Sharma Dalai, H.N., *Bhāratakośa* (*Assamese*), Barpeta, Assam, 1947.

Sharma A.N., *Bhārata Manīṣā* (Assamese) Publication Board, Gauhati 1965.

Sharma, U.C., *The Viśvāmitras and the Vasiṣṭhas*, Veveka Publications, Aligarh, July, 1975.

Shastri, Kapiladev, *Vaidika Ṛṣi: Ek Pariśīlana*, Kurukshetra, 1978.

Shastri, A.M., *India as Seen in Bṛhat Saṁhitā of Varāhamihira*, Motilal Banarsidass, Varanasi, 1969.

Shastri, K.C., *Bengal's Contribution to Sanskrit Grammar in the Pāṇinian and Cāndra Systems*, Part I, Calcutta, 1972.

Shendge, N.J., *The Religion and Philosophy of the Atharvaveda*, BORI, Poona, 1952.

Shenge, Malati, J., *The Civilized Demons: the Harappans in the Ṛgveda*, New Delhi, 1977.

Siddantalankar, S., *Heritage of Vedic Culture*, Bombay, 1969.

Singer, Milton, ed. *Kṛṣṇa: Myths, Rites and Attitudes*, Honolulu, 1966.

Smith, H. Daniel, *A Descriptive Bibliography of the Printed Texts of the Pañcarātrāgama*, Oriental Institute, Baroda, 1975.

Smith, R.M., *Dates and Dynasties in the Earliest India*, Motilal Banarsidass, Delhi, 1973.

Smith, Vincent, *A Early History of India*, 4th Edn., Oxford, 1924.

Sörensen, S., *An Index to the Names in the Mahābhārata* (reprint) Delhi, 1963.

Tilak, B.G., *Vedic Chronology and Vedāṅga Jyotiṣa*, Poona, 1952.

Tripathi, K.S., *A Cultural Study of the Śrīmad Bhāgavata*. B.H.U. Sanskrit Series, Vol. IV, Varanasi, 1969.

Triveda, D.S., *Indian Chronology*, Bombay, 1963.

Upadhayaya Baladeva, *Ācārya Sāyaṇa aur Mādhava* (Hindi), Prayaga, 1949.

Purāṇa Vimarśa, Varanasi, 1965.

Vaidya, C.V., *History of Sanskrit Literature,* (Vedic Period), Poona, 1930.

Varma, Siddheshwar, *Critical Studies in the Phonetic Observations of Indian Grammarian,* Delhi, 1961.

Velankar, H.D., *Ṛgveda Maṇḍala II* (Eng. tr.), University of Bombay, 1966.

Ṛgveda Maṇḍala III (Eng. tr), University of Bombay, 1968.

Ṛgveda Maṇḍala VII (text., tr., annotation and Introduction), Bharatiya Vidya Bhavan, Bombay-7, 1963.

Venkatasubbia, A., *Satyaloka in the Ṛgveda,* A Study, VI Series 48, Hoshiarpur, 1974.

Vishva Bandhu, *Vedic Word Concordance,* (16 Volumes) VVRI, Lahore and Hoshiarpur, pub. between 1942-65.

Brāhmaṇic Citations, Hoshiarpur, 1966.

Upaniṣadic Citations, Hoshiarpur, 1972.

Weber, A., *Indische Studien,* Berlin, Vols. I-II, 1950.

Wheeler, Mortimer, *Early India and Pakistan,* (Revised Edn). London, 1968.

Whitney, W.D., *Atharvaveda Saṁhitā* (tr. 2 Vols) reprint Delhi, 1962.

Wilhelm. F., *Politische Polemiken in Steaatslehrbuch des Kautīlya,* Wiesvaden 1960.

Wilson & Others, *Matsya Purāṇa* (tr.) Orient Publishers, Delhi, 1972.

Wilson, H.H., *Viṣṇu Purāṇa* (tr.) 1864.

Ṛgveda (translation 6 Vols. 1-6) Poona, 1925-28, reprint, Delhi, 1977.

Winternitz, *A History of Indian Literature,* translated into English by Mrs. Ketkar, S. University of Calcutta, 1927.

Some Problems of Indian Literature, Delhi, 1977.

Zimmer *Altindisches Leben,* Berlin, 1879.

(C) *Articles*

(Arranged according to Roman alphabetical order)

Altekar, A.S., "Can we Reconstruct Pre-Bhārata War History?" Presidential Address, Archaic and Early Cultural History Section, PIHS, Third Session, Calcutta 1939, pp. 33-37.

Atkins, S.D., "Pūṣan in the Sāma, Yajur and Atharva Vedas" JAOS-67, pp. 274-95.

Chapekar, N.G., "Bharadvāja", ABORI Vol. XXXI, 1950, pp. 292-96.

"Gṛtsamada", Prasada, January, 1951.

"Viśvāmitra and the Kuśikas", Potdar Comm. Vol.

"Kaṇva in the Ṛgveda", JBBRAS, 27.

"Agastya", JBBRAS, 28.

"Kakṣīvān", Kevalananda Saraswati Comm. Vol.

"Uśanā Kāvya", Prasada, September, 1950.

Dandekar, R.N., "The Antecedents and Early Beginning of the Vedic Period", Presidential Address, Ancient Period, PIHS, 10th Session, Bombay, 1947.

Devasthali, G.V., "Śleṣa as a means of economy in the Bharadvāja Maṇḍala", Journal of Poona University, Humanities Section, 23, 1965, pp. 39-44.

Diwekar, H.R., "Chronology of the Ṛgvedic hymns", Saradapitha Patrika, Dwaraka, 6(2), Aug. 1966, pp. 1-18.

Goyatonde, S.N. (Mrs), "The Sāmans II", BUJ, XXXII, New Series, No. 38(2) September 1963, pp. 89-126.

Handiqui, K.K., "Women-poets of the Ṛgveda", IA, 59.

Hariyappa, "Ṛgvedic Legends through the Ages", BDCRI, 11, 1951.

Iyer, Sakuntala, A., "The Sāmans, I", BUJ. Vol. XXXI, New Series, No. 37(2) September, 1962, pp. 35-61. (See Goyatonde above).

Jog, K.P., "The Aśvins in the Ṛgveda and their traces in the later literature", JUB, 33(2) September, 1964, pp. 1-50; 34(2), September, 1965, pp. 1-65.

Kangle R.P., "Bharadvāja: An Ancient Teacher of Political Science", Munshi Indological Vol. BV. Vol. XX-XXI, pp. 333-39.

Kashikar, C.G., "Survey of the Śrauta Sūtras", BUJ, Vol. XXXV, New Series No. 41(2) September, 1966.

Koparkar, D.G., "Bharadvāja munince Vaimānika Śāstra" (in Marathi) Navabharat, Vol. 29, No. 7, April, 1976.

Kosambi, D.D., "The Study of Ancient Indian Tradition", Indica, IHRI, Silver Jubilee Vol., pp. 196-214.

Kramrish, Stella, "Pūṣan", JAOS, 81, 1961, pp. 104 ff.

Patel, Manilal, "Bharadvāja's Hymns to Agni", BV 2-3, May-November, 1941.

Pusalkar, A.D., "Rājarṣis or Royal sages", Aryan Path, 29(4), pp. 147-52.

"Brāhmaṇa Tradition and Kṣatriya Tradition", Hiriyanna Comm. Vol. 1952, pp. 151-55.

"Dāśarājña, A New approach", BV 10.

Rahurkar, V.G., "Ṛgvedāntila Mudgala va Mudgalāni" (Marathi), Chitrav Comm. Vol. 1954, pp. 85-97.

"The Ṛṣikās (Female Seers), of the Ṛgveda", Dandekar Fel. Vol. 1969, pp. 41-55.

"Ṛgvedāntila Bharadvāja va tatkulīya ṛṣi" (Marathi), Sanskrit Saugandha, 1970, pp. 1-7.

Raja, C. Kunhan, "The Authors of the Ṛgveda" K.V., Rangaswami Ayangar Comm. Vol., Madras, 1940.

Sarmah, T., "Ṛjiśvan", CASS. Studies Series, V, 1979, pp. 111-18.

"Saṁyu Bārhaspatya", BV, XLIII, 1-3, 1983, pp. 80-86.

"Bharadvāja(s) in the Ṛgveda," Glory of India, Vol. VIII, Nos. 1-4, 1984, pp 37-44.

"Vaidik Sāhityat Hariyūpiyār Yuddha" (Assamese) Prakash, Publication Board, Guwahati, Assam Vol. XIII, No. 5, March, 1988: pp. 61-67

Shende, N.J. "The Foundations of the Atharvedic Religion", BDCRI, Poona-6, Vol. 9.

Seth, H.C., "Certain Vedic, Avestan and Greek Traditions and the Age of the Ṛgveda", ABORI, 23, 1942, pp. 451-64.

Sukhtankar, "The Bhṛgus and the Bharata", ABORI XVIII.

Upadhyaya, S.A., "Hymns to Pūṣan", BV 25(1-2), 1965, pp. 38-50.

Velankar, H.D., "Hymns to Agni in Maṇḍala VI", BUJ, 24(2) September 1955, pp. 36-64.

"Hymns to Indra" (Published in parts in JUB, Nos. 3, 6, 8, 9, 10, 11, 13, 28 etc).

"Family hymns in the Family Maṇḍalas", JBBRAS, 18, 1942.

"Emotional Simile in the Ṛgveda and Concept of Bhakti", BV, Vol. 25 (3-4), 1965.

"Divodāsa Atithigva and Atithigvas", ABORI Vol. XXIII, 1942, pp. 657-68.

INDEX

(Abb. S.O. Son of
D.O. Daughter of
P.O. Protege of)